Production and Inventory Management

ARNOLDO C. HAX
Massachusetts Institute of Technology

DAN CANDEA
Polytechnic Institute of Cluj-Napoca

PRENTICE-HALL, INC., *Englewood Cliffs, New Jersey* 07632

Library of Congress Cataloging in Publication Data

HAX, ARNOLDO C.
    Production and inventory management.

    Bibliography: p.
    Includes index.
    1. Production control.   2. Inventory control
I. Candea, Dan.   II. Title.
TS155.8.H38 1983   658.5   83-9612
ISBN 0-13-724880-6

Editorial/production supervision
    and interior design: LINDA C. MASON
Cover design: BEN SANTORA
Manufacturing buyer: ED O'DOUGHERTY

To: Neva M., Andres, and Neva P. Hax
                    and
        Rodica and George Candea

Printed in the United States of America

10 9 8 7 6 5 4 3 2 1

ISBN 0-13-724880-6

Prentice-Hall International, Inc., *London*
Prentice-Hall of Australia Pty. Limited, *Sydney*
Editora Prentice-Hall do Brasil, Ltda., *Rio de Janeiro*
Prentice-Hall Canada Inc., *Toronto*
Prentice-Hall of India Private Limited, *New Delhi*
Prentice-Hall of Japan, Inc., *Tokyo*
Prentice-Hall of Southeast Asia Pte. Ltd., *Singapore*
Whitehall Books Limited, *Wellington, New Zealand*

Contents

Preface

This book is intended to be a text for a course dealing with the effective design of production and inventory management systems. Throughout the book we have emphasized the role the operations research methodology plays in the development of these systems. At the same time, we have attempted to provide conceptual frameworks and pragmatic recommendations, based on our professional experience, which we hope will complement the theoretical methodology presented.

The book surveys, in a fairly exhaustive way, the most important model-based contributions to the central themes of production and inventory management: facilities design (Chapter 2), aggregate production planning (Chapter 3), inventory control (Chapter 4), forecasting methods (Chapter 4), and operations scheduling (Chapter 5). In addition, it presents an up-to-date review of the methodology, developed principally at M.I.T., for the design of hierarchical production planning systems (Chapter 6). Finally, it analyzes the question of diagnostic analysis of a production and distribution system (Chapter 7), an important topic which has received little attention in the literature.

Throughout the book the emphasis has been to present a clear formulation of the basic issues, to describe the most relevant methodologies to address these issues in some detail, and to facilitate the further research of more advanced topics by providing comprehensive reference material.

The level of the book is that of the advanced undergraduate or graduate in business administration, industrial engineering, or operations research. We assume the reader is familiar with the fundamental methodologies of operations research, such as mathematical programming, probability theory, and basic statistical concepts.

We have tried to motivate the reader by offering some broad conceptual frameworks of production-inventory systems (Chapter 1), as well as by introducing each chapter with a clear statement of the problems to be discussed. Therefore, no necessary prerequisite in production and inventory management is required. However, a practical exposure of the operations management function will greatly enhance the reader's understanding of the methodologies discussed in the book.

This book has evolved through many years of research work in operations management conducted at M.I.T. Many of our colleagues and graduate students have contributed greatly to the research ideas. The primary thrust of our research focus was the development of an appropriate methodology for the design of hierarchical production planning systems, which is described in Chapter 6. We would like to express our most sincere thanks to some of those who have helped us in shaping many of these concepts: Michael Bosyj, Maqbool Dada, Raymond Fisher, Henry Gabbay, John Golovin, Stephen Graves, Elizabeth Haas, Uday Karmarkar, John Little, Thomas Magnanti, Nicolas Majluf, William Martin, Silvia Pariente, Mark Pendrock, Joseph Valor-Sabatier, Thomas Victor, and Roy Welsch.

We would like to single out two persons, Gabriel Bitran and Harlan Meal, who have been central architects of the hierarchical planning methodology and whose inputs were crucial both for its initial development and its subsequent extensions and refinements.

Moreover, we would like to acknowledge the exhaustive review of the manuscript being done by Li Chang, who has given us invaluable comments.

Edward Silver provided much inspiration as well as making constructive comments on several chapters. We also wish to acknowledge our reviewers Morris A. Cohen, University of Pennsylvania, and Robert Haessler, University of Michigan.

In the production of the book we owe our deep thanks to Deborah Cohen for an outstanding job of typing, editing, and proofreading the many versions of the original manuscript.

And finally we would like to thank the Office of Naval Research, through the auspices of Dr. Marvin Denicoff, for its research support throughout this effort under contract N00014-75-C-0556.

1

Introduction

1.1 The Nature of the Production-Inventory Management Systems

Production-inventory systems are concerned with the effective management of the total flow of goods, from the acquisition of raw materials to the delivery of finished products to the final customer. A production-inventory system is composed of a large number of elements which have to be managed effectively in order to deliver the final products in appropriate quantities, where they are required, at the desired time and quality, and at a reasonable cost. In a general situation, the most important elements are the following:

- Multiple plants, possibly containing a wide variety of equipment that represents the manufacturing capabilities of the firm.
- Multiple warehouses (distribution centers, local, regional, and factory warehouses) that might define a complicated distribution network.
- Multiple products (including raw materials, supplies, semifinished and finished products) to be purchased, manufactured, and distributed by the organization. The product structure could be fairly complex, involving several production stages of fabricating and assembly operations. The total number of individual items, representing varieties of product specification, color, dimensions, and so on, could exceed several thousands.
- Transportation and local delivery means, either owned, leased, or contracted, by the firm.
- Communication and data processing equipment.
- People, representing a wide variety of skills covering all the organizational echelons.

1

The acquisition and utilization of these elements are subject to a wide variety of constraints. Examples are the following:

- productivity constraints
- equipment capacity constraints
- labor availability
- technological constraints
- purchasing, manufacturing, and distribution lead times
- demand uncertainties and seasonalities
- service requirements
- other constraints (institutional, financial, marketing, and so on)

In order to determine effective ways to acquire and use the logistics elements subject to these constraints, several cost components have to be taken into consideration. The most important factors contributing to cost are the following:

- production and purchasing costs
- setup or changeover costs
- transportation and handling costs
- hiring and firing costs
- overtime costs
- inventory-related costs
- promotional and advertising costs
- subcontracting costs
- renting and leasing costs
- overhead
- capital investments and depreciation
- taxes

From the mere enumeration of these production-inventory system components, it is clear that the underlying decision process can be extremely difficult. Decisions involve comparisons of a large number of alternatives with complex interactions among system components. They cover several organization echelons, forcing a great deal of coordination both vertically and among functional areas. The exclusive use of conventional managerial wisdom, based largely on experience and intuition, may not be adequate in assuring effective decision making. In this book we will emphasize the role of operations research methodology in the development of support systems to manage production and inventory decisions.

To identify the characteristics that a sound support system should have, we will start by reviewing three different frameworks that have been proposed to classify production-inventory decisions (Hax [1976]). These frameworks provide simple taxonomies, stressing the relative differences of some aspects of the logistics process. At times, they tend to oversimplify and overgeneralize the inherent complexities of the process. However, we feel important inferences can be drawn from these frameworks which we are going to exploit in setting up design criteria for logistics support systems.

1.2   Anthony's Framework: Strategic, Tactical, and Operational Decisions

The first of these frameworks was proposed by Robert N. Anthony [1965]. He classified decisions into three categories: strategic planning, management control (tactical planning), and operations control. Let us briefly comment on the characteristics of each of these categories and review their implications for a model-based approach to support production-inventory management decisions.

1.2.1   Strategic Planning: Facilities Design

Strategic planning is concerned mainly with establishing managerial policies and with developing the necessary resources the enterprise needs to satisfy its external requirements in a manner consistent with its specific goals. Anthony defines *strategic planning* as "the process of deciding on the objectives of the organization, on changes in these objectives, on the resources used to attain these objectives, and on the policies that are to govern the acquisition, use, and disposition of these resources."

In the area of production and inventory management, the most important decisions that can be supported by model-based systems are those concerned with the design of production and distribution facilities. These decisions are on facilities, involving major capital investments for the development of new capacity, either through the expansion of existing capacity or the construction or purchase of new facilities and equipment. They include the determination of location and size of new plants and warehouses, the acquisition of new production equipment, the design of working centers within each plant, and the design of transportation facilities, communication equipment, data processing means, and so on.

These decisions are extremely important because, to a great extent, they are responsible for maintaining the competitive capabilities of the firm, determining its rate of growth, and eventually defining its success or failure. An essential characteristic of these strategic decisions is that they have long-lasting effects, thus forcing long planning horizons in their analysis. This, in turn, requires the consideration of uncertainties and risk attitudes in the decision-making process.

Moreover, investments in new facilities and expansions of existing capacities are resolved at fairly high managerial levels, and are affected by information which is both external and internal to the firm. Thus, any form of rational analysis of these decisions has of necessity a very broad scope, requiring information to be processed in a very aggregate form to allow inclusion of all the dimensions of the problem and to prevent top managers from being distracted by unnecessary operational details.

Chapter 2 of this book provides a comprehensive analysis of the mathematical models available to support facilities design decisions.

1.2.2 Management Control (Tactical Planning): Aggregate Capacity Planning

Anthony defines *management control* as "the process by which managers assure that resources are obtained and used effectively and efficiently in the accomplishment of the organization's objective." The emphasis of management control is on the resource utilization process.

Once the physical facilities have been decided upon, the basic problem to be resolved is the effective allocation of resources (e.g., production, storage and distribution capacities, work force availabilities, financial, marketing, and managerial resources) to satisfy demand and technological requirements, taking into account the costs and revenues associated with the operation of the resources available to the firm. These decisions are far from simple when we deal with several plants, many distribution centers, many regional and local warehouses, with products requiring complex multistage fabrication and assembly processes, that serve broad market areas affected by strong randomness and seasonalities in their demand patterns. They usually involve the consideration of a medium-range time horizon, divided into several periods, and require significant aggregation of the relevant managerial information. Typical decisions to be made within this context are utilization of regular and overtime work force, allocation of aggregate capacity resources to product families, accumulation of seasonal inventories, definition of distribution channels, and selection of transportation and transshipment alternatives. The most common vehicle to communicate the management control decision of the firm is the company's budget.

Chapter 3 surveys extensively the various modeling approaches to support aggregate production planning decisions.

1.2.3 Operational Control: Detailed Production Scheduling

After making an aggregate allocation of the resources of the firm, it is necessary to deal with the day-to-day operational and scheduling decisions. This stage of the decision-making process is called *operational control*. Anthony defines it as "the process of assuring that specific tasks are carried out effectively and efficiently." The operational control decisions require the complete disaggregation of the information generated at higher levels into the details consistent with the managerial procedures followed in daily activities. Typical decisions at this level are:

- the assignment of customer orders to individual machines
- the sequencing of these orders in the work shop
- inventory accounting and inventory control activities
- dispatching, expediting, and processing of orders
- vehicular scheduling

The systems to support operational inventory control decisions are discussed in Chapter 4. Chapter 5 is devoted to the analysis of detailed production scheduling issues.

The three types of decisions identified in Anthony's Framework—strategic planning, management control, and operational control—differ

TABLE 1.1   Differentiating Factors of the Three Decision Categories

FACTOR	STRATEGIC PLANNING	MANAGEMENT CONTROL (TACTICAL PLANNING)	OPERATIONAL CONTROL
Purpose	Management of change, resource acquisition	Resource utilization	Execution, evaluation, and control
Implementation instruments	Policies, objectives, capital investments	Budgets	Procedures, reports
Planning horizon	Long	Medium	Short
Scope	Broad, corporate level	Medium, plant level	Narrow, job shop level
Level of management involvement	Top	Middle	Low
Frequency of replanning	Low	Medium	High
Source of information	Largely external	External and internal	Largely internal
Level of aggregation of information	Highly aggregated	Moderately aggregated	Detailed
Required accuracy	Low	Medium	High
Degree of uncertainty	High	Medium	Low
Degree of risk	High	Medium	Low

markedly in various dimensions. The nature of these differences, expressed in relative terms, is summarized in Table 1.1.

1.3   Implications of Anthony's Framework: A Hierarchical Integrative Approach

There are significant conclusions that can be drawn from Anthony's classification regarding the nature of a decision support system. First, strategic, tactical, and operational decisions cannot be made in isolation because they interact strongly with one another. Therefore, an integrated approach is required if one wants to avoid the problems of suboptimization. Second, this approach, although essential, cannot be made without decomposing the elements of the problem in some way, within the context of a hierarchical system that links higher level decisions with lower level ones in an effective manner. Decisions that are made at higher levels provide constraints for lower level decision making: in turn, detailed decisions provide the necessary feedback to evaluate the quality of aggregate decision making.

This hierarchical approach recognizes the distinct characteristics of the type of management participation, the scope of the decision, the level of aggregation of the required information, and the time framework in which the decision is to be made. In our opinion, it would be a serious mistake to attempt to deal with all these decisions simultaneously, via a monolithic system or model. Even if computer and methodological capabilities would permit the solution of a large detailed integrated logistics model, which is clearly not the case today, this approach is inappropriate because it is not responsive to the management needs at each level of the organization, and would prevent the interactions between models and managers at each organization echelon.

The basic question to be resolved when designing a hierarchical system are:

- How to partition the decision process into modules or subproblems which properly represent the various levels of decision making in the organizational structure?
- How to aggregate and disaggregate the information through the various hierarchical levels?
- How to solve each of the subproblems identified by the partitioning procedure?
- What linking mechanisms should be used among the subproblems?
- How to evaluate the overall performance of the system, particularly with regard to issues of suboptimization introduced by the hierarchical design?

These questions are not easy to answer. Some factors which have to be taken into consideration are:

- The organizational structure of the firm that establishes the hierarchical breakdown of responsibilities, identifies the decision makers the system is intended to support, and provides the basis for a preliminary decomposition of the overall decision process.

- The nature of the resulting subproblems, which suggest the methodology that might be applicable to solve each of the system modules. Naturally, it is preferable to define subproblems which lend themselves to easy and effective solutions.
- The nature of the product structure, which is helpful in identifying ways in which information regarding individual items can be aggregated into families and product types.
- The degree of interaction and transfer of information from each of the hierarchical levels of the system. An effective design should facilitate the specification of the constraints that higher level decisions impose on the lower hierarchical echelons, and the control feedback that is transferred from the lower to the higher level decisions. In addition, the feasibility of disaggregation of information should be guaranteed throughout the process, and measures of performance should be available to assess the overall quality of decision making.

M.I.T. has devoted a significant effort in the last ten years to the development of an appropriate methodology for the design of hierarchical production planning systems. Chapter 6 reviews the most essential contributions resulting from this effort.

1.4   The Product Structure Framework

Another fundamental input to the determination of a production-inventory support system is the nature of the product structure of the firm. The most general product structure can be represented by Figure 1.1. The logistics activities associated with the various elements of the product structure can be grouped into three major categories: purchasing, production (including fabrication and assembly), and distribution.

Purchasing deals with the procurement of raw materials, tools, supplies, maintenance parts and purchased parts, subassemblies, and finished products. These are the basic inputs to the production and/or distribution activities obtained from external sources.

Production encompasses the fabrication and assembly operations and represents the process of converting raw materials into finished goods. It is useful to distinguish between fabrication and assembly activities since the manufacturing characteristics and the managerial decisions associated with these two processes are quite different. Table 1.2 provides a comparison of fabrication and assembly operations. It is worth noting that the fabrication and assembly activities can overlap in a given manufacturing situation. The resulting production process could then consist of several stages with alternating fabrication and assembly operations.

Job shops are further classified into open and closed job shops. In an *open job shop*, all products are made to order, which means that normally no

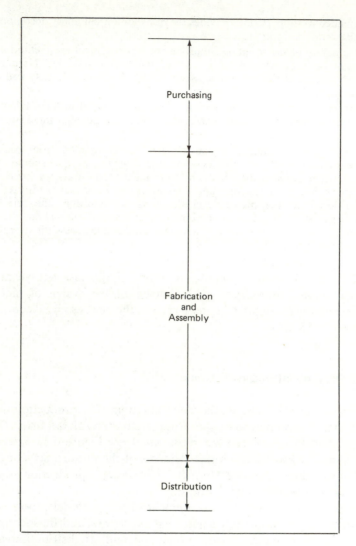

FIGURE 1.1   Product structure.

TABLE 1.2   Production Process Taxonomy

DIFFERENTIATING FACTORS	FABRICATION	ASSEMBLY
Type of process	Intermittent	Continuous
Process configuration	Job shop	Assembly line
Locus of decision making	Decentralized	Centralized
Equipment	Flexible	Specialized
Labor	High skilled	Low skilled
Scheduling	Dispatching	Permanent design

inventory is accumulated (for example, a repair maintenance shop). In a *closed job shop*, routine demand for finished products can be forecast, production run in batch sizes, and inventories carried.

Distribution deals with the allocation of finished products from production or supply centers to customers or intermediate destinations. The product structure and the associated logistics activities have important implications that we will now examine.

1.5 Implications of the Product Structure Framework: A Classification of Production-Inventory Systems

Obviously, not every firm possesses every element of the product structure identified above, nor is it engaged in all of the activities listed. For example, most retail or wholesale firms are concerned only with purchasing activities; many production plants have a production process with exclusively fabrication operations; most manufacturing firms are not involved directly with distribution operations; and so on.

In order to prescribe a production-inventory support system to a firm, it is imperative to resolve two basic issues related to the product structure.

What elements are present in the product structure of the firm, and what degree of complexity is involved in making the corresponding purchasing, production, and distribution decisions? To answer these questions we will propose a classification of logistics systems based on the product structure and the logistics activities undertaken by the firm.

How can we aggregate the final items produced and distributed by the firm, which may amount to several thousands, so that proper planning and control procedures are defined? This question will be answered by suggesting a classification scheme based on the product structure characteristics.

1.5.1 Types of Production-Inventory Systems

To deal systematically with the first issue raised, it is useful to classify the production-inventory systems into four categories that are suggested by the types of activities the firm is engaged in (Buffa and Taubert [1972], Buffa and Miller [1979], and Johnson and Montgomery [1974]).

1. *Pure inventory systems*. Pure inventory systems represent the simplest form of decision support systems in the logistics field. They are normally used whenever there is only a procurement activity, with no production or complex distribution interactions. They are applicable to raw material purchasing

decisions, and simple retail or wholesale operations when items are purchased from outside vendors.

A comprehensive discussion of pure inventory systems is conducted in Chapter 4.

2. *Continuous production systems.* Continuous production systems normally involve the manufacturing of a few families of technologically related products in large quantities through fixed routings. In those cases it becomes economically desirable to design and lay out a special facility dedicated exclusively to the manufacturing of those products. The resulting facility is called a *fabrication line*, if the production process involves fabrication; or an *assembly line,* if it involves assembly.

Balancing the production capacities of the various stages of the production line represents the central problem of continuous systems. This is the issue discussed in section 5.4 of this book.

3. *Intermittent production systems.* Intermittent production systems are usually present when the manufacturing function involves batch production of many products which share several processing centers. Machines are time-shared among many different items being switched from one product to another according to some pattern governed by the demand process, the technology of manufacturing, and the relevant economic factors.

Normally, the decision support systems dealing with intermittent production are composed of two different planning stages: an aggregate capacity planning effort (which is discussed in Chapter 3), and a detailed job shop scheduling effort (which is addressed in section 5.2). The integration of these planning stages is the subject of Chapter 6.

4. *Project management.* A special, and important, case of intermittent systems is the project management system, where the production effort is done infrequently, often only once. In general, project management involves the coordination of a large number of complex items that must be scheduled according to specified precedence requirements in order to minimize cost, minimize the total project completion time, or achieve a logical tradeoff between these two objectives.

Section 5.3 is dedicated to reviewing the methodology pertaining to project management.

Except for issues pertaining to facilities design (Chapter 2) and comments regarding diagnostic questions (Chapter 7), we will not deal formally in this book with the integration of production and distribution systems.

1.5.2 Aggregation of Items

Another critical question that can be resolved by analyzing the product structure of the firm is related to ways in which individual items can be aggregated into families or types for purposes of aggregate capacity planning.

Proper aggregation of information is of crucial importance in the design of hierarchical production-inventory systems.

This issue will be first addressed in Chapter 3, and more formally explored in Chapter 6.

1.6   The Diagnostic Process

Most of the work reported in the production and inventory management literature is heavily biased toward a problem-solving approach, often with a quantitative, model-based orientation. A long and sustained effort in this direction has resulted in remarkable accomplishments, making production one of the most mature managerial functions. Most of our book is devoted to reviewing this work.

However, we feel our book would be incomplete if we were not to cover an equally significant issue for problem solving, that of problem identification. We believe that what really distinguishes a good production management practitioner from a naive one is the ability to recognize what are the meaningful areas in which to concentrate managerial attention. This is the essence of the diagnostic process, which demands a new perspective from which to look at production and inventory issues because the methodology available for problem solving is not appropriate for diagnostic purposes. We need simpler tools, smaller models, more aggregate and less data-hungry, to support diagnostic exploratory analyses. Chapter 7 reports on an actual diagnostic study, which we believe represents a contribution to this field.

BIBLIOGRAPHY

ANTHONY, R. N., *Planning and Control Systems: A Framework for Analysis*, Harvard University Press, Cambridge, Mass., 1965.

BUFFA, E. S. and J. G. MILLER, *Production-Inventory Systems: Planning and Control*, Irwin, Homewood, Ill., 1979

BUFFA, E. S. and W. H. TAUBERT, *Production-Inventory Systems: Planning and Control*, Irwin, Homewood, Ill., 1972.

HAX, A. C., "The Design of Large Scale Logistics Systems: A Survey and an Approach," in W. Marlow (editor), *Modern Trends in Logistics Research*, M.I.T. Press, Cambridge, Mass., 1976, pp. 59–96.

JOHNSON, A. J. and D. C. MONTGOMERY, *Operations Research in Production Planning, Scheduling, and Inventory Control*, Wiley, New York, 1974.

2

Facilities Design

2.1 Introduction

This chapter treats the facilities design problem as the problem of determining the number, sizes, and locations of the facilities that a firm needs in order to serve its markets. The most common objective used in the design of the whole system is to minimize the total cost of transportation within the system, and the cost of setting up and operating the facilities. The solution to the problem must also specify the flow between all relevant points in the system. The facilities can be as varied as plants, distribution centers (warehouses), departments in an organization, telephone exchanges, and so on, and the flow can carry material goods, documents, electrical signals, services, and so on. In order to be specific, this chapter treats problems related to systems for the production and distribution of material goods; in general, however, problem formulations and solution methods encountered in this context have a wider range of applicability.

The primary objective of this chapter is to develop an understanding of the types of mathematical models that are available to help managers with the facilities design problem. Prior to providing a formulation of the problem, it is important to single out some of its characteristics that influence significantly the problem representation.

1. *Exclusion of strategic as well as operational decisions*. The facilities design problem does not include either high-level strategic decisions (such as policy formulation and definition of product line) or low-level operational decisions (such as inventory replenishment rules, detailed vehicular scheduling, data processing and order filling systems, etc.). These issues are left outside the

analysis because:

- They require decision variables, constraints, information, and timing that are different from those used in the basic sizing and location problem; the inclusion of these additional considerations would make the formulation extremely complex and computationally infeasible.
- The formalization of high-level strategic decisions is still not developed to the point where they could be satisfactorily included in a mathematical model. However, proper sensitivity analyses conducted with the type of models to be described herein for the facilities design problem can clearly contribute to a better understanding of the impact of strategic decisions.

2. *Explosive combinatorial nature of the problem.* Normally, the number of alternatives to be considered in deciding location of facilities and allocation of the flow of goods from those facilities to customer areas is so large that an exhaustive examination of those alternatives is out of the question. For instance, if a problem with 10 plants, 20 products, 50 possible distribution center sites, and 100 customer areas is considered, there are 1 million feasible product–plant–warehouse–customer combinations to be analyzed. Therefore, models can play an important role in improving managers' abilities to deal with such explosive problems.

3. *Long planning horizons.* The impact of a facilities design decision could be felt several years into the future. This forces long planning horizons to be part of an effective model formulation, which can capture the dynamic implications of the decision. Two approaches have been pursued in dealing with this aspect: one in which the dynamic implications are explicitly recognized, and another in which a "snapshot" view of the problem is taken. With the former approach, a long planning horizon is divided into multiple periods and an appropriate measure of performance, such as the net present value (Klein and Klimpel [1967]), or the total discounted cost (Ballou [1973], Wesolowsky and Truscott [1975]) is optimized based on forecasts for demands, selling prices, requirements, and operating costs, subject to the constraint that demands should be met throughout the planning horizon. Allowance can be made for the possibility of expanding, closing, or opening new facilities over the length of the planning horizon. With the latter approach, the model contains only a single period representation. The dynamic implications are analyzed by repeatedly solving one-period models, covering a desired planning horizon. Every one-period model represents the conditions predicted to prevail at that particular time period, including opening of new facilities or closing of old ones. A sequence of period-by-period snapshots can provide alternative scenarios for a subsequent dynamic analysis that would encompass the corresponding multiperiod planning horizon.

The vast majority of the literature adopts the snapshot view of the problem because of four important reasons:

- In multiperiod models inventories provide the fundamental linking between consecutive time periods (see Chapter 3). In the facilities design problem, however, a time period has a length of one or more years and, therefore, inventories lose this linking attribute. For instance, it is hard to conceive that a manager would start stockpiling inventories in one year only because the available forecast shows a likely surge in demand in a subsequent year. Hence, the problem itself loses much of the dynamic features that warrant the use of complex and costly models.
- The severe uncertainties that affect the forecasts needed in building a multiperiod model make the usefulness of the dynamic approach questionable.
- The difficulty of obtaining the necessary data and computational difficulties brought about by the size of the problem prohibit considering the dynamic aspect.
- The snapshot approach, as mentioned earlier, still allows for a dynamic treatment.

2.1.1   A Simple Model Formulation

As a way of completing our introductory discussion to the facilities design problem, let us present the mathematical formulation of a simplified version of such a problem: one dealing with a single product and a one-stage distribution process. The problem can be formulated as follows:

$$\text{Minimize} \qquad Z = \sum_{i=1}^{m} f_i Y_i + \sum_{i=1}^{m} \sum_{j=1}^{n} c_{ij} X_{ij} \qquad (2.1)$$

subject to:

$$\sum_{i=1}^{m} X_{ij} = d_j \qquad\qquad j = 1,\dots,n \qquad (2.2)$$

$$\sum_{j=1}^{n} X_{ij} \leqslant Y_i \sum_{j=1}^{n} d_j \qquad i = 1,\dots,m \qquad (2.3)$$

$$X_{ij} \geqslant 0 \qquad\qquad \begin{cases} i = 1,\dots,m \\ j = 1,\dots,n \end{cases} \qquad (2.4)$$

$$Y_i = 0,1 \qquad\qquad i = 1,\dots,m, \qquad (2.5)$$

where:

c_{ij} = the cost of supplying one unit of merchandise from warehouse site i $(i = 1,2,\dots,m)$ to customer j $(j = 1,2,\dots,n)$; c_{ij} may include the unit operating cost at warehouse i

Y_i = the $0-1$ variable that takes on a value of 1 if the decision is made to open a warehouse at site i, and a value of 0 otherwise

f_i = the fixed cost associated with opening a warehouse at site i
X_{ij} = the level of material flow from warehouse at site i to customer j
d_j = the demand of customer j over the time span of the analysis.

Constraints (2.2) state that the demands of all customers have to be met no matter from which warehouse(s); constraints (2.3) merely show that if no warehouse is opened at site i then no flow can take place between site i and any of the customers' locations. If, on the other hand, a warehouse is opened at site i, constraint (2.3) will be nonbinding since in no case can the flow from site i to all customers be larger than the sum of their demands. A capacity constraint might be added in equation (2.3) if so needed, in which case the term $\sum_{j=1}^{N} d_j$ should be replaced by k_i, the total capacity available at warehouse i.

Although model (2.1)–(2.5) is simple in that it handles only one product in a one-stage distribution system (warehouse $\rightarrow$ customer), it is, however, of a general nature in that it involves making decisions on both important aspects of the facilities design issue: the location aspect (where to put the new facilities) and the allocation aspect (what should be the item movement associated with every warehouse–customer pair)—(2.1)–(2.5) is thus called a location–allocation problem.

In the sections that follow, a broader picture and basic formulations of the facilities design problem is presented; solution procedures are provided and discussed for some of the models, and references are indicated for all.

2.2   Issues and Assumptions in Modeling the Facilities Design Problem

In general, the facilities design problem is broader than what was implied by the definition and illustration of section 2.1. There, a *macro* view of the system was offered. At a *micro* level, one would consider more detailed aspects such as the location of departments in a building, of machines in a shop, of merchandise in a warehouse, and so on. This is known as the *facility layout problem*.

A variety of different problems can be formulated in the area of facilities design. Depending on the assumptions made and on the specific issues addressed, the characteristics of the resulting models and the methodologies used in solving them can vary a great deal. Thus, it is useful to develop a framework to classify the various types of facilities design problems. The most important dimensions of this framework are:

- the nature of the set of possible facility locations (continuous or discrete)
- the optimization criterion to use (minimization of total cost, maximization of benefits, or minimization of maximum distance)

- the nature of the problem (location, allocation, or location–allocation problem)
- the number of facilities to be located (single or multifacility problem)
- the number of distribution stages (one- or two-stage problem)
- the nature of capacity restrictions (uncapacitated or capacitated problem)
- the number of products distributed (single or multiproduct problem)

We will now analyze each one of these dimensions of the problem in more detail.

2.2.1 Nature of the Set of Possible Facility Locations

There are two opposite approaches that have been proposed regarding the nature of the possible facility locations: the *infinite set* or *continuous space* approach, and the *feasible set* or *discrete space* approach. The first allows for a facility to be located anywhere in the two-dimensional space, which is equivalent to considering an infinite number of possible sites. The second alternative limits the number of possible locations to a finite set of predetermined sites.

There are certain features associated with the two approaches just mentioned:

- The infinite set approach is more general in that it does not require a set of "attractive" locations to be prespecified. However, due to its general nature, it normally assumes that the transportation costs are proportional to distance (rectilinear, Euclidean, or squared Euclidean), and the optimal solution might call for opening a warehouse in some infeasible location, like the middle of a lake.
- The feasible set approach requires that a list of possible feasible location sites be provided, together with the associated costs. The costs can be much more realistic than with the infinite set approach in that they can be related to the specific geographical location of the contemplated sites, and the transportation costs do not have to be functions of distance. We believe the feasible set approach to be more appropriate for the majority of practical applications.

2.2.2 Optimization Criteria and Cost Structure

In most cases the optimization involves *minimizing* an objective function that can be:

- The total cost associated with building and operating the new facilities, and with supporting the item flow within the system.
- The sum of distances or times to be traveled by the item flow. The distance considered between two points can be: the rectilinear distance (when movement takes place parallel to the two axes that define the two-dimensional space) and

the Euclidean distance (straight-line distance) or the squared Euclidean distance.

- The number of facilities to be located.

Other cases involve *maximizing* an objective function (as in the partial covering problem—see section 2.4.2.2), while in other situations the *minimax* solution is sought (for instance, the placement of schools in a given residential area such that the maximum distance to be traveled by any student between home and school be minimized). Minimax formulations often occur when dealing with emergency facilities location, such as firehouses, police stations, hospitals, and so on.

2.2.3   *Nature of the Problem*

There are three generic types of problems associated with facilities design: the location problem, the allocation problem, and the location–allocation problem. In general, there could be existing facilities and new facilities to be located in desirable sites. A flow of goods (information, services, etc.) is provided from these facilities to predetermined customer areas. The allocation problem involves the determination of the best possible flow patterns from existing and/or new facilities to the customer areas.

It is customary to use the terms *interaction* or *interchange* to denote the transfer of goods among facilities, or between facilities and customer areas.

Table 2.1 presents a general taxonomy of the three types of problems mentioned above, pertaining to the facilities design. In addition to these, the facility layout problem constitutes a fourth type.

In what follows, a brief account is given of each type of problem. Further details are provided in subsequent sections.

(a)   The *location problem* deals with the question of where to locate new facilities, assuming that the transfer of flow of goods between them and the customer areas is known and given.

If the feasible set approach is used and there are no interactions between pairs of new facilities, the location problem generates an *assignment problem*. This problem is labeled *bottleneck assignment problem* when the objective is to minimize the maximum of some overall penalty. Whenever exchange of goods does exist between pairs of new facilities, a quadratic *assignment problem* results.

As mentioned previously, the use of the infinite set approach normally leads to the definition of cost functions which are functions of the distance between facilities and customer areas (Euclidean, rectilinear, or squared Euclidean distances).

(b)   The *allocation problem* assumes that the number and locations of all facilities are given, so that the only remaining issue is how to allocate the item movement to the existing routes linking the facilities. Models relevant to this topic are of the *transportation*, *transshipment*, and *network flow* type, which have been developed and treated extensively in the operations research literature. They will not be dealt with here, as they are beyond the scope of this chapter; some references that cover them include: Bradley, Hax, and Magnanti [1977, chap. 8], Wagner [1969, chaps. 6 and 7], Ford and Fulkerson [1962], Hu [1969], Magnanti and Golden [1978], and Christofides [1975].

The minimax version of the allocation problem is known as the *bottleneck transportation problem*.

(c)   In the *location–allocation problem* the number of facilities, their locations, and the amount of interaction with existing facilities and customer areas all become decision variables. Some representative models and solution methods will be treated in more detail in a subsequent section. We will mention at this point that by making some special assumptions the location–allocation problem leads into specific models that have received considerable attention:

- The *covering problem* (or *set covering problem*) considers *n* customers and *m* possible location sites for new facilities. Every customer should be covered by at least one new facility. It might be possible to cover a given customer from a given facility location. If the cost of locating a new facility is site-dependent, the objective would be the minimization of the *total cost* of constructing the required number of facilities. If the cost is site-invariant, the objective becomes one of minimizing the *total number* of facilities, and the problem is called the total covering problem. It is to be pointed out that there is no cost directly associated with the amount of interaction between the new facilities and the customers, nor is there any decision variable related to the level of those interactions and to the sizes of the facilities. However, the problem still contains the allocation aspect because the location solution will implicitly define which facility(ies) covers which customer(s). If it is desired that a customer be covered by exactly one new facility, rather than by at least one, the covering problem becomes a *partitioning problem*. It is more difficult, and sometimes impossible, to solve a partitioning rather than a covering problem.
- The *partial covering problem* deals with cases where it is not possible to set up enough facilities to "totally cover" all customers. Therefore, the objective becomes to locate the given number of new facilities in such a way as to cover the maximum number of customers. A variant of the partial covering problem is the problem in which at most a given number of facilities have to be opened such as to minimize the distances traveled by the customers, all customer demands having to be met.

(d)   The *facility layout problem* has been mentioned earlier as another type of facilities design problem. Arrangements of production shops and storerooms in a plant, of offices and departments in an administrative building, of various sorts of merchandise in a warehouse, of machine tools and other pieces of equipment in a fabrication shop, are all instances of the facility layout problem. It should be pointed out that while in plant or warehouse location problems the facilities are normally regarded as dimensionless points, in layout problems the facilities are considered as areas whose locations need to be determined. The facility layout problem is outside the scope of this book. The interested reader is directed to Francis and White [1974], Reed [1961, 1967], Muther [1955, 1961], Treson [1952], and Moore [1962] for a specialized treatment of this subject.

However, it is often the case that in some layout situations (e.g., the location of one or more new machines in a production shop, the assignment of rooms to various offices and divisions in a building, etc.), some less specialized models, such as those used for general facility location problems, would apply.

2.2.4   Number of Facilities to Be Located

The primary dichotomy to consider in the facilities design problem regarding the number of facilities to be located is single versus multiple facilities.

- *Single-facility* problems are normally location problems, since the allocation aspect is automatically taken care of by the uniqueness of the facility (it has to cover all customers with the type of services it provides). If, however, the situation calls for a partial covering formulation (to be seen later) the resulting problem becomes a location–allocation problem. This problem would also arise in cases where there already exist several other facilities of the same specialization as the facility in question, and along with locating the new facility a reassignment of customers to all facilities would be contemplated.
- *Multifacility* problems can result in both location and location–allocation models.

2.2.5   Number of Distribution Stages

The largest majority of the models include only one stage of distribution: *warehouse* → *customer*. A greater generality is achieved when a two-stage system is considered (of course, if the real situation warrants such a model): *plant* → *warehouse* → *customer*.

2.2.6   Capacity Restrictions

The vast majority of the models reported in the literature are *uncapacitated*, explainable in part by the computational difficulties already inherent in the 0–1 programs associated with the location or location–allocation problems. *Capacities* can be imposed, in the more general case, at plant level, warehouse level, or upon the transportation channels, with due increase in model complexity, but with a substantial gain in the model representation.

2.2.7   Number of Products Being Distributed

In many cases there is only a *single product* handled by the system. More realism is added when *multiproducts* are considered, at the expense of added computational difficulty.

2.3   General Discrete Location–Allocation Problems

From the discussion on the issues and assumptions of the facilities design modeling it is obvious that a large number of models can be conceived. Of these, the discrete location–allocation problem deserves special attention due to its versatility and appropriateness in describing the majority of plant and warehouse location problems encountered in practice.

It should be mentioned that the finite set approach also parallels the most general managerial practice. In locating new facilities, like plants or warehouses, a number of requirements have to be observed, such as geographical and infrastructure conditions, natural resource and labor availabilities, distance to potential markets, local industry and tax regulations, competitive conditions, and public interests. Normally, there are a limited number of locations that would meet all the requirements reasonably well, thus becoming potential location sites for the new facilities.

TABLE 2.1   Modeling the Facilities Design Problem

APPROACH	NATURE OF PROBLEM	TYPES OF PROBLEMS	NUMBER OF FACILITIES TO BE LOCATED
Feasible Set Approach (discrete space formulations)	Location problems	General location problems Assignment problems Quadratic assignment problems	Multifacility problems
		Minimax location problems Bottleneck assignment problems	Single-facility problems Multifacility problems
	Allocation problems	Transportation problems Transshipment problems Network flow problems Bottleneck (minimax transportation problems)	Multifacility problems
	Location–allocation problems	General location–allocation problems Covering problems Partitioning problems Total covering problems Partial covering problems Minimax location–allocation problems	Multifacility problems
Infeasible Set Approach (continuous space formulations)	Location problems	Euclidean—distance problems Rectilinear—distance problems Squared Euclidean—distance problems	Single–facility problems Multifacility problems with prespecified number of new facilities
	Location–allocation problems	Euclidean—distance problems Rectilinear—distance problems Squared Euclidean—distance problems	Multifacility problems with prespecified number of new facilities

Of the location–allocation models listed in Table 2.1 under the discrete space formulations, we will treat only the general problem in this section. The other problem types will be addressed in a later section.

2.3.1 Features and Formulations

The simplest case of a location–allocation problem in discrete space has been presented as model (2.1)–(2.5) and will be repeated here for convenience:

Minimize
$$Z = \sum_{i=1}^{m} f_i Y_i + \sum_{i=1}^{m} \sum_{j=1}^{n} c_{ij} X_{ij} \qquad (2.1)$$

subject to:

$$\sum_{i=1}^{m} X_{ij} = d_j \qquad\qquad j = 1, \ldots, n \qquad (2.2)$$

$$\sum_{j=1}^{n} X_{ij} \leqslant Y_i \sum_{j=1}^{n} d_j \qquad i = 1, \ldots, m \qquad (2.3)$$

$$X_{ij} \geqslant 0 \qquad \begin{cases} i = 1, \ldots, m \\ j = 1, \ldots, n \end{cases} \qquad (2.4)$$

$$Y_i = 0, 1 \qquad\qquad i = 1, \ldots, m. \qquad (2.5)$$

The problem requires that an unspecified number of facilities, limited only by the number of available sites, be located among m possible (or feasible) sites in order to supply n customers. The decision to locate a facility at site i is associated with a fixed charge f_i and a cost c_{ij} of supplying one unit of merchandise to customer j. A total minimum cost design is desired.

This is considered to be a simple model because it handles only a single product in an uncapacitated one-stage (warehouse → customer) distribution system, under a cost function which is linear with the exception of the discontinuity (fixed charge) at the origin.

Certainly, to make the model more realistic, a number of additional features should be included, if possible, into the formulation. At the same time, the resulting model should lend itself to solution by some reasonably efficient computational technique. These issues, analyzed by Geoffrion [1975] and Geoffrion, Graves, and Lee [1978], are discussed in the next sections.

2.3.1.1 Features to Be Modeled

1. *Multiple products* are often necessary to be modeled since in most situations several products or product groups are made and distributed. When they share the available production or distribution capacities, it becomes necessary to treat them explicitly in the model.

2.   *Two stages of distribution*: *plants* → *warehouses* → *customers*, *with the preservation of the identity of the plant where the shipment originated*. Since large firms normally utilize distribution centers (or warehouses) between plants and customers, it is useful to build two-stage models in order to achieve a more realistic representation of this situation. Also, when the price or demand structure depends upon the identity of the originating plant, or when the total transit time from plant to customer in the case of deteriorating merchandise should be controlled, it becomes necessary to build into the model the capability of keeping track of the plant origin of transit commodities all the way to the customer.

Modeling 1 and 2

Notations:

subscript i specifies the plant, $i = 1, \ldots, I$
subscript j denotes the warehouse location site, $j = 1, \ldots, J$
subscript k specifies the customer area, $k = 1, \ldots, K$
subscript l specifies the product, $l = 1, \ldots, L$
X_{ijkl} = amount of product l shipped from plant i to customer k via the warehouse location at j
c_{ijkl} = cost of supplying one unit of x_{ijkl}
d_{kl} = customer k's demand for product l.

The new formulation is:

Minimize
$$Z = \sum_j f_j Y_j + \sum_i \sum_j \sum_k \sum_l c_{ijkl} X_{ijkl} \tag{2.6}$$

subject to:

$$\sum_i \sum_j X_{ijkl} = d_{kl} \qquad \begin{cases} k = 1, \ldots, K \\ l = 1, \ldots, L \end{cases} \tag{2.7}$$

$$\sum_i \sum_k X_{ijkl} \leqslant Y_j \sum_k d_{kl} \qquad \begin{cases} j = 1, \ldots, J \\ l = 1, \ldots, L \end{cases} \tag{2.8}$$

$$X_{ijkl} \geqslant 0 \qquad \begin{cases} i = 1, \ldots, I \\ j = 1, \ldots, J \\ l = 1, \ldots, L \end{cases} \tag{2.9}$$

$$Y_j = 0, 1 \qquad j = 1, \ldots, J. \tag{2.10}$$

3.   *Productive capacity limits for plants and size limits for warehouses.* Lower and upper bounds for plant or warehouse size are useful in ensuring that the assumed cost structure will be a reasonable representation of the reality. Indeed, below a certain operating level the existence of the facility

might be unjustified, while above a given threshold major changes, like an expansion or the opening of a new facility, might be required.

Modeling 3

Notations:

P_{il} = maximum capacity available for the production of product l at plant i

$\overline{W}_j$ = maximum allowed throughput for a warehouse at site j

$\underline{W}_j$ = minimum allowed throughput for a warehouse at site j.

Two sets of constraints will have to be appended to model (2.6)–(2.10):

$$\sum_j \sum_k X_{ijkl} \leqslant P_{il} \qquad \begin{cases} i = 1,\ldots,I \\ l = 1,\ldots,L \end{cases} \qquad (2.11)$$

$$\underline{W}_j Y_j \leqslant \sum_i \sum_k \sum_l X_{ijkl} \leqslant \overline{W}_j Y_j \qquad j = 1,\ldots,J. \qquad (2.12)$$

The left-hand side of (2.11) is the total output of product l at plant i; constraints (2.12) state that the total throughput of warehouse at location j can be nonzero if and only if a warehouse has been opened at site j ($Y_j = 1$). Evidently, in the presence of (2.12), constraints (2.8) are no longer needed.

4.   *Two stages of distribution*: *plants* → *warehouses* → *customers*, *without preserving the identity of the plant where the merchandise originated.*

Modeling 4

Notations:

Z_{ijl} = amount of product l shipped from plant i to the warehouse located at site j

X_{jkl} = amount of product l supplied to customer k by the warehouse at site j

d_{ijl} = cost of supplying one unit of Z_{ijl}

c_{jkl} = cost of supplying one unit of X_{jkl}.

In the formulation (2.6)–(2.10), constraints (2.7) and (2.8) have to be replaced by:

$$\sum_j X_{jkl} = d_{kl} \qquad j = 1,\ldots,J \qquad (2.13)$$

$$\sum_k X_{jkl} = \sum_i Z_{ijl} \qquad \begin{cases} j = 1,\ldots,J \\ l = 1,\ldots,L \end{cases} \qquad (2.14)$$

$$\sum_k X_{jkl} \leqslant Y_j \sum_k d_{kl} \qquad \begin{cases} j = 1,\ldots,J \\ l = 1,\ldots,L, \end{cases} \qquad (2.15)$$

and the appropriate nonnegativity constraints will also be required. Constraints (2.14) state that the warehouse at site j neither piles up inventory nor produces commodity l; rather, it distributes to customers all available amounts of product l received from the supplying plants. By (2.15), if no warehouse is open at site j ($Y_j = 0$), no customers are served from j; also, by (2.14), no deliveries from plants to site j can take place. The objective function (2.6) has to be replaced by

Minimize $$\sum_i f_i Y_i + \sum_i \sum_j \sum_l d_{ijl} Z_{ijl} + \sum_j \sum_k \sum_l c_{jkl} X_{jkl}$$

5. *Each customer served by a single warehouse.* In many cases it is advantageous for the distributing firm to service each customer from a single warehouse in order to simplify accounting and marketing, and to achieve economies of scale in transportation. Such a practice is also to the advantage of the customer, who would have to deal with only one supply center for all his needs in one or several lines of products.

Modeling 5

A binary variable V_{jk} will be introduced and defined as follows:

$$V_{jk} = \begin{cases} 1 & \text{if customer } k \text{ is assigned to the warehouse located at site } j \\ 0 & \text{otherwise} \end{cases}$$

In formulation (2.6)–(2.10) constraints (2.7) are replaced by:

$$\sum_i X_{ijkl} = d_{kl} V_{jk} \qquad \begin{cases} j = 1, \ldots, J \\ k = 1, \ldots, K \\ l = 1, \ldots, L. \end{cases} \tag{2.16}$$

Obviously, additional constraints should be imposed to ensure that each customer is assigned to one warehouse only:

$$\sum_j V_{jk} = 1 \qquad k = 1, \ldots, K. \tag{2.17}$$

6. *Various desired constraints on the distribution system configuration.*

6a. *Minimum service levels.* Service consideration could be of utmost importance in defining constraints in the configuration of distribution facilities. Very often it is mandatory to reach prescribed customer areas within a specified time limit to assume a satisfactory service level. It might also be desirable to limit the traveling time of some specific commodities which are subject to deterioration.

Modeling 6a

One approach to enforce a minimum level of service for a given customer area k is to require that all warehouses serving that area should be located within a maximum acceptable distance $\bar{t}_k$. Let t_{jk} be the distance between the potential site of warehouse j and the customer area k. The service constraint can be expressed as follows:

$$\sum_i \sum_j X_{ijk} \frac{t_{jk}}{d_{kl}} \leqslant \bar{t}_k \qquad \begin{cases} k = 1, \ldots, K \\ l = 1, \ldots, J. \end{cases} \tag{2.18}$$

Notice that if there is only one warehouse j supplying product to customer area k, then

$$\sum_i X_{ijkl} = d_{kl}$$

and (2.18) merely forces the distance between j and k to be within the prescribed radius, that is,

$$t_{jk} \leqslant \bar{t}_k.$$

Whenever there is more than one warehouse serving area k, the right-hand side of (2.18) can be interpreted as a weighted average of the distance from all active warehouses to customer area k.

If we would like to prevent any shipment from any location j to a customer k outside the allowable distance $\bar{t}_k$, we can make use of the acceptability coefficients a_{jk}:

$$a_{jk} = \begin{cases} 1 & \text{if } t_{jk} \leqslant \bar{t}_k \\ 0 & \text{if } t_{jk} > \bar{t}_k. \end{cases} \qquad \begin{cases} j = 1, \ldots, J \\ k = 1, \ldots, K \end{cases}$$

The following constraints

$$\sum_i X_{ijkl} \leqslant a_{jk} d_{kl} \qquad \begin{cases} j = 1, \ldots, J \\ k = 1, \ldots, K \\ l = 1, \ldots, L \end{cases} \tag{2.19}$$

will guarantee that nothing can be shipped from j to k if $t_{jk} > \bar{t}_k$. For those (j, k) pairs for which $a_{jk} = 1$, constraint (2.19) merely states that the shipment from location j to customer k cannot exceed the customer's total demand. Finally, whenever each customer is being served by a single warehouse, the service constraint can simply be stated as:

$$\sum_j t_{jk} V_{jk} \leqslant \bar{t}_k \qquad k = 1, \ldots, K,$$

the variable V_{jk} being 1 if customer k is served from warehouse at site j; and 0, otherwise.

In all the above expressions the terms t_{jk} and $\bar{t}_k$ can be interpreted as traveling time rather than distances.

Modeling 6b   *Upper and lower bounds on the number of warehouses to be opened.*

If $\underline{N}$ and $\overline{N}$ denote, respectively, the lower and upper bounds for the number of warehouses, the following additional constraint should be introduced:

$$\underline{N} \leqslant \sum_i Y_i \leqslant \overline{N}. \qquad (2.20)$$

6c.   *Subsets of location sites where at least one (or at most one) warehouse should operate.*

Modeling 6c

Let S be a subset of location sites where at least one warehouse should be opened; then:

$$\sum_{i \in S} Y_i \geqslant 1 \qquad (2.21)$$

would impose this constraint. The reserved inequality ($\leqslant$) would ensure that at most one warehouse will be operated.

Although the features discussed in this section represent some of the most important and useful elements to be considered in the formulation of a facilities design model, they by no means exhaust all the important characteristics of the problems encountered in practice. Occasionally, it might be desirable to enrich the objective function representation incorporating economies of scale and other nonlinearities.* A more general distribution structure might be appropriate to characterize additional stages of the production–distribution process. It could be important to take into account changes in the demand pattern through a given year, due to promotional and seasonality effects. All of those additional features can also be incorporated in the model formulation, at the price of increasing both data collection and computational costs.

2.3.1.2 Features Normally Excluded from Model Formulation

1.   *Multiple time periods.* With a few exceptions, as mentioned in section (2.1), most models are one-period models based on the "snapshot" approach.

2.   *Alternative modes of transportation and different unit rates that apply to shipments of different weights and composition.* The best transportation mode is normally considered, and weighted averages for each product and each route (computed externally to the location–allocation model) are used as shipment rates.

3.   *Simultaneous consideration of plant location, plant expansions, and warehouse location problems.* Although two-stage location–allocation problems take the plants into consideration, it is not the plant location or expansion

---

*Economies of scale can be approximated by a piecewise linear function to any degree of accuracy. The formulation, however, forces additional integer variables to be introduced which expand the computational difficulty of the resulting model (see Bradley, Hax, and Magnanti [1977, chap. 13.5]).

problem which is addressed; rather, the plants are fixed and given, and are looked upon only as supply sources. A plant location and investment problem is a strategic issue, given the size of the capital investment required as well as the normally long economic life of a plant. A warehouse location problem is more on a tactical level. It is recommended that these two issues be approached separately to avoid the joint treatment of strategic and tactical decisions (see Anthony [1965] and Hax [1976]).

4.   *Treatment of uncertainties.* The rather long planning horizon normally associated with a facility location problem brings the uncertainties of the relevant parameters into the picture. All of the formulations presented before contain no stochastic parameters; however, they are already computationally complex problems. An attempt to incorporate uncertainties directly into the location problem formulation would most likely preclude finding a feasible solution procedure. Therefore, under these circumstances, the overall problem is normally decomposed into two problems:

(a)   the location–allocation problem solved under the certainty assumption
(b)   the optimal solution, or several "good" solutions provided by (a) then treated as investment problems under uncertainty in order to assess their profitability (Hax and Wiig [1976], Candea, Hax and Karmarkar [1978])

Figure 2.1 gives a graphical description of the approach just described.

5.   *Inventory cost, and data processing and communication costs.* Figure 2.2 gives a qualitative picture of the major categories of costs as functions of the number of warehouses in the distribution system. The inventory cost, the freight cost, and the data processing and communication cost are nonlinear and depend on the distribution system configuration, degree of centralization, and nature of the inventory replenishment policies. Although these costs are not included in the location–allocation model formulation, they should be computed "a posteriori" and added to the cost of the solution produced by the model, thus enabling the analyst to get an estimate of the overall cost of the contemplated distribution system design.

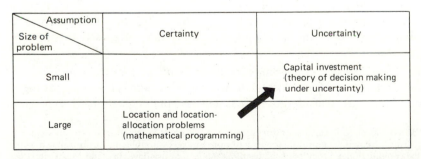

Size of problem ╲ Assumption	Certainty	Uncertainty
Small		Capital investment (theory of decision making under uncertainty)
Large	Location and location-allocation problems (mathematical programming)	

FIGURE 2.1   A two-step approach in solving facilities design problems under uncertainty.

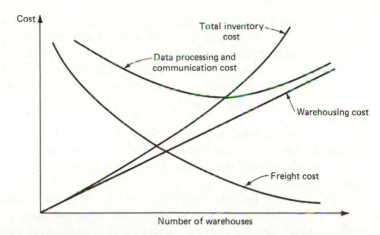

FIGURE 2.2   Qualitative picture of major categories of costs as functions of number of warehouses in distribution system.

2.3.2   Computational Methods

Geoffrion [1975] considers that a computational method has to satisfy three requirements in order to be fully acceptable:

1. *It should be an optimizing method* for important reasons:

   - To prevent missing important opportunities for savings.
   - To permit answering "what if...?" questions, in order to rank various scenarios posed by the user; clearly, nonoptimizing methods make it meaningless to attempt comparative runs.
   - In case of data input errors, optimizing methods lend themselves better to tracking down the sources of error.

2. *It should require moderate computer costs.*
3. *It should be fast, reliable, and easy to use in order to permit repeated secondary optimization runs.* The secondary runs are necessary to answer "what if...?" questions, to perform sensitivity analysis, and so on.

A large number of solution procedures and computer packages to solve location–allocation problems exist, and some will be presented below within the following framework:

- general mixed integer linear programming computer codes
- specialized branch-and-bound procedures
- Benders decomposition approach
- heuristics
- simulation

There were some early approaches that fall under none of the above categories, in that they tried to derive approximate formulations solvable by linear programming rather than solving the problem under the original formulation. Thus, Balinski and Mills [1960] linearize the problem; they replace the piecewise linear warehousing cost function (which has a fixed charge at the origin) with the average unit cost of operating the facility at some high level. This high level is either the upper bound on the warehouse throughput, or the total flow of merchandise through the system, whichever is smaller. In this way a transportation problem is obtained, which is simple to solve; the solution to the transportation problem is a lower bound to the original problem.

Prior to the Balinski and Mills model, the Baumol and Wolfe [1958] approximation technique was published. They treat one product in a two-stage (plant → warehouse → customer) distribution system, with upper bounds on warehouse sizes. Their cost function is strictly concave with a fixed cost at the origin. The algorithm is an iterative procedure that solves a transportation problem at each stage. The transportation solution sets a tentative operation level for the warehouses, at which level the warehousing concave cost functions are approximated by their derivatives, and the transportation costs are modified accordingly. The algorithm does not guarantee optimality; also, although the assumed cost function permits a fixed charge for every warehouse, the algorithm does not appear to handle these fixed costs.

While only of historical interest, the above techniques have been mentioned in order to provide a better picture of the difficulties posed by the location–allocation problems, as well as to point to the considerable progress that has been made in this area to the extent that "a point has now been reached where almost any one or two stage distribution system, no matter how large, can be dealt with effectively" (Geoffrion et al. [1978]).

2.3.2.1 General Mixed Integer Linear Programming Computer Codes

Every major computer company offers some mixed integer programming (MIP) code, of which the following are well known: IBM's MPSX-MIP, CDC's OPHELIE, and Univac's UMPIRE (for a survey, see Geoffrion and Marsten [1972]).

Among the advantages of using such a code are the following:

- They are readily available.
- They offer great flexibility in handling fixed costs, economies of scale, and constraints involving integer variables (such as the requirement that every customer be served by one and only one warehouse).

But they are too general to be efficient enough; they cannot take advantage of the special structure of the location–allocation problems, so that their performance is likely to be about two orders of magnitude worse than the performance of the best specialized codes (Geoffrion [1975, p. 31]). Also, the number of integer variables that can be handled effectively is small (a few dozen) and, because of computer time and memory bounds (they all use branch-and-bound), true optimality is rarely achieved; rather, a certain degree of suboptimization is usually accepted, as defined by the difference between some lower bound and the best available solution. To conclude, it has to be mentioned that general codes require the development of matrix generators and report writers; also, the user should be experienced enough with the specific MIP code in order to take best advantage of the various user options provided.

2.3.2.2 Specialized Branch-and-Bound Procedures

Branch-and-bound (see Bradley, Hax, and Magnanti [1977, chap. 9.6]) is an enumerative algorithm that searches the set of all possible integer solutions, without having to consider all of them individually. The key idea is to partition the original problem into subproblems; each subproblem constitutes a node of the enumeration tree. At each node a relaxation of the subproblem is solved (usually a linear programming relaxation). Depending on the solution, one of two decisions can be reached at a node:

- The node is *fathomed* — the search at that node should not go deeper into the tree. This occurs when the optimal solution to the original problem has been found (and the search stops completely), or when there are indications that by continuing from the fathomed node either no feasible solution may be found or, even if it were found, it would be no better than the best integer solution available so far. The search will have to go over to another node not fathomed so far.
- The node is not fathomed — the search will continue along some branch emanating from the nonfathomed node.

The existence of binary variables associated with the fixed cost in location–allocation problems makes the use of branch-and-bound appropriate. A number of papers have been published on this approach. Some address the uncapacitated problem (Efroymson and Ray [1966], Khumawala [1972], Atkins and Shriver [1968], Spielberg [1969a, 1969b], and Erlenkotter [1978]), while other papers like Davis and Ray [1969], Soland [1974], and Akinc and Khumawala [1977] treat the problem with upper bound constraints on the warehouse throughput.

The balance of this section will present the algorithms of Efroymson and Ray, and Khumawala as an illustration of the application of branch-and-bound methods to the location–allocation problem.

The formulation Efroymson and Ray started with is a slightly changed version of formulation (2.1)–(2.5) given earlier, obtained by making the following transformation of variables:

$$X'_{ij} = \frac{X_{ij}}{d_j} \qquad \begin{cases} i = 1, \ldots, m \\ j = 1, \ldots, n. \end{cases}$$

Maximize
$$Z = \sum_{i=1}^{m} f_i Y_i + \sum_{i=1}^{m} \sum_{j=1}^{n} c'_{ij} X'_{ij} \tag{2.22}$$

subject to:

$$\sum_{i=1}^{m} X'_{ij} = 1 \qquad\qquad j = 1, \ldots, n \tag{2.23}$$

$$0 \leqslant X'_{ij} \leqslant Y_i \qquad\qquad \begin{cases} i = 1, \ldots, m \\ j = 1, \ldots, n \end{cases} \tag{2.24}$$

$$Y_i = 0, 1 \qquad\qquad i = 1, \ldots, m, \tag{2.25}$$

where:

X'_{ij} = the fraction of customer j's demand supplied from the warehouse at site i

$c'_{ij} = c_{ij} d_j$ = the cost of supplying the entire demand of customer j from the warehouse at site i.

Branch-and-bound can be applied directly to (2.22)–(2.25) by branching on the values of Y_i and solving a linear program at every node. Clearly, the first step is to solve (2.22)–(2.25) as a linear program with all Y_i's continuous variables and such that $0 \leqslant Y_i \leqslant 1$. If the solution has all Y_i's integral, then the problem is solved; otherwise, the search would have to be continued by branching deeper into the tree.

Since Y_i is binary, two branches would diverge from a node; that is, at every node one location site i is selected whose Y_i is neither 0 nor 1. One of the branches leaving the node would consider that a warehouse is open at site i, hence $Y_i = 1$; the other branch would assume that no warehouse exists at site i, or $Y_i = 0$. The value of Y_i may not be changed after leaving the decision node and going deeper into the search tree.

The linear program solved at each node observes the values of those Y variables that have been set either to zero or 1 at higher level nodes; all other Y's are constrained to lie within the interval $[0, 1]$.

A reformulation of (2.22)–(2.25) permits avoiding solving the linear program at every node by means of the simplex method; rather, after the reformulation the solution is immediate by simple inspection.

At some node in the branch-and-bound tree the set of indices of Y's can be partitioned into three subsets:

$K_1 = \{i: Y_i = 1\} = $ set of location sites where a facility is open,

$K_0 = \{i: Y_i = 0\} = $ set of location sites where no facility is open,

$K_2 = \{i: Y_i \text{ unassigned}\} = $ set of location sites for which a decision is yet to be made. K_2 contains those location sites for which the linear programming solution produced fractional Y's.

Let P_i be the set of indices of those customers that can be supplied from facility site i; n_i is the number of elements in P_i. Let N_j be the set of indices of those facility sites that can supply customer j.

Formulation (2.22)–(2.25) becomes, then:

Minimize
$$Z = \sum_{i=1}^{m} f_i Y_i + \sum_{i=1}^{m} \sum_{j=1}^{n} c'_{ij} X'_{ij} \qquad (2.26)$$

subject to:

$$\sum_{i \in N_j} X'_{ij} = 1 \qquad\qquad j = 1,\ldots,n \qquad (2.27)$$

$$0 \leqslant \sum_{j \in P_i} X'_{ij} \leqslant n_i Y_i \qquad\qquad i = 1,\ldots,m \qquad (2.28)$$

$$Y_i = 0, 1 \qquad\qquad i = 1,\ldots,m. \qquad (2.29)$$

The optimal solution to the linear programming problem (2.26)–(2.29) with $0 \leqslant Y_i \leqslant 1$ can be proven to be:

$$
\begin{cases}
X'_{ij} = \begin{cases} 1 & \text{if } c'_{ij} + \dfrac{g_i}{n_i} = \min\limits_{k \in K_1 \cup K_2} \left[c'_{kj} + \dfrac{g_k}{n_k} \right] \\[2mm] 0 & \text{otherwise,} \end{cases} \\[8mm]
Y_i = \dfrac{\sum\limits_{j \in P_i} X'_{ij}}{n_i} \quad \text{if } i \in K_2,
\end{cases}
\qquad (2.30)
$$

where:

$$g_k = \begin{cases} f_k & \text{if } k \in K_2 \\ 0 & \text{if } k \in K_1. \end{cases}$$

The above solution is complete since:

$$X'_{ij} = 0 \quad \text{for } i \in K_0$$
$$Y_i = 1 \quad \text{for } i \in K_1 \text{ (by definition)}$$
$$Y_i = 0 \quad \text{for } i \in K_0 \text{ (by definition).}$$

Clearly, (2.30) is much more efficient than solving (2.22)–(2.25) by the simplex method, so that the entire tree search gains in efficiency.

The authors introduce three simplifications that can be used to speed up the algorithm by reducing the number of evaluations required to solve (2.26)–(2.29). Extensions are also provided to cover cases in which there is a variable cost at facility i related to the level of output (if the facility is a plant), or throughput (if it is a warehouse).

The computational experience reported in the paper shows an average computer time of about 10 minutes on an IBM 7094 for problems involving 50 location sites and 200 customers. According to the authors [p. 367], it appears that "the most difficult problem in computation is the storage of the terminal nodes."

Khumawala [1972] has developed and improved the branch-and-bound algorithm of Efroymson and Ray. Three kinds of efficiencies have been added.

(a) Efficient branching decision rules for selecting, at every node of the search tree, a yet unassigned warehouse to be constrained open and closed.
(b) An improved method for solving the linear program at each step of the branch-and-bound algorithm.
(c) Improvements in the computer code for the branch-and-bound algorithm, including increased efficiency in the use of computer storage.

Before the branching rules can be discussed, the following quantities will have to be defined:

- Let ∇_{ij} be the minimum cost savings for customer j that can be achieved if a warehouse is opened at site i, when considered over all nonclosed sites at that node of the branch-and-bound tree (nonclosed means either open or yet undecided upon):

$$\nabla_{ij} = \min_{\substack{k \in K_1 \cup K_2 \\ k \in N_j \\ k \neq i}} \left[\max(c'_{kj} - c'_{ij}, 0) \right], \quad i \in K_2, j \in P_i \qquad (2.31)$$

where all notations are the same as in the discussion on Efroymson and Ray's paper.

Compute:

$$\nabla_i = \sum_{j \in P_i} \Delta_{ij} - f_i, \quad i \in K_2. \qquad (2.32)$$

Δ_i shows by how much the sum of the minimum savings for a warehouse at site i, over all customers that it can supply, exceeds its fixed cost f_i. If $\Delta_i \geqslant 0$, a warehouse is fixed open at site i for all branches emanating from the node.

- Let ω_{ij} be the maximum bound on the cost reduction for opening a warehouse. It is similar to ∇_{ij} except that the comparisons are only made over all the fixed open warehouses, rather than over all nonclosed warehouses. Thus:

$$\omega_{ij} = \min_{\substack{k \in K_1 \\ k \in N_j}} \left[\max(c'_{kj} - c'_{ij}, 0) \right], \quad i \in K_2, j \in P_i, \tag{2.33}$$

and:

$$\Omega_i = \sum_{j \in P_i} \omega_{ij} - f_i, \quad i \in K_2, \tag{2.34}$$

where Ω_i is the excess of the sum of the maximum savings for a warehouse at site i (over all customers it can supply) over the fixed charge f_i. If $\Omega_i \leqslant 0$ the site i will not contain a warehouse in the branches emanating from the decision node.

Eight branching rules are defined and tested; they show how to select, from set K_2, the warehouse to be set closed and open:

- *Delta rules*. Select from K_2 the warehouse site which has:

1. the largest Δ among all negative Δ's,
2. the smallest Δ among all negative Δ's.

- *Omega rules*. Select from K_2 the warehouse site which has:

3. the largest Ω among all positive Ω's,
4. the smallest Ω among all positive Ω's.

- *Y rules*. The location sites in subset K_2 have fractional Y's. If Y is close to 1 that site is more likely to contain a warehouse; if Y is close to zero that site is more likely to stay closed in the terminal solution reached from the node. Thus, the two Y rules are to select from K_2 the warehouse which has:

5. the largest fractional Y value,
6. the smallest fractional Y value.

- *Demand rules*. If the sum of the demands of customers which can be supplied from site i is very large, the decision whether to open a warehouse at that site or to keep the site closed might have an important impact, which might reduce the search. Thus:

7. *Largest demand rule*. Select from K_2 the site from which the largest total demand can be supplied.
8. *Smallest demand rule*. Select from K_2 the site from which the smallest total demand can be supplied.

Sixteen test problems with 25 location sites and 50 customers have been solved by each branching decision rule. The computational results indicate that the largest Ω rule proved to be the most efficient in all but one problem. Coupled with the features described in (b) and (c) above, the algorithm solved most of the problems in less than 10 seconds on a CDC 6500 (the times on the IBM 360/65 are reported to have been found almost the same).

Probably the major disadvantage of the special branch-and-bound algorithms mentioned above is that they have been designed to solve simple models, which are not always acceptable representations of real life situations.

2.3.2.3 Benders Decomposition Approach

The Benders method (Benders [1962]) provides an alternative to branch-and-bound for solving mixed integer programs. In essence, it decouples the original problem into separate problems, one having a linear programming structure and the other being an integer programming problem. For a brief presentation of the method, consider the following mixed integer program:

$$Z^* = \min Z = cX + dY \tag{2.35}$$

subject to:

$$AX + DY \geqslant b \tag{2.36}$$

$$X \geqslant 0 \tag{2.37}$$

$$Y \geqslant 0 \text{ and integer,} \tag{2.38}$$

where X is a vector of continuous variables, Y a vector of integer variables, c and d are row vectors of objective coefficients, A and D are matrices of constraint coefficients, and b is a vector of right-hand side terms. It is assumed that the problem is feasible and that its objective function is bounded from below over the feasible region.

For a fixed Y, problem (2.35)–(2.38) reduces to a linear program:
Primal:

$$Z(Y) = \min[cX + dY] \tag{2.39}$$

subject to:

$$AX \geqslant b - DY \tag{2.40}$$

$$X \geqslant 0 \tag{2.41}$$

$$(Y \text{ fixed}). \tag{2.42}$$

One is interested in values of Y that would satisfy two requirements:

- Y combined with X should give a feasible solution to (2.35)–(2.38); call this choice a feasible Y.
- Y should be selected such as to minimize $Z(Y)$.

Formally, the two requirements may be written as finding:

$$Z^* = \min Z(Y) \tag{2.43}$$

subject to:

$$Y \geqslant 0, \text{ integer and feasible} \tag{2.44}$$

The dual of (2.39)–(2.42) is:

Dual:

$$\text{Maximize } \left[U(b - DY) + dY \right] \tag{2.45}$$

subject to:

$$UA \leqslant c \tag{2.46}$$

$$U \geqslant 0, \tag{2.47}$$

where U is a row vector of dual variables associated with the constraints set (2.40). As Y is fixed, $(b - DY)$ are known coefficients for the dual problem, and dY is a constant.

The assumption that the original problem (2.35)–(2.38) is feasible and bounded, implies that the primal problem (2.39)–(2.42) is also feasible and bounded. Consequently, by invoking the weak duality theorem of linear programming, a feasible solution to the primal problem provides an upper bound for the objective function (2.45) of the dual problem. Therefore, the choice of a feasible Y is reduced to finding a vector such that (2.45) is bounded from above. To perform this task it is useful to represent the dual vector U in terms of the K extreme points $E = \{ p^1, p^2, \ldots, p^K \}$ and the L extreme rays $R = \{ r^1, r^2, \ldots, r^L \}$ of the dual feasible region. The representation property of linear programming* allows U to be expressed as follows:

$$U = \alpha_1 p^1 + \alpha_2 p^2 + \cdots + \alpha_K p^K + \beta_1 r^1 + \beta_2 r^2 + \cdots + \beta_L r^L \tag{2.48}$$

where $\alpha_1, \alpha_2, \ldots, \alpha_K$, and $\beta_1, \beta_2, \ldots, \beta_L$ are nonnegative weights and

$$\alpha_1 + \alpha_2 + \cdots + \alpha_K = 1. \tag{2.49}$$

By substitution, the dual can be written in terms of extreme points and extreme rays as follows:

Maximize
$$\{ \alpha_1 \left[p^1(b - DY) \right] + \cdots + \alpha_K \left[p^K(b - DY) \right]$$
$$+ \beta_1 \left[r^1(b - DY) \right] + \cdots + \beta_L \left[r^L(b - DY) \right] + dY \} \tag{2.50}$$

subject to:

$$\alpha_1 + \cdots + \alpha_K = 1 \tag{2.51}$$

$$\alpha_j \geqslant 0 \qquad\qquad j = 1, \ldots, K \tag{2.52}$$

$$\beta_i \geqslant 0 \qquad\qquad i = 1, \ldots, L. \tag{2.53}$$

---

*For a discussion of the representation property, see Bradley, Hax, and Magnanti [1977, chap. 12].

In this version of the dual, the variables are the weights α_j and β_i.

The only way (2.50) could become unbounded from above would be if some $r^i(b - DY) > 0$, in which case, by letting the corresponding $\beta_i \to +\infty$, the objective function would approach $+\infty$. If all $r^i(b - D) \leqslant 0$, then (2.50) is bounded and the solution to the dual is trivial, that is, take each $\beta_i = 0$ and select $\alpha_r = 1$ where:

$$p^r(b - DY) = \max\left[\, p^j(b - DY)\right] \qquad j = 1, \ldots, K.$$

Thus, a value of Y is feasible if $r^i(b - DY) \leqslant 0$, $i = 1, \ldots, L$, and when Y is feasible the optimum value of the dual objective function is

$$\max_{1 \leqslant j \leqslant K}\left[\, p^j(b - DY) + dY\right].$$

By linear programming duality, this value must equal Z^*, the optimal value of the primal objective function. Consequently, problem (2.43)–(2.44), which defines the choice of Y, becomes:

$$Z^* = \min\left\{\max_{1 \leqslant j \leqslant K}\left[\, p^j(b - DY) + dY\right]\right\} \qquad (2.54)$$

subject to:

$$r^i(b - DY) \leqslant 0 \qquad i = 1, \ldots, L \qquad (2.55)$$

$$Y \geqslant 0 \text{ and integer.} \qquad (2.56)$$

To obtain a linear program out of (2.54)–(2.56) (whose objective function is not linear because of the inner maximization), define:

$$W = \max_{1 \leqslant j \leqslant K}\left[\, p^j(b - DY) + dY\right]$$

or, equivalently,

$$W \geqslant p^j(b - DY) + dY \qquad j = 1, \ldots, K.$$

Then, (2.54)–(2.56) can be written as:

$$Z^* = \min W \qquad (2.57)$$

subject to:

$$W \geqslant p^j(b - DY) + dY \qquad j = 1, \ldots, K \qquad (2.58)$$
$$r^i(b - DY) \leqslant 0 \qquad i = 1, \ldots, L \qquad (2.59)$$
$$y \geqslant 0 \quad \text{and integer.} \qquad (2.60)$$

Thus, the solution to the original problem (2.35)–(2.38) can be obtained in two steps:

1. First, solve (2.57)–(2.60) as an integer program and find Z^* and an optimal Y.
2. Then substitute this value of Y into (2.39)–(2.42) and solve the corresponding linear program to find the optimal X.

Step 1, however, is impossible to solve due to the need to identify from the outset all extreme points p^j and rays r^i, and the enormous number of constraints these extreme points would produce. Since most of the constraints would be nonbinding in the optimal solution, it is possible to bypass this computational difficulty by generating extreme points and rays, and their corresponding constraints, as needed. Thus, problem (2.57)–(2.60) can be restated as follows:

Minimize $\hspace{8em} W \hspace{10em}$ (2.61)

subject to:

$$W \geqslant p^j(b - D) + dY \quad p^j \in E' \hspace{4em} (2.62)$$

$$r^i(b - DY) \leqslant 0 \quad r^i \in R' \hspace{4em} (2.63)$$

$$Y \geqslant 0 \text{ and integer,} \hspace{6em} (2.64)$$

where $E' \subseteq E$ and $R' \subseteq R$; E', R' are small subsets of all extreme points (E), and all extreme rays (R), respectively. The solution strategy to be followed is:

1. Initiate the process by specifying few (or no) constraints (2.62) and (2.63); this implies defining initial subsets E' and R'.
2. Solve the resulting problem (2.61)–(2.64) to find the optimal solution Y^*.
3. Check whether this value Y^* is optimal over the entire set of extreme points E and extreme rays R. If not, redefine E' and R' and return to Z.

To accomplish step 3, the following linear program, called the *subproblem*, is to be solved:

Maximize $V \hspace{6em} (b - DY^*) \hspace{8em}$ (2.65)

subject to:

$$VA \leqslant c \hspace{10em} (2.66)$$

$$V \geqslant 0. \hspace{10em} (2.67)$$

This subproblem is identical to the dual (2.45)–(2.47).

If there is an optimal solution it will be an extreme point of the feasible region of the dual; call this extreme point $\bar{p}$. The solution $\bar{p}$ is such that constraints (2.59) are not violated, since in the maximization at optimality all coefficients $(b - DY^*) \leqslant 0$, hence $\bar{p}(b - DY^*) \leqslant 0$ as $\bar{p} \geqslant 0$. If also $\bar{p}(b - DY^*) \leqslant W^* - d\delta^*$, then problem (2.57)–(2.60) has been solved. Otherwise, the extreme point $\bar{p}$ is added to E' and the approximation problem is re-solved.

If (2.65)–(2.67) is unbounded the solution is an extreme ray $\bar{r}$, having a positive objective value $\bar{r}(b - DY^*) > 0$, which is in violation of (2.63). Therefore, the extreme ray $\bar{r}$ is added to R' and the approximation problem is re-solved.

Since both E and R contain finite numbers of elements, the convergence of the Benders method is guaranteed.

When using iterative procedures, like the one described above, it is useful to derive upper and lower bounds on the (unknown) optimal objective value Z^*. The bounds will help one assess the effect of terminating with a suboptimal solution by indicating how far the current solution is removed from Z^*.

Thus, every time the approximation problem is solved, its optimal solution W^* is a lower bound on Z^* because the approximation problem is less constrained than (2.57)–(2.60); $W^* \leqslant Z^*$.

It has been shown earlier that a Y which keeps the dual objective function bounded is also feasible in the primal. This means that whenever subproblem (2.65)–(2.67) solves at an extreme point $\bar{p}$ its objective value $\bar{p}(b - DY^*)$ is bounded, which implies that the dual is bounded and, consequently, Y^* is feasible in the primal. By strong duality theorem $Z(Y^*) = \bar{p}(b - DY^*) + dY^*$. As Y^* is only one potential choice for Y, it immediately follows that $\bar{p}(b - D\delta^*) + dY^* \geqslant Z^*$.

At optimality the two bounds are pinched together: $W^* = \bar{p}(b - DY^*) + dY^*$.

Geoffrion and Graves [1974] applied Benders decomposition to the following two-stage facilities design problem:

Minimize
$$\sum_{i,j,k,l} c_{ijkl} X_{ijkl} + \sum_{j} \left[f_j Y_j + v_j \sum_{k,l} d_{kl} Z_{jk} \right] \qquad (2.68)$$

subject to:

$$\sum_{j,k} X_{ijkl} \leqslant p_{il} \qquad \begin{cases} i = 1,\ldots,I \\ l = 1,\ldots,L \end{cases} \qquad (2.69)$$

$$\sum_{i} X_{ijkl} = d_{kl} Z_{jk} \qquad \begin{cases} j = 1,\ldots,J \\ k = 1,\ldots,K \\ l = 1,\ldots,L \end{cases} \qquad (2.70)$$

$$\sum_{j} Z_{jk} = 1 \qquad k = 1,\ldots,K \qquad (2.71)$$

$$\underline{w}_j Y_j \leqslant \sum_{k,l} d_{kl} Z_{jk} \leqslant \overline{w}_j Y_j \qquad j = 1,\ldots,J \qquad (2.72)$$

$$X_{ijkl} \geqslant 0 \qquad \begin{cases} i = 1,\ldots,I \\ j = 1,\ldots,J \\ k = 1,\ldots,K \\ l = 1,\ldots,L \end{cases} \qquad (2.73)$$

$$Y_j = 0, 1 \qquad j = 1,\ldots,J \qquad (2.74)$$

$$Z_{jk} = 0, 1 \qquad \begin{cases} j = 1,\ldots,J \\ k = 1,\ldots,K. \end{cases} \qquad (2.75)$$

Linear configuration constraints on Y's and/or Z's, $\qquad (2.76)$

where:

i = index for plants

j = index for possible location sites for warehouses (or distribution centers)

k = index for customer demand zones

l = index for commodities

p_{il} = production capacity for commodity l at plant i

d_{kl} = demand for commodity l in customer zone k

$\underline{w}_j, \overline{w}_j$ = minimum, maximum allowed total annual throughput for a warehouse at site j

f_j = fixed annual cost associated with a warehouse at site j

v_j = variable unit cost of throughput for a warehouse at site j

c_{ijkl} = average unit cost of producing and shipping commodity l from plant i through warehouse j to customer zone k

X_{ijkl} = amount of commodity l shipped from plant i through warehouse j to customer zone k

Y_j = a binary variable that takes on a value of 1 if a warehouse is open at site j, and 0 otherwise

Z_{jk} = a binary variable that is 1 if customer zone k is served by a warehouse located at site j, and 0 otherwise.

All summations run over the allowable combinations of indices; some combinations are either physically impossible, or obviously uneconomical. (2.69) is the capacity constraint at plant i for product l. (2.70) specifies that all demands have to be met; however, if customer k is not allocated to the warehouse at site j no shipment can take place from j to k. Constraints (2.71) require that each customer must be supplied by a single warehouse, and (2.72) are the lower and upper bounding constraints on the annual throughput of the warehouse at site j. Constraints (2.72) state that the total throughput at warehouse j can be positive only if a warehouse has been open at site j. Once a warehouse is open, its throughput is constrained by the lower and upper bounds ($\underline{w}_j$ and $\overline{w}_j$, respectively).

The linear configuration constraints (2.76) are designed to give the model more flexibility. Some other features that can be modeled have been discussed in section 2.3.1.1 and additional refinements are indicated by Geoffrion, Graves, and Lee [1978]. Constraints (2.76) have to be linear and not involve any X variables.

It is to be pointed out that the model shown above could have been formulated with a smaller number of constraints. For instance, (2.70) can be replaced with the following equivalent set of equations:

$$
\begin{cases}
\sum\limits_{i,j} X_{ijkl} = d_{kl}, & \begin{cases} k = 1,\ldots,K \\ l = 1,\ldots,L \end{cases} \\[2em]
\sum\limits_{i,l} X_{ijkl} = \left[\sum\limits_{l} d_{kl}\right] Z_{jk}, & \begin{cases} j = 1,\ldots,J \\ k = 1,\ldots,K. \end{cases}
\end{cases}
\tag{2.77}
$$

While (2.70) has KJL equations, (2.77) has only $K(J+L) < KJL$. However, it turns out that it is not necessarily true that a reduction in the number of constraints would help the algorithm become more efficient. The efficiency of Benders' approach depends on whether the problem can be solved before the number of extreme points in E', and extreme rays in R', in (2.61)–(2.64), becomes so large as to make the solution computationally prohibitive. Therefore, certain formulations, even with a larger number of constraints, might prove advantageous in terms of algorithm efficiency.

Benders' method has been specialized to solve problem (2.68)–(2.76); the interested reader can find in Geoffrion and Graves [1974], Geoffrion [1976], McDaniel and Devine [1977], and Geoffrion, Graves, and Lee [1978] detailed information on the algorithm, implementation issues, and computational experience.

One important point, however, is noteworthy: when the binary variables Y, Z are temporarily fixed, the corresponding primal problem separates into as many independent transportation problems as there are commodities. Indeed, if the warehouses are considered fixed and given, as well as the warehouse–customer assignments, the remaining problem is simply to decide from which plant to ship how much to which customer in order to satisfy demand and to observe plant capacity restrictions for every product. This can be seen by fixing Y, Z in (2.68)–(2.76), thus obtaining the following model:

Minimize
$$
\sum_{i,k,l} c_{ij(k)kl} X_{ij(k)kl}
\tag{2.78}
$$

subject to:

$$
\sum_{k} X_{ij(k)kl} \leq p_i l \qquad \begin{cases} i = 1,\ldots,I \\ l = 1,\ldots,L \end{cases}
\tag{2.79}
$$

$$
\sum_{i} X_{ij(k)kl} = d_{kl} \qquad \begin{cases} k = 1,\ldots,K \\ l = 1,\ldots,L \end{cases}
\tag{2.80}
$$

$$
X_{ij(k)kl} \geq 0 \qquad \begin{cases} i = 1,\ldots,I \\ k = 1,\ldots,K \\ l = 1,\ldots,L. \end{cases}
\tag{2.81}
$$

$j(k)$ shows which warehouse site j serves customer k or, put differently, j is such that for the given k we have $Z_{jk} = 1$.

(2.78)–(2.81) decomposes immediately by subscript l into a number of transportation problems equal to the number of products L. Therefore, the important feature is that virtually any number of products can be included in model (2.68)–(2.76).

The application of Benders decomposition to the facilities design problem provides an effective iterative procedure to select trial warehouse configurations and distribution assignments and to evaluate their corresponding performance, until improvements appear small relative to the computational burden of continuing the calculations. Geoffrion and his colleagues have tested the method on a variety of practical applications, including up to 100 products, 100 warehouses, and 400 customer areas. They report typical industrial applications to have 2–50 products, several plants, 40–60 warehouses, 125–250 customer areas, and 1,000–4,000 binary variables. Computer runs within a few tenths of 1% of global optimality require 2 to 4 major iterations, and several minutes of cpu time on an IBM 360/91 computer, which is remarkably efficient for a problem of such complexity. On the disadvantages side, it should be mentioned that a major programming effort is required by such an application; the algorithm has to be specialized for each application in order to ensure a high efficiency.

2.3.2.4 Heuristics

In general, heuristics may be thought of as educated rules-of-thumb that bring in common-sense approaches to problem solving.

Heuristics were popular methods to use in the solution of facilities design problems during the sixties, when computational limitations prevented the application of optimization procedures. Heuristics were designed in early model formulations to reduce the search for alternative configurations, and to obtain "good," but not necessarily optimal, solutions. Kuehn and Hamburger [1963] and Wiest [1966] provide good expositions of the philosophy of the heuristic approach.

Of the many heuristics available in the literature, the often quoted work of Kuehn and Hamburger and the heuristics proposed by Manne [1964] will be briefly described in this section.

Kuehn and Hamburger were among the first to apply heuristic programming techniques to the facilities design problem. They solve a two-stage (plant → warehouse → customer) location–allocation problem, with multiple products and capacitated plants and warehouses. The heuristic program has two parts:

1. *The main program*, which locates one warehouse at a time until an increase in the total system cost is observed.

2.   *The bump and shift routine*, which tries to change the solution obtained by the main program by dropping existing warehouses, or by shifting their current location.

The main program uses three principal heuristics:

- Consider only few geographical locations as promising sites for a warehouse, namely, those at or near concentrations of demand.
- Locate warehouses one at a time, adding at each stage of the analysis the warehouse producing the greatest cost savings for the entire system.
- To determine which warehouse to add, evaluate only a small number of the entire set of possible warehouse sites at each stage of the procedure. These sites are chosen such that, considering only their local demand, they would produce the largest cost savings if supplied by local warehouses rather than by the system existing in the previous stage.

After all potential location sites are either eliminated from consideration an uneconomical, or are assigned warehouses, the bump and shift routine is entered. This routine is designed to modify solutions arrived at in the course of the main program, as follows:

- Any warehouse which has become uneconomical because some of the customers originally assigned to it have been subsequently allocated to warehouses located later, is eliminated (bumped) from further consideration.
- Warehouses are shifted around to other potential sites within their territories, so as to insure the servicing of the demand zones established during the bump routine in the most economical way.

The heuristics have been applied to 12 sample problems and required an average of 6 minutes on an IBM-650. The authors report solutions very close to the optimum in most instances.

In the heuristics developed by Kuehn and Hamburger, the economies of scale associated with warehouse operations are represented only by the fixed charge incurred when a warehouse is opened. Feldman, Lehrer, and Ray [1966] extend that work by allowing economies of scale to be present over the entire range of warehouse sizes. They characterize warehousing cost by means of strictly concave cost functions, and develop additional heuristics for assigning customer areas to opened warehouses and to drop warehouses from a trial configuration.

Shortly after Kuehn and Hamburger's paper, Manne [1964] proposed a somewhat similar approach for solving a class of fixed charge problems. His assumptions are more restrictive, assuming a single product, one stage of distribution, and no capacity limitations. A model of type (2.1)–(2.5) results from these assumptions. He acknowledges at the outset [p. 213] that "it remains to be seen whether the performance of this technique is seriously downgraded as a result of introducing more realistic assumptions." Manne's algorithm is called the Steepest Ascent One Point Move Algorithm, SAOPMA. Manne points out that the uncapacitated structure of his formulation makes it an easy matter to calculate the X_{ij}'s of the problem, given any set of warehouses that are fixed open or closed ($Y_j = 1$ or 0). Demand center j is simply supplied by that warehouse with the minimum value of c_{ij}.

Formally, let:

$$c_{i*j} = \underset{1 \leqslant j \leqslant n}{\text{Minimum}} \left(c_{ij} | Y_i = 1 \right).$$

Then:

$$X_{i*j} = d_j,$$

where $i*$ denotes the optimal location from where customer j is to be served.

Manne adopts two heuristics comparable to Kuehn and Hamburger's. He assumes that it is enough to consider only a small subset of all possible location sets from which to select the final solutions. He assumes further that a reasonably good solution can be obtained by only considering the status of one particular warehouse at a time. Here, however, his algorithm diverges from that of Kuehn and Hamburger.

A geometric insight into the problem is helpful. Each of the possible combinations of open or closed warehouses may be considered as one of the vertices of a unit hypercube (i.e., for m possible locations, there are 2^m possible warehouse location vectors $[Y_1, Y_2, \ldots, Y_m]$ where each Y_j can take on values of either 0 or 1). As mentioned previously, for a given vertex it is trivial to allocate the demand concentrations among the open warehouses and to compute the associated value of the objective function at that vertex. For large m, the 2^m possible combinations make a complete enumeration impossible. As is the case with other heuristics, SAOPMA attempts to reduce the number of vertices examined before a good solution is obtained.

SAOPMA starts at an arbitrary vertex and evaluates all possible one-point moves to adjacent vertices. It selects that move which offers the greatest total cost reduction, or terminates if no improvement is found. By a one-point move is meant a single element alteration of the m-element location vector. For example, take $m = 3$. If one starts at vertex $(1, 0, 1)$ warehouses 1 and 3 are open. Possible one-point moves are to $(0, 0, 1)$, $(1, 1, 1)$, and $(1, 0, 0)$, but no others.

Manne concludes from his computational experience that SAOPMA is capable, under the present assumptions, of obtaining solutions within 2 to 6% of optimum.

It is interesting to note the chronology of the papers presented so far:

- 1963: Kuehn and Hamburger ⎫
- 1964: Manne   ⎬ Heuristics
- 1966: Efroymson and Ray   ⎫ Branch-and-bound and some
- 1972: Khumawala   ⎬ heuristics
- 1974: Geoffrion and Graves ⎬ Benders decomposition

A shift from nonoptimal methods toward optimal algorithms is obvious, due to the progress witnessed especially in the integer and mixed integer programming field.

Heuristic programming was used extensively before any integer programming algorithm was developed or made computationally feasible. The main drawback of the heuristic approach is that it leads to a "good" solution, with no assurance or feeling for optimality. Often it is necessary to have the absolute standard of performance which is provided by the optimal solution, especially when it is desired to evaluate several alternatives before making a decision, to perform sensitivity analyses, or to pose "what if...?" questions. Potentially attractive saving opportunities can be missed when important facilities design decisions are based exclusively on approximations.

However, an advantage of the heuristic approach is that it imposes, in theory, no limitations to the model. It gives a high degree of flexibility to the model designer, allowing nonlinearities and more realistic representations to be introduced.

Perhaps the most appropriate modeling approach to complex problems, such as those described in this chapter, is to use a combination of heuristics and optimization procedures. A good example of exploiting this combination is using a preprocessor to suggest good starting solutions to a mathematical programming model. The preprocessor is designed to accept heuristic inputs from analysts and decision makers, which greatly improve both the realism of the model and its computational effectiveness.* Another example is provided by Khumawala [1972], who introduced several heuristic rules in the branching part of his branch-and-bound algorithm, obtaining much improved computational time.

2.3.2.5 Simulation

The heart of the simulation approach to facilities design is not to *generate* distribution systems (neither optimal nor suboptimal), but to provide a mechanism to *evaluate* in great detail a fully specified design alternative supplied from outside the simulation model. Rather than proceeding systematically from a starting point toward an optimum solution, simulation provides a means to look at proposed alternatives in the distribution system. The decision maker must provide these alternatives and decide when he is satisfied with the solution obtained.

While the inability to optimize is a serious limitation, there is, however, an important advantage: the evaluation of the proposed distribution system

---

*For an illustration of this point, the reader is referred to Chapter 6 in Bradley, Hax, and Magnanti [1977].

can be done at a micro level, by taking detailed account of such data as:

- individual ordering patterns of customers
- transportation rates structure and vehicle scheduling
- order filling policies
- stock allocation in the system, replenishment and transshipment policies, interwarehouse movement of inventory

Also, simulation models permit the consideration of a virtually unlimited number of products, plants, warehouses, and customers. Shycon and Maffei [1963] mention that they have analyzed distribution systems as large as 12 plants, 25 commodities, 100 warehouse locations, and 5,000 customers.

There are currently a number of computer simulation packages for studying distribution systems, of which the Distribution System Simulator, or DSS (Connors et al. [1972]), marketed by IBM, and LREPS, are perhaps the most outstanding. Also, simulation programs have been designed by many firms using either special simulation languages like GPSS And SIMSCRIPT, or programming languages of larger generality. Advertisements for packages may be found regularly in such journals as *Computer World*, *Modern Data*, and *Datamation*.

The *Distribution System Simulator* was designed with the idea of facilitating the development of a customized model to serve specific users' needs, presented via a questionnaire; such an idea is a viable and interesting one, very much worth exploring. The system is organized in terms of an external Answer Sheet, and internal Source Library, Decision Tables, and Editor and Output Generator.

DSS produces the computer program required to perform the simulation, and specifies the data input to be provided by the user. DSS is attractive and represents a step in the right direction to help an educated user in formulating a model-based approach to improve the quality of the decision making in a logistics environment.

However, the critiques by Hax [1974] and Aggarwal [1973] point to some important limitations and deficiencies present in the DSS, of which the most serious are shown here:

1. It fails to support plant and warehouse location decisions, as well as decisions regarding expansions or improvements in the production and distribution facilities. By approaching the problem only from a simulation point of view, instead of using an optimization approach, DSS is very limited in this respect.
2. The production process and its interactions with the distribution system are ignored. The plant is assumed to maintain an unlimited inventory that can satisfy any demand.

3. DSS also ignores the raw material stages and the in-process inventories. Therefore the simulation output, when implemented, is likely to result in adverse effects upon the manufacturing and raw material acquisition stages.

4. It treats each stocking point in isolation as if it were independent from the rest of the system, thus failing to provide an integrative approach to the logistics decision process. This is a serious shortcoming because in a multiechelon distribution system it is crucial to deal specifically with the issue of interdependence of inventories of items at various stocking points throughout the system.

5. It fails to support decisions that are made on an infrequent basis, such as introduction or discontinuance of items, promotional campaigns, handling of slow-moving items, and so on.

6. In its present form, DSS seems inappropriate to deal with the day-to-day decisions at the operational level, which require much more detailed information.

The critical aspects shown above with respect to the simulation approach in general and the DSS in particular are not meant to show that simulation should not be used in making decisions on the facilities design problem. The ability of the simulation technique to deal with very detailed information can be exploited by combining optimization and simulation:

- An optimization model could be used first, to solve the problem under various scenarios at a macro level, by taking into account the dominant cost components and the major interdependencies. Inevitably, certain detail aspects (such as the allocation of stock in the system) have to be disregarded for lack of adequate computational power.
- A simulation model could then consider the optimum solutions generated by the optimization, as design alternatives, and evaluate them in greater detail.

The process may be viewed as an iterative procedure, with information passed up and down between optimization and simulation. The optimization model provides the alternatives (which, in complex problems, are bound to be better than the alternatives guessed by an analyst or by management), while the simulation model can explore the merits of each alternative in an environment that closely resembles the actual operational setting.

In concluding, a word of caution: simulation is expensive (Atkins and Shriver [1968, p. 72]). Geoffrion [1975, p. 36] suggests that, if a firm is willing to spend the large amount of money and effort required by simulation, it should be reasonable to spend the relatively small additional amount required to have the optimization feature also included in the package. Optimization would improve the choice of alternatives. Moreover, the data required by the simulation would include most, if not all, of the data needed to run the optimization model.

2.4   Other Discrete Space Formulations

As already mentioned in 2.2.4, single facility problems under the feasible set approach are computationally trivial, since they can be solved by complete enumeration of the alternative location sites. The multifacility problems are much richer, but also much more difficult to solve.

This section will be devoted to three categories of problems: multifacility location problems, special location–allocation models, and minimax problems.

2.4.1   Location Problems

In the location problem the number of new facilities to be set up, as well as the interactions between them and the customers, are known and given. There are m facilities to be located; each facility will require one site from among n available sites, with $m \leqslant n$; it is not possible to locate more than one facility at any given site. Assume that there are no interactions within the set of new facilities; the interactions are only between the new facilities and the set of customers.

There are two types of costs involved here:

- a fixed cost associated with locating the new facility i at site j
- costs associated with operating facility i at site j and supporting the item movement between facility i and site j and every customer in the system

A cost c_{ij} can be associated with every facility i–site j pair ($i = 1, 2, \ldots, m$, $j = 1, 2, \ldots, n$). The objective is to locate the m new facilities in such a way as to minimize the total cost of setting up and operating the system.

If Y_{ij} is a variable that takes on a value of 1 if the ith facility is located at the jth site, and a value of zero otherwise, the location problem can be formulated as follows:

Minimize
$$Z = \sum_{i=1}^{m} \sum_{j=1}^{n} c_{ij} Y_{ij} \tag{2.82}$$

subject to:

$$\sum_{j=1}^{n} Y_{ij} = 1 \qquad\qquad i = 1, \ldots, m \tag{2.83}$$

$$\sum_{i=1}^{m} Y_{ij} \leqslant 1 \qquad\qquad j = 1, \ldots, n \tag{2.84}$$

$$Y_{ij} = 0, 1 \qquad\qquad \begin{cases} i = 1, \ldots, m \\ j = 1, \ldots, n. \end{cases} \tag{2.85}$$

Constraints (2.83) require that every new facility be located at one of the sites, while constraints (2.84) enforce the requirement that at most one facility may be located at any given site j.

When the number of facilities is equal to the number of sites, constraints (2.84) should hold at equality since precisely one facility has to be located at every site. The resulting model is then the well-known *assignment problem* (Bradley, Hax, and Magnanti [1977, chap. 8.2], Garfinkel and Nemhauser [1972a, chap. 3], Hung and Rom [1980], and Barr, Glover, and Klingman [1977]). Since the assignment problem may be viewed as a special case of the uncapacitated transportation model, it can be shown that constraints $Y_{ij} = 0, 1$ are superfluous. Therefore, for $m = n$ the location problem can be reformulated as a linear program:

Minimize
$$Z = \sum_{i=1}^{n} \sum_{j=1}^{n} c_{ij} Y_{ij} \tag{2.86}$$

subject to:

$$\sum_{j=1}^{n} Y_{ij} = 1 \qquad i = 1, \ldots, n \tag{2.87}$$

$$\sum_{i=1}^{n} Y_{ij} = 1 \qquad j = 1, \ldots, n \tag{2.88}$$

$$Y_{ij} \geqslant 0 \qquad \begin{cases} i = 1, \ldots, n \\ j = 1, \ldots, n. \end{cases} \tag{2.89}$$

If $m < n$, which is often the case, a number n-m dummy facilities will have to be created. Their corresponding costs in the objective function: $c_{m+1, j}$, $c_{m+2, j}, \ldots, c_{n, j}$ ($j = 1, 2, \ldots, n$) are all set to zero, which means that when a dummy facility is assigned to some location site j no cost is incurred.

In addition to facility location problems, other situations can be formulated as assignment problems: setting up schedules for assignment of classes to classrooms, assignment of work jobs to work teams, and so on. For solution methods the references indicated above will prove helpful; also, most operations research textbooks offer a treatment of this topic.

Another model of wide interest in the operations research literature is the *quadratic assignment problem*, in which there are m sites and m facilities to be located, and there are interactions (known and given) between pairs of new facilities. It costs c_{ijkl} to support the interactions between facility i located at j and facility k located at l*; $c_{ijkl} = c_{klij}$.

---

*Thus, for instance, suppose there is a fixed cost f_{ij} to locate facility i at site j, and similarly f_{kl} for facility k at site l. As mentioned, the interactions (e.g., flow of goods) between i and site j and k at site l are known; let c'_{ijkl} be the cost of producing (if it is the case), handling, and transporting all the goods between the two facilities. Then, the total cost c_{ijkl} is:

$$c_{ijkl} = f_{ij} + f_{kl} + c'_{ijkl}.$$

Let δ_{ij} be a binary variable defined as:

$$\delta_{ij} = \begin{cases} 1 \text{ if facility } i \text{ is located at site } j \\ 0 \text{ otherwise.} \end{cases}$$

Then, the problem is to assign each facility to one of the sites (no site can have more than one facility) in such a way as to minimize the total system cost:

Minimize
$$Z = \frac{1}{2} \sum_{\substack{i,k=1 \\ i \neq k}}^{m} \sum_{\substack{j,l=1 \\ j \neq l}}^{m} c_{ijkl} Y_{ij} Y_{kl} \tag{2.90}$$

subject to:

$$\sum_{i=1}^{m} Y_{ij} = 1 \qquad\qquad j = 1, \ldots, m \tag{2.91}$$

$$\sum_{j=1}^{m} Y_{ij} = 1 \qquad\qquad i = 1, \ldots, m \tag{2.92}$$

$$Y_{ij} = 0, 1 \qquad\qquad \begin{cases} i = 1, \ldots, m \\ j = 1, \ldots, m. \end{cases} \tag{2.93}$$

The objective function is quadratic, hence the name of the problem. The cost term c_{ijkl} is incurred if and only if facility i is located at site j and facility k at site l. The factor $1/2$ has been included to avoid the double counting which would occur because of the symmetry $c_{ijkl} = c_{klij}$. Constraints (2.91) ensure that precisely one facility is located at each site; constraints (2.92) guarantee that each facility is assigned to some site.

As with the assignment problem (2.86)–(2.89), if the number of potential sites exceeds the number of new facilities, dummy facilities will have to be considered to force equality. Also, it is to be noted that formulation (2.90)–(2.93) permits the inclusion of already existing facilities, in case there are interactions between these and the new facilities to be located. The existing facilities and their sites will be included in the total number m; then, whenever at some site i there already exists a facility, say j, the corresponding Y_{ij} will have to be fixed at a value of 1 in the statement of the problem.

Quadratic assignment problems arise in a variety of situations: location of a group of interconnected plants that contribute jointly to the production of a line of items, assignment of offices and departments to rooms in an office building, design of control panels where operations (adjustment of control knob or valve positions, reading of displays) are performed in sequences, and so on. For solution algorithms, a good treatment is given in Francis and White [1974, chap. 8], Burkard and Stratmann [1978], and Bazaraa and Sherali [1980].

2.4.2 Location–Allocation Problems

Section 2.3 has focused upon the general location–allocation problem. This section will concentrate on some special location–allocation models known as covering and partial covering problems.

The *covering problem* normally arises under circumstances in which a number (unspecified) of similar facilities have to be located, such as to serve (or "cover") n customers. At most, one facility can be located at each of m possible sites. It might not be possible to cover a given customer j from a location site i; this is specified by a matrix of covering coefficients a_{ij} that take on the value of 1 if customer j can be covered from site i, and the value of zero, otherwise. There is a cost c_i if a facility is located at site i. The objective is to minimize the total cost while serving all customers.

Minimize
$$Z = \sum_{i=1}^{m} c_i Y_i \qquad (2.94)$$

subject to:

$$\sum_{i=1}^{m} a_{ij} Y_i \geqslant 1 \qquad\qquad j = 1,\ldots,n \qquad (2.95)$$

$$Y_i = 0,1 \qquad\qquad i = 1,\ldots,m \qquad (2.96)$$

where:

$$Y_i = \begin{cases} 1 \text{ if a facility is located at site } i \\ 0 \text{ otherwise.} \end{cases} \qquad (2.97)$$

Constraints (2.95) indicate that every customer must be covered by at least one new facility.

It is of interest to point to two aspects of the problem:

- Although, apparently, the problem is only a location problem it also performs the allocation of customers to sites. For instance, suppose that for customer $j = 7$ of all the covering coefficients $a_{17}, a_{27}, a_{37}, \ldots$ only the following are equal to 1:

$$a_{17} = 1, \qquad a_{37} = 1, \qquad a_{47} = 1, \qquad a_{67} = 1.$$

Then, a particular solution to (2.94)–(2.96) with, say, $Y_1 = 0$, $Y_3 = 1$, $Y_4 = 1$, $Y_6 = 0$ would indicate that customer number 7 will have to be served from locations 3 and 4, and from no other location.

- The model cannot address the issue of what portion of a customer's requirements should be satisfied from a particular facility. Also, there is nothing in the model formulation to distinguish among facilities, nor is there any decision made with respect to the sizes of the various facilities; therefore, they are assumed to be all the same. For these reasons, the covering problem is useful in modeling such situations as locating emergency facilities.

The *partitioning problem* has the same general setting as the covering problem; however, it is more restrictive in the sense that any given customer j has to be covered by exactly one new facility:

Minimize
$$Z = \sum_{i=1}^{m} c_i Y_i \tag{2.98}$$

subject to:

$$\sum_{i=1}^{m} a_{ij} Y_i = 1 \qquad\qquad j = 1, \ldots, n \tag{2.99}$$

$$Y_i = 0, 1 \qquad\qquad i = 1, \ldots, m. \tag{2.100}$$

Let the $n \times m$ matrix A be defined as $A = (a_{ji})$. For the covering problem the necessary and sufficient condition for the existence of a feasible solution is that A has no row of zeros; that is, every customer should be coverable from at least one location site (Garfinkel and Nemhauser [1972a, p. 301]). In the case of the partitioning problem, however, for a given A one cannot say, in general, whether (2.98)–(2.100) will have a feasible solution, which implies that there are situations where partitions may not exist.

What is sometimes called the *total covering problem*, to be contrasted later with the partial covering problem, is a particular instance of (2.94)–(2.96) for the case of site-invariant costs. Thus, $c_j = c$ ($j = 1, \ldots, n$), and the problem becomes:

Minimize
$$Z = \sum_{i=1}^{m} Y_i \tag{2.101}$$

subject to:

$$\sum_{i=1}^{m} a_{ij} Y_i \geqslant 1 \qquad\qquad j = 1, \ldots, n \tag{2.102}$$

$$Y_i = 0, 1 \qquad\qquad i = 1, \ldots, m, \tag{2.103}$$

having the objective of serving all customers with the minimum number of facilities.

In applying the total covering problem to locating fire stations, Plane and Hendrick [1977] partition the set of m possible locations in preferred sites $i = 1, \ldots, k$, $(1 < k < m)$, and nonpreferred sites $i = k + 1, \ldots, m$. Then, instead of the objective function (2.101), they use a hierarchical objective function,

Minimize
$$Z = \sum_{i=1}^{k} Y_i + \sum_{i=k+1}^{m} (1 + \varepsilon) Y_i,$$

where ε is any number between 0 and $1/m$. The result is the simultaneous minimization of the number of fire stations and the maximization of the number of preferred fire stations within the minimum total number of stations.

It is conceivable that, due to certain limitations such as an insufficient budget, it might be impossible to acquire the total number of facilities required by the solution to (2.101)–(2.103); rather, a more limited number N of new facilities can be made available. In this situation, a good idea would be to try to locate the N facilities among the m sites in such a way as to serve the maximum number of customers. The *partial covering problem* is thus obtained:

Maximize $$Z = \sum_{j=1}^{n} \max_{i} a_{ij} Y_i \qquad (2.104)$$

subject to:

$$\sum_{i=1}^{m} Y_i \leqslant N \qquad (2.105)$$

$$Y_i = 0, 1 \qquad\qquad i = 1, \ldots, m. \qquad (2.106)$$

As a_{ij} are the zero-one covering coefficients and Y_i are zero-one variables, $\max a_{ij} Y_i$ can take on one of two values: a value of 1 when facilities are open to at least one site from which customer j can be served, or a value of zero when customer j cannot be served from any of the currently open facilities. The value of the objective function shows the number of covered customers.

Coefficients a_{ij} can be made more general. Thus, for instance, let:

$$a_{ij} = \begin{cases} 2 \text{ if it is preferable that customer } j \text{ be served from site } i \\ 1 \text{ if customer } j \text{ can be served from site } i \\ 0 \text{ otherwise,} \end{cases}$$

in which case the maximization will tend to choose preferential sites.

A variation of the partial covering problem is obtained as follows: every customer j can be served from any site i; the distance between i and j is D_{ij}, and the maximum number of facilities that can be set up is N. The objective is to locate the facilities in such a way as to minimize the sum of distances between customers and the facilities to which they are assigned.

Minimize $$Z = \sum_{j=1}^{n} \min_{i} \Delta_{ij} \qquad (2.107)$$

subject to:

$$\sum_{i=1}^{m} Y_i \leqslant N \qquad (2.108)$$

$$Y_i = 0, 1 \qquad\qquad i = 1, \ldots, m, \qquad (2.109)$$

where Y_i has been defined in (2.97), and

$$\Delta_{ij} = \begin{cases} D_{ij} \text{ if } Y_i = 1, \\ \infty \text{ otherwise.} \end{cases} \qquad (2.110)$$

The minimization inside the objective function requires that every customer j be covered by the closest open facility. By the way Δ_{ij} has been defined, the distances to the location sites at which no facilities have been opened are excluded from consideration. Constraints (2.108) impose a limit on the total number of facilities that may be set up.

It is to be noted that no fixed charge has been included in the formulation, which means that the cost of building a facility is site-invariant.

The solution to (2.107)–(2.109) indicates, via the vector of Y_i's, at which sites facilities should be located. At the same time, the requirement that every customer be supplied by the closest facility specifies the allocation of customers to facilities.

In the case where the n customers differ from each other (e.g., their demands are different), the model can be made to reflect this by assigning weights to customers in the objective function (e.g., the weights can be the demands themselves). In this case, let:

$$d_j = \text{demand of customer } j \qquad (j = 1, \dots, n)$$

$$Z_{ij} = \begin{cases} 1 \text{ if customer } j \text{ is served from site } i \\ 0 \text{ otherwise.} \end{cases}$$

If the demand is, for instance, in tons, and the distance in kilometers, the objective will be the minimization of tons × kilometers transported in the system:

Minimize
$$Z = \sum_{i=1}^{m} \sum_{j=1}^{n} D_{ij} Z_{ij} d_j Y_i \qquad (2.111)$$

subject to:

$$\sum_{i=1}^{m} \sum_{j=1}^{n} Z_{ij} d_j Y_i = \sum_{j=1}^{n} d_j \qquad (2.112)$$

$$\sum_{i=1}^{m} Z_{ij} = 1 \qquad\qquad j = 1, \dots, n \qquad (2.113)$$

$$\sum_{i=1}^{m} Y_i \leqslant N \qquad\qquad (2.114)$$

$$Z_i, Y_{ij} = 0, 1 \qquad\qquad \begin{cases} i = 1, \dots, m \\ j = 1, \dots, n. \end{cases} \qquad (2.115)$$

Constraints (2.112) ensure that all demands are served; clearly, in the left-hand side term of (2.112) both Y_i and Z_{ij} must be equal to 1 in order for location site i to participate in satisfying the demand of customer j. Constraints (2.113) require that every customer j be assigned to one and only one facility site, and (2.114) imposes the upper bound on the total number of facilities to be set up.

The particular feature of this model, not found in any of the formulations presented before, is the set of nonlinear (quadratic) constraints (2.112); coupled with the nonlinear objective function and with the binary variables, they render the problem difficult to solve.

A large number of situations, other than warehouse or plant location, are amenable to formulations of the covering problem type, such as: political districting, airline crew scheduling, location of emergency service facilities, truck dispatching, file organization for information retrieval from computer systems, and so on (see Francis and White [1974, chap. 10.3] for detailed references).

As far as the solution procedures are concerned for the classes of covering problems discussed in this section, a large number of approaches have been taken and are reported in the literature: branch-and-bound, dynamic programming, cutting plane, and heuristic methods. The interested reader is directed to the following titles, in which further bibliographical references may be found:

- Garfinkel and Nemhauser [1972b]
- Garfinkel and Nemhauser [1972a, chap. 8]
- Christofides and Korman [1975]
- Francis and White [1974, chap. 10.3]
- Curry and Skeith [1969] and Shannon and Ignizio [1970] for (2.111)–(2.114)

We conclude this section by mentioning yet another alternative to modeling both uncapacitated and capacitated location–allocation problems: the generalized assignment problem (Ross and Soland [1975, 1977]), which appears to offer "a good combination of modeling flexibility and reasonable computational requirements" (Ross and Soland [1977, p. 354]).

2.4.3 Minimax Location and Location–Allocation Problems

In a minimax problem the objective function is to minimize the maximum of some overall penalty such as total cost incurred, or distance to be traveled, time to complete a certain set of assignments, and so on. The purpose of the model is to accomplish this minimax objective subject to a number of constraints.

Among the typical situations leading to minimax formulations are cases of emergency facilities location such as fire extinguishers in a building, fire houses in a metropolitan area, police stations, hospitals in a city, and so on. In many of these examples the decision maker might consider that fast response to an emergency call is more important than the minimization of total cost, in which cases the facilities will be located so as to minimize the maximum distance or travel time between any potential "trouble spot" and the nearest facility.

The simplest example is a one-facility minimax location problem, where there are m possible locations, n customers, and one facility to locate. The problem can be solved by hand by inspection of the matrix D of distances, or traveling times, or convenience of access:

$$D = \begin{vmatrix} D_{11} & D_{12},\ldots, & D_{1n} \\ D_{21} & D_{22},\ldots, & D_{2n} \\ \vdots & & \vdots \\ D_{m1} & D_{m2} & D_{mn} \end{vmatrix} \tag{2.116}$$

Since the objective is to:

$$\underset{i=1,\ldots,m}{\text{minimize}} \left[\underset{j=1,\ldots,n}{\text{max}} D_{ij} Y_i \right] \tag{2.117}$$

where Y_i has been defined by (2.97), one would scan every row i (location i) for the maximum D_{ij} and, then, the row with the smallest maximum will be chosen.

An example with an added degree of difficulty would be one in which several facilities have to be located. Consider n possible location sites, and m specialized new facilities (for instance, one city hospital, one fire station, and one police station). The area to be served by the facilities is divided into a number of zones. If facility i $(i=1,\ldots,m)$ is located at site j $(j=1,\ldots,n)$ define the inefficiency coefficient α_{ij} associated with the (i, j) assignment. For example, the inefficiency can be a function of:

- the distance between facility i at site j and the most distant zone to be served, or the sum of distances to all zones to be served
- the importance of the service to be provided (for instance, speed of providing medical assistance could be judged as twice as important as speed of answering a fire alarm)
- the risk attributed to the zones served

A minimax problem would then result if one wanted to minimize the maximum inefficiency of the system to be designed. To cast the problem in the "standard" form, n-m dummy facilities are created, with the corresponding inefficiencies $\alpha_{m+1, j}, \alpha_{m+2, j},\ldots,\alpha_{nj}$ $(j=1,\ldots,n)$ equal to zero; it is thus ensured that the "max" function will select inefficiencies associated with the real facilities. Also, define the binary variable Y_{ij} to be 1 when facility i is located at site j and zero otherwise. The formulation is:

Minimize $$Z = \max_{\substack{i=1,\ldots,n \\ j=1,\ldots,n}} \left[\alpha_{ij}Y_{ij}\right] \qquad (2.118)$$

subject to:

$$\sum_{j=1}^{n} Y_{ij} = 1 \qquad\qquad i = 1,\ldots,n \qquad\qquad (2.119)$$

$$\sum_{i=1}^{n} Y_{ij} = 1 \qquad\qquad j = 1,\ldots,n \qquad\qquad (2.120)$$

$$Y_{ij} = 0,1 \qquad\qquad \begin{cases} i = 1,\ldots,n \\ j = 1,\ldots,n. \end{cases} \qquad (2.121)$$

Constraints (2.119) ensure that every facility is assigned to some site; by (2.120) every location site will have one and only one facility. The set of constraints are the same as in the assignment problem (2.86)–(2.89); clearly, if one changed the objective to minimizing the total system inefficiency the assignment problem would be immediately recovered.

In the operations research literature formulation, (2.118)–(2.121) is known as the *bottleneck assignment problem* (an application in a production environment, where inefficiency creates bottlenecks, has brought about the name of the model).

Formulation (2.118)–(2.121) does not include any allocation aspects; it is a pure location problem. At the expense of added complexity, the allocation side of the problem may also be included. Suppose that a large metropolitan area is partitioned into n zones and a number of fire houses have to be located in the area; the city council has designated m possible location sites for the fire houses and has decided that every fire house will serve q zones (n is an integral multiple of q). The problem is twofold: to locate the facilities and to allocate the zones to the facilities in such a way as to minimize the maximum distance (or time) the fire trucks would have to travel when answering a fire alarm. Assume the established rule is that whenever a fire alarm is placed from zone j ($j = 1,\ldots,n$) it will be directed to the fire house located at site i ($i = 1,\ldots,m$) to which the zone was assigned; also, the distance D_{ij} considered is measured from the location site i to the foremost extreme of zone j.

Variable Y_i is associated with the location aspect: Y_i is 1 if a fire house is located at site i, and zero otherwise. Variable Z_{ij} helps with the allocation aspect: Z_{ij} is 1 if zone j is assigned to site i, and zero otherwise. The formulation is then:

Minimize $$Z = \max_{i,j} \left[D_{ij}Y_iZ_{ij}\right] \qquad (2.122)$$

subject to:

$$\sum_{j=1}^{n} Z_{ij} = qY_i \qquad\qquad i = 1, \ldots, m \qquad\qquad (2.123)$$

$$\sum_{i=1}^{m} Z_{ij} = 1 \qquad\qquad j = 1, \ldots, n \qquad\qquad (2.124)$$

$$Y_i, Z_{ij} = 0, 1 \qquad\qquad \begin{cases} i = 1, \ldots, m \\ j = 1, \ldots, n. \end{cases} \qquad\qquad (2.125)$$

Constraints (2.123) require that q zones be served from location site i if a facility is placed there; by (2.124) each zone is assigned to one fire house.

It is interesting to note that for a fixed and given assignment vector $(Y_1, Y_2, \ldots, Y_m)$, the minimax location–allocation model yields what has come to be known as the *bottleneck transportation problem*. This is important because if an enumeration scheme is used to solve (2.122)–(2.125), the resulting subproblems will be of the bottleneck transportation type, solvable by the threshold algorithm of Garfinkel and Rao [1971].

Minimax formulations for continuous space will not be presented here, but may be found in Francis and White [1974, chap. 9], together with solution procedures and references. For solutions to the bottleneck assignment problem the reader is directed to Garfinkel [1971].

2.5 Continuous Space Formulations

As mentioned in 2.2.1, the continuous space or infinite set approach allows for a facility to be located anywhere in the two-dimensional space, which is equivalent to considering an infinite number of possible location sites.

This section will consider first single-facility location problems, and then will move to multifacility location cases.

2.5.1 Single-Facility Location Models

Under the discrete space approach, single-facility location problems were computationally trivial since they could be solved by complete enumeration of the alternative location sites. Of course, this is no longer the case under the continuous space approach.

The general statement of the problem is the following: there are n customers located at known points in the two-dimensional space $(x_1, y_1), (x_2, y_2), \ldots, (x_n, y_n)$; a new facility is to be placed at some point (X_0, Y_0) yet to be determined. The interactions between the new facility and every customer are known; the costs incurred in the system are of a transportation nature, proportional to the distance D_{0j}, $j = 1, 2, \ldots, n$, between point (X_0, Y_0) and customer j. The objective is to locate the new facility such as to minimize the total cost.

Minimize
$$Z = \sum_{j=1}^{n} c_j D_{0j} \tag{2.126}$$

where:

Z = the total cost function

c_j = cost parameter that shows how much it costs per unit distance to support the interactions between the new facility and customer j over some period of time (one month, one year, the entire planning horizon, etc.).

A number of situations can lead to models of this sort, such as the location of a new machine in a fabrication shop, an elevator in a warehouse, a warehouse in a new market district, and so on.

D_{0j} can be represented as the Euclidean distance between two points:

$$D_{0j} = \left[\left(X_0 - x_j \right)^2 + \left(Y_0 - y_j \right)^2 \right]^{1/2} \tag{2.127}$$

However, it is customary in plant shops or warehouses to have a rectangular network of aisles, in which case the rectilinear or rectangular distances are relevant:

$$D_{0j} = |X_0 - x_j| + |Y_0 - y_j| \tag{2.128}$$

where $|\cdot|$ is used to denote an absolute value.

Another case arises when the warehouse has radial aisles, like the one treated by White [1973].

In other situations the cost grows faster than the straight-line distance. Of particular interest is the problem where the cost is proportional to the square of the Euclidean distance, expressed by:

$$D_{0j} = \left(X_0 - x_j \right)^2 + \left(Y_0 - y_j \right)^2 \tag{2.129}$$

Solutions to (2.126) can be obtained by calculus, graphical, or analog techniques. Since (2.126) has no constraints, the rectangular and the square Euclidean distance problems can be decoupled into two problems optimizing x_0 and y_0 separately. The solution to the square Euclidean distance problem is known as the center-of-gravity solution, because the coordinates X_0, Y_0 for the new facility turn out to be weighted averages of the corresponding coordinates of the existing facilities.

2.5.2 Multifacility Location and Location– Allocation Models

The general statement of the unconstrained version of this problem is slightly changed as compared to the single-facility case: there are n customers located at known points in the two-dimensional space $(x_1, y_1), (x_2, y_2), \ldots, (x_n, y_n)$; m

new facilities are to be located at some points, unknown yet $(X_0^1, Y_0^1), (X_0^2, Y_0^2), \ldots, (X_0^m, Y_0^m)$. The interactions (e.g., flow of goods) between any facility i ($i = 1, 2, \ldots, m$) and the customers are known and given; a transportation cost proportional to the distance D_{ij} is associated with the flow of goods between i and j. The objective is to locate the m new facilities such as to minimize the total transportation cost:

Minimize
$$Z = \sum_{i=1}^{m} \sum_{j=1}^{n} c_{ij} D_{ij} \tag{2.130}$$

where:

$\quad c_{ij} =$ cost parameter that shows how much is costs per unit distance to support the interactions between the new facility i and customer j over some specified time interval.

The expressions for the distance D_{ij} in the Euclidean, rectangular, and square Euclidean cases are simple extensions of (2.127), (2.128), (2.129). Notice that the cost function (2.130) does not include a fixed charge (as was the case under the feasible set approach). Therefore, it is crucial that the number of new facilities be specified in advance; otherwise, the obvious solution would be to open a new facility at every demand point to minimize the transportation cost down to zero. However, if a fixed charge were to be introduced, an immediate difficulty would arise: the fixed charge would have to be expressed as a function of the planar coordinates.

More realism can be added to the formulation if the allocation feature is also included. In this case, let:

$\quad Q_{ij} =$ quantity shipped from facility i to customer j

$\quad c_{ij} =$ cost per unit distance of supplying a unit quantity to the j-th customer from facility i

$\quad D_{ij} =$ the appropriate distance between i and j,

and the resulting problem is:

Minimize
$$Z = \sum_{i=1}^{m} \sum_{j=1}^{n} c_{ij} Q_{ij} D_{ij} \tag{2.131}$$

subject to:

$$\sum_{i=1}^{m} Q_{ij} = d_j \qquad\qquad j = 1, \ldots, m \tag{2.132}$$

$$Q_{ij} \geqslant 0 \qquad\qquad \begin{cases} i = 1, \ldots, m \\ j = 1, \ldots, n. \end{cases} \tag{2.133}$$

Constraints (2.132) ensure that demand is satisfied at all customer locations.

It is evident that, since (2.131)–(2.133) has no capacity constraints, in the optimal solution every customer will be served by one facility only. Under these circumstances (2.131)–(2.133) can be easily transformed into an alternative formulation that might lend itself to the development of better solution algorithms. To do this, let:

$$\frac{Q_{ij}}{d_j} = Y_{ij}$$

where:

$$Y_{ij} = \begin{cases} 1 \text{ if the customer } j \text{ is served by facility } i \\ 0 \text{ otherwise.} \end{cases}$$

Then, (2.131)–(2.133) becomes:

Minimize
$$Z = \sum_{i=1}^{m} \sum_{j=1}^{n} c_{ij} d_j D_{ij} Y_{ij} \qquad (2.134)$$

subject to:

$$\sum_{i=1}^{m} Y_{ij} = 1 \qquad j = 1,\ldots,n \qquad (2.135)$$

$$Y_{ij} = 0,1 \qquad \begin{cases} i = 1,\ldots,m \\ j = 1,\ldots,n. \end{cases} \qquad (2.136)$$

The solution of (2.134)–(2.136) will specify the location (X_0^i, Y_0^i) of every new facility $i = 1,\ldots,m$, and the assignment of the customer to the new facilities.

The imposition of capacity constraints upon the new facilities is easily achieved if one starts from (2.131)–(2.133). Let r_i be the available capacity (or resource) at the new facility i; then, the capacitated version of the location–allocation problem is:

Minimize
$$Z = \sum_{i=1}^{m} \sum_{j=1}^{n} c_{ij} Q_{ij} D_{ij} \qquad (2.137)$$

subject to:

$$\sum_{i=1}^{m} Q_{ij} = d_j \qquad j = 1,\ldots,n \qquad (2.138)$$

$$\sum_{j=1}^{n} Q_{ij} \leqslant r_i \qquad i = 1,\ldots,m \qquad (2.139)$$

$$Q_{ij} \geqslant 0 \qquad \begin{cases} i = 1,\ldots,m \\ j = 1,\ldots,n. \end{cases} \qquad (2.140)$$

Unlike the uncapacitated model, in (2.137)–(2.140) it might be optimal to serve customer j's demand from more than one facility.

Extensions of the formulations presented above can be provided to cover a variety of situations, such as:

(a)   two-stage distribution systems (plant → warehouse → customer)

(b)   cases where interactions exist not only between the set of new facilities and the customers but also between pairs of new facilities

(c)   particular forms of the cost parameter c_{ij}. Thus, c_{ij} could be:

- constant: $c_{ij} = c$; that is, the locations of the supply and destination bear no influence upon the unit cost;

- dependent only on the location of the customer being served: $c_{ij} = c_j$, which might be justified when specific means of transportation are used, or when different merchandise is supplied to various customers;

- invariant with respect to the distance; c_{ij} will then be simply the cost per unit quantity transported. For instance, if the supply source is on the east coast and the customer on the west coast it might make no difference where on the east coast and where on the west coast they are located.

The interested reader can find a number of such extensions in: Francis and White [1974, chap. 5], and Eilon et al. [1971, chap. 4]. For solution procedures good starting references are: Francis and White [1974, chaps. 5, 6], and Eilon et al. [1971, chaps. 3, 4]. Problem (2.134)–(2.136) has been treated by Cooper [1963, 1964], and problem (2.137)–(2.140) by Cooper [1972]. An extension of the problem (2.130) has been treated by Calamai and Charalambous [1980].

BIBLIOGRAPHY

AGGARWAL, S., "A Critique of 'The Distribution System Simulator' by M. M. Connors et al.," *Management Science*, Vol. 20, No. 4, Part I, December 1973, pp. 482–486.

AKINC, U. and B. M. KHUMAWALA, "An Efficient Branch and Bound Algorithm for the Capacitated Warehouse Location Problem," *Management Science*, Vol. 23, No. 6, February 1977, pp. 585–594.

ALCOUFFE, A. and G. MURATET, "Optimal Location of Plants," *Management Science*, Vol. 23, No. 3, November 1976, pp. 267–274.

ANTHONY, R. N., *Planning and Control Systems: A Framework for Analysis*, Harvard University Press, Boston, 1965.

ARMOUR, G. C. and E. S. BUFFA, "A Heuristic Algorithm and Simulation Approach to the Relative Location of Facilities," *Management Science*, Vol. 9, No. 1, January 1963, pp. 294–309.

ATKINS, R. J. and R. H. SHRIVER, "New Approach to Facilities Location," *Harvard Business Review*, May–June 1968, pp. 70–79.

BALINSKI, M. L. and H. MILLS, "A Warehouse Problem," Prepared for the Veterans Administration, *Mathematica*, Princeton, N.J., April 1960.

BALLOU, R. H., *Business Logistics Management*, Prentice-Hall, Englewood Cliffs, N.J., 1973.

BARR, R. E., F. GLOVER, and D. KLINGMAN, "The Alternating Basis Algorithm for Assignment Problems," *Mathematical Programming*, Vol. 13, No. 1, August 1977, pp. 1–13.

BAUMOL, W. J. and P. WOLFE, "A Warehouse Location Problem," *Operations Research*, Vol. 6, No. 2, March–April 1958, pp. 252–263.

BAZARAA, M. S. and H. D. SHERALI, "Benders' Partitioning Scheme Applied to a New Formulation of the Quadratic Assignment Problem," *Naval Research Logistics Quarterly*, Vol. 27, No. 1, March 1980, pp. 29–41.

BENDERS, J. F., "Partitioning Procedures for Solving Mixed-Variables Programming Problems," *Numerische Mathematik*, Vol. 4, 1962, pp. 238–252.

BRADLEY, S. P., A. C. HAX, and T. L. MAGNANTI, *Applied Mathematical Programming*, Addison-Wesley, Reading, Mass., 1977.

BUFFA, E. S., G. C. ARMOUR, C. GORDON, and T. E. VOLLMAN, "Allocating Facilities with Craft," *Harvard Business Review*, March–April 1964, pp. 136–159.

BURKARD, R. E. and K. H. STRATMANN, "Numerical Investigation on Quadratic Assignment Problem," *Naval Research Logistics Quarterly*, Vol. 25, No. 1, March 1978, pp. 129–148.

CALAMAI, P. and C. CHARALAMBOUS, "Solving Multifacility Location Problems Involving Euclidean Distances," *Naval Research Logistics Quarterly*, Vol. 27, No. 4, December 1980, pp. 609–620.

CANDEA, D. I., A. C. HAX, and U. S. KARMARKAR, "Economic and Social Evaluation of Capital Investment Decisions—An Application," in A. C. Hax (editor), *Studies in Operations Management*, North Holland, New York, 1978.

CHRISTOFIDES, N., *Graph Theory — An Algorithm Approach*, Academic Press, London, 1975.

CHRISTOFIDES, N. and S. KORMAN, "A Computational Survey of Methods for the Set Covering Problem," *Management Science*, Vol. 21, No. 5, January 1975, pp. 591–599.

CONNORS, H. M., C. CORAY, C. J. CUCCARO, W. K. GREEN, D. W. LOW, and H. H. MARKOWITZ, "The Distribution System Simulator," *Management Science*, Vol. 18, No. 8, April 1972, pp. B452–B453.

COOPER, L., "Location–Allocation Problems," *Operations Research*, Vol. 11, No. 3, 1963, pp. 331–344.

COOPER, L., "Heuristic Methods for Location–Allocation Problems," *SIAM Review*, Vol. 6, No. 1, 1964, pp. 37–52.

COOPER, L., "The Transportation–Location Problem," *Operations Research*, Vol. 20, No. 1, January–February 1972, pp. 94–108.

CURRY, G. L. and R. W. SKEITH, "A Dynamic Programming Algorithm for Facility Location and Allocation," *AIIE Transactions*, Vol. 1, No. 2, June 1969, pp. 133–138.

DAVIS, P. S. and T. L. RAY, "A Branch-Bound Algorithm for the Capacitated Facilities Location Problem," *Naval Research Logistics Quarterly*, Vol. 16, No. 3, November 1969, pp. 331–343.

DEARING, P. M. and R. L. FRANCIS, "A Minimax Location Problem on a Network," *Transportation Science*, Vol. 8, 1974, pp. 333–343.

DEARING, P. M. and R. L. FRANCIS, "A Network Flow Solution to a Multi-Facility Minimax Location Problem Involving Rectilinear Distances," *Transportation Science*, Vol. 8, 1974, pp. 126–141.

DEARING, P. M., R. L. FRANCIS, and T. J. LOWE, "Convex Location Problems on Tree Networks," *Operations Research*, Vol. 24, No. 4, July–August 1976, pp. 628–642.

DUTTON, R., G. HINMAN, and C. B. MILLHAM, "The Optimal Location of Nuclear-Power Facilities in the Pacific Northwest," *Operations Research*, Vol. 22, No. 3, May–June 1974, pp. 478–487.

EFROYMSON, M. A. and T. L. RAY, Branch-Bound Algorithm for Plant Location," *Operations Research*, Vol. 14, No. 3, May–June 1966, pp. 361–368.

EILON, S., C. D. T. WATSON-GANDY, and N. CHRISTOFIDES, *Distribution Management: Mathematical Modelling and Practical Analysis*, Hafner, New York, 1971.

ERLENKOTTER, D., "A Dual-Based Procedure for Uncapacitated Facility Location," *Operations Research*, Vol. 26, No. 6, November–December 1978, pp. 992–1009.

FELDMAN, E., F. A. LEHRER, and T. L. RAY, "Warehouse Location Under Continuous Economies of Scale," *Management Science*, Vol. 12, No. 9, May 1966, pp. 670–684.

FORD, L. R., JR. and D. R. FULKERSON, *Flows in Networks*, Princeton University Press, Princeton, N.J., 1962.

FRANCIS, R. L. and J. M. GOLDSTEIN, "Location Theory: A Selective Bibliography," *Operations Research*, Vol. 22, No. 2, March–April 1974, pp. 400–410.

FRANCIS, R. L. and J. A. WHITE, *Facility Layout and Location — An Analytical Approach*, Prentice-Hall, Englewood Cliffs, N.J., 1974.

FURMAN, G. G. and H. J. GREENBERG, "Optimal Weapon Allocation with Overlapping Area Defenses," *Operations Research*, Vol. 21, No. 6, November–December 1973, pp. 1291–1308.

GARFINKEL, R. S., "An Improved Algorithm for the Bottleneck Assignment Problem," *Operations Research*, Vol. 19, No. 7, November–December 1971, pp. 1747–1751.

GARFINKEL, R. S. and G. L. NEMHAUSER, *Integer Programming*, Wiley, New York, 1972a.

GARFINKEL, R. S. and G. L. NEMHAUSER, "Optimal Set Covering: A Survey," in A. M. Geoffrion (editor), *Perspectives on Optimization*, Addison-Wesley, Reading, Mass., 1972b.

GARFINKEL, R. S. and M. R. RAO, "The Bottleneck Transportation Problem," *Naval Research Logistics Quarterly*, Vol. 18, No. 4, December 1971, pp. 465–472.

GEOFFRION, A. M., "A Guide to Computer-Assisted Methods for Distribution Systems Planning," *Sloan Management Review*, Vol. 16, No. 2, Winter 1975, pp. 17–41.

GEOFFRION, A. M., "Better Distribution Planning with Computer Models," *Harvard Business Review*, July–August 1976, pp. 92–104.

GEOFFRION, A. M. and G. W. GRAVES, "Multicommodity Distribution System Design by Benders Decomposition," *Management Science*, Vol. 20, No. 5, January 1974, pp. 822–844.

GEOFFRION, A. M., G. W. GRAVES, and S. LEE, "Strategic Distribution System Planning: A Status Report," in A. C. Hax (editor), *Studies in Operations Management*, North Holland, New York, 1978.

GEOFFRION, A. M. and R. E. MARSTEN, "Integer Programming: A Framework and State-of-the-Art Survey," *Management Science*, Vol. 18, No. 9, May 1972, pp. 465–491.

HANAN, M. and J. KURTZBERG, "A Review of the Placement and Quadratic Assignment Problems," *SIAM Review*, Vol. 14, 1972, pp. 324–342.

HAX, A. C., "Planning a Management Information System for a Distributing and Manufacturing Company," *Sloan Management Review*, Vol. 14, No. 3, Spring 1973, pp. 85–98.

HAX, A. C., "A Comment on the 'Distribution System Simulator,'" *Management Science*, Vol. 21, No. 2, October 1974, pp. 233–236.

HAX, A. C., "The Design of Large Scale Logistics Systems: A Survey and an Approach," in W. Marlow (editor), *Modern Trends in Logistics Research*, M.I.T. Press, Cambridge, Mass., 1976, pp. 59–96.

HAX, A. C. and K. M. WIIG, "The Use of Decision Analysis in Capital Investment Problems," *Sloan Management Review*, Vol. 17, No. 2, Winter 1976, pp. 19–48.

HU, T. C., *Integer Programming and Network Flows*, Addison-Wesley, Reading, Mass., 1969.

HUNG, M. S. and W. O. ROM, "Solving the Assignment Problem by Relaxation," *Operations Research*, Vol. 28, No. 4, July–August 1980, pp. 969–982.

HURTER, A. P., JR., M. K. SCHAEFER, and R. E. WENDELL, "Solutions of Constrained Location Problems," *Management Science*, Vol. 22, No. 1, September 1975, pp. 51–56.

KHUMAWALA, B. M., "An Efficient Branch and Bound Algorithm for the Warehouse Location Problem," *Management Science*, Vol. 18, No. 12, August 1972, pp. B718–B731.

KHUMAWALA, B. M., "An Efficient Heuristic Procedure for the Uncapacitated Warehouse Location Problem," *Naval Research Logistics Quarterly*, Vol. 21, No. 1, March 1973, pp. 109–121.

KLEIN, M. and R. R. KLIMPEL, "Application of Linearly Constrained Nonlinear Optimization to Plant Location and Sizing," *Journal of Industrial Engineering*, Vol. 18, No. 1, January 1967, pp. 90–95.

KOLESAR, P. and W. E. WALKER, "An Algorithm for the Dynamic Relocation of Fire Companies," *Operations Research*, Vol. 22, No. 2, March–April 1974, pp. 249–274.

KUEHN, A. A. and M. J. HAMBURGER, "A Heuristic Program for Locating Warehouses," *Management Science*, Vol. 9, No. 4, July 1963, pp. 643–666.

LEA, A. C., "Location–Allocation Systems: An Annotated Bibliography," Discussion Paper No. 13, Department of Geography, University of Toronto, Toronto, May 1973.

MAGNANTI, T. L. and B. L. GOLDEN, "Transportation Planning: Network Models and Their Implementation," in A. C. Hax (editor), *Studies in Operations Management*, North Holland, New York, 1978.

MANNE, A. S., "Plant Location Under Economies-of-Scale—Decentralization and Computation," *Management Science*, Vol. 11, No. 2, November 1964, pp. 213–235.

MCDANIEL, D. and M. DEVINE, "A Modified Benders' Partitioning Algorithm for Mixed Integer Programming," *Management Science*, Vol. 24, No. 3, 1977, pp. 312–319.

MEYER, C. F., "A Long-Range Selection and Timing Analysis System for Facility Location: Implementation," *Management Science*, Vol. 20, No. 3, November 1973, pp. 261–273.

MOORE, J. M., *Plant Layout and Design*, Macmillan, New York, 1962.

MUTHER, R., *Practical Plant Layout*, McGraw-Hill, New York, 1955.

MUTHER, R., *Systematic Layout Planning*, Industrial Education Institute, Boston, 1961.

PINKUS, C. E., D. GROSS, and R. M. SOLAND, "Optimal Design of Multiactivity Multifacility Systems by Branch and Bound," *Operations Research*, Vol. 21, No. 1, January–February 1973, pp. 270–283.

PLANE, D. R. and T. E. HENDRICK, "Mathematical Programming and the Location of Fire Companies for the Denver Fire Department," *Operations Research*, Vol. 25, No. 4, July–August 1977, pp. 563–578.

PLANE, D. R. and C. MCMILLAN,   *Discrete Optimization*, Prentice-Hall, Englewood Cliffs, N.J., 1971.

REED, R.,   *Plant Layout: Factors, Principles, and Techniques*, Irwin, Homewood, Ill., 1961.

REED, R.,   *Plant Location, Layout and Maintenance*, Irwin, Homewood, Ill., 1967.

REVELLE, C., D. MARKS, and J. LIEBMAN,   "An Analysis of Private and Public Sector Location Models," *Management Science*, Vol. 16, No. 11, July 1970, pp. 692–708.

ROSS, G. T. and R. M. SOLAND,   "A Branch and Bound Algorithm for the Generalized Assignment Problem," *Mathematical Programming*, Vol. 8, 1975, pp. 91–105.

ROSS, G. T. and R. M. SOLAND,   "Modeling Facility Location Problems as Generalized Assignment Problems," *Management Science*, Vol. 24, No. 3, November 1977, pp. 345–357.

SCOTT, A. J.,   "Location–Allocation Systems: A Review," *Geographical Analysis*, Vol. 2, No. 2, 1970, pp. 95–119.

SCOTT, A. J.,   "Dynamic Location–Allocation Systems: Some Basic Planning Strategies," *Environment and Planning*, No. 3, 1971, pp. 73–82.

SHANNON, R. E. and J. P. IGNIZIO,   "A Heuristic Programming Algorithm for Warehouse Location," *AIIE Transactions*, Vol. 2, No. 4, December 1970, pp. 334–339.

SHYCON, H. N. and R. B. MAFFEI,   "Simulation—Tool for Better Distribution," *Harvard Business Review*, November–December 1960, pp. 65–75.

SHYCON, H. N. and R. B. MAFFEI,   "Remarks on the Kuehn–Hamburger Paper," *Management Science*, Vol. 9, No. 4, July 1963, pp. 667–668.

SOLAND, R. M.,   "Optimal Defensive Missile Allocation: A Discrete Min-Max Problem," *Operations Research*, Vol. 21, No. 2, March–April 1973, pp. 590–596.

SOLAND, R. M.,   "Optimal Facility Location with Concave Costs," *Operations Research*, Vol. 22, No. 2, March–April 1974, pp. 373–382.

SPIELBERG, K.,   "Algorithm for the Simple Plant-Location Problem with Some Side Conditions," *Operations Research*, Vol. 17, No. 1, January–February 1969a, pp. 85–111.

SPIELBERG, K.,   "Plant Location with Generalized Search Origin," *Management Science*, Vol. 16, No. 3, November 1969b, pp. 165–178.

SWEENEY, D. J. and R. L. TATHAM,   "An Improved Long-Run Model for Multiple Warehouse Location," *Management Science*, Vol. 22, No. 7, March 1976, pp. 748–758.

TAPIERO, C. S.,   "Transportation—Location–Allocation Problems Over Time," *Journal of Regional Science*, Vol. 11, No. 3, December 1971, pp. 377–386.

TRESON, W. G.,   *Factory Planning and Plant Layout*, Prentice-Hall, Englewood Cliffs, N.J., 1952.

TUCKER, J. V. and R. C. CARLSON,   "The Simple Plant-Location Problem Under Uncertainty," *Operations Research*, Vol. 24, No. 6, November–December 1976, pp. 1045–1054.

WAGNER, H. M.,   *Principles of Operations Research with Applications to Managerial Decisions*, Prentice-Hall, Englewood Cliffs, N.J., 1969.

WAGNER, H. M.,   "The Design of Production and Inventory Systems for Multifacility and Multiwarehouse Companies," *Operations Research*, Vol. 22, No. 2, March–April 1974, pp. 278–291.

WALKER, W. E.,   "Using the Set-Covering Problem to Assign Fire Companies to Fire Houses," *Operations Research*, Vol. 22, No. 2, March–April 1974, pp. 275–277.

WALKER, W. E., "A Heuristic Adjacent Extreme Point Algorithm for the Fixed Charge Problem," *Management Science*, Vol. 22, No. 5, January 1976, pp. 587–596.

WESOLOWSKY, G. O., "Dynamic Facility Location," *Management Science*, Vol. 19, No. 11, July 1973, pp. 1241–1248.

WESOLOWSKY, G. O. and W. G. TRUSCOTT, "The Multiperiod Location–Allocation Problem with Relocation of Facilities," *Management Science*, Vol. 22, No. 1, September 1975, pp. 57–65.

WHITE, J. A., "On the Optimum Design of Warehouses Having Radial Aisles," *AIIE Transactions*, Vol. 4, No. 4, December 1972, pp. 333–336.

WIEST, J. D., "Heuristic Programs for Decision Making," *Harvard Business Review*, September–October 1966, pp. 129–143.

3

Aggregate Production Planning

3.1 Introduction

Production planning is concerned with the determination of production, inventory, and work force levels to meet fluctuating demand requirements. Normally, the physical resources of the firm are assumed to be fixed during the planning horizon of interest and the planning effort is oriented toward the best utilization of those resources, given the external demand requirements. A problem usually arises because the times and quantities imposed by the demand requirements seldom coincide with the time and quantities which use the firm's resources efficiently. Whenever the conditions affecting the production process are not stable in time (due to changes in demand, cost components, or capacity availability), production should be planned in an aggregate way to obtain effective resource utilization. The time horizon of this planning activity is dictated by the nature of the dynamic variations; for example, if demand seasonalities are present, a full seasonal cycle should be included into the planning horizon. Commonly the time horizon varies from six to 18 months, 12 months being a suitable figure for most planning systems.

Since it is usually impossible to consider every fine detail associated with the production process while maintaining such a long planning horizon, it is mandatory to aggregate the information being processed. This aggregation can take place by consolidating similar items into product groups, different machines into machine centers, different labor skills into labor centers, and individual customers into market regions. The type of aggregation to be performed is suggested by the nature of the planning systems to be used, and the technical as well as managerial characteristics of the production activities. Aggregation forces the use of a consistent set of measurement units. It is common to express aggregate demand in production hours.

Once the aggregate plan is generated, constraints are imposed on the detailed production scheduling process which decide the specific quantities to be produced of each individual item. These constraints normally specify production rates or total amounts to be produced per month for a given product family. In addition, crew sizes, levels of machine utilization, and amounts of overtime to be used are determined.

When demand requirements do not change with time, and costs and prices are also stable, it may be feasible to bypass entirely the aggregate planning process, provided the resources of the firm are well balanced to absorb the constant requirements. However, when these conditions are not met, serious inefficiencies or even infeasibility might result from attempting to plan production, responding only to immediate requirements and ignoring the future consequences of present decisions. To illustrate this point, consider what happens when an order point–order quantity inventory control system (see Chapter 4) that treats every item in isolation, is applied in the presence of strong demand seasonalities. First, at the beginning of the peak season demand starts increasing rapidly and a large number of items simultaneously trigger the order point, demanding production runs of the amount specified by the order quantities. Being unable to satisfy all these orders while maintaining an adequate service level, management may react by reducing the production run lengths, thereby creating multiple changeovers of small quantities. This, in turn, reduces the overall productivity (because of the high percentage of idle machine time due to the large number of changeovers), increases costs, and deteriorates customer service levels. Second, items at the end of the season are produced in normal order quantities (typically large). Since demand is low, capacities tend to be idle, replenishment times decrease, order points get lower, fewer items trigger leading to increasing idle time, and so on. Inventory is created that is inactive until the beginning of the next season or that must be liquidated at salvage values. An effective aggregate capacity planning system would prevent such inefficiencies.

3.1.1   Ways to Absorb Demand Fluctuations

There are several methods that managers can use to absorb changing demand patterns. These ways can be combined to create a large number of alternative production planning options.

1. Management can change the size of the work force by hiring and laying off, thus allowing changes in the production rate to take place. Excessive use of these practices, however, can create severe labor problems.
2. While maintaining a uniform regular work force, management can vary the production rate by introducing overtime and/or idle time, or relying on outside subcontracting.
3. While maintaining a uniform production rate, management can anticipate future demand by accumulating seasonal inventories. The tradeoff between

the cost incurred in changing production rates and holding seasonal inventories is the basic question to be resolved in most practical situations.

4. Management can also resort to planned backlogs whenever customers may accept delays in filling their orders.

5. An alternative which has to be resolved at a higher planning level is the development of complementary product lines with demand patterns which are counterseasonal to the existing products. This alternative is very effective in producing a more even utilization of the firm's resources, but it does not eliminate the need for aggregate planning.

3.1.2 Costs Relevant to Aggregate Production Planning

Relevant costs can be categorized as follows:

1. *Basic production costs.* Included here are material costs, direct labor costs, and overhead costs. It is customary to divide these costs into variable and fixed costs, depending on whether the amount of the incurred cost over a certain time span is or is not a function of the corresponding production volume.

2. *Costs associated with changes in the production rate.* Typically, this category includes the costs of increasing the production rate above the level that can be achieved during the regular work schedule with the available work force. Since this objective can be accomplished either by varying the size of the work force and/or working overtime, this category includes costs involved in hiring, training, and laying off personnel, as well as overtime compensations. For some companies outside subcontracting represents a third alternative, in which case the cost of subcontracting will also fall in this category.

3. *Inventory related costs.* In the most general sense, inventories can take on both positive and negative values. In the first case, there will be inventory holding costs incurred, in which the major component is the cost of capital tied up in inventory; other components are storing, insurance, taxes, spoilage, and obsolescence. In the second case, shortage costs occur; they are usually very difficult to measure and include costs of expediting, loss of customer goodwill, and loss of sales revenues resulting from the shortage situation.

For more extensive discussions on the above cost elements, the reader can consult McGarrah [1963], Holt et al. [1960], and Buffa [1972].

3.1.3 The Role of Models in Aggregate Production Planning

Models have played an important role in supporting management decisions in aggregate production planning. Anshen et al. [1958] indicate that models are of great value in helping managers to:

1. Quantify and use the intangibles which are always present in the background of their thinking but which are incorporated only vaguely and sporadically in scheduling decisions.
2. Make routine the comprehensive consideration of all factors relevant to scheduling decisions, thereby inhibiting judgments based on incomplete, obvious, or easily handled criteria.
3. Fit each scheduling decision into its appropriate place in the historical series of decisions and, through the feedback mechanism incorporated in the decision rules, automatically correct for prior forecasting errors.
4. Free themselves from routine decision-making activities, thereby giving them greater freedom and opportunity for dealing with extraordinary situations.

In order to describe the different types of models that can be used in supporting aggregate planning decisions, we found it useful to classify the models according to the assumptions they make about the structure of the cost components. In the following sections, first linear cost models will be analyzed, followed by quadratic cost models, fixed cost models, and then general nonlinear cost models. Our discussion will closely follow Hax [1978].

3.2 Linear Cost Models

Some of the very first models proposed to guide aggregate planning decisions assume linearity in the cost behavior of the decision variables. These kinds of models are very popular even today because of the computational conveniences associated with linear programming. Moreover, these models are less restrictive than they first appear because nonlinear cost functions can be approximated to any degree of accuracy by piecewise linear segments (Bradley, Hax, and Magnanti [1977, chap. 13.5]); these approximations result in linear programs whenever a convex cost function is minimized, or a concave cost function is maximized.

The linear cost models can be divided into two categories, depending on how management goals are incorporated into the formulation:

- classical linear programming formulations, where the objective function represents a unique goal (such as minimizing the total production cost)
- goal programming formulations, in which several goals appear explicitly, and tradeoffs among these goals are worked out based on a set of priorities, rather than specific numerical cost factors

3.2.1 Classical Linear Programming Models

Depending on whether hiring and firing are considered to be decision variables two types of models will result: fixed work force and variable work force models.

3.2.1.1   Fixed work force models

The case where the work force is fixed will be considered first. Hirings and layoffs to absorb demand fluctuations during the planning horizon are disallowed. Production rates can fluctuate only by using overtime from the regular work force.

The following notation is used to describe the model in mathematical terms.

Parameters:

v_{it} = unit production cost for product i in period t (exclusive of labor costs)

c_{it} = inventory carrying cost per unit of product i held in stock from period t to $t + 1$

r_t = cost per manhour of regular labor in period t

o_t = cost per manhour of overtime labor in period t

d_{it} = forecast demand for product i in period t

k_i = manhours required to produce one unit of product i

$(rm)_t$ = total manhours of regular labor available in period t

$(om)_t$ = total manhours of overtime labor available in period t

I_{io} = initial inventory level for product i

W_o = initial regular work force level, in manhours

T = time horizon, in periods

N = total number of products.

Decision variables:

X_{it} = units of product i to be produced in period t

I_{it} = units of product i to be left over as inventory in period t

W_t = manhours of regular labor used during period t

O_t = manhours of overtime labor used during period t.

A simple version of the fixed work force–linear cost model is:

$$\text{Minimize } Z = \sum_{i=1}^{N} \sum_{t=1}^{T} (v_{it} X_{it} + c_{it} I_{it}) + \sum_{t=1}^{T} (r_t W_t + o_t O_t) \qquad (3.1)$$

subject to:

$$X_{it} + I_{i,t-1} - I_{it} = d_{it} \qquad \begin{cases} t = 1, \ldots, T \\ i = 1, \ldots, N \end{cases} \qquad (3.2)$$

$$\sum_{i=1}^{N} k_i X_{it} - W_t - O_t = 0 \qquad t = 1, \ldots, T \qquad (3.3)$$

$$0 \leqslant W_t \leqslant (rm)_t \qquad t = 1, \ldots, T \qquad (3.4)$$

$$0 \leqslant O_t \leqslant (om)_t \qquad t = 1, \ldots, T \qquad (3.5)$$

$$X_{it}, I_{it} \geqslant 0 \qquad \begin{cases} i = 1, \ldots, N \\ t = 1, \ldots, T. \end{cases} \qquad (3.6)$$

The objective function (3.1) expresses the minimization of variable production, inventory, and regular and overtime labor costs. If the marginal production costs are invariant over time, $v_{it} = v_i$, the terms $v_i X_{it}$ do not need to be included in the objective function. Due to the cost minimization objective, there will be no inventory left at the end of period T; therefore, total production over the planning horizon is a constant equal to the total demand less the initial inventory:

$$\sum_{i=1}^{N} \sum_{t=1}^{T} v_i X_{it} = \sum_{i=1}^{N} v_i \left(\sum_{t=1}^{T} d_{it} - I_{io} \right) = \text{Constant}.$$

Similarly, if the payroll of the available regular work force $(rm)_t$ constitutes a fixed commitment (that is, employees get full pay whether they are fully employed or idle), the term $\sum_{t=1}^{T} r_t W_t$ becomes $\sum_{t=1}^{T} r_t (rm)_t = \text{Constant}$, hence it should be deleted from (3.1).

Constraints (3.2) represent the typical production-inventory balance equation, in which both the amount of inventory I_{it} to be left in stock at the end of period t and the demand d_{it} in period t are supplied by: the amount $I_{i,t-1}$ of product i in stock at the end of period $(t-1)$, and the production X_{it} in period t. Notice that (3.6) implies that no backordering is allowed. The next model will show how backorders can be incorporated. Moreover, (3.2) assumes a deterministic demand, d_{it}, for every item in every time period. One way to allow for uncertainties in the demand forecast is to specify a lower bound for the ending inventory in each period, that is, $I_{it} \geqslant ss_{it}$, where ss_{it} is the safety stock associated with item i in period t (safety stocks depend on the demand forecast errors and the level of customer service to be provided; see Chapter 4).

Constraints (3.3) define the total manpower to be used in every period. This model formulation assumes that manpower availability is the only constraining resource of the production process. It is straightforward to expand the number of resources being considered, provided that the linearity assumptions are maintained.

Constraints (3.4) and (3.5) impose lower and upper bounds on the use of regular and overtime manhours in every time period.

It has been already indicated how constraints (3.6) could be changed to incorporate safety stocks. One should bear in mind that, if no terminal conditions are imposed upon the inventories at the end of the planning horizon, the model will drive them to zero. If total depletion of inventories is undesirable, a target inventory constraint should be added in the model. An additional constraint should also be attached if there are storage requirements that cannot be exceeded; for example, the constraint

$$\sum_{i=1}^{N} I_{it} \leqslant (sc)_t \qquad t = 1, \ldots, T$$

implies that the total inventory in each period cannot be greater than the total storage capacity $(sc)_t$.

When it is necessary to assign products to different work centers with limited capacities, the decision variables are redefined to identify those decisions explicitly. For example, X_{ict} may denote the amount of product i produced at working center c during period t. It is straightforward to carry out the resulting transformations in the overall model.

Even the very simple model described by expressions (3.1)–(3.6) could present enormous computational difficulties if the individual items to be scheduled are not grouped in broad product categories. If one ignores constraints (3.4), (3.5), and (3.6), which merely represent upper and lower bounds for the decision variables, the model consists of $T \cdot (N + 1)$ effective constraints. When dealing with complex production situations, the total number of individual items, N, may be several thousands. For example, if the planning model has 12 time periods and the production planning process involves 5,000 items, the model would have about 60,000 constraints, which exceed the capabilities of a regular linear programming code.

In most practical applications, however, it would not be functional to plan the allocations of the production resources at this level of detail. First, a detailed scheduling program should take into account a large number of technological and marketing considerations which cannot be included in the overall model due to their highly qualitative nature. Second, as has been mentioned before, many of the planning issues to be resolved within the model deal with broad allocations of resources, and excessively detailed information would obscure rather than enlighten these decisions. Third, aggregate forecasts are more accurate than detailed forecasts.

It is common practice, therefore, to aggregate items in product types. The criteria for aggregation are evident from the model structure: members of a single product type should share similar demand patterns (d_{it}), have similar cost characteristics (v_{it}, c_{it}), and require similar unit production times (k_i). Once the aggregate planning decisions are made, these decisions impose constraints that must be observed when performing detailed item scheduling (see Chapter 6).

Notice that this model, as well as any other dynamic planning model, requires the definition of a planning horizon T and the partitioning of this time horizon into multiple time periods. One might assume that this partitioning results in T equally spaced time periods; this does not need to be the case. Many operational planning systems are better designed if this partitioning generates uneven time periods, so that the more recent time periods carry more detailed information.

Due to the uncertain environment in which this planning effort is being conducted, a widely adopted strategy is planning with a rolling horizon. Under this strategy the T period model (3.1)–(3.6) is repeatedly solved, usually at the end of every time period, as new information becomes available and is used to update the model parameters. Although, in principle, the solution to model (3.1)–(3.6) provides decisions to be carried out over all periods in the model, only the plan for the upcoming period is actually implemented before the model is rerun. Of course, questions could be raised with respect to how good a finite horizon strategy is in an infinite horizon environment. There are two reasons why the finite horizon strategy is appropriate (Baker [1975]):

- In general, the optimal solution to an infinite horizon model requires parameter estimations for an infinite number of future periods. The only exception occurs when planning horizon theorems are applicable (see sections 3.4.1 and 3.5.1.1). Because of the limited information available about the future, and because of the computational problems associated with increasingly large models, in the general case the finite horizon strategy imposes itself as the only viable alternative.
- The quality of forecasts tends to deteriorate with the distance into the future of the period for which they are made. Therefore, the value to the planning process of forecasts made for periods beyond a certain planning horizon T is questionable.

Broad technological, institutional, marketing, financial, and organizational constraints can also be included in the model formulation. This flexibility, characteristic of the linear programming approach to problem solving, has made this type of model very useful and popular.

A simple version of the fixed work force linear programming model, having a transportation problem structure, was first proposed by Bowman [1956].

3.2.1.2 Variable work force models

Whenever it is feasible to change the work force during the planning horizon as a way to counteract demand fluctuations, the composition of the work force becomes a decision variable whose values can change by hiring and laying off personnel. Therefore, the corresponding hiring and layoff costs should be part of the objective function. Moreover, the corresponding model presented below allows for shortages to be included; thus a backordering cost is also part of the formulation.

Besides the decision variables and parameters introduced in the previous model, the following additional notations are needed:

H_t = manhours of regular work force hired in period t

F_t = manhours of regular work force laid off in period t

I_{it}^+ = units of ending inventory of product i in period t

I_{it}^- = units of product i backordered at the end of period t

b_{it} = cost per unit of backorder of product i carried from period t to $t+1$

h_t = cost of hiring one manhour in period t

f_t = cost of laying off one manhour in period t

p = overtime allowed as a fraction of the regular hours.

A simple version of the variable work force model can be formulated as follows:

Minimize
$$Z = \sum_{i=1}^{N} \sum_{t=1}^{T} \left(v_{it} X_{it} + c_{it} I_{it}^+ + b_{it} I_{it}^- \right)$$

$$+ \sum_{t=1}^{T} \left(r_t W_t + o_t O_t + h_t H_t + f_t F_t \right) \tag{3.7}$$

subject to:

$$X_{it} + I_{i,t-1}^+ - I_{i,t-1}^- - I_{it}^+ + I_{it}^- = d_{it} \qquad \begin{cases} i = 1, \ldots, N \\ t = 1, \ldots, T \end{cases} \tag{3.8}$$

$$\sum_{i=1}^{N} k_i X_{it} - W_t - O_t \leqslant 0 \qquad t = 1, \ldots, T \tag{3.9}$$

$$W_t - W_{t-1} - H_t + F_t = 0 \qquad t = 1, \ldots, T \tag{3.10}$$

$$- pW_t + O_t \leqslant 0 \qquad t = 1, \ldots, T \tag{3.11}$$

$$X_{it}, I_{it}^+, I_{it}^- \geqslant 0 \qquad \begin{cases} i = 1, \ldots, N \\ t = 1, \ldots, T \end{cases} \tag{3.12}$$

$$W_t, O_t, P_t, H_t, F_t \geqslant 0 \qquad t = 1, \ldots, T. \tag{3.13}$$

The objective function is self-explanatory.

Constraints (3.8) represent the production-inventory balance equation. Notice that this is equivalent to the old balance equation

$$X_{it} + I_{i,t-1} - I_{it} = d_{it},$$

except that now:

$$I_{it} = I_{it}^+ - I_{it}^-   t = 1, \ldots, T.$$

In the present model the ending inventory, I_{it}, can be either positive ($I_{it}^+ > 0$ indicates that stock remains at the end of the period) or negative ($I_{it}^- > 0$ indicates an accumulation of backorders at the end of the period). Since there is a cost attached to both I_{it}^+ and I_{it}^- those variables will never be positive simultaneously. Attention should be drawn to the real meaning of I_{it}^- in model (3.7)–(3.13): I_{it}^- represents backorders that accumulate from period to period, which means that if demand cannot be satisfied in some period it can be satisfied at a later time; of course, a penalty will be incurred for any backordering of this sort. A different situation, which can also be easily modeled, arises when stockouts result in lost sales rather than backorders; in this case constraints (3.8) would become $X_{it} + I_{i,t-1}^+ - I_{it}^+ + I_{it}^- = d_{it}$, where I_{it}^- is the amount of demand for item i in period t that cannot be served, consequently resulting in lost sales.

Constraints (3.9) limit production to available manpower. Since a cost is associated with hirings and layoffs it is possible that at some point in time the regular work force W_t will be partially idle, therefore the $\leqslant$ sign in (3.9) is perfectly justified.

Constraints (3.10) define the change in the work force size during period t, that is, $W_t - W_{t-1} = H_t - F_t$. Labor is added whenever $H_t > 0$, or is subtracted whenever $F_t > 0$. Once again, since costs are attached to both hirings and layoffs, H_t and F_t will never have positive values simultaneously in a given time period.

Constraints (3.11) impose an upper bound on the total overtime available in period t as a function of the regular work force size; that is, $O_t \leqslant pW_t$, where p is the overtime allowed as a fraction of the regular hours.

Many of the comments made for the fixed work force model regarding ways to expand or simplify the models and ways to aggregate items in product types are applicable here and are not repeated. One remark, however: if safety stocks are imposed ($I_{it}^+ \geqslant ss_{it}$), situations could develop in which backorders are planned along with carrying positive inventories in the form of safety stocks. This turns out to be no contradiction when one thinks that safety stocks are not intended to be used inside the planning model (3.7)–(3.13) to serve forecasted demand or to fill in accumulated backorders; rather, safety stocks are held to meet unexpected contingencies arising outside the model from uncertain demand.

The first of this type of models was proposed by Hanssmann and Hess [1960]. Several alternative approaches have been suggested, particularly those by Haehling von Lanzenaur [1970a], and O'Malley, Elmaghraby, and Jeske [1966].

Lippman et al. [1967a] have analyzed the form of the optimal policies for a single-product problem assuming convex production costs, V-shaped manpower fluctuation costs, and increasing holding costs. In reference [1967b] the authors provide an efficient algorithm to solve the special case where all the cost functions are linear and demand requirements are either monotone decreasing or increasing. The algorithm is an iterative procedure that starts by guessing the value of W_T, the regular manpower at the end of the planning horizon. It provides, next, an optimum policy for this value of W_T, and checks this policy against an optimality test. If an improvement is possible the algorithm yields a better value of W_T and the process is repeated. Convergence is guaranteed in a finite number of iterations.

Whenever costs are linear and demand requirements are nondecreasing, there exists an optimum policy such that

$$
\begin{aligned}
W_{t+1} &\geqslant W_t & t &= 1, \ldots, T-1 \\
O_{t+1} &\geqslant O_t & t &= 1, \ldots, T-1 \\
\frac{O_{t+1}}{W_{t+1}} &\geqslant \frac{O_t}{W_t} & t &= 1, \ldots, T-1 \\
(W_T - W_t)O_t &= 0 & t &= 1, \ldots, T.
\end{aligned}
$$

This result is used throughout the computational process. Yuan [1967] extended this approach to a multiproduct problem.

In an early work, Hoffman and Jacobs [1954] and Antosiewicz and Hoffman [1954] considered a linear cost model for a single product, allowing for changes in the production rate to be represented in the objective function. They analyzed the qualitative properties of the optimum solution, and proposed simple procedures to compute that solution when demand requirements are monotone increasing. This work was extended by Johnson and Dantzig [1955].

Linear programming models can be expanded easily to cover production processes with several stages. A comprehensive discussion of multistage linear programming models including multiple routings, multiple sources, product mix decisions, and multiple production and distribution decisions is presented by Johnson and Montgomery [1974]; a survey and a reformulation of the multistage production planning problem are given by Candea [1977].

3.2.2   Goal Programming Models

One important shortcoming of the classical linear programming formulations is that they can treat explicitly only one objective. This objective is expressed as the optimization of a function that must be homogeneous; this means that all relevant decision variables have to be converted such as to become measurable by a common unit (most often, the dollar).

In many cases, however, managerial decisions require the consideration of several goals, which can often conflict with each other and might be incommensurable. There are various ways of approaching the problem:

- Select the most important of these objectives, make it into the objective function of the optimization model, and incorporate the others into the constraint set so as to generate a minimum level of achievement of those objectives.
- Establish a global objective function by heuristic means: weight the various objectives and add them up to obtain the global objective. A method to perform this unification of multiple objectives is suggested by Briskin [1966].

These two approaches, although relatively straightforward to implement, are arbitrary and pragmatic, and do not necessarily resolve the basic issues behind the multiple objective question.

- A third approach is to use utility theory, which requires the direct assessment of the multiattribute preference function of the decision maker (Keeney and Raiffa [1976]). This is conceptually extremely attractive but requires a great deal of work to be implemented (Hax and Wiig [1976]); also, there are still methodological limitations in developing utility functions for either individuals or groups.
- Another approach is goal programming, which will be discussed in this section.

Goal programming, as defined by Lee [1972, p. 21], is "a modification and extension of linear programming. The goal programming approach allows a simultaneous solution of a system of complex objectives rather than a single objective."

To formulate a problem as a goal programming model one has to specify a set of goals along with the priority level associated with each of them. The set of constraints is set up, in general, of two kinds of relationships: regular constraints (like in any LP) representing dependencies among decision variables and parameters, and goal constraints relating the decision variables to goals. The deviational variables, which are always part of the goal constraints, will show the extent to which the goals are met in the optimal solution. To complete the model the objective function has to be defined. The objective is to achieve to the fullest possible extent every specified goal, in order of its priority. Therefore, the objective function has a multilevel structure; each level contains the sum (possibly weighted) of the deviational variables associated with the goals at that priority level.

During the solution procedure, first the deviations from the goal with the highest level of priority are minimized as much as possible, then the deviations for the goal with the second priority level, and so on. Once a higher priority goal is optimized, the optimization of a lower priority goal cannot possibly improve the higher goal, nor is it allowed to worsen the accomplishment level of the higher priority goal.

It is clear from the above considerations that a goal programming model is, by its nature, always a minimization problem.

The general form of a goal constraint is:

$$\sum_{j=1}^{n} a_{ij} X_j + D_i^- - D_i^+ = b_i \qquad i = 1, \ldots, m,$$

where b_i can be regarded as the target level of the ith goal, and:

X_j = the jth decision variable, $j = 1, \ldots, n$

a_{ij} = coefficient relating the jth decision variable to the ith goal

D_i^- = deviational variable denoting the amount by which the ith goal is underachieved

D_i^+ = deviational variable denoting the amount by which the ith goal is overachieved.

With respect to the ith goal, three important types of objective functions can be distinguished:

1. Minimize $(D_i^+ + D_i^-)$—this minimizes the absolute value of $(\sum_{j=1}^{n} a_{ij} X_j - b_i)$, by searching for that vector of X_j's that would meet the goal $\sum_{j=1}^{n} a_{ij} X_j = b_i$ exactly, in which case $D_i^+ = D_i^- = 0$. It is not always possible to find such X_j's; therefore, either D_i^+ or D_i^- (but not both) can be positive. If, in the optimal solution $D_i^+ > 0$, then $D_i^- = 0$ and $\sum_{j=1}^{n} a_{ij} X_j > b_i$; similarly, if $D_i^- > 0$, then $D_i^+ = 0$ and $\sum_{j=1}^{n} a_{ij} X_j < b_i$.
2. Minimize D_i^+—this minimizes the positive deviation from the target value, which is equivalent to stating that deviations of $\sum_{j=1}^{n} a_{ij} X_j$ above b_i are undesirable. However, no penalty is attached to underachieving the ith goal, which implies that underachievements are regarded as acceptable. For example, overtime operation hours should be limited, if possible, to no more than a specified level.
3. Minimize D_i^-—this minimizes the negative deviation from the target level of the goal. Deviations of $\sum_{j=1}^{n} a_{ij} X_j$ below b_i are not desirable, while overachievements are not penalized. For example, it is wished that profits be at least as high as a prespecified figure.

Other objective functions are also possible, although not very often used:

4. Minimize $(D_i^- - D_i^+)$—it is equivalent to the minimization of D_i^- with b_i set sufficiently large.
5. Minimize $(D_i^+ - D_i^-)$—equivalent to the minimization of D_i^+ if b_i is made very small.

A variant of "Minimize $(D_i^+ + D_i^-)$" is obtained when different weights are attached to the two variables:

$$\text{Minimize } (w_1 D_i^+ + w_2 D_i^-)$$

For example: Suppose the target inventory is zero with D_i^+, D_i^- representing inventory and storage, respectively; then the two weights are either the costs or are proportional to the costs of carrying inventory and incurring shortages, respectively.

To illustrate the goal programming approach, consider an aggregate production planning problem with a fixed work force. N products are manufactured, the planning horizon is T period long, there is only one binding resource, the work force, which is fixed, and regular hours have to be paid for whether employees are idle or not. Suppose the management has specified the following priorities associated with its aggregate planning goal structure:

$P_1 =$ the highest priority assigned to the satisfaction of demand; the fewer the backorders, the higher the service level.

$P_2 =$ the second priority level associated with the minimization of both overtime hours and idle time. The minimization of over-time is desired since one hour of overtime costs 50% more than an hour of regular time. The minimization of idle time is sought because, although the regular hours constitute a fixed commitment, idle time is considered detrimental to workers' discipline and morale.

$P_3 =$ the third priority assigned to the minimization of end-of-the-month inventories.

The model is:

$$\text{Minimize } Z = P_1 \sum_{i=1}^{N} \sum_{t=1}^{T} p_i D_{it}^- + P_2 \sum_{t=1}^{T} \left(1.5R_t^+ + R_t^-\right) + P_3 \sum_{i=1}^{N} \sum_{t=1}^{T-1} c_i D_{it}^+$$

$$(3.14)$$

subject to:

$$I_{i0} + X_{i1} - D_{i1}^+ + D_{i1}^- = d_{i1} \qquad i = 1,\ldots,N \qquad (3.15)$$

$$D_{i,t-1}^+ + X_{it} - D_{it}^+ + D_{it}^- - D_{i,t-1}^- = d_{it} \qquad \begin{cases} t = 2,\ldots,T-1 \\ i = 1,\ldots,N \end{cases} \qquad (3.16)$$

$$D_{i,T-1}^+ + X_{iT} + D_{iT}^- - D_{i,T-1}^- = d_{iT} \qquad i = 1,\ldots,N \qquad (3.17)$$

$$\sum_{i=1}^{N} k_i X_{it} + R_t^- - R_t^+ = (rm)_t \qquad t = 1,\ldots,T \qquad (3.18)$$

$$R_t^+ \leqslant (om)_t \qquad t = 1,\ldots,T \qquad (3.19)$$

$$X_{it}, D_{it}^-, R_t^+, R_t^- \geqslant 0 \qquad \begin{cases} i = 1,\ldots,N \\ t = 1,\ldots,T \end{cases} \qquad (3.20)$$

$$D_{it}^+ \geqslant 0 \qquad \begin{cases} i = 1,\ldots,N \\ t = 1,\ldots,T-1. \end{cases} \qquad (3.21)$$

The notations we have used are:

Parameters:

p_i = profit per unit of product i

c_i = unit cost of product i

d_{it} = forecast demand for product i in period t

k_i = manhours required to produce one unit of product i

$(rm)_t$ = total manhours of regular labor available in period t

$(om)_t$ = total manhours of overtime labor available in period t

I_{i0} = initial inventory of product i.

Decision variables:

X_{it} = amount of product i to be produced in period t

D_{it}^+ = ending inventory of product i in period t

D_{it}^- = backorders of product i at the end of period t

R_t^+ = hours of overtime in period t

R_t^- = hours of idle time in period t.

The objective function (3.14) shows that the highest priority goal is the minimization of the backorders. Since the N products differ in terms of profitability, their backorders have been weighted by the corresponding profit margins.

The second level of priority involves the minimization of overtime and idle time. The overtime variable is weighted by its relative cost compared to regular time.

The lowest priority goal aims at minimizing ending inventories. It has been considered appropriate to weight the inventory variables by the unit costs of the items because the unit cost determines the investment in inventories; also, in most cases, the unit inventory carrying cost is proportional to the unit cost.

Constraints (3.15)–(3.17) are the inventory balance equations in which the deviational variables indicate by how much the availability of product i in period t exceeds or misses the forecast level of demand. In period 1 there are no initial backorders. In constraint (3.17) the deviational variable D_{iT}^+ is omitted in order to avoid piling up excess inventory solely for the sake of minimizing idle time.

Constraints (3.18) stipulate that, if insufficient, the available regular manhours can be supplemented by overtime R_t^+. It is also possible, however, to underutilize the regular manhours by R_t^-.

Constraint (3.19) places an upper bound on the amount of overtime that can be scheduled.

P_1, P_2, P_3 are nonquantitative parameters. They are ranking coefficients that show goal priorities. The meaning of this hierarchy is that the decision variables have to be chosen such as to have the backorders minimized, disregarding the second and third priority goals. Only after the highest priority goal has been achieved is one supposed to consider the overtime and idle time issue, and so on.

From the above, it is apparent that the simplex algorithm can be modified to solve goal programming problems: start by finding the optimum solution to the linear program whose objective function is the highest priority (P_1) portion of the original objective function. After this is done, solve another linear program whose objective function is the next highest priority (P_2) portion of the original objective function, and so on.

The interested reader can find a good treatment of the entire topic together with the modified simplex method for solving goal programming models in Lee [1972].

3.2.3 Advantages and Disadvantages of Linear Cost Models

The overwhelming advantage of linear cost models is that they generate linear programs which can be solved by readily available and efficient computer codes. Linear programs permit models with a large number of decision variables and constraints to be solved expediently and cheaply. In addition, linear programming lends itself very well to the performance of parametric and sensitivity analyses; this feature can be helpful in making aggregate planning decisions. The shadow price information can be of assistance in identifying opportunities for capacity expansions, marketing penetration strategies, new product introductions, and so on.

As indicated before, the linearity assumptions which are implicit in these models are less restrictive than they appear. First, cost structures might behave linearly within the range of interest of the decision variables under consideration. Second, general convex separable functions can be treated with piecewise linear approximation. Moreover, with some ingenuity certain functions which at first seem to present nonlinear characteristics can be linearized, as indicated in the cited references of Hanssmann and Hess [1960] and Haehling von Lanzenauer [1970a].

Goal programming models bring in added capability to deal explicitly with multiple, and often conflicting and incommensurable, goals. They also allow one to better handle decision variables whose associated costs might prove difficult, or even impossible, to estimate (such as, for instance, the cost of backorders).

The most serious disadvantage of linear programming models is their failure to deal with demand uncertainties explicitly. However, this can be corrected by introducing safety stocks, as explained in subsection 3.2.1.1. Moreover, Dzielinski, Baker, and Manne [1963] have reported favorable experiences in using linear programming models under fairly uncertain and dynamic environments.

3.3   Quadratic Cost Models (Linear Decision Rules)

Holt, Modigliani, Muth, and Simon [1960] found that quadratic functions could provide good approximations to the actual costs involved in planning production and employment. Also, a good reason behind using quadratic cost models in solving aggregate capacity planning problems is that the decision rules that are generated possess a linear structure (because the differentiation of a quadratic function produces a linear function); therefore, the decision rules are easy to use. Thus, these models are also known as *linear decision rules*. The first model of this kind was developed by Holt, Modigliani, Muth, and Simon (HMMS). Subsequently, several extensions have been offered. The original HMMS model will be briefly discussed below.

The HMMS model calls for a complete aggregation of all product types into a single category. This might require the use of appropriate compatible units that allow the transformation to be made. Thus, there are essentially two decision variables:

$$X_t = \text{aggregate production rate for period } t$$

$$W_t = \text{work force size in period } t.$$

The remaining decision variable,

$$I_t = \text{ending inventory in period } t,$$

is specified automatically by the values of X_t and W_t, and the relationship that exists among the three variables and the demand d_t in period t.

The optimum decision rules, therefore, will have to specify the levels of the aggregate production and work force such as to minimize a cost function (which will turn out to be quadratic in this case).

3.3.1   Cost Components

The components of the quadratic cost function that have been identified in the HMMS model are:

1. *Regular payroll costs.* These costs are assumed to increase linearly with the work force size, according to the following relationship:

$$c_1 W_t + c_{13},$$

where c_1 and c_{13} are cost coefficients to be determined externally to the model. Since c_{13} is a constant, it can be eliminated from further consideration.

2. *Hiring and layoff costs.* Both hiring and layoff costs are assumed quadratic in the work force variation ($W_t - W_{t-1}$), thus allowing an increasing cost rate to be incorporated. The specific relationship is a U-shaped curve given by:

$$c_2(W_t - W_{t-1} - c_{11})^2$$

where c_2 and c_{11} are constants to be evaluated. c_{11} is introduced to allow for asymmetry in the cost function.

3. *Overtime and idle costs.* Given a work force size W_t there is a desirable production rate of $c_4 W_t$. If the production rate exceeds that amount, there will be overtime cost; if it is lower than that amount, there will be a cost of idle time. The exact nature of these cost relationships is given by the expression

$$c_3(X_t - c_4 W_t)^2 + c_5 X_t - c_6 W_t + c_{12} X_t W_t$$

where the last three terms are given to improve the accuracy of the cost relationships.

4. *Inventory and backorder costs.* The relationship which characterizes the inventory related costs is assumed to be of the following form:

$$c_7[I_t - (c_8 + c_9 d_t)]^2$$

where:

d_t = expected unit of aggregate product demand in period t.

The target inventory level is $c_8 + c_9 d_t$; when deviations from this target occur, either carrying or backorder costs are incurred which increase with the square of these deviations. In the original HMMS work, c_9 was set to zero.

The estimation of the cost coefficients is an expensive and time-consuming activity requiring statistical analysis, accounting information, and managerial inputs. Extensive work has been done to improve the quality of these estimates (Van dePanne and Bosje [1962], Kriebel [1967]), and to develop aggregate cost functions which represent the cost characteristics of the individual items (Bergstrom and Smith [1970], Krajewski et al. [1973]).

3.3.2   Model Formulation

Given the cost structure discussed above, the aggregate capacity planning model can be formulated as:

$$\text{Minimize } Z = \sum_{t=1}^{T} \left[(c_1 - c_6)W_t + c_2(W_t - W_{t-1} - c_{11})^2 + c_3(X_t - c_4 W_t)^2 \right.$$

$$\left. + c_5 X_t + c_{12} X_t W_t + c_7(I_t - c_8 - c_9 d_t)^2 + c_{13} \right] \qquad (3.22)$$

subject to:

$$X_t + I_{t-1} - I_t = d_t \qquad\qquad t = 1, \ldots, T \qquad\qquad (3.23)$$

$$X_t, W_t \geqslant 0 \qquad\qquad t = 1, \ldots, T. \qquad\qquad (3.24)$$

One of the interesting features of the model is that it does not assume demand d_t to be deterministic. Simon [1956] proved that if the demand forecasts are unbiased and represent expected values, the linear decision rules resulting from the minimization of (3.22) subject to constraints (3.23) and (3.24) provide minimum expected costs. Therefore, the objective functions (3.22) should be regarded as the minimization of expected costs.

3.3.3 The Linear Decision Rules

The above model has a unique global minimum if the objective function is strictly convex. This condition is usually met by many cost functions encountered in practice since the cost components often have increasing marginal costs.

Optimal solutions to the model are found by the use of Lagrangians. Several applications have been reported which illustrate the nature of the resulting rules (see Buffa and Taubert [1972]). In general, the form of the rules can be characterized by equations of the following type:

$$X_t = a_0 d_t + a_1 d_{t+1} + \cdots + a_{T-t} d_T + b W_{t-1} + c - d I_{t-1} \qquad (3.25)$$

$$W_t = e_0 d_t + e_1 d_{t+1} + \cdots + e_{T-t} d_T - f W_{t-1} + g - h I_{t-1}. \qquad (3.26)$$

Equation (3.25) describes the nature of the aggregate production rate which is dependent on future demand forecasts, previous work force size, and beginning inventory. The same comments apply to expression (3.26), which illustrates the form of the aggregate work force decision. The weights given to the demand forecasts (the a's and e's) decrease rapidly with time (see, for instance, the example in Holt, Modigliani, Muth, and Simon [1960, pp. 60–63]).

3.3.4 Extensions to the HMMS Model

Several extensions of the initial HMMS model have been reported in the literature. Bergstrom and Smith [1970] generalized the approach to a multiproduct formulation and incorporated diminishing marginal revenues in the objective function. Their work was, in turn, further expanded by Hausman and McClain [1971] to allow for randomness in the items' demand. Chang and Jones [1970] also dealt with the multiproduct problem; they suggested procedures to solve situations when production cannot be started and completed in a given time period. Sykpens [1967] included plant capacity as an additional decision variable. Peterson [1971] proposed an extension of the HMMS model to allow the manufacturer, at a cost, to smooth distribution orders to achieve less pronounced fluctuations in work force, production, and inventory levels. Welam [1978] developed an HMMS type interactive model where a manager can establish an appropriate tradeoff between the hiring and layoff costs and other costs. Gaalman [1978] proposed a method for aggregating items under the HMMS setting.

3.3.5 Advantages and Disadvantages of Quadratic Cost Models

The major advantages of quadratic cost models are that they allow for a more realistic cost structure in the planning process, provide linear decision rules which are easy to solve and implement, and allow uncertainties to be handled directly since the linear decision rules minimize the expected cost, provided that unbiased expected demand forecasts are given.

There are, however, serious drawbacks: the strong need for aggregation, the elaborate estimation procedures that are required to assess the numerical values of the cost coefficients, and the numerical difficulties encountered when the number of decision variables and constraints increase, which limits the model dimensions to a small size.

Computational results (Van dePanne and Bosje [1962]) seem to indicate that decision rules are fairly insensitive to large errors in estimating cost parameters. This is a very attractive property, due to the difficulty in providing accurate cost values.

In spite of the encouraging results reported on large savings obtained by applying linear decision rules to actual managerial situations, these techniques have not been adopted by practicing managers. Probably the disadvantages listed outweigh the advantages that linear decision rules have vis-à-vis linear programming models. Comparisons made by Kolenda [1970] between HMMS and Hanssmann–Hess types of models rank these two approaches very close in overall efficiency. If one adds to this the enormous computational capabilities of linear programming, the result is the more widespread use of linear cost models.

3.4   Lot Size Models (Fixed Cost Models)

Whenever the manufacturing process is characterized by batch-type production operations (as opposed to continuous production), a cost is incurred when setting up the production facilities for a given run. Including the setup cost in the planning process creates many problems. First, every item that generates a setup (or a family of items sharing a common setup) has to be identified and treated independently, as opposed to the case where setups are ignored in the planning process and, consequently, the aggregation of items can take place to a larger extent. This expands the number of variables and constraints, thus leading to large-scale systems that can be coped with only by using special computational techniques. Second, the inclusion of setup costs produces the problem of lot size indivisibility, since a single setup has to be incurred for each batch. This introduces integer variables in the model formulation. Finally, setup costs give rise to fixed cost components in the objective function, and the downtime, which is characteristic of every setup operation, introduces nonlinearities in the constraint set. The resulting large-scale, integer, nonlinear programming model is hard to resolve computationally. Some of the most effective approaches that have been suggested to handle this problem will be reviewed in what follows.

3.4.1   Uncapacitated Lot Size Models

The standard economic lot size formula, also known as the EOQ (economic order quantity) formula,* determines the production amount for an individual item when setup and inventory holding costs identify the cost tradeoffs. This formula does not account for any interaction that exists among the individual items to be scheduled for production. In particular, it ignores the capacity limitations which impose some of the more critical constraints to production planning.

Moreover, the EOQ formula assumes the demand to be constant and known over the planning horizon. When the demand is known but changing during the various time periods of the planning horizon (i.e., exhibiting seasonalities), the EOQ formula can provide very misleading recommendations. Wagner and Whitin [1958] suggested a dynamic programming model to solve the dynamic version of the economic lot size problem. Their approach will be reviewed here because of its important role in the capacitated lot size models to be discussed later.

A simple version of the uncapacitated lot size problem can be described as follows:

$$\text{Minimize } Z = \sum_{t=1}^{T} \left[s_t \delta(X_t) + c_t I_t \right] \tag{3.27}$$

subject to:

$$X_t + I_{t-1} - I_t = d_t \qquad\qquad t = 1, \ldots, T \tag{3.28}$$

$$X_t \geqslant 0 \qquad\qquad t = 1, \ldots, T \tag{3.29}$$

$$I_t \geqslant 0 \qquad\qquad t = 1, \ldots, T \tag{3.30}$$

---

*For a discussion on the various types of EOQ formulas that have been proposed in the literature, see Chapter 4, section 4.2.

where:

$$\delta(X_t) = \begin{cases} 0 \text{ if } X_t = 0 \\ 1 \text{ if } X_t > 0 \end{cases} \tag{3.31}$$

X_t = amount to be produced in period t

I_t = ending inventory in period t

s_t = setup cost in period t

c_t = inventory holding cost per unit held in period t

d_t = demand during period t.

No backorders are allowed, and the variable costs are assumed to be time-invariant; consequently, the variable cost component did not have to be included in the objective function.

A dynamic programming solution to this problem is straightforward. The functional equation that represents the minimum cost policy (including only setup and inventory holding costs) for periods t through $T-1$ is:

$$f_t(I_{t-1}) = \min_{\substack{X_t \geqslant 0 \\ X_t + I_{t-1} \geqslant d_t.}} \left[s_t \delta(X_t) + c_t(X_t + I_{t-1} - d_t) + f_{t+1}(X_t + I_{t-1} - d_t) \right]$$

In the last period T the minimization of the costs requires that no inventory be left over; hence, the functional equation becomes:

$$f_T(I_{T-1}) = \min_{\substack{X_T \geqslant 0 \\ X_T + I_{T-1} = d_T.}} \left[s_T \delta(X_T) \right]$$

A backward induction process can be applied, in conjunction with the above functional equation, to compute the optimum lot sizes during the planning horizon. However, this is not the best way to approach the problem. Wagner and Whitin proved four important results about the nature of the optimal solution to (3.27)–(3.31), which enabled them to find a more efficient solution algorithm.

Assuming no initial inventory (that is, $I_0 = 0$),* the four results are:

1. There is always an optimal policy such that:

$$I_{t-1} X_t = 0 \qquad \text{for } t = 1, \ldots, T.$$

Therefore, costs can never be reduced by using a policy that carries stock into some period and at the same time schedules production in the same period.

---

* If the initial inventory is not zero, subtract it from the demand requirements in the first period to obtain an adjusted requirement for that period. If the initial inventory exceeds the first-period demand, continue with this adjustment process until all the inventory is used up. Thus, a problem with initial inventory can be easily transformed into one with no initial inventory.

2.   It is enough to consider optimal policies such that for all t:

$$X_t = 0, \text{ or } X_t = \sum_{j=t}^{k} d_j; \text{ for some } k, \qquad t \leqslant k \leqslant T.$$

This implies that in any given period the production is either zero or equal to the sum of consecutive demands for some number of periods into the future.

3.   Whenever it is optimal to have $I_t = 0$ for some period t, periods 1 through t and $t+1$ through T can be considered by themselves. Indeed, in formulation (3.27)–(3.31) the inventory is the only link between periods; hence, when the inventory at the end of some period is zero, the link in time at that point disappears and the original planning horizon can be partitioned.

It is advantageous at this point to reformulate the dynamic programming approach as a forward process. The functional equation that characterizes the forward induction procedure can be specified by letting $f(t)$ be the minimal cost program from period 1 to t; then:

$$f(t) = \min\left\{ \min_{1 \leqslant j < t} \left[s_j + \sum_{h=j}^{t-1} \sum_{k=h+1}^{t} c_h d_k + f(j-1) \right], s_t + f(t-1) \right\}$$

$$(3.32)$$

where $f(1) = s_1$, and $f(0) = 0$. s_j represents the setup cost in period j, and $\sum_{h=j}^{t-1}\sum_{k=h+1}^{t} c_h d_k$ provides the inventory carrying cost for periods $j+1$ through t.

The last and most important result of Wagner and Whitin is the following:

4.   *The planning horizon theorem.* If in period t^* the minimum of (3.32) occurs at $j = t^{**} \leqslant t^*$, then in periods $t > t^*$ it is sufficient to consider only $t^{**} \leqslant j \leqslant t$. In particular, if $t^* = t^{**}$ it is sufficient to consider policies with $X_{t^*} > 0$.

Thus, by theorem 4, for every new period $t > t^*$ a planning horizon t^{**} through t, rather than 1 through t, has to be considered in (3.32); the implication is that for t large enough the time interval $[t^{**}t]$ is usually substantially shorter than $[1, t]$.

The above results have a decisive impact in terms of reducing the computational effort required to solve (3.27)–(3.31). Indeed, it is clear that with a planning horizon of T periods, and by considering results 1 and 2, there are a number of 2^{T-1} possible candidates for the optimal solution to the model (in period 1 production has to take place, assuming a positive demand for period 1, while in any other period t, $1 < t \leqslant T$, a setup may or may not occur; hence, 2^{T-1} sequences of setups result). These 2^{T-1} possible solutions are called *dominant production sequences* or schedules (Manne [1958]). Then, results

1, 2, and 3 immediately suggest the formulation of the forward dynamic programming algorithm, which has to consider only $1 + 2 + \cdots + T = T(T + 1)/2$ of the 2^{T-1} sequences. Finally, theorem 4 leads to a further reduction in the amount of computations, by allowing the decomposition of the original problem into a succession of smaller problems.

Numerical examples illustrating how to carry out the forward induction procedure are provided in the original reference of Wagner and Whitin [1958].

Wagner [1960] expanded this approach to include changing purchasing or manufacturing costs during the multiperiod planning horizon. Eppen, Gould, and Pashigian [1969] and Zabel [1964] made significant extensions to the planning horizon theorem. Zangwill [1969] showed how to treat backordering costs and provided a network representation of the problem. Another approach for the inclusion of backorders was suggested by Elmaghraby and Bawle [1972], who analyzed the uncapacitated problem when ordering must be in batches greater than one with and without setup costs. Kao [1979] considered a multiproduct dynamic lot size problem where, in addition to a separate setup cost for each product ordered, a joint setup cost is incurred when one or more products are ordered.

The concept of dominant production sequences has been exploited greatly for computational purposes when dealing with capacitated lot size models. This is shown in subsequent sections.

3.4.2   Capacitated Lot Size Models

The capacitated lot size model deals with a multi-item production planning problem under changing demand requirements during the multiperiod planning horizon. The items are competing for limited capacity and setup costs become an important element of the total cost to be minimized.

As before, the fixed work force problem is analyzed first, when only overtime can be added to expand the manhour availability; subsequently the variable work force problem is presented, where hirings and layoffs are permitted in order to change the total production rate.

3.4.2.1   Fixed work force, capacitated lot size models

Using the notations of section 3.2.1.1, a simple version of the fixed work force, capacitated, fixed cost model can be formulated as follows:

$$\text{Minimize} \quad Z = \sum_{i=1}^{N} \sum_{t=1}^{T} \left[s_{it} \delta(X_{it}) + v_{it} X_{it} + c_{it} I_{it} \right] + \sum_{t=1}^{T} \left(r_t W_t + o_t O_t \right) \quad (3.33)$$

subject to:

$$X_{it} + I_{i,t-1} - I_{it} = d_{it} \qquad \begin{cases} t = 1, \ldots, T \\ i = 1, \ldots, N \end{cases} \qquad (3.34)$$

$$\sum_{i=1}^{N} [a_i \delta(X_{it}) + k_i X_{it}] - W_t - O_t = 0 \qquad t = 1, \ldots, T \qquad (3.35)$$

$$0 \leqslant W_t \leqslant (rm)_t \qquad t = 1, \ldots, T \qquad (3.36)$$

$$0 \leqslant O_t \leqslant (om)_t \qquad t = 1, \ldots, T \qquad (3.37)$$

$$X_{it}, I_{it} \geqslant 0 \qquad \begin{cases} i = 1, \ldots, N \\ t = 1, \ldots, T \end{cases} \qquad (3.38)$$

where:

$$\delta(X_{it}) = \begin{cases} 0 \text{ if } X_{it} = 0 \\ 1 \text{ if } X_{it} > 0, \end{cases} \qquad (3.39)$$

s_{it} = cost of a setup for product i in period t

a_i = manhours consumed by a setup operation for product i.

This model does not allow backorders, although it is easy to incorporate this added feature in the formulation. Most of the comments made for the fixed work force, linear cost model are also applicable here and will not be repeated. The feature which is different, however, is the presence of $\delta(X_{it})$ both in the objective function (3.33) and in the constraints (3.35); this completely breaks the linearity of the objective function and the constraints set, and makes the computation of this formulation much more difficult. In what follows some of the methods that have been proposed to solve the model will be examined.

(A) Fixed cost models

Whenever the downtime consumed by the setup operation is negligible, $a_i = 0$ in (3.35) and the lot size fixed work force model becomes a fixed cost linear programming model, also known as the *fixed charge model*. Since the objective function of the fixed charge model is concave and the constraint set is convex, the global minimum will occur at an extreme point. However, generally, many local minima exist at extreme points, and therefore a simplex type algorithm is not very effective to use since it might terminate at a local minimum.

Several approaches have been suggested to deal with this problem. Exact solution methods can be classified in two different categories: extreme point ranking procedures (Gray [1971] and Murty [1968]), and branch-and-bound solutions to mixed integer programming formulations of the problem (Jones and Soland [1962] and Steinberg [1970]). Exact methods are computationally limited to relatively small size problems, and therefore have little practical value at the present. As a result of this limitation, several heuristic approaches have been proposed that generate near-optimal solutions. Generally, these heuristics start by producing a good extreme point solution, and then by examining the adjacent extreme points a local minimum is determined. Afterward, a move is made to an extreme point away from this local minimum, and the process is repeated until either no further improvement is obtained or a specified number of iterations are completed. Effective heuristics have been provided by Balinski [1961], Cooper and Drebes [1967], Cooper [1975], Denzler [1969], Rousseau [1973], Steinberg [1970], and Walker [1976].

(B)   The linear programming approach

When the downtimes, a_i, required to set up production runs are not negligible, the resulting large-scale nonlinear capacitated lot size model becomes extremely hard to solve in a direct way. In response to these computational difficulties, Manne [1958] suggested a reformulation of the problem as a linear programming model. This approach was subsequently refined by Dzielinski, Baker, and Manne [1963], Dzielinski and Gomory [1965], and Lasdon and Terjung [1971].

The approach consists of having each column of the linear programming planning model represent a possible production schedule. A production schedule (or sequence) for product i specifies in which periods the facility should be set up for the production of i, and how much of product i to make every time the setup takes place, so as to meet the demand requirements over the T period planning horizon.

To illustrate how these dominant schedules can be constructed define:

X_{ijt} = amount of item i to be produced by means of production
sequence j in period t; $i = 1, \ldots, N$, $j = 1, \ldots, J$; $t = 1, \ldots, T$,

and as usual, let

d_{it} = forecast demand for item i in period t.

Consider, for simplicity, a planning horizon of $T = 3$ periods. There is a number of $2^{3-1} = 4$ dominant sequences for each item i as shown in Table 3.1.

It is easy to compute the total production, inventory holding and setup costs, t_{ij}, for every sequence; Table 3.2 shows the costs of all dominant sequences developed in Table 3.1.

In general,

$$t_{ij} = \sum_{t=1}^{T} \left[s_{it} \delta(X_{ijt}) + v_{it} X_{ijt} + c_{it} I_{it} \right]. \tag{3.40}$$

TABLE 3.1 Dominant Sequences: Production of Item *i* in Every Time Period

SEQUENCE NO.	TIME PERIOD		
	$t=1$	$t=2$	$t=3$
$j=1$	$X_{i11}=d_{i1}+d_{i2}+d_{i3}$	$X_{i12}=0$	$X_{i13}=0$
$j=2$	$X_{i21}=d_{i1}+d_{i2}$	$X_{i22}=0$	$X_{i23}=d_{i3}$
$j=3$	$X_{i31}=d_{i1}$	$X_{i32}=d_{i2}+d_{i3}$	$X_{i33}=0$
$j=4$	$X_{i41}=d_{i1}$	$X_{i42}=d_{i2}$	$X_{i43}=d_{i3}$

Let l_{ijt} be the amount of resource (in this case, labor) required in period t for the production of item i by schedule j; then,

$$l_{ijt} = a_i \delta(X_{ijt}) + k_i X_{ijt}. \tag{3.41}$$

If, as before, $(rm)_t$ is the available number of manhours, the fixed work force lot size model can be formulated as:

Minimize
$$Z = \sum_{i=1}^{N} \sum_{j=1}^{J} t_{ij}\theta_{ij} \tag{3.42}$$

subject to:

$$\sum_{i=1}^{N} \sum_{j=1}^{J} l_{ijt}\theta_{ij} \leqslant (rm)_t \qquad t=1,\ldots,T \tag{3.43}$$

$$\sum_{j=1}^{J} \theta_{ij} = 1 \qquad i=1,\ldots,N \tag{3.44}$$

$$\theta_{ij} \geqslant 0 \qquad \begin{cases} i=1,\ldots,N \\ j=1,\ldots,J, \end{cases} \tag{3.45}$$

where J = the total number of dominant production sequences, which is 2^{T-1}.

Variables θ_{ij} require some explanation. If the solution to the above model turned out, by mere chance, to have all θ_{ij}'s integers, clearly those integral values would have to be either 0 or 1 (by constraints [3.44] and [3.45]). The interpretation that would be attached to a $\theta_{ij}=1$ is that the jth production

TABLE 3.2 Total Cost of Dominant Sequences of Table 3.1

SEQUENCE NO.	t_{ij}
$j=1$	$t_{i1} = s_{i1} + v_{i1}(d_{i1}+d_{i2}+d_{i3}) + c_{i1}(d_{i2}+d_{i3}) + c_{i2}(d_{i3})$
$j=2$	$t_{i2} = (s_{i1}+s_{i3}) + v_{i1}(d_{i1}+d_{i2}) + v_{i3}d_{i3} + c_{i1}d_{i2}$
$j=3$	$t_{i3} = (s_{i1}+s_{i2}) + v_{i1}d_{i1} + v_{i2}(d_{i2}+d_{i3}) + c_{i2}d_{i3}$
$j=4$	$t_{i4} = (s_{i1}+s_{i2}+s_{i3}) + v_{i1}d_{i1} + v_{i2}d_{i2} + v_{i3}d_{i3}$

sequence has been chosen by the model to satisfy the demands of the ith item; of course, a $\theta_{ij} = 0$ would show that the jth sequence is not active in relation to product i. If some θ_{ij}'s are fractional, constraints (3.44) require that they add up to unity, which is equivalent to saying that all demands for item i must be met.

We have to realize, however, that (3.42)–(3.45) is only an approximation of the capacitated lot size problem because the optimal schedule may not be among the "pure strategies" represented by the set of dominant sequences of production. The possible deviation from these patterns is due to the presence of constraints on the available capacity of production. Worse still, when the solution contains fractional θ_{ij}'s no physical meaning can be attached to them (for instance, a $\theta_{ij} = 1/3$ would imply that only $1/3$ of the cost of the setups called for by the jth production sequence, and only $1/3$ of the setup time, are spent). Therefore, one would be tempted to insist on restricting θ_{ij} to be either 0 or 1. Although the resulting solution may be suboptimal with respect to the capacitated lot size problem, it would be at least meaningful.

Unfortunately, the integrality constraints would most likely render any real life problem computationally infeasible.

In practical applications, however, solving the linear program of equations (3.42)–(3.45) provides a good approximation of the integer solution. Indeed, given the $T + N$ constraints of the model, there will be at most $T + N$ positive variables in the optimal linear programming solution. Having only N products, there will be at most T of them for which more than one θ_{ij} is positive and, by (3.44), fractional. Since in most practical applications N is much larger than T, the fractional θ_{ij}'s represent a small percentage of the total number of variables, and thus does not have much significance.

The model formulated above does not need too much additional explanation: expression (3.42) states the objective of the model as the minimization of variable production, setup, and inventory holding costs. It is possible to expand the model to include regular and overtime labor costs, shortage costs, and hiring and layoff costs. Constraints (3.43) force the total manpower consumed in the production schedules not to exceed the maximum labor availability in each time period. It is a simple matter to consider several types of production resources, and to include a variable work force as a decision variable with overtime capabilities (see Dzielinski, Baker, and Manne [1963], Dzielinski and Gomory [1965], and Gorenstein [1970], for these model extensions). Constraints (3.44), as explained above, ensure that the demand requirements for the ith item will be met either by one or by a combination of several production sequences for that item. Finally, conditions (3.45) are the usual nonnegativity requirements for all decision variables.

As already mentioned, the model can be expanded to include capacity constraints due not only to manpower availability but also to any number, K, of limited resources. In this case the problem of fractional θ_{ij}'s will not be of significance whenever N (the number of items to be scheduled) is much larger than $K \times T$ (the number of resources times the number of time periods). This condition is usually satisfied in practice.

From the computational point of view, real life applications of the linear program (3.42)–(3.45) pose difficult problems because of its size. In some situations the number of items to be scheduled runs into the thousands; a model with that many rows requires capabilities that the current linear programming codes, based on the regular simplex procedure, cannot provide. In addition, there is the problem of the tremendous number of columns; each item generates 2^{T-1} dominant production sequences. If $T = 12$, there will be $2^{12-1} = 2,048$ variables for each item, and if there are 1,000 items to schedule, the model will have more than 2 million θ_{ij} variables.

To bypass these difficulties, Dzielinski and Gomory [1965] suggested a Dantzig–Wolfe [1960] decomposition approach where the subproblem led to uncapacitated lot size models of the Wagner–Whitin type. These subproblems, which can be solved quite simply, are used to generate "attractive" entering production sequences so that there is no need to specify all the columns of coefficients from the very beginning.

The decomposition approach, however, has one severe limitation for this type of problem. As is well known, the decomposition technique finds a near-optimum solution relatively fast, but a large number of iterations might be required to obtain the optimum. In most applications it is not very critical to get the optimum. Lower bounds can be evaluated to determine how good an approximation to the optimum the current solution is, and stopping rules can be designed accordingly. In this problem, however, it is important to obtain the optimum, because only an extreme point can guarantee that there will be at most T fractional θ_{ij}'s, and, as has been shown earlier, it is critical to limit the number of fractional values of the θ_{ij} variables.

To resolve this limitation, Lasdon and Terjung [1971] maintained the column generation procedure suggested by Dzielinski and Gomory (thus bypassing the computational problem introduced by the large number of columns); but instead of defining a decomposition master program, they solved the original linear programming formulation using generalized upper bounding techniques (Dantzig and Van Slyke [1967]), thereby taking advantage of the special structure of the constraints (3.44) (generalized upper bounding constraints).

Given the importance of the column generation procedure in solving large-scale systems, the way it has been applied by Lasdon and Terjung to problem (3.42)–(3.45) will be briefly discussed here.

As a first step, a reduced version of the original problem is solved:

Minimize
$$Z = \sum_{i=1}^{N} \sum_{j=1}^{J'} t_{ij}\theta_{ij} \qquad (3.42')$$

subject to:

$$\sum_{i=1}^{N} \sum_{j=1}^{J'} l_{ijt}\theta_{ij} \leqslant (rm)_t \qquad\qquad t = 1,\dots,T \qquad\qquad (3.43')$$

$$\sum_{j=1}^{J'} \theta_{ij} = 1 \qquad\qquad i = 1,\dots,N \qquad\qquad (3.44')$$

$$\theta_{ij} \geqslant 0 \qquad\qquad \text{all } i, j. \qquad\qquad (3.45')$$

This version is obtained by considering a smaller number of columns, namely, by taking into account only a small subset J' of production sequences for every item i ($J' \ll J$).* Suppose (3.42')–(3.45') is solved. Let $\pi_t, t = 1,\dots,T$, be the set of dual variables associated with constraints (3.43'), and $\pi_{T+i}, i = 1,\dots,N$, be the dual variables associated with constraints (3.44'). The reduced costs in problem (3.42')–(3.45') are given by the expression:

$$\overline{t_{ij}} = t_{ij} - \sum_{t=1}^{T} \pi_t l_{ijt} - \pi_{T+i}. \qquad\qquad (3.46)$$

To choose the entering variable one has to find

$$\min_{i} \min_{j} \overline{t_{ij}}.$$

By replacing t_{ij} and l_{ijt} in (3.46) by their expressions (3.40) and (3.41), and by rearranging terms, the inner minimization becomes

$$\min_{j} \sum_{t=1}^{T} \left\{ \left[(s_{it} - \pi_t a_i)\delta(X_{ijt}) + (v_{it} - \pi_t k_i)X_{ijt} + c_{it}I_{it} \right] \right\}. \qquad (3.47)$$

Since $\pi_t \leqslant 0$, the coefficients in (3.47) are all positive. (3.47) requires that, for item i, a sequence of setups and production levels X_{ijt} be found that would minimize the sum of setup, variable manufacturing and inventory carrying costs, and, at the same time, satisfy the demand requirements for item i over the T period planning horizon. But this is precisely a single-item uncapacitated lot size problem that can be efficiently solved by the dynamic programming approach of Wagner and Whitin [1958] and Wagner [1960]. Notice that subindex j in expression (3.47) is somehow irrelevant since the minimization does not require an enumeration of production sequences j, but the generation of a new production sequence. The application of the Wagner–Whitin approach will generate the optimum production schedule for each item i, by determining the X_{ijt}'s.

At this point there are N new columns, or production sequences, generated (one for each item i). To determine which column is to be appended to (3.42')–(3.45'), and thus enter the basis, π_{T+i} is subtracted from the optimum

---

*Lasdon and Terjung [1971, p. 954] suggested an effective initialization procedure to identify the subject of J' production sequences.

value of expression (3.47) corresponding to item i. The minimum of the resulting differences (if it is negative) identifies the entering column, which is appended to the reduced linear program. The new larger program (3.42′)–(3.45′), thus generated, is solved by the standard generalized upper bounding technique, a new set of dual variables is obtained, and the whole procedure is reiterated. If the minimum reduced cost found is nonnegative, no cost reduction can be achieved by considering additional production schedules, and one would conclude that the optimal solution to (3.42)–(3.45) has just been found.

Gorenstein [1970] used a similar model to support long-range production decisions in a tire company. In addition, he linked the output of that model to a short-range scheduling plan, and introduced precedence relationships in the production of finished and semifinished tires and their components. An alternative approach to the capacitated fixed cost problem was developed by Kortanek, Sodaro, and Soyster [1968].

As already mentioned, Manne's approximate formulation is useful only when $N \gg T$. To eliminate this shortcoming, Newson [1975a] suggested a heuristic procedure which is independent of column generation techniques and treats the lot size problem as a shortest route problem.

3.4.2.2   Variable work force, capacitated lot size models

In this model the work force size also becomes a decision variable. Using the notations defined previously, the model can be formulated as follows:

Minimize
$$Z = \sum_{i=1}^{N} \sum_{t=1}^{T} \left[s_{it}\delta(X_{it}) + v_{it}X_{it} + c_{it}I_{it} \right]$$
$$+ \sum_{t=1}^{T} (r_t W_t + o_t O_t + h_t H_t + f_t F_t) \tag{3.48}$$

subject to:

$$X_{it} + I_{i,t-1} - I_{it} = d_{it} \qquad \begin{cases} i = 1,\dots,N \\ t = 1,\dots,T \end{cases} \tag{3.49}$$

$$\sum_{i=1}^{N} [a_i\delta(X_{it}) + k_i X_{it}] - W_t - O_t \leqslant 0 \qquad t = 1,\dots,T \tag{3.50}$$

$$W_t - W_{t-1} - H_t + F_t = 0 \qquad t = 1,\dots,T \tag{3.51}$$

$$- pW_t + O_t \leqslant 0 \qquad t = 1,\dots,T \tag{3.52}$$

$$X_{it}, I_{it} \geqslant 0 \qquad \begin{cases} i = 1,\dots,N \\ t = 1,\dots,T \end{cases} \tag{3.53}$$

$$W_t, O_t, H_t, F_t \geqslant 0 \qquad t = 1,\dots,T \tag{3.54}$$

where:

$$\delta(X_{it}) = \begin{cases} 0 \text{ if } X_{it} > 0 \\ 1 \text{ if } X_{it} = 0. \end{cases} \tag{3.55}$$

The interpretation of the model should now be straightforward to the reader. One could easily extend the formulation to include backorders, following the procedure suggested in the linear cost, variable work force model.

The solution procedures used to deal with this model are identical to those employed with the lot size, fixed work force model; that is, a fixed cost model is generated whenever the downtime incurred in manufacturing setup (a_i) is negligible; otherwise the linear programming approximation suggested by Manne, with solution by Dzielinski and Gomory, or Lasdon and Terjung, can be applied.

Newson [1975b] proposed to attack the problem in two stages. The first stage deals with the detailed scheduling decision for each individual item over the multiperiod planning horizon, neglecting the manpower constraints. For a given product i this stage can be formulated as follows:

Minimize
$$z_i = \sum_{t=1}^{T} \left[s_{it} \delta(X_{it}) + v_{it} X_{it} + c_{it} I_{it} \right]$$

subject to:

$$\begin{aligned} X_{it} + I_{i,t-1} - I_{it} = d_{it} & \qquad t = 1, \ldots, T \\ X_{it}, I_{it} \geqslant 0 & \qquad t = 1, \ldots, T. \end{aligned}$$

After this model is solved for each of the N items, the capacity required by the detailed schedule for each time period t is computed as:

$$\hat{P}_t = \sum_{i=1}^{N} \left[a_i \delta(X_{it}) + k_i X_{it} \right] \qquad t = 1, \ldots, T.$$

Then the second-stage model dealing with the aggregate capacity decisions is solved. The model is defined as follows:

Minimize
$$z(\underline{\hat{P}}) = \sum_{t=1}^{T} \left(r_t W_t + o_t O_t + h_t H_t + f_t F_t \right)$$

subject to:

$$\begin{aligned} W_t + O_t - \hat{P}_t \geqslant 0 & \qquad t = 1, \ldots, T \\ W_t - W_{t-1} - H_t + F_t = 0 & \qquad t = 1, \ldots, T \\ - pW_t + O_t \leqslant 0 & \qquad t = 1, \ldots, T \\ W_t, O_t, H_t, F_t \geqslant 0 & \qquad t = 1, \ldots, T. \end{aligned}$$

Newson suggested a heuristic iterative process that relates the two models sequentially until a terminal criterion is met.

3.4.3 Advantages and Disadvantages of Lot Size Models

The primary advantage of these models is that they incorporate the scheduling issues associated with lot size indivisibilities into the capacity planning decisions. This, however, creates the need for a great deal of detailed information throughout the planning horizon, which is costly to gather and process.

An alternative approach to coordinate the aggregate capacity planning and detailed scheduling decisions is represented by the construction of hierarchical planning systems (see Chapter 10).

Before closing this section on lot size models, it should be recalled that solving mixed integer programs with a fixed charge cost function was also the focus of Chapter 2 on the facilities design problem. The efficient techniques presented there were specialized to take advantage of the structure of the location–allocation problems, and therefore are not applicable to the production-inventory models shown above. As for Benders' method, which is more general, not too much can be said about how effective it could be, since too little computational experience exists, and also because its performance efficiency is apparently crucially influenced by the structure of the constraints set (Geoffrion and Graves [1974, pp. 837–842]). Finally, the current state of the art of the general mixed integer programming codes is totally inadequate to solve production problems of any realistic size, given that they can handle only a small number of integral variables.

3.5   General Cost Models

The linear models, quadratic models, and lot size models analyzed so far, although appropriate for a great number of applications, impose several restrictions on the nature of the cost functions to be used. Some authors have argued that realistic industrial situations tend to exhibit cost functions which are nonlinear and discontinuous and, therefore, cannot be treated by any of the methods previously outlined. Buffa and Taubert [1972] report the following factors as mainly responsible for this cost behavior: supply and demand interactions, manufacturing or purchasing economies of scale, learning curve effects, quantum jumps in costs with the addition of a new shift, technological and productivity changes, and labor slowdowns.

Several aggregate capacity planning methods have been suggested, which attempt to be more responsive to the complexities introduced by the specific decision environment. Generally, these more realistic approaches do not guarantee that an optimum solution will be found. They can be classified roughly according to the following categories:

- Nonlinear analytical models, which provide a mathematical treatment of general nonlinear cost structures.
- Heuristic decision rules, which attempt to bring in the decision maker's intuition about the problem under consideration, by incorporating "rules-of-thumb" that contribute to the solution of the problem.
- Search decision rules, which consist of the application of hill-climbing techniques to the response surface defined by the nonlinear cost function and the problem constraints.
- Simulation decision rules, which represent the problem under consideration by a set of programmed instructions. The decision maker is able to test various approaches in an iterative fashion, where the outcome of each run suggests what the subsequent run might be. Simulation is particularly suitable to treat the uncertainties present in the decision-making process.

The following sections will review the major contributions that have been proposed in each of the above categories.

3.5.1   Nonlinear Analytical Models

During the last twenty years, a significant amount of work has been devoted to the analytical treatment of production planning models with general nonlinear cost functions. Much of this work has attempted to decompose the multiperiod planning problem by using dynamic programming principles. Due to the inherent complexities of the problem under consideration and the computational limitations of dynamic programming, these models can seldom be implemented to support period-to-period planning decisions. However, they are effective in analyzing qualitative properties of the optimum solutions. Most of the models to be discussed in this section will be single-product models.

Two types of single-product models are covered in the literature. The *first type* does not penalize for changes in the production rate, and can be formulated as follows:

Minimize
$$Z = \sum_{t=1}^{T} \left[v_t(X_t) + c_t(I_t) \right] \tag{3.56}$$

subject to:

$$X_t + I_{t-1} - I_t = d_t \qquad t = 1, \ldots, T \tag{3.57}$$

$$\underline{I_t} \leqslant I_t \leqslant \overline{I_t} \qquad t = 1, \ldots, T \tag{3.58}$$

$$\underline{X_t} \leqslant X_t \leqslant \overline{X_t} \qquad t = 1, \ldots, T, \tag{3.59}$$

where $v(X)$ and $c(I)$ are, respectively, the nonlinear production and inventory carrying cost functions. $I_t, \bar{I}_t$, and $X_t, \bar{X}_t$ are lower and upper bounds imposed on the total amount of inventory and production in every time period. By choosing $I_t = 0$ for all t, all backlogging is eliminated. Optimum solutions to this model can be obtained by using standard dynamic programming methods.

The *second type* of model introduces production change costs that depend on both the current as well as the past production levels. In this case, the objective function (3.56) is substituted by the following expression:

$$\text{Minimize} \qquad Z = \sum_{t=1}^{T} \left[v_t(X_t) + c_t(I_t) + p_t(X_{t-1}, X_t) \right]. \qquad (3.60)$$

The production change cost function p is assumed to be zero whenever $X_{t-1} = X_t$, and nonnegative otherwise.

A number of different functional forms have been proposed to characterize the production change costs (Johnson and Montgomery [1974, chap. 4–4.2]):

$$p_t(X_{t-1}, X_t) = p_t |X_t - X_{t-1}| \qquad (3.61)$$

$$p_t(X_{t-1}, X_t) = p_t(X_t - X_{t-1})^+ + p_t'(X_t - X_{t-1})^- \qquad (3.62)$$

$$p_t(X_{t-1}, X_t) = p_t(X_t - X_{t-1})^2 \qquad (3.63)$$

$$p_t(X_{t-1}, X_t) = \begin{cases} p_t, & \text{if } X_t > 0 \text{ and } X_{t-1} = 0 \\ 0, & \text{otherwise,} \end{cases} \qquad (3.64)$$

$$p_t(X_{t-1}, X_t) = \begin{cases} p_t, & \text{if } X_t > 0 \text{ and } X_{t-1} = 0 \\ p_t', & \text{if } X_t = 0 \text{ and } X_{t-1} > 0 \\ 0, & \text{otherwise.} \end{cases} \qquad (3.65)$$

In (3.62) the following notations have been used:

$$(X_t - X_{t-1})^+ = \begin{cases} X_t - X_{t-1} & \text{if } X_t > X_{t-1} \\ 0 & \text{otherwise,} \end{cases}$$

$$(X_t - X_{t-1})^- = \begin{cases} X_{t-1} - X_t & \text{if } X_t < X_{t-1} \\ 0 & \text{otherwise.} \end{cases}$$

Notice that when $p = p'$, function (3.62) is identical to (3.61).

Functions (3.61) and (3.62) can be treated as linear functions (see, for example, Hanssmann and Hess [1960]). Expression (3.63) is a simple quadratic convex cost. (3.64) defines a startup cost function; (3.65) includes startup as well as shutdown costs.

Models with production change costs do not lend themselves to solution by standard dynamic programming techniques since there are two state variables, and it is well known that, in general, dynamic programs with two or more state variables are computationally infeasible. However, other more

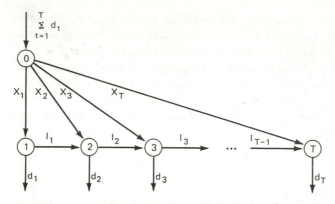

FIGURE 3.1   The network interpretation of the inventory balance equations.

efficient algorithms have been published for special cases: Zangwill [1966c] for a production change cost function which is (piecewise) concave on ($[-\infty, 0]$ and $[0, +\infty]$), and Sobel [1970b] for a production change cost function involving both startup and shutdown costs.

It is important to mention that constraints (3.57)–(3.59) can be interpreted as governing the flow in a network (Figure 3.1). Nodes $1, 2, \ldots, T$ represent the various time periods in the planning horizon. Node 0 is an artificial source to provide a flow balance condition. Zangwill [1969] suggested this network representation and extended it to allow for backlogging. The network analogy has generated several important contributions to the production planning problem (Kalymon [1972], Veinott [1969], Zangwill [1968, 1969]).

To facilitate an organized discussion of the nonlinear analytical models, three broad categories will be identified: convex cost models, concave cost models, and optimum control and feedback models.

3.5.1.1 Convex cost models

In practice, convex cost functions do not create difficult problems. These cost functions can be approximated, to any desired degree of accuracy, by means of piecewise linear functions and the resulting production planning problem can be solved by linear programming procedures. Direct analytical treatment of convex cost models, however, provides important insights with regard to the nature of the optimum decision rules.

Veinott [1964] considered the problem of determining the optimum production quantities of a single product over a finite number of time periods so as to minimize convex production and inventory costs [expression (3.56)] subject to the constraints represented by expressions (3.57), (3.58), and (3.59). When the total cost function is strictly convex, the optimum production quantities are unique. Veinott performed a parametric analysis to study the changes in the optimum production levels resulting from variations in demand requirements, and in inventory and production bounds. His findings can be summarized as follows:

1. The optimum production in a given period is a nondecreasing function of:

   - the demand requirements $(d_1, d_2, \ldots, d_T)$ in any given period of the planning horizon
   - the upper and lower production capacity bounds in the given period $(\overline{X}_t, \underline{X}_t)$
   - the upper and lower inventory bounds in the given period and all succeeding periods $(\overline{I}_k, \underline{I}_k,$ for $k = t, t + 1, \ldots, T)$

2. The optimum production in a given period is a nonincreasing function of:

   - the upper and lower production capacity bounds in every other period $(\overline{X}_k, \underline{X}_k,$ for $k = 1, 2, \ldots, t - 1, t + 1, \ldots, T)$
   - the upper and lower inventory bounds in any preceding period $(\overline{I}_k, \underline{I}_k,$ for $k = 1, 2, \ldots, t - 1)$

Veinott exploited these results to develop simple and intuitive computational procedures for finding optimum production schedules for a range of parameter values. Karush [1958] suggested a dynamic programming approach to this problem.

Johnson [1957] studied a special case of this problem where no backlogging is allowed, no storage limits are permitted, and inventory carrying costs are linear. For this case, Johnson proved a very simple optimum rule: requirements should be satisfied in order of their due dates by the cheapest available means.

Modigliani and Hohn [1955] analyzed the problem for a convex and nondecreasing production cost function, and linear inventory holding cost without production capacity or storage limits. In addition, they assumed that the cost function is time-invariant over the planning horizon. The problem, then, can be stated as follows:

Minimize
$$Z = \sum_{t=1}^{T} \left[v(X_t) + cI_t \right] \qquad (3.66)$$

subject to:

$$X_t + I_{t-1} - I_t = d_t \qquad t = 1, \ldots, T \qquad (3.67)$$

$$I_t \geq 0, \, X_t \geq 0 \qquad t = 1, \ldots, T \qquad (3.68)$$

where:

$v(X_t) =$ the production cost function

$c =$ inventory carrying cost per unit of product per period.

The derivative of $v(X_t)$, to be denoted $v'(X_t)$, is assumed to be nonnegative, nondecreasing, and continuous. In order to characterize the properties of the optimum solution to this problem, it is helpful to view the cumulative production, $P_t = \sum_{k=1}^{t} X_k$, and the cumulative demand requirements, $D_t = \sum_{k=1}^{t} d_k$, as piecewise linear functions of time formed by straight lines joining adjacent points. Also, let K_t be the upper envelope of the cumulative demand requirements, D_t, and at moment $t = 0$ let $P_0 = D_0 = K_0 = 0$.

If P_t^* denotes an optimum production plan, the following properties can be shown to be true (Modigliani and Hohn [1955], Klein [1961]):

1. $P_T^* = D_T$.
2. $D_t \leqslant P_t^* \leqslant K_t$, $t = 1, 2, \ldots, T$.
3. For any $t = 1, \ldots, T$, if $K_t = D_t$, then $P_t^* = D_t$. The periods in which this property holds are called *planning horizons*.
4. If D_t is concave, then $P_t^* = D_t$, $1 \leqslant t \leqslant T$.
5. If D_t is convex, then P_t^* is convex.
6. A *fundamental solution* to the problem is the set of production quantities X_t that minimizes the objective function (3.66), subject only to constraint (3.67). The fundamental solution satisfies the following condition on the marginal costs:

$$v'(X_{t+1}) = v'(X_1) + tc.$$

When the nonnegativity constraints are also observed, the optimal solution to (3.66)–(3.68) will satisfy the inequalities:

$$v'(X_{t+1}) \leqslant v'(X_L) + tc.$$

Modigliani and Hohn proposed an algorithm based on fundamental solutions, which can be implemented graphically. However, the qualitative properties associated with planning horizons are the most important results of Modigliani and Hohn's work. They proved that the total planning interval can be partitioned into subintervals, defined by the planning horizons, within which the optimal plan is independent of requirements and costs during periods not contained in the corresponding subinterval. Furthermore, if inventory holding costs are negligible, a constant rate of production within each interval is optimum.

There are important practical implications that can be drawn. In production planning decisions affected by strong seasonalities, the relevant horizon is unlikely to extend beyond the period of seasonally high sales of the current cycle, unless sales over the next seasonal cycle tend to be substantially higher than in the current one. Moreover, if the relevant horizon extends beyond the current cycle, this extension is likely to proceed by whole seasonal cycles.

Charnes, Cooper, and Mellon [1955] extended the Modigliani–Hohn results for slightly more general production cost structures and indicated that more than one product could be included in the model, provided that suitable surrogates for total costs be utilized instead of output (for example, labor hours).

Klein [1961] combined the works of Modigliani and Hohn [1955] and Hoffman and Jacobs [1954] to introduce piecewise linear costs associated with production rate changes. In an earlier work, Klein [1957] offered some insightful comments on the general shape of the optimum production schedules under a variety of costs and requirements conditions. Lee and Orr [1977] extended the works of Modigliani and Hohn to a more complicated case where an inventory stage constraint exists. McClain and Thomas [1977] examined the effect of planning horizon length and explored the use of ending conditions in order to shorten a long planning horizon in an aggregate planning model.

More recently, Lippman et al. [1967a] have studied the form of optimum policies for a single-product problem assuming convex production costs, linear hiring and layoff costs, and nondecreasing inventory costs. In a subsequent paper [1967b], the authors proposed a computational algorithm for the case where the cost functions are linear and demand is either monotone increasing or decreasing. Yuan [1967] extended the algorithm to cover convex production costs and arbitrary demand requirements.

3.5.1.2 Concave cost models

Concave costs can result from setup charges, discounting, and economies of scale in the production process. Since these situations occur frequently in practice, the study of production planning under concave cost functions has attracted significant attention in the past.

Consider first the uncapacitated, single-product, concave cost problem, ignoring production change costs. This problem can be formulated as:

Minimize
$$Z = \sum_{t=1}^{T} \left[v_t(X_t) + c_t(I_t) \right]$$

subject to:

$$X_t + I_{t-1} - I_t = d_t \qquad t = 1, \ldots, T$$
$$X_t \geqslant 0 \qquad\qquad\quad t = 1, \ldots, T.$$

If backorders are not allowed, constraints

$$I_t \geqslant 0 \qquad t = 1, \ldots, T$$

should be added.

Zangwill [1966b] proved that it can be assumed without loss of generality that $I_0 = I_T = 0$. Several algorithms proposed to solve the problem assume this condition.

The minimum of a concave function subject to linear constraints occurs at an extreme point of the convex set determined by the linear constraints.

Concave cost functions could be minimized, therefore, by performing an exhaustive analysis of the extreme points of the constraint set. However, complete enumeration is seldom feasible for the general problem. Fortunately, the optimum solution satisfies some important properties that can be exploited to develop effective dynamic programming algorithms for this problem.

When no backorders are allowed, the optimum solution is such that (Wagner and Whitin [1958]):

$$I_{t-1}X_t = 0 \qquad t = 1, \dots, T.$$

This result was extended to the backordering case (Zangwill [1969], Veinott [1969]), where the optimum solution satisfies the following conditions:

$$
\begin{aligned}
I_{t-1}^+ > 0 \quad &\text{implies} \quad X_t = 0 \\
X_t > 0 \quad &\text{implies} \quad I_t^- = 0, \text{ and} \\
I_{t-1}^+ > 0 \quad &\text{implies} \quad I_t^- = 0.
\end{aligned}
$$

These properties, together with the concept of dominant production schedules and planning horizons (see section 3.4.1), have played a fundamental role in the analysis of concave cost models.

A specially important class of concave cost production planning problems is represented by the lot size problem, where the objective function is characterized by the presence of setup costs and linear variable production and inventory costs. This problem has been discussed extensively in section 3.4 and will not be repeated here. In particular, section 3.4.1 considered the single-product uncapacitated problem and described forward and backward dynamic programming algorithms to solve this problem. These dynamic approaches can be expanded easily to the general concave cost function (Johnson and Montgomery [1974, pp. 212–224]).

Zangwill [1966b] suggested a backward dynamic programming algorithm for a single-product problem with or without backlogging. Backlogs are assumed to be filled at most α periods after the scheduled delivery date. This condition can be expressed as follows:

$$I_t \geq - \sum_{k=t-\alpha+1}^{t} d_k,$$

where $d_k = 0$ for $k \leq 0$. If $\alpha = 0$ no backlogging is allowed. If $\alpha > T$, backlogging becomes unrestricted since the time horizon is limited to T time periods.

Zangwill considered concave production costs and piecewise concave inventory cost, allowing for a discontinuity at the origin so as to distinguish between backlogging and inventory carrying costs. These results were expanded by Zangwill [1966a] to include multiple facilities in parallel and in series. The lot size problem with multiple facilities was treated as a network problem by Zangwill [1969] and Kalymon [1970]. Kalymon has analyzed the case of arborescent structured production systems, in which each facility requires input from a unique immediate predecessor. A general discussion of the network approach for single-product concave cost models is given by Zangwill [1968]. This approach can be extended to multiple product single-resource models.

Veinott [1969], using the characterization of extreme points of Leontief substitution systems, presented a unified theory to deal with single-product concave cost problems, and extended Zangwill's results to an arborescent multiechelon structure.

Adding capacity constraints to the concave cost model:

$$X_t \leqslant \overline{X_t} \qquad t = 1, \ldots, T,$$

creates serious computational difficulties in the dynamic programming algorithms, since these restrictions break the structure of the uncapacitated optimum solution.

Florian and Klein [1971] studied the capacitated single-product concave cost case under no backordering, and when backordering is limited to at most α periods. They analyzed the properties of the extreme points of the constraint set, and used these properties to develop a dynamic programming—shortest route algorithm for problems in which the production capacities are the same in every period. Florian and Robillard [1971] proposed a branch-and-bound procedure to solve the capacitated network problem when the cost of sustaining the flow over an arc is concave; the procedure can be applied to solve production planning problems with concave costs. Baker, Dixon, Magazine, and Silver [1978] explored the properties of the optimal solution of the capacitated single-product concave cost problem.

Some work has been devoted to study the single-commodity production planning problem, including concave production costs, concave inventory costs, and piecewise concave costs of changing the production level from period to period. Zangwill [1966c] analyzed the case of no backordering and nondecreasing demand requirements (i.e., $d_t \leqslant d_{t+1}$, $t = 1, \ldots, T$). He studied the properties of the optimum solution under these conditions, and proposed dynamic programming algorithms for special cost structures. Sobel [1970b] made a similar analysis of problems with smoothing startup and shutdown costs.

3.5.1.3   Optimum control and feedback models

Two important additional issues regarding production planning decisions have been studied by means of general cost analytical models. These are:

- continuous time (rather than discrete time periods) formulations for production planning models
- analysis of the stability conditions for production decision rules

The basic concepts that have been applied in dealing with these issues are Pontryagin's optimum principle (Pontryagin et al. [1962]) and feedback and servomechanism theory (Holt et al. [1960, chap. 19], Forrester [1961], and Simon [1952]). This section will briefly review the implications of this work.

Several approaches have been proposed in the literature to deal with aggregate production planning through continuous time. As with the previous nonlinear analytical models examined earlier, these approaches do not lead in general to practical computational procedures. They require a high level of aggregation (normally leading to single-product models), and their usefulness relies primarily on the characterization of the structure of optimal policies. Continuous time models are important in applications that involve high-speed control and where dynamic responses need to be examined.

One of the first studies dealing with a continuous time production model was proposed by Arrow, Karlin, and Scarf [1958, chaps. 4, 5]. They suggested a continuous formulation of the problem of balancing inventory and production costs. Let:

$I(t)$ = inventory level at time t

$X(t)$ = production rate at time t

$d(t)$ = demand requirements at time t

$v(X)$ = production cost, per unit time, when the rate of production is X

$c(I)$ = cost, per unit time, associated with holding the inventory I.

The problem can be formulated as follows:

Minimize
$$\int_0^t \{v[X(t)] + c[I(t)]\}\, dt$$

subject to:

$$I(t) = I(O) + \int_0^t X(t)\, dt - \int_0^t d(t)\, dt.$$

An equivalent statement of the above inventory balance equation is:

$$\frac{dI(t)}{dt} = X(t) - d(t).$$

If no shortages are allowed, the following constraint should be added:

$$I(t) \geqslant 0.$$

The problem was studied under the assumptions of linear inventory holding costs, and production change costs that are proportional to the change when the variation is upward, and zero when the change is downward. The properties of the optimum solution were analyzed for various forms of the demand functions.

Hwang and Fan [1966] and Hwang, Fan, and Erickson [1967] applied Pontryagin's optimum principle to the continuous time production problem. In the production planning context the optimum control actions correspond to the optimum level of the production quantities, and the state variables refer to the inventory levels. The problem can be stated as follows:

Minimize $\int_0^T \{c_x[X(t)-X^*]^2 + c_i[I(t)-I^*]^2\}\,dt$

subject to:

$$\frac{dI(t)}{dt} = X(t) - d(t).$$

Both the production cost and the inventory holding and stockout cost have been approximated by quadratic functions, in which c_x and c_i are constants. The above integral yields the total cost incurred between time 0 and time T. X^* and I^* are target levels for production and inventory; they are assumed known, and can be functions of time t.

The application of Pontryagin's principle produces the following optimum solution to the problem:

$$I(t) = A_1 e^{\lambda t} + A_2 e^{-\lambda t} + [I(t)]_p$$

$$X(t) = A_1 \lambda e^{\lambda t} - A_2 e^{-\lambda t} + \frac{dI(t)p}{dt} + d(t)$$

where:

$$\lambda^2 = C_i / C_x,$$

A_1 and A_2 are to be determined by initial conditions, and $I(t)p$ is the particular solution of an equation to be decided by the forms and/or the values of I^* and d (Hwang, Fan, and Erickson [1967]).

Nelson [1966] applied Pontryagin's principle to obtain necessary and sufficient conditions for optimality in a problem of manpower assignment in a labor and machine constrained production system.

Concepts such as feedback, lagged responses, types of control devices, and stability of the production system over time play a fundamental role in the design and operation of ongoing production planning systems. Servomechanism theory provides the basis for a formal analysis of these concepts in the production environment. Holt and Simon [1954] and Hanssmann [1962, pp. 132–136] proved that the production rules derived by differentiating a quadratic cost function can generate a very unstable system, creating unacceptable fluctuations in production and inventory levels unless demand forecasts during the planning horizon are perfect. Vassian [1955] proposed ways to construct stable feedback rules for this situation, and Holt and Simon [1954] and Simon [1952] indicated how the unstable rules can suggest the definition of stable classes of rules. However, as Hanssmann stated, there appears to be no general theory available today to provide the practitioner with a complete understanding of the stability of a proposed set of decision rules. This is particularly valid whenever external forecasts are introduced in the production planning model. At the present time, simulation seems to be the only way to explore exhaustively the degree of stability of the production planning decision rules.

For further discussion on this subject, the reader is referred to Holt et al. [1960, chap. 19].

3.5.2 Heuristic Decision Rules

Perhaps the most important attempt to incorporate management behavior in a systematic fashion into the aggregate capacity planning problem is Bowman's management coefficient approach [1963]. Bowman suggested that managers' decisions on production rates, inventory levels, and work force levels tend to be responsive to the costs that are relevant to making those decisions. However, managers might overreact to the daily pressures of their work, occasionally making erratic decisions with expensive outcomes, decisions which vary from their average pattern of past behavior. On the other hand, since most cost functions exhibit a flat shape around the optimum, small deviations from the optimum are not going to generate heavy penalties.

From this, Bowman concluded that decision rules with coefficients estimated from management's past performance should produce better results than existing operating schedules, and better results than those generated from analytical studies. Thus, he postulated a certain functional form for the production scheduling decision rules, and then calculated all the coefficients involved.

The actual structure of the decision rule to be used can be derived either from analytical considerations (like the linear decision rules obtained from quadratic cost functions), or from intuitive reasoning, or from a combination of both. Bowman suggested the following example of a production scheduling rule:

$$X_t = \sum_{i=t}^{t+T-1} a_i d_i + x(X_{t-1} - d_t) + y(I_N - I_{t-1})$$

where:

X_t = production scheduled in period t

d_t = sales forecast for period t

x, y = smoothing constants $(0 \leqslant x \leqslant 1), (0 \leqslant y \leqslant 1)$

I_N = "normal" inventory level

I_{t-1} = inventory at the end of period $t - 1$

a_i = weighting coefficient for sales forecast S_i

$\qquad a_t > a_{t+1} > \cdots > a_{t+T-1}$

T = the number of time periods in the planning horizon.

The numerical values of the coefficients a_i, x, and y are obtained not by analytical methods (as in the HMMS models) or by simulation techniques, but by performing regression analyses on past management behavior.

Bowman reported encouraging results by comparing the performance of his approach against linear decision rules and actual past costs in four industries. Mellichamp and Love [1978] suggested a random walk production-inventory heuristic which generates very good results.

3.5.3 Search Decision Rules

Jones [1967] combined the heuristic approach with search techniques to develop a method for aggregate capacity planning that was called Parametric Production Planning. In a heuristic manner, he started by postulating the existence of two linear decision rules to be used in making work force and production level decisions. Then, by search, he found the optimal values of the parameters in the decision rules.

In what follows, assume that the upcoming time period is denoted as period t. The decision maker is, then, at the end of period $t - 1$.

The work force decision rules take the form of a smoothing expression:

$$W_t = W_{t-1} + A(W_D - W_{t-1})$$

where:

W_{t-1} = current work force level

W_t = planned work force level for the upcoming period

W_D = desired work force level to meet forecasted future demands

A = coefficient determining the fraction of desired change of work force to be implemented in the upcoming period; $0 \leqslant A \leqslant 1$.

The desired work force W_D is expressed as a weighted sum of the work force required to meet future sales during the T-period planning horizon.

$$W_D = \sum_{i=1}^{T} b_i K(d_{t+i-1})$$

where:

b_i = weighting coefficient for sales forecast d_{t+i-1}

$K(d_t)$ = number of workers required to produce d_t units at minimum total cost.

After experimenting with several weighting functions, Jones suggested the following expression to determine the values of the b_i coefficients:

$$b_i = \frac{B^i}{\sum_{i=1}^{T} B^i}$$

where:

> B = coefficient between 0 and 1 such that its ith power, B^i, determines the relative weight to be given to the demand forecast for period i.

Note that all the b_i coefficients, $i = 1, \ldots, T$, are expressed as a function of a single parameter B. Also notice that the average value of the b_i coefficients is $(\sum_{i=1}^{T} b_i / T) = (1/T)$.

Moreover, Jones included a term to prevent consistent inventory depletion or buildup because of the needs to smooth production. Jones suggested the following corrective term to be added to the work force decision rule:

$$b_1 K (I_t^* - I_{t-1})$$

where:

> I_t^* = optimal inventory level at the end of the upcoming period, computed so as to balance off the cost of stockouts and backorders against the cost of holding inventory.

The same $K(\cdot)$ function that was involved in computing the desired work force level, is again used here to convert the inventory discrepancy $(I_t^* - I_{t-1})$ into the number of workers who can offset it at the lowest total cost. The weight attached to the inventory discrepancy term is b_1, which is also the weight that has been placed on the demand forecast for the upcoming period t. In this way, the excess or deficit of inventory is subtracted from or added to the first period forecast, thus generating an effective (or net) demand forecast for that period.

The resulting work force decision rule becomes:

$$W_t = W_{t-1} + A \left[\sum_{i=1}^{T} b_i K (d_{t+i-1}) - W_{t-1} + b_1 K (I_t^* - I_{t-1}) \right].$$

The production decision rule is similar to the work force rule:

$$X_t = K^{-1}(W_t) + C \left[\sum_{i=1}^{T} e_i d_{t+i-1} - K^{-1}(W_t) + e_1 (I_t^* - I_{t-1}) \right]$$

where:

> $K^{-1}(W_t)$ = number of units that can be produced by W_t workers at minimum cost; $K^{-1}(\cdot)$ is the inverse of function $K(\cdot)$.

> C = coefficient between 0 and 1 indicating the fraction of the desired production increase or decrease to be achieved

> e_i = weighting coefficient for sales forecast d_{t+i-1}.

The e_i coefficients are defined as an expression similar to the one used for the b_i coefficients:

$$e_i = \frac{D^i}{\sum_{i=1}^{T} D^i},$$

where:

$D =$ coefficient between 0 and 1 such that its ith power, D^i, determines the relative weight to be given to the demand forecast for period i.

The numerical values of the four coefficients A, B, C, and D are obtained by applying search techniques in the five-dimensional space determined by the firm's cost function and the four parameters. The cost function is determined by taking into account the cost structure and the production relationships relevant to the firm under consideration; it can be much more diverse, and hence closer to reality, than in the case of the analytical models.

There are a large number of different search techniques available for optimization purposes. An extensive coverage of these techniques has been given by Wilde [1964]. Among them, the one that seems most promising is the Direct Search procedure developed by Hooke and Jeeves [1961]. Jones suggested that the response surface determined by the four coefficients and the associated profitability measure is unimodal, shallow, and smooth; these are highly desirable attributes for the search techniques to be applied. Jones reported some encouraging results after testing the performance of his approach on four different examples.

Another important application of search to aggregate capacity planning was developed by Taubert [1968]. There are some basic differences between Taubert's and Jones' approaches. Taubert searches for the values of production rates, work force, and inventory levels during each time period, while Jones searched only for the values of the four coefficients. The dimensionality of the search depends on the number of time periods included in the planning horizon. In Taubert's search there were 20 independent variables; the computational results showed an average of 19 seconds per run on an IBM 7094/7044.

Taubert also suggested the possibility of combining search with a branch-and-bound procedure. Branch-and-bound consists of partitioning the original problem into a number of simpler problems, which, when solved, yield information about the feasible region and bounds on the original problem. Search would be used, in the author's view, to solve the simpler problems resulting at the nodes of the branch-and-bound tree. This approach, attractive in its potential, has not been tested yet.

Another simple application of search to aggregate capacity planning was done by Goodman [1973].

In concluding, it has to be mentioned that, like any other technique, search is also affected by "the curse of dimensionality" (Bellman [1957]). "The vastness of hyperspace" (Wilde [1964]) makes the computational effort increase very rapidly with the number of variables considered in the problem. Therefore, a tradeoff has to be achieved between dimensionality and the cost of conducting the search.

3.5.4 Simulation Decision Rules

For a long time, simulation has been recognized as an important modeling tool to deal with situations where analytical models either become computationally infeasible or provide too simplified a representation of the real problem.* Vergin [1966] developed a general purpose simulator able to capture some of the special aspects present in practical scheduling problems but ignored, by necessity, in the analytical approaches to the capacity planning problem. The simulation can be adjusted to incorporate special conditions of a particular firm.

The simulation process starts with an initial schedule which is suggested by experience or represents the current practice in the firm. An objective function, which has no restrictions in terms of its structure, is used to evaluate the performance of each schedule. A change is introduced in employment levels, overtime, inventories, subcontracting, and so on until a local minimum is achieved.

Vergin [1966] conducted a study of three manufacturing firms affected by strong seasonalities; he reported that simulation schedules performed much better than both existing operating schedules and linear decision rules schedules.

3.5.5 Advantages and Disadvantages of General Cost Models

One of the greatest advantages of the general cost models is their added realism. They can reflect more accurately the production planning environment, including uncertainties, and special cost structure and constraints. In addition, they are more closely associated with the actual decision process, which makes them more acceptable by managers and easier to explain and justify.

However, these advantages have a price. Usually the models are expensive to develop and run, and the computational procedures used to solve them seldom guarantee overall optimality. Some of the models require a high degree of aggregation; this creates problems of implementation when decisions need to be disaggregated at lower levels. Moreover, general cost models are not suitable for handling a large number of interactive constraints, as opposed to linear programming models that can easily do this.

---

*For good references on simulation see Emshoff and Sisson [1970], Naylor et al. [1966], and Silver [1977].

Analytical models are helpful in determining qualitative properties of the optimum solutions but seldom generate practical algorithmic procedures.

Lee and Khumawala [1974] tested, in a realistic environment, the performance of the Linear Decision Rule model against Bowman's Management Coefficient Model, Jones' Parametric Production Planning Model, and Taubert's Search Decision Rule. They concluded that the Search Decision Rule clearly outperformed the other three models evaluated; they also provided a synthesis for implementing aggregate capacity planning models. Moskowitz and Miller [1975] compared Bowman's Management Coefficient Model with the Linear Decision Rule model in an aggregate production planning context. Their experimental results support Bowman's model.

BIBLIOGRAPHY

ANSHEN, M., C. C. HOLT, F. MODIGLIANI, F. J. MUTH, and H. A. SIMON, "Mathematics for Production Scheduling," *Harvard Business Review*, March–April 1958, pp. 51–58.

ANTHONY, R. N., *Planning and Control Systems: A Framework for Analysis*, Graduate School of Business Administration, Harvard University, Boston, 1965.

ANTOSIEWICZ, H., and A. J. HOFFMAN, "A Remark on the Smoothing Problem," *Management Science*, Vol. 1, No. 1, October 1954, pp. 92–95.

ARMSTRONG, R. J. and A. C. HAX, "A Hierarchical Approach for a Naval Tender Job Shop Design," Operations Research Center, M.I.T., September 1974.

ARROW, K. J., S. KARLIN, and H. SCARF, *Studies in the Mathematical Theory of Inventory and Production*, Stanford University Press, Stanford, Calif., 1958.

BAKER, K. R., "An Experimental Study of the Effectiveness of Rolling Schedules in Production Planning," Graduate School of Business Administration Paper No. 138, Duke University, Durham, N.C., October 1975.

BAKER, K. R., P. DIXON, M. J. MAGAZINE, and E. A. SILVER, "An Algorithm for the Dynamic Lot-Size Problem with Time-Varying Production Capacity Constraints," *Management Science*, Vol. 24, No. 16, December 1978, pp. 1710–1720.

BAKER, K. R. and D. W. PETERSON, "An Analytic Framework for Evaluating Rolling Schedules," Graduate School of Business Administration Paper No. 177, Duke University, Durham, N.C., March 1976.

BALINSKI, M. L., "Fixed Cost Transportation Problem," *Naval Research Logistics Quarterly*, Vol. 8, January 1961, pp. 41–54.

BELLMAN, R., *Dynamic Programming*, Princeton University Press, Princeton, N. J., 1957.

BERGSTROM, G. L. and B. E. SMITH, "Multi-Item Production Planning—An Extension of the HMMS Rules," *Management Science*, Vol. 16, No. 10, June 1970, pp. B614–B629.

BITRAN, G. R. and A. C. HAX, "On the Design of Hierarchical Production Planning Systems," *Decision Sciences*, Vol. 8, No. 1, January 1977, pp. 28–55.

BOWMAN, E. H., "Production Scheduling by the Transportation Method of Linear Programming," *Operations Research*, Vol. 4, No. 1, February 1956, pp. 100–103.

BOWMAN, E. H., "Consistency and Optimality in Managerial Decision Making," *Management Science*, Vol. 9, No. 2, January 1963, pp. 310–321.

BRADLEY, S. P., A. C. HAX, and T. L. MAGNANTI, *Applied Mathematical Programming*, Addison–Wesley, Reading, Mass., 1977.

BRISKIN, L. E., "A Method of Unifying Multiple Objective Functions," *Management Science*, Vol. 12, No. 10, June 1966, pp. B406–B416.

BROWN, R. G., *Decision Rules for Inventory Management*, Holt, Rinehart and Winston, New York, 1967.

BUFFA, E. S., *Operations Management: Problems and Models*, Wiley, New York, 1972.

BUFFA, E. S. and W. H. TAUBERT, *Production-Inventory Systems: Planning and Control*, Irwin, Homewood, Ill., 1972.

CANDEA, D., "Issues of Hierarchical Planning in Multistage Production Systems," Technical Report No. 134, Operations Research Center, M.I.T., Cambridge, Mass., July 1977.

CHANG, R. H. and C. M. JONES, "Production and Workforce Scheduling Extensions," *AIIE Transactions*, Vol. 2, No. 4, December 1970, pp. 326–333.

CHARNES A., W. W. COOPER, and B. MELLON, "A Model for Optimizing Production by Reference to Cost Surrogates," *Econometrica*, Vol. 23, No. 3, July 1955, pp. 307–323.

CHARNES, A., W. W. COOPER, R. J. NIEHAUS, and A. STEDRY, "Static and Dynamic Assignment Models with Multiple Objectives, and Some Remarks on Organization Design," *Management Science*, Vol. 15, No. 8, April 1969, pp. B365–B375.

COOPER, L., "The Fixed Charge Problem—I: A New Heuristic Method," *Computers and Mathematics with Applications*, Vol. 1, 1975, pp. 89–95.

COOPER, L. and C. DREBES, "An Approximate Solution Methods for the Fixed Charge Problem," *Naval Research Logistics Quarterly*, Vol. 14, No. 1, March 1967, pp. 101–113.

DAMON, W. W. and R. SCHRAMM, "A Simultaneous Decision Model for Production, Marketing and Finance," *Management Science*, Vol. 19, No. 2, October 1972, pp. 161–172.

DANTZIG, G. B. and R. M. VAN SLYKE, "Generalized Upper Bounding Techniques," *Journal of Computer System Sciences*, Vol. 1, 1967, pp. 213–226.

DANTZIG, G. B. and P. WOLFE, "Decomposition Principle for Linear Programs," *Operations Research*, Vol. 8, No. 1, January–February 1960, pp. 101–111.

DENZLER, D. R., "An Approximate Algorithm for the Fixed Charge Problem," *Naval Research Logistics Quarterly*, Vol. 16, No. 3, September 1969, pp. 411–416.

DZIELINSKI, B. P., C. T. BAKER, and A. S. MANNE, "Simulation Tests of Lot Size Programming," *Management Science*, Vol. 9, No. 2, January 1963, pp. 229–258.

DZIELINSKI, B. P. and R. E. GOMORY, "Optimal Programming of Lot Sizes, Inventory and Labor Allocations," *Management Science*, Vol. 11, No. 9, July 1965, pp. 874–890.

EILON, S., *Elements of Production Planning and Control*, Macmillan, New York, 1962.

ELMAGHRABY, S. E., *The Design of Production Systems*, Reinhold, New York, 1966.

ELMAGHRABY, S. E., "Some Recent Developments in Aggregate Production Planning and Scheduling: An Abbreviated Bibliography," OR Report No. 85, North Carolina State University, Raleigh, January 1973.

ELMAGHRABY, S. E., and V. Y. BAWLE, "Optimization of Batch Ordering Under a Deterministic Variable Demand," *Management Science*, Vol. 18, No. 9, May 1972, pp. 508–517.

EMSHOFF, J. R. and R. L. SISSON, *Computer Simulation Models*, Macmillan, New York, 1970.

EPPEN, G. D. and F. J. GOULD, "A Lagrangian Application to Production Models," *Operations Research*, Vol. 16, No. 4, July–August 1968, pp. 819–829.

EPPEN, G. D., F. J. GOULD, and B. P. PASHIGIAN, "Extensions of the Planning Horizon Theorem in the Dynamic Lot Size Model," *Management Science*, Vol. 15, No. 5, January 1969, pp. 268–277.

EVANS, J. P. and F. J. GOULD, "Application of Generalized Lagrange Multiplier Technique to a Production Planning Problem," *Naval Research Logistics Quarterly*, Vol. 18, No. 1, March 1971, pp. 59–74.

EVANS, J. P. and F. J. GOULD, "A Generalized Lagrange Multiplier Algorithm for Optimum or Near Optimum Production Scheduling," *Management Science*, Vol. 18, No. 5, January 1972, pp. 229–311.

EVERETT, H., "Generalized Lagrange Multiplier Method for Solving Problems of Optimum Allocation of Resources," *Operations Research*, Vol. 11, No. 3, May–June 1963, pp. 339–417.

FLORIAN, M. and M. KLEIN, "Deterministic Production Planning with Concave Costs and Capacity Constraints," *Management Science*, Vol. 18, No. 1, September 1971, pp. 12–20.

FLORIAN, M. and P. ROBILLARD, "An Implicit Enumeration Algorithm for the Concave Cost Network Flow Problem," *Management Science*, Vol. 18, No. 3, November 1971, pp. 184–193.

FORRESTER, J., *Industrial Dynamics*, M.I.T. Press, Cambridge, Mass., 1961.

GAALMAN, G. J., "Optimal Aggregation of Multi-Item Production Smoothing Models," *Management Science*, Vol. 24, No. 16, December 1978, pp. 1733–1739.

GALBRAITH, J. R., "Solving Production Smoothing Problems," *Management Science*, Vol. 15, No. 12, August 1969, pp. B665–B674.

GEOFFRION, A. M. and G. W. GRAVES, "Multicommodity Distribution Systems Design by Benders Decomposition," *Management Science*, Vol. 20, No. 5, January 1974, pp. 822–844.

GOODMAN, D. A., "A New Approach to Scheduling Aggregate Production and Work Force." *AIIE Transactions*, Vol. 5, No. 2, June 1973, pp. 135–141.

GOODMAN, D. A., "A Goal Programming Approach to Aggregate Planning of Production and Work Force," *Management Science*, Vol. 20, No. 12, August 1974, pp. 1569–1575.

GORENSTEIN, S., "Planning Tire Production," *Management Science*, Vol. 17, No. 2, October 1970, pp. B72–B82.

GRAY, P., "Exact Solution of the Fixed-Charge Transportation Problem," *Operations Research*, Vol. 19, October 1971, pp. 1529–1538.

GREEN, P., "Heuristic Coupling of Aggregate and Detailed Models in Factory Scheduling," unpublished Ph.D. thesis, M.I.T., Cambridge, Mass., 1971.

GROFF, G. K. and J. F. MUTH, *Operations Management: Analysis for Decisions*, Irwin, Homewood, Ill., 1972.

HADLEY, G. and T. M. WHITIN, *Analysis of Inventory Systems*, Prentice-Hall, Englewood Cliffs, N.J., 1963.

HAEHLING VON LANZENAUER, C., "Production and Employment Scheduling in Multi-Stage Production Systems," *Naval Research Logistics Quarterly*, Vol. 17, No. 2, June 1970a, pp. 193–198.

HAEHLING VON LANZENAUER, C., "A Production Scheduling Model by Bivalent Linear Programming," *Management Science*, Vol. 17, No. 1, September 1970b, pp. 105–111.

HANSSMANN, F., *Operations Research in Production and Inventory Control*, Wiley, New York, 1962.

HANSSMANN, F. and S. W. HESS, "A Linear Programming Approach to Production and Employment Scheduling," *Management Technology*, No. 1, January 1960.

HAUSMAN, W. H. and J. D. McClain, "A Note on the Bergstrom–Smith Multi-Item Production Planning Model," *Management Science*, Vol. 17, No. 11, July 1971, pp. 783–785.

HAX, A. C., "Integration of Strategic and Tactical Planning in the Aluminum Industry," Technology Report Operations Research Center, M.I.T., Cambridge, Mass., September 1973.

HAX, A. C. "A Comment on the Distribution System Simulator," *Management Science*, Vol. 21, No. 2, October 1974, pp. 223–236.

HAX, A. C., "The Design of Large Scale Logistics Systems: A Survey and an Approach," in W. Marlow (editor), *Modern Trends in Logistics Research*, M.I.T. Press, Cambridge, Mass., 1976, pp. 59–96.

HAX, A. C., "Aggregate Production Planning," in J. Moders and S. Elmaghraby (editors), *Handbook of Operations Research*, Van Nostrand Reinhold, New York, 1978.

HAX, A. C. and H. C. MEAL, "Hierarchical Integration of Production Planning and Scheduling," *North Holland/TIMS, Studies in Management Sciences, Vol. 1, Logistics,* North Holland/American Elsevier, 1975, pp. 53–69.

HAX, A. C. and K. M. WIIG, "The Use of Decision Analysis in Capital Investment Problems," *Sloan Management Review*, Vol. 17, No. 2, Winter 1976, pp. 19–48.

HOFFMAN, A. J. and W. JACOBS, "Smooth Patterns of Production," *Management Science*, Vol. 1, No. 1, October 1954, pp. 86–91.

HOLSTEIN, W. R., "Production Planning and Control Integrated," *Harvard Business Review*, Vol. 46, No. 3, May–June 1968, pp. 121–140.

HOLT, C. C., F. MODIGLIANI, and J. F. MUTH, "Derivation of a Linear Decision Rule for Production and Employment Scheduling," *Management Science*, Vol. 2, No. 2, January 1956, pp. 159–177.

HOLT, C. C., F. MODIGLIANI, J. F. MUTH, and H. A. SIMON, *Planning Production, Inventories, and Work Force*, Prentice-Hall, Englewood Cliffs, N.J., 1960.

HOLT, C. C., F. MODIGLIANI, and H. A. SIMON, "Linear Decision Rule for Production and Employment Scheduling," *Management Science*, Vol. 2, No. 1, October 1955, pp. 1–30.

HOLT, C. C. and H. A. SIMON, "Optimal Decision Rules for Production and Inventory Control," *Proceedings of the Conference on Operations Research in Production and Inventory Control*, Case Institute of Technology, January 1954.

HOOKE, R. and T. A. JEEVES, "Direct Search Solution of Numerical and Statistical Problems," *Journal of the Association for Computing Machinery*, Vol. 8, April 1961, pp. 212–229.

HWANG, C. L. and L. T. FAN, "The Application of the Maximum Principle to Industrial and Management Systems," *Journal of Industrial Engineering*, Vol. 17, No. 11, November 1966, pp. 589–593.

HWANG, C. L., L. T. FAN, and L. E. ERICKSON, "Optimum Production Planning by the Maximum Principle," *Management Science*, Vol. 13, No. 9, May 1967, pp. 751–755.

JAGANNATHAN, R. and M. M. RAO, "Class of Deterministic Production Planning Problems," *Management Science*, Vol. 19, No. 11, July 1973, pp. 1295–1300.

JOHNSON, L. A. and D. C. MONTGOMERY, *Operations Research in Production Planning, Scheduling, and Inventory Control*, Wiley, New York, 1974.

JOHNSON, S. M., "Sequential Production Planning over Time at Minimum Cost," *Management Science*, Vol. 3, No. 4, July 1957, pp. 435–437.

JOHNSON, S. M. and G. B. DANTZIG, "A Production Smoothing Problem,"

Proceedings of the Second Symposium in Linear Programming, Washington, D.C., January 1955.

JONES, A. P. and R. M. SOLAND, "A Branch-and-Bound Algorithm for Multi-Level Fixed-Charge Problems,"*Management Science*, Vol. 16, No. 1, September 1969, pp. 67–76.

JONES, C. H., "Parametric Production Planning," *Management Science*, Vol. 13, No. 11, July 1967, pp. 843–866.

KALYMON, B. A., "A Decomposition Algorithm for Arborescence Inventory Systems," *Operations Research*, Vol. 20, No. 4, July–August 1972, pp. 860–874.

KAO, E. P. C., "A Multi-Product Dynamic Lot-Size Model with Individual and Joint Set-Up Costs," *Operations Research*, Vol. 27, No. 2, March–April 1979, pp. 279–289.

KARUSH, W., "On a Class of Minimum Cost Problems," *Management Science*, Vol. 4, No. 2, January 1958, pp. 136–153.

KEENEY, R. L. and H. RAIFFA, *Decisions with Multiple Objectives; Preferences and Value Tradeoffs*, Wiley, New York, 1976.

KLEIN, M., "Some Production Planning Problems," *Naval Research Logistics Quarterly*, Vol. 4, No. 4, December 1957, pp. 269–286.

KLEIN, M., "On Production Smoothing," *Management Science*, Vol. 7, No. 3, April 1961, pp. 286–293.

KOLENDA, J. F., "A Comparison of Two Aggregate Planning Models," unpublished master's thesis, Wharton School of Finance and Commerce, Philadelphia, Penn., 1970.

KORTANEK, K. O., D. SODARO, and A. L. SOYSTER, "Multi-Product Production Scheduling via Extreme Point Properties of Linear Programming," *Naval Research Logistics Quarterly*, Vol. 15, 1968, pp. 287–300.

KORTANEK, K. O. and A. L. SOYSTER, "On the Status of Some Multi-Product Multi-Period Production Scheduling Models," *Management Science*, Vol. 17, No. 8, April 1971, pp. B560–B561.

KRAJEWSKI, L. J., V. A. MABERT, and H. E. THOMPSON, "Quadratic Inventory Cost Approximations and the Aggregation of Individual Products," *Management Science*, Vol. 19, No. 11, July 1973, pp. 1229–1240.

KRIEBEL, C. H., "Coefficient Estimation in Quadratic Programming Models," *Management Science*, Vol. 13, No. 8, April 1967, pp. B473–B486.

KUHN, H. W. and W. J. BAUMOL, "An Approximative Algorithm for the Fixed-Charge Transportation Problem," *Naval Research Logistics Quarterly*, Vol. 9, No. 1, 1962, pp. 1–15.

LASDON, L. S. and R. C. TERJUNG, "An Efficient Algorithm for Multi-Item Scheduling," *Operations Research*, Vol. 19, No. 4, July–August 1971, pp. 946–969.

LEE, D. R. and D. ORR, "Further Results on Planning Horizons in the Production Smoothing Problem," *Management Science*, Vol. 23, No. 5, January 1977, pp. 490–498.

LEE, S. M., *Goal Programming for Decision Analysis*, Auerbach, Philadelphia, 1972.

LEE, W. B. and B. M. KHUMAWALA, "Simulation Testing of Aggregate Production Planning Models in Implementation Methodology," *Management Science*, Vol. 20, No. 6, February 1974, pp. 903–911.

LEVITAN, R. E., "A Note on Professor Manne's Dominance Theorem," *Management Science*, Vol. 5, No. 3, April 1959, pp. 332–334.

LIPPMAN, S. A., A. J. ROLFE, H. M. WAGNER, and J. S. C. YUAN, "Optimal Production Scheduling and Employment Smoothing with Deterministic Demands," *Management Science*, Vol. 14, No. 3, November 1967a, pp. 127–158.

LIPPMAN, S. A., A. J. ROLFE, H. M. WAGNER, and J. S. C. YUAN, "Algorithm for Optimal Production Scheduling and Employment Smoothing," *Operations Research*, Vol. 15, No. 6, November–December 1967b, pp. 1011–1029.

MAGEE, J. F. and D. M. BOODMAN,   *Production Planning and Inventory Control*, McGraw-Hill, New York, 1967.

MANNE, A. S.,   "A Note on the Modigliani–Hohn Production Smoothing Model," *Management Science*, Vol. 3, No. 4, July 1957, pp. 371–379.

MANNE, A. S.,   "Programming of Economic Lot Sizes," *Management Science*, Vol. 4, No. 2, January 1958, pp. 115–135.

McCLAIN, J. and J. THOMAS,   "Horizon Effects in Aggregate Production Planning with Seasonal Demand," *Management Science*, Vol. 25, No. 7, March 1977, pp. 728–736.

McGARRAH, R. E.,   *Production and Logistics Management*, Wiley, New York, 1963.

MELLICHAMP, J. M. and R. M. LOVE,   "Production Switching Heuristics for the Aggregate Planning Problem," *Management Science*, Vol. 24, No. 12, August 1978, pp. 1242–1251.

MIZE, J. H., C. R. WHITE, and G. H. BROOKS,   *Operations Planning and Control*, Prentice-Hall, Englewood Cliffs, N.J., 1971.

MODIGLIANI, F. and F. E. HOHN,   "Production Planning over Time and the Nature of the Expectation and Planning Horizon," *Econometrica*, Vol. 23, No. 1, January 1955, pp. 46–66.

MORIN, F.,   "Note on an Inventory Problem Discussed by Modigliani and Hohn," *Econometrica*, Vol. 23, No. 4, October 1955, pp. 447–450.

MOSKOWITZ, H. and J. G. MILLER,   "Information and Decision Systems for Production Planning," *Management Science*, Vol. 22, No. 3, November 1975, pp. 359–370.

MURTY, K. G.,   "Solving the Fixed Charge Problem by Routing Extreme Points," *Operations Research*, Vol. 16, No. 2, March–April 1968, pp. 268–279.

NADDOR, E.,   *Inventory Systems*, Wiley, New York, 1966.

NAYLOR, T. et al.,   *Computer Simulation Techniques*, Wiley, New York, 1966.

NELSON, R. T.,   "Labor Assignment as a Dynamic Control Problem," *Operations Research*, Vol. 14, No. 3, May–June 1966, pp. 369–376.

NEWSON, P. E. F.,   "Multi-Item Lot Size Scheduling by Heuristic. Part I: With Fixed Resources," *Management Science*, Vol. 21, No. 10, June 1975a, pp. 1186–1193.

NEWSON, P. E. F.,   "Multi-Item Lot Size Scheduling by Heuristic. Part II: With Variable Resources," *Management Science*, Vol. 21, No. 10, June 1975b, pp. 1194–1203.

O'MALLEY, R. L., S. E. ELMAGHRABY, and J. W. JESKE,   "An Operational System for Smoothing Batch-Type Production," *Management Science*, Vol. 12, No. 10, June 1966, pp. B433–B449.

ORRBECK, M. G., D. R. SCHUETTE, and H. E. THOMPSON,   "The Effect of Worker Productivity on Production Smoothing," *Management Science*, Vol. 14, No. 6, February 1968, pp. B332–B342.

PETERSON, R.,   "Optimal Smoothing of Shipments in Response to Orders," *Management Science*, Vol. 17, No. 9, May 1971, pp. 597–607.

PONTRYAGIN, L. S., V. G. BOLTGANSKII, R. V. GAMKSELIDZE, and E. F. MISHCHENKO,   *The Mathematical Theory of Optimal Processes*, Wiley, New York, 1962.

ROUSSEAU, J. M.,   "A Cutting Plane Method for the Fixed Cost Problem," unpublished Ph.D. thesis, Sloan School of Management, M.I.T., August 1973.

SHWIMER, J.,   "Interaction Between Aggregate and Detailed Scheduling in a Job Shop," unpublished Ph.D. thesis, M.I.T., 1972.

SILVER, E. A., "A Tutorial on Production Smoothing and Work Force Balancing," *Operations Research*, Vol. 15, No. 6, November–December 1967, pp. 985–1010.

SILVER, E. A., "A Tutorial on Simulation," OR Report No. 32, Département de Mathématiques, Ecole Polytechnique Fédérale de Lausanne, Lausanne, Switzerland, April 1977.

SIMON, H. A., "On the Application of Servomechanism Theory in the Study of Production Control," *Econometrica*, Vol. 20, No. 2, April 1952, pp. 247–268.

SIMON, H. A., "Dynamic Programming Under Uncertainty with a Quadratic Criterion Function," *Econometrica*, Vol. 24, No. 1, 1956, pp. 74–81.

SOBEL, M. J., "Smoothing Start-up and Shut-down Costs in Sequential Production," *Operations Research*, Vol. 17, No. 1, January–February 1969a, pp. 133–144.

SOBEL, M. J., "Production Smoothing with Stochastic Demand I: Finite Horizon Case," *Management Science*, Vol. 16, No. 3, November 1969b, pp. 195–207.

SOBEL, M. J., "Making Short-Run Changes in Production when the Employment Level Is Fixed," *Operations Research*, Vol. 18, No. 1, January–February 1970a, pp. 35–51.

SOBEL, M. J., "Smoothing Start-up and Shut-down Costs: Concave Case," *Management Science*, Vol. 17, No. 1, September 1970b, pp. 78–91.

SOBEL, M. J., "Production Smoothing with Stochastic Demand II: Infinite Horizon Case," *Management Science*, Vol. 17, No. 11, July 1971, pp. 724–735.

STARR, M. K., *Production Management — Systems and Procedures*, Prentice-Hall, Englewood Cliffs, N. J., 1972.

STEINBERG, D. I., "The Fixed Charge Problem," *Naval Research Logistics Quarterly*, Vol. 17, No. 2, June 1970, pp. 217–235.

SYKPENS, H. A., "Planning for Optimal Plant Capacity," unpublished master's thesis, Sloan School of Management, M.I.T., Cambridge, Mass., 1967.

TAUBERT, W. H., "A Search Decision Rule for the Aggregate Scheduling Pattern," *Management Science*, Vol. 14, No. 6, February 1968, pp. B343–B359.

THOMAS, J., "Linear Programming Models for Production–Advertising Decisions," *Management Science*, Vol. 17, No. 8, April 1971, pp. B474–B484.

VAN DE PANNE, C. and P. BOSJE, "Sensitivity Analysis of Lost Coefficient Estimates: The Case of Linear Decision Rules for Employment and Production," *Management Science*, Vol. 9, No. 1, October 1962, pp. 82–107.

VASSIAN, H. J., "Application of Discrete Variable Servo Theory to Inventory Control," *Operations Research*, Vol. 3, No. 3, August 1955, pp. 272–289.

VEINOTT, A. F., "Production Planning with Convex Costs: A Parametric Study," *Management Science*, Vol. 10, No. 3, April 1964, pp. 441–460.

VEINOTT, A. F., "Minimum Concave-Cost Solution of Leontief Substitution Models of Multi-Facility Inventory Systems," *Operations Research*, Vol. 17, No. 2, March–April 1969, pp. 262–291.

VEINOTT, A. F. and H. M. WAGNER, "Optimal Capacity Scheduling—I and II," *Operations Research*, Vol. 10, No. 4, July–August 1962, pp. 518–546.

VERGIN, R. C., "Production Scheduling Under Seasonal Demand," *Journal of Industrial Engineering*, Vol. 7, May 1966, pp. 260–266.

WAGNER, H. M., "A Postscript to Dynamic Problems in the Theory of the Firm," *Naval Research Logistics Quarterly*, Vol. 7, No. 1, March 1960, pp. 7–12.

WAGNER, H. M., *Statistical Management of Inventory Systems*, Wiley, New York, 1962.

WAGNER, H. M., *Principles of Operations Research*, Prentice-Hall, Englewood Cliffs, N.J., 1969.

WAGNER, H. M. and T. M. WHITIN, "A Dynamic Version of the Economic Lot Size Model," *Management Science*, Vol. 5, No. 1, October 1958, pp. 89–96.

WALKER, W. E., "A Heuristic Adjacent Extreme Point Algorithm for the Fixed Charge Problem," *Management Science*, Vol. 22, No. 5, January 1976, pp. 587–596.

WELAM, U. P., "An HMMS Type Interactive Model for Aggregate Planning," *Management Science*, Vol. 24, No. 5, January 1978, pp. 564–575.

WILDE, D. J., *Optimum Seeking Methods*, Prentice-Hall, Englewood Cliffs, N.J., 1964.

WINTERS, P. R., "Constrained Inventory Rules for Production Smoothing," *Management Science*, Vol. 8, No. 4, July 1962, pp. 470–481.

YUAN, S. C., "Algorithms and Multi-Product Model in Production Scheduling and Employment Smoothing," Technical Report No. 22, NSF GS-552, Stanford University, Stanford, Calif., August 1967.

ZABEL, E., "Some Generalizations of an Inventory Planning Horizon Theorem," *Management Science*, Vol. 10, No. 3, April 1964, pp. 465–471.

ZANGWILL, W. I., "A Deterministic Multiproduct, Multifacility Production and Inventory Model," *Operations Research*, Vol. 14, No. 3, May–June 1966a, pp. 486–587.

ZANGWILL, W. I., "A Deterministic Multi-Period Production Scheduling Model with Backlogging," *Management Science*, Vol. 13, No. 1, September 1966b, pp. 105–119.

ZANGWILL, W. I., "Production Smoothing of Economic Lot Sizes with Non-Decreasing Requirements," *Management Science*, Vol. 13, No. 3, November 1966c, pp. 191–209.

ZANGWILL, W. I., "Minimum Concave Cost Flows in Certain Networks," *Management Science*, Vol. 14, No. 7, March 1968, pp. 429–450.

ZANGWILL, W. I., "A Backlogging Model and Multi-Echelon Model of a Dynamic Economic Lot Size Production System—A Network Approach," *Management Science*, Vol. 15, No. 9, May 1969, pp. 506–527.

ZOLLER, K., "Optimal Disaggregation of Aggregate Production Plans," *Management Science*, Vol. 17, No. 8, April 1971, pp. B533–B549.

4

Inventory Management

4.1 Introduction

Production planning has among its objectives the determination of inventory levels. In this chapter we are primarily concerned with inventories that are involved in industrial production—namely, inventories of raw materials, purchased and manufactured parts, subassemblies, assemblies, and finished products. However, many of the decision rules presented below are also valid for managing inventories in other kinds of operations, such as retailing, distribution, service operations, and so on.

4.1.1 Inventories and Their Functions

Since inventories normally represent a sizable investment in a logistic system, legitimate questions can be raised with respect to the causes for the existence of inventories as well as the functions that they perform. In general, one can think of five categories of stocks:

1. pipeline stocks
2. cycle stocks
3. seasonal stocks
4. safety stocks
5. stock held for other reasons

Pipeline stocks. Inventories in this category are a consequence of the finiteness of the production and transportation rates in any industrial environment. The pipeline stock, also called process stock, consists of materials actually being worked on, or moving between work centers, or being in transit to distribution centers and customers.

Cycle stocks. In the majority of cases, industrial production and materials procurement take place in batches. This can happen because of two reasons:

- *Economies of scale.* If the average cost of producing, purchasing, or moving stock decreases as the lot size increases it is advantageous to operate with larger quantities at a time. A typical example is when a fixed setup or an administrative cost is incurred whenever an item has to be produced or ordered from an outside vendor. A larger order quantity results in a reduced fixed cost per unit of item.
- *Technological requirements.* The design of the process may impose certain batch sizes. For instance, in a chemical reactor processing by tankfuls might be necessary in order to achieve desired reaction parameters.

Cycle inventory, also called lot size inventory, exhibits a time behavior that alternates between a high point, corresponding to the delivery of the batch to stock, and a low point that immediately precedes delivery to stock.

Seasonal stocks. When the requirements for the items vary with time, it may become economical to build inventory during periods of low demand to ease the strain of peak demand periods upon the production facilities. The extent to which this policy should be used is determined by balancing the cost of carrying seasonal inventories against the cost of changing the production rate and of not meeting demand entirely. This problem has been dealt with extensively in Chapter 3.

Safety stocks. Inventories may be carried because of uncertainties of future requirements. Future requirements are estimated by forecasting, but forecasts are always accompanied by errors. If planning is done disregarding the possible forecasting errors, shortages may be incurred when materialized requirements exceed the forecast. To prevent the losses normally associated with shortages, safety stocks have to be held in the form of extra inventories above the level that would result from planning on the basis of the demand forecasts alone.

Safety stocks can offer protection not only against demand uncertainties. Whenever the quantities delivered vary from what is ordered, or when procurement lead times exhibit a probabilistic behavior, safety stocks are effective tools in hedging against supply uncertainties.

Stock held for other reasons. Inventories can perform the important function of decoupling the various stages of production. By deliberately creating stocking points between adjacent stages, a certain degree of independence can be achieved in operating the stages. Without such decoupling inventories, any disturbance at some stage would shortly affect the entire system. Stocks may be carried for a number of other reasons: to take advantage of a favorable raw material price or quantity discounts, to anticipate an expected rise in price, and so on (Morgan [1963]).

4.1.2 Classification of Inventory Systems

An inventory system is composed of a large number of elements and has to perform functions of major significance to the company (Hax [1976]). In order to prescribe an inventory system to support the organization's logistics process it is important in the first place to identify the type of system called for, based on the elements that are present in the product structure of the firm and the degree of complexity involved in making the logistics decisions. To this purpose four categories of inventory systems can be identified:

Pure inventory systems.   These systems are intended to support decisions regarding the replenishment of inventories for individual items. The decision rules associated with these systems are statistically based and specify for each item an order point (that determines when the item should be ordered) and an order quantity (that determines how much to order). Each item is treated independently from any other item except, perhaps, to allow for joint ordering of families of items, and to account for simple aggregate constraints reflecting storage and financial or other limitations.

Pure inventory systems are normally applicable to raw material purchasing decisions, and retail or wholesale activities, where items are purchased from outside vendors and, possibly, minor production operations are performed such as cutting and packaging. Pure inventory systems can also be used to control production of finished goods in very simple manufacturing environments which are not affected by significant fluctuations in demand requirements and where ample production capacity is available. As these conditions are rarely met in most production environments, pure inventory systems are basically used to support only purchasing decisions.

Production-inventory systems.   These systems apply to situations where the firm manufactures the finished products internally rather than procuring them externally. The manufactured items normally compete for production capacity; therefore simple order point–order quantity rules, which ignore item interactions, are no longer effective control tools. Higher level decisions have to be made for the allocation of scarce resources among the competing items. The specific methodologies vary significantly with the type of production process involved in the manufacturing activities. In particular, a fabrication or intermittent process has to be controlled quite differently from an assembly or continuous process.

Obviously, the development of a production-inventory system is much more of a complex task than the design of a pure inventory system. Chapter 3 has given an in-depth coverage of various approaches to modeling the allocation of production capacity and labor at the aggregate level. Chapter 6 will consider the integration of aggregate and detailed level decisions in production-inventory systems.

Distribution-inventory systems and *production-distribution-inventory systems.* The added feature, the distribution, involves the allocation of available inventory (purchased from outside vendors in distribution-inventory systems, or manufactured internally in a production-distribution-inventory system) among a set of stocking points located in a possibly complex network. In practice, sound applicable management science support is not available for these types of decisions. There are two basically different procedures that are used to deal with the inventory allocation aspect. In the first one, referred to as a *push system*, the allocation of inventory is decided centrally for the whole system, taking into account all the distribution requirements and stock availabilities throughout the distribution network. Mathematical programming models are instrumental in supporting push systems. By the second procedure, referred to as the *pull system*, the individual warehouses generate requests for inventory replenishment independently, based on their own inventory status and demand requirements. Statistically based inventory models have been associated with pull systems.

An important issue, which has hardly been tackled by researchers, is that of the integration of distribution, production, and scheduling into a coherent, coordinated planning system. Although attempts have been made to approach this problem (e.g., Hax [1973], Hax and Meal [1975], and Krauss [1977]), answers of a more general nature, to questions like, how and at what level should distribution planning interact with production planning and scheduling, are yet to be provided. As Karmarkar [1975, p. 199] points out, while the hierarchical framework holds promise for a solution to the problem, the issues of aggregation and disaggregation of items may prove to be difficult since the bases for aggregation may not be the same for production and distribution.

In this chapter we are primarily concerned with pure inventory systems.

4.1.3 Objectives and Structure of Inventory Management System

Brown [1978a, p. 173] suggested that there have been two streams of development in the field of inventory operations. One is represented by mathematical abstractions of the inventory system in which the major effort went into modeling the process and searching for optimal policies in terms of minimizing relevant costs. There is a large and still growing literature on inventory theory, in which papers such as Arrow et al. [1953] and Dvoretzky et al. [1952, 1953], and books like Whitin [1953], Arrow et al. [1958], Scarf et al. [1963], and Hadley and Whitin [1963] have already become classics. The other school of thought is primarily concerned with practical issues such as demand and costs measurement, system design, relations among logistics and other industrial management functions, system management, and so on (Magee [1968], Magee and Boodman [1967], and Brown [1967, 1977]). It is this practical viewpoint that will be developed in this chapter.

An *inventory system* can be defined as a coordinated set of rules and procedures that allow for routine decisions on *when* and *how much* to order of each item needed in the manufacturing or procurement process to fill customer demand, which call attention to the nonroutine situations the rules do not cover, and which provide managers with the necessary information to make these decisions effectively. The objective of a well-designed procedure should be the minimization of the costs incurred in the inventory system, attaining at the same time the customer service level specified by the company policies. We will deal with the inventory management problem from an implementable system perspective. While the theoretical developments have to be given full credit for the insights they bring into the problem and for the establishment of the form of optimal policies, the design of the system has to rely on decision rules that represent some implementable form of the theoretically derived optimal policies.

An inventory management system can be viewed as being structured of subsystems or modules:

- the transactions and file maintenance module
- the decision rules module
- the system integrative module
- the system–management interaction and evaluation module

The *transactions and file maintenance module* concerns the bookkeeping of inventory control—namely, the entry, auditing, control, and processing of inventory transactions, as well as the file maintenance functions. Files have to be continuously updated in order to provide accurate information on available stock (on hand and on order) and often customer order status. The data base should be posted for any changes that may occur in the cost of items, delivery lead times, source of acquisition, ordering restrictions, and so on. As expressed by Brown [1978, p. 174]: "The major system-design problem is to assure the efficiency and reliability of the system." This is the primary concern of the transactions and file maintenance module.

The *decision rules module* is concerned with the fundamental components of inventory planning and control procedures. The main decision rules are aimed at answering *when* and *how much* to order of each item in order to maintain inventories at the "right" level. At the same time, any forward-looking system should also include *forecasting* capabilities. Moreover, because of the unavoidable forecast inaccuracies, *safety stocks* decision rules are needed in order to guarantee some desired level of customer service.

The *system integrative module* brings the decision rules together with distinct inventory policies. The various items being controlled, depending on their inherent characteristics, require specific degrees of management attention and service levels that can be achieved by using some appropriate stock policy.

The *system–management interaction and evaluation module* is intended to provide management with such information as to permit an evaluation of the operating performance, to identify problem areas, and to allow for management selection of policy variables (system parameters).

In the sections that follow, we present in some detail each of the modules with the exception of the transactions and file maintenance module, whose development concerns almost exclusively the area of data processing.

4.2   Economic Order Quantity Decision Rules

4.2.1   Costs in an Inventory System

As stated previously, the objective of an inventory system is the minimization of the costs involved in the operations. Therefore, at this point we find it useful to discuss briefly the costs relevant to a pure inventory system.

Obviously, the only costs that should be considered are the ones which vary as the stock policy is changed. We can group these costs in three categories:

- procurement costs
- costs associated with the existence of inventories (supply exceeds demand)
- costs associated with stockouts (demand exceeds supply)

Procurement costs can be seen as composed of two parts: the cost that has to be paid by the system to the supplier of the ordered items, and the cost incurred by the system in the procurement process, also called ordering cost. The ordering cost itself can have a number of components: administrative (paperwork, computer processing, telephone calls, postage, etc.), transportation of the items ordered, and handling and inspection of the shipment when it arrives.

For the purpose of future development, it is important to regroup the procurement costs into two categories: costs per unit of item that depend on the amount ordered, and unit costs that do not depend on the order size. An example of the former category is the case where the cost of ordering an amount Q is A for any positive value of Q, and therefore the unit ordering cost is A/Q; this is highly relevant because it thus becomes an incentive for purchasing the item in large batches with the obvious purpose of lowering the per unit share of the ordering cost. An instance of the latter category of costs is the constant purchasing unit price (i.e., no economies or diseconomies of scale). Since these kinds of costs cannot influence the decision on order size, they can be dropped from consideration in the analysis.

It should be mentioned that the assumption of a fixed ordering cost, regardless of the order size, is common in inventory systems research, and we also use it throughout the chapter. We should be aware, however, that this is an approximation. Indeed, if we consider the transportation, handling, and inspection costs per batch, they are invariant only within a limited range of lot sizes. With a radical change in order size, one might reconsider the mode of transportation and the handling and inspection equipment and techniques. On the other hand, part of the annual administrative costs does not vary if the total number of orders stays within certain limits. Beyond those limits, the number of purchasing agents, phone lines, cost of supporting services, and so on changes, which leads to a cost chart as shown in Figure 4.1 (Hadley and Whitin [1963]).

Costs associated with the existence of inventories are due to a number of causes: storage and handling, property taxes, insurance, spoilage, obsolescence, pilferage, rent if the inventory system does not own the storing facilities, and capital costs. The capital cost represents either direct expenditures for funds (interest) or the rate of return that could be obtained by investing elsewhere the capital tied up in inventory.

Of all the above components, only those which change as the level of inventory changes should be brought into the analysis. For instance, the amounts spent on heating, lighting, and security services for the warehouse tend to be invariable with the stock level, and if so they should be disregarded.

The diversity in the inventory carrying cost components is undoubtedly reflected in their functional relationships to the inventory level, which creates serious difficulties in modeling these costs in a satisfactory manner. The usual simplifying assumption made in inventory management is that carrying costs are proportional to the size of the investment in inventory. Thus, if r is the carrying charge (or holding cost) expressed in dollars per year per dollar of inventory investment, and C is the unit cost of the item in dollars, then the

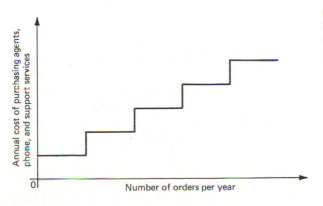

FIGURE 4.1
Effect of number of orders upon some administrative costs.

annual inventory carrying cost H for that item, in dollars per year per unit, is:

$$H = rC.$$

r can also be interpreted as the percentage of the unit cost of the item to be charged as inventory holding cost.

A special class of costs associated with the existence of inventories are the salvage costs. Such costs occur when, at the end of a limited sales season or after some operation is shut down, there is inventory left over. Depending on the action taken with respect to the excess inventory, the salvage cost can be either the carrying cost until the next season, or the difference between the cost of the item to the inventory system and the price at which it can be disposed of (this price may be negative if there is a cost for disposal of the surplus).

Costs associated with stockouts.   A stockout situation arises whenever demand occurs and the system is out of stock. Depending on the circumstances, a stockout may result in one of the following conditions:

- To meet demand, a priority special order is released; the stockout cost is represented in this case by the additional cost of the special order as compared to normal operation.
- Demand is backordered and filled when stock becomes available by routine replenishment. Stockout costs of a less tangible nature occur in this situation, such as loss of customer's goodwill, lowering of the degree of military readiness if a military supply system is involved, and so on.
- Demand which cannot be met is lost (the lost sales case). The stockout costs would have to account, besides the loss of customer's goodwill, for lost profit on the units which were requested but which were unavailable.

Other costs may apply to either of the stockout situations described above, such as penalties stemming from failure to meet legal contractual obligations, cost of getting information on the customer's belated order, contacting and relaying the information to the customer, and so on.

The problem of quantifying the stockout costs has long been a difficult and unsatisfactorily resolved question in inventory theory, especially because of the intangible components. There are two aspects that require consideration: the functional form of the mathematical expression describing the stockout costs, and the estimation of the parameters once the functional form is established. The most widely used simplifying assumption is that the stockout cost is proportional either to the number of units out of stock, to the maximum duration of the shortage, or to the product of the number of units times the duration of the stockout (Holt et al. [1960, chap. 12-2]). The simplest way—but not necessarily a good one—to assess the unit stockout cost is to consider it equal to the lost profit, or to the cost of expenditure on a rush order. If, however, a stockout influences customers to transfer some of their ensuing business to competitors, the lost profit on the later business should also be captured. Along this line and by considering a decision tree model in which all possible outcomes of a stockout situation are included, Oral et al. [1972] have conducted a statistical study for a company with the objective of determining expected unit shortage costs. Their results show that, for the company under study, the unit shortage cost bears an exponential functional relationship to the gross profit for the item. Schwartz [1966, 1970] approaches the loss of customer's goodwill by modeling its effect upon the future demand pattern.

For the purpose of this chapter, costs are considered time-invariant. Also, given that the planning horizon relevant to inventory problems is sufficiently short, discounting of costs to account for the time value of money is unimportant, and hence is not used. The reader interested in more extensive discussions on costs can consult such references as: McGarrah [1963, chaps. 1.4, 5.4], Hadley and Whitin [1963, chap. 1], and Arrow et al. [1958, chap. 2].

4.2.2 Single Item Economic Order Quantity Decision Rules

4.2.2.1 Economic order quantity for fast-moving items

When dealing with stocked items, the question regarding how much to order is answered by the economic order quantity (EOQ). The EOQ provides the proper lot size by minimizing the cost components involved—that is, the ordering cost, the inventory carrying cost, and the stockout cost (if shortages are permitted).

The simple classical economic lot size model.   If the following assumptions apply, then what has come to be known as the standard Wilson lot size formula provides the economic order quantity:

(a) Demand is continuous at a constant rate.

(b) The process continues infinitely.

(c) No constraints are imposed (on quantities ordered, storage capacity, available capital, etc.).

(d) Replenishment is instantaneous (the entire order quantity is received all at one time as soon as the order is released).

(e) All costs are time-invariant.

(f) No shortages are allowed.

(g) Quantity discounts are not available.

The following notations are used:

D = demand rate, units per year

A = ordering cost, dollars per order

C = unit cost, dollars per unit of item (the value of the item immediately after it is delivered to stock)

r = inventory carrying charge, dollars per dollar of inventory per year

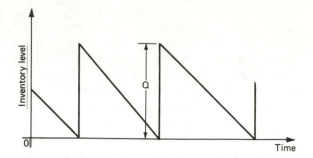

FIGURE 4.2
Simple classical inventory model.

H = annual inventory holding cost, dollars per unit of item per year; $H = rC$

TC = total annual cost of operating the system, dollars per year

Q = order quantity, units per lot.

Figure 4.2 shows the behavior of an inventory system which operates by the assumptions listed above.

There are D/Q orders placed during one year, and the average inventory is $Q/2$; hence, the total annual cost of ordering and carrying inventory is:

$$TC = A\frac{D}{Q} + rC\frac{Q}{2}.$$

The optimum Q^* is obtained by setting $d(TC)/dQ = 0$; the solution is

$$Q^* = \sqrt{\frac{2AD}{rC}} = \sqrt{\frac{2AD}{H}}. \tag{4.1}$$

It is easy to see that Q^* is the global minimum. Indeed, $d^2(TC)/dQ^2 > 0$ for any finite $Q > 0$.

Graphically, the cost components can be presented as follows:

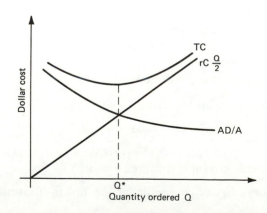

The reader can verify that the optimal lot size Q^* occurs at the intersection of the ordering cost AD/Q and the inventory holding cost $rCQ/2$.

Formula (4.1) was first derived in 1915 by F. W. Harris of the Westinghouse Corporation. However, the expression is widely known as the *Wilson lot size formula* since R. H. Wilson, a consultant, used such a formula in his work on inventory management in many companies.

The annual demand D is obtained by a forecast based upon the demand history for the item under consideration. Parameters A and H are either derived by some statistical estimation technique or are inferred by management from past experience. Solomon [1959] showed that total inventory cost in the neighborhood of the optimum lot size is relatively insensitive to moderately small variations in the amount ordered. Brown [1977, p. 212] recommends rounding off lot sizes to reasonable values; his argument is that if the lot is within the range 70 to 140% of the true optimum, the total annual costs rise less than 6% above the true minimum. Also, by a sensitivity test, Zimmermann and Sovereign [1974, p. 359] conclude that the sensitivity of total cost with respect to errors in ordering and inventory holding costs is very small if the errors are in the same direction. This makes unnecessary a great deal of accuracy in estimating the parameters involved in the calculations (i.e., D, A, r, and C). These characteristics of the Wilson lot size formula have made it widely used in practice.

The ordering cost A used in the EOQ calculations should be the marginal ordering cost. However, inventory carrying costs should be based on the total purchasing cost of the item, since it is this total cost that determines the capital invested in inventory. In the American economy, a typical value of r used in practice ranges from 0.25 to 0.30.

We will now proceed to relax some of the assumptions used to derive the simple economic lot size formula in order to enrich the applicability of the model.

The classical economic lot size model with finite supply rate.   The first assumption to be relaxed is assumption (d) mentioned in 4.2.2.1, dealing with instantaneous replenishment. In many situations, the amount ordered is not delivered all at once, but becomes available at a given supply rate. This would be the case of an order being filled by a machine, which has a finite production rate. We will assume that the supplying process is continuous and takes place at a constant rate until Q units are delivered to stock—then it stops.

Let:

$$P = \text{production (supply) rate, units per year.}$$

We will assume that $P > D$; that is, the supply rate exceeds the demand rate.

In this case the time behavior of the inventory level is depicted in Figure 4.3. In this picture T represents the cycle time; t_s is the period of time over which a batch of size Q is supplied to inventory. During t_s stock is input to inventory at a rate P and simultaneously removed from inventory at a rate D; thus stock accumulates at a rate of $(P - D)$ units per year. The highest

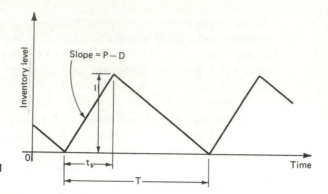

FIGURE 4.3
Classical inventory model
with finite supply rate.

inventory position is $I = t_s(P - D)$, where t_s is the time necessary to process the Q units at a rate of P—that is, $t_s = Q/P$. As the average inventory is $I/2$, it is a simple matter to express the total annual cost:

$$TC = A\frac{D}{Q} + H\frac{Q}{2}\left(1 - \frac{D}{P}\right). \tag{4.2}$$

The global minimum of TC is Q^*:

$$Q^* = \sqrt{\frac{2AD}{H\left(1 - \frac{D}{P}\right)}}.$$

Notice that when $P \to \infty$ (i.e., we reach an instantaneous replenishment), $Q \to \sqrt{2AD/H}$, which is the simple classical lot size described by expression (4.1).

On the other hand, if $D \to P$ (demand and supply rates are equal), $Q \to \infty$. The interpretation is that in this case the supplying source has to be fully devoted to the demand requirement. No inventory builds up, and there is just one initial setup or ordering; consequently, the cost minimization requires the lot size to be extremely large.

The classical economic lot size model with backlogging allowed. For this case we relax assumption (f), allowing for shortages to take place, and keep the other assumptions stated in 4.2.2.1 unchanged. Figure 4.4 describes the variation of inventory level with time. The stock positions range from a low of $-B$ (amount of demand deliberately unsatisfied and put on the backorder list) to a high of $Q - B$ which represents the amount on hand immediately after a lot of size Q is delivered. Notice that B units out of Q are never carried in stock; as soon as delivery takes place the backlog of orders is filled. Clearly, a low stockout cost is an incentive for backordering demand, since this yields savings on the inventory holding cost.

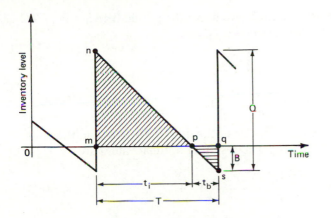

FIGURE 4.4
The backordering case.

Assume the backordering cost incurred by the inventory system is proportional both to the number B of units short and the duration t_b of the shortage.

Let:

$b =$ the cost to have one unit backordered for one year, dollars per unit per year.

From Figure 4.4 it is easy to see that time t_i, when positive inventory is available, is given by:

$$t_i = \frac{Q - B}{D}.$$

Also, the total cycle time T is determined by:

$$T = \frac{Q}{D}.$$

The average inventory on hand can be computed by dividing the area under the triangle map of Figure 4.4 by the duration T of the cycle. Therefore:

$$\text{Average inventory} = \frac{1}{T} \cdot \frac{(Q - B)t_i}{2} = \frac{(Q - B)^2}{2Q}.$$

Similarly, the time during which backorders are incurred, t_b, is given by:

$$t_b = \frac{B}{D}.$$

Therefore:

$$\text{Average backorder level} = \frac{1}{T} \cdot \frac{Bt_b}{2} = \frac{B^2}{2Q}.$$

The total annual cost is:

$$TC = A\frac{D}{Q} + H\frac{(Q - B)^2}{2Q} + b\frac{B^2}{2Q}.$$

To obtain the optimal value Q^+ and B^+ we make the partial derivatives of TC with respect to Q and B equal to zero, that is,

$$\begin{cases} \dfrac{\partial(TC)}{\partial Q} = 0 \\[2mm] \dfrac{\partial(TC)}{\partial B} = 0. \end{cases}$$

These represent necessary conditions for optimality. Sufficient conditions are given by Luenberger [1973, p. 114]. The resulting optimal values are:

$$Q^* = \sqrt{\frac{2AD}{H}}\ \sqrt{\frac{H+b}{b}} \tag{4.3}$$

$$B^* = \frac{HQ^*}{H+b} = \sqrt{\frac{2AD}{b}}\ \sqrt{\frac{H}{H+b}}. \tag{4.4}$$

Expressions (4.3) and (4.4) are defined only for $b > 0$. Of course, $b = 0$ does not make sense if stockouts are permitted. Indeed, in such a case, $B^* = Q^* \to \infty$. This means that, with no charge for backorders, one would keep piling up unfilled demand until the backlog gets infinitely large. Then one single order would be released to satisfy all accumulated demand, thus driving the per unit share of the ordering cost to zero. Notice that if $b \to \infty$ no backorders may be carried in the optimum solution, and (4.3) becomes the Wilson lot size formula.

The classical economic lot size model with lost sales.   A different case exists whenever the demand that takes place during a shortage period is lost. This situation is illustrated in Figure 4.5, where t_l denotes the duration of the shortage period. The time period when positive inventory accumulates is

FIGURE 4.5
The lost sales case.

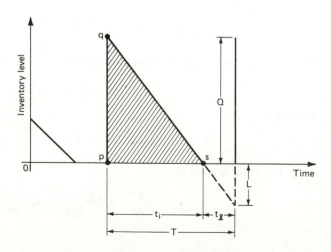

$t_i = Q/D$. The lost sales per cycle are L units, and the cycle time is $T = (Q + L)/D$. There are $D/(Q + L)$ cycles per year.

To calculate the average inventory, we use the inventory triangle pqs on Figure 4.5:

$$\text{Average inventory} = \frac{1}{T} \cdot \frac{Qt_i}{2} = \frac{Q^2}{2(Q + L)}.$$

Assume that for each unit of demand which occurs during the stockout situation a cost c_l is incurred by the system. Then:

$$\text{Annual shortage cost} = c_l L \cdot \frac{1}{T} = c_l \frac{LD}{Q + L}.$$

The total annual cost is:

$$TC = A\frac{D}{Q + L} + H\frac{Q^2}{2(Q + L)} + c_l\frac{LD}{Q + L}.$$

Necessary conditions for optimality are:

$$\begin{cases} \dfrac{\partial(TC)}{\partial Q} = 0 \\[2mm] \dfrac{\partial(TC)}{\partial L} = 0 \end{cases}$$

or:

$$\begin{cases} \tfrac{1}{2}HQ^2 + HQL - c_l DL - AD = 0 & (4.5) \\[2mm] \tfrac{1}{2}HQ^2 - c_l DQ + AD = 0. & (4.6) \end{cases}$$

Equation (4.6) yields:

$$Q^* = \frac{c_l D \pm \sqrt{(c_l D)^2 - 2HAD}}{H}. \tag{4.7}$$

For Q^* to take on real values, the expression under the square root has to be nonnegative:

$$(c_l D)^2 \geqslant 2HAD \tag{4.8}$$

$$c_l D > \sqrt{(c_l D)^2 - 2HAD}. \tag{4.9}$$

When (4.8) is satisfied, Q^* is always positive. Q^* takes on one positive value when (4.8) holds at equality, or two distinct positive values when (4.8) is an inequality.

To calculate the optimum value of L, consider first the case where (4.8) holds as strict inequality: $(c_l D)^2 > 2HAD$. Then, by substituting (4.7) into (4.5), the optimum lost sales position is:

$$L^* = -\frac{c_l D \pm \sqrt{(c_l D)^2 - 2HAD}}{H}. \tag{4.10}$$

From (4.7) and (4.10), it follows that $L^* = -Q^* < 0$, that is, L^* is not contained in the interval $0 < L^* < \infty$. Therefore, the optimal operating value is $L^* = 0$, since nothing can be gained from running the system with any positive amount of lost sales, and the optimal lot size is given by Wilson's formula (4.1).

Consider now the case when (4.8) is an equality:

$$(c_l D)^2 = 2HAD. \tag{4.11}$$

Under this setting, $Q^* = c_l D/H$; substitute it into (4.5):

$$\frac{1}{2} \cdot \frac{(c_l D)^2}{H} + c_l DL - c_l DL - AD = 0. \tag{4.12}$$

Given (4.11), (4.12) is an identity, hence any value of L^* is optimal. It is also a simple matter to check that, when (4.11) holds, the total cost TC at $Q = Q^*$ is independent of L, that is, $TC = c_l D$. Hadley and Whitin [1963, p. 50] give the following intuitive interpretation to this last result: the time sequence of events in Figure 4.5 can be arranged by consolidating an arbitrary number of lost sales periods. Thus, the new graph would present a region similar to Figure 4.1, where there are no lost sales for a long time, and then another region where for a long time there is nothing but lost sales. This does not change the average cost per year.

The conclusion is that, for the given stockout cost structure and because constraint (4.8) has to be observed, nothing can be gained by allowing shortages to develop, and therefore it is at least as economical to run the system without any stockouts as to run the system with any positive quantity of stockouts.

The lot size model with quantity discounts.   Frequently, when deciding upon a purchasing quantity vendor's discount, schedules are available and have to be considered. Quantity discounts are usually offered in one of the following two forms (Hadley and Whitin [1963, chap. 2]):

1. all units discounts
2. incremental quantity discounts

Consider that all assumptions made at the beginning of section 4.2.2.1, except (g), are in effect; that is, we will allow for quantity discounts.

1. The Lot Size Model with Quantity Discounts for All Units

In this form the discount price applies to all units purchased (see Figure 4.6). There are a number of price breaks $b_0 = 0, b_1, b_2, \ldots, b_i, \ldots$ such that if the ordered amount Q is within discount interval i, $b_{i-1} \leq Q < b_i$, then the unit price for each of the Q units is c_i, where $c_i < c_{i-1}$.

For discount level i the total annual cost function is:

$$TC_i = c_i D + A\frac{D}{Q} - rC_i\frac{Q}{2} \tag{4.13}$$

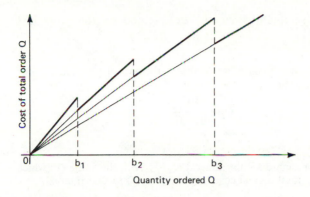

FIGURE 4.6
All units quantity discounts.

defined for $b_{i-1} \leqslant Q < b_i$. In Figure 4.7 a case with four discount levels is illustrated ($b_4 = \infty$). It is easy to show that these cost curves do not intersect and that $TC_i < TC_{i-1}$ for all Q.

Let us define $TC(Q)$ as follows:

$$TC(Q) = TC_i \qquad \text{if } b_{i-1} \leqslant Q < b_i, \ i = 1, 2, \ldots \qquad (4.14)$$

The solid lines in Figure 4.7 represent the total annual cost function $TC(Q)$ for $0 \leqslant Q < \infty$. The broken line segments depict functions TC_i outside their corresponding discount intervals.

The problem is then to find the order quantity Q^* that leads to the global optimum of $TC(Q)$. By inspecting Figure 4.7 it is apparent that Q^* can take on one of the following values:

- the EOQ which minimizes the annual cost for some discount level
- one of the two extreme points of some discount interval

In the case shown in Figure 4.7 the optimum order quantity is $Q^* = b_3$.

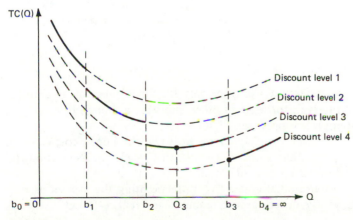

Discount level 1
Discount level 2
Discount level 3
Discount level 4

FIGURE 4.7   Four discount levels.

The optimum purchase quantity can be determined by the procedure given below:

Step I.   Determine the minimum point of the mathematical function TC_i for $0 \leqslant Q < \infty$; denote it Q_i:

$$Q_i = \sqrt{\frac{2AD}{rC_i}} \, .$$

Notice that $Q_{i-1} < Q_i$, since $C_{i-1} > C_i$.

Step II. Determine for each discount interval i, $[b_{i-1}, b_i]$, the value Q_i^* which minimizes the total annual cost function $TC(Q)$ in that interval:

$$Q_i^* = \begin{cases} b_i - 1 & \text{if } Q_i < b_{i-1} \\ Q_i & \text{if } b_{i-1} \leqslant Q_i \leqslant b_i \\ b_i & \text{if } b_i < Q_i. \end{cases}$$

Thus, for the case of Figure 4.7, we have:

$$Q_1^* = b_1; \qquad Q_2^* = b_2; \qquad Q_3^* = Q_3; \qquad Q_4^* = b_3.$$

Step III. Out of the set of all $Q_i^* = Q_i$ (there is at least one such Q_i^*), choose the one with the largest subscript i; call it Q_k^*. The global optimum order quantity Q^* cannot lie in a discount interval $i < k$; this follows from the property that for $i < k$, $TC_i > TC_k$ for all Q.
          Compute the total cost function at Q_k:

$$TC(Q_k) = C_k D + A \frac{D}{Q_k} + rC_k \frac{Q_k}{2} \, .$$

Step IV. Test all other discount levels $j > k$. Compute the total cost function at the corresponding Q_j^*:

$$TC(Q_j^*) = C_j D + A \frac{D}{Q_j^*} + rC_j \frac{Q_j^*}{2} \, .$$

The optimum discount level is given by that value of j for which $TC(Q_k) - TC(Q_j^*)$ is positive and a maximum. The optimal overall Q^* is then set equal to the corresponding Q_j^*.
          If all $TC(Q_j)$ are larger than $TC(Q_k)$, then $Q^* = Q_k$.

2.   The Lot Size Model with Incremental Quantity Discounts

This form of discount offers a lower price only for the number of units in the particular discount interval; for units in other intervals, although belonging to the same order, other prices apply (see Figure 4.8).

Thus, the first b_1 units cost C_1 each, the next $(b_2 - b_1)$ units cost C_2 each; the units in the $[b_{i-1}, b_i]$ interval cost C_i each, with $C_i < C_{i-1}$. Assumptions (a) through (f) specified in 4.2.2.1 are still valid.

To derive the total annual cost $TC(Q)$ of operating the system assume $b_{i-1} \leqslant Q < b_i$. The yearly ordering cost amounts to $A(D/Q)$. Let P_i be the

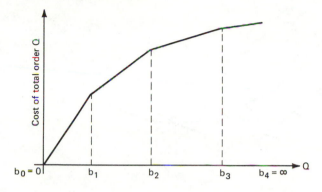

FIGURE 4.8
Incremental quantity discounts.

purchase price of a lot of size Q in the ith discount interval:

$$P_i = \sum_{k=1}^{i-1} C_k(b_k - b_{k-1}) + C_i(Q - b_{i-1}) \qquad \text{for } b_{i-1} \leqslant Q < b_i.$$

The annual purchase cost is $(D/Q)P_i$.

The annual inventory holding cost is given by $r(P_i/2)$.

Then the annual cost corresponding to the ith discount interval is:

$$TC_i = A\frac{D}{Q} + \frac{D}{Q}\sum_{k=1}^{i-1} C_k(b_k - b_{k-1}) + \frac{D}{Q}C_i(Q - b_{i-1})$$

$$+ \frac{r}{2}\sum_{k=1}^{i-1} C_k(b_k - b_{k-1}) + \frac{r}{2}C_i(Q - b_{i-1}) \text{ for } b_{i-1} \leqslant Q \leqslant b_i. \quad (4.15)$$

The annual cost function $TC(Q)$ is defined as:

$$TC(Q) = TC_i \qquad \text{if } b_{i-1} \leqslant Q < b_i, \quad i = 1, 2, \ldots \quad (4.16)$$

By grouping terms in (4.15) one obtains:

$$TC_i = \left[A + \sum_{k=1}^{i-1} C_k(b_k - b_{k-1}) - C_i b_{i-1} \right]\frac{D}{Q} + rC_i\frac{Q}{2}$$

$$+ \left[C_i D + \frac{r}{2}\sum_{k=1}^{i-1} C_k(b_k - b_{k-1}) - \frac{r}{2}C_i b_{i-1} \right]. \quad (4.17)$$

Functional form (4.17) immediately suggests a curve of the same shape as in the classical economic lot size model, with a unique global minimum. Figure 4.9 illustrates the fact; cost function $TC(Q)$ is represented by the solid.

As opposed to the all units discount case, the $TC(Q)$ curve is continuous [it can be shown that $TC_i(Q = b_i) = TC_{i+1}(Q = b_i)$].

An aspect we are interested in is the nature of the price break points b_i, $i = 1, 2, \ldots$. As Hadley and Whitin [1963, p. 67] mention, the slope of TC_i at

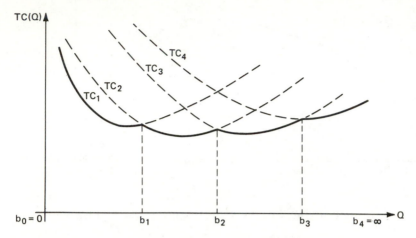

FIGURE 4.9 Annual cost functions under incremental quantity discounts.

$Q = b_i$ is larger than the slope of TC_{i+1} at $Q = b_i$. Indeed:

$$\frac{d(TC_i)}{dQ} = -\left[A + \sum_{k=1}^{i-1} C_k(b_k - b_{k-1}) - C_i b_{i-1}\right]\frac{D}{Q^2} + \frac{1}{2}rC_i$$

$$\frac{d(TC_{i+1})}{dQ} = -\left[A + \sum_{k=1}^{i} C_k(b_k - b_{k-1}) - C_{i+1} b_i\right]\frac{D}{Q^2} + \frac{1}{2}rC_{i+1}.$$

Then, for $Q = b_i$:

$$\frac{d(TC_i)}{dQ}(Q = b_i) = -\left[A + \sum_{k=1}^{i-1} C_k(b_k - b_{k-1})\right]\frac{D}{b_i^2} + C_i b_{i-1}\frac{D}{b_i^2} + \frac{1}{2}rC_i$$

$$\frac{d(TC_{i+1})}{dQ}(Q = b_i) = -\left[A + \sum_{k=1}^{i-1} C_k(b_k - b_{k-1})\right]\frac{D}{b_i^2} - C_i(b_i - b_{i-1})\frac{D}{b_i^2}$$

$$+ C_{i+1}\frac{D}{b_i} + \frac{1}{2}rC_{i-1}.$$

It is clear that $\frac{1}{2}rC_i > \frac{1}{2}rC_{i+1}$.
Also:

$$C_i b_{i-1}\frac{D}{b_i^2} > -C_i(b_i - b_{i-1})\frac{D}{b_i^2} + C_{i+1}\frac{D}{b_i} = C_i b_{i-1}\frac{D}{b_i^2} - (C_i - C_{i+1})\frac{D}{b_i}.$$

Hence:

$$\frac{d(TC_i)}{dQ}(Q = b_i) > \frac{d(TC_{i+1})}{dQ}(Q = b_i).$$

Hence, the global minimum of $TC(Q)$ cannot occur at a price break point b_i.

The optimum of $TC(Q)$ can be determined as follows:

Step I.   Compute the optimal lot size for every discount level:

$$Q_i = \sqrt{\frac{2D\left[A + \sum_{k=1}^{i-1} C_k(b_k - b_{k-1}) - C_i b_{i-1}\right]}{rC_i}}. \quad (4.18)$$

Step II.   If $b_{i-1} \leqslant Q_i < b_i$ compute $TC_i(Q_i)$.

Step III.   The overall optimum Q^* equals the Q_i corresponding to the smallest $TC_i(Q_i)$.

4.2.2.2   Economic order quantity for slow-moving items

With slow-moving items, demand can no longer be assumed continuous at a constant rate, and consequently the classical EOQ formula fails, because this condition violates assumption (a), as stated in 4.2.2.1.

In order to study this case, assume that one unit of demand occurs at constant time intervals known with certainty. All other assumptions may be maintained as previously.

Cost minimization obviously requires the order quantity Q to be a positive integer and to arrive exactly at the moment when demand for one unit of item occurs. Therefore, the inventory level varies between zero and $Q-1$.

As the annual requirement is D units/year the interval between two consecutive demands is $t = 1/D$. Then, during time interval $[0, t]$ there are $Q-1$ units in stock, in time interval $[t, 2t]$ there are $Q-2$ units in stock, and so on. The inventory holding cost for one cycle is:

$$Ht\left[(Q-1) + (Q-2) + \cdots + 1 + 0\right] = \frac{H}{D} \cdot \frac{Q(Q-1)}{2}.$$

The total annual cost can be expressed as:

$$TC(Q) = A\frac{D}{Q} + \frac{D}{Q} \cdot \frac{H}{D} \cdot \frac{Q(Q-1)}{2} = A\frac{D}{Q} + \frac{H}{2}(Q-1). \quad (4.19)$$

For Q^* to be the optimum lot size it is necessary that:

$$TC(Q^*) < TC(Q^*-1) \quad (4.20)$$

and

$$TC(Q^*) < TC(Q^*+1). \quad (4.21)$$

By substituting (4.19) into (4.20), one gets:

$$\frac{H}{2} < \frac{AD}{Q^*(Q^*-1)}. \quad (4.22)$$

Similarly, (4.21) yields:

$$\frac{H}{2} > \frac{AD}{Q^*(Q^*+1)}. \quad (4.23)$$

Inequalities (4.22) and (4.23) can be combined into:

$$Q^*(Q^*-1) < \frac{2AD}{H} < Q^*(Q^*+1). \qquad (4.24)$$

Hanssmann [1962, p. 21] suggests that Q^* is one of the two integers bracketing the real number

$$Q_0 = \sqrt{\frac{2AD}{H}}.$$

4.2.2.3 *Economic order quantity for items with limited sales period*

In this case the item whose inventory is to be controlled presents a demand pattern with a limited sales period, its demand being a random variable with a known probability distribution, rather than a constant demand rate, as previously assumed. The item can be procured only once at the beginning of the period. After the sales period terminates, there is a cost associated with the stock left over at the end of the period. The stock either has to be discarded because of spoilage or obsolescence (e.g., newspapers), has to be sold at a reduced price (e.g., fashions), or has to be stored until the next season (e.g., Christmas decorations, snow tires, etc.). At the same time there is a cost for running out of stock while the sales season is still on. The problem is known in the operations research literature as the "newsboy problem" or as the "single-period inventory model with stochastic demand."

The following notations are used:

$D =$ demand during the sales period; it is a continuous random variable

$f(D) =$ probability density function of D, assumed known

$c_0 =$ cost associated with having one unit of item in stock at the end of the sales period, dollars per unit

$c_u =$ cost incurred by the system for each unit of demand which occurs when the system is out of stock, dollars per unit.

To derive the decision rule we seek the amount Q^* that has to be purchased at the beginning of the season (assume no initial inventories) such as to minimize the expected cost incurred by the system at the end of the sales period.

There are two kinds of costs:

$$\text{Cost of excess inventory} = \begin{cases} c_0(Q-D), & \text{if } D < Q \\ 0, & \text{if } D \geqslant Q. \end{cases}$$

$$\text{Cost of stockout} = \begin{cases} 0, & \text{if } D \leqslant Q \\ c_u(D-Q), & \text{if } D > Q. \end{cases}$$

The total expected cost $TC(Q)$ is:

$$TC(Q) = \int_0^Q c_0(Q - D)f(D)\, dD + \int_Q^\infty c_u(D - Q)f(D)\, dD.$$

The necessary condition for Q^* to be optimal is:[1]

$$\frac{d[TC(Q)]}{dQ} = c_0 \int_0^{Q^*} f(D)\, dD - c_u \int_{Q^*}^\infty f(D)\, dD = 0.$$

As $\int_Q^\infty f(D)\, dD = 1 - \int_0^Q f(D)\, dD$, it follows that:

$$\int_0^{Q^*} f(D)\, dD = \frac{c_u}{c_u + c_0}. \tag{4.25}$$

If we let $F(D)$ be the cumulative probability distribution of D, then (4.25) yields:

$$F(Q^*) = \frac{c_u}{c_u + c_0}. \tag{4.26}$$

If we check the second derivative, it shows that A^* is a global minimum:

$$\frac{d^2[TC(Q)]}{dQ^2} = c_0 f(Q) + c_u f(Q) > 0.$$

The problem can have alternative formulations by including revenues from sales (Hadley and Whitin [1963, chap. 6-2]) or by using discrete probability distributions (if applicable). In the latter case, a formula similar to (4.26) can be derived or payoff (or loss) tables can be used for solution (Schlaifer [1959, chaps. 4.1, 7.2]).

4.2.3 Multiple Items Economic Order Quantity Decision Rules

4.2.3.1 Economic order quantity for multiple items sharing same equipment

This problem is also known as the "multiproduct cycling problem" or "the economic lot scheduling problem," and is already bordering the production-inventory systems. Assume that one piece of equipment is used to process m items on a cyclical basis. Unless there is plenty of idle time, the independent lot sizing and scheduling of items for runs on the equipment is likely to lead to interference between different products. Therefore, some cycling policy is necessary in order to avoid the risk of an infeasible schedule.

The simplest way to solve the problem is to impose the rule by which every item is produced once in each cycle (Hanssmann [1962]), which is

---

[1]See Sokolnikoff and Redheffer [1958, pp. 261–262] for the derivative of a definite integral.

tantamount to requiring that the number of runs per year be the same for all items, say, N. Given the nature of the problem, a finite production rate of P_i units/year has to be assumed for each item i.

The total annual cost under this policy is:

$$TC = N \sum_{i=1}^{m} A_i + \frac{1}{2N} \sum_{i=1}^{m} H_i D_i \left(1 - \frac{D_i}{P_i}\right) \tag{4.27}$$

where D_i is the annual demand for the ith item; the other notations are used as before.

In (4.27) subscript $_i$ denotes each of the m items. The derivation of (4.27) is similar to that of (4.2) except that the lot size is expressed as $Q = D/N$.

The optimum number of annual production cycles N^* has to satisfy the first-order condition:

$$\frac{d(TC)}{dN} = \sum_{i=1}^{m} A_i - \frac{1}{2N^2} \sum_{i=1}^{m} H_i D_i \left(1 - \frac{D_i}{P_i}\right) = 0.$$

Then:

$$N^* = \sqrt{\frac{\sum_{i=1}^{m} H_i D_i \left(1 - \dfrac{D_i}{P_i}\right)}{2 \sum_{i=1}^{m} A_i}} \tag{4.28}$$

and, of course, the optimum lot size for the ith item is:

$$Q_i^* = \frac{D_i}{N^*}. \tag{4.29}$$

It is reasonable to require N^* to be an integer; therefore, if it is not, we check the two bracketing integers and choose the one yielding the lowest total cost. It is important to make sure that the cycle time $T = 1/N$ is feasible in the sense that it is long enough to allow for setting up and producing one lot of each item.

Clearly, Q_i^* of (4.29) is in general different from the lot size determined independently by (4.2). If Q_i^* is much smaller than the independently determined EOQ, then it might be economical not to run item i every cycle. A rule-of-thumb is proposed by Magee and Boodman [1967, p. 70]: if the minimum-cost number of runs for the product alone, for any one or more products, is less than half the value for all products, the product is a possible candidate for only occasional runs. Such a case may arise, for instance, when the item exhibits a low sales rate and high setup costs. Then, by the rule-of-thumb mentioned above, the item would be made only occasionally, such as once every second or third cycle.

A related problem is the treatment of a family of m items. Consider that in order to run any one item of the family (or all of them) a major setup cost A

(or, if items are purchased, a major ordering cost) has to be incurred. Within the family, however, only a minor cost a_i is involved in changing over from some item to item i. Because of the significant setup for the family, it is reasonable to coordinate the individual lot sizes so that when one item runs out of stock, all other items in the family or most of them also run out of stock; then, the large setup cost A would be justified.

If T years is the family cycle, by the above argument the cycle T_i for the ith item should be an integral multiple of T:

$$T_i = k_i T, \qquad k_i > 0 \text{ and integer.} \tag{4.30}$$

Since there are $1/T$ family cycles per year, the total annual cost is:

$$TC = \frac{1}{T}A + \sum_{i=1}^{m} a_i \frac{D_i}{Q_i} + \sum_{i=1}^{m} H_i \frac{Q_i}{2}. \tag{4.31}$$

By (4.30) the number of item i cycles per year is $D_i/Q_i = 1/T_i = 1/k_i T$. It also follows that $Q_i = D_i k_i T$. After substituting in (4.31):

$$TC = \frac{1}{T}\left(A + \sum_{i=1}^{m} \frac{a_i}{k_i} \right) + \frac{T}{2} \sum_{i=1}^{m} k_i H_i D_i. \tag{4.32}$$

The necessary optimality condition for T is $d(TC)/dT = 0$, from which it follows that:

$$T^* = \sqrt{\frac{2\left(A + \sum_{i=1}^{m} \dfrac{a_i}{k_i} \right)}{\sum_{i=1}^{m} k_i H_i D_i}}. \tag{4.33}$$

Brown [1967, p. 48] offers a heuristic iterative procedure to search for the optimum values of k_i and T^*.

Certainly, the above discussion suggests the fact that different cycles for different items can also be used in the first problem presented in this section, where the m items were not members of a family. Bomberger [1966] has approached this case by requiring that each individual cycle T_i be an integer multiple, k_i, of some fundamental cycle T, and that the sum of the times required to set up and produce a lot of each item be less than the fundamental cycle. Dynamic programming is used to find the multiples.

Other approaches have also been proposed in the literature (see, for instance, Goyal [1974], and Silver [1975]). The interested reader is referred to Elmaghraby [1978] for a review of the economic lot scheduling problem.

The work illustrated above has consistently assumed deterministic demand; the difficulty encountered in the optimization process relates to the combinatorial nature of the search for optimal cycle multiples. Consideration of stochastic demand is bound to render the problem even more difficult. The literature is sparse with respect to this issue (Goyal [1973], Graves [1977]).

Brown [1971, p. 206] takes a pragmatic view of the problem; his rule calls for the production of one item until some maximum inventory is reached, after which the facility is switched over to another item even if it has not yet run short.

4.2.3.2 Economic order quantity for multiple items under aggregate constraints

Unconstrained optimization of economic order quantities is often an unrealistic assumption because of such reasons as limited storage space availability, a fixed budget for inventory investment, and so on. Aggregate constraints also arise in hierarchical production planning systems, where the determination of individual production runs has to observe inventory target levels set by the aggregate plan; this issue, however, will be discussed later in Chapter 6.

Suppose the warehouse capacity is W and the storage space required per unit of item i is w_i. Assuming that the simple classical inventory system of section 4.2.2.1 is used, the following constraint has to be observed:

$$\sum_{i=1}^{m} w_i Q_i \leqslant W \tag{4.34}$$

where m is the total number of items controlled. By this constraint we make sure that even if all items reached their maximum inventory positions simultaneously, the warehouse would still be able to contain them all.

The problem is then:

Minimize
$$TC = \sum_{i=1}^{m} A_i \frac{D_i}{Q_i} + \frac{1}{2} \sum_{i=1}^{m} H_i Q_i \tag{4.35}$$

subject to:

$$\sum_{i=1}^{m} w_i Q_i - W \leqslant 0 \tag{4.36}$$

$$-Q_i \leqslant 0 \qquad i = 1, 2, \ldots, m. \tag{4.37}$$

The objective function is convex. This can be shown by examining its Hessian $\mathcal{H}$. The Hessian is a diagonal matrix with all positive elements on its main diagonal. Therefore, for all nonzero vectors x it is true that $x^T \mathcal{H} x > 0$, hence the Hessian is positive definite and TC is convex (Luenberger [1973, p. 118]). The total cost reaches its minimum within the confines of constraints (4.36)–(4.37), and this is a global minimum.

The Kuhn–Tucker conditions (Mangasarian [1969]) are necessary and sufficient for optimality in this case. Let λ be the nonnegative Lagrange multiplier for (4.36) and γ_i for each of (4.37). The Lagrangian is:

$$L = \sum_{i=1}^{m} A_i \frac{D_i}{Q_i} + \frac{1}{2} \sum_{i=1}^{m} H_i Q_i + \lambda \left(\sum_{i=1}^{m} w_i Q_i - W \right) - \sum_{i=1}^{m} \gamma_i Q_i. \tag{4.38}$$

The Lagrangian can be simplified when we realize that, given the nature of the problem, in the optimum solution $Q_i > 0$ and, therefore, $\gamma_i = 0$. Then the last term in L can be dropped and the Kuhn–Tucker conditions are:

$$\frac{\partial L}{\partial Q_i} = 0, \qquad i = 1, \ldots, m \qquad (4.39)$$

$$\sum_{i=1}^{m} w_i Q_i - W \leqslant 0 \qquad (4.40)$$

$$\lambda \left(\sum_{i=1}^{m} w_i Q_i - W \right) = 0 \qquad (4.41)$$

$$\lambda \geqslant 0. \qquad (4.42)$$

The solution can be obtained by trying both $\lambda = 0$ and $\lambda > 0$. For $\lambda = 0$ the solution is given by:

$$\frac{\partial L}{\partial Q_i} = 0, \qquad i = 1, \ldots, m \qquad (4.43)$$

and must be checked against (4.40).

For $\lambda \neq 0$ the solution can be obtained from:

$$\frac{\partial L}{\partial Q_i} = 0, \qquad i = 1, \ldots, m \qquad (4.44)$$

$$W - \sum_{i=1}^{m} w_i Q_i = 0. \qquad (4.45)$$

Obviously, the case $\lambda = 0$ means that the storage capacity limitation is not binding and, therefore, the optimal solution is to use the economic lot sizes determined for each item independently.

For $\lambda \neq 0$:

$$-A_i \frac{D_i}{Q_i^2} + \frac{1}{2} H_i + \lambda w_i = 0, \qquad i = 1, \ldots, m \qquad (4.46)$$

$$\sum_{i=1}^{m} w_i Q_i = W. \qquad (4.47)$$

After solving (4.46) for Q_i, and substituting for Q_i in (4.47) we obtain:

$$Q_i = \sqrt{\frac{2 A_i D_i}{H_i + 2\lambda w_i}} \,, \qquad i = 1, \ldots, m \qquad (4.48)$$

$$\sum_{i=1}^{m} w_i \sqrt{\frac{2 A_i D_i}{H_i + 2\lambda w_i}} = W. \qquad (4.49)$$

Equation (4.49) has to be solved for λ and, in general, this cannot be done analytically. Holt et al. [1960, chap. 10] and Candea [1975] provide discussions of the topic and suggest solutions by graphical methods and search techniques.

4.3 Forecasting

Throughout the previous chapters of this book, future demand (or requirements) has been playing a leading role in the process of making decisions with respect to planning production, inventories and work force, and economic lot sizing. To reach these kinds of decisions, demand projections have to be made covering moderate planning horizons into the future. For facilities design problems, demand information has been again a major input; this time, however, our knowledge about demand has to be much more far reaching, extending over periods of several years.

Information about future requirements is obtained by the process of forecasting. Demand forecasts can span a large variety of planning horizons, ranging from days (e.g., the "newsboy problem") to years and decades (e.g., capital investment problems). Certainly forecasts can be made for many other purposes (weather forecasts, costs forecasts, technological forecasts, etc.). In this chapter, however, we will be concerned only with demand forecasts for short- and medium-range horizons, to be used in production and inventory control.

Brown [1977, p. 73] considers that there are two broad approaches to forecasting: the "descriptive" approach and the "explanatory" approach.

In the *descriptive approach*, the basic assumption is that the underlying process that has generated demand in the past continues into the future. Statistical models are applicable in this case. The time series (or the demand history) is analyzed for components (such as the base or constant component, trends, and seasonalities) and then it is extrapolated into the future. A word of caution: Forecasts based on mathematical models should constitute only the

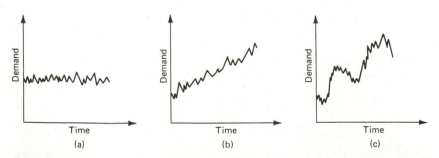

FIGURE 4.10   Demand patterns: (a) Base, (b) Trend, (c) Trend and seasonalities.

starting point for decision making. Managerial inputs, information on special facts (for instance, knowledge about an impending promotional campaign by the owned company or a competitor's firm) should interact with the forecasting system and appropriately alter future estimates of demand.

The *explanatory approach* tries to build causal relationships into the model. A large variety of models can be found in the literature, ranging from large econometric models (economy-wide, sectoral, industry, etc.) to special models, such as predicting the buying patterns of certain groups of consumers.

This chapter concentrates on descriptive models which are particularly useful in inventory management, and which account for the following demand patterns (see Figure 4.10):

1. The *base* (or constant) pattern presents a central tendency of the time series at any given time.
2. The *trend* process exhibits a consistent long-run shift of the average. The linear trend is the most common of such trends.
3. The *seasonal* pattern shows a cyclic variation, usually with a one-year periodicity. Seasonalities can be superimposed upon a background of constant annual average demand, or can be associated with a process in which the annual average features a trend.

In all cases, a random error component (noise) is present, which is the unexplained deviation of the data from the basic generating process.

Other demand patterns exist (Johnson and Montgomery [1974, p. 403]) such as step functions, impulse function, and so on, but they are not treated here.

Once an appropriate model is identified, the forecasting problem is threefold:

- estimation of all unknown parameters of the model
- computation of a forecast by projecting the model into the future
- updating the parameter estimates as new data become available

With respect to the task of updating the model parameters by incorporating fresh data, two approaches can be pursued. In one approach the time origin is fixed and, therefore, every time the forecast is updated, the parameters have to be recomputed from scratch in order to incorporate the latest observations. The other approach, called direct smoothing or adaptive smoothing (Brown [1963, p. 168]), assumes the time origin to be at the end of the current period, and updates the parameters by combining the old estimates and the latest forecast error recorded. Obviously, direct smoothing requires the time origin to be shifted every time the forecast is updated.

To date, a sizable number of forecasting techniques have been perfected; it is beyond the scope of this chapter to present them all. Books and papers have been published on the topic and some starting references are indicated below:

- *Regression methods* fit some hypothesized model, linear in its coefficients, to the time series. Least-square estimators are used for the coefficients. Multiple regression can also be used as an explanatory method of forecasting when a causal relationship between the dependent variable and the independent variables is present (Montgomery and Johnson [1976, chap. 2], Wheelwright and Makridakis [1977, chap. 7]).

- *Moving average* computes an average of a constant number N of past observations in order to eliminate the random variations or noise. As a new observation becomes available, the oldest observation is dropped (in order to keep their number constant) and a new average is computed (Montgomery and Johnson [1976, chap. 2], Makridakis and Wheelwright [1978, chaps. 4, 11]).

- *Exponential smoothing* has become a very popular method of forecasting. It is discussed in detail in the next sections.

- *Bayesian methods* are useful when one is faced with a lack of historical data at the beginning of the forecasting process. The approach is then to start with some initial subjective estimates of the parameters in the model, and use of Bayes' theorem to modify them in light of the actual data observed (Cohen [1966], Montgomery and Johnson [1976, chap. 10]; for Bayesian theory see Raiffa and Schlaifer [1961], Raiffa [1970]).

- The *Box – Jenkins models* are a set of autoregressive models in which successive observations are highly dependent. Three classes of models are considered; the autoregressive process, the moving average (of the errors) process, and the mixed autoregressive–moving average process. The choice of the correct model is made by examining the autocorrelation coefficients (Box and Jenkins [1976], Makridakis and Wheelwright [1978, chap. 10], Wheelwright and Makridakis [1977, chap. 8]).

4.3.1 Exponential Smoothing Methods
for Fast-Moving Items

Distinct forecasting procedures have to be used in forecasting fast- and slow-moving items. Slow-moving items are treated in a later section. Exponential smoothing techniques for fast-moving items are presented in this section, with the understanding that forecasts are updated once every time period. The length of the period can vary depending on the characteristics of the controlled items, but four weeks is a usual period length in many inventory systems.

Out of the multitude of forecasting techniques we choose exponential smoothing because it is relatively simple, reasonably accurate, and efficient from the computational point of view. These reasons certainly account for the widespread use of exponential smoothing.

4.3.1.1 Exponential smoothing for the base (constant) pattern

The base pattern (Figure 4.10a) has a stationary demand distribution. The mean demand is time-invariant, although unknown.

Let:

A_t = actual demand observed in period t

a = the true, unknown, constant demand which generates the observed demand pattern

ε_t = random noise component associated with period t, having $E(\varepsilon_t) = 0$ and constant variance σ_ε^2.

Thus:

$$A_t = a + \varepsilon_t. \tag{4.50}$$

In order to forecast A_t, we have to produce an estimate $\hat{a}$ of the constant component a.

Assume that $(T-1)$ periods have gone by and now we are in a position to produce a forecast for period T. First, we try to obtain an estimate of the constant term which we will use as the forecast of next period's demand:

$$F_T^b = \hat{a}. \tag{4.51}$$

The superscript ^{b} denotes the base model.

Being concerned with the forecast errors, we choose as an estimation criterion the minimization of the sum of weighted squared forecasting errors. Since recent errors are more relevant to the forecasting procedure than earlier errors, recent errors receive a greater weight than earlier ones:

$$\text{Minimize} \sum_{t=1}^{T-1} \beta^t (A_{T-t} - \hat{a})^2, \qquad 0 < \beta \leqslant 1. \tag{4.52}$$

Clearly, the weight β^t decreases with the age of the data.

Setting the first derivative equal to zero one gets:

$$\sum_{t=1}^{T-1} \beta^t A_{T-t} - \hat{a} \sum_{t=1}^{T-1} \beta^t = 0.$$

But:

$$\sum_{t=1}^{T-1} \beta^t = \beta + \beta^2 + \cdots + \beta^{T-1} = \frac{1-\beta^T}{1-\beta} - 1 = \beta \frac{1-\beta^{T-1}}{1-\beta}.$$

Thus:

$$F_T^b = \hat{a} = \frac{1-\beta}{\beta(1-\beta^{T-1})} \sum_{t=1}^{T-1} \beta^t A_{T-t}. \tag{4.53}$$

Going through a similar process, we can reconstruct our forecast F_{T-1}^b for period $T-1$ made at the end of period $T-2$:

$$F_{T-1}^b = \frac{1-\beta}{\beta^2(1-\beta^{T-2})} \sum_{t=2}^{T-1} \beta^t A_{T-t}. \tag{4.54}$$

If T is large enough $\beta^{T-1} \to 0$ and $\beta^{T-2} \to 0$; therefore, F_T^b and F_{T-1}^b get simplified:

$$F_T^b = \frac{1-\beta}{\beta} \sum_{t=1}^{T-1} \beta^t A_{T-t}. \tag{4.55}$$

$$F_{T-1}^b = \frac{1-\beta}{\beta^2} \sum_{t=2}^{T-1} \beta^t A_{T-t}. \tag{4.56}$$

(4.55) can be expressed as:

$$F_T^b = (1-\beta) A_{T-1} + \frac{1-\beta}{\beta} \sum_{t=2}^{T-2} \beta^t A_{T-t}.$$

and, from expression (4.56), we obtain:

$$F_T^b = (1-\beta) A_{T-1} + \beta F_{T-1}^b \tag{4.57}$$

Let $\alpha = 1 - \beta$; then:

$$F_T^b = \alpha A_{T-1} + (1-\alpha) F_{T-1}^b \tag{4.58}$$

F_T^b is the forecast for period T made at the end of period $T-1$. By the nature of the model, it is also the forecast for any other time period in the future.

Equation (4.58) can be given an intuitive interpretation: the forecast for period T can be obtained by combining the previous forecast (for period $T-1$) with the latest actual demand observed. The forecast for period T is thus composed of a fraction $(1-\alpha)$ of the previous forecast plus a fraction α of the actual demand A_{T-1}. The mix is controlled by monitoring parameter α.

The origin of time is continuously updated; thus, the time period for which we have recorded the most recent observation is always labeled $T-1$, while the upcoming period is always called T.

Equation (4.58) defines what is called forecasting by exponential smoothing, and α is the smoothing constant. The term "exponential" originates in the exponential decay with time t of the β^t coefficients.

A heuristic intuitive development of (4.58) was proposed by Brown [1959, p. 46]. To get the new forecast of demand, adjust the previous forecast by a fraction α of the amount by which demand exceeded forecast in the last period. That is:

$$F_T^b = F_{T-1}^b + \alpha \left(A_{T-1} - F_{T-1}^b \right) \tag{4.59}$$

By rearranging the terms:

$$F_T^b = \alpha A_{T-1} + (1-\alpha) F_{T-1}^b \tag{4.60}$$

which is precisely equation (4.58). Equation (4.59), however, allows us to see better the meaning of the smoothing constant. If α is large, the system is "nervous" in reacting to forecast errors, while with a smaller α more of a smoothing effect is obtained (slower response to forecast errors).

Forecast F_T^b is an asymptomatically unbiased estimator of a. To show this, (4.60) can be expanded recursively as follows:

$$F_T^b = \alpha A_{T-1} + \beta F_{T-1}^b$$
$$= \alpha A_{T-1} + \alpha\beta A_{T-2} + \beta^2 F_{T-2}^b$$
$$= \alpha A_{T-1} + \alpha\beta A_{T-2} + \alpha\beta^2 A_{T-3} + \beta^3 F_{T-3}^b.$$

Thus, yielding:

$$F_T^b = \alpha \sum_{t=1}^{T-1} \beta^{t-1} A_{T-t} + \beta^{T-1} F_1^b. \tag{4.61}$$

Then, the expected value of F_T^b in a stabilized system ($T \to \infty$) is:

$$E[F_T^b] = E\left[\alpha \sum_{t=1}^{\infty} \beta^{t-1} A_{T-t}\right] = \alpha \sum_{t=1}^{\infty} \beta^{t-1} E[A_{T-t}].$$

As $E[A_{T-t}] = a$, it follows:

$$E[F_T^b] = a\alpha \sum_{t=1}^{\infty} \beta^{t-1} = a\alpha \frac{1}{1-\beta} = a. \tag{4.62}$$

Therefore, our decision to use F_T^b to forecast the unknown a appears to have been reasonable.

Two issues have to be resolved before (4.59) or (4.60) is used to predict demand: the initialization of the model, and the appropriate choice of the smoothing constant.

Brown [1963, p. 102] recommends the use of the simple average of the most recent N observations as the initial value of the smoothed statistic:

$$\left(F_{T-1}^b\right)_{\text{initial}} = \frac{\sum_{t=1}^{N} A_t}{N} \tag{4.63}$$

When no demand history is available $(F_{T-1}^b)_{\text{initial}}$ is made equal to a subjective prediction of the average, based on the judgment of marketing people or derived from similarities with other products.

Call period 1 the first period of the forecasting horizon, period 2 the second period, and so on. Then, when we start forecasting for the first time, our forecast F_1^b is precisely the initial value $(F_{T-1}^b)_{\text{initial}}$. At the end of the first period, after the actual demand A_1 will have been observed, (4.60) will generate a forecast F_2^b for period 2:

$$F_2^b = \alpha A_1 + (1-\alpha) F_1^b.$$

It is important to realize that the initial forecast $(F_{T-1}^b)_{\text{initial}}$ soon gets strongly discounted in the forecasting process by a weight β^t (after t observations), as indicated by (4.61). Therefore, any reasonable estimate can be used as an initial condition.

The rate of response of the forecasting model is certainly influenced by the choice of the smoothing constant. A higher value for α improves the ability of the model to track a fluctuating pattern of demand, but reduces its function of filtering out random variations. The choice of α is also affected by the reliability of the initialization procedure. If the initial estimate $(F_{T-1}^b)_{\text{initial}}$ is questionable, a larger α will help discount its influence faster. Contrarily, if there is a strong confidence in the prediction of initial conditions, a smaller α will prevent any quick and undesired change by smoothing out the random component of the demand generating process. The forecast update period is still another factor, in that over a longer period conditions are more likely to change and, therefore, a larger smoothing constant is required in order to incorporate the change into the updated forecast.

From the above discussion, it is clear that there are contradictory issues involved in choosing the appropriate value of the smoothing constant. On the one hand, we want the forecast to be sensitive enough in order to respond to the real changes in the demand pattern. On the other hand, forecast stability is desirable as a protection against the system overreacting to random variations. The ultimate criterion should be to improve the accuracy of the forecasts (Brown [1963, p. 118]). As a general rule, the literature recommends values for α within the range 0.01 to 0.3, a value of 0.1 being a satisfactory compromise between a very stable system and a "nervous" system (Brown [1963], Johnson and Montgomery [1974]). Simulation can also be of assistance in choosing a proper value of α (Holt et al. [1960]). If demand history is available, it can be partitioned into two sets of data. The first set is used to initialize the model; the model is then run with different smoothing constants over the first part of the series, in order to reduce the effect of initial conditions, and then over the remaining data, considering the second set as fresh demand observations. Select that value of α which optimizes some criterion (e.g., minimizes the sum of squared errors). If a rather large value of α seems to be required (especially if over 0.3), this should be regarded as a strong indication that a different model might be necessary.

It is conceivable that more than one value of the smoothing constant might have to be used if circumstances change. If the initial estimate of the average is unreliable we can start out with a large α; after a few periods of running the model, when the effect of initial conditions has worn off and the true process has "taken over," the smoothing constant can be decreased to provide a greater stability.

A somewhat similar line of thinking has led to the development of the adaptive control smoothing models for automatically adjusting the value of the smoothing constant. A tracking signal, representative of the forecasting system's performance, is continuously monitored (section 4.3.5). When the tracking signal exceeds some appropriately chosen bounds, indicating unacceptably large forecasting errors, the value of the smoothing constant is increased accordingly, in order to give more weight to recent data and thus bringing the system faster into line with the changed pattern of demand. When the out-of-control condition disappears, the smoothing constant can be restored to its "normal" value. Basically, this is the essence of the adaptive control model proposed by Trigg and Leach [1967]. Other techniques have been proposed by Eilon and Elmaleh [1970], Montgomery [1970], and Chow [1965] with extensions by Roberts and Reed [1969].

4.3.1.2 *Exponential smoothing for demand patterns with linear trend*

The linear trend pattern is illustrated in Figure 4.10b and can be represented by a polynomial of degree one:

$$A_t = a + bt + \varepsilon_t, \tag{4.64}$$

where:

A_t = demand observed in period t

a = base component, from which the linear trend starts

b = trend

ε_t = random noise sample in period t; with $E(\varepsilon_t) = 0$ and constant variance σ_ε^2.

Also, let F_T^{tr} be the forecast made at the end of period $T-1$ for period T; the superscript ^{tr} denotes the trend model.

We approach the task of producing F_T^{tr} in two ways: by using two smoothing constants, or by using only one smoothing constant but, instead, resorting to double smoothing.

Forecasting the linear trend pattern with two smoothing constants.   First, let us see what would happen if we were to use the simply smoothed statistic F_T^b of 4.3.1.1 to forecast the linear trend pattern. The forecast would be given by:

$$F_T^b = \alpha A_{T-1} + (1-\alpha) F_{T-1}^b$$

or by (4.61):

$$F_T^b = \alpha \sum_{t=1}^{T-1} \beta^{t-1} A_{T-t} + \beta^{T-1} F_1^b.$$

Let us compute the expected value of F_T^b:

$$E\left[F_T^b\right] = \alpha \sum_{t=1}^{T-1} \beta^{t-1} E\left[A_{T-t}\right] + \beta^{T-1} E\left[F_1^b\right]$$

$$= \alpha \sum_{t=1}^{T-1} \beta^{t-1} \left[a + b(T-t)\right] + \beta^{T-1} E\left[F_1^b\right]$$

$$= a\alpha \sum_{t=1}^{T-1} \beta^{t-1} + bT\alpha \sum_{t=1}^{T-1} \beta^{t-1} - b\alpha \sum_{t=1}^{T-1} t\beta^{t-1} + \beta^{T-1} E\left[F_1^b\right].$$

If we let $T \rightarrow \infty$ in order to stabilize the system (i.e., discount to zero initial conditions or any transient response), we get:

$$E\left[F_T^b\right] = a\alpha \sum_{t=1}^{\infty} \beta^{t-1} + bT\alpha \sum_{t=1}^{\infty} \beta^{t-1} - b\alpha \sum_{t=1}^{\infty} t\beta^{t-1}$$

$$= a\alpha \frac{1}{1-\beta} + bT\alpha \frac{1}{1-\beta} - b\alpha \frac{1}{(1-\beta)^2}$$

$$= a + bT - b\frac{1}{\alpha}. \tag{4.65}$$

However, the expected value of the observed demand A_T is (from 4.64):

$$E(A_T) = a + bT.$$

It follows from (4.65) that in the case of a linear trend pattern the steady state response of the simple exponential smoothing forecast F_T^b for period T lags the expected demand of period T by a constant $b(1/\alpha)$.

An equivalent result (Brown [1963, p. 128]), states that simple exponential smoothing develops a lag of $b(1-\alpha)/\alpha$ behind $a + b(T-1)$, which is immediately apparent from (4.65).

The larger the smoothing constant, the smaller the lag; however, even with a high value of α the bias persists, therefore requiring corrections for trend.

Let $\mathfrak{T}_T$ be the estimate of the trend, computed at the end of period $T-1$ —that is, the projected trend for period T. Since $\mathfrak{T}_T$ will also be updated by exponential smoothing, we want to distinguish between the smoothing constant used in computing F_T^b, call it α_1, and the smoothing constant used in trend calculations, let it be α_2. The trend is smoothed as follows:

$$\mathfrak{T}_T = \alpha_2 \left(F_T^b - F_{T-1}^b\right) + (1-\alpha_2)\mathfrak{T}_{T-1} \tag{4.66}$$

which expresses the fact that the trend forecast for period T is obtained as a linear combination between the previous trend forecast (for period $T-1$) and the current change in the average demand forecast (constant process) $F_T^b - F_{T-1}^b$.

Equation (4.66) yields:

$$\mathfrak{T}_T = \alpha_2 \sum_{t=0}^{T-2} (1-\alpha_2)^t \left(F_{T-t}^b - F_{T-t-1}^b\right) + (1-\alpha_2)^{T-1}\mathfrak{T}_1 \tag{4.67}$$

The expected value of $\mathfrak{T}_T$ is:

$$E\left[\mathfrak{T}_T\right] = \alpha_2 \sum_{t=0}^{T-2} (1-\alpha_2)^t E\left[F_{T-t}^b\right] - \alpha_2 \sum_{t=0}^{T-2} (1-\alpha_2)^t E\left[F_{T-t-1}^b\right]$$

$$+ (1-\alpha_2)^{T-1} E\left[\mathfrak{T}_1\right] \tag{4.68}$$

By (4.65) we have:

$$E\left[F_{T-t}^b\right] = a + b(T-t) - b\frac{1}{\alpha_1} \qquad (4.69)$$

and

$$E\left[F_{T-t-1}^b\right] = a + b(T-t-1) - b\frac{1}{\alpha_1}. \qquad (4.70)$$

Let T grow very large; then the last term in (4.68) tends to zero, so it can be disregarded. From (4.68), (4.69), and (4.70) it follows that:

$$E\left[\mathfrak{I}_T\right] = b, \qquad (4.71)$$

that is, the trend computed by (4.66) is an asymptomatically unbiased estimator of the real trend.

By (4.64), (4.65), and (4.70) we can compute:

$$E\left[F_T^b + \frac{1}{\alpha_1}\mathfrak{I}_T\right] = a + bT - b\frac{1}{\alpha_1} + \frac{1}{\alpha_1}b = a + bT = E[A_T] \qquad (4.72)$$

and, therefore, expression $F_t^b + 1/\alpha_1(\mathfrak{I}_T)$ is an unbiased demand forecast for period T.

The response of the system to the linear trend process is stable, although it tends to overshoot slightly a sudden jump in demand such as an impulse or a step input. Eventually, it settles down to the correct value (Brown [1959, chap. 2]).

Here is a summary of the formulae for forecasting a linear trend process:

$$F_T^{tr} = F_T^b + \frac{1}{\alpha_1}\mathfrak{I}_T$$

$$F_T^b = \alpha_1 A_{T-1} + (1 - \alpha_1)F_{T-1}^b \qquad (4.73)$$

$$\mathfrak{I}_T = \alpha_2\left(F_T^b - F_{T-1}^b\right) + (1 - \alpha_2)\mathfrak{I}_{T-1}.$$

F_T^{tr} is the demand forecast made at the end of period $T-1$ for period T. For any other period more distant in the future—say, $T+\tau$—the forecast is obtained with $F_T^{tr} + \tau\mathfrak{I}_T$.

The forecasting system (4.73) is used as follows:

- At the end of the current period (period $T-1$), a record of the actual sales A_{T-1} of the product is obtained.
- The previous forecast F_{T-1}^b is known, hence F_T^b can be computed.
- The trend is updated to yield $\mathfrak{I}_T$. F_{T-1}^b and $\mathfrak{I}_{T-1}$ are known from the previous time period, and F_T^b has just been calculated.
- With all elements available, F_T^{tr} is fully determined.

The same comments made in the previous section for the selection of α apply for the choice of the smoothing constants α_1, α_2.

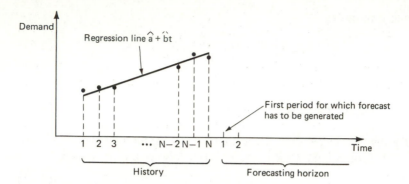

FIGURE 4.11   Initialization by use of regression.

The initialization procedure has to provide two starting values: F_1^b and $\mathcal{T}_1$ [or $(F_{T-1}^b)_{\text{initial}}$ and $(\mathcal{T}_{T-1})_{\text{initial}}$] for the first period of the forecasting horizon. Suppose that N periods of demand history are available. Fit, by regression, a line $a + bt$ to the data (Figure 4.11); the regression yields two estimates $\hat{a}$ and $\hat{b}$. Then:

$$F_1^b = \left(F_{T-1}^b\right)_{\text{initial}} = \hat{a} + \hat{b}N$$

$$\mathcal{T}_1 = \left(\mathcal{T}_{T-1}\right)_{\text{initial}} = \hat{b}$$

The forecast for the first period of the forecasting horizon is: $F_1^{tr} = F_1^b + \mathcal{T}_1$. After the first period is over, the value of the actual demand A_1 becomes known, and the smoothing process can start:

$$F_2^b = \alpha_1 A_1 + \left(1 - \alpha_1\right) F_1^b$$

$$\mathcal{T}_2 = \alpha_2 \left(F_2^b - F_1^b\right) + \left(1 - \alpha_2\right) \mathcal{T}_1$$

$$F_2^{tr} = F_2^b + \frac{1}{\alpha_1} \mathcal{T}_2.$$

Obviously, a few periods are necessary for the smoothing process to reach the steady state.

When several years of history are available, the initial estimate of the trend can also be computed as follows: calculate the average monthly demand in the first year and in the last year; then, $\mathcal{T}_1$ is the average trend between the first and last years (Holt et al. [1960, p. 265]).

With 7 to 11 months of history, Brown [1977, p. 104] recommends the least-square fit for initialization.

In other cases, when the available demand history is short or when there is not a clear understanding of the demand pattern, it is generally better to start by using an initial trend of zero. To compensate use fast smoothing, at the beginning, with $\alpha_2 = 0.3$, which guarantees a rapid adjustment of the model to

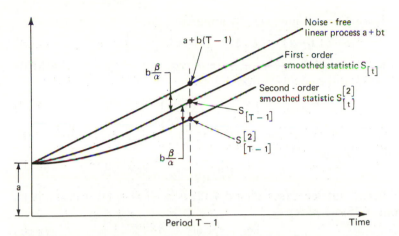

FIGURE 4.12 Original data, first-order, and second-order smoothed statistics for a noise-free linear trend process.

the existing trend. Then lower the smoothing constant to a "normal" level like $\alpha_2 = 0.1$.

Forecasting the linear trend pattern with double exponential smoothing. We have shown that F_T^b of equation (4.58) is an exponentially smoothed statistic whose value is computed at the end of period $T-1$ and used to make predictions for period T. For the purpose of this section and for unity of exposure, let us think now of F_T^b not as a forecast but as a statistical entity whose smoothed value* $S_{[T-1]}$ at the end of period $T-1$ is obtained by:

$$S_{[T-1]} = \alpha A_{T-1} + (1-\alpha) S_{[T-2]}. \tag{4.74}$$

In (4.74) $S_{[T-2]}$ is the smoothed statistic computed at the end of period $T-2$, and A_{T-1} is the actual demand recorded in period $T-1$; α is the smoothing constant.

If exponential smoothing is applied to the results of smoothing the original data, the second-order smoothed statistic $S_{[T-1]}^{[2]}$ is obtained. This process is called double exponential smoothing and is defined by:

$$S_{[T-1]}^{[2]} = \alpha S_{[T-1]} + (1-\alpha) S_{[T-2]}^{[2]}. \tag{4.75}$$

In (4.75) $S_{[T-1]}^{[2]}$ is the second-order smoothed statistic computed at the end of period $T-1$.

It has been shown earlier that $S_{[T-1]}$ develops a bias of $b(\beta/\alpha)$ behind A_{T-1}; similarly, the steady state response of $S_{[T-1]}^{[2]}$ is biased by the same $b(\beta/\alpha)$ behind $S_{[T-1]}$ (see Figure 4.12).

---

*Brackets around the subscript indicate that the statistic is computed *at the end* of the bracketed period; contrast with nonbracketed statistics, e.g., F_T^b, or with observed values *during* some time period, e.g., A_{T-1}.

From Figure 4.12 it is immediately apparent that:

$$a + b(T - 1) = 2E\left[S_{[T-1]}\right] - E\left[S_{[T-1]}^{[2]}\right].\tag{4.76}$$

Since the "distance" between $S_{[T-1]}$ and $S_{[T-1]}^{[2]}$ is $b(\beta/\alpha)$, the estimate $\hat{b}_{[T-1]}$ of the trend at the end of period $T - 1$ is:

$$\hat{b}_{[T-1]} = \frac{\alpha}{\beta}\left(S_{[T-1]} - S_{[T-1]}^{[2]}\right).\tag{4.77}$$

Hence, the unbiased demand forecast F_T^{tr} for period T, produced at the end of period $T - 1$, is given by:

$$F_T^{tr} = 2S_{[T-1]} - S_{[T-1]}^{[2]} + \hat{b}_{[T-1]}.\tag{4.78}$$

The "current" intercept (see Figure 4.12) is $a + b(T - 1)$; if $\hat{a}_{[T-1]}$ is its estimate, from (4.76) we have:

$$\hat{a}_{[T-1]} = 2S_{[T-1]} - S_{[T-1]}^{[2]},\tag{4.79}$$

and therefore (4.78) could also be written as $F_T^{tr} = \hat{a}_{[T-1]} + \hat{b}_{[T-1]}$.

Forecasts made at the end of period $T - 1$ for any future period $T + \tau$ are computed by $F_T^{tr} + \tau\hat{b}_{[T-1]}$.

To start the forecasting procedure two initial values, for $S_{[T-1]}$ and $S_{[T-1]}^{[2]}$, have to be provided. Equations (4.76) and (4.77) suggest that the initial conditions $S_{[0]}$ and $S_{[0]}^{[2]}$ can be derived from the estimates $\hat{a}_{[0]}$ and $\hat{b}_{[0]}$ of the base and trend at time zero; thus, by making $T = 1$ one gets:

$$\begin{cases} \hat{a}_{[0]} = 2S_{[0]} - S_{[0]}^{[2]} \\ \hat{b}_{[0]} = \dfrac{\alpha}{\beta}\left(S_{[0]} - S_{[0]}^{[2]}\right). \end{cases}$$

$\hat{a}_{[0]}$ and $\hat{b}_{[0]}$ can be obtained by fitting a regression line to past data, if available. Otherwise, subjective estimates of the coefficients have to be produced. Afterward:

$$\begin{cases} S_{[0]} = \hat{a}_{[0]} - \dfrac{\beta}{\alpha}\hat{b}_{[0]} \\ S_{[0]}^{[2]} = \hat{a}_{[0]} - 2\dfrac{\beta}{\alpha}\hat{b}_{[0]}. \end{cases}$$

The forecast for the first period of the forecasting horizon is: $F_1^{tr} = 2S_{[0]} - S_{[0]}^{[2]} + \hat{b}_{[0]}$. After period 1 the system of equations (4.74), (4.75), (4.77), and (4.78) can take over.

Brown [1963, Chap. 10] shows that the value of the smoothing constant used in double exponential smoothing, call it α_{double}, should be related to the value of the smoothing constant used in simple smoothing—call it α_{simple}—by the following equation:

$$1 - \alpha_{\text{simple}} = \left(1 - \alpha_{\text{double}}\right)^2$$

Thus, the equivalent of a small "simple" smoothing constant $\alpha_{\text{simple}} = 0.01$ is $\alpha_{\text{double}} = 0.005$, while a large smoothing constant equivalent to $\alpha_{\text{simple}} = 0.3$ is $\alpha_{\text{double}} = 0.163$.

4.3.1.3 *Exponential smoothing for demand patterns with trend and seasonalities*

Demand patterns with trend and seasonalities (Figure 4.10c) can exhibit, in general, two seasonal behaviors:

1. The multiplicative seasonal effect, by which the amplitude of the seasonal swing is proportional to the sales level:

$$\text{Demand}_t = (\text{Base} + \text{Trend}) \cdot (\text{Seasonal factor})_t.$$

2. The additive seasonal effect, in which case the amplitude of the seasonal pattern does not depend on the level of sales:

$$\text{Demand}_t = \text{Base} + \text{Trend} + (\text{Seasonal factor})_t.$$

Since in most cases the amplitude of the seasonal pattern is proportional to the level of sales (Makridakis and Wheelwright [1978, p. 199]), we develop in this section the multiplicative model. Its form is given by Winters [1960]:

$$A_t = (a + bt)c_t + \varepsilon_t, \tag{4.80}$$

where all notations have been explained previously except c_t which is the seasonal factor associated with period t. The amount between parentheses contains no seasonal effects and can be, therefore, forecast by a system similar to (4.73):

$$F_T^{tr} = F_T^b + \frac{1}{\alpha_1} \mathfrak{J}_T \tag{4.81}$$

$$F_T^b = \alpha_1 \frac{A_{T-1}}{SF_{[T-1-L]}} + (1 - \alpha_1) F_{T-1}^b \tag{4.82}$$

$$\mathfrak{J}_T = \alpha_2 (F_T^b - F_{T-1}^b) + (1 - \alpha_2) \mathfrak{J}_{T-1}. \tag{4.83}$$

The above equations are written at the end of period $T - 1$.

In (4.82) $SF_{[T-1-L]}$ is the smoothed seasonal factor for period $T - 1$ updated L periods ago, where L is the length of the seasonal cycle. In many cases the seasonal cycle is one year, which makes $L = 12$ months or $L = 13$ four-week periods. By dividing in (4.82) the actual demand A_{T-1} by $SF_{[T-1-L]}$ the seasonal component is removed; hence, only the permanent component and the trend enter the smoothing process of F_T^{tr}.

At the end of period $T - 1$, the estimate of the seasonal factor has to be updated. Its new value $SF_{[T-1]}$ is given by:

$$SF_{[T-1]} = \alpha_3 \frac{A_{T-1}}{F_T^b + \dfrac{1 - \alpha_1}{\alpha_1} \mathfrak{J}_T} + (1 - \alpha_3) SF_{[T-1-L]} \tag{4.84}$$

This value will be used to deseasonalize the observed data one cycle (L periods) later (e.g., the updated seasonal factor computed at the end of May this year, $SF_{[\text{May}]}$, will be used to deseasonalize the actual demand A_{May} recorded during May next year).

In (4.84) the fraction $A_{T-1}/\{F_T^b - [(1-\alpha_1)/\alpha_1]\mathfrak{I}_T\}$ represents the current observed seasonal variation since, as shown in 4.3.1.2, the denominator is an asymptotically unbiased estimate of $a + b(T-1)$.

α_3 is the smoothing constant used for seasonal factor updating.

If F_T^{tr+s} is the demand forecast made at the end of period $T-1$ for period T, then:

$$F_T^{tr+s} = \left(F_T^{tr}\right)\cdot\left(SF_{[T-L]}\right). \tag{4.85}$$

For any other more distant period $T + \tau$ the forecast is obtained with:

$$F_{T+\tau}^{tr+s} = \left(F_T^{tr} + \tau\mathfrak{I}_T\right)\cdot\left(SF_{[T+\tau-L]}\right). \tag{4.86}$$

Thus, we need the seasonal factor for period $T + \tau$, which was last updated at the end of period $T + \tau - L$. If $\tau \geqslant L$ the appropriate seasonal factor has to be reused cyclically.

Initialization procedures, which are all quite similar, have been proposed by Winters [1960], Johnson and Montgomery [1974, chap. 6-4], and Montgomery and Johnson [1976, chap. 5]. Starting values $(F_{T-1}^b)_{\text{initial}}$, $(\mathfrak{I}_{T-1})_{\text{initial}}$, and $(SF_{[T-1-L]})_{\text{initial}}$ have to be provided.

Suppose that a demand history of L periods is available for the last N seasonal cycles (Figure 4.13). Let $\bar{A}_i$ be the per period average of the observations during the ith season, $i = 1, \ldots, N$.

This initial estimate of the trend can be computed from the formula:

$$\left(\mathfrak{I}_{T-1}\right)_{\text{initial}} = \frac{\bar{A}_N - \bar{A}_1}{(N-1)L} \tag{4.87}$$

FIGURE 4.13   Initialization of forecasting process for trend and seasonalities.

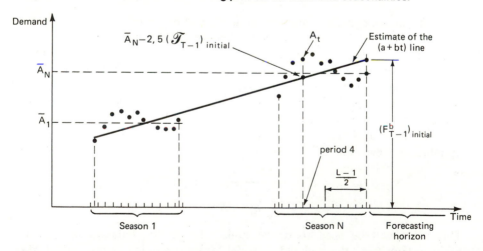

From Figure 4.13 it is apparent that (4.87) gives the slope of the line estimating $a + bt$.

The starting value for the permanent (base) component can be computed from:

$$\left(F_{T-1}^b\right)_{\text{initial}} = \bar{A}_N + \frac{L-1}{2}\left(\mathfrak{I}_{T-1}\right)_{\text{initial}}. \tag{4.88}$$

For each of the $N \cdot L$ periods, a seasonal factor is calculated as the ratio of actual sales for the period to the height of the corresponding point on the estimated $(a + bt)$ line:

$$SF_t = \frac{A_t}{\bar{A}_i - [(L+1)/2 - j](\mathfrak{I}_{T-1})_{\text{initial}}}, \qquad t = 1, \ldots, NL, \tag{4.89}$$

where $\bar{A}_i$ is the average for the season which includes period t, and j is the position of the period within the season. In Figure 4.13 the case with $i = N$ and $j = 4$ is illustrated.

By (4.89) N values of the seasonal factor are produced for each period of the season. Their average is then taken to obtain a single estimate for each period:

$$\overline{SF}t = \frac{1}{N} \sum_{k=0}^{N-1} SF_{t+kL}, \qquad t = 1, \ldots, L.$$

Finally, the seasonal factors have to be normalized so that they add up to L. By this step we make sure that the seasonal factors produce only seasonal adjustments, without increasing or decreasing the average level of demand:

$$\left(SF_t\right)_{\text{initial}} = \overline{SF}_t \cdot \frac{L}{\sum_{t=1}^{L} \overline{SF}_t}.$$

The forecast for the first period of the forecasting horizon is:

$$F_1^{tr+s} = \left[\left(F_{T-1}^b\right)_{\text{initial}} + \left(\mathfrak{I}_{T-1}\right)_{\text{initial}}\right]\left(SF_1\right)_{\text{initial}} \tag{4.90}$$

where $(SF_1)_{\text{initial}}$ is the initial estimate of the seasonal factor appropriate for period 1 of the forecasting horizon.

After the actual demand in period 1 A_1 becomes known, the forecasting can be automatically produced by using equations (4.81)–(4.86). In equation (4.84), used here to update the seasonal factor at the end of period 1, the value to use for $SF_{[T-1-L]}$ is $(SF_1)_{\text{initial}}$.

An alternative way for initializing the forecasting procedure is shown in the original paper by Winters [1960].

McClain [1974] and McClain and Thomas [1973] found that, under changing conditions, exponentially smoothing models, like Winters', can possibly induce instability of the forecast, especially if the trend smoothing constant α_2 is large. In order to avoid the oscillatory behavior, Peterson and Silver [1979] recommend α_2 values not in excess of 0.05; they also suggest that the set of smoothing constants $\alpha_1 = 0.2$, $\alpha_2 = 0.05$, $\alpha_3 = 0.1$ has proven reasonable in many cases.

It is important to mention that special care should be given to the initialization of the seasonal factors because they are reestimated only once a cycle; therefore the effect of their starting values is felt longer, especially when the smoothing constants are small.

Seasonal demand and more complex shapes of pattern can be described by appropriately combining polynomial, trigonometric, and exponential functions of time.

Thus, a simple sinusoidal model

$$A_t = a_1 + a_2 \sin \frac{2\pi t}{12} + \varepsilon_t$$

can represent a sales pattern observed 12 times during the seasonal cycle. The origin of the sine wave may be shifted t_0 periods by using:

$$A_t = a_1 + a_2 \sin \frac{2\pi}{12}(t - t_0) + \varepsilon_t,$$

which is equivalent to:

$$A_t = a_1 + a_2' \sin \frac{2\pi t}{12} + a_3 \cos \frac{2\pi t}{12} + \varepsilon_t.$$

If, besides seasonalities, a linear trend is also present, a simple 12-point model to reflect this is:*

$$A_t = a_1 + a_2 t + a_3 \sin \frac{2\pi t}{12} + a_4 \cos \frac{2\pi t}{12} + \varepsilon_t.$$

In many cases, as the level of sales increases with time, the seasonal effect also grows, so that:

$$A_t = a_1 + a_2 t + (a_3 + a_4 t) \sin \frac{2\pi t}{12} + (a_5 + a_6 t) \cos \frac{2\pi t}{12} + \varepsilon_t.$$

Including harmonics of the basic wave forms allows us to increase the descriptive accuracy of the models.

In dealing with these more complex types of forecasting models, as well as the simpler cases presented earlier, one has to find an iterative procedure for updating the estimates of the coefficient values with each new observation.

Brown [1963, chaps. 11, 12] develops a procedure, called the general exponential smoothing, by which the vector of coefficients in the model is updated directly, by taking linear combinations of the old coefficient estimates (made at the end of the previous period) and the most recently observed one period forecast error. Similar to the exponential smoothing techniques seen earlier, the approach is to gradually discount the data in time; the criterion observed in estimating and updating the coefficient values is the minimization

---

*Unless models are derived from each other, coefficients $a_1, a_2, \ldots$ used in some expression are in no way connected with coefficients with the same notation involved in another expression.

of squared residuals. Unlike the smoothing presented before, however, the model coefficients are smoothed directly rather than through the use of exponentially smoothed statistics.

The discount factor β_k (where k is the number of coefficients in the forecasting model), $0 < \beta_k \leqslant 1$, is taken as $\beta_k = 1 - \alpha_k$ where α_k is the smoothing constant. The larger the number of coefficients (terms) in the model, the more descriptive or tracking built-in ability it has and, therefore, the smoothing constant can take on smaller values. If α_1 is the smoothing constant used in simple exponential smoothing the following should hold:

$$(1 - \alpha_k)^k = 1 - \alpha_1. \tag{4.91}$$

The direct revision of coefficients is shown to be generally appropriate for all forecasting models which consist of time functions generated by a transition matrix—that is, functions whose values at time period $t + 1$ are linear combinations of the same functions evaluated at the previous time t.*

When the forecasting model contains only polynomial functions of time, and after the transient effect of initial conditions becomes negligible, general exponential smoothing produces forecasts identical to multiple smoothing. Thus, for instance, general exponential smoothing (in steady state) produces for the linear trend model (Brown [1963, p. 172]) the same coefficients we have seen earlier resulting from double exponential smoothing [expressions (4.77), (4.79)].

4.3.2 Forecasting over Lead Times

In production and inventory systems the lead time starts when a replenishment order is triggered or a shop order is released, and it ends whenever the order is filled. Since there is always the possibility that available inventory will not last through the lead time, it is important to forecast demand over lead times in order to be able to set appropriate order points.

We have shown in the preceding section how to produce forecasts for future periods. Then, if we are now at the end of period $T - 1$, the forecast of cumulative demand for a lead time of l periods is:

$$(F_l)_T = \sum_{\tau = 0}^{l-1} F_{T+\tau}^{\cdot}, \tag{4.92}$$

where:

$(F_l)_T$ = forecast over an l period lead time extending from period T through period $T + l - 1$

$F_{T+\tau}^{\cdot}$ = forecast made at the end of $T - 1$ for period $T + \tau$. The appropriate forecasts have to be used depending on the demand pattern (base, trend, seasonalities).

---

*This class of functions includes polynomials, sinusoids, exponentials, and sums and products of them.

If the lead time is slightly variable, we should consider an interval long enough to include all reasonable cases.

If the lead time is highly and unpredictably variable, we should measure the demand during the lead time directly and then forecast demand per lead time rather than per period.

If the inventory is reviewed after each transaction, the lead time is exactly the time required to deliver the item to stock. However, if the inventory is reviewed on a regular schedule, we must add one review period to the delivery lead time, the review period being the interval between regular reviews.

4.3.3 Forecast Errors

The random elements in the demand pattern generate errors in the forecast of the expected demand. The noise in the demand process means that the observed demand does fluctuate around the average process and these fluctuations in turn create errors in our estimate of what the average process is. We define the forecast error E_T in period T as the observed discrepancy between the forecast F_T for period T and the actual observation A_T for that period:*

$$E_T = F_T^{\cdot} - A_T. \tag{4.93}$$

$F_T^{\cdot}$ is the forecast for the next period; therefore, we called E_T the one period forecast error.

As forecast errors are a reflection of the uncertainties inherent in the demand process, knowledge of forecast errors' characteristics is central to setting safety stocks (order points) to provide protection against stockouts during the lead time.

4.3.3.1 One-period forecast errors

In manufacturing environments, where consumer demand has to be fed through several levels of distribution, forecast errors are generally normally distributed. In a retail business, where ultimate consumer demand is served, forecast errors are more likely to be exponentially distributed (Brown [1977, p. 146]).

Since we have repeatedly stressed the use of asymptomatically unbiased statistics in predicting future demand, we should expect the mean of the forecast to be the mean of the observed demand and the mean forecast error to be zero.

The dispersion of the forecast errors is measured by the variance of the distribution of errors. With a mean error of zero, the variance is estimated by

---

*As mentioned earlier, the appropriate forecast F_T used depends on the underlying demand pattern.

the mean square error (MSE). In most applications we may assume the distribution of errors to be stationary and, therefore, we can consider that the squared error fluctuates around a constant level. This immediately suggests using simple exponential smoothing to update the mean square error:

$$(MSE)_T = \alpha_k E_{T-1}^2 + (1-\alpha_k)(MSE)_{T-1}, \qquad (4.94)$$

where:

$(MSE)_T =$ mean square error forecast for period T made at the end of period $T-1$

$E_{T-1} =$ current forecast error, observed in period $T-1$

$\alpha_k =$ smoothing constant corresponding to the model used for forecasting; for a model with k coefficients α_k conforms to relation (4.91).

When a history of demand is available for the item under consideration, an initial value for MSE can be computed by simulating the adopted forecast model over the historical data. The simulated errors (i.e., residuals) are squared and summed. The sum is divided by the number of degrees of freedom to yield the initial MSE. The number of degrees of freedom is given by the difference between the number of errors in the sum and the number of terms in the forecast model.

If the item has no demand history (or the history is too short), an initial value of MSE can be estimated from the variance law (Brown [1977]). The variance law shows that the standard deviation of the forecast errors σ_T and the level of the forecast are related. In the two more common forms of the law, the standard deviation is proportional to some power of the forecast: $\sigma_T = a(F_T)^b$, with values for b frequently between 0.7 and 0.9, or the variance can be expressed by some polynomial function of the forecast: $\sigma_T^2 = c(F_T) + d(F_T)^2$ (Burgin and Wild [1967], Stevens [1974]). Parameters a, b, c, d are particular of all the items that come from a homogeneous population (e.g., items in a product line). Consequently, in systems where forecast models are available and currently used, the variance law can be established by regression by families of items and stored in the data base. When products with no history are introduced, first an initial forecast is generated and then, from the appropriate variance law, the initial estimate of the variance of the forecast errors can be obtained.

For safety stock calculations, one needs an updated forecast of the standard deviation of the errors $\hat{\sigma}_T$ for the upcoming period T; this is given by:

$$\hat{\sigma}_T = \sqrt{(MSE)_T}. \qquad (4.95)$$

In earlier treatments of forecasting, the standard deviation of errors was estimated by multiplying the mean absolute deviation by a factor of 1.25

(Brown [1963, chap. 19], Montgomery and Johnson [1976, chap. 7]). The mean absolute deviation was updated by simple exponential smoothing:

$$(MAD)_T = \alpha_k |E_{T-1}| + (1 - \alpha_k)(MAD)_{T-1},$$

where $(MAD)_T$ is the mean absolute deviation (i.e., the average value of the absolute forecast error) updated at the end of period $T - 1$. For initialization of the smoothing equation, see Montgomery and Johnson [1976, chap. 7-4]. α_k is the smoothing constant corresponding to a k-term model.

Even though the procedure is only an approximation, it was initially used because it held computational advantages relevant at the time when computing equipment was still in an incipient stage (it avoids storing numbers with numerous digits resulting from squaring observed errors, and it does not involve extracting square roots). Later, then, it became rooted as a tradition in the literature and in the computerized inventory systems. However, with the new power acquired by the large modern computers, the quest for this sort of computational simplicity is no longer justified and, therefore, the more accurate procedure based on MSE calculations may be adopted.

4.3.3.2 *Errors in forecasting over lead times*

The value of $\hat{\sigma}_T$ provides a measure of the accuracy of the one-period demand forecast. As mentioned earlier, however, our interest is to forecast the demand over the lead time and, therefore, it is the dispersion of the forecast error over the lead time which is significant to measure.

When the lead time is known with certainty, encompassing l periods, the estimated standard deviation $(\hat{\sigma}_l)_T$ of the forecast errors over the lead time* is expressed, in most practical applications, in terms of the updated standard deviation estimate $\hat{\sigma}_T$ of the one-period errors.

By definition:

$$(E_l)_T = \sum_{\tau=0}^{l-1} F_{T+\tau,[T-1]} - \sum_{\tau=0}^{l-1} A_{T+\tau}$$

$$= \sum_{\tau=0}^{l-1} \left(F_{T+\tau,[T-1]} - A_{T+\tau} \right), \tag{4.96}$$

where:

$(E_l)_T =$ the cumulative forecast error over an l period lead time extending from period T through period $T + l - 1$

$F_{T+\tau,[T-1]} =$ demand forecast for period $T + \tau$ made at the end of period $T - 1$

$A_{T+\tau} =$ Actual demand during period $T + \tau$.

---

*Estimate $(\hat{\sigma}_l)_T$ is computed at the end of period $T - 1$ and refers to a lead time of length l spanning periods $T, T + 1, \ldots, T + l - 1$.

If all noise samples ε_t are serially independent (i.e., demands in nonoverlapping time periods are independent), $F'_{T+\tau,[T-1]}$ and $A_{T+\tau}$ are also independent because $F'_{T+\tau,[T-1]}$ is based on demand outcomes up to and including period $T-1$ and $A_{T+\tau}$ is independent of the demand in any other time period. Therefore:

$$(\sigma_l)^2_T = \mathrm{Var}\left(\sum_{\tau=0}^{l-1} F'_{T+\tau,[T-1]}\right) + l\sigma_\varepsilon^2. \tag{4.97}$$

Equation (4.97) shows that the variation in the cumulative forecast error comes from two sources: the variation in the forecast resulting from noise samples in the observations before period T, and the noise that affects the true process throughout the lead time. We should observe that even though the cumulative forecast over the lead time is the sum of l period forecasts, the cumulative forecast variance is not the sum of the period forecast variances. The reason is that all forecasts $F_{T+\tau,[T-1]}$ are based upon the same demand information and therefore are serially correlated.

To illustrate let us consider the constant demand pattern (Figure 4.10a) for which the forecasting is done with the exponential smoothing model (4.60):

$$F_T^b = \alpha A_{T-1} + (1-\alpha) F_{T-1}^b.$$

Forecast F_T^b is also the forecast for every period of the lead time. By (4.61) and for a large enough T:

$$F_T^b = \frac{\alpha}{\beta} \sum_{t=1}^{\infty} \beta^t A_{T-t}.$$

The variance of the forecast is then:

$$\mathrm{Var}\left[F_T^b\right] = \frac{\alpha^2}{\beta^2}\left(\beta^2 + \beta^4 + \beta^6 + \cdots\right)\sigma_\varepsilon^2 = \frac{\alpha^2}{\beta^2}\cdot\frac{\beta^2}{1-\beta^2}\sigma_\varepsilon^2$$

$$\mathrm{Var}\left[F_T^b\right] = \frac{\alpha}{1+\beta}\sigma_\varepsilon^2$$

The cumulative forecast is:

$$\sum_{\tau=0}^{l-1} F_{T+\tau,[T-1]}^b = \sum_{\tau=0}^{l-1} F_T^b = lF_T^b.$$

Hence, the variance of the cumulative forecast is $l^2(\alpha/1+\beta)\sigma_\varepsilon^2$.

By (4.97) the variance of the forecast error over the lead time is given by:

$$(\sigma_l)^2_T = \left(l^2\frac{\alpha}{1+\beta} + l\right)\sigma_\varepsilon^2. \tag{4.98}$$

Table 4.1 lists the values of $(l^2(\alpha/1+\beta)+l)$ for four levels of the smooth-constant α.

TABLE 4.1   Variance of Cumulative Forecast Error as Function of σ_ε^2 for Constant Demand Pattern

LEAD TIME l	$\alpha = 0.3$	$\alpha = 0.2$	$\alpha = 0.1$	$\alpha = 0.05$
1	1.1765	1.1111	1.0526	1.0256
2	2.7059	2.4444	2.2105	2.1026
3	4.5882	4.0000	3.4737	3.2308
4	6.8235	5.7778	4.8421	4.4103
5	9.4118	7.7778	6.3158	5.6410
6	12.3529	10.0000	7.8947	6.9231
7	15.6471	12.4444	9.5789	8.2564
8	19.2941	15.1111	11.3684	9.6410
9	23.2941	18.0000	13.2632	11.0769
10	27.6471	21.1111	15.2632	12.5641
11	32.3529	24.4444	17.3684	14.1026
12	37.4118	28.0000	19.5789	15.6923

In order to use Table 4.1, one has to have an estimate of the noise variance σ_ε^2. First, we recall that the mean square error is an estimate of the one-period forecast error variance:

$$\hat{\sigma}_T^2 = (MSE)_T. \tag{4.99}$$

Then (4.98) provides the relationship between σ_T^2 (make $l = 1$) and σ_ε^2 in the following form:

$$\sigma_T^2 = c_1 \sigma_\varepsilon^2 \tag{4.100}$$

where constant c_1 is found in the first row of Table 4.1.

An estimate of σ_ε^2 can be obtained by:

$$\hat{\sigma}_\varepsilon^2 = \frac{(MSE)_T}{c_1}. \tag{4.101}$$

As mentioned earlier, however, it is customary to compute the standard deviation $(\sigma_l)_T$ of the cumulative forecast error in terms of the standard deviation σ_T of the one-period errors. The relationship can be expressed by a coefficient k_l:

$$k_l = \frac{(\sigma_l)_T}{\sigma_T} = \sqrt{\frac{l^2 \dfrac{\alpha}{1+\beta} + l}{\dfrac{\alpha}{1+\beta} + 1}}. \tag{4.102}$$

Coefficients k_l are given in Table 4.2 for various values of the smoothing constant.

TABLE 4.2   Standard Deviation of Cumulative Forecast Error as Function of σ_T for Constant Demand Pattern

LEAD TIME l	$\alpha = 0.3$	$\alpha = 0.2$	$\alpha = 0.1$	$\alpha = 0.05$
1	1.0000	1.0000	1.0000	1.0000
2	1.5166	1.4832	1.4491	1.4318
3	1.9748	1.8974	1.8166	1.7748
4	2.4083	2.2804	2.1448	2.0736
5	2.8284	2.6458	2.4495	2.3452
6	3.2404	3.0000	2.7386	2.5981
7	3.6469	3.3466	3.0166	2.8373
8	4.0497	3.6878	3.2863	3.0659
9	4.4497	4.0249	3.5496	3.2863
10	4.8477	4.3589	3.8079	3.5000
11	5.2440	4.6904	4.0620	3.7081
12	5.6391	5.0200	4.3128	3.9115

A similar sort of analysis can be conducted for any forecasting model; the algebra, however, tends to become very tedious. The general exponential smoothing approach mentioned earlier, having been developed in matrix form, offers the important advantage of being a systematic way of proceeding through the computations.*

Thus, for the linear trend model $A_t = a + b_t + \varepsilon_t$ general exponential smoothing (which in steady state yields the same coefficients as double exponential smoothing) leads to the following variance of the cumulative forecast error:

$$\mathrm{Var}\left(\sum_{\tau=0}^{l-1} F^{tr}_{T+\tau,[T-1]} \right) = l^2 \frac{\alpha_2}{2(1+\beta_2)^3}\left[5(1+2\beta_2+\beta_2^2)+4(1-\beta_2^2)l + \alpha_2^2 l^2\right]\sigma_\varepsilon^2$$

where $F^{tr}_{T+\tau,[T-1]}$ is the forecast for period $T+\tau$ made at the end of period $T-1$, and α_2 denotes the smoothing constant to be used in the two-coefficient forecasting model. By (4.97) one can compute the variance of the cumulative forecast error:

$$(\sigma_l)^2_T = \left\{ l^2 \frac{\alpha_2}{2(1+\beta_2)^3}\left[5(1+2\beta_2+\beta_2^2)+4(1-\beta_2^2)l+\alpha_2^2 l^2\right]+l\right\}\sigma_\varepsilon^2.$$

From the above equation it is apparent, as it also was in the case of the constant demand pattern, that the variance of the cumulative forecast error is linearly related to the variance of the noise. This holds true, in general, for

---

* General exponential smoothing is not reproduced here since the interested reader can find its full development in a number of references like Brown [1963], Montgomery and Johnson [1976], and Johnson and Montgomery [1974].

forecasting models of any complexity if general exponential smoothing procedures can be applied. If c_l stands for the proportionality coefficient, then:

$$(\sigma_l)_T^2 = c_l \sigma_\varepsilon^2.$$

Table 4.3 shows the values of c_l for the linear trend model for various combinations of lead times and smoothing constants, and Table 4.4 contains the standard deviation of the cumulative forecast error $(\sigma_l)_T$ as a function of the standard deviation σ_T of the one-period error. The smoothing constant α_2 conforms to relation (4.91):

Simple smoothing constant α_1	0.3	0.2	0.1	0.05
Equivalent smoothing constant α_2	0.16334	0.10557	0.05132	0.02532

From inspecting tables 4.1–4.4 it is apparent that with smaller smoothing constants the effect of the variance of the cumulative forecast is diminished, and the variance of the cumulative error is dominated by the accumulated noise. This is to say that, along with the reduction in the serial correlation of demand forecasts over the lead time, coefficient c_l tends toward the limiting case $c_l = l$, or $(\sigma_l)_T = l^{0.5}\sigma_T$.

As mentioned at the beginning, the above results depend on exact independence of the random variation in demand. However, in reality one can expect to find some (unknown) serial correlation in the noise, which makes the variation of the cumulative forecast error depend on lead time somewhat differently than inferred from the previous theoretical results. However, the qualitative findings, like the impact of the smoothing constant on the serial correlation of the forecasts, will still stay valid.

TABLE 4.3   Variance of Cumulative Forecast Error as Function of σ_ε^2 for Linear Trend Pattern

LEAD TIME l	$\alpha_2 = 0.16334$	$\alpha_2 = 0.10557$	$\alpha_2 = 0.05132$	$\alpha_2 = 0.02532$
1	1.2385	1.1456	1.0672	1.0324
2	3.0215	2.6083	2.2746	2.1309
3	5.4566	4.4285	3.6307	3.2975
4	8.6597	6.6487	5.1445	4.5342
5	12.7554	9.3133	6.8251	5.8432
6	17.8765	12.4691	8.6817	7.2264
7	24.1644	16.1646	10.7239	8.6861
8	31.7688	20.4506	12.9614	10.2242
9	40.8479	25.3801	15.4041	11.8432
10	51.5684	31.0078	18.0624	13.5449
11	64.1054	37.3908	20.9466	15.3319
12	78.6425	44.5882	24.0672	17.2061

TABLE 4.4   Standard Deviation of Cumulative Forecast Error as Function of σ_T for Linear Trend Pattern

LEAD TIME l	$\alpha_2 = 0.16334$	$\alpha_2 = 0.10577$	$\alpha_2 = 0.05132$	$\alpha_2 = 0.02632$
1	1.0000	1.0000	1.0000	1.0000
2	1.5619	1.5089	1.4599	1.4367
3	2.0990	1.9661	1.8445	1.7872
4	2.6443	2.4091	2.1956	2.0957
5	3.2092	2.8512	2.5289	2.3790
6	3.7992	3.2991	2.8521	2.6457
7	4.4171	3.7563	3.1699	2.9006
8	5.0647	4.2251	3.4849	3.1470
9	5.7430	4.7068	3.7992	3.3870
10	6.4527	5.2026	4.1139	3.6222
11	7.1945	5.7130	4.4302	3.8537
12	7.9686	6.2387	4.7488	4.0824

Empirically, the following expression has been found to give a fairly accurate representation in many inventory systems:

$$(\sigma_l)_T = l^B \sigma_T \tag{4.103}$$

where B is a power that expresses the relationship between the cumulative forecast error and the duration of the lead time. B is a constant characteristic of all items that come from a homogeneous population, like items in a product line, and can be obtained by regression. Experience shows that for most demand behavior B lies between 0.5 and 1.0. Notice that $B = 0.5$ is the limiting case which implies that the one-period forecast errors are independent random variables.

For practical inventory control purposes the theoretical results can also be approximated quite well, in the range $1 \leqslant l \leqslant 12$, by the following linear function (Brown [1967, p. 144]):

$$(\sigma_l)_T = (0.659 + 0.341 l) \sigma_T. \tag{4.104}$$

For comparison, Figure 4.14 presents the variation of the $[(\sigma_l)_T]/[\sigma_T]$ ratio with lead time l. Brown's function (4.104) approximates fairly well the theoretical results derived for the constant demand process (see Table 4.2) with a moderate smoothing constant $\alpha = 0.1$ (the approximation is equally good for the linear trend pattern). The limiting case $(\sigma_l)_T = \sqrt{l}\,\sigma_T$ is also shown. As the power of l is increased ($l^{.7}$ in Figure 4.14) relation (4.103) can be used to reflect the effect of the serial correlation of the forecasts upon the variation of the cumulative forecast errors.

When lead times are variable, forecasting should be done per lead time directly rather than by period. The errors over the lead time can be measured

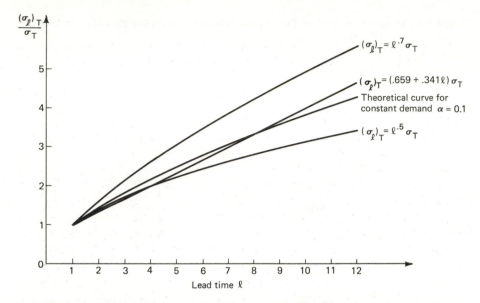

FIGURE 4.14   Theoretical and empirical functions for standard deviation of cumulative forecast error.

and the mean square error can be updated by (4.94) to obtain estimates of the standard deviation of the errors. Starting values in the smoothing equation (4.94) can be produced by use of the variance law applied to the demand forecast for the upcoming lead time.

4.3.4   Forecasting Slow-Moving Items

Slow-moving items are those which have a low level of demand and frequent periods of no usage. It is difficult to define a threshold above which an item would be classified as a fast mover and below which as a slow mover mainly because the threshold depends on the nature of the item: what would be low demand (in units) for some item might very well represent a high demand for some other item. In any case, it seems very unlikely that the separation point between high and low usage should ever be higher than 100 units per year and more likely it should be around 50 units per year. Peterson and Silver [1979] recommend classifying items according to their demand over the replenishment lead time: an expected lead time demand of 10 units or larger puts the item in the fast movers' class, while an expected lead time demand of less than 10 units defines a slow mover.

Slow-moving items tend to exhibit a lumpy demand pattern; thus, there may be several consecutive periods in which there is no demand at all, followed by one or several periods during which transactions of various sizes take place. Of course, not all lumpy demand items are slow movers and not all slow movers have lumpy demand. In assembly operations, component parts often present lumpy requirements induced by the batch-type production normally encountered in manufacturing; this does not mean, though, that all these parts are slow movers. Conversely, some very specific foodstuff carried by a supermarket and purchased by the members of an ethnic community might exhibit continuous sales, but in small overall amounts; thus, that foodstuff can be a slow mover without having a lumpy demand.

In this section we are interested in slow movers with lumpy demand, since the discontinuities in requirements invalidate the use of the forecasting methods presented before. Indeed, if ordinary exponential smoothing is used, demand forecasts will tend to be much lower than the average demand per period at the time just before an order is received, and much higher than the average demand per period just after an order has been received. This tends to increase the forecast errors.

In order to establish whether an item is lumpy or not, Brown [1977, chap. 12.3] suggests the following procedure: a forecast model is fit and then simulated over historical data. The residual differences between the data and the model are recorded and their standard deviation is calculated. If that standard deviation is greater than the level in the forecast model, the item is said to have lumpy demand.

Various forecasting methods have been proposed for slow-moving items, ranging from simple exponential smoothing to more elaborate techniques. They involve different system costs, and to choose one or another depends very much on the importance and value of the controlled item.

4.3.4.1 Exponential smoothing for slow-moving items

Since any one period's demand carries limited information and also, as a way of eliminating the instability of the forecast, the exponential smoothing should be conducted with very small values of the smoothing constant α—say, between 0.01 and 0.05. As small values of α imply that the initial conditions used to start the computations carry a considerable weight for a long time, these initial values should represent the average usage for a period of at least one year. Simple exponential smoothing (section 4.3.1.1) should be employed because the high level of noise in the demand of slow-moving items usually obscures any sort of basic pattern. Therefore, it does not make too much sense trying to discern trends or seasonal variations.

A small value of α should also be used to update the estimates of the mean square error (see 4.3.3.1).

Using exponential smoothing for slow movers is essentially the same procedure as for fast-moving items. This could constitute an important practical advantage for the implementation stage.

4.3.4.2   Forecasting the demand transactions size and the time between transactions

Croston [1972] argues that simple exponential smoothing in the case of intermittent demand items is biased and has a rather large variance. He proposes that the two components, the magnitude of individual demand occurrences and the time between consecutive transactions, be forecast.

Suppose that we are at the end of period T, during which a demand of size s_T (possibly zero) has been observed. The time elapsed since the last transaction is p_T periods. For normally distributed demand magnitudes, Croston [1972] proposes the following forecasting procedure:

- If $s_T > 0$ (i.e., in period T a demand transaction occurs), the following updating is performed:

$$\hat{s}_{[T]} = \alpha s_T + (1 - \alpha) \hat{s}_{[T-1]} \tag{4.105}$$

$$\hat{p}_{[T]} = \alpha p_T + (1 - \alpha) \hat{p}_{[T-1]} \tag{4.106}$$

  where:

  $\hat{s}_{[T]}$ = the estimate, at the end of period T, of the average demand transaction size

  $\hat{p}_{[T]}$ = the estimated number of periods until the next nonzero demand occurrence, computed at the end of period T.

- If $s_T = 0$ (i.e., in period T no demand occurs), the estimates are kept the same as they were at the end of the previous period.

The procedure yields unbiased estimates and a variance lower than the exponential smoothing.

The updating of the mean square error is done only in those periods in which a nonzero demand occurs; the updating is by exponential smoothing [see equation (4.94)].

4.3.4.3   Alternative ways of estimating parameters of theoretical probability distributions of demand

Because of the relatively few transactions occurring with slow-moving items during a year, we can assume, in general, that the probability distribution of demand over the lead time is fairly stationary. Based on the item's history or on some initial subjective assessments, we can estimate the probability distribution of demand and then use it to determine safety stocks and order points (to be seen later).

Empirically, the Poisson distribution has been found to represent reasonably well the distribution of demand for a slow-moving item. The Poisson distribution* is completely defined by a single parameter, the mean

---

* For a presentation of the Poisson distribution and its properties, see Hastings and Peacock [1975].

value of the random variable. If the mean value is λ and the standard deviation is σ, then:

$$\sigma = \sqrt{\lambda}.$$

For a slow-moving item let the random Poisson variable be the demand over the lead time. At each receipt of replenishment stock, the estimate of the lead time demand can be revised by exponential smoothing:

$$(F_l)_{\text{new}} = \alpha(A_l) + (1-\alpha)(F_l)_{\text{old}} \tag{4.107}$$

where:

$(F_l)_{\text{new}}$ = the revised forecast for the lead time demand

$(F_l)_{\text{old}}$ = the old forecast for the lead time demand

A_l = actual demand during the lead time just ended

α = the smoothing constant.

The mean square lead time demand (MS_l) can also be updated by exponential smoothing (Brown [1977, chap. 12]):

$$(MS_l)_{\text{new}} = \alpha(A_l)^2 + (1-\alpha)(MS_l)_{\text{old}} \tag{4.108}$$

where "new" and "old" denote the revised estimate and the previous estimate, respectively.

The standard deviation of lead time is estimated by:*

$$(STD_l) = \sqrt{(MSL)_{\text{new}} - (F_l)_{\text{new}}^2}. \tag{4.109}$$

Another possibility is to estimate the expected lead time demand by an average (or moving average) of historical lead time data; similarly, the standard deviation can be computed from actually observed data rather than from smoothed statistics.

Peterson and Silver [1979, chap. 9] recommend that lead time demand be considered as Poisson distributed if:

$$0.9\sqrt{(F_l)} \leqslant (STD_l) \leqslant 1.1\sqrt{(F_l)}, \tag{4.110}$$

that is, if the standard deviation is within 10% of $\sqrt{(F_l)}$. When (4.110) is not satisfied, the Poisson model is inappropriate and the Laplace distribution[†] is suggested for use. The Laplace distribution holds the advantage of being a continuous function, and it is often easier to work analytically with models of inventory systems if the variables can be treated as continuous. This allows one to eliminate the problems caused by discreteness and to take derivatives instead of working with differences.

---

*The variance σ^2 of a random variable x can be computed as: $\sigma^2 = E(x^2) - (E[x])^2$.

[†]The Laplace distribution is also known as the "bilateral exponential" (Feller [1971, Vol. 2, p. 49]) since it is a two-sided, symmetric exponential function. Some of its important properties are shown by Peterson and Silver [1979, p. 767].

In general, the Poisson distribution can raise computational problems if it is used for a large number of items. Therefore, Peterson and Silver recommend the use of the Poisson distribution only for expensive items, and the exclusive use of the Laplace distribution for all other items in inventory.

The test imposed by relation (4.110) is just a crude and simple way of checking on the goodness of the Poisson assumption. In some cases distributions other than Poisson and Laplace might be recommended. For instance, demand transactions can be generated by a Poisson process while the number of units requested when a demand occurs can vary randomly from demand to demand.* Statistical theory provides goodness-of-fit tests (see Hoel et al. [1971]) to check whether a sample of observed lead time demands are likely to have been generated by some hypothesized stochastic process. However, complicated distributions and sophisticated goodness-of-fit tests should be used with extreme caution; normally, they bring about an increased system cost that might not be justified unless the item is extremely important or expensive, thus presenting the opportunity of a substantial reduction in overall operating costs coming from an improved inventory policy.

When a new item is introduced on the system or when adequate data are unavailable to estimate the probability distribution of lead time demand, Bayesian forecasting can be resorted to. One starts out with some prior assessments in the form of a probability distribution placed over the possible values of one or several parameters that define the stochastic process generating lead time demands. As new data become available they are blended with prior information, by means of the Bayes rule, to revise our knowledge about the uncertain parameters. The interested reader is directed, as a starting reference, to the book by Montgomery and Johnson [1976, chap. 10].

4.3.4.4 *Empirically determined probability distributions of lead time demand*

So far we have been concerned with fitting some theoretical distribution to the available demand data. Consider now the case where we make use of an empirically determined distribution. To keep things simple, assume that the lead time is a constant l. If a demand history is available, divide it into nonoverlapping time intervals of length l and establish how many units have been requested in each such time interval. The range of possible lead time demands has to be partitioned into a number of n classes by the following class limits:

$$A_l(0) < A_l(1) < \cdots < A_l(n-1) < A_l(n),$$

---

*A simple case of such a demand process is presented by Hadley and Whitin [1963, chap. 3-7]; they call it the "stuttering Poisson" process, in which a Poisson distribution generates the demands, and the number of units requested when a demand occurs has a geometric distribution.

where A_l denotes actual demand in lead time interval of length l. The class limits should be set so that each observation can be assigned to only one class. A histogram can be constructed to represent the frequency with which the observed lead time demands are falling in each class. The frequency thus determined for the ith class, having limits $A_l(i-1)$ and $A_l(i)$, $i=1,\ldots,n$, is a good estimate of the probability $p(i)$ that a lead time demand will lie in this class (Figure 4.15).

If no adequate history is available, one should start with some initial subjective prediction (similar to the Bayesian prior estimate) of the various probabilities $p(i)$, $i=1,\ldots,n$.

Brown [1963, chap. 13] presents a very simple method for updating probabilities $p(i)$ as new data become available, under the assumption that the probability distribution of lead time demands is stationary or changing very slowly with time.

Thus, suppose that a time interval of l periods has just concluded and a demand of A_l units has been recorded such that:

$$A_l(i-1) < A_l \leqslant A_l(i),$$

that is, A_l lies in the ith class.

At this time old estimates of the probabilities $p(i)$ exist:

$$\mathcal{P}_{\text{old}} = \begin{bmatrix} \hat{p}_{\text{old}}(1) \\ \hat{p}_{\text{old}}(2) \\ \vdots \\ \hat{p}_{\text{old}}(n) \end{bmatrix} \tag{4.111}$$

where $\mathcal{P}_{\text{old}}$ is the $n \times 1$ column vector of estimates.

FIGURE 4.15   Empirical density.

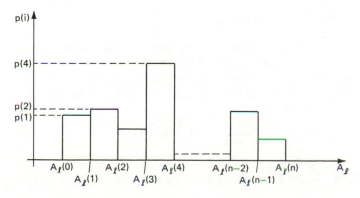

Our problem is to revise these estimates in the light of the latest information. To do this define first the following function of A_l:

$$u(i) = \begin{cases} 1 & \text{if } A_l(i-1) < A_l \leqslant A_l(i) \\ 0 & \text{otherwise,} \end{cases} \tag{4.112}$$

and then construct the n-component column vector $\mathcal{U}$:

$$\mathcal{U} = \begin{bmatrix} u(1) \\ u(2) \\ \vdots \\ u(n) \end{bmatrix}$$

The element of $\mathcal{U}$ whose value is equal to 1 shows the class interval in which the latest recorded actual lead time demand A_l has fallen; all other elements are zero.

The blending of old and current information is done by vector smoothing according to the rule:

$$\mathcal{P}_{\text{new}} = \alpha\mathcal{U} + (1-\alpha)\mathcal{P}_{\text{old}} \tag{4.113}$$

where α is the exponential smoothing constant.

Since in our case A_l lay in the ith class, the updated vector $\mathcal{P}_{\text{new}}$ has the following components:

$$\hat{p}_{\text{new}}(1) = (1-\alpha)\hat{p}_{\text{old}}(1)$$

$$\vdots \qquad\qquad \vdots$$

$$\hat{p}_{\text{new}}(i-1) = (1-\alpha)\hat{p}_{\text{old}}(i-1)$$
$$\hat{p}_{\text{new}}(i) = (1-\alpha)\hat{p}_{\text{old}}(i-1) + \alpha \tag{4.114}$$
$$\hat{p}_{\text{new}}(i+1) = (1-\alpha)\hat{p}_{\text{old}}(i-1)$$

$$\vdots \qquad\qquad \vdots$$

$$\hat{p}_{\text{new}}(n) = (1-\alpha)\hat{p}_{\text{old}}(n)$$

All elements of $\mathcal{P}_{\text{new}}$ are nonnegative; also, from (4.114) it follows that $\sum_{k=1}^{n} \hat{p}_{\text{new}}(k) = 1$. Therefore, $\mathcal{P}_{\text{new}}$ is a probability vector.

It may be shown that the exponential vector smoothing yields unbiased estimates of the true probabilities, and that the variance of the forecast for the ith probability is:

$$\text{Var}[\hat{p}_{\text{new}}(i)] = \frac{\alpha}{2-\alpha} p(i)[1-p(i)] \tag{4.115}$$

From (4.115) it is obvious that in order to reduce the variance of the forecast, the class limits should be set so that $p(i)$ is either large (close to one) or small (close to zero). Since in most cases in inventory systems the right tail of the distribution is relevant (to be seen later when safety stocks are discussed), Brown recommends that near the tail class limits be set so that class probabilities result in very small values (of the order of 0.02); the rest of the distribution can be considered one event, having a large probability (of the order of 0.9).

The choice of the smoothing constant α goes by reasons similar to the ones put forth in section 4.3.1.1. If the probability distribution is believed constant in time and the initial conditions are reliable, a small α should be used in order to reduce the variance of the forecast and thus to obtain a more stable system. Otherwise, if conditions are likely to change with time and questionable estimates have to be used to initialize the forecasting procedure, a larger smoothing constant is preferred in order to discount starting values faster and to track real changes closer.

The use of empirical distributions looks straightforward and vector smoothing is rather simple to apply. However, because of the scarcity of historical data that plagues many inventory systems (especially manual systems), it might be extremely difficult (if not utterly impossible) to represent reliably the tail of the distribution for the purpose of setting order points. In such cases, the only way out is to use a theoretical distribution whose parameters have to be estimated or guessed at from whatever information can be put together.

4.3.5 Tracking Signals to Monitor the Forecasts

Through the use of unbiased forecast models, the mean of the forecast errors should be zero as long as the assumptions on which the forecast is generated are valid. Therefore, so long as the model and the demand generating process are consistent with each other we should expect the forecast errors to fluctuate within reasonable limits around zero. However, if the process changes, thus invalidating the model, the forecast errors will tend to have repeatedly the same sign, thus moving the average error away from zero. In such cases, either automatic procedures are applied to bring the system in line with the changed conditions (see references on adaptive control smoothing, section 4.3.1.1) or personal intervention is required (to be discussed later).

The purpose of a tracking signal is to detect the situation where the model produces biased forecasts and, thus, to initiate corrective action.

The technique to be presented in this section, suggested by Trigg [1964] and called the *smoothed error tracking signal,** computes the expected forecast error by simple exponential smoothing and then tests the hypothesis that this

---

*An alternative technique based on the cumulative forecast error was developed by Brown [1959] but presents weaknesses that make it nonrecommended for use; see criticism by Brown [1967, p. 163] himself.

value is zero. If the hypothesis is rejected, this constitutes the signal that the forecast model is biased.

Suppose that a forecast model with k coefficients is currently in use, and we are at the end of period $T-1$. The smoothed error at this point in time, which also represents the error forecast for the upcoming period T, is:

$$(SE)_T = \alpha_k E_{T-1} + (1 - \alpha_k)(SE)_{T-1} \tag{4.116}$$

where:

$(SE)_T =$ error forecast (i.e., smoothed error) for period T, computed at the end of $T-1$

$E_{T-1} =$ forecast error actually observed in period $T-1$ [for definition see equation (4.93)]

$\alpha_k =$ smoothing constant corresponding to the k coefficient model [see equation (4.91)].

When the smoothing process is started, the initial value of the smoothed error in (4.116) is set to zero; this reflects our assumption that the model is correct and that the initial parameter estimates are unbiased.

If the forecasts were unbiased one would expect the value of the smoothed error $(SE)_T$ to fluctuate around zero with a constant variance σ_{SE}^2. The derivation of σ_{SE}^2 involves tedious algebra because the errors are not independent random variables; this is because demand forecasts are computed as combinations of past data and, therefore, the resulting forecast errors are serially correlated.

For an exponentially smoothed constant demand model Brown [1967, p. 165] derived analytically the expression for the variance of the smoothed error:

$$\sigma_{SE}^2 = \frac{\alpha}{(2 - \alpha)^2} \sigma^2 \tag{4.117}$$

where σ^2 is the variance of the forecast errors, and α is the simple smoothing constant used for the constant demand pattern. As σ^2 is unknown, an estimate of it has to be used. At the end of period $T-1$ the estimate is $\hat{\sigma}_T = (MSE)_T$ [see equations (4.94)–(4.95)]; consequently, the standard deviation of the smoothed error is estimated by:

$$(\hat{\sigma}_{SE})_T = \frac{\sqrt{\alpha}}{(2 - \alpha)} \sqrt{(MSE)_T}. \tag{4.118}$$

In the case of forecast models with a larger number of terms, the only practical way to approach the estimation of σ_{SE} is by simulation. Brown [1967, chap. 12] did so for a six-term model describing trend and seasonalities.

Brown [1977, p. 156] and Montgomery and Johnson [1976, p. 166] suggest that the result given in equation (4.118) could be used as a reasonable approximation also for models other than the constant demand pattern, for which it had been originally developed.

We can now define the tracking signal for period T as:

$$(TS)_T = \frac{(SE)_T}{(\hat{\sigma}_{SE})_T}. \qquad (4.119)$$

The tracking signal measures, in multiples of the standard deviation, how far removed from zero is the updated smooth error. The tracking signal is considered to be satisfactory if it falls between two limits $-K$ and $+K$:

$$-K \leqslant (TS)_T \leqslant K. \qquad (4.120)$$

If the tracking signal is outside this range, this should be an indication that the forecast is unacceptably biased and some intervention is required to correct the deficiencies.

The value of the detection limit K is subject to management policies; usually it is between 2 and 5. For expensive or important items, the limits have to be set quite tight (i.e., $K = 2$) to be sure that real changes are detected early in their development; in this case, however, one has also to accept the risk of getting a few false alarms when some unlikely (but possible) large errors trigger the signal, but nothing has really happened. For cheap items, where the processing of false reports might constitute an unacceptable system cost in view of the low value of the items, the limits should be set wider so that when the tracking signal triggered, it would be very likely that some real problems have taken place. Low-cost items, that normally do not entail close management attention, can be protected against stockouts by large safety stocks since inventory investment is insignificant. Therefore, even if a real change in the demand pattern has gone on for a while before triggering the signal, the safety stock might still prevent a shortage from occurring.

Certainly, the limits can be changed any time during the operation of the system. If there are too many reports, the limits can be widened; if, on the contrary, it turns out that the system is too slow in detecting real changes, they can be set tighter.

4.4 Safety Stock Decision Rules

In an inventory system whenever the available inventory reaches a certain level, called the order point, a production or purchasing order, depending on whether the item is manufactured or purchased, should be released. By available inventory we mean the sum of the stock on hand and the stock already on order, less any unfilled customer demand (if it had been backlogged).

The order point should represent sufficient inventory to last through the lead time. When demand is uncertain (as it is in most cases), it is obvious that the order point should be set equal to the forecast of the maximum reasonable demand over the lead time. One way of estimating the maximum reasonable demand is to forecast the expected demand during the lead time (see section

4.3.2) and then to add an allowance for protection against the uncertainty inherent in any forecast. This allowance is called the safety stock.

The setting of safety stocks, order points, and other parameters of the inventory system should conform to the characteristics of the controlled items (usage rate and cost). Some items are expensive or are considered very important and, therefore, we like to devote more careful and close attention to them, while low-cost products are dealt with on a rather routine basis. From a technical point of view, inventory control procedures that are adequate to manage high-usage items do not work satisfactorily with low-usage items and vice-versa (we have already made this distinction when we differentiated between forecasting for fast movers and for slow movers). For these reasons, inventory items have to be classified into groups that should be homogeneous with respect to the control procedures that apply. Since investment in the inventory of any given item is proportional to two of the item's most important characteristics, the item's usage and its cost, a commonly used method of classification is the so-called ABC inventory classification, according to the annual dollar usage.

4.4.1 The ABC Inventory Classification

The annual dollar usage is obtained by multiplying the yearly usage of the item by its unit cost. Observations of a large number of multi-item inventories have revealed that a small fraction of the items accounts for a high percentage of the cumulative annual dollar usage, while another large percentage of the items represents only a small fraction of the total annual value. This suggests the need to classify the items into three categories, called A, B, and C.

We present an example to illustrate how the classification is constructed, as well as some of its features.

Suppose that we are managing an inventory of 3,000 items and, because the system is not computerized, it would be too costly to consider every single record for analysis. Therefore, we decide to use a 1% random sample,* by picking every one hundredth stock record; from every record, the annual dollar usage is read and listed in descending sequence. Assume that the sample is as shown in Table 4.5.

To simplify the analysis, we group the sampled items by annual usage intervals, and then compute cumulative percentages as in Table 4.6.

From Table 4.6 it is immediately apparent that there are a few items (10% of total inventory) that account for the most substantial portion of the total annual dollar usage (about 67%); these are class A items.

---

* As becomes clear later, all we need are percentage distributions. As we believe the sample to be representative of the entire inventory population, the sample percentages will be used as estimates of the population percentages.

TABLE 4.5　The 1 Percent Random Sample

ITEM NUMBER	ANNUAL DOLLAR USAGE	ITEM NUMBER	ANNUAL DOLLAR USAGE	ITEM NUMBER	ANNUAL DOLLAR USAGE
1	334,369	11	15,835	21	1,495
2	189,094	12	11,271	22	1,451
3	53,104	13	6,634	23	1,394
4	49,514	14	6,374	24	863
5	43,045	15	5,324	25	788
6	33,860	16	4,964	26	384
7	26,903	17	3,533	27	221
8	26,370	18	3,134	28	189
9	18,215	19	2,143	29	122
10	17,501	20	1,926	30	84

At the other extreme, there is a large group (60% of all items) which contributes a very small percentage (about 5%) to the total annual usage; these are class C items.

The intermediate group, class B items, is more balanced in that it contains a fairly large number of items (30%) and also represents an important proportion of total annual usage (about 28%).

Although the break points between these classes vary according to each individual business' conditions, a common breakdown might be as follows:

Class	Percentage of items	Percentage of total annual dollar usage
A	5–15	50–60
B	20–30	25–40
C	55–75	5–15

In highly technological industries, such as computer or aircraft production, class A tends to have a small percentage of items while producing a large share of total annual sales. In contrast, inventories of consumer products at the retail level have a more numerous A class—that is, it takes a larger portion of items to provide the same large fraction of total annual sales. Industrial producers are in an intermediate position.

If the cumulative fraction of total annual usage is represented against the cumulative percentage of items, the points follow a Pareto curve (Figure 4.16).

An alternative way of plotting the data in Table 4.6 is to use a horizontal axis representing the natural logarithms of the annual dollar usages, and a vertical axis with a normal probability ruling (lognormal graph paper). Two curves are graphed: cumulative fraction of items versus annual usage, and cumulative fraction of total annual usage versus annual usage (Figure 4.17). Each set of points falls nearly along a straight line (the solid lines in Figure

TABLE 4.6 Inventory Analysis

INTERVAL OF ANNUAL DOLLAR USAGES	NUMBER OF ITEMS IN INTERVAL	CUMULATIVE NUMBER OF ITEMS	CUMULATIVE % OF ITEMS	ANNUAL DOLLAR USAGE OF ITEMS IN INTERVAL	CUMULATIVE ANNUAL DOLLAR USAGE	CUMULATIVE % OF USAGE	INVENTORY CLASSIFICATION
Over 200,000	1	1	3.33	334,369	334,369	38.88	A
100,000.01–200,000	1	2	6.67	189,094	523,463	60.87	
50,000.01–100,000	1	3	10.00	53,104	576,567	67.04	
20,000.01–50,000	5	8	26.67	179,692	759,259	87.94	B
10,000.01–20,000	4	12	40.00	62.822	819,081	95.24	
5,000.01–10,000	3	15	50.00	18,332	837,413	97.37	
2,000.01–5,000	4	19	63.33	13,774	851,187	98.97	C
1,000.01–2,000	4	23	76.67	6,166	857,353	99.69	
500.01–1,000	2	25	83.33	1,651	859,004	99.88	
200.01–500	2	27	90.00	605	859,609	99.95	
100.01–200	2	29	96.67	311	859,920	99.99	
100 and less	1	30	100.00	84	860,004	100.00	

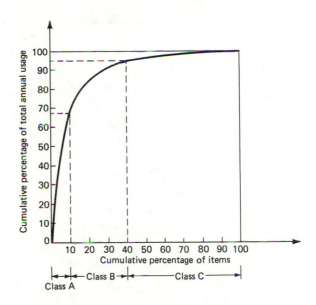

FIGURE 4.16
Pareto curve of *ABC*
classification.

FIGURE 4.17 Percentage distributions versus annual usage.

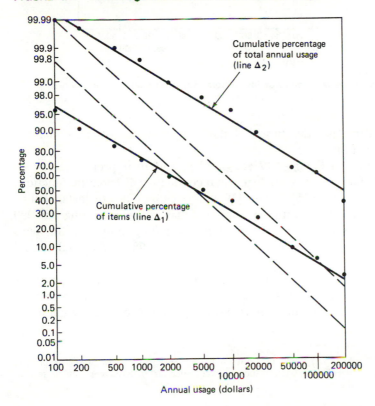

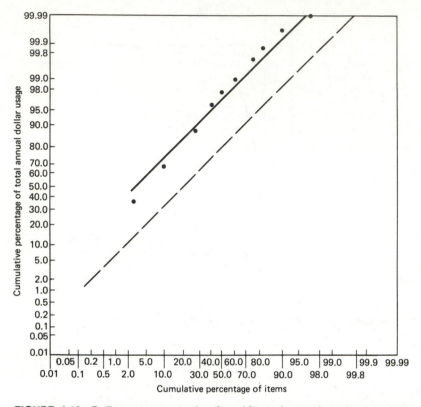

FIGURE 4.18   Dollar usage versus fraction of items for two inventory populations.

4.17), which means that the annual dollar usages in our inventory have a lognormal distribution.

The two lines in Figure 4.17 are parallel, and their properties can be derived from the fact that they are lognormal cumulative distribution functions (Hastings and Peacock [1975], Brown [1959, Appendix C]). For instance, line Δ_1 tells us that the items with an annual dollar usage exceeding $50,000 represent 10% of the total inventory. Similarly, according to line Δ_2, the items whose annual dollar usage is over $2,000 contribute 99% to the total annual usage.

It is, in general, true for all industries that the annual dollar usage across an inventory of items is lognormally distributed.* If an inventory is nonhomogeneous (i.e., contains two or more separate inventory populations),

---

*Brown [1977, chap. 9.1] shows that not only usage in terms of cost or selling price is lognormal, but other inventory related values as well, such as material cost, cubic feet of warehousing space, weight, etc.

each population has its own lognormal distribution curves. For instance, in Figure 4.17 the two dashed parallel lines represent a different group of items than the inventory sample in Table 4.5 and described by the solid lines Δ_1 and Δ_2. This sort of stratification in an inventory is important because each separate population may require different inventory management and marketing policies.

An alternative way of plotting the distribution is to graph the cumulative percentage of total annual usage against the cumulative percentage of items, using two axes, both with normal probability scales. Given that the two cumulative distribution lines in Figure 4.17 are parallel, the new graph results in another line with a 45° slope (Figure 4.18). Both inventory populations of Figure 4.17 are represented in Figure 4.18 with a solid line and, respectively, a dashed line.

Thus, whenever the attempt to draw a 45° line through the scatter of points, as in Figure 4.18, results in a bad fit, we would suspect the existence of more than one inventory population; it might also mean that the distribution is not lognormal, which is, however, unlikely. A careful investigation should reveal the causes for such an occurrence.

4.4.2 Safety Stocks for Fast-Moving Items

As mentioned earlier, when demand is uncertain the order point has to be set such as to provide sufficient stock to meet any reasonable demand over the lead time:*

$$\text{Order point} = \text{Maximum reasonable demand during lead time}$$

$$= (\text{Demand forecast over lead time}) + (\text{Safety stock}).$$

$$(4.121)$$

Since the value of the standard deviation σ_l of the forecast errors over the lead time[†] provides a measure of the accuracy of lead time demand forecasts, it is generally accepted that the safety stock SS is related to σ_l through a multiplying factor k, called the safety factor:

$$SS = k\sigma_l \qquad (4.122)$$

---

*In a periodic review system (to be seen later), where inventory decisions are made at fixed intervals, intervals called review periods, the concept of lead time has to be enlarged to include not only the replenishment lead time but also one review period. This is necessary because, after an inventory decision has been made, the next opportunity to influence the stock level, and thus avert a possible stockout, appears only after a review period (when the new decision is made), plus a replenishment lead time (when the order actually arrives).

[†] When it comes to actually computing safety stocks, an estimate of σ_l is needed. If we are at the end of period $T - 1$, beginning of period T, the most recently updated estimate is $(\hat{\sigma}_l)_T$ (see section 4.3.3.2) and the safety stock for the l-period lead time starting with period T is:

$$(SS)_T = k(\hat{\sigma}_l)_T.$$

Thus, an inaccurate forecast exposes us to a higher risk of running out of stock during the lead time; at the same time, however, it is reflected in an increased σ_l, which leads to a larger safety stock as protection against the risk.

We should mention that, throughout the development of the safety stock decision rules, we make the assumption that the average demand is a constant or is changing very slowly with time; this ensures the stability of the order point with time. The issue of time-varying uncertain demand patterns is postponed to a later section. We also consider the lead time to be constant; in case it is not, we should forecast demand as suggested in section 4.3.2. Attempts to estimate lead time distributions are bound, in most cases, to remain just academic exercises because of the computational difficulties brought about and because, usually, the additional data required are just not available (Hadley and Whitin [1963, chap. 9-6]). Therefore, with highly variable lead times it is always advisable to try to negotiate with the suppliers in order to cut down the variability.

The safety stock factor k is the control that reflects what management considers to be reasonable in protecting service to the customers. "Reasonable" is understood here in terms of a tradeoff: poor service results in tangible costs (such as the cost of expediting, foregone profit on sales lost because of stockout situations, etc.) and intangible costs (such as loss of goodwill), while improved service means that additional safety stock has to be carried which implies that extra inventory investment is needed.

Thus, the safety stock should correspond to a compromise between too costly shortages and too expensive inventories. One approach to computing safety stocks is to assess the cost incurred in a shortage situation and, then, to minimize the total relevant costs associated with the inventory system. Although appealing and rather easy to apply from the optimization point of view, this approach has a serious drawback in that, in general, it is extremely difficult to provide estimates for the cost of stockouts. Another approach, which avoids this thorny problem, starts from a prespecified service level that has to be achieved by appropriately setting the safety stock. The desired service level is established by management; this implies that some tradeoff between conflicting factors is implicitly worked out and imbedded in the value of the service level. In what follows, examples are presented for both approaches.

4.4.2.1   Setting Safety Stocks When Stockout Cost Is Proportional to Number of Units Short

In this case the system incurs a charge c_s for every unit short (i.e., demanded but out of stock) such as, for instance, when items are manufactured on overtime or bought from a competitor at extra cost in order to avert an impending stockout situation.

The model and the derivation to be presented are governed by the following assumptions:

- the demand rate, although uncertain, is constant or changing very slowly with time
- the lead time is deterministic and time-invariant
- the order quantity Q is assumed to have been predetermined
- an order of size Q is released precisely when available inventory reaches the order point
- average shortages are considered negligibly small when compared with the average inventory*

The relevant costs are: the ordering, inventory holding, and stockout costs; we determine the size of the safety stock (i.e., the value of k) such as to minimize the sum of the costs over a time span of one year. As no aggregate constraints are imposed, each item is treated independently of the others.

The following notations are used:

D = average demand rate, units per year

A = ordering cost, dollars per order

C = unit cost, dollars per unit of item

r = inventory carrying charge, dollars per dollar of inventory per year

H = annual inventory holding cost, dollars per unit of item per year; $H = rC$

TC = total expected annual cost, dollars per year.

The expected annual ordering cost is easily computed given that, with an average annual demand of D and replenishment of size Q, we have:

$$\text{Expected number of replenishments per year} = \frac{D}{Q}.$$

Hence,

$$\text{Expected annual ordering cost} = A\frac{D}{Q}. \tag{4.123}$$

As mentioned above, a replenishment order is placed when the available inventory reaches the order point. Until the replenishment arrives, the inventory level drops by an amount equal to the demand over the lead time. Since we assumed that shortages are, on the average, too small to influence the average on-hand inventory level, the expected inventory level just before a replenishment arrives is:

$$\begin{array}{c}\text{Expected on-hand inventory just} \\ \text{before replenishment arrives}\end{array} = \left(\begin{array}{c}\text{Order} \\ \text{point}\end{array}\right) - \left(\begin{array}{c}\text{Expected demand} \\ \text{over lead time}\end{array}\right).$$

---

*This assumption is reasonable because practice shows that safety stocks are carried with the purpose of keeping shortages at a low level, which by no means should compare in size with the average level of positive stock.

From (4.121), and from the assumption that an unbiased forecasting system is in use, it follows that:

$$\text{Expected on-hand inventory just} \atop \text{before replenishment arrives} = \text{Safety stock} = k\sigma_l. \qquad (4.124)$$

It is obvious that immediately after a replenishment of size Q arrives the inventory level changes:

$$\genfrac{}{}{0pt}{}{\text{Expected on-hand inventory just}}{\text{after replenishment arrives}} = \left(\genfrac{}{}{0pt}{}{\text{Order}}{\text{quantity}}\right) + \left(\genfrac{}{}{0pt}{}{\text{Safety}}{\text{stock}}\right)$$

$$= Q + k\sigma_l. \qquad (4.125)$$

Since the demand rate has a constant mean, inventory varies, on the average, linearly between a maximum of $Q + k\sigma_l$ and a minimum of $k\sigma_l$; therefore:

$$\genfrac{}{}{0pt}{}{\text{Expected annual}}{\text{inventory holding cost}} = \left(\frac{Q}{2} + k\sigma_l\right) rC. \qquad (4.126)$$

The expected annual shortage cost can be computed as follows:

$$\genfrac{}{}{0pt}{}{\text{Expected annual}}{\text{shortage cost}} = c_s \cdot \left(\genfrac{}{}{0pt}{}{\text{Expected number of}}{\genfrac{}{}{0pt}{}{\text{units short per}}{\text{replenishment cycle}}}\right) \cdot \left(\genfrac{}{}{0pt}{}{\text{Expected number of}}{\genfrac{}{}{0pt}{}{\text{replenishment}}{\text{cycles per year}}}\right).$$

$$(4.127)$$

If $\tilde{d}_l$ is the demand over the lead time and d_l is the expected demand over the lead time, the number of units short per replenishment cycle is:

$$\genfrac{}{}{0pt}{}{\text{Shortage}}{\text{per cycle}} = \begin{cases} \tilde{d} - (d_l + k\sigma_l) & \text{if } \tilde{d}_l > (d_l + k\sigma_l) \\ 0 & \text{if } \tilde{d}_l \leqslant (d_l + k\sigma_l). \end{cases} \qquad (4.128)$$

To calculate the expected value of (4.128) one needs the probability density of $\tilde{d}_l$. It is important to mention that, with unbiased forecasts, we see demand $\tilde{d}_l$ distributed around the forecast, according to the same distribution function as the forecast errors over lead time. The spread of $\tilde{d}_l$ is characterized by the standard deviation σ_l.

In the case of fast movers, if the random noise of demand is normally distributed and the successive noise samples have no serial correlation, the cumulative (over the lead time) forecast errors are also normally distributed. More generally, however, Brown [1963, chap. 19] shows by analysis and simulation that for forecasts based upon a linear, discrete, time-invariant system (as is the case with multiple smoothing or general exponential smoothing models) forecast errors are approximately normal for a wide range of distributions of demand data (simulations were run with data sampled from normal, uniform, and triangular distributions). Therefore, the normality of lead time forecast errors is a generally accepted practice with fast movers.

Thus, let $f(\tilde{d}_l)$ be the normal density function for the lead time demand, having mean d_l and standard deviation σ_l. Then,

$$\begin{array}{l} \text{Expected number of} \\ \text{units short per} \\ \text{replenishment cycle} \end{array} = \int_{d_l + k\sigma_l}^{\infty} \left[\tilde{d}_l - (d_l + k\sigma_l) \right] f(\tilde{d}_l) d(\tilde{d}_l).$$

To normalize the distribution we make a change of variable: $u = (\tilde{d}_l - d_l)/\sigma_l$; afterward, we obtain:

$$\begin{array}{l} \text{Expected number of} \\ \text{units short per} \\ \text{replenishment cycle} \end{array} = \sigma_l \int_k^{\infty} (u - k) f(u)\, du \qquad (4.129)$$

where $f(u)$ is the normalized normal density (with zero mean and a standard deviation equal to 1).

The integral above is the partial expectation of the normally distributed u; we call it $G(k)$ and it will be useful in some later developments:

$$G(k) = \int_k^{\infty} (u - k) f(u)\, du, \quad u \sim N(0,1). \qquad (4.130)$$

In concise form:

$$\begin{array}{l} \text{Expected number of} \\ \text{units short per} \\ \text{replenishment cycle} \end{array} = \sigma_l G(k). \qquad (4.131)$$

Since the expected number of replenishment cycles per year is D/Q, the annual cost associated with the stockouts is given by:

$$\text{Expected annual shortage cost} = \sigma_l G(k) \frac{D}{Q} c_s. \qquad (4.132)$$

The total expected annual cost results from the sum of (4.123), (4.126), and (4.132):

$$TC = A\frac{D}{Q} + \left(\frac{Q}{2} + k\sigma_l \right) rC + \sigma_l G(k) \frac{D}{Q} c_s. \qquad (4.133)$$

As TC is convex in k, the necessary and sufficient condition for a minimum is the null value of the first derivative:*

$$\frac{d(TC)}{dk} = r\sigma_l C - c_s \sigma_l \frac{D}{Q} \int_k^{\infty} f(u)\, du = 0.$$

Let $P(k)$ be the complement of the cumulative distribution function:

$$P(k) = \int_k^{\infty} f(u)\, du, \quad u \sim N(0,1). \qquad (4.134)$$

---

*See Sokolnikoff and Redheffer [1958, pp. 261–262] for the derivative of a definite integral.

The optimal value of the safety factor k must be set so as to satisfy:

$$P(k) = \frac{QrC}{Dc_s}.$$ (4.135)

Values of the $P(k)$ function can be found tabulated in any statistics text.

Equation (4.135) makes sense only for $QrC/Dc_s < 1$. If $QrC/Dc_s > 1$ or when k results from (4.135) with some negative value which is considered unacceptable, the safety factor should be set at the smallest allowable value established by management.

When using optimal lot sizing policies faster moving items have Q/D smaller than slower moving items; consequently, under similar costs, faster moving items tend to be allotted larger safety stocks. This result, however, is in no way an endorsement of the still widely used practice by which safety stocks are set as equal time supplies for all items in an inventory. First, it is apparent that k is not linearly related to the demand rate. Second, the safety stock is influenced by the cost structure and the accuracy of the forecasts.

4.4.2.2   Setting safety stocks to achieve prespecified service level

As mentioned earlier, setting safety stocks so as to achieve a prespecified service level skirts the difficult issue of explicitly determining the shortage cost. We treat in this section two measures of service level:

- the expected number of stockout occasions (irrespective of size) per year
- the fraction of demand to be served routinely from stock

We choose these two measures of service because practice shows that in many cases they reflect the managerial way of thinking in terms of what constitutes poor or good service to the customer.

Safety stocks for specified average number of stockout occasions per year. The significance of this measure of service level is probably best described by Brown [1977, p. 176]: "In any manufacturing process it is practical to expedite one order and get it delivered sooner than normal. It is practical to expedite two orders. It is not practical to expedite half the open orders—nothing gets done then."

Thus, to the extent that expediting does not become a way of living, it is normal now and then to have to move a few orders ahead in the schedule; for this, the average number of shortage occurrences has to be kept below a prespecified threshold. The idea is that part of the service is provided by being able to satisfy part of the demand directly from the shelf; this service is further improved by expediting.

Let (SO) be the acceptable average number of shortage occasions per year. Our problem is to find a value for the safety factor k so as to achieve the prespecified value of (SO). The assumptions upon which the model is built are similar to the ones in the previous section 4.4.2.1, except that in the lost sales case the shortages affect the inventory level (to be seen).

With a lead time demand normally distributed around a mean d_l with a standard deviation σ_l, and having a safety stock of $k\sigma_l$, the probability of a stockout at the end of the lead time is given by the $P(k)$ function of (4.134):

$$P(k) = \int_{d_l + k\sigma_l}^{\infty} f(\tilde{d}_l) d(\tilde{d}_l) = \int_k^{\infty} f(u) \, du, \quad u \sim N(0,1).$$

The expected number of replenishments per year is D/Q; consequently:

$$\begin{array}{c} \text{Expected number of} \\ \text{shortage occurrences per year} \end{array} = \frac{D}{Q} P(k) = (SO). \qquad (4.136)$$

The best value of the safety factor k is so as to conform to the following equation:

$$P(k) = \frac{Q}{D}(SO). \qquad (4.137)$$

If a small number of shortages (i.e., high service level) are desired, $P(k)$ should be small and k results large. Thus, decision rule (4.137) provides the safety stock with the intuitive and desirable feature by which good service requires larger safety stocks, while smaller safety stocks are associated with poorer service, all other things being equal.

We should mention that the above developments leading to (4.137) assume that any unfilled demand is backordered and served as soon as the replenishment arrives. If, however, in the case of a shortage customers are not willing to wait, unfilled demand is lost. By (4.131) an amount of $\sigma_l G(k)$ units result, on the average, in lost sales per cycle. The consequence is the following: if, in the backorders case, where eventually all demand is served, a demand of Q units is recorded on the average during a replenishment cycle, in the lost sales case $Q + \sigma_l G(k)$ units are demanded on the average in a cycle, of which Q are served and the others lost. Therefore, a system with lost sales with larger inventories and fewer cycles, namely:

$$\begin{array}{c} \text{Expected annual number of} \\ \text{replenishment cycles in} \\ \text{the lost sales case} \end{array} = \frac{D}{Q + \sigma_l G(k)}. \qquad (4.138)$$

The decision rule (4.137) can be modified accordingly. The resulting equation, however, is by no means trivial to solve.

Safety stocks for specified fraction of demand to be served directly from stock. Here, management considers the service level to be satisfactory if a given percentage, $\mathscr{F}$, of the annual demand is served directly from stock; the remaining fraction $(1-\mathscr{F})$ that cannot be satisfied directly from shelf is either backordered or expedited to be moved faster through the replenishment process.

The same assumptions as those in the previous section stay valid here too.

With a lead time demand which is normally distributed (mean d_l, and standard deviation σ_l) and a safety stock $k\sigma_l$, the expected quantity short per order cycle is $\sigma_l G(k)$ [see equation (4.131)]. During the year an average of D/Q orders are placed and, therefore, the expected amount to be backordered annually is

$$\text{Expected number of units short per year} = \sigma_l G(k)\frac{D}{Q}. \tag{4.139}$$

According to the definition of the customer service level, it is still satisfactory if $(1-\mathscr{F})D$ cannot be served promptly from stock. Equating this with (4.139), one obtains the condition to be satisfied by the safety factor k we are seeking:

$$G(k) = \frac{Q}{\sigma_l}(1-\mathscr{F}). \tag{4.140}$$

Selected values of the partial expectation function are shown in Table 4.7; they should be sufficient for any practical work in inventory systems. More values may be found in Peterson and Silver [1979, pp. 779–786].

TABLE 4.7   Values of Partial Expectation Function $G(k)$ for Normal Distribution

k	$G(k)$	k	$G(k)$
0.0	0.3989	1.8	0.01428
0.1	0.3509	1.9	0.01105
0.2	0.3069	2.0	0.008491
0.3	0.2668	2.1	0.006468
0.4	0.2304	2.2	0.004887
0.5	0.1978	2.3	0.003662
0.6	0.1687	2.4	0.002720
0.7	0.1429	2.5	0.002004
0.8	0.1202	2.6	0.001464
0.9	0.1004	2.7	0.001060
1.0	0.08332	2.8	0.000761
1.1	0.06862	2.9	0.000542
1.2	0.05610	3.0	0.000382
1.3	0.04553	3.1	0.000267
1.4	0.03667	3.2	0.000185
1.5	0.02931	3.3	0.000127
1.6	0.02324	3.4	0.000087
1.7	0.01829	3.5	0.000058

From (4.140) it is clear that, for a specified service level, safety stocks depend on both the order quantity and the accuracy of the forecasts.

Thus, the larger the value of Q, the larger the value of $G(k)$, and therefore the smaller the safety factor needed for a given customer service. This is so because when the order quantity is large there are fewer shipments per year; hence, there are fewer opportunities to backorder.

Similarly, the smaller the standard deviation σ_l of the forecast errors, the larger $G(k)$ and the smaller the safety factor. Thus, with an accurate forecasting system, the standard deviation is low and, at the same time, one needs fewer standard deviations as safety stock—a double saving in safety stock investment.

Let us note that, according to this decision rule, faster moving items need higher safety stocks than do slower moving items. Indeed, under optimal lot sizing, the ratio D/Q tends to increase the higher the usage of the item (Q grows slower than D does); at the same time, the variance law (see section 4.3.3.1) tells us that the standard deviation of the forecast errors tends to increase with the usage D. Consequently, for a specified $\mathcal{F}$, faster moving items command a lower value for $G(k)$ and, therefore, a larger safety factor k.

Decision rule (4.140) has been worked out for the backordering situation. In the lost sales case the expected number of cycles per year is not D/Q, but $D/[Q + \sigma_l G(k)]$, as shown in (4.138).

Then,

$$\begin{matrix} \text{Expected number of} \\ \text{units short per year} \end{matrix} = \sigma_l G(k) \frac{D}{Q + \sigma_l G(k)} = \sigma_l G(k) \frac{D}{Q} \cdot \frac{Q}{Q + \sigma_l G(k)}.$$

The ratio $Q/[Q + \sigma_l G(k)]$ is precisely the fraction $\mathcal{F}$ of demand satisfied promptly from stock. Hence:

$$\begin{matrix} \text{Expected number of} \\ \text{units short per year} \end{matrix} = \sigma_l G(k) \frac{D}{Q} \mathcal{F}. \tag{4.141}$$

By definition of the service level, (4.141) has to be equated with $(1 - \mathcal{F})D$; then, the safety factor k has to satisfy the following condition:

$$G(k) = \frac{Q}{\sigma_l} \frac{1 - \mathcal{F}}{\mathcal{F}}. \tag{4.142}$$

Since, normally, fraction $\mathcal{F}$ is close to 1, from comparing (4.140) and (4.142) it is evident that the safety factor is affected in no significant way by whether unfilled demand can be backordered or lost.

The value of the service level $\mathcal{F}$ differs with the category of items for which inventory control has to be implemented:

- A items should be handled with relatively low service level (a value of $\mathcal{F} = 0.8$ seems reasonable). This results in lower safety stocks and, therefore, in smaller inventory investments for these relatively expensive items. However, this apparent lack of service is overcome by tight control procedures and efficient expediting throughout the manufacturing and procurement process that will, in practice, increase the aimed service level to a high performance without having to pay the penalty of expensive safety stocks. It is in the control of these items where most of management judgment, attention, and intervention is concentrated, using automatic inventory rules to provide only a sound guideline for these management decisions.

- B items should be handled fairly routinely, with service levels on the order of $\mathcal{F} = 0.95$. The inventory control system has to provide sound replenishment decisions, and normally there should be no need for extensive expediting, management intervention, or tight external control.
- C items should be present in ample supply and handled with a minimum of records, controls, and procedures. Normally, their replenishment decisions should be completely mechanized, being assigned a very high service level (between 0.95 and 0.98).

A number of alternative measures of service level can be found: their use is determined by the way in which managers identify best parallel targets for customer service. Some of these measures are presented below, accompanied by brief qualifications; for all of them, the control is the safety factor k which yields the safety stock in the form of $k\sigma_l$.

The expected number of units short per replenishment cycle is given by $\sigma_l G_k$ [see equation (4.131)] and, in Brown's [1977, p. 176] opinion, is a primary measure of service (as is also the expected number of stockout occasions per year) in that it serves in deriving other measures like the fraction of demand to be served routinely from stock.

The probability of stockout during a replenishment cycle can be computed as $P(k)$, the complement of the cumulative distribution function of lead time demand [equation (4.134)]. This and the previous measure of service focus management's attention on every individual cycle, thus avoiding the pitfalls of service levels calculated as averages. For instance, while the annual average service, expressed as a fraction of demand to be satisfied directly from stock, might look really good, the corresponding value k of the safety factor could still yield, on a cycle-by-cycle basis, an unacceptably large chance $P(k)$ of shortage occurrence.

At the same time, however, the cycle oriented service measures tend to lose sight of the general picture. Thus, if one item is replenished ten times annually and another item only once, and if k is set so as to produce for both items a probability of 0.10 of stockout per cycle, then we expect the first item to run out of stock once a year [see equation (4.136)] but the second item only once every 10 years. Although the safety factor is the same for both items, it is questionable whether the customer service is the same.

For these reasons, it is advantageous to assess service performance simultaneously with measures of different emphasis: replenishment cycle oriented and annual average oriented.

The probability that n_0 cycles develop shortages during a year ($n_0 = 1, 2, \ldots, D/Q$) can be easily computed by defining the occurrence of a stockout situation in a replenishment cycle as a Bernoulli trial having a probability of success (i.e., occurrence) of $P(k)$ [see equation (4.134)] and a probability of failure $[1 - P(k)]$. A binomial process with a total number of D/Q trials takes place; n_0 stockout situations occur during a year with a probability of

$$\frac{\left(\dfrac{D}{Q}\right)!}{\left(\dfrac{D}{Q} - n_0\right)!n_0!} P(k)^{n_0}[1 - P(k)]^{D/Q - n_0}.$$

The mean of this distribution is a measure of service discussed earlier: the expected number of shortage occurrences per year $D/QP(k)$. If one wants to know *the chance of at least one cycle having shortages during one year* the answer is given by computing $1 - [1 - P(k)]^{D/Q}$.

The fraction of time the system has on-hand positive stock is often called the ready rate of the system. As shown earlier, in the backorders case, the average demand over a replenishment cycle is Q, and in the lost sales case it is $Q + \sigma_l G(k)$. In both instances, the expected number of units short per cycle is $\sigma_l G(k)$. Since we assumed that the average demand rate is constant, the ratio of time short in a cycle to the total duration of the replenishment cycle (i.e., the fraction of time the system is out of stock) is the same as the ratio of the expected amount short to the average demand over the cycle:

$$\text{Fraction of time system is out of stock} = \begin{cases} \dfrac{\sigma_l G(k)}{Q}, & \text{backorders case} \\[3mm] \dfrac{\sigma_l G(k)}{Q + \sigma_l G(k)}, & \text{lost sales case.} \end{cases} \tag{4.143}$$

Since the lost sales case produces higher inventories, the fraction of time out of stock results are smaller than in the backorders case.

The ready rate is then computed as $1 - $ (fraction of time out of stock):

$$\text{Fraction of time system has on-hand positive stock} = \begin{cases} \dfrac{Q - \sigma_l G(k)}{Q}, & \text{backorders case} \\[3mm] \dfrac{Q}{Q + \sigma_l G(k)}, & \text{lost sales case.} \end{cases} \tag{4.144}$$

Notice that under the assumption of unit-sized demand transactions, which has been imbedded in the calculation of the expected amount short per cycle, it is apparent from (4.144) that the ready rate is equivalent to the fraction $\mathcal{F}$ of demand served directly from stock. With non-unit-sized demands there is the possibility of overshooting the order point, which leaves the two measures of service only approximately equivalent.

4.4.2.3   Allocation of safety stocks under aggregate constraints

In the previous two sections, safety stock decisions have been analyzed by considering every inventory item in isolation. It is very often the case, however, that some aggregate constraints apply such as a limited budget for inventory investment, limited warehousing space, and so on, in which case items interact by competing for the scarce resource.

A large variety of decision rules can be developed by optimizing various objective functions within the bounds imposed by the aggregate constraints (Gerson and Brown [1970]).

Suppose, then, that we have an inventory of n items, a limited budget for annual inventory investment I; we want to allocate this budget among the n items so as to minimize the total expected number of units short per year; subscript $_i$ denotes the ith item.

Assume that the average demand rate is constant (although demand is probabilistic), the lead time is time-invariant and known with certainty, and an order of size Q_i (which is determined independently and prior to establishing the safety stocks) is released as soon as the available inventory of the ith item reaches the corresponding order point. One unit of item i costs c_i dollars. Unfilled demand is backordered.

By use of relations (4.126) and (4.139), the formal representation of the problem is:

Minimize
$$Z = \sum_{i=1}^{n} \sigma_{li} G(k_i) \frac{D_i}{Q_i}$$

subject to:

$$\sum_{i=1}^{n} \left(\frac{Q_i}{2} + k_i \sigma_{li} \right) C_i \leq I.$$

Two observations are in order here:

- Given the nature of the problem, the solution will always have the constraint held at equality.
- As Q_i are predetermined constants, the constraint can be simplified by expressing it only in terms of the required investment in safety stocks I_s.

Hence, the problem we have to solve is:

Minimize
$$Z = \sum_{i=1}^{n} \sigma_{li} G(k_i) \frac{D_i}{Q_i} \qquad (4.145)$$

subject to:

$$\sum_{i=1}^{n} k_i \sigma_{li} C_i = I_s. \qquad (4.146)$$

The objective function is convex, which can be shown by looking at the Hessian of Z. As the objective function is separable in the k_i's, the Hessian $\mathcal{H}$

is an $n \times n$ diagonal matrix with all positive elements on its main diagonal of the form:* $a_{ii} = \sigma_{li}(D_i/Q_i)f(k_i)$, $i = 1, \ldots, n$, where $f(k_i)$ is the normal density function (with zero mean, and a standard deviation of 1) evaluated at k_i. For all nonzero vectors x, the Hessian satisfies $x^T \mathcal{H} x > 0$, hence it is positive definite, Z is convex (Luenberger [1973, p. 118]), and the Lagrangian multiplier technique can be applied.

The Lagrangian is:

$$L = \sum_{c=1}^{n} \sigma_{li} G(k_i) \frac{D_i}{Q_i} + \lambda \left(\sum_{i=1}^{n} k_i \sigma_{li} C_i - I_s \right), \qquad (4.147)$$

where λ is the nonnegative Lagrange multiplier.

To find the minimum of Z, subject to the constraint on investment, set $\partial L / \partial k_i = 0$, which yields:

$$P(k_i) \cdot \frac{D_i}{Q_i} \cdot \frac{1}{C_i} = \lambda, \qquad i = 1, \ldots, n, \qquad (4.148)$$

where $P(k_i)$ is given by (4.134).

Gerson and Brown [1970] solve a similar problem in which the expected value of the total annual shortages $\sum_{i=1}^{n} \sigma_{li} G(k_i)(D_i/Q_i)C_i$ is minimized subject to (4.146). The optimal solution satisfies:

$$P(k_i) \frac{D_i}{Q_i} = \lambda, \qquad i = 1, \ldots, n, \qquad (4.149)$$

which means that safety factors k_i should be chosen so as to produce the same expected number, λ, of shortage occurrences per year for each item.

By varying λ in (4.148) or (4.149), one obtains different values of the required inventory investment; the solution is that λ which leads to equality in (4.146).

As mentioned earlier, other objectives can be optimized, subject to aggregate constraints, such as the expected number of shortage occurrences per year $\sum_{i=1}^{n} (D_i/Q_i)P(k_i)$. For models minimizing the total of ordering, inventory carrying, and stockout costs under aggregate inventory constraint, see Holt et al. [1960, chap. 12].

4.4.2.4   Simultaneous determination of safety stocks and order quantities

In this section we relax the assumption of predetermined order quantities; our concern is to determine lot sizes and safety stocks jointly. Decision rules

---

*

$$\frac{\partial Z}{\partial k_i} = -\sigma_{li} \frac{D_i}{Q_i} \int_{k_i}^{\infty} f(u) \, du \cdot \frac{\partial^2 Z}{\partial k_i^2} = \sigma_{li} \frac{D_i}{Q_i} f(k_i).$$

are derived for both the case of the individual product and the case of optimization under aggregate constraints.

Order quantity and safety stock for a single product. To illustrate, consider the total cost function of section 4.4.2.1; the optimal Q and k are sought so as to minimize the sum of ordering, inventory holding, and stockout costs:

Minimize $$TC = A\frac{D}{Q} + \left(\frac{Q}{2} + k\sigma_l\right)rC + \sigma_l G(k)\frac{D}{Q}c_s. \qquad (4.150)$$

The first-order conditions for a minimum are given by $\partial(TC)/\partial Q = 0$ and $\partial(TC)/\partial k = 0$. It is interesting, however, to find out more about the shape of TC; if it is convex, it has a minimum which is a global minimum.

The Hessian of TC is:

$$\mathcal{H} = \begin{vmatrix} \dfrac{\partial^2(TC)}{\partial Q^2} & \dfrac{\partial^2(TC)}{\partial Q\,\partial k} \\[2mm] \dfrac{\partial^2(TC)}{\partial k\,\partial Q} & \dfrac{\partial^2(TC)}{\partial k^2} \end{vmatrix} = \begin{vmatrix} \dfrac{2AD}{Q^3} + \dfrac{2\sigma_l c_s DG(k)}{Q^3} & \dfrac{\sigma_l c_s DP(k)}{Q^2} \\[2mm] \dfrac{\sigma_l c_s DP(k)}{Q^2} & \dfrac{\sigma_l c_s Df(k)}{Q} \end{vmatrix}$$

$\mathcal{H}$ is a symmetric matrix of the form $\begin{pmatrix} a & b \\ b & c \end{pmatrix}$; the necessary and sufficient conditions for such a matrix to be positive definite are: $a > 0$ and $\det\mathcal{H} = ac - b^2 > 0$. In our case clearly $a > 0$. Then:

$$\det\mathcal{H} = \frac{1}{Q^4}\left[2A\sigma_l c_s D^2 f(k) + 2\sigma_l^2 c_s^2 D^2 G(k)f(k) - \sigma_l^2 c_s^2 D^2 P^2(k)\right]$$

Q^4 is always positive. With respect to k we notice that:

$$\lim_{k \to \infty} (\det\mathcal{H}) = 0$$

Also:

$$\frac{\partial(\det\mathcal{H})}{\partial k} = \frac{1}{Q^4}\left[2A\sigma_l c_s D^2 f'(k) + 2\sigma_l^2 C_s^2 D^2 G(k)f'(k)\right], \quad (4.151)$$

where $f'(k)$ is short for $df(k)/dk$.

Evidently, if $f'(k) < 0$, then (4.151) is negative. This means that, with increasing k, the determinant of the Hessian tends to decrease monotonely to zero. Hence, $\det\mathcal{H}$ is positive.

We conclude that, for $f'(k) < 0$, the Hessian of TC is positive definite, so TC is convex. The restriction $f'(k) < 0$ is satisfied for $k > 0$; thus, we would only accept positive safety stocks.

The first-order conditions are:

$$\begin{cases} \dfrac{\partial(TC)}{\partial Q} = \dfrac{rC}{2} - \dfrac{AD + \sigma_l c_s DG(k)}{Q^2} = 0 \\[4mm] \dfrac{\partial(TC)}{\partial k} = r\sigma_l C - \dfrac{\sigma_l c_s DP(k)}{Q} = 0. \end{cases} \qquad (4.152)$$

Solve to get:

$$Q = \sqrt{\frac{2[AD + \sigma_l c_s DG(k)]}{rC}} \qquad (4.153)$$

$$P(k) = \frac{QrC}{c_s D}. \qquad (4.154)$$

If there is no uncertainty involved (i.e., $\sigma_l = 0$), the optimal order quantity becomes the classical Wilson's formula (4.1). Otherwise, the presence of uncertainty requires a larger Q in order to diminish the number of replenishment cycles per year and thus reduce the exposure to the risk of running out of stock.

Combining (4.153) and (4.154) yields:

$$\sqrt{2rC[AD + \sigma_l c_s DG(k)]} - c_s DP(k) = 0, \qquad (4.155)$$

which can be solved by search technique or by table lookup and trial and error. Once k is known, (4.153) produces the optimal Q. One can also find a solution by an iterative scheme that moves between equations (4.153) and (4.154) (see, for instance, Hadley and Whitin [1963, chap. 4-4]).

Order quantities and safety stocks under aggregate constraints. Here we reconsider the problem of section 4.4.2.3: find, for the n items in the system, the best order quantities Q_i and safety factors k_i, $i = 1, \ldots, n$, so as to minimize the total expected number of units short per year, subject to a total inventory budget I.

Minimize
$$Z = \sum_{i=1}^{n} \sigma_{li} G(k_i) \frac{D_i}{Q_i} \qquad (4.156)$$

subject to:

$$\sum_{i=1}^{n} \left(\frac{Q_i}{2} + k_i \sigma_{li} \right) C_i = I. \qquad (4.157)$$

In order to apply the Lagrange multiplier method, we have to make sure that the Hessian of Z is positive definite (the Hessian of the constraint is a zero matrix, so it cannot affect the second-order conditions for optimality (Luenberger [1973, p. 226]).

Z is a function of $2n$ variables; it separates in n functions, each related to one item only:

$$Z(k_1, Q_1; k_2, Q_2; \ldots; k_n, Q_n) = \sum_{i=1}^{n} z_i(k_i, Q_i).$$

The Hessian $\mathcal{H}$ of Z displays a succession of n symmetric two-by-two matrices on its main diagonal; the ith two-by-two matrix is the Hessian $\mathcal{h}_i$ of z_i;

all other elements in $\mathcal{H}$ are zero.

$$\mathcal{H} = \begin{pmatrix} \dfrac{\partial^2 Z}{\partial k_1^2} & \dfrac{\partial^2 Z}{\partial k_1 \partial Q_1} & 0 & 0 & \cdots \\[2ex] \dfrac{\partial^2 Z}{\partial k_1 \partial Q_1} & \dfrac{\partial^2 Z}{\partial Q_1^2} & 0 & 0 & \cdots \\[2ex] 0 & 0 & \dfrac{\partial^2 Z}{\partial k_2^2} & \dfrac{\partial^2 Z}{\partial k_2 \partial Q_2} & \cdots \\[2ex] 0 & 0 & \dfrac{\partial^2 Z}{\partial k_2 \partial Q_2} & \dfrac{\partial^2 Z}{\partial Q_2^2} & \cdots \\[2ex] \vdots & \vdots & \vdots & \vdots & \vdots \end{pmatrix}$$

$$= \begin{pmatrix} \hbar_1 & 0 & \cdots & 0 \\ 0 & \hbar_2 & \cdots & 0 \\ & & \ddots & \\ 0 & 0 & \cdots & \hbar_n \end{pmatrix}.$$

We want to show that for all nonzero vectors X it is true that $X^T \mathcal{H} X > 0$. Vector X has $2n$ elements and we regard it as being made of n vectors with 2 elements each:

$$X = \begin{pmatrix} x_1 \\ x_2 \\ \vdots \\ x_n \end{pmatrix}.$$

Therefore:

$$X^T \mathcal{H} X = x_1^T \hbar_1 x_1 + x_2^T \hbar_2 x_2 + \cdots + x_n^T \hbar_n x_n. \qquad (4.158)$$

We have:

$$\hbar_i = \begin{pmatrix} \dfrac{\sigma_{li} D_i f(k_i)}{Q_i} & \dfrac{\sigma_{li} D_i P(k_i)}{Q_i^2} \\[2ex] \dfrac{\sigma_{li} D_i P(k_i)}{Q_i^2} & \dfrac{2\sigma_{li} D_i G(k_i)}{Q_i^3} \end{pmatrix}.$$

Since the upper left element is positive, $\hbar_i$ is positive definite if its determinant is positive.

$$\det \hbar_i = \dfrac{\sigma_{li}^2 D_i^2}{Q_i^4} \left[2f(k_i) G(k_i) - P^2(k_i) \right]$$

$$\lim_{k_i \to \infty} (\det \hbar_i) = 0 \qquad (4.159)$$

$$\dfrac{\partial (\det \hbar_i)}{\partial k_i} = \dfrac{2\sigma_{li}^2 D_i}{Q_i^4} f'(k_i) G(k_i). \qquad (4.160)$$

Under the restriction of using only positive safety factors, we have $f'(k_i) < 0$, the derivative (4.160) is negative and, by (4.159), det $\hbar_i > 0$. Hence, $\hbar_i$ is positive definite, making $x_i^T \hbar_i x_i > 0$.

From (4.158) it immediately follows that $\mathcal{H}$ is positive definite.

Form the Lagrangian function L using a nonnegative multiplier λ and apply the first-order conditions for optimality: $\partial L / \partial Q_i = 0$, $\partial L / \partial k_i = 0$, and they yield:

$$Q_i = \sqrt{\frac{2\sigma_{li} D_i G(k_i)}{\lambda C_i}} \tag{4.161}$$

$$Q_i = \frac{D_i P(k_i)}{\lambda C_i}. \tag{4.162}$$

Together, (4.161) and (4.162) lead to an equation whose solution is the optimal k_i for a given λ:

$$P(k_i) = \sqrt{\frac{2\lambda\sigma_{li} C_i G(k_i)}{D_i}}. \tag{4.163}$$

The Q_i corresponding to the given λ and k_i can be calculated from either (4.161) or (4.162).

A search over the values of λ has to be performed in view of the inventory constraint (4.157).

Developments of decision rules for other objective functions are conducted by Holt et al. [1960, chap. 13], Gerson and Brown [1970].

It is apparent that consideration of the joint determination of lot sizes and safety stocks brings considerable computational complexity into the system and, therefore, might be warranted only for the most expensive or important of the class A items. For the case of the single product for which Q and k are derived by minimizing the total cost of equation (4.150), Peterson and Silver [1979, p. 367] find that the cost penalty for computing Q and k independently rather than jointly is larger when ratio Q/σ_l is small. They show that low values of Q/σ_l are more likely with class A items than with B or C items and, consequently, they recommend that use of the more sophisticated approach of joint determination be limited to some A items.

4.4.3 Safety Stocks for Slow-Moving Items

The philosophy behind setting safety stocks for slow movers is the same as in the case of fast-moving items: when placing an order, sufficient stock should be available (on hand plus already on order) to meet the maximum reasonable demand over the lead time.

If the forecast model in use fits a theoretical distribution to data (e.g., the normal, Poisson, Laplace, or gamma distribution) by estimation of the appropriate parameters, then the safety stock is made equal to some multiple k

of the standard deviation σ_l of the forecast errors over the lead time, and the order point follows from (4.121). Another approach is to work with and determine directly the order point s. Evidently, in view of the definition (4.121) of the order point, the two approaches are equivalent.

If, alternatively, the empirical cumulative probability distribution of lead time demand is determined (section 4.3.4.4), the order point is read directly off the cumulative curve.

A few examples and comments are provided below to illustrate the two approaches.

4.4.3.1 *Safety stocks based on theoretical distributions*

This approach is essentially the same procedure used to determine order points for fast-moving items, except that the expected lead time demand and σ_l would be estimated by procedures specific to slow movers. As mentioned in section 4.3.4.3, use of complicated probability distributions should be limited to expensive or very important items, where the increased system cost is balanced by the possible substantial reduction in inventory investment or by the improved service brought about by the more accurate estimates. For cheap and unimportant items, the normality of forecast errors may still be considered as a reasonable approximation; therefore, the safety factor k should be selected from the same tables for fast-moving items, which could constitute an important practical advantage for the implementation stage.

To substantiate the statements made above, consider the case where the system incurs a charge c_s for every unit short, and lead time demand is generated by a Poisson process.

The following assumptions hold:

- Although demand rate is uncertain, its average of D units/year is a constant.
- Demand is discrete and units are demanded one at a time.
- An order of size Q is released exactly when available inventory hits the order point.*
- Order point s and replenishment quantity Q are discrete.
- Lead time is a constant l.
- Any unfilled demand is backordered.

The ordering cost is A dollars/order, the cost of the item is C dollars/unit, and the inventory carrying charge is r dollars/dollar·year.

---

*Given the discreteness of demand, if transaction sizes are random, overshoots of the order point may occur, and the order point–order quantity system might no longer be appropriate. Indeed, if an unusually large overshoot takes place, the regular replenishment lot of size Q might not even bring the inventory level back to the order point. Systems that can cope with this sort of situation are discussed in later sections.

We determine the optimal order size Q and order point s so as to minimize the total of the average annual costs (ordering, holding, and backorders costs).

The basic proofs are derived by Hadley and Whitin [1963, chap. 4-7], and we extract here only the results relevant to our problem.

The expected annual ordering cost is $A(D/Q)$.

Lead time demand is Poisson with mean (and variance) equal to Dl. Let the mean lead time demand be denoted by $d_l = Dl$, and let $\tilde{d}_l$ be the probabilistic demand over the lead time. The, $p(\tilde{d}_l; d_l)$ is the Poisson probability that $\tilde{d}_l$ units are demanded during a lead time of l periods, given that the process generates on the average d_l units per lead time.

Now, we are interested in the expected on-hand inventory $\bar{I}$ that costs us $rC\bar{I}$ to hold. By definition:

$$\begin{pmatrix} \text{Available} \\ \text{inventory} \end{pmatrix} = \begin{pmatrix} \text{On-hand} \\ \text{inventory} \end{pmatrix} + \begin{pmatrix} \text{Amount} \\ \text{on order} \end{pmatrix} - \begin{pmatrix} \text{Amount} \\ \text{on backorder} \end{pmatrix}.$$

Then:

$$\bar{I} = \begin{pmatrix} \text{Expected available} \\ \text{inventory} \end{pmatrix} - \begin{pmatrix} \text{Expected amount} \\ \text{on order} \end{pmatrix} + \begin{pmatrix} \text{Expected number} \\ \text{of backorders} \\ \text{at any time} \end{pmatrix}.$$

We have:

$$\frac{\text{Expected available}}{\text{inventory}} = \frac{Q+1}{2} + s$$

$$\frac{\text{Expected amount}}{\text{on order}} = d_l = Dl$$

$$\begin{matrix} \text{Expected number} \\ \text{of backorders} \\ \text{at any time} \end{matrix} = \frac{1}{Q}[b(s) - b(s+Q)]$$

where function $b(v)$ is defined by:

$$b(v) = \frac{(Dl)^2}{2}P(v-1; d_l) - (Dl)vP(v; d_l) + \frac{v(v+1)}{2}P(v+1; d_l).$$

$$(4.164)$$

In (4.164) function $P(u; d_l)$ is the complement of the Poisson cumulative distribution function, that is:

$$P(u; d_l) = \sum_{\tilde{d}_l = u}^{\infty} p(\tilde{d}_l; d_l).$$

$$(4.165)$$

The expected on-hand inventory is:

$$\bar{I} = \frac{Q+1}{2} + s - Dl + \frac{1}{Q}[b(s) - b(s+Q)].$$

$$(4.166)$$

The last cost component is the backorders cost.

$$\text{Expected number of units backordered per year} = \frac{D}{Q}[a(s) - a(s+Q)] \qquad (4.167)$$

where function $a(v)$ is:

$$a(v) = DlP(v; Dl) - vP(v+1; Dl).$$

The total expected annual cost function TC is constructed from (4.166), (4.167), and the ordering cost:

$$TC = A\frac{D}{Q} + rc\left\{\frac{Q+1}{2} + s - Dl + \frac{1}{Q}[b(s) - b(s+Q)]\right\}$$
$$+ c_s\frac{D}{Q}[a(s) - a(s+Q)]. \qquad (4.168)$$

When it is rather costly to incur backorders, the minimization of TC acts so as to make shortages improbable. Then the terms $a(s+Q)$ and $b(s+Q)$ become negligibly small and can be removed from the cost function, thus simplifying TC substantially.

Minimizing (4.168) requires a computer and use of a search technique; minimizing the simplified version, with $a(s+Q)$ and $b(s+Q)$ neglected, requires somewhat less computational effort (Hadley and Whitin [1963, chap. 4-8]), but it still takes a number of back-and-forth iterations between successive values of Q and s.

The complicated way in which total costs depend on Q and s, aggravated by the discreteness of the variables (which precludes use of derivatives in optimization) explains the reserve management scientists show in recommending the Poisson distribution for practical work. It is not uncommon to find inventory control systems in which for all items lead time demand is assumed to vary normally; the differentiation among items, such as ABC classification and fast-moving versus slow-moving classification, is made when deciding upon the appropriate forecasting technique, the level of service, and the amount of managerial attention to be assigned to various groups of items.

It was mentioned earlier [relation (4.110)] that lead time demand can be considered Poisson distributed if the standard deviation of lead time demand is within 10% of $\sqrt{\text{Lead time demand forecast}}$. Otherwise, Peterson and Silver [1979, chap. 9] recommend the use of the Laplace distribution.

The Laplace distribution, also called the bilateral exponential, is composed of two symmetric back-to-back exponential functions. Let the Laplace variable be the probabilistic lead time demand $\tilde{d}_l$; the distribution is characterized by the mean value d_l and the standard deviation σ_l:

$$f(\tilde{d}_l) = \frac{1}{\sqrt{2}\,\sigma_l}e^{-\sqrt{2}/\sigma_l|\tilde{d}_l - d_l|}. \qquad (4.169)$$

An illustration of Laplace density function is provided in Figure 4.19.

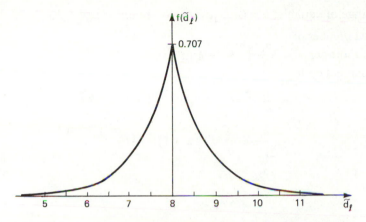

FIGURE 4.19 Laplace density function with mean $d_l = 8$ units and $\sigma_l = 1$ unit.

Let us reconsider now the problem of section 4.4.2.1, where the stockout cost is proportional to the number of units short. The following assumptions hold:

- Lead time demand is Laplace distributed.
- The average demand rate is a constant, D units/year.
- Order of size Q is released precisely when the available inventory reaches the order point.
- Lead time is a constant l.
- Unfilled demand is backordered; for each unit backordered, a charge c_s is incurred.
- Average shortages are considered negligibly small when compared with the average inventory.

Consider that both the safety factor k and the lot size Q are unknown. We restrict our attention only to nonnegative values for k.

Similarly to equation (4.133), we can write the expression of the total expected annual cost:

$$TC = A\frac{D}{Q} + \left(\frac{Q}{2} + k\sigma_l\right)rC + c_s\frac{D}{Q}\left(\begin{array}{c}\text{Expected number of}\\ \text{units short per}\\ \text{replenishment cycle}\end{array}\right)$$

$$\begin{array}{c}\text{Expected number of}\\ \text{units short per}\\ \text{replenishment cycle}\end{array} = \int_{d_l + k\sigma_l}^{\infty}\left[\tilde{d}_l - (d_l + k\sigma_l)\right]f(\tilde{d}_l)\,d(\tilde{d}_l).$$

Make a change of variable: $u = (\tilde{d}_l - d_l)/\sigma_l$ to obtain:

Expected number of
units short per $= \dfrac{\sigma_l}{\sqrt{2}} \displaystyle\int_k^\infty (u - k) e^{-\sqrt{2}u}\, du$
replenishment cycle

$$= \dfrac{\sigma_l}{\sqrt{2}} \int_k^\infty u e^{-\sqrt{2}u}\, du - \dfrac{\sigma_l}{\sqrt{2}} k \int_k^\infty e^{-\sqrt{2}u}\, du$$

$$= \dfrac{\sigma_l}{2\sqrt{2}} e^{-\sqrt{2}k}(\sqrt{2}\,k + 1) - \dfrac{\sigma_l}{2} k e^{-\sqrt{2}k}$$

$$= \dfrac{\sigma_l}{2\sqrt{2}} e^{-\sqrt{2}k}.$$

Hence:

$$TC = A\frac{D}{Q} + \left(\frac{Q}{2} + k\sigma_l\right) rC + c_s \frac{D}{Q} \cdot \frac{\sigma_l}{2\sqrt{2}} e^{-\sqrt{2}k}. \qquad (4.170)$$

It is easy to show that TC is convex (its Hessian is positive definite) under our restriction that $k \geqslant 0$. Setting $\partial(TC)/\partial Q = 0$ and $\partial(TC)/\partial k = 0$ yields:

$$Q = \sqrt{\dfrac{2\left(AD + \sigma_l c_s D \dfrac{e^{-\sqrt{2}k}}{2\sqrt{2}}\right)}{rC}} \qquad (4.171)$$

$$k = \frac{1}{\sqrt{2}} \ln \frac{c_s D}{2QrC}. \qquad (4.172)$$

Again, as seen in earlier developments, the optimal lot size tends to be larger than that given by Wilson's formula (4.1), thus reducing the exposure to the risk of running out of stock over the year.

As is often the case, Q can be determined independently of k without incurring too severe a penalty for missing the mathematical optimum. Then, we are left with finding the best safety factor k from (4.172).

Following the general lines of reasoning used so far, a large variety of results* can be further developed for slow-moving items under various service level considerations (see measures of service in section 4.4.2.2) for either joint or sequential determination of the order quantity and the safety stock. However, as already mentioned, the choice among models for practical applications has to strike a balance between the need for accurately capturing the observed item's characteristics, the system cost brought about by the model complexity, and the managerial considerations regarding service to customers.

*Hadley and Whitin [1963, chap. 4] and Peterson and Silver [1979, chaps. 7, 9, and 11].

4.4.3.2 Safety stocks based on empirical distributions

Suppose that, based on the item's history, we have empirically determined the cumulative probability distribution of lead time demand $\tilde{d}_l$.

The order point s is determined by reading it right off the probability curve (Figure 4.20) so as to satisfy certain service requirements:

$$\text{Prob}\left(\tilde{d}_l \leqslant s\right) = \text{SERVICE} \tag{4.173}$$

or

$$\text{Prob}\left(\tilde{d}_l > s\right) = 1 - \text{SERVICE}. \tag{4.174}$$

The value to be assigned to what we symbolically call SERVICE should result from managerial considerations. Technically, any method that was presented in section 4.4.2 for setting safety stocks can be used, as long as it yields a control parameter in the form of either a cumulative probability value or the complement of the cumulative probability.

To illustrate, consider that the cost of backordering is proportional to the number of units short (section 4.4.2.1). Then, assuming Q and the order point s to be continuous variables, we write the total expected annual cost by similarity to expression (4.133):

$$TC = A\frac{D}{Q} + \left(\frac{Q}{2} + s - d_l\right)rC + c_s\frac{D}{Q}\int_s^\infty \left(\tilde{d}_l - s\right)f\left(\tilde{d}_l\right)d\left(\tilde{d}_l\right).$$

Density $f(\tilde{d}_l)$ is analytically unknown but this affects us in no way.

For a predetermined Q set $d(TC)/ds = 0$ to get the best s; the first order condition yields:

$$\int_s^\infty f\left(\tilde{d}_l\right)d\left(\tilde{d}_l\right) = \frac{QrC}{Dc_s}. \tag{4.175}$$

FIGURE 4.20
Empirical probability distribution curve of demand over lead time.

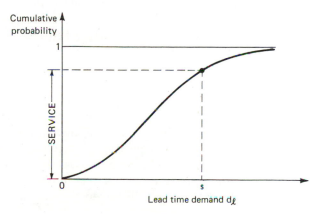

Then, set $1 - \text{SERVICE}$ equal to the calculated value of (4.175) and read the optimal s off the cumulative probability curve.

For other measures of the service level like a specified average number of stockout occasions per year, the probability of stockout during a replenishment, and so on, the value of SERVICE can be derived similarly. However, we would not use measures like the expected number of units short per replenishment cycle, or a specified fraction of demand to be served directly from stock, because we cannot reliably determine empirical partial expectations.

If we have to work with integer numbers for the order point, then s becomes the smallest integer such that $\text{Prob}\,(\tilde{d}_l \leqslant s) \geqslant \text{SERVICE}$.

4.5   The System Integrative Module

The system integrative module assembles the decision rules derived in the previous chapters into inventory control policies. An inventory control policy should be able to provide answers to two basic questions: *when* to order a replenishment batch, and *how much* to order of the particular item controlled. Throughout the section on safety stocks an order point–order quantity policy (i.e., an order of size Q is released when the available inventory reaches the order point s) has been assumed because it best suits the presentation and development of the topic. Occasionally it was hinted, however, that, for cases not meeting all the assumptions made there, other policies might be appropriate.

Before putting an inventory control system together, we still have to deal with the decision whether to make a particular item to order or to stock it.

4.5.1   *Made-to-Order Versus Stock Items*

If an item is made to order (or purchased to order), its production (or purchase) should be limited to the amount generated by a specific customer order received, and should start at a date compatible with the required or promised delivery date. If, on the contrary, we are dealing with a stock item, we are expected to be able to fill the item's demand directly from stock, at least to the extent made possible by the service level considerations built into the inventory control system.

In section 4.1.1 several reasons for holding inventories have been discussed, and we have seen that stocks perform certain functions. In order to decide on making to order or stocking an item, we concentrate on two essential aspects: inventories are held to attend customer service requirements or to provide cost savings. Consequently, to determine whether or not an item should be stocked we should analyze, first, if service considerations force us to keep the item in stock, regardless of cost implications, and, second, if this is not the case, whether we should still stock it due to cost considerations.

Made-to-order versus stock classification based on service considerations.
We can associate with each product a quantity called "desired maximum
promised delivery lead time," which is the maximum period of time we still
consider acceptable for the customer to wait for the delivery of the ordered
merchandise. This delivery time can be evaluated by taking into account the
previous delivery history of the product, the customers' requests, and the
competitors' delivery policies. Also, determine for each product the
"manufacturing (or purchasing) lead time" as the length of time that elapses
from the moment at which a manufacturing order (or purchasing requisition) is
released until the product is physically available for delivery. The lead time can
be determined from previous history or by estimates provided by foremen and
dispatchers (or purchasing agents).

Then the decision rule is as follows: if the manufacturing (or purchasing)
lead time is larger than the desired maximum promised delivery lead time,
classify the product as a stock item; otherwise, there is no need to stock the
product based on service considerations, and an economic analysis of the
consequences of the made-to-order versus stock decision has to be performed.

One point to be emphasized: an item may be exceedingly important to
make the production or logistics process of a firm feasible. In such a case,
although service considerations, measured in terms of the desired delivery lead
time, may not force us to stock the item, the constraints imposed by the
process itself may require us to do so.

*Made-to-order versus stock classification based on economic
considerations.* We have seen that even if the result of the previous analysis
indicates that the product need not be stocked for service reasons, it still might
be desirable to stock it for economic reasons. Thus, we have to compare the
cost incurred if the item is made to order with the cost resulting if it is stocked.

The assumptions and the data of the problem* are as follows:

- The expected annual demand for the item D units/year; it is expected that a
  number of N orders are received annually from customers.
- There is a fixed charge of A dollars/order for the manufacturing setup (or for
  placing a purchasing order).
- If the item is stocked, it is ordered in economic order quantities Q; also, to
  protect against uncertainties a safety stock (SS) is held.
- It costs C_{STOCK} dollars/unit to procure the item for stock; it costs C_{MTO}
  dollars/unit when the item is made to order; the two costs are established by
  assuming that in the made-to-order case the expected order size is D/N units,
  and in the stock case it is Q units.
- Stock is carried at a charge of r dollars/dollar·year.
- Service level is high enough so as to make the backorders cost negligible.

---

*Under somewhat different assumptions, the problem was also worked out by Popps [1965].

The expected annual made-to-order cost TC_{MTO} is determined by the total ordering cost and the cost of the items themselves:

$$TC_{MTO} = NA + DC_{MTO}. \tag{4.176}$$

When the product is stocked, the expected annual cost TC_{STOCK} is:

$$TC_{STOCK} = \frac{D}{Q}A + \left[\frac{Q}{2} + (SS)\right]rC_{STOCK} + DC_{STOCK} + C_{syst}$$

where C_{syst}, dollars/year, is the system cost (the item's share) of having the item stocked.

Since, if stocked, the item is ordered in economic order quantities $Q = \sqrt{2AD/rC_{stock}}$ the expression of TC_{STOCK} becomes:

$$TC_{STOCK} = \sqrt{2DArC_{STOCK}} + (SS)rC_{STOCK} + DC_{STOCK} + C_{syst} \tag{4.177}$$

Certainly, if quantity discounts are available, items are replenished jointly, or situations other than the conditions of the classical economic lot size model occur, the appropriate formula from section 4.2 has to be used.

The decision rule to be applied is then: if $TC_{MTO} < TC_{STOCK}$ classify the item as made-to-order; otherwise, classify it as a stock item.

By comparing (4.176) and (4.177), some qualitative qualifications can be expressed. As the ordering cost A increases, TC_{MTO} grows faster than TC_{STOCK} and thus the system tends to the stocking situation. A small number of orders per year tends to favor the made-to-order situation; this supports the intuitive feeling that the made-to-order versus stock question is more likely to be raised with slow movers rather than with fast-moving items. Obviously, if the carrying charge r is large, holding inventories becomes disadvantageous and we are pushed toward the made-to-order decision.

Note that in order to compute the total costs we need estimates for all the parameters involved (yearly demand, number of orders, etc.). The required safety stock can be taken from historical records, if the product was previously stocked; if not, an approximation can be used in the following form:

$$(SS) = k\sqrt{l\frac{D}{12}}$$

where k is the safety factor, and l is the lead time, in months. This approximation assumes that demand during the lead time l is Poisson; after all, this assumption is not that bad when we recall that the slow-moving items are the ones that are more likely to be involved in made-to-order versus stock decisions.

One final point: Because of the statistical variations in the underlying data, there are induced fluctuations in the estimates of the parameters in cost expressions (4.176) and (4.177). It is conceivable that, when parameters' values are revised, an item which was previously made-to-order might be pushed into the stock items class, or vice-versa, solely because of the random fluctuations in data. To prevent this kind of unstable behavior, Johnson [1962] suggests that, as long as the difference between the values of TC_{MTO} and TC_{STOCK} do not exceed a certain threshold, the sense of the inequality between TC_{MTO} and TC_{STOCK} may be allowed to change without changing the classification the item had before running the test.

4.5.2 Continuous Versus Periodic Review Systems

The order point–order quantity control policy presented earlier assumes that the stock level is exactly known at every point in time; this is the only way in which we can tell when the order point s is reached and then place a replenishment order for an amount Q. This policy is known under the short name of (s, Q).

In general, a continuous review system is one in which the stock status has to be always known.* In practice, rather than continuously surveying the inventory level, an equivalent approach is adopted: each transaction (taking orders from customers, shipping, receiving stock, placing orders to suppliers) triggers an immediate updating of the inventory status. For this reason, the continuous review system is also known as the transactions reporting system.

It is easy to think of situations where a continuous review system is obviously not a good choice. For instance, if the supplier of a line of items accepts orders only once a week there is no reason why we should review the stock of those items more often, and when we review it we should do it right before placing the order. Such a system, as opposed to the previous one, is called periodic review system because the stock status is determined periodically. The time between two stock reviews is the review period; it spans R periods of time.

Before taking a closer look at the various policies that can be operated under the two systems, a few more qualitative considerations are in order here. Besides conditions of the sort shown above, there are also economic considerations that can make one system look more attractive than the other.

If the review costs are small (i.e., the processing of transactions is inexpensive compared with ordering costs and the annual number of transactions is small relative to annual demand for the item) a continuous review system is preferred because it leads to lower overall inventories than a periodic system. Indeed, when working with an (s, Q) policy sufficient safety stock must be provided to offer protection over the l-period replenishment lead time. In a periodic review system, the situation is different because replenishment decisions are made R periods apart. Suppose the current decision is made at time t (of course, taking into account all outstanding orders); everything ordered up to and including moment t is delivered to stock until $t + l$. The next replenishment decision is made at $t + R$, with delivery time

*Zimmerman [1966] calls it "perpetual inventory control system."

$t + R + l$. Clearly, then, in time interval $[t, t + R + l)$ our only opportunity to influence the stock level and, hence, the performance of the system, is the current replenishment decision. It follows that, in a periodic review system, the safety stock must be large enough to provide protection for a length of time $l + R$. Thus, to achieve the same service level, it takes less safety stock in a continuous system than in a periodic system. This is certainly advantageous when:

- inventory carrying charges are high either because the cost of the controlled item is high or because the item requires special conditions that make stocking expensive
- the required safety stock is relatively large due to either a high service level desired by management or because of severely fluctuating demand which results in relatively inaccurate forecasts.

If the cost of operating a transactions reporting system is significant, the alternative is a periodic review system. Basically, during every R period the stock status is reviewed and a decision is made about how much to order (possibly nothing). If ordering is expensive compared with the review costs, one would place an order only if the inventory level were really low at the time of the review. If, on the contrary, ordering costs are small relative to review costs, one might want to order a positive quantity every time a review is conducted in order to avoid having wasted the costly review.

In what follows several basic policies are examined; each is characterized by a number of control parameters and the purpose of the presentation is to show how to determine their values:

- Continuous review systems

  - (s, Q) policy—when available inventory* reaches level s order Q units
  - (s, S) policy—when available inventory becomes equal to or less than s order up to level S
- Periodic review systems

  - (nQ, s, R) policy—If, at a review time, the available inventory is less than or equal to s, an amount nQ is ordered ($n = 1, 2, 3, \ldots$); multiple n should be such that, after the order is placed, the available inventory reaches a level in the interval $(s, s + Q)$. If available inventory is greater than s no order is placed.
  - (S, R) policy—At each review time, a sufficient quantity is ordered to bring the level of the available inventory up to a level S.
  - (s, S, R) policy—If, at a review time, the available inventory is less than or equal to s a sufficient quantity is ordered to bring the level of the available inventory up to S; otherwise, no order is placed.

*Recall that the available inventory is defined as the inventory on hand plus the amount on order less the number of units backordered.

Clearly, under the assumption of continuous and deterministic demand, there is no difference between the two systems; differences appear, however, for stochastic demands.

Discussions on these policies are conducted under the assumption that the probability distribution of demand is stationary.

Note on multiechelon systems and on control policies for the case of dynamic demand patterns are included in section 4.5.5.

In general, the exact formulation of the operation of an inventory system tends to lead to rather involved models that require, in most cases, a computer and appropriate search routines or iterative schemes to obtain the optimal values of the control variables. We have already seen it in the case of an (s, Q) policy, the simplest of all control policies, where the Poisson generated demands (section 4.4.3.1) yielded a fairly complicated cost function. Even if we treat the simpler case of normally distributed demands, the exact formulation still raises computational problems (see Hadley and Whitin [1963, chap. 4-9]); the situation becomes more serious as these problems are amplified by the number of items in the controlled inventory. Moreover, some problems, like the lost sales case, when more than one order is outstanding, still lack a satisfactory exact treatment.

For these reasons we hold the view that, for routine use, heuristic approximate formulations, which yield operational decision rules with minimum cost penalties for missing the mathematical optimum, are recommended. At the same time we have to acknowledge the basic theoretical body of work on inventory control policies since, although the results might be too sophisticated for day-to-day use by most companies, their value is qualitative in that they show the structure of the optimal solution to be followed and how various parameters affect the system's controls.

4.5.3 Continuous Review Systems

4.5.3.1 Order point–order quantity, (s, Q), policy

We are already familiar with this policy since it has been extensively assumed in our treatment of the safety stocks. Figure 4.21 gives a graphical representation of how the available (AI) and on-hand (OH) inventory vary with time under an (s, Q) policy.

The setting of the two control variables s and Q has been discussed in sections 4.4.2 and 4.4.3—that is, either Q is computed as the economic order quantity and the order point s is determined afterward, or Q and s are calculated jointly.

One form of physical materialization of the (s, Q) model is the "two-bin system," largely applicable to class C items. The stock of an item is stored in two bins. One of them, usually larger, is the working bin from which demand is currently served without requisitions or paperwork. The second bin is opened

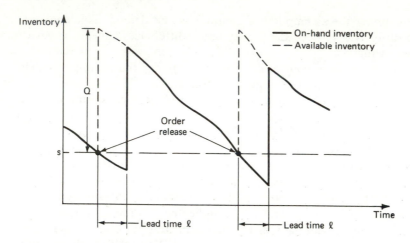

FIGURE 4.21   Inventory pattern under (s, Q) policy.

when the working bin becomes empty; at the same time, when this second bin is opened, a replenishment order for the item is released. Clearly, the amount of stock in the second bin materializes the order point. When the order comes in the second bin is refilled first, and the excess amount is put into the working bin. Since this system works properly only if there is no more than one order outstanding at any point in time, it is recommended that the order quantity should last much longer than the replenishment lead time. The order point should be set so as to offer a high-service level (recall that C items are cheap) to compensate for the rather loose control.

Before closing this problem we want to reiterate the idea that, when the integrality of demand is taken into account, the (s, Q) policy works properly only if demand occurs one unit at a time. If the size of the demand transactions is random, it is possible to overshoot the order point. It is conceivable that, in the case of an unusually large overshoot, the placing of an order of size Q might not be able to raise the available inventory level above s. Hence, the available inventory will never cross the order point again, no order will ever be released any more, and the operation of the inventory system will be seriously disturbed.

4.5.3.2 (s, S) policy

For situations in which the number of units-per-demand transaction is a random variable the (s, S) policy is preferred to (s, Q). This is so because, even if an overshoot occurs at the time when the need to replenish is recognized, the order-up-to-S system restores the deficit. The replenishment quantity varies depending on how large the overshoot is; in Figure 4.22 the placing of two replenishment orders, of differing sizes Q_1 and Q_2, is illustrated.

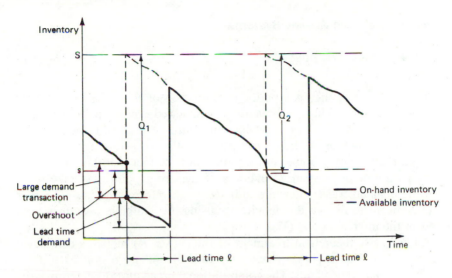

FIGURE 4.22   Inventory pattern under (s, S) policy.

A case in which an (s, S) policy is the obvious choice of a continuous review system is the replenishment control for lumpy items.

The (s, S) policy receives considerable attention by Arrow et al. [1958]. One of the difficulties associated with modeling it is finding the probability distribution of the overshoots, as this depends on the $S-s$ difference and on the probability distribution of the number of units in a demand transaction. Karlin [1958] derives the distribution of overshoots under the reasonable assumption that the average demand transaction size is substantially smaller than the amount $S-s$. Once this is established, the two controls s and S can be determined along lines similar to safety stock calculations.* This procedure may be justified when we are dealing with fairly expensive items.

Real world inventory systems tend to operate heuristic versions of the (s, S) policy. While retaining the essence of (s, S)—namely, that to make up for overshooting the order point one orders up to S—the two control variables s and S are determined using the (s, Q) model. The basic assumption of this approach, which in most cases turns out to be correct, is that large overshoots are quite improbable and, therefore, neglecting the overshooting phenomenon is a reasonable approximation.

Thus, Q is set equal to the economic order quantity (section 4.2), then the order point s is calculated according to section 4.4, and finally the value of S is determined by: $S = s + Q$. If more precision is required and the added sophistication is warranted, Q and s are computed jointly rather than sequentially.

---

*Peterson and Silver [1979, chap. 14-2] develop an approximate formulation of the problem and its solution.

4.5.4   *Periodic Review Systems*

4.5.4.1   *(nQ, s, R) policy*

The (nQ, s, R) policy is a periodic adaptation of the order point–order quantity (s, Q) model. Thus, the inventory is reviewed every R periods of time (rather than continuously); if the available inventory is less than or equal to s, an order of size nQ ($n = 1, 2, 3, \dots$) is placed, otherwise nothing is ordered. Ordering a multiple of Q comes in recognition of the fact that, because of the periodic nature of the system, overshoots of the order point may take place even if the demand transactions are unit sized. Therefore, ordering nQ rather than Q is meant to restore the deficit by raising the available inventory level above s in the interval $(s, s + Q)$.

An extensive theoretical treatment of the (nQ, s, R) model is conducted by Hadley and Whitin [1963, chaps. 5-3 to 5-5] under Poisson as well as normally distributed demands. The computational procedures to determine the optimal control parameters Q, s, and R turn out to be quite complicated, requiring a computer and appropriately designed search procedures.

In general, in the real world the (nQ, s, R) policy has gained much less acceptance than the (s, S, R) and (S, R) models. One reason can be that an (s, S, R) type of control policy, although by no means computationally simple, is expected in general to yield a lower average annual cost than (nQ, s, R). Secondly, the (S, R) policy is easier computationally than both (nQ, s, R) and (s, S, R). Moreover, when ordering costs are relatively low compared to review costs, one would tend to order every time a review is made and, therefore, in such a case the (S, R) policy is essentially optimal besides being computationally easier.

4.5.4.2   *(S, R) policy*

In practical applications, (S, R) is the most largely used periodic review policy. It works as follows: every R period of time the inventory is reviewed and an order is placed so as to make the available inventory level equal to S.

Its wide acceptance is due to several advantages:

- Its operation is simple and, therefore, it is easily understood by clerical personnel.
- The computation of the controls, S and R, is simpler than with other periodic review policies, especially in the heuristic version of the policy.
- It results in a predictable work load on the purchasing or production scheduling departments as opposed to the (nQ, s, R) and (s, S, R) policies where the number of orders released at a review time fluctuates depending on the relative positions of the available inventories with respect to the order points.

As mentioned earlier, however, the (S, R) policy is not universally recommended. Indeed, if ordering cost is high one may save by not placing an order at every review time, but only then when inventory is low and a replenishment is required in order to avoid a stockout situation.

Figure 4.23 pictures the time behavior of inventories resulting from an (S, R) policy. Clearly, the size of each replenishment order is equal to the demand during the preceding review interval (see point N).

The order placed at time t (point M) arrives at $t + l$. The next order will arrive at $t + l + R$. Hence, whether a stockout condition develops between $t + l$ and $t + l + R$ depends on the replenishment decision made at t. The problem is, then, very much similar to the setting of safety stocks in an (s, Q) system—that is, for a given time R between reviews find the order-up-to-level S which provides adequate protection against stockouts over a time span of $l + R$ periods, without building unneeded inventory.

The exact cost equations for the (S, R) policy are formulated by Hadley and Whitin [1963, chap. 5-6] for two cases: Poisson and normally distributed demands. Both cases are shown to be particular instances of the (nQ, s, R) models: for the Poisson demand, make $Q = 1$ and $s + 1 = S$ in the corresponding (nQ, s, R) equations, and for the normal case set $s = S$ and take the limit as $Q \to 0$. The resulting relations for the determination of the two controls, S and R, are too complicated to be of real practical use for routine applications.

We present below an approximate heuristic treatment of the (S, R) policy which yields simpler results under a set of reasonable assumptions.

FIGURE 4.23 **Inventory pattern under (S, R) policy.**

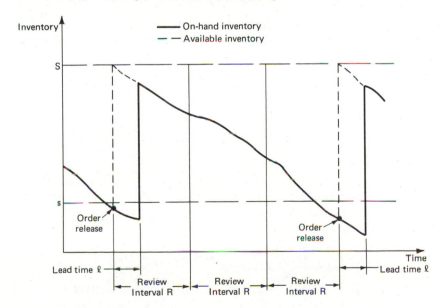

Thus, assume that:

- demand is a continuous variable whose probability distribution is stationary
- the replenishment lead time is a constant
- units demanded and out of stock are backordered; backorders, however, are expensive and, therefore, average shortages are considered negligibly small relative to the on-hand inventory
- the cost of making a review or, in general, the cost of the control system, is independent of the values of the control variables S and R

The following notations are used:

D = average demand rate, units per year

A = ordering cost, dollars per order

J = cost of making a review, dollars per review

C = unit cost, dollars per unit of item (no quantity discounts)

r = inventory carrying charge, dollars/dollar·year

c_s = shortage cost incurred by the system for every unit backordered, dollars/unit

$\tilde{d}_{l+R}$ = demand over the replenishment lead time plus review interval; it is a random variable having the density function $f(\tilde{d}_{l+R})$ with a mean d_{l+R} and a standard deviation of the forecast errors over a replenishment lead time plus a review interval of σ_{l+R}. Evidently, density $f(\tilde{d}_{l+R})$ depends on both l and R.

The relevant costs are: the ordering, review, inventory carrying, and backordering costs; we seek to minimize their total over a span of one year by appropriately setting S and R.

Since demand has a continuous density function, the probability of no demand occurring during a review interval is zero; therefore, an order is placed with each review and:

$$\text{Expected annual costs of ordering and review} = \frac{A+J}{R}, \qquad (4.178)$$

where R is expressed in years.

As the demand rate has a constant mean, inventory varies on the average linearly between a maximum (just after a replenishment arrives) and a minimum (just before a replenishment arrives).

Point W in Figure 4.23 illustrates a maximum:

$$\text{Expected inventory just after a replenishment arrives} = S - d_{l+R} + D \cdot R \qquad (4.179)$$

where the product $D \cdot R$ yields the demand during the review interval.

Point v illustrates a minimum:

$$\text{Expected inventory just} \atop \text{before a replenishment arrives} = S - d_{l+R}. \qquad (4.180)$$

By neglecting the backorders, according to one of our assumptions, the half way between the above maximum and minimum can be regarded as closely approximating the average on-hand inventory; then:

$$\text{Expected annual} \atop \text{inventory holding cost} = \left(S - d_{l+R} + \frac{D \cdot R}{2} \right) rC. \qquad (4.181)$$

Backorders occur whenever demand during the replenishment lead time plus a review interval exceeds S. Then (see section 4.4.2.1):

$$\text{Expected annual} \atop \text{backordering costs} = \frac{c_s}{R} \int_S^\infty \left(\tilde{d}_{l+R} - S \right) f\left(\tilde{d}_{l+R} \right) d\left(\tilde{d}_{l+R} \right). \qquad (4.182)$$

The total annual cost TC is the sum of (4.178), (4.180), and (4.182). If the review interval R is given, the optimal order-up-to-level S results from:

$$\frac{d(TC)}{dS} = rC - \frac{c_s}{R} \int_S^\infty f\left(\tilde{d}_{l+R} \right) d\left(\tilde{d}_{l+R} \right) = 0. \qquad (4.183)$$

Let $\Pi(S) = \int_S^\infty f(\tilde{d}_{l+R}) d(\tilde{d}_{l+R})$, that is, the complement of the cumulative of $f(\tilde{d}_{l+R})$. Then S_0, the optimal value of S, is the solution of:

$$\Pi(S) = \frac{rCR}{c_s}. \qquad (4.184)$$

This result is strikingly similar to (4.135) in which Q/D, the duration of a cycle, is the analog of the review interval.

The review interval R could be the result of conditions external to the model; for example, our vendor can accept our orders only every second Monday.

If this is not the case, R can be derived from the economic order quantity EOQ expressed as a time supply: $R = EOQ/D$. When computing the value of the EOQ, the fixed cost J of making a review must be added to the ordering cost A. Of course, the resulting value of R should be adjusted so as to fit the modus operandi of the department which is in charge of inventory control.

Still another alternative is to determine the optimal R and S jointly. This requires the simultaneous solution of (4.184) and $\partial(TC)/\partial R = 0$. Since density $f(\tilde{d}_{l+R})$ depends on the review interval R, this case is computationally more involved than the previous situation in which R was exogenously determined. To solve it some numerical techniques are used. A simple approach is the following: for each of a set of values $R_1, R_2, R_3, \ldots$, calculate the optimal S_0 by use of (4.184). Plot the total cost TC as a function of R, using the corresponding S_0 for the given R to compute TC. From the plot find the optimal R.

To treat the lost sales case we have to rewrite the inventory holding cost equation (4.181). In the backorders situation, when shortages developed, part of the incoming replenishment was used to satisfy the unfilled orders. This is not the case under the lost sales assumption as shortages are not backlogged; therefore, on-hand inventories are larger by the average amount of units of stock in a review cycle.

$$\text{Expected number of units short per review interval} = \int_S^\infty (\tilde{d}_{l+R} - S) f(\tilde{d}_{l+R}) d(\tilde{d}_{l+R}) \quad (4.185)$$

Expected annual inventory holding cost

$$= \left[S - d_{l+R} + \frac{D \cdot R}{2} + \int_S^\infty (\tilde{d}_{l+R} - S) f(\tilde{d}_{l+R}) d(\tilde{d}_{l+R}) \right] rC. \quad (4.186)$$

Continue to consider c_s as the cost of one unit out of stock. Then the total annual cost TC is obtained by summing up (4.178), (4.182), and (4.186). For a given R, the optimal value of S is a solution to the first-order condition:

$$\frac{d(TC)}{dS} = rC - rC \int_S^\infty f(\tilde{d}_{l+R}) d(\tilde{d}_{l+R}) - \frac{c_s}{R} \int_S^\infty f(\tilde{d}_{l+R}) d(\tilde{d}_{l+R}) = 0 \quad (4.187)$$

which yields:

$$\Pi(S) = \frac{rCR}{c_s + rCR} \quad (4.188)$$

where, as defined earlier, $\Pi(S)$ is the complementary cumulative of $f(\tilde{d}_{l+R})$.

In order to avoid costing out shortages explicitly, the order-up-to-level S can be determined by means of prespecified service level considerations. For this purpose it is advantageous to think of the expected inventory just before a replenishment arrives as a safety stock for a time span of $l + R$. Then, from (4.180) it follows that:

$$S = d_{l+R} + SS, \quad (4.189)$$

where SS stands for the safety stock. By analogy with (4.121), from (4.189) we conclude that S should be set equal to the maximum reasonable demand during a replenishment lead time plus a review interval.

It is again reasonable to link the safety stock to the standard deviation σ_{l+R} of the forecast errors over a lead time plus a review interval through a safety factor k:

$$SS = k\sigma_{l+R}.$$

Thus:

$$S = d_{l+R} + k\sigma_{l+R}, \quad (4.190)$$

and the general expression (4.185) changes to:

Expected number of units
short per review interval

$$= \int_{d_{l+R} + k\sigma_{l+R}}^{\infty} \left[\tilde{d}_{l+R} - (d_{l+R} + k\sigma_{l+R}) \right] f(\tilde{d}_{l+R}) d(\tilde{d}_{l+R}). \qquad (4.191)$$

For fast-moving items under normally distributed forecast errors (see section 4.4.2.1), we obtain the particular expression:

$$\begin{array}{l} \text{Expected number of} \\ \text{units short per review} \\ \text{interval under normal distribution} \end{array} = \sigma_{l+R} G(k). \qquad (4.192)$$

For slow-moving items, if the Laplace distribution applies (see section 4.4.3.1), (4.191) becomes:

$$\begin{array}{l} \text{Expected number of} \\ \text{units short per review} \\ \text{interval under Laplace distribution} \end{array} = \frac{\sigma_{l+R}}{2\sqrt{2}} e^{-\sqrt{2}k}. \qquad (4.193)$$

By similarity with the developments of section 4.4.2.2, for a given review interval R and a prespecified measure of the service level, the value of the safety factor k can be determined, and the order-up-to-level S can be set accordingly by equation (4.190).

Extensions of the (S, R) policy to cover the case of stochastic replenishment lead times are provided by Hadley and Whitin [1963, chap. 5-2] under the assumption that orders cannot cross, that is, the lower, $l_{\min}$, and the upper, $l_{\max}$, limits to the possible range of lead time values are such that $l_{\max} < l_{\min} + R$.

4.5.4.3 (s, S, R) policy

When placing of an order is expensive, it may be advantageous not to order at every review time, with the purpose of saving on ordering costs. The way the (s, S, R) policy works is then: at every review time, the level of the available inventory is compared with s; if less than or equal to s a sufficient quantity is ordered to raise the available inventory up to S, if greater than s no order is released (Figure 4.24).

The optimality of this policy is studied by Scarf [1960], following earlier work by Arrow, Harris, and Marschak [1951], and by Dvoretzky, Kiefer, and Wolfowitz [1953]; see also Zabel [1962]. Recent papers include Ehrhardt [1979], Iwaniec [1979], and Freeland and Porteus [1980].

Under the assumptions of a constant replenishment lead time l, backordering of unfilled demand, and constant unit cost for the controlled item, Scarf [1960] proves that the (s, S, R) policy is optimal if function $g(x; R)$

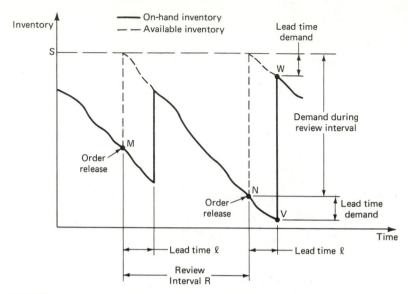

FIGURE 4.24 Inventory pattern under (s, S, R) policy.

is convex and differentiable everywhere with respect to x. Function $g(x; R)$ is defined as follows: given a given review interval R, if t is a review time for the system and x is the available inventory after ordering a quantity $Q \geqslant 0$, $g(x; R)$ is the sum of the expected carrying and backorder costs incurred in the period from $t + l$ to $t + l + R$ and discounted to time t by a positive interest rate. The vehicle of the study is a dynamic programming model developed over an n-period planning horizon (for convenience, a period is redefined as spanning the time of a review interval). We present the results briefly below.

Consider, then, that t is a review time for the system; also, t marks the beginning of period j.

$$F_j(y + Q; R) = \min_{Q \geqslant 0} \left[J + A\delta(Q) + CQ + g_j(y + Q; R) \right.$$

$$\left. + a \int_0^\infty F_{j+1}(y + 0 - \tilde{d}_R; R) f(\tilde{d}_R) d(\tilde{d}_R) \right], \quad (4.194)$$

with $j = 1, 2, \ldots, n$; $F_{n+1}(\cdot) = 0$; $\delta(0) = 0$, $\delta(Q) = 1$ when $Q > 0$.

The recurrence relationship (4.194) calculates the total discounted costs if an optimal policy, to be discussed later, is used at time t and at all future review times. y is the available inventory at time t before any order is placed; after ordering, the inventory level becomes $y + Q$.

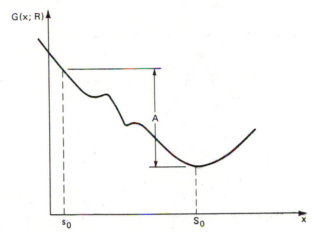

FIGURE 4.25
An A-convex curve.

The discount factor a, $0 \leqslant a \leqslant 1$, gives the present worth at time t of the costs evaluated at $t + R$.

$\tilde{d}_R$ is the demand occurring in a period of length R; its probability distribution is described by the density $f(\tilde{d}_R)$.

All other notations are the same as in section 4.5.4.2.

Scarf's proof is based on showing inductively that the following function is A-convex if $g(x; R)$ is convex in x and differentiable everywhere:

$$G(x; R) = Cx + g(x; R) + a \int_0^\infty F(x - \tilde{d}_R) f(\tilde{d}_R) d(\tilde{d}_R). \quad (4.195)$$

$G(x; R)$ is A-convex* in x (A is the cost of placing an order) if for any $\alpha \geqslant 0$:

$$A + G(\alpha + x; R) - G(x; R) - \alpha G'(x; R) \geqslant 0, \quad (4.196)$$

where G' indicates the derivative with respect to x.

Notice that (4.196) does not imply convexity for $G(x; R)$. Therefore, $G(x; R)$ can have a shape as shown in Figure 4.25, with several local minima. s_0 and S_0 denote the optimum control variables of the (s, S, R) policy.

In the n-period dynamic programming model a $G_j(x; R)$ function can be written for each period $j = 1, 2, \ldots, n$; the optimal policy in period j is characterized by two numbers s_{oj}, S_{0j}. Then, if available inventory y_j prior to the placing of any order is less than or equal to s_{0j} order up to S_{0j} because $G_j(y_j; R) \geqslant G_j(S_{0j}) + A$; if $y_j > s_{0j}$ do not order since $G_j(y_j; R) < G_j(S_{0j}) + A$.

Although local minima and maxima may exist, an A-convex function may not display a behavior like that of Figure 4.26. It is easy to show that

---

*A function $f(x)$ is convex if for any x_1, x_2 and any β, $0 \leqslant \beta \leqslant 1$, the following holds: $f[\beta x_1 + (1 - \beta) x_2] \leqslant \beta f(x_1) + (1 - \beta) f(x_2)$. An equivalent definition of convexity is that for any $\alpha \geqslant 0$ we have: $f(\alpha + x) - f(x) - \alpha f'(x) \geqslant 0$, where f' is the derivative of $f(x)$ with respect to x.

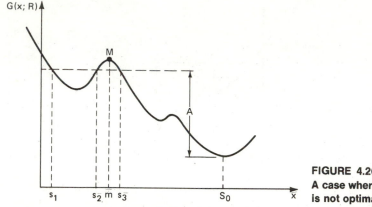

FIGURE 4.26
**A case where (s, S, R) policy
is not optimal.**

point M, a local maximum, leads to a violation of the A-convexity property. Indeed, set $x = m$ and $\alpha = S_0 - m$; as $G'(m; R) = 0$ relation (4.196) becomes $A + G(S_0; R) \geqslant G(m; R)$, which is obviously a contradiction. More generally, if $S_{\min}$ is a local minimum of $G(x; R)$, there may be no local maximum at a point $x_{\max} < S_{\min}$ if $G(x_{\max}; R) > A + G(S_{\min}; R)$.

Notice that in the case of Figure 4.26 an (s, S, R) policy would not be optimal. Rather, the best ordering policy would be: if $y \leqslant s_1$ order up to S_0; if $s_1 < y < s_2$ do not order; if $s_2 \leqslant y \leqslant s_3$ order a quantity $S_0 - y$; if $y > s_3$ do not order.

In general, function $g(x; R)$ is convex* and, therefore, we expect an (s, S, R) policy to be optimal.

However, if the unit cost of the item is not a constant (e.g., quantity discounts) it is not true that (s, S, R) should still be optimal.

The above results make it clear why the (S, R) policy is not an optimal policy unless $A = 0$. From Figure 4.25 it is apparent that the optimal S_0 is the minimizing value of x in (4.195) and the reorder point s_0 is such that $G(s_0) = G(S_0) + A$. Then, for $A = 0$ we have $s_0 = S_0$ which yields an (S, R) policy.

For the infinite period problem (which can be obtained as a limiting case by letting the number of periods $n \to \infty$), under Scarf's assumptions and if demands are independent identically distributed random variables in each period, there is an optimal stationary (s, S, R) policy, that is, $s_j = s$ and $S_j = S$ in all periods (Iglehart [1963a, 1963b]).

---

*We expect $g(x; R)$ to be convex for the following reason: if the initial inventory is low, the expected costs tend to be high because of the relatively large number of backorders. As x increases, the backorders situation improves and costs go down. But, beyond a certain point, a further rise in x causes the inventory holding charges to go up and eventually to outweigh the reduction in backorder penalty, thus inducing an increase in $g(x; R)$.

Theoretically, one would find the solution to the recurrence equation (4.194), for a given R and discount rate a, to obtain the amount to be ordered Q_0 as a function of the initial inventory y. In the steady state case with an infinite number of periods, the ensuing functional equation has to be solved or, if an approximation is acceptable, an n-period system (with n large) can be used instead. The optimal function $Q_0(y:R)$ then yields the optimal s_0 and S_0 (see, for instance, Hadley and Whitin [1963, chap. 8-5]). To also optimize with respect to R, different values of the review interval have to be tried. In the real world the choice of values for R is limited by organizational considerations, relations with suppliers and customers, and so on.

An alternative approach to computing the optimal values of s and S under stationary demand is to minimize the expected costs (review and ordering plus inventory holding and backorder costs) per unit time. Markov chain theory or renewal processes are used by various authors to obtain average cost formulas: Arrow, Harris, and Marschak [1951], Karlin [1958], Wagner, O'Hagan, and Lundh [1965], and Veinott and Wagner [1965]. Hadley and Whitin [1963, chap. 5-9] derive the average annual cost by computing the expected cost per replenishment cycle (i.e., the time between the placing of two consecutive orders) and then dividing by the average length of a cycle. Thus, they make use of a basic result of renewal theory (Karlin and Taylor [1975, chap. 5]), by which the long-run expected costs per unit time = (expected costs per cycle)/(expected length of the cycle).

As a general rule, solving whichever approach is taken is difficult computationally,* especially when thinking in terms of systems of realistic size (thousands or even more items to be controlled). As with other ordering policies, this has encouraged the development of approximate heuristic approaches: Wagner, O'Hagan, and Lundh [1965], Snyder [1974], Nahmias [1975, 1979], Naddor [1975], Peterson and Silver [1979, chap. 8.9], and Ehrhardt [1981].

The two control variables s and S should have some safety and economic features and, in principle, can be thought of, from a pragmatic point of view, as follows: the order point s represents an inventory level which, if at the current review time no order is placed, should be large enough to satisfy the maximum reasonable demand during a review interval R plus a replenishment lead time. When an order is released it has to satisfy an economic criterion and, therefore, the amount ordered is some sort of economic order quantity. The time span covered on the average by this quantity has to be an integer number of review intervals. Then the order-up-to-level S is obtained by adding to s the economic order quantity.

---

*Under the assumption of exponentially distributed demand per time period Karlin [1958] obtains simple expressions for s and S. Thus, $S = s + Q$, where Q is given by the classical Wilson lot size formula, and s results from an exponential expression. However, the result presents interest rather from a theoretical point of view, because the exponential distribution is not a good match for the probability distribution of demand per period.

In industrial settings it is often true that review costs are relatively high and, therefore, it is common to find review intervals large enough so that an order is placed at every review time with either an (S, R) or (s, S, R) policy. Hence, also considering the computational advantage, one would expect to find that for practical implementations the (s, S, R) policy is replaced by the (S, R) policy without important deviations from optimality.

On the other hand, if ordering costs are high relative to the review costs, in which case an (s, S, R) policy is definitely more economical than (S, R), the question can still be raised whether it is not advantageous to switch over to a continuous review system rather than using periodic review.

4.5.5   *Other Issues in Inventory Control Systems*

In the preceding sections we have confined our presentation to some fundamental problems in single-item, single stocking point, stationary demand inventory control systems, emphasizing the need for operational replenishment policies which, while skirting undue computational difficulties, would still maintain the essence of theoretically proved optimal decisions.

As soon as the aforementioned assumptions are relaxed other control policies emerge. In section 4.2.3 we have seen some cases of multiple items sharing the same equipment or replenished under aggregate constraints. Other joint replenishment systems are possible. For example, consider a family of m items; in order to replenish any one item of the family, a major setup cost A is incurred at the family level and a minor setup cost a_i is involved in including item i in the order. Suppose a periodic review system is used, with *coordinated* (s_i, S_i, R) *ordering policies*, according to which each item has its individual order point s_i and order-up-to-level S_i, but the review interval R is the same for all items. For any given R the control variables s_i and S_i, $i = 1, 2, \ldots, m$, have to be optimal, as discussed in section 4.5.4.3. The best R is determined by search so as to minimize the total expected costs of the system (review, ordering, inventory holding, and shortage costs).

A special type of continuous review (s, S) system developed for the case of a family of coordinated items is the *can-order* (s, c, S) *policy* (Balintfy [1964], Maher et al. [1973], and Silver [1974]). If an item has to be ordered, the major family setup is incurred in excess of the minor setup a_i charge if item i is included in the replenishment. Each item has its individual controls $s_i < c_i < S_i$, $i = 1, 2, \ldots, m$. (s, c, S) operates as follows: when the available inventory of some item i becomes equal to or smaller than s_i an order is released for an amount sufficient to bring the inventory level up to S_i. At the same time, if any other item j of the family has its available inventory at or below c_j it is included in the order with a quantity large enough to raise the inventory level to S_j. Hence, c_j is called the "can-order point" and the policy is named accordingly. The idea is then evident: if at the time when a major setup is incurred item j's inventory is at c_j or lower, this is a signal that pretty soon item j itself will reach its order point* s_j and trigger a replenishment order and the associated major setup. Thus, in order to avoid an excessive number of major setups the (s, c, S) policy allows an item to be ordered even if it has not reached the order point s.

If the single stocking point assumption is dropped, *the multiechelon situation* has to be modeled. Multiechelon distribution networks and multistage production systems are the two broad classes of problems under this heading, and their vastness prohibits any attempt to treat the topic in this chapter; rather, a few notes are made and starting references are provided for the interested reader.

A "stage," "location," or "echelon" is any physical point at which inventories may be held. In the field of production systems, the terms "stage," "facility," and sometimes "station" are used interchangeably. A multiechelon distribution system involves transfers of goods between locations, exogenous sources, and customers. A multistage production system can be thought of as being a production process in which component parts have to be obtained by manufacturing or by purchasing, then assembled into subassemblies, assemblies, and finally into the finished good. It is useful, for modeling purposes, to conceptualize the system as a network in which a node is a location or stage; an arc connecting two nodes is used to represent an activity involving both nodes, and is usually directed. The node from which an arc leaves is the predecessor; the node where it ends is the successor. In multistage models we can identify two kinds of demands for the product stocked or manufactured at a stage: independent demand coming from customers (or market demand), and dependent demand generated by successor stages.

A number of multistage configurations may be distinguished:

- *Serial system*. Each stage can have no more than one successor and one predecessor.

- *Parallel system*. Each stage is single, and serves only independent demands (it has no predecessor or successor); however, stages may share costs.

- *Pure assembly system*. Each stage can have any number of predecessor stages, but at most one successor stage; the corresponding network converges toward a node which, in a manufacturing setting, represents the assembling of the final product to be delivered to the customer.

- *Arborescent system*. Each stage has a single predecessor but any number of successors; the associated network has a single supply location.

- *Acyclic system*. Each stage can have any number of predecessors and successors but the network representation contains no cycles, that is, it is not possible to make a sequence of shipments such that material starts and ends at the same location.

- *General system*. The associated network allows transfers of goods between any two locations; the structure is arbitrary with no restrictions on the relationship between stages.

---

*s_j is also called "must-order point" to contrast with the "can-order point" c_j.

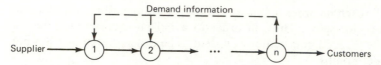

FIGURE 4.27   Serial system with *n* stages.

Because of the dependent demand, the treatment of multiechelon situations is bound to differ markedly from the single stocking point problem. In general, dependent demand does not lend itself to statistical forecasting and, therefore, the methods of statistical inventory control are no longer appropriate.

In the area of distribution systems, comprehensive surveys have been written by Veinott [1966], Clark [1972], Aggarwal [1974], and Karmarkar [1975]. We choose to present briefly in this section an important concept in multistage inventory control, developed by Simpson [1958], namely, the base stock system.

Consider *n* stages in series, where the material flow takes place from stage 1 to stage 2, then from stage 2 to stage 3, and so on. The characteristic of the base stock system is that information on actual customer demand is fed back directly to each stage. Each stage controls its ordering policy independently, based on demand information rather than reacting to its successor's ordering policy. Thus, the system acquires much more stability than in the case where each stage sees only the demand generated by its successor and where small changes in end-item demand can lead to large oscillations in the replenishment orders and in the levels of inventories upstream.*

In Simpson's work, a base stock level B_i is associated with each stage $i = 1, 2, \ldots, n$. When an order is received at one of the stages i a replenishment order is immediately placed with the predecessor stage $i - 1$ for an equal amount. When a stage is out of stock any demand which occurs then at that stage is backordered; however, the reorder is still placed with the predecessor immediately when the demand arrives. Thus, the on-hand inventory minus the amount backordered plus the quantity on order is always maintained constant and equal to the base stock level. Note that when end-items are withdrawn from the final stage *n*, a process of explosion takes place throughout the system.

The performance at stage *i* is characterized by the service time T_i defined as the maximum time needed to fill an order placed against inventory *i*. Evidently, if inventories are high, smaller service times are achieved and vice-versa. The determination of the optimum service times and, hence, the optimal base stock levels depends on a policy variable set by management: the probability α_i that the service time at stage *i* exceeds the value of T_i.

*The phenomenon is described by Forrester [1961, chap. 2].

Given the α_i's ($i = 1, 2, \ldots, n$), the base stock levels are calculated so as to minimize the expected inventory holding cost per unit time for the entire system. Simpson also imposes the conditions that $T_1 = 0$, which means that the raw material inventory (stage 1) is never empty, and $T_n = 0$, that is, delivery to the customer should take place without delay. The optimal solution is that each stage should carry either no inventory at all or the maximum reasonable level of stock which assures that the stage's inventory is never empty (the equivalent of $T_i = 0$).

In the original development of the base stock system, the ordering or setup cost is left out of consideration. However, when it becomes so important that neglecting it would affect the economics of our decisions, the operation of the base stock control should be modified accordingly. Certainly, one would not place a replenishment order after each demand; rather, ordering should be made in economic order quantities or, if demand is not unit sized, a minimum amount should accumulate before an order is released. Thus, an (s, Q) or (s, S) policy would be used at each stage. However, the essence of the base stock system must still be retained, namely, that the system is driven by actual customer demand. Therefore, the values of Q_i and s_i for stage i are based on end-time demand forecasts and the associated forecast errors over the replenishment lead time corresponding to stage i (Peterson and Silver [1979, chap. 12]).

In the area of multistage production systems, the assumption about the planning horizon appears to determine two different approaches to the problem. The infinite horizon models are of the economic order quantity type; they start by evaluating in-process inventories, and then minimize the total of setup and inventory holding costs. In the finite horizon, models demand occurs by time periods, can be deterministic or stochastic, varying or constant in time; usually, these models are of the mathematical programming sort. Some features of a general nature are reviewed below; for a more detailed view of the literature, the interested reader is directed to Johnson and Montgomery [1974, chaps. 3-8 and 4-7], and Candea [1977].

In the multistage lot size problem demand is, in most cases, deterministic and occurring at a constant rate, costs are time-invariant, and the system is assumed to be in operation indefinitely into the future. In this static environment the assumption of time-invariant economic order quantities is reasonable. Schwarz and Schrage [1975] show that under the stated conditions, time-invariant lot sizes are optimal. If production is instantaneous and there are no capacity constraints, Crowston and Wagner [1970] and Crowston et al. [1973] prove that in pure assembly systems it is optimal to set the lot size at stage s equal to an integral multiple of the lot size at a stage immediately succeeding s. This is not necessarily true when production is noninstantaneous (see Jensen and Khan [1972]), or when the structure of the process is not pure assembly. Candea [1977] finds the optimal lot sizing policy for the latter case, when the process is assembly leading to the production of an end-item;

however, a stage is no longer restricted to having at most one successor, it can have several successors (e.g., a component part produced at some stage goes into two or more subassemblies assembled at successor stages). Whenever lot sizing in integral multiples is assumed to be or is optimal, the multiples are computed by dynamic programming procedures, by branch-and-bound algorithms, or even by considering all possible combinations of lot sizes if the problem is small enough (Taha and Skeith [1970]). To reduce the search space, many procedures start out by developing heuristic bounds on the range of lot size multiples to be considered.

In the finite horizon models, in every period of the planning horizon a demand for a nonnegative amount of the product (or products) under consideration occurs. If the production process structure under study is facilities in series, the problem can be represented as a network flow problem of the transshipment type. If the cost structure is linear, network algorithms of the dynamic programming type exist (Zangwill [1969] for the single product case; Veinott [1969] extends Zangwill's approach to arborescent and assembly line structures).

When an assembly system is modeled, the result is no longer a network flow problem; it becomes a combinatorial problem, and either dynamic programming or branch-and-bound algorithms are fit for solution. The authors who have studied this kind of problem put considerable effort into:

- exploiting the characteristics of the optimal solution in order to provide good formulations for the recurrence equations in the dynamic programming algorithms
- finding good bounds in the branch-and-bound algorithms
- finding "reasonable" restrictive assumptions upon the cost functions, which would thus enable them to develop better bounds and more efficient algorithms

In general, the multistage production problem is still in an incipient stage in terms of results applicable to real world systems. The general case is pruned by assumptions until its structure allows solution by an existing technique. For instance, capacity constraints are more often than not disposed of* in order to allow solution by concave cost network techniques, and setup costs are neglected to permit formulation and solution by linear programming.

While discussing multistage systems, and since we have already touched upon the area of production, we should also mention the topic of *M*aterial *R*equirements *P*lanning (MRP). Conceptualized for a manufacturing environment, MRP deals with the problems of determining the requirements of components (parts, subassemblies, assemblies), establishing the points in time

*Capacitated formulations may be found but, usually, other simplifications are brought in: Dorsey et al. [1974, 1975] study the simpler problem of stages in parallel; Haehling von Lanzenauer [1970] waives the setup charges and obtains a linear programming model; Klingman et al. [1977] develop a formulation for a parallel system with a planning horizon of one time period; Gabbay [1975] tackles the serial system with multiple products under restrictive assumptions on the cost structure.

when the components are needed, and scheduling the manufacturing or purchasing of the components so that they become available at the time of usage and not much earlier. The starting point for MRP is the assembly schedule, by time period, for the end-items (or final products); this is called the "master schedule." Working backward from the master schedule, by a process called "explosion," the planned production quantities of end-product are projected into the appropriate amounts of required components. The book by Orlicky [1975] should make a good starting reference. The increase in computing capability brought about by the advent of the large-scale random access computer has encouraged and made possible the adoption of the method. Its popularity is due, in part, to its straightforwardness and its orderly and systematic approach to timed requirements planning. However, a big problem has still not been convincingly solved: how to draw a good (leave aside optimal) feasible master schedule? MRP assumes the master schedule as given, while we have seen earlier that optimizing efficient techniques for production planning in multistage systems has yet to be developed.

As mentioned at the outset of section 4.5.5, the inventory replenishment policies developed earlier assumed stationary demand. When this assumption is dropped, we have to deal with *dynamic models for time-varying demand*. Dynamic models usually have a finite planning horizon consisting of T time periods, and the demand is given in the form of $d_i, i = 1, 2, \ldots, T$ to be served in period i; thus, the demand can vary from period to period. Demand can be deterministic or stochastic.

If demand is deterministic and time-invariant, one would order an economic order quantity precisely one lead time before the existing stock would vanish. When demand is deterministic and time-varying, a similar policy should be used, except that the order quantity will also change with time. An extensive treatment of this topic has been given in the Aggregate Production Planning chapter of this book. In the single-product case, for which the optimizing algorithm of Wagner–Whitin is presented in the aforementioned chapter, a number of heuristics are proposed, coming mainly from the research work done in connection with lot sizing in an MRP context. Silver and Meal [1973] propose a heuristic that sets the economic order quantity such as to minimize total relevant costs per unit time for the duration of the replenishment quantity. Other procedures are presented by Plossl and Wight [1971] and Orlicky [1975, chap. 6]. Berry [1972] suggests an experimental framework for systematically comparing the various lot sizing procedures.

In the case of stochastic demand, any attempt to use inventory control policies of the types described in sections 4.5.3 and 4.5.4 should take account of the time variability of demand and, consequently, one would expect that the values of the control parameters (order quantity Q, order point s, order-up-to-level S) also become functions of time. We have seen the computational problems already encountered in designing control policies under stationary demand assumptions. Therefore, with dynamic stochastic demand an optimization of the policy control variables is out of the question for any implementation purposes, and one has to resort to heuristics (see, for example, Peterson and Silver [1979, chap. 8.9]). Unfortunately, this might not be of too much help either, as the problem might prove extremely difficult for reasons other than computational. Recall that, to develop a dynamic model with stochastic demand, one needs to know the distribution of demand in each future period. Or, in the real world, simply predicting what the mean demand will be for each future period could be a very tough job, not to speak of forecasting the exact nature of the probability distribution.

4.6   The System–Management Interaction and Evaluation Module

This module is intended to provide management with such information as to allow the selection of policy variables, to permit an evaluation of system performance, and to assist in the identification of problem areas where managerial intervention is required.

4.6.1   Exchange Curves

In section 4.2.1 a discussion on costs in inventory systems was carried out. If we refer, for instance, to the inventory carrying costs (storage and handling, property taxes, insurance, spoilage, obsolescence, pilferage, rent for storing facilities, and capital costs), it is apparent that some components represent out-of-pocket expenditures (e.g., rent for leased storage space, or interest paid for capital borrowed from banks), other components are foregone opportunities for return that could be earned by alternative uses of internal funds (e.g., company-owned storage space could be used for other productive activities, or internal funds tied up in inventories might be put to work in alternative investments and produce a certain rate of profit), and some have both features.

Also, it is important to realize that costs used in production and inventory control problems may differ from the accounting costs as the bases of their definition can differ. Finally, many cost elements cannot be determined accurately, so accounting rules have to be employed which may change as a matter of company policy.

The idea emerging from these considerations is that some costs, to the extent that they include foregone opportunities or that their definition is subject to arbitrary rules, can be adjusted so as to help achieve certain objectives. Therefore, they can be thought of as representing management policy variables.

Other noncost parameters involved in designing an inventory control system are policy variables, such as the prespecified service measures used in setting safety stocks (section 4.4.2.2).

An exchange curve shows the tradeoffs that can be achieved between two or more aggregate measures of performance of the inventory system as the policy variable's value is varied. Thus, for instance, a large value for the inventory carrying charge r generates smaller inventories* with more frequent replenishments and higher total ordering costs. A small r encourages the buildup of inventories and reduces the annual replenishment expenses.

If for a population of n stocked items we consider that the charge r is the same for all of them, although unknown yet, we can graph an exchange curve in terms of the total (i.e., across all items) average inventory investment versus the total annual ordering cost, having r as a parameter and assuming that all items are replenished in economic order quantities.

The economic order quantity Q_i^* for the ith item is given by Wilson's lot size formula (4.1). It is straightforward to derive the two aggregate measures mentioned above:

$$Y = \frac{\text{Total average}}{\text{inventory investment}} = \sum_{i=1}^{n} \frac{1}{2} Q_i^* C_i = \frac{1}{\sqrt{2r}} \sum_{i=1}^{n} \sqrt{A_i D_i C_i}$$

$$X = \frac{\text{Total annual}}{\text{ordering cost}} = \sum_{i=1}^{n} \frac{A_i D_i}{Q_i^*} = \frac{\sqrt{r}}{\sqrt{2}} \sum_{i=1}^{n} \sqrt{A_i D_i C_i} \,.$$

The equation of the exchange curve is a hyperbola:

$$XY = \frac{1}{2} \left(\sum_{i=1}^{n} \sqrt{A_i D_i C_i} \right)^2 .$$

It is also true that:

$$\frac{Y}{X} = \frac{1}{r}$$

and this helps us pinpoint various values of the inventory carrying charge in the exchange curve.

If management does not want a total investment in inventory larger on the average than, say, $650,000 the exchange curve (Figure 4.28) shows that the inventory carrying charge should not exceed $r = 0.27$; for this value of r the total annual ordering cost is $175,628. A value of $r = 0.20$ (which is most commonly cited in the literature on inventory control as being typical of the American manufacturing industry) implies a total average inventory investment of $755,784 and ordering costs of $151,157.

When exchange curves for safety stocks are derived, the policy variable can be, for example, the safety factor k (see section 4.4) and the aggregate measures may be chosen: the total safety stock investment versus the expected annual value of backordered demand. For details see Brown [1967, chaps. 14 and 17] or Peterson and Silver [1979, chaps. 6 and 7].

---

*By inventories we are referring here to cycle or working stock. Safety stocks, for a given level of customer service, tend to increase as *EOQ* decreases as a result of a high r (see section 4.4).

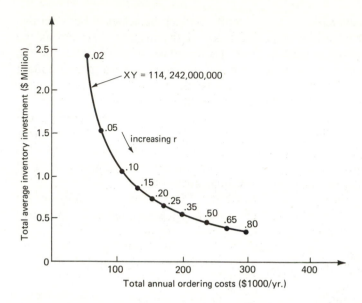

FIGURE 4.28   Exchange curve for value of $\sum_{i=1}^{n} \sqrt{A_i D_i C_i} = 478,000$, and replenishment by *EOQ*.

4.6.2   How Much to Order?

We have presented in section 4.2 decision rules on economic order quantities under various assumptions. However, it is important to impose both upper and lower limits to the economic order quantity beyond the recommendations resulting from EOQ calculations.

Since we cannot trust usage rates over very long periods of time, it is wise to allow for a maximum order quantity of at most one year. Of course, this maximum amount is a management decision that can be revised any time this seems advisable. It can also take into account other considerations, such as the shelf life of the item. Thus, if the EOQ is larger than a one-year supply or the supply over the allowable shelf life, the smallest of the three quantities should be used as a replenishment order.

It also makes sense to define a minimum amount to order; for instance, the equivalent of one month of demand. This would prevent ordering in such small sizes that one setup would follow after the other.

Minimum order quantities may also be required by outside suppliers, for whom it might be uneconomical to process an order unless a minimum amount is requested.

In some production processes, such as in the chemical industry, the size of the production batch could be imposed by the capacity of certain reaction tanks or of some special containers.

Finally, for lumpy demand items, Brown [1977, p. 248] recommends that the economic order quantity should be rounded upward to be at least as large as the standard deviation of the lead time demand.

4.6.3   Updating Frequency of System Parameters

The frequency of updating the system parameters depends on several factors such as whether the item is fast moving or slow moving, and whether it is an A, B, or C class item.

A very important parameter is the length of the review period; that is, the length of the time interval between regular reviews of the available inventory. For the important A items, continuous close surveillance is recommended, that is, stock status should be updated after each transaction. The C class items warrant the least attention and, therefore, large safety stocks and a simple control system (e.g., the two-bin system) should be employed. For all other items it seems reasonable to recommend the use of one week as a review period, as a proxy for a continuous review system.

Since demand forecasts are used primarily to define order points and order quantities, the updating frequency of the forecasting is directly related to the updating of EOQs and order points. Monthly updating of order points and quarterly updating of EOQs for fast-moving items are normally considered appropriate. This implies that demand forecasting should be updated monthly, and that the lead times should be expressed in months. However, for important A items, the EOQ and order point should be reviewed every time an order is placed.

In the case of slow-moving items, if demand forecasts and order points are based on empirical distributions, we suggest that the order points and EOQs be updated only once a year. However, when exponential smoothing with a very small α is used for forecasting, it is necessary to update demand forecasts and order points once a month, and EOQs once a quarter.

For lumpy demand items, where an (s, S) ordering policy is appropriate, the maximum and minimum levels are revised once a year or after at least 30 demand transactions, whichever occurs earlier (Brown [1977, p. 248]).

4.6.4   Actions to Be Taken When Tracking Signal Is Triggered

Section 4.3.5 has dealt with the issue of tracking signals to monitor forecast errors, and a test based on the smoothed forecast error, to check whether the forecast is biased, was developed there. Discussions were also presented in section 4.3 on adaptive control techniques, by which the value of the smoothing constant was regarded as a parameter and its value changed automatically in response to indications from the tracking signal of an out-of-control situation.

We should be aware, however, that forecasting may not be left entirely under the supervision of automated systems, as sometimes fundamental changes occur in the demand pattern that require human intervention. It is also true that if we are dealing with a large number of items, it could be impractical to study the demand behavior of every item whose tracking signal triggers and, therefore, some mixed system, that combines automatic control with managerial action, is needed.

The procedure we present here attempts to correct the disturbance the first time it occurs by automatically increasing the smoothing constant, thus making the forecast respond faster to actual demand changes. After a specified number of months, the computations switch back to the normal value of α, if the forecast agrees with the demand. But if the tracking signal is triggered while using the fast smoothing constant, a report is printed containing the demand history for the past 12 months (or more if available and desired) and external intervention is requested to correct the forecast. Since in many cases the increase of α is sufficient to correct the forecasting inaccuracies,* this procedure only signals for management analysis of those cases requiring external judgment.

Particular values of α which correspond to normal smoothing have been discussed in section 4.3. To decide whether to use normal smoothing or fast smoothing, we need to keep track of a smoothing rate counter, COUNT, for each stock item. If the forecast model was initiated by using one year or more of previous data, or if we are fairly confident of the values used to initialize the forecasting model, the counter COUNT is set to zero. If, however, we are dealing with a new item or one with a very short history, the counter is set equal to the number of months we think is needed for the forecast to track the demand properly, by using the fast smoothing coefficient. Let us say, for the sake of being specific, that we let COUNT = 6. Actually, any number from 4 to 9 seems to be appropriate, depending on the item's demand pattern. Each month, in the process of revising the forecast, the counter value is reduced by one, until it reaches zero.

Whenever the tracking signal is not triggered and the counter is zero, the normal smoothing coefficient should be used; and whenever the tracking signal is not triggered and the counter is positive, the fast smoothing constant should be used.

Whenever the tracking signal is triggered and the counter is zero, automatically the counter is increased, say to COUNT = 6, and the smoothing

*Sometimes errors in recording data may slip through and, if large enough, when processed in revising the forecasts might trip the tracking signal. These one-time errors are normally corrected by the automatic procedure outlined above. However, to prevent this sort of situation, or at least to detect the big outliers, the concept of "demand filters" was developed. Thus, any actual demand which is more than 4 or 5 current standard deviations away from the forecast should be called to the attention of an appropriate management person, as a possible outlier.

rate takes on the fast value. In this form, during the coming six months the forecast will be based more on current demand and less on past history.

Whenever the tracking signal is triggered and the counter has a positive value, this indicates that the faster smoothing is not adequate to compensate for the change in demand pattern, and management should exercise judgment to incorporate the proper corrections into the model. The computer should generate a report containing the item code number, its cost (to measure the importance of its contribution to inventory investment), the value of the tracking signal detection limit, the type of forecasting model used (with or without trend), and historical information of the past 12 months regarding actual demand, forecast level, trend (if available), demand forecast, forecast error, and the standard deviation or variance of the forecast errors. When the necessary corrections have been made, the smoothed error is set to zero and the smoothing rate counter is set to zero or 6 (say), depending on whether normal or fast smoothing is used, respectively.

The types of corrective actions management can take to improve the forecasting procedures are basically the following:

- change the forecast level
- change the forecast trend, if corrections for trends are used
- incorporate trend, if corrections for trends are not used
- cancel trend, if corrections for trend were used but that seems inappropriate
- modify the value of the smoothing constants
- modify the value of the tracking signal factor

These modifications are self-explanatory. It may take some time until management develops the proper skill to deal with this problem. At least until the learning process is well established, it could pay off to keep track of the forecast errors resulting from the modified forecasts and the unchanged forecasts, in order to encourage the types of changes which seem to result in significant improvement.

4.6.5 *Management Adjustments to Statistical Forecasts*

The statistical forecasting methods that we have incorporated in the inventory control system are designed to detect and extrapolate consistent patterns in past demand data including base, trends, and seasonalities. However, there are many instances where information is available about changes in the demand pattern that have not yet taken place, which could effectively improve the statistical forecast provided by the system. Price change development of new items, advertising promotions, competitor policies known in advance, changes in the national economy, and opening of new markets are just a few examples of events that could greatly affect the demand of all or a few items. These events can be recognized by management long before they actually modify the demand pattern of a given item. Thus, it becomes important that management introduces these subjective elements into the forecasting system, by adjusting the statistical forecast provided by the computer. Figure 4.29 illustrates the demand forecasting system when external management adjustments are combined with the statistical forecast computations to create the final forecast.

The actions that management could take to adjust the statistical forecast are essentially the same actions that are available when the demand tracking signal is triggered, namely:

- Change the value of the forecast for the present period with or without carrying this change into the forecast model.
- Modify some or all of the parameters involved in the forecasting model, that is, smoothing coefficients, level, trend, and tracking signal factor.
- Modify the type of forecasting model used, that is, forecasting with or without trend and consideration of seasonal cycles.

Whatever the change may be, when a forecast adjustment results exclusively from management intervention, it is important to keep track separately of the forecast errors incurred by the adjusted forecast and by the unchanged statistical forecast. In this way, a measure of performance can be

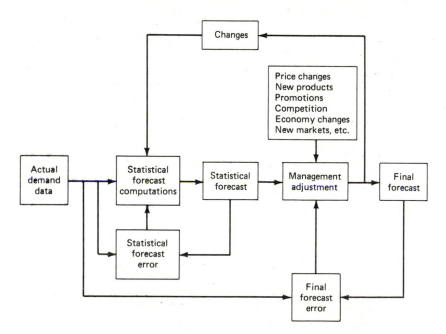

FIGURE 4.29　Demand forecasting system with management adjustment.

attached to external adjustments and a learning process can be established, by encouraging the continuation of those kinds of changes which usually improve the forecast and by discouraging changes in the wrong direction.

4.6.6 Production and Inventory Control System Outputs*

The purpose of this section is to provide a very general discussion on the type of outputs we could expect to generate from a production and inventory control system. The system outputs can be divided into four categories:

A. operating documents, which include shop orders, purchase requisitions, and finished product final assembly orders
B. routine status reports
C. management exception reports
D. analysis reports

The operating documents are those which direct the production operations. The primary purpose of the production and inventory control system is to issue these documents at the appropriate times for the required quantities. The routine status reports are used for reference purposes and, to some extent, for management review to check that the system is operating satisfactorily. The management exception reports are intended to draw attention to particular problem areas and usually require some management intervention or judgment. The analysis reports periodically summarize various operating statistics and, therefore, permit an evaluation of the operating performance in the recent past. These reports can be used to identify more general problem areas than are specified in the management exception reports and also provide data which serve as a basis for management selection of system parameters.

We now provide brief comments regarding each type of output that we may consider appropriate in a production and inventory control system:

A. *Operating Documents*

1. *Shop orders*. Shop orders are the documents which direct the in-plant production of manufactured products.
2. *Purchase requisitions*. These documents generate a request to initiate the replenishment of a particular purchased item for a specific quantity.

B. *Routine Status Reports*

1. *Inventory status*. The inventory status report is prepared once every review period and show the various status information for each item for which there

---

*Although this chapter was primarily concerned with pure inventory systems, as our book also addresses the production function in other chapters and because we do not intend to include another section on system outputs, we chose to enlarge the scope of this section so as to cover the more general production and inventory control systems.

is some physical inventory or for any item which is designated as a stocked item but which may not have any inventory at that time.

2. *Nonstock items requirement status.* The nonstock items requirement status report shows the level of known requirements based on open orders by the date of requirements in the future. It shows whether a shop order or a purchase requisition has been released as yet to cover the requirements or, if not, the date on which the document will be generated.

3. *Shop order and purchase requisition status.* This report is primarily intended to show the degree of completion of partially completed open orders.

4. *Finished product requirement status.* This report shows the level of future customer order commitments for each finished product. It shows the number of customer orders for which shipment is past due for each finished product.

5. *Open customer order status.* This report lists each open customer order, that is, all of the items included in the order which have not been shipped and the status of each item.

C. *Management Exception Reports*

1. *Customer order edit rejects.* This report lists the customer orders and order changes which were entered into the system, but which were rejected because of some type of validity check error.

2. *Inventory shortage.* It may be decided to have inventory shortages reported in two different ways. One report lists the inventory shortages by items—that is, it identifies each shop order number for which each item is backordered, the date the backorder occurred, and the quantity unfilled. This report is a quick indication of how great the need is for a particular item. The other version of the inventory shortage report would organize the information by shop order. Listing all components required for the shop order which are not available and specifying the quantity required of each. This report is useful to determine which items are holding up production of the particular shop order.

3. *Past due report.* This report lists all of the open shop orders which have not been completed by the specified due date, the open purchase requisitions for which the material has not been received by the specified due date, and the open customer orders which have not been shipped by the specified promised shipping date.

4. *Forecast tracking error signals.* Whenever the forecasting procedures are not tracking demand in a satisfactory way, a message is automatically released indicating the forecast tracking error. According to the magnitude of this error and the frequency in which this error occurred, an automatic correction is made by the system or a notice is released indicating the need of outside management intervention (just discussed in section 4.6.4).

D. *Analysis Reports*

1. *Shipping on time/delay performance.* This report analyzes the shipping performance for customer orders.

2. *Vendor on time delivery/quality performance.* This report would contain an analysis of the purchase orders placed.

3. *Vendor and shop lead time analysis.* This report contains an analysis of the manufacturing lead time on shop orders and purchase delivery lead times on purchase requisitions on all such actions in the past quarter.

4. *Production rate report.* The production rate for an item is the rate at which units are finished once the first unit in a lot has been completed. It is determined by dividing the total number of units in a lot by the elapsed time between the date the first unit is completed and the date the last unit is completed.

5. *Inventory service performance.* This report shows for each stocked item the number of purchase/manufactured lots completed in the past quarter, the completion performance on this lot—that is, the number that were completed on time and the number of days late for any late orders—the total usage over the past quarter, and the total number of units backordered over the period.

6. *Usage cost rank listing.* This report lists all products ranked in order of their usage during the past year, to be used as the basis for the ABC item classification (see section 4.4.1).

7. *Inactive stock report.* This report lists all of the items which did not have any usage during the past year, but for which there is some stock in inventory.

8. *Suggested classifications for made-to-order versus stock.* This report is the result of the made-to-order versus stock analysis performed on each finished product (section 4.5.1). For each finished product, the report indicates one of the following four classifications as the result of the analysis:

   - stock because of delivery service requirement
   - stock because of economic justification
   - made-to-order because of economic justification
   - no clear economic advantage

9. *Finished product minimum promised delivery time.* This report specifies the minimum delivery time that can be provided for each finished product based on the total manufacturing lead time of the finished product.

BIBLIOGRAPHY

AGGARWAL, S. C., "A Review of Current Inventory Theory and Its Applications," *International Journal of Production Research*, No. 12, 1974, pp. 443–472.

ARROW, K. J., T. E. HARRIS, and J. MARSCHAK, "Optimal Inventory Policy," *Econometrica*, Vol. 19, 1951, pp. 250–272.

ARROW, K. J., S. KARLIN, and H. SCARF (editors), *Studies in the Mathematical Theory of Inventory and Production*, Stanford University Press, Stanford, Calif., 1958.

BALINTFY, J. L., "On a Basic Class of Multi-Item Inventory Problems," *Management Science*, Vol. 10, No. 2, January 1964, pp. 287–297.

BELLMAN, R., I. GLICKSBERG, and O. GROSS, "On the Optimal Inventory Equation," *Management Science*, Vol. 2, No. 1, October 1955, pp. 83–104.

BENLI, O. and P. NANDA, "A Solution Procedure for Location–Allocation–Production Problems," Department of Industrial Engineering and Operations Research, College of Engineering, Syracuse University, Syracuse, N.Y., 1977.

BERRY, W. L., "Lot Sizing Procedures for Requirements Planning Systems: A Framework for Analysis," *Production and Inventory Management*, Vol. 13, No. 2, 1972, pp. 19–34.

BOMBERGER, E. E.,   "A Dynamic Programming Approach to a Lot Size Scheduling Problem," *Management Science*, Vol. 12, No. 11, July 1966, pp. 778–784.

BOX, G. E. P. and G. M. JENKINS, *Time Series Analysis*, Holden-Day, San Francisco, 1976.

BROWN, R. G., *Statistical Forecasting for Inventory Control*, McGraw-Hill, New York, 1959.

BROWN, R. G., *Smoothing, Forecasting and Prediction of Discrete Time Series*, Prentice-Hall, Englewood Cliffs, N.J., 1963.

BROWN, R. G., *Decision Rules for Inventory Management*, Holt, Rinehart and Winston, New York, 1967.

BROWN, R. G., *Management Decisions for Production Operations*, Dryden Press, Hinsdale, Ill., 1971.

BROWN, R. G., *Materials Management Systems*, Wiley, New York, 1977.

BROWN, R. G., "Inventory Control," in J. J. Moder and S. E. Elmaghraby (editors), *Handbook of Operations Research — Models and Applications*, Van Nostrand Reinhold, New York, 1978a.

BROWN, R. G., "Forecasting," in J. J. Moder and S. E. Elmaghraby (editors), *Handbook of Operations Research — Models and Applications*, Van Nostrand Reinhold, New York, 1978b.

BUFFA, E. S., *Modern Production Management*, Wiley, New York, 1969.

BUFFA, E. S. and W. H. TAUBERT, *Production-Inventory Systems: Planning and Control*, Irwin, Homewood, Ill. 1972.

BURGIN, T. A. and A. R. WILD, "Stock Control-Experience and Usable Theory," *Operational Research Quarterly*, Vol. 18, No. 1, March 1967, pp. 35–52.

CANDEA, D. I., "A Comparative Study of Solutions to the Holt, Modigliani, Muth and Simon Disaggregation Model by Search Techniques," Working Paper No. 814-75, Sloan School of Management, M.I.T., Cambridge, Mass., October 1975.

CANDEA, D. I., "Issues of Hierarchical Planning in Multi-Stage Production Systems," Technical Report No. 134, Operations Research Center, M.I.T., Cambridge, Mass., July 1977.

CHOW, W. M., "Adaptive Control of the Exponential Smoothing Constant," *Journal of Industrial Engineering*, Vol. 16, No. 5, 1965, pp. 314–317.

CLARK, A. J., "An Informal Survey of Multi-Echelon Inventory Theory," *Naval Research Logistics Quarterly*, Vol. 19, 1972, pp. 621–650.

COHEN, G. D., "Bayesian Adjustment of Sales Forecasts in Multi-Item Inventory Control Systems," *Journal of Industrial Engineering*, Vol. 17, No. 9, 1966, pp. 474–479.

CROSTON, J. D., "Forecasting and Stock Control for Intermittent Demands," *Operational Research Quarterly*, Vol. 23, No. 3, September 1972, pp. 289–303.

CROSTON, J. D., "Stock Levels for Slow-Moving Items," *Operations Research Quarterly*, Vol. 25, No. 1, March 1974, pp. 123–130.

CROWSTON, W. B. and M. WAGNER, "Lot Size Determination in Multi-Stage Assembly Systems," Working Paper No. 508-71, Alfred P. Sloan School of Management, M.I.T., Cambridge, Mass., September 1970.

CROWSTON, W. B., M. WAGNER, and J. F. WILLIAMS, "Economic Lot Size Determination in Multi-Stage Assembly Systems," *Management Science*, Vol. 19, No. 5, January 1973, pp. 517–527.

DORSEY, R. C., T. J. HODGSON, and H. D. RATLIFF, "A Production Scheduling Problem with Batch Processing," *Operations Research*, Vol. 22, No. 6, November–December 1974, pp. 1271–1279.

DORSEY, R. C., T. J. HODGSON, and H. D. RATLIFF, "A Network Approach to a Multi-Facility, Multi-Product Production Scheduling Problem without Backordering," *Management Science*, Vol. 21, No. 7, March 1975, pp. 813–822.

DVORETZKY, A., J. KIEFER, and J. WOLFOWITZ, "The Inventory Problem: I, Case of Known Distributions of Demand; II, Case of Unknown Distributions of Demand," *Econometrica*, Vol. 20, 1952, pp. 187–222.

DVORETZKY, A., J. KIEFER, and J. WOLFOWITZ, "On the Optimal Character of the (s, S) Policy in Inventory Theory," *Econometrica*, Vol. 21, 1953, pp. 586–596.

DYER, D., "To Stock or Not to Stock? That Is the Question," *Modern Distribution Management*, Vol. 7, No. 5, March 23, 1973, pp. 3–7.

EHRHARDT, R., "The Power Approximation for Computing (s, S) Inventory Policies," *Management Science*, Vol. 25, No. 8, August 1979, pp. 777–786.

EHRHARDT, R., "Analytic Approximations for (s, S) Inventory Policy Operating Characteristics," *Naval Research Logistics Quarterly*, Vol. 28, No. 2, June 1981, pp. 255–266.

EILON, S. and J. ELMALEH, "Adaptive Limits in Inventory Control," *Management Science*, Vol. 16, No. 8, April 1970, pp. B533–B548.

EILON, S. and J. ELMALEH, "An Evaluation of Alternative Inventory Control Policies," *International Journal of Production Research*, Vol. 7, No. 1, 1968, pp. 3–14.

ELMAGHRABY, S. E., "The Economic Lot Scheduling Problem (ELSP): Review and Extensions," *Management Science*, Vol. 24, No. 6, February 1978, pp. 587–598.

FELLER, W., *An Introduction to Probability Theory and Its Applications*, Vol. 2, Wiley, New York, 1971.

FORRESTER, J. W., *Industrial Dynamics*, M.I.T. Press, Cambridge, Mass., 1961.

FREELAND, J. R. and E. PORTEUS, "Evaluating the Effectiveness of a New Method for Computing Approximately Optimal (s, S) Inventory Policies," *Operations Research*, Vol. 28, No. 2, March–April 1980, pp. 353–364.

GABBAY, H., "A Hierarchical Approach to Production Planning," Technical Report No. 120, Operations Research Center, M.I.T., Cambridge, Mass., December 1975.

GEISLER, M., "A Test of a Statistical Method for Computing Selected Inventory Model Characteristics by Simulation," *Management Science*, Vol. 10, No. 4, July 1964, pp. 709–715.

GERSON, G. and R. G. BROWN, "Decision Rules for Equal Shortage Policies," *Naval Research Logistics Quarterly*, Vol. 17, No. 3, 1970, pp. 351–358.

GOYAL, S. K., "Analysis of Joint Replenishment Inventory Systems with Resource Restrictions," *Operational Research Quarterly*, Vol. 26, No. 1, April 1975, pp. 197–203.

GOYAL, S. K., "Determination of Optimum Packaging Frequency of Items Jointly Replenished," *Management Science*, Vol. 21, No. 4, December 1974, pp. 436–443.

GOYAL, S. K., "Lot Size Scheduling on a Single Machine for Stochastic Demand," *Management Science*, Vol. 19, No. 11, July 1973, pp. 1322–1325.

GRAVES, S. C., "The Multi-Product Production Cycling Problem," unpublished dissertation, University of Rochester, October 1977.

GROFF, G. K. and J. F. MUTH, *Operations Management: Analysis for Decisions*, Irwin, Homewood, Ill., 1972.

HADLEY, G. and T. M. WHITIN, *Analysis of Inventory Systems*, Prentice-Hall, Englewood Cliffs, N.J., 1963.

HAEHLING VON LANZENAUER, C. H., "Production and Employment Scheduling in Multi-Stage Production Systems," *Naval Research Logistics Quarterly*, Vol. 17, No. 2, June 1970, pp. 193–198.

HANSSMANN, F., *Operations Research in Production and Inventory Control*, Wiley, New York, 1962.

HASTINGS, N. A. J. and J. B. PEACOCK, *Statistical Distributions*, London Butterworths, London, 1975.

HAX, A. C., "Integration of Strategic and Tactical Planning in the Aluminum Industry," Working Paper No. 026-73, Operations Research Center, M.I.T., Cambridge, Mass., September 1973.

HAX, A. C., "The Design of Large Scale Logistics Systems: A Survey and an Approach," in W. H. Marlow (editor), *Modern Trends in Logistics Research*, M.I.T. Press, Cambridge, Mass., 1976.

HAX, A. C. and H. C. MEAL, "Hierarchical Integration of Production Planning and Scheduling," in M. A. Geisler (editor), *Studies in Management Sciences*, Vol. I, *Logistics*, North Holland-American Elsevier, Amsterdam, Holland, 1975.

HOEL, P. G., S. C. PORT, and C. J. STONE, *Introduction to Statistical Theory*, Houghton Mifflin, Boston, 1971.

HOLT, C. C., F. MODIGLIANI, J. F. MUTH, and H. A. SIMON, *Planning Production, Inventories, and Work Force*, Prentice-Hall, Englewood Cliffs, N.J., 1960.

IGLEHART, D., "Optimality of (s, S) Policies in the Infinite Horizon Dynamic Inventory Problem," *Management Science*, Vol. 9, No. 2, January 1963a, pp. 259–267.

IGLEHART, D., "Dynamic Programming and Stationary Analysis of Inventory Problems," in H. E. Scarf, D. M. Gilford, and M. W. Shelly (editors), *Multistage Inventory Models and Techniques*, Stanford University Press, Stanford, Calif., 1963b.

IWANIEC, K., "An Inventory Model with Full Load Ordering," *Management Science*, Vol. 25, No. 4, April 1979, pp. 374–384.

JENSEN, P. A. and H. A. KHAN, "Scheduling in a Multi-Stage Production System with Setup and Inventory Costs," *AIIE Transactions*, Vol. 4, No. 2, 1972, pp. 126–133.

JOHNSON, J., "On Stock Selection at Spare Parts Stores Sections," *Naval Research Logistics Quarterly*, Vol. 9, No. 1, March 1962, pp. 49–59.

JOHNSON, L. A. and D. C. MONTGOMERY, *Operations Research in Production Planning, Scheduling, and Inventory Control*, Wiley, New York, 1974.

KARLIN, S., "The Application of Renewal Theory to the Study of Inventory Policies," in K. J. Arrow, S. Karlin, and H. Scarf (editors), *Studies in the Mathematical Theory of Inventory and Production*, Stanford University Press, Stanford, Calif., 1958.

KARLIN, S., "Steady State Solutions," in K. J. Arrow, S. Karlin, and H. Scarf (editors), *Studies in the Mathematical Theory of Inventory and Production*, Stanford University Press, Stanford, Calif., 1958.

KARLIN, S. and H. M. TAYLOR, *A First Course in Stochastic Processes*, Academic Press, New York, 1975.

KARMARKAR, U. S., "Multilocation Distribution Systems," Technical Report No. 117, Operations Research Center, M.I.T., Cambridge, Mass., September 1975.

KLINGMAN, D. D., R. M. SOLAND, and G. T. ROSS, "Optimal Lot-Sizing and Machine Loading for Multiple Products," in *The Problems of Disaggregation in Manufacturing and Service Organizations — Conference Proceedings*, Ohio State University, Columbus, Ohio, March 10–11, 1977.

KRAUSS, G. H., "An Approach to the Analysis of Integrated Production–Distribution Systems," in *The Problems of Disaggregation in Manufacturing and Service Organizations — Conference Proceedings*, Ohio State University, Columbus, Ohio, March 10–11, 1977.

LEVY, J., "Optimum Inventory Policy When Demand Is Increasing," *Operations Research*, Vol. 8, No. 6, November–December 1960, pp. 861–863.

LUENBERGER, D. C., *Introduction to Linear and Nonlinear Programming*, Addison-Wesley, Reading, Mass., 1973.

MAGEE, J. F., *Industrial Logistics*, McGraw-Hill, New York, 1968.

MAGEE, J. F. and D. M. BOODMAN, *Production Planning and Inventory Control*, McGraw-Hill, New York, 1967.

MAHER, M., J. GITTINS, and R. MORGAN, "An Analysis of a Multi-Line Re-Order System Using a Can-Order Policy," *Management Science*, Vol. 19, No. 7, March 1973, pp. 800–808.

MAKRIDAKIS, S. and S. C. WHEELWRIGHT, *Forecasting — Methods and Applications*, Wiley, New York, 1978.

MAKRIDAKIS, S. and S. C. WHEELWRIGHT, *Interactive Forecasting*, Holden-Day, San Francisco, 1978.

MANGASARIAN, O. L., *Nonlinear Programming*, McGraw-Hill, New York, 1969.

McCLAIN, J. O., "Dynamics of Exponential Smoothing with Trend Seasonal Terms," *Management Science*, Vol. 20, No. 9, May 1974, pp. 1300–1304.

McCLAIN, J. O. and L. J. Thomas, "Response Variance Tradeoffs in Adaptive Forecasting," *Operations Research*, Vol. 21, No. 2, March–April 1973, pp. 554–568.

McGARRAH, R. E., *Production and Logistics Management: Text and Cases*, Wiley, New York, 1963.

MONTGOMERY, D. C., "Adaptive Control of Exponential Smoothing Parameters by Evolutionary Operation," *AIEE Transactions*, Vol. 2, No. 3, 1970, pp. 268–269.

MONTGOMERY, D. C. and L. A. JOHNSON, *Forecasting and Times Series Analysis*, McGraw-Hill, New York, 1976.

MORGAN, J. I., "Question for Solving the Inventory Problem," *Harvard Business Review*, Vol. 41, No. 4, July–August 1963, pp. 95–110.

NADDOR, E., "Optimal and Heuristic Decisions in Single- and Multi-Item Inventory Systems," *Management Science*, Vol. 21, No. 11, July 1975, pp. 1234–1249.

NAHMIAS, S., "On the Equivalence of Three Approximate Continuous Review Inventory Models," *Naval Research Logistics Quarterly*, Vol. 23, No. 1, March 1976, pp. 31–36.

NAHMIAS, S., "On the Equivalence of Three Approximate Continuous Review Inventory Models," *Naval Research Logistics Quarterly*, Vol. 23, No. 1, March 1976, pp. 31–36.

NAHMIAS, S., "Simple Approximations for a Variety of Dynamic Leadtime Lost-Sales Inventory Models," *Operations Research*, Vol. 27, No. 5, September–October 1979, pp. 904–924.

ORAL, M., M. S. SALVADOR, A. REISMAN, and B. V. DEAN, "On the Evaluation of Shortage Costs for Inventory Control of Finished Goods," *Management Science*, Vol. 18, No. 6, February 1972, pp. B344–B351.

ORLICKY, J., *Material Requirements Planning*, McGraw-Hill, New York, 1975.

PETERSON, R. and E. A. SILVER, *Decision Systems for Inventory Management and Production Planning*, Wiley, New York, 1979.

PLOSSL, G. W. and O. W. WIGHT, "Material Requirements Planning by Computer," Special Report of the American Production and Inventory Control Society, Washington, D.C., 1971.

POPP, W., "Simple and Combined Inventory Policies, Production to Stock or to Order," *Management Science*, Vol. 11, No. 9, July 1965, pp. 868–873.

PRATT, J. W., H. RAIFFA, and R. SCHLAIFER, *Introduction to Statistical Decision Theory*, McGraw-Hill, New York, 1965.

RAIFFA, H., *Decision Analysis — Introductory Lectures on Choices Under Uncertainty*, Addison-Wesley, Reading, Mass., 1970.

RAIFFA, H., AND R. SCHLAIFER, *Applied Statistical Decision Theory*, Harvard University Press, Cambridge, Mass., 1961.

ROBERTS, S. D. and R. REED, "The Development of a Self-Adaptive Forecasting Technique," *AIIE Transactions*, Vol. 1, No. 4, 1969, pp. 314–322.

SCARF, H. E., "The Optimality of (*S, s*) Policies in the Dynamic Inventory Problem," in K. J. Arrow, S. Karlin, and P. Suppes (editors), *Mathematical Methods in the Social Sciences*, Stanford University Press, Stanford, Calif., 1960.

SCARF, H. E., "A Survey of Analytical Techniques in Inventory Theory," in H. E. Scarf, D. M. Gilford, and M. W. Shelly (editors), *Multistage Inventory Models and Techniques*, Stanford University Press, Stanford, Calif., 1963.

SCARF, H. E., D. M. GILFORD, and M. W. SHELLY (editors), *Multistage Inventory Models and Techniques*, Stanford University Press, Stanford, Calif., 1963.

SCHLAIFER, M. J., "The Use of an Economic Lot Range in Scheduling Production," *Management Science*, Vol. 5, No. 4, July 1959, pp. 434–442.

SCHWARTZ, B. L., "A New Approach to Stockout Penalties," *Management Science*, Vol. 12, No. 12, August 1966, pp. B538–B544.

SCHWARTZ, B. L., "Optimal Inventory Policies in Perturbed Demand Models," *Management Science*, Vol. 16, No. 8, April 1970, pp. B509–B518.

SCHWARZ, L. B. and L. SCHRAGE, "Optimal and System Myopic Policies for Multi-Echelon Production/Inventory Assembly Systems," *Management Science*, Vol. 21, No. 11, July 1975, pp. 1285–1294.

SILVER, E. A., "A Control System for Coordinated Inventory Replenishment," *International Journal of Production Research*, Vol. 12, No. 6, 1974, pp. 647–671.

SILVER, E. A., "Modifying the Economic Order Quantity (EOQ) to Handle Coordinated Replenishments of Two or More Items," *Production and Inventory Management*, Vol. 16, No. 3, 1975, pp. 26–38.

SILVER, E. A. and H. C. MEAL, "A Heuristic for Selecting Lot Size Requirements for the Case of a Deterministic Time-Varying Demand Rate and Discrete Opportunities for Replenishment," *Production and Inventory Management*, Vol. 14, No. 2, 1973, pp. 64–74.

SIMPSON, K. S., "In-Process Inventories," *Operations Research*, Vol. 6, No. 6, November 1958, pp. 863–873.

SNYDER, R., "Computation of (*S, s*) Ordering Policy Parameters," *Management Science*, Vol. 21, No. 2, October 1974, pp. 223–229.

SOKOLNIKOFF, I. S. and R. M. REDHEFFER, *Mathematics of Physics and Modern Engineering*, McGraw-Hill, New York, 1958.

SOLOMON, M. J., "The Use of an Economic Lot Range in Scheduling Production," *Management Science*, Vol. 5, No. 4, July 1959, pp. 434–442.

STEVENS, C. F., "On the Variability of Demand for Families of Items," *Operational Research Quarterly*, Vol. 25, No. 3, September 1974, pp. 411–419.

TAHA, H. A. and R. W. SKEITH, "The Economic Lot Sizes in Multi-Stage Production Systems," *AIIE Transactions*, June 1970, pp. 157–162.

TRIGG, D. W., "Monitoring a Forecast System," *Operational Research Quarterly*, Vol. 15, No. 3, September 1964, pp. 271–274.

TRIGG, D. W. and A. G. LEACH, "Exponential Smoothing with an Adaptive Response Rate," *Operational Research Quarterly*, Vol. 18, No. 1, 1967, pp. 53–59.

VEINOTT, A. F., JR., "Minimum Concave-Cost Solution of Leontief Substitution Models of Multi-Facility Inventory Systems," *Operations Research*, Vol. 17, March–April 1969, pp. 262–291.

VEINOTT, A. F., JR., "The Status of Mathematical Inventory Theory," *Management Science*, Vol. 12, No. 11, July 1966a, pp. 745–777.

VEINOTT, A. F., JR., "On the Optimality of (*s, S*) Inventory Policies: New Conditions and a New Proof," *SIAM Journal on Applied Mathematics*, Vol. 14, No. 5, September 1966b, pp. 1067–1083.

VEINOTT, A. F., JR. and H. WAGNER, "Computing Optimal (s, S) Inventory Policies," *Management Science*, Vol. 11, No. 5, March 1965, pp. 525–552.

WAGNER, H., M. O'HAGAN, and B. LUNDH, "An Empirical Study of Exactly and Approximately Optimal Inventory Policies," *Management Science*, Vol. 11, No. 7, May 1965, pp. 690–723.

WHEELWRIGHT, S. C. and S. MAKRIDAKIS, *Forecasting Methods for Management*, Wiley, New York, 1977.

WHITIN, T. M., *The Theory of Inventory Management*, Princeton University Press, Princeton, N.J., 1953.

WINTERS, P. R., "Forecasting Sales by Exponentially Weighted Moving Averages," *Management Science*, Vol. 6, No. 3, November 1960, pp. 324–342.

ZABEL, E., "A Note on the Optimality of (S, s) Policies in Inventory Theory," *Management Science*, Vol. 9, No. 1, October 1962, pp. 123–125.

ZANGWILL, W. I., "A Backlogging Model and a Multi-Echelon Model of a Dynamic Economic Lot Size Production System—A Network Approach," *Management Science*, Vol. 15, No. 9, May 1969, pp. 506–527.

ZIMMERMANN, H. J., "Periodic vs. Perpetual Inventory Control Systems," *Production and Inventory Management*, Vol. 7, No. 4, October 1966, pp. 66–79.

ZIMMERMANN, H. J. and M. G. SOVEREIGN, *Quantitative Models for Production Management*, Prentice-Hall, Englewood Cliffs, N.J., 1974.

5

Operations Scheduling

5.1 Introduction

As we discussed in Chapter 1 of this text, the hierarchical nature of the managerial process warrants the use of hierarchical production planning and inventory control systems in which decisions are made in sequence, with each set of decisions at an aggregate level providing constraints within which more detailed decisions are made. This approach is instrumental in bringing about computational feasibility in large real world planning models, and at the same time facilitates management involvement at the various stages of the decision-making process.

If we are to refer to the industrial manufacturing environment, a typical set of decision levels consists of facilities design, assignment of products to manufacturing plants and distributing warehouses, aggregate planning, production scheduling and inventory control, and operations scheduling. The lower one gets in the hierarchy, the narrower is the scope of the plan, the lower is the management level involved, the more detailed is the information needed, and the shorter is the planning time horizon. Thus, operations scheduling is at the bottom of the hierarchical planning system. Its purpose is to make the most detailed scheduling decisions, involving the assignment of the operations to specific machines and operators during a given time interval.

Considering the relationship between the production process and the demand process, production systems can be broken down into two categories: intermittent systems and continuous systems, each category imposing certain characteristics upon the operations scheduling process.

In *intermittent systems* the production rate that may be achieved with existing capacity is much higher than the demand rate and, therefore, items are normally produced in batches. Machines are time-shared among many different items, being switched from one product to another according to some pattern governed by the demand process. In the case of customer made-to-order production, the manufacturing lot size may be as small as one unit, and almost no processing patterns are ever repeated.

Typically, in a manufacturing environment the intermittent production system generates the *job shop scheduling* problem. The job shop is the set of all machines that are associated with a given set of jobs, and the problem is to order the operations to be performed on each machine subject to routing and shop constraints, such that some measurable function of the ordering is optimized (Salvador [1978]).

A special case of the intermittent systems is the large-scale one-time project, in which all productive resources are fully devoted to the realization of some usually complex task (a power plant, a spaceship, and R&D project, etc.) over an extended period of time (months or even years). Scheduling for the large-scale one-time project is known as the *project management* problem. In such a problem the activities involved in the project are represented as a network, and scheduling and resource allocations are performed by specialized network planning techniques.

In *continuous systems*, demand for the product is very large and reasonably stable, thus making it economical for the manufacturing facility to be designed and physically laid out by product in the form of a production line (or assembly line for assembly processes). The line produces at a rate which is virtually equal to the rate at which the item is consumed, thus making it necessary for the item* to be produced continuously.

The continuous system gives rise to the *line balancing* problem, where there is a very close relationship between the design of the line and the scheduling issue. The tasks to be performed along the line should be defined and grouped in such a way that smooth flow of the product is obtained with maximum labor and equipment utilization. Once the line is designed and set up, its internal working is no longer a matter of concern to the scheduler; for the purpose of production scheduling, the line may be regarded as just a single large integrated machine.

This chapter is structured according to the three classes of scheduling problems above: job shop scheduling, project management, and line balancing.

5.2 Job Shop Scheduling

Before proceeding further, several basic notions have to be defined; we will adopt the definitions given in the classical book of Conway et al. [1967].

An *operation* is an elementary task to be performed. The amount of

---

*There are many instances in which the line produces not one but a group of items that have different sizes but similar design and essentially the same sequence of production operations. In this case we speak about group technology (Starr [1978]).

processing required by an operation is called *processing time*; in most cases setup times are independent of job sequence and are included in the processing times. A *job* is a set of operations that are interrelated by precedence restrictions derived from technological constraints. The precedence restrictions define the *routing*, which is the ordering of the operations onto jobs. A *machine* is a piece of equipment, a device, or a facility capable of performing an operation.

An operation has three attributes: it is associated with a job, is identified with a specific machine, and requires a processing time on the machine.

The *ready time*, *release time*, or *arrival time* of a job is the time at which the job is released to the shop floor; it is the earliest time at which the first operation of the job could begin processing. In some applications the start time of the job must be contained in some interval determined by an early and a late start time (Fisher and Jaikumar [1978]). The *due date* is the time by which the last operation of the job should be completed. The *completion time* of a job is the time at which processing of the last operation of the job is completed.

A *schedule* is an ordering of the operations onto machines. A schedule has to observe routing relationships, and possibly other restrictions (e.g., no overlap of operations in a time interval).

To illustrate, consider Table 5.1, which contains data on three jobs that are released at various times to the shop. The first job has two operations; the second, four operations; and the third, one operation. The numbering of the operations is such that they are to be performed in the same sequence as they are numbered.

Figure 5.1 shows one of the many possible schedules that may be generated for the given set of jobs. The graphical technique used in a Gantt chart. A Gantt chart (first suggested by Henry Laurence Gantt in 1903) has a time scale along the abscissa and a horizontal line for each machine. Each operation is represented by a segment whose beginning indicates the planned start time, and whose length is proportional to the processing time. Time periods with no segment yet drawn indicate available capacity on that particular machine in which other jobs may be scheduled.

From the schedule of Figure 5.1 it is apparent that job 1 is early, job 2 is completed right on time, and job 3 is tardy. By manipulating the line segments associated with the operations one may generate other schedules.

Since operations scheduling is the lowest level in a hierarchical structure, it uses decisions made at higher planning levels with respect to two important issues:

1. The productive resources (facilities with machines and workers) are fully specified. It is not within the scope of scheduling to add production capacity.
2. The jobs to be performed are given to the operations scheduling process and they all must be completed.

These two issues were addressed in chapters 2 and 3, respectively. The interactions among these decisions will be further discussed in Chapter 6.

TABLE 5.1 Data on Set of Three Jobs

JOB #	ARRIVAL TIME	DUE DATE	OPERATION 1		OPERATION 2		OPERATION 3		OPERATION 4	
			MACHINE	PROC'G* TIME	MACHINE	PROC'G TIME	MACHINE	PROC'G TIME	MACHINE	PROC'G TIME
1	0	11	1	3	3	2	—	—	—	—
2	1	10	3	1	2	3	3	3	1	2
3	3	8	3	1	—	—	—	—	—	—

*Proc'g = Processing.

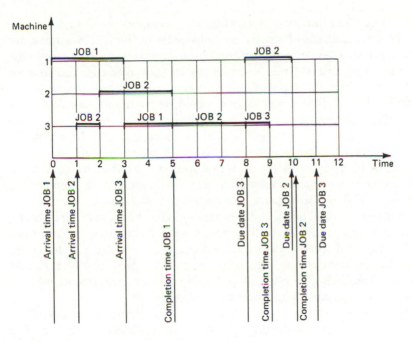

FIGURE 5.1   A schedule for set of three jobs.

It is useful to distinguish two different types of intermittent systems: the *open job shop* and the *closed job shop*. In an open job shop all products are made to order and, normally, no inventory is carried. In a closed job shop, routine demand for finished products can be forecasted, production run in batch sizes, and inventories are carried.

In an *open shop*, or made-to-order business, the forecasts that drive the aggregate plan are made in terms of work load (hours of machine or labor utilization). Since one does not produce for stock, the emphasis is on the readiness of the work force and equipment to absorb fluctuating demands. This implies that, when incoming business is affected by seasonalities, the manufacturer has to be ready to vary the work force accordingly (assuming that enough machine capacity exists to meet the peak season), or to resort to subcontracting to meet high demand. The value of the aggregate plan lies in detecting the periods when capacity changes are required in view of the available forecasts, and thus enables the managers to take the appropriate preparatory steps well before the tide has arrived. As customer orders come in, the scheduling function tries to accommodate them within the available capacity of the various work centers required for processing. The better the forecast and the aggregate planning, the better the match between capacity and work load, and the fewer the difficulties with scheduling the operations to be performed.

It is rare to find pure open shops because managers try to find ways to alleviate the disadvantages of strictly made-to-order business. Thus, there are cases where a made-to-order manufacturer also produces some stock items that are used in a compensatory role to make up for the difference (positive or negative) between available capacity and incoming made-to-order requests. Or, if the competitive conditions permit, one would negotiate delivery due dates such as to allow the release rate of customer orders to the shop to match the production rate that can be achieved with the existing capacity. In multistage production systems,* another alternative is quite often at work: the final product comes in a large variety of configurations obtained by combining standard components (parts, subassemblies, assemblies) in a number of different ways. This is, for instance, the situation of the automobile industry where a combination of standard components—engine, body, seats, upholstery, and so on, and options: power steering, power brakes, automatic transmission, air conditioning, and so on—yield the final configuration that is sold to the customer. In such cases the assembly shop may produce to customer specifications, thus being an open shop, while standard components may be produced for stock, making fabrication a closed shop.

In the case of a *closed shop* customers are served from inventory; thus, the emphasis is on the availability of stock or readiness to deliver. The aggregate plan is drawn in terms of product types (see Chapter 3). We realize, however, that what is actually produced in the shop are individual items; product-type units are just abstractions. Therefore, we have to disaggregate the aggregate plan into manufacturing batches of individual items. In the disaggregation process the decisions pertaining to *which* item to produce and in what *quantity* are made in the context of inventory replenishment rules. Each manufacturing lot thus established, with its set of interrelated operations, becomes a job that will be taken up by the operations scheduling procedure.

Although disaggregation techniques will be fully analyzed in Chapter 6, it might be helpful to discuss here the simplest of such techniques: "the equalization of runout times." As its name implies, the production amount established at the aggregate level for a given type is allocated among member items in such a way as to equalize their runout times.

Let P5 be one of the product types, the fifth considered in the aggregate plan. Suppose that this type includes six items: P5I1, P5I2,..., P5I6. For P5, Table 5.2 shows the production and inventory levels, by period, as they result from an aggregate planning model run over a 13-period planning horizon. The product type has an initial inventory of 16,825.

Table 5.3 gives detailed information on each of the six individual items: initial inventories, and demands for the first two periods.

---

*A multistage production system is a production process in which component parts have to be obtained by manufacturing or by purchasing, then assembled into subassemblies and assemblies, and finally into the finished good.

TABLE 5.2   Aggregate Information on Product Type P5
Initial inventory = 16,825

PERIOD	DEMAND	PRODUCTION LEVEL	END-OF-PERIOD INVENTORY
1	18,544	10,871	9,152
2	13,233	12,788	8,707
3	12,254	9,712	6,165
4	11,933	7,979	2,211
5	9,200	6,989	0
6	7,428	7,428	0
7	9,651	9,651	0
8	7,638	7,638	0
9	3,353	3,353	0
10	3,691	3,691	0
11	5,398	5,398	0
12	6,434	6,434	0
13	8,630	9,630	0

Assume aggregate planning takes place on a rolling horizon basis; then we only disaggregate and implement the production plan for the upcoming period, that is, period 1 in our example.

Given the demand for P5 in period 2, its inventory at the end of period 1 is depleted (i.e., runs out) in $9,152/13,233 \approx 0.6916$ periods. In order to realize a good synchronization of the production planning system, we tend to keep the inventories of all six individual items in balance. Therefore, we require the end-of-period-1 inventories of P5I1, P5I2,..., P5I6 to cover the future demands of the same 0.6916 periods.

Consequently, we should plan for item P5I1 to have an inventory of $2,000 \cdot 0.6916 \approx 1,383$ at the end of period 1, for P5I2 an inventory of $1,400 \cdot 0.6916 \approx 968$, and so on. The corresponding planned production levels for the

TABLE 5.3   Detailed Information on Member Items of Product Type P5

ITEM	PERIOD 1 DEMAND	PERIOD 2 DEMAND	INITIAL INVENTORY
P5I1	2,900	2,000	2,685
P5I2	2,100	1,400	1,100
P5I3	4,200	3,000	3,940
P5I4	3,200	2,200	3,200
P5I5	3,800	2,700	3,800
P5I6	2,344	1,933	2,100
Total for type P5	18,544	13,233	16,825

TABLE 5.4   Detailed Production Plan Resulting from Disaggregation of Type P5

ITEM	INITIAL INVENTORY	PERIOD 1 DEMAND	INVENTORY PLANNED FOR END OF PERIOD 1	PLANNED PRODUCTION FOR PERIOD 1
P5I1	2,685	2,900	1,383	1,598
P5I2	1,100	2,100	968	1,968
P5I3	3,940	4,200	2,075	2,335
P5I4	3,200	3,200	1,522	1,522
P5I5	3,800	3,800	1,867	1,867
P5I6	2,100	2,344	1,337	1,581
Total for type P5	16,825	18,544	9,152	10,871

upcoming period follow immediately, and are shown in Table 5.4. Notice that the sum of the planned production for the member items resulting from this disaggregation equals the amount (10,871) to be produced for product type P5, determined by the aggregate planning model.

The batch of 1598 units of P5I1 with its associated operations, routing, due date, and so on constitutes a job; similarly for the other five manufacturing lots. The disaggregation of the aggregate type P5 has thus generated a set of six jobs.

In the most general job shop problem, there are *m* machines on which a number of jobs have to be processed. Each job is released to the shop floor at a time known with certainty or unknown, and has its specific operations, routing, due date, and other attributes. The problem is to draw a plan for time-phasing the individual jobs so as to optimize some job- or shop-related measure of performance.

In the literature, the terms "scheduling" and "sequencing" are associated with the job shop problem. *Scheduling* is assigning each operation of each job a start time and a completion time onto a time scale of a machine, within the precedence relations postulated (see, for example, Figure 5.1). Under uncertainty a schedule cannot be determined because the arrival time of the job, operation processing times, as well as other attributes, might not be fully known. Then all one can do is sequencing. *Sequencing* means that, for each machine in the shop, one has to establish the order in which the jobs waiting in the queue in front of that particular machine have to be processed.

In this chapter we use scheduling as the more general term, also including the meaning of sequencing. However, if it becomes necessary to point specifically to the use of job ordering, we will resort to the term sequencing.

Traditionally, much of the research literature in the field of scheduling was motivated by problems arising in manufacturing shops; hence, the frequent use of manufacturing vocabulary. By generalization, however, many of the results apply in other fields as diverse as services, communication, and so on.

5.2.1 The Job Shop Process—Issues and Assumptions

The job shop process includes the machines, the jobs with their operations, the job- and shop-related constraints, and the rules by which operations are assigned to the corresponding machines (Conway et al. [1967]).

The job shop process has elicited an impressive body of research, as is obvious from such extensive survey papers as those by Elmaghraby [1968], Day and Hottenstein [1970], Panwalkar and Iskander [1977], Salvador [1978], and Moore and Wilson [1967]. Why the job shop scheduling problem has generated this amount of literature is hard to answer. It would certainly be an overstatement to say that industrial managers, and people in industry whose work is related to operations scheduling, are conscious of the potential benefits that exist in better scheduling and anxious to see new solution procedures coming along (Mellor [1969]). Moreover, Pounds [1963, p. 8] reports that he was unable "to elicit any recognition of a scheduling problem from people who schedule ... because for them, in most cases, no scheduling problem exists. That is, there is no scheduling problem for them because the organization which surrounds the schedulers reacts to protect them from strongly interdependent sequencing problems."

For certain, one reason that motivated the large body of research work produced in the field is the continuous challenge to operations researchers raised by the job shop scheduling problems. Their combinatorial nature, which is readily apparent from the small example of Table 5.1 and Figure 5.1, makes them inherently difficult. Optimal schedules have so far been produced only for small or specially structured cases, while the realistic general job shop process remains combinatorially locked.

Recent work in complexity theory* applied to scheduling problems appears to offer new guidance to researchers. According to this theory, combinatorial problems may be classified as "P-time" class or "NP-time" class (also known as "NP-complete") problems. The P-time problems are the "easy" ones, in the sense that efficient algorithms may be found for their optimal solution. In this context, an algorithm is efficient when it requires a solution time that is bounded by a polynomial function of the problem size (Karp [1975]). The NP-complete problems are the "hard" ones, because it is unlikely to find for them a polynomially bounded optimizing algorithm. Unfortunately,

---

*The reader interested in this topic could consult, for references, the book by Coffman [1976] and the special issue on scheduling published in *Operations Research*, Vol. 26, No. 1, 1978.

most scheduling problems are NP-complete. Nevertheless, knowledge of the fact that a problem is NP-complete is highly valuable because then the effort should be directed toward finding efficient approximation techniques for generating good feasible schedules, rather than searching for possibly inefficient algorithms that hold some promise of optimality. How good or how close to optimality is the schedule thus produced is still another question. Garey et al. [1978] and Gonzalez and Sahni [1978] have presented a new approach to analyzing this issue by developing bounds on the worst case behavior of approximation algorithms.

The scheduling literature contains a large variety of models ranging from the simplest single-machine shop to the most general job shop with m machines. The assumptions made and the restrictions imposed upon the job shop process are equally diverse. However, most of the research work has centered on a basic job shop process characterized by the following assumptions (Conway et al. [1967]):

1. Each machine is continuously available for assignment, without consideration of shifts, holidays, shutdowns for maintenance, or accidental breakdowns.

2. Jobs consist of strictly serially ordered operations. This means that the job's routing is given and must be adhered to fully. Also, a given operation may have at most one other operation immediately preceding or succeeding it; thus, no nested assembly operations are permitted.

3. There is only one of each type of machine in the shop.

4. Each operation can be performed by only one machine in the job shop; that is, machines are not interchangeable.

5. Operations preemption is not allowed; that is, once an operation is started on a machine, it must be completed before another operation can begin on that machine.

6. Operation overlapping is not allowed; that is, a given operation of a job may be started only if the operations that precede it, if any, are completed.

7. A machine can process at most one operation at a time.

8. There is only one limiting resource in the shop: the machine; that is, an operation requires only one machine for its processing; labor, tools, materials, and so on are in ample supply.

Although the basic job shop process is a simplification of most real shops, its investigation can bring many useful insights into the scheduling problem. Obviously, one can build representations closer to real life situations by relaxing the above assumptions, but the price paid is increased model complexity.

Within the general structure defined by assumptions 1–8, various issues concerning the job shop process can be considered in the model. These issues, singled out below, determine the dimensions along which we will review some representative job shop models available in the literature.

5.2.1.1 Nature of the job arrival process

The job arrival process can be classified as *static* or *dynamic*. In the static case all the jobs that are to be processed in the shop arrive simultaneously at some time T (the time T may be arbitrarily set to zero); no further jobs will arrive after time T to the end of the scheduling horizon. In the dynamic shop jobs arrive intermittently. The literature treats the case in which a finite number of jobs, n, arrive at known future times, and the other case in which jobs arrive continuously according to some probabilistic process.

Most production environments feature dynamic job shops as new orders are periodically released to the shop floor while others get completed. Static situations may also occur, for instance when jobs are processed in batches with no batch being released for processing before the previous one clears the facility (e.g., batch processing of jobs in some computer systems).

5.2.1.2 Deterministic versus probabilistic job shop process

A *deterministic* job shop process has all job- and shop-related attributes fixed and known with certainty, that is, jobs are either all available at time zero (the static case) or arrive at various known future times (the dynamic case), and processing times are known when the jobs reach the shop. The scheduling problem is then solved by the generation of a schedule in which each operation is associated with an exact start time and an exact processing time onto the time axis of the corresponding machine.

In a *probabilistic* job shop model, job arrival times or operation processing times, or both, are random variables described by probability distributions. The job shop becomes a queueing system in which one can no longer generate a schedule, rather, as mentioned earlier, one would resort to sequencing. The typical assumptions are:

- Jobs arrive in a random fashion, which follows a Poisson distribution.
- Operations have exponentially distributed processing times. If the problem requires processing times to be known at the time jobs arrive in the shop, the exponential probability distributions are sampled and the results are made available to the scheduling procedure.

5.2.1.3 Shop configuration

The simplest configuration is the *single-machine shop*. Each job has a single operation that is to be performed on the single machine existing in the shop. Scheduling in this context means, in essence, finding a sequence in which the jobs have to be processed. The importance of the single-machine shop is twofold. On the theoretical side, it is the elementary cell in investigating and understanding scheduling principles in more complex job shops. On the practical side, many complex situations may be quite rightfully modeled as single-machine shops. An assembly line or other integrated process, whose inner working is set by the physical design and layout, can be viewed for scheduling purposes as just one big machinery; or if in a multistage process one machine constitutes a bottleneck, scheduling can be done taking into account only this machine, and so on.

The more complex job shop models allow for a number of $m > 1$ machines. According to the flow pattern of the jobs through the shop, three types of job shops are distinguished in the literature: the parallel machine shop, the flow shop, and the general job shop.

The *parallel machine shop* can be regarded as an extension of the single machine case, in the sense that the jobs still consist of only one operation. There are m machines that work in parallel. In general, a given job can be processed on several of the m machines, possibly on any of them; however, different processing times may be required if the machines are not identical.

The *flow shop* contains m machines, and jobs consist of strictly ordered sequences of operations (assumption 2 of section 5.2.1). All movement between machines within the shop must be in a uniform direction. An example is the assembly line with the work stations standing for the machines. Let us note, however, that in the general flow shop some jobs may have less than m operations. If this is the case, not all jobs have to begin processing on the same machine or have to be completed at the same machine, nor should two sequentially numbered operations of a job require two adjacent machines. A flow shop can be described by a job transfer matrix of the type shown in Figure 5.2 which can have positive entries in row j and column k only for

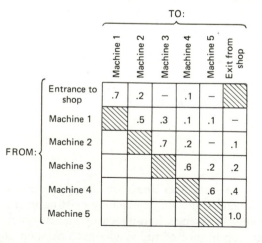

	TO:					
FROM:	Machine 1	Machine 2	Machine 3	Machine 4	Machine 5	Exit from shop
Entrance to shop	.7	.2	—	.1	—	
Machine 1		.5	.3	.1	.1	—
Machine 2			.7	.2	—	.1
Machine 3				.6	.2	.2
Machine 4					.6	.4
Machine 5						1.0

FIGURE 5.2
Transfer matrix for five-machine flow shop.

			TO:			
	Machine 1	Machine 2	Machine 3	Machine 4	Machine 5	Exit from shop
Entrance to shop	.3	–	.2	.1	.4	
Machine 1		–	.3	–	.5	.2
Machine 2	.1		–	.6	–	.3
Machine 3	.5	–		.1	.1	.3
Machine 4	–	.2	.2		–	.6
Machine 5	.1	.1	.1	.6		.1

FROM:

FIGURE 5.3
Transfer matrix for five-machine general job shop.

$k \geqslant j$. Entries show the fraction of jobs transferred from machine j to machine k. The first row shows that work can enter the shop at machines 1, 2, and 4. The last column indicates that jobs can leave the shop from machines 2, 3, 4, and 5.

It is often convenient to treat the jobs as all having exactly m operations; in case a job has fewer than m, it will be assigned zero processing times correspondingly.

The *general job shop* has m machines; jobs are in general multistage and can have any number of operations. However, an assumption common to most models available in the literature is that each job has exactly m operations and requires each machine only once. The work flow in the general job shop has an arbitrary pattern, as is apparent from the transfer matrix of Figure 5.3.

5.2.1.4 Optimization Criteria

In the previous chapters, the majority of models evaluate decisions with respect to their cost performance. With job shop scheduling models, things are different in that costs no longer constitute the universal optimization criterion. Rather, most of the time schedules are judged in terms of performance measures that relate to the individual job. However, sometimes researchers find it convenient to assess schedules with respect to performance measures relating to the shop. As for the costs associated with scheduling decisions, there are many fewer references to them in the literature. Of course, other optimization criteria may be found, although they appear less frequently. For instance, Gertsbakh and Stern [1978] treat the problem of n jobs processed on parallel identical machines. The problem is to determine the starting time of each job, within its prespecified starting interval, so as to minimize the number of machines required to process all jobs.

At this point, we have to adopt some notations for the terms we have introduced at the beginning of section 5.2:

$_i$ = subscript to identifying the job

$_j$ = subscript to identifying the operation

o_i = number of operations of job i

$_k$ = subscript identifying the machine; $k = 1, \ldots, m$

a_i = arrival time of job i

d_i = due date of job i

p = processing time; p will take various subscripts depending on the situation to be described.

Performance measures relating to the individual job.   Since in any industrial concern, meeting due dates is a prerequisite for gaining or maintaining the competitive advantage, an important piece of information for the evaluation of schedules is the *completion time C_i* of job i. It was defined earlier as the time at which processing of the last operation of the job is completed.

The time elapsed between the arrival and completion of job i is the total time that the job spends in the shop; it is called *flow time F_i*:

$$F_i = C_i - a_i.$$

The flow time F_i is actually composed of two elements: one is the processing time p_i, during which job i is processed by machines, and the other is the *waiting time W_i*, during which job i waits before different operations begin. Thus:

$$F_i = C_i - a_i = W_i + p_i. \tag{5.1}$$

In general, processing time represents a small portion of the flow time; during the majority of the flow time a job waits in queues for other jobs to be processed.

With respect to the due date, a job can be early if $C_i < d_i$; it can be tardy if $C_i > d_i$; or it can be right on time if $C_i = d_i$ (see example of Table 5.1 and Figure 5.1). Therefore, the *lateness L_i* of job i:

$$L_i = C_i - d_i, \tag{5.2}$$

can be positive, zero, or negative. If job i is completed after its due date, we are recording *tardiness T_i* (positive lateness):

$$T_i = \max(0, L_i). \tag{5.3}$$

If job i is completed ahead of its due date, we are in the presence of *earliness E_i* (negative lateness):

$$E_i = \max(0, -L_i). \tag{5.4}$$

In general, earliness is not an interesting variable because, in most cases, it has no direct benefits associated with it. However, tardiness is an important scheduling concern since, normally, penalties result from jobs missing their due dates.

In a job shop, every job is associated with a specific value for each of the variables defined above. In order to characterize the overall performance, these individual values have to be merged into some aggregate performance measures. The measures most often used are the average (mean), the maximum, or sometimes the variance of flow time, lateness, tardiness, or completion times. The schedule which minimizes one of these measurements is optimum with respect to it. If jobs are not equal in importance, they are assigned corresponding weighting factors which are then incorporated into the performance measure.

Example

If we have n jobs with flow times F_i, $i = 1, \ldots, n$, the mean flow time $\bar{F}$ is:

$$\bar{F} = \frac{1}{n} \sum_{i=1}^{n} F_i.$$

If jobs are of differing importance, reflected by a set of weighting factors v_i, $i = 1, \ldots, n$, the mean weighted flow time $\bar{F}_v$ is:

$$\bar{F}_v = \frac{\sum_{i=1}^{n} v_i F_i}{\sum_{i=1}^{n} v_i}.$$

In some instances we are concerned with delivering most of the orders by their due dates, in which cases schedules are sought so as to minimize the number of proportion of tardy jobs.

Except for the variance, all other measures of performance introduced above belong to the widely used class of regular measures of performance. A performance measure is regular if:

- it is a function of the job completion times
- its value has to be minimized
- its value increases only if at least one of the completion times in the schedule increases

Another aggregate performance measure is the makespan M, which is the length of time required to complete all the n jobs in the shop. If all n jobs are simultaneously available, the makespan is the maximum flow time: $M = F_{\max} = \max F_i$, and is regular in the sense shown above.

Under some uncertain conditions (random processing times unknown at the time operations begin processing, probabilistic due dates), one would resort to probabilistic versions of the performance measures, such as the expected value of the mean flow time, the probability of being tardy, or the expected lateness.

Performance measures relating to the shop.   One of the main themes of scheduling research is shop congestion since a congested shop implies that large work-in-process inventories exist, delivery times are long, and service tends to be poor. Work-in-process inventory (or pipeline stocks, as termed in section 4.1.1) can be measured, in principle, in two ways:

- If jobs are similar in terms of their cost or if it is important to get as many jobs as possible out of the shop, one can take a count of the number of jobs in the shop.
- If jobs are dissimilar, one can take a record of the work content of the jobs in the shop. This is done on the assumption that the cost of inventories is related to their work content.

Work-in-process may also be viewed differently, depending on the nature of the planning and control process being used. For planning work force or for loading machine centers, the work content (in standard hours) is relevant; while for determining storage space requirements, the number of orders on the shop floor is pertinent.

In scheduling research, several measures of performance are used to reflect work-in-process inventory:

- The mean number of jobs in the system, the average being taken over some time interval. For instance, in the static single machine shop with n jobs, the average number of jobs is usually computed over the maximum flow time (or makespan).
- The work content of the jobs, which can be expressed in several ways depending on the situation to be modeled. Conway et al. [1967, chap. II-2] propose that:
  - total work content = the sum of the processing times of all jobs in the shop
  - work completed = the sum of the processing times of all completed operations of all jobs in the shop
  - work remaining = (total work content) − (work completed)
  - imminent operation work content = the sum of the processing times of the particular operations for which jobs are waiting in queue

Costs as a performance measure are approached in the literature mostly from the analytical point of view. In most cases costs are nondecreasing and nonnegative functions of the completion time (Picard and Queyranne [1978], Schrage and Baker [1978]), thus imposing a penalty on job tardiness. This acknowledges the general concern shown by schedulers for excessive lateness of shop orders. Or, costs may depend on the amount of resources used, as reported in the work of Abdel-Wahab and Kameda [1978], where one unit of cost is charged for each resource unit involved in the performance of the job.

Other cost structures may include the cost of idle machines, cost of work-in-process inventory, cost of long production lead times, or cost of missed due dates (Jones [1973]).

In general, scheduling decisions affect (Conway et al. [1967, chap. 2-5]):

- the work-in-process inventory level and, thus, system inventory costs
- the completion of jobs on time, hence, service quality and the competitive edge in the market
- aggregate costs via the efficient or inefficient utilization of the existing capacity. More efficient, intensive use of the capacity will free part of it, thus making it possible for additional work to be done; this tends to make every unit of work cheaper in terms of capital costs. Efficient, intensive use of the capacity increases system responsiveness, thus reducing the need for large safety stocks and the employment of overtime, subcontracting, and additional shifts

In general, scheduling to optimize some job- or shop-related measure of performance will not minimize total costs. Gupta and Dudek [1971] have shown this experimentally in a study conducted for the flow shop problem. However, Manne [1960] indicates that by reducing the time spent in the shop by all jobs one can reduce total costs.

Flow relationships.   It is obvious that there should be some relationship among the performance measures related to the job, the shop, and costs, as all are connected with the same job shop process. In particular, the relationship between flow time and inventory has been given special attention, and positive results have been obtained that reinforce the intuitive feeling that the shorter the flow time, the lower the inventory; that is, the more rapid the turnaround of orders, the smaller the number of jobs in the shop.

We state here the results without proofs. Proofs may be found in Conway et al. [1967, chap. 2-4].

Consider first the static case of a job shop where n jobs are simultaneously available at time zero. As time goes on, jobs complete their processing and leave the shop one by one. Consequently, the number of jobs in the shop decreases with time and becomes zero after F_{max}. Let $N(t)$ be the number of jobs in the shop at time t. Then, the average number $\overline{N}$ of jobs in the shop* over the time span F_{max} is computed by:

$$\overline{N} = \frac{1}{F_{max}} \int_0^{F_{max}} N(t)\, dt.$$

*The significance of $\overline{N}$ is that it gives a measure of the average congestion during time interval $[0, F_{max}]$. Note that a job is considered to be in the shop during the entire interval between its arrival time and its completion time. In this interval it can be either waiting in a queue, or it can be on a machine undergoing processing. Consequently, $\overline{N}$ consists of two components: the mean number of jobs which are in queue awaiting processing, and the mean number of jobs which are actually being processed. We are interested in reducing the mean number of jobs in queue because the time spent there is nonproductive.

$\overline{N}$ is related to the mean flow time as follows:

$$\frac{\overline{F}}{F_{\max}} = \frac{\overline{N}}{n}. \tag{5.5}$$

Equation (5.5) shows that, for a given makespan, the average number of jobs in the shop is proportional to the average flow time.

Consider now the dynamic case of a job shop where jobs arrive continuously over time at an average arrival rate of λ jobs per time unit. If the job shop process is in steady state* the following equation holds[†]

$$\overline{F} = \frac{\overline{N}}{\lambda}. \tag{5.6}$$

Result (5.6) states that the mean flow time is linearly related to the mean number of jobs in the system. Consequently, a scheduling strategy which minimizes $\overline{F}$ also minimizes $\overline{N}$ and, therefore, mean flow time has been used frequently as a measure of shop congestion.

Also, from definitions (5.1) and (5.2) it follows that:

$$\overline{F} = \overline{C} - \overline{a} = \overline{W} + \overline{p} = \overline{L} + (\overline{d} - \overline{a}) \tag{5.7}$$

where:

$\overline{C}, \overline{W}, \overline{L}$ = the mean completion time, mean waiting time, and mean lateness, respectively

$\overline{a}, \overline{d}, \overline{p}$ = the average job arrival time, the average job due date, and the average job processing time, respectively.

As $\overline{a}, \overline{d}, \overline{p}$ are given to the scheduling problem, a schedule which is optimal for mean flow time $\overline{F}$ is also optimal with respect to mean completion time $\overline{C}$, mean waiting time $\overline{W}$, and mean lateness $\overline{L}$.

5.2.1.5 *Jobs with restrictions*

In most scheduling studies the jobs to be processed in the shop are *independent*, that is, there are no technological precedence restrictions among jobs, and operation processing times on a given machine do not depend on the sequence in which jobs follow each other on that particular machine.

When jobs are dependent, different cases may arise. One instance is that of the *sequence-dependent setup times* in which the setup time required for job i

---

*In this context the process is in steady state when the long-run average rate at which jobs leave the shop (i.e., the average completion rate) is equal to the average arrival rate λ. Under steady state, the number of jobs in the system is finite at all times.

[†]To compute $\overline{N}$ a time interval is selected during which a large number n of jobs should arrive at the shop. Then, $\overline{N}$ is the average number of jobs over the time interval required for the n jobs to be completed. $\overline{F}$ is the mean flow time for the n jobs.

depends on the job which immediately precedes it on the machine. This problem has been extensively studied in the context of the single machine shop by modeling it as a traveling salesman problem.

Other cases involve *precedence relations* among jobs imposed by technological restrictions on their sequence. Thus, a set of jobs forms a *chain* (*jobs in series*) if each job has at most one immediate predecessor and at most one immediate successor (Conway et al. [1967, chap. 4-3]). A set of jobs forms an *assembly tree* (Baker [1974, chap. 3]) if each job may have at most one immediate successor. In Figure 5.4 an assembly tree structure is shown, with the nodes of the graph representing the jobs, and the arrows the precedence constraints.

More general, *arbitrary precedence* structures have also been treated in the literature but only limited results have been obtained because of problem complexity; see Muntz and Coffman [1969] with the case of two identical processors.

The precedence restrictions result in a reduction in the number of feasible schedules, which may be considered an advantage. On the other hand, however, the optimization tends to be more difficult than with independent jobs.

Sometimes technological restrictions occur with respect to the timing of the operations of the job. Thus, there are cases in which, once the processing of the job begins, subsequent operations are not allowed to wait. They must be processed with no delays in their sequence. This instance is called by Baker [1974, chap. 6] *shop without intermediate queues* and the traveling salesman problem formulation has been used for its solution.

It is clear from the above discussion that a number of models can be and have been built by combining the various features of sections 5.2.1.1–5.2.1.5. For example, Table 5.5 presents the kinds of job shops that may be encountered from the point of view of the job arrival process and the nature of the operation processing times. Of course, not all possible models have received equal attention from researchers, some because they are not acceptable representations of a job shop process, others because of their complexity. Still, the number of models available in the literature is very large.

In what follows we will review some representative scheduling problems which, we feel, can contribute to the understanding of basic scheduling

FIGURE 5.4
An assembly tree with five jobs.

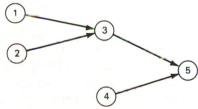

TABLE 5.5   Ways of Modeling Job Shop

ARRIVAL PROCESS	NATURE OF PROCESSING TIMES	CASE DESCRIPTION
Static	Deterministic	*n* jobs available at time zero; all processing times are known with certainty when jobs arrive in the shop.
Static	Probabilistic	*n* jobs available at time zero; processing times not known with certainty when jobs arrive in the shop (described by probability distributions).
Dynamic deterministic	Deterministic	*n* jobs arrive at known future times; processing times known when jobs arrive in the shop.
Dynamic deterministic	Probabilistic	*n* jobs arrive at known future times; processing times not known with certainty when jobs arrive in the shop (described by probability distributions).
Dynamic probabilistic	Deterministic	Poisson arrivals (continuous, infinite horizon process); processing times known when jobs arrive in the shop.
Dynamic probabilistic	Probabilistic	Poisson arrivals (continuous, infinite horizon process); processing times not known with certainty when jobs arrive in the shop (described by probability distributions).

concepts. In concluding the job shop scheduling section, Table 5.11 will take an overall view of them.

For the sake of brevity, proofs will be, in general, omitted. However, the reader will be directed to appropriate sources for the missing proofs. References will also be provided for the reader interested in a closer look at more specific issues.

5.2.2   The Single-Machine Shop

This shop contains a single machine on which jobs, consisting of a single operation, have to be processed. In this context, scheduling is literally the same as sequencing. The problem has received the greatest theoretical attention of all scheduling problems.

In the investigation of the single machine shop, as well as other shop configurations, an important class of schedules is the class of permutation schedules. A *permutation schedule* is fully determined by specifying the order in which the jobs have to be processed; it means that, if jobs are numbered from 1 to *n*, such a schedule is simply a permutation of these numbers.

Another class constitutes schedules with preemption. *Preemption* refers to interrupting a job's processing on the machine before completion in order to process another job. *Preempt – resume* means that a job has the same total processing time regardless of the number of interruptions, that is, processing may resume where it left off and no additional work is required because of the preemption(s). *Preempt – repeat* means that all processing up to the interruption is lost and, therefore, all of the job's processing must be repeated when the job returns to the machine.

A third category of schedules are *schedules with inserted idle time*, in which the machine is kept idle although in the shop there is at least one job whose processing could be started. Note that in the static shop neither the preemptive schedules nor the schedules with inserted idle time may be described by a permutation of the jobs' numbers. Indeed, with preemption, a job may appear several times in the job sequence, while in the case of idle time the amount of inserted idle time has to be specified besides the job ordering.

5.2.2.1 The single-machine static deterministic shop

By assumption, there are n jobs available simultaneously at time zero; all processing times are known with certainty at the time of scheduling.

If the scheduling objective is to optimize a regular measure of performance, it is sufficient to consider only permutation schedules since they constitute a dominant set vis-à-vis preemptive schedules and schedules with inserted idle time (Conway et al. [1967, p. 24]). Then, obviously, the total elapsed time to complete the n jobs—that is, the makespan—is sequence-independent. The simplest and best known results are given as follows:

- For minimizing the mean flow time, the shortest processing time sequencing is optimal.
- For minimizing the maximum job tardiness and the maximum job lateness, the earliest due date sequencing is optimal.

Let us denote the position in sequence by a subscript between square brackets. For instance, $p_{[3]}$ is the processing time of the job which occupies the third position in sequence.

The Shortest Processing Time (SPT) rule minimizes the mean flow time $\overline{F}$ by constructing a sequence in which jobs are arranged in order of nondecreasing processing time (Smith [1956]):

$$p_{[1]} \leqslant p_{[2]} \leqslant \cdots \leqslant p_{[n]}.$$

SPT sequencing minimizes, then, shop congestion.

A graphical representation is often used to demonstrate intuitively the optimality of the SPT rule with respect to the minimization of $\overline{F}$. Any schedule

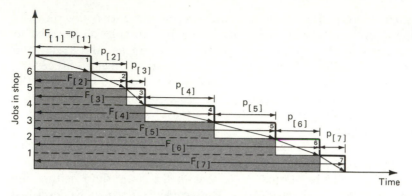

FIGURE 5.5   An arbitrary schedule for set of seven jobs.

can be represented as a graph in which the number of jobs in the shop is plotted against time (Figure 5.5). The processing time and the flow time of each job are shown on the graph. Each nonshaded block is associated with a vector on its diagonal, and is numbered in the upper right corner.

As each step in the graph has a height equal to unity, the total area under the heavy line represents the sum of job flow times $\sum_{i=1}^{n} F_i$. It follows that $\bar{F}$ is minimized by a job sequence which minimizes the total area of the graph. To achieve this, one should order the n jobs so that the aforementioned vectors form a convex curve, which amounts to placing the steepest vector (i.e., the shortest processing time) to the left, then the next steepest vector (i.e., the next shortest processing time), and so on, as shown in Figure 5.6. But this is nothing but SPT sequencing.

If jobs do not have equal importance (e.g., they have different dollar values and, therefore, have different shares in the work-in-process inventory) each job may be assigned a weighting factor v_i. Then, in order to minimize the mean weighted flow time, it is optimal to sequence the jobs in order of

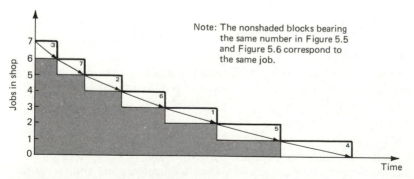

FIGURE 5.6   The *SPT* schedule for set of seven jobs.

nondecreasing weighted processing time (Smith [1956]):

$$\frac{p_{[1]}}{v_{[1]}} \leqslant \frac{p_{[2]}}{v_{[2]}} \leqslant \cdots \leqslant \frac{p_{[n]}}{v_{[n]}}.$$

This is the Shortest Weighted Processing Time (SWPT) rule.

By the flow relationships of section 5.2.1.4, SPT sequencing also minimizes mean completion time, mean waiting time, mean lateness, and mean number of jobs in the shop.

The Earliest Due Date (EDD) rule consists of sequencing the jobs in order of nondecreasing due dates:

$$d_{[1]} \leqslant d_{[2]} \leqslant \cdots \leqslant d_{[n]},$$

which is optimal with respect to minimizing the maximum job tardiness and maximum job lateness (Conway et al. [1967, chap. 3-3]).

The interesting part of it is that if there is no way in which all jobs can be completed on time, the EDD sequence guarantees that the job performing worst in terms of meeting its due date is at least as close or even closer to its due date than the worst performing job in any other sequence.

A development of EDD sequencing by Moore [1968] leads to an algorithm for *minimizing the number of tardy jobs.* Thus, the n jobs are first ordered by the EDD rule, and then this sequence is modified by sequentially selecting certain jobs and moving them to the end of the original sequence (see also Maxwell [1970]). Fisher and Jaikumar [1978] adapted Moore's algorithm to minimize the number of late missions in the space shuttle program.

We should notice that the distribution of lateness values can be fairly well controlled: SPT sequencing enables one to minimize its mean, thus shifting the weight of the distribution to the left, while use of the EDD rule reduces the upper tail of it by minimizing the maximum lateness.

Nevertheless, of much more interest to schedules is the distribution of tardiness (positive lateness). We have shown above that EDD sequencing minimizes the maximum job tardiness. Minimizing the mean (or weighted) tardiness, however, is a much more difficult task, as tardiness is not linear in completion times, thus requiring combinatorial techniques for solution.

For the *tardiness problem,* the general form of the performance measure Z is:

$$Z = \sum_{i=1}^{n} z_i T_i,$$

where z_i are coefficients. The objective is to minimize Z. The case with $z_i = 1$ for all i yields the total tardiness problem, the case with $z_i = 1/n$ for all i yields the mean tardiness problem, and the case with $z_i = v_i/(\sum_{i=1}^{n} v_i)$ for all i, where v_i are specific job weights, yields the weighted tardiness problem. Karp [1972] and Lenstra et al. [1977] show that the problem is NP-complete.

The one-machine tardiness problem has been considered by many researchers using a variety of research techniques. To name just a few: branch-and-bound techniques by Fisher [1976], Rinnooy Kan et al. [1975], Picard and Queyranne [1978], Shwimer [1972a]; dynamic programming by Baker and Schrage [1978], and Schrage and Baker [1978]; hybrid algorithms based on dynamic programming by Emmons [1969] and Srinivasan [1971]; the heuristic neighborhood search by Wilkerson and Irwin [1971]; random sampling (or probabilistic dispatching) in Baker [1974, chap. 3]. The dynamic programming approach of Schrage and Baker [1978] appears to be very efficient in terms of computational time requirements.

As mentioned in section 5.2, when setup times are independent of job sequence, they are usually absorbed in the processing times. There are cases, however, when the time required to set up the machine for the next job also depends on the job which precedes it in the sequence (e.g., as in color changes in injection molding). This is known as the problem of *sequence-dependent setup times*. Formally, the setup time notation becomes doubly subscripted, $s_{[i-1],[i]}$, denoting the time to change over from the job which occupies position $(i-1)$ in the sequence to the job in the ith position.

For this problem, the usual measure of performance is the makespan M. This is no longer a constant, but a function of the order in which jobs are processed.

$$M = F_{\max} = F_{[n]} = \sum_{i=1}^{n} s_{[i-1],[i]} + \sum_{i=1}^{n} p_{[i]}.$$

$s_{[0],[1]}$ represents the time to set up the machine for the first job in the schedule, state 0 being the idle state.

As the sum of the processing times is a constant, minimizing the makespan is equivalent to minimizing the sum of the setup times. In this form the sequence-dependent setup times problem can be interpreted as the well-known "traveling salesman problem," for whose solution many approaches are available (branch-and-bound algorithms, dynamic programming, integer programming formulations, and heuristics). Karp [1972] has shown that the problem is NP-complete. For an extensive survey of solution procedures see Bellmore and Nemhauser [1968]; for more recent references see Papadimitriou and Steiglitz [1978]; and for applications to sequencing problems see Conway et al. [1967, chap. 4-1] and Baker [1974, chap. 4].

5.2.2.2 The single-machine dynamic shop

As is apparent from Table 5.5, the dynamic shop encompasses several instances depending on whether jobs arrive at deterministic times in the future or the arrival process is stochastic, and on whether processing times are known constants or are probabilistically described at the moment jobs arrive in the

shop. It is obvious that in a shop in which arrivals occur over time one has two ways to go in sequencing; nonpreemptive and preemptive sequencing.

Whenever one does not seek to build a schedule (with precise starts and completion times), because it is not possible or necessary, one should instead try to specify the order in which the jobs waiting in the queue in front of the machine are to be processed. This may be achieved by the use of priority or selection disciplines. A *priority discipline* is a rule which selects one of the jobs waiting in the queue to go onto the machine next. There are two instances in which implementing a priority discipline can be called for:

- when the machine becomes idle after completing the processing of a job
- when a new job arrives in the shop (if preemption is permitted)

This type of decision making is called *dispatching*; it requires no look-ahead information. With dispatching, decisions on start times are made as they are needed, just before the job being concerned goes onto the machine. Consequently, the start times result in an increasing sequence of numbers.

To illustrate, let us consider a shop with *dynamic deterministic arrivals* and *deterministic job processing times*. Suppose we are concerned with minimizing shop congestion, so we seek the minimum flow time. Job attributes are shown in Figure 5.7a.

First, consider the nonpreemptive sequencing; two situations may arise:

- A situation in which, for some reason, the machine may not be held idle; in this case, the mean flow time minimizer is the Shortest Processing Time discipline (Conway et al. [1967, chap. 8-6]). SPT rule is applied to all jobs in the queue at the moment some job completes processing, to select the next job to start processing (Figure 5.7b).
- A situation in which the scheduler, taking advantage of the knowledge of future arrivals, is allowed to plan on keeping the machine idle until some future job arrives, in order to process that job before any of the jobs already waiting in the queue. This way a *schedule with inserted idle time* is generated. The idleness is used with the purpose of improving on the measure of performance (Figure 5.7c). Unfortunately, there has been very little headway in developing specialized techniques for constructing schedules with inserted idle time; there has still been reliance on general combinatorial methods.

Note that scheduling with inserted idle time is not a dispatching procedure, while the SPT discipline is.

Now let us examine the preemptive sequencing. We have to consider preempt–resume and preempt–repeat disciplines.

If preempt–resume is possible, one does not need and would not use any advance knowledge. Rather, whenever a new job arrives in the shop, the priority discipline is enacted on the spot and a decision is made on whether to continue the ongoing processing or to preempt and start on the newcomer. The

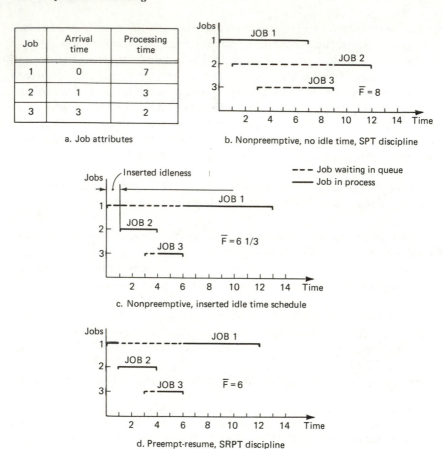

FIGURE 5.7   **Scheduling for dynamic, deterministic single-machine shop.**

optimal selection discipline for minimizing the mean flow time is a generalization of the SPT rule of the static shop, namely, the Shortest Remaining Processing Time (SRPT) discipline. It also minimizes the mean queue length. By SRPT, when a new job arrives in the shop, the machine is always assigned to the job having the smallest amount of processing still to be carried out (rather than the original processing time as with SPT); see Figure 5.7d. SRPT discipline is a dispatching procedure.

If preempt–repeat prevails, one should operate as if preemption were not permitted at all. Indeed, having the advance knowledge of future arrivals, processing of a job should not be started if it cannot be completed before another job arrives which would be given priority by the selection discipline and cause preemption. Thus, preempt–repeat does not make sense with deterministic arrivals and constant processing times.

If we are concerned with meeting due dates, a generalization of EDD sequencing of the static shop has proven to be optimal (Conway et al. [1967, chap. 8-8]): *earliest due date discipline under preempt – resume* minimizes the maximum lateness. The way this rule works is to preempt the job being processed when another job with a closer due date arrives in the shop. The newly arriving job is started on the machine.

If we want to *minimize the number of tardy jobs* under the most general assumptions, we will find that there is no generalization of Moore's algorithm of the static shop; rather, the problem has been shown to be NP-complete (Lenstra et al. [1977]). Solutions have been offered to particular instances of the problem under restrictive assumptions (Kise et al. [1978]).

We should mention that, although the preemptive disciplines have been given extensive treatment and, as already seen, can bring improvement to the measure of performance, they seldom constitute a desirable alternative in industrial environments because of the difficulties associated with managing a preemptive scheduling system.

A more realistic case is the *dynamic probabilistic shop*, in which job arrivals are generated by a stochastic process. Since precise advance information about future arrivals is not available, sequencing may be done only by dispatching procedures, using priority disciplines.

The most extensive treatment has been given to the processing time-dependent disciplines. By an intuitive extension of the results obtained for the deterministic shop (both static and dynamic deterministic), it was felt that, by ordering jobs with the help of processing time-related rules, one can reduce flow times, the number of jobs in the queue, and thus the congestion in the shop.

Before showing some of these results, we should mention that under uncertainty the mean flow time takes on a probabilistic connotation because the flow time of any job becomes a stochastic variable. This is clear from the following considerations: suppose job i is waiting in the queue while the machine is busy processing another job; then:

1. While job i is waiting, higher priority jobs may join the queue and cause the selection of job i to be delayed. The delay is probabilistic.

2. Even if no new job arrives, the waiting time of job i depends on the (possibly nondeterministic) processing times of the higher priority jobs already in the queue.*

3. After job i goes onto the machine, its processing time is sampled from the corresponding probability distribution and, therefore, its own contribution to the flow time is nondeterministic.

*Statements 2 and 3 refer to the cases in which processing times are not known with certainty when jobs arrive in the shop.

It follows that, with each sampling of the arrival process and of the processing time distributions, a different value of the overall mean flow time may result. Thus, the overall mean flow time is associated with a probability distribution. It is the expected value of this distribution (the expected mean flow time or the grand mean of flow time) whose minimum is sought.

Nonpreemptive sequencing.   If processing times are precisely known when jobs arrive in the shop, the Shortest Processing Time discipline minimizes the mean flow time, as it did in the dynamic deterministic job.

We should mention that, although SPT minimizes the average of the flow times, there might be individual jobs with long processing times (and, therefore, low priority) experiencing very long flow times. This is regarded as a basic disadvantage of SPT. Remedies have been proposed and tested, one of which is to alternate SPT with a selection discipline which would force jobs with low priority under SPT out of the shop (the problem of correcting SPT for its deficiency is taken up later in section 5.2.5.2). The alternate rule is the First Come, First Served (FCFS) a nonpreemptive discipline by which jobs are processed in order of their arrival. FCFS was shown by Schrage [1966] to produce a variance of flow time substantially lower than SPT in heavily loaded single machine shops.

If processing times are known when jobs arrive at the machine, being probabilistically described, out of all jobs in the queue the highest priority should be given to the job with the Shortest Expected Processing Time (SEPT). This selection discipline guarantees the minimization of the expected mean flow time.

The weighted versions of SPT and SEPT are also applicable (Conway et al. [1967, chap. 8-6]).

Preemptive sequencing.   For a more in-depth study, the reader is directed to Conway et al. [1967, chap. 8-7], Schrage [1968], and Smith [1978]. The remarkable finding is that, when processing times are known, under preempt–resume the Shortest Remaining Processing Time discipline is still optimal with respect to minimizing the mean flow time.

For tardiness oriented measures of performance, there are far fewer results. Research has been conducted (Jackson [1960, 1961, 1962]) which suggests that sequencing related to job due dates influences the distribution of the maximum expected lateness. The conjecture is that EDD sequencing minimizes the upper bound on lateness. Extensions to Jackson's work are provided by Holtzman [1971] and Goldberg [1977].

5.2.3   The Parallel Machine Shop

The parallel machine shop is an important generalization of the single-machine problem: jobs still consist of a unique operation, but instead of a single machine there are m machines working in parallel. Much of the research has been elicited in computer system environments in connection with scheduling various jobs to be performed on a number of simultaneously available processors.

Two distinct kinds of parallel machine shops have been considered in the literature:

- The static parallel machine shop with deterministic processing times. The machines may be identical or not. If they are not identical, a given job may require different processing times, depending on which machine processes it. A distinction can be made between the case where a job must be processed on a single machine (nonpreemptable jobs), and the case in which an individual job may be divided among two or more machines (preemptable jobs). Also, jobs can be independent or interrelated by precedence restrictions (see Dogramaci and Surkis [1979] and Sahni [1979]).

- The dynamic parallel machine shop with Poisson distributed arrivals and exponentially distributed processing times at each machine, and all identical machines. For this case, limited analytical results have been obtained under restrictive assumptions (Conway et al. [1967, chap. 10]); see also Su and Sevcik [1978].

In what follows we will refer to some basic problems of the static deterministic shop.

As opposed to the single-machine problem, in the parallel machine shop *minimizing the makespan M* is an important concern. Unfortunately, nonpreemptive scheduling of n independent jobs is NP-complete for $m \geqslant 2$ (Lenstra and Rinnooy Kan [1978]). Therefore, approximation algorithms have to be employed. We present two such heuristics (nonpreemptive), for which bounds on their worst case behavior have been developed (Garey et al. [1978]).

The Largest Processing Time (LPT) algorithm starts by arranging the n jobs in order of nonincreasing processing time. Then assign each job in order to the machine with the smallest load of processing already scheduling. Figure 5.8 shows both the LPT scheduling and the optimal schedule for a two-parallel-machine, five-job shop.

The MULTIFIT heuristic starts by setting some deadline D, by which time all jobs should be completed. Let each machine have an ordinal number between 1 and m. Then:

1. Construct an LPT ordering of the jobs.
2. Assign the first job on the LPT list to the lowest numbered machine which would complete it by deadline D. If none of the machines can complete the job by D, the algorithm has failed.
3. If step 2 can be carried out, remove the job from the list. If the list becomes empty, the algorithm has succeeded.
4. If the list is not empty, go back to step 2.

Clearly, for a given D, the algorithm either succeeds or fails. In either case another value for D can be determined, using binary search: in case the algorithm fails the value should be larger, and in case it succeeds the value should be smaller. The whole procedure is repeated with the new D. The goal is to find the smallest D for which the algorithm can still build a feasible schedule. For the set of jobs in Figure 5.8a, for any $D \geqslant 17$ the MULTIFIT heuristic would succeed, and it would fail for any $D < 17$.

In case preemption is allowed, McNaughton [1959] develops an optimal algorithm that minimizes the makespan for m identical machines under preempt–resume.

If the objective is to *minimize the mean flow time* when jobs are nonpreemptable and the machines are identical, building a schedule requires resolution of two issues: the n jobs have to be partitioned among the m machines, and an appropriate permutation schedule has to be determined for each machine. Given our experience with the single-machine shop, it comes as no surprise to find that a simple sorting procedure, similar to the SPT rule for the one machine shop, is optimal.

Job	Processing time
1	5
2	10
3	8
4	4
5	6

a. Job processing times

Position in LPT order	[1]	[2]	[3]	[4]	[5]
Job number	2	3	5	1	4
Processing time	10	8	6	5	4

b. LPT ordering of jobs

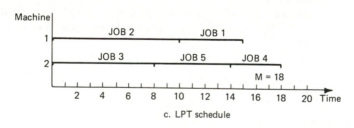

c. LPT schedule

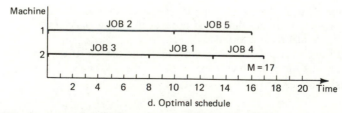

d. Optimal schedule

FIGURE 5.8   The *LPT* algorithm for minimizing makespan.

To develop the procedure, suppose that the kth machine, $k = 1, \ldots, m$, is allotted n_k jobs to process. Clearly, $\sum_{k=1}^{m} n_k = n$. Denote by $k[i]$ the job which is in the ith position in sequence on the kth machine. Then the flow times on the kth machine can be written as:

$$F_{k[1]} = p_{k[1]}; \quad F_{k[2]} = p_{k[1]} + p_{k[2]};$$
$$\cdots \quad F_{k[n_k]} = p_{k[1]} + p_{k[2]} + \cdots + p_{k[n_k]}.$$

The mean flow time for the entire set of n jobs is:

$$\bar{F} = \frac{1}{n} \left[\sum_{i=1}^{n_1} (n_1 - i + 1) p_{1[i]} + \sum_{i=1}^{n_2} (n_2 - i + 1) p_{2[i]} + \cdots + \sum_{i=1}^{n_m} (n_m - i + 1) p_{m[i]} \right].$$

Each processing time appears precisely once; the sequences of coefficients and corresponding processing times are:

$$\text{Machine 1} \begin{cases} n_1 & n_1 - 1 & \cdots & 2 & 1 \\ p_{1[1]} & p_{1[2]} & \cdots & p_{1[n_1 - 1]} & p_{1[n_1]} \end{cases}$$

$$\text{Machine 2} \begin{cases} n_2 & n_2 - 1 & \cdots & 2 & 1 \\ p_{2[1]} & p_{2[2]} & \cdots & p_{2[n_2 - 1]} & p_{2[n_2]} \end{cases}$$

$$\vdots \qquad \vdots \qquad \qquad \vdots \qquad \vdots$$

$$\text{Machine } m \begin{cases} n_m & n_m - 1 & \cdots & 2 & 1 \\ p_{m[1]} & p_{m[2]} & \cdots & p_{m[n_m - 1]} & p_{m[n_m]} \end{cases}$$

The sum of products that constitutes $\bar{F}$ is minimized by matching the coefficients in decreasing order with processing times in nondecreasing order. Thus, the m coefficients of 1 should be associated with the m largest processing times (which means that each of the m longest jobs is placed at the end of a machine sequence), then the m coefficients of 2 should be paired with the next m longest processing times, and so on.

Therefore, to construct a schedule which minimizes the mean flow time (McNaughton [1959]), proceed as follows:

1. Construct an SPT ordering of the jobs:

$$p_{[1]} \leqslant p_{[2]} \leqslant \cdots \leqslant p_{[n]}$$

2. Assign the jobs from the SPT list to the m machines in rotation:

Jobs in SPT sequence	[1]	[2]	$\cdots$	[m]	[m+1]	[m+2]	$\cdots$	[2m]	[2m+1]	[2m+2]	$\cdots$
Machine	1	2	$\cdots$	m	1	2	$\cdots$	m	1	2	$\cdots$

A dispatching version of the above algorithm can easily be envisioned: construct an SPT list of the jobs; start processing the first m jobs on the SPT list, each on one machine; then, as soon as a machine completes a job it is assigned the first of the remaining jobs on the list.

When the machines are not identical, Horn [1973] shows how to reduce the mean flow time problem to a linear assignment problem.

As for the weighted mean flow time problem, it is much more difficult to produce a solution, and the results of the single machine shop cannot be generalized. It is possible to give the problem an m-dimensional dynamic programming formulation (Rothkopf [1966]) which, however, is computationally infeasible, even for moderate cases, because of its dimensionality. Eastman et al. [1964] show how to compute a lower bound on the minimum value of th weighted mean flow time, and Baker and Merten [1973] propose and test several heuristics for this problem.

For mean flow time problems with precedence constraints, see Sethi [1977] and Morton and Dharan [1978].

For *tardiness* oriented measures of performance not too much progress has been made. Root [1965] gives an algorithm for the minimization of the mean tardiness in the special case when all jobs have the same due date. Other search algorithms for special cases are developed by Elmaghraby and Park [1974], Barnes and Brennan [1977], and Nunnikhoven and Emmons [1977]; and Lawler [1964] formulates the case in which identical machines and jobs have the same processing time as a transportation problem.

For the problem of scheduling m parallel machines under precedence constraints, for various measures of performance, it is suggested that the reader start by consulting the paper of Lenstra and Rinnooy Kan [1978].

The case of sequence-dependent setups can be interpreted as an m vehicle routing problem. Parker et al. [1977] use this interpretation to find heuristics to minimize the total changeover time.

5.2.4 The Flow Shop

The flow shop consists of m machines arranged in series, and of jobs that require m operations,* each operation being performed on a different machine. The flow of work is unidirectional; thus, each job must visit each machine in the prescribed order.

Although the flow shop problem is the simplest multistage scheduling problem, it turns out to be disappointingly difficult due to the inherent combinatorial aspects. Except for Johnson's [1954] optimizing procedure for the static two-machine flow shop with makespan criterion, no constructive algorithms exist for larger general flow shops or for other measures of performance. An explanation for this lack of success comes from the relatively

---

*In case a job has fewer operations, it may still be treated as an m operation job with zero processing times assigned correspondingly.

recent finding that nonpreemptive scheduling for the flow shop problem is NP-complete when the makespan or the mean flow time is minimized (Garey et al. [1976]); with preemptive scheduling, Gonzalez and Sahni [1978] prove NP-completeness for the makespan criterion.

Since the vast majority of research has been conducted for the static flow shop, we are limiting our presentation to this class of problems. Some of the few theoretical results for the dynamic probabilistic flow shop are given by Conway et al. [1967, chap. 10]. Magee and Boodman [1967, pp. 263–272] describe a procedure for balancing work load on processing centers in flow shop–like manufacturing situations under dynamic order arrivals. Their approach expresses the practitioner's point of view, which is concerned with finding feasible schedules. No single measure of performance is considered; rather, improved global shop performance is sought in terms of lower work-in-process inventories, reduced lead times and delayed orders, and uniform utilization of labor.

If one considers an arbitrary sequence of jobs on each machine, then with m machines and n jobs a total number of $(n!)^m$ schedules may be constructed. There are, however, two important theorems that serve to reduce the number of schedules that have to be considered (proofs may be found in Conway et al. [1967, chap. 5] or Baker [1974, chap. 6]).

Theorem 1

- When scheduling to minimize any regular measure of performance in the static deterministic flow shop, it is sufficient to consider only schedules in which the same job ordering is imposed on the first two machines.

Theorem 2

- When scheduling to minimize makespan in the static deterministic flow shop, it is sufficient to consider only schedules in which the same job ordering is imposed on machines 1 and 2, and the same job ordering on machines $m - 1$ and m.

A *permutation schedule* for a flow shop is a schedule in which the order of jobs is identical on all machines. By the above theorems, the following consequences result:

1. In a two-machine flow shop, the optimal schedule with respect to any regular measure of performance is a permutation schedule. For an example, see Figure 5.9 where two regular measures of performance are considered: makespan and mean flow time.
2. In a three-machine flow shop, the makespan is minimized by a permutation schedule (Johnson [1954]).

Unfortunately, this second dominance property does not extend either to other measures of performance or to larger flow shops ($m \geqslant 4$). Indeed, in

M1 ───▶ M2

Job number	Processing time on machine	
	M1	M2
1	1	4
2	2	1

a. Processing times on machines M1 and M2

Schedule number	Job sequence on machine		Makespan	Mean flow time
	M1	M2		
1	1 - 2	1 - 2	⑥	5.5
2	1 - 2	2 - 1	8	6
3	2 - 1	1 - 2	8	7.5
4	2 - 1	2 - 1	7	⑤

b. All possible nonpreemptive schedules

FIGURE 5.9   A two-machine, two-job flow shop.

Figure 5.10 an example is developed in which the makespan, in a three-machine flow shop, is minimized by permutation schedule #1, while the best schedule with respect to mean flow time is #2, which is not a permutation schedule. Then the illustration of Figure 5.11 shows that, in a four-machine flow shop, the best schedule with respect to both makespan and mean flow time is the nonpermutation schedule #4.

5.2.4.1   Johnson's two-machine flow shop problem (makespan criterion)

Probably the most important and the best known result for the flow shop problem is Johnson's [1954] nonpreemptive algorithm for optimizing the makespan in the general two-machine static flow shop.

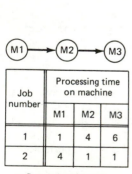

M1 ───▶ M2 ───▶ M3

Job number	Processing time on machine		
	M1	M2	M3
1	1	4	6
2	4	1	1

a. Processing times on machines M1, M2, M3

Schedule number	Job sequence on machine			Makespan	Mean flow time
	M1	M2	M3		
1	1 - 2	1 - 2	1 - 2	⑫	11, 5
2	1 - 2	1 - 2	2 - 1	13	⑩
3	1 - 2	2 - 1	1 - 2	17	16, 5
4	1 - 2	2 - 1	2 - 1	16	11, 5
5	2 - 1	1 - 2	1 - 2	16	15, 5
6	2 - 1	1 - 2	2 - 1	17	14
7	2 - 1	2 - 1	1 - 2	16	15, 5
8	2 - 1	2 - 1	2 - 1	15	10, 5

b. All possible nonpreemptive schedules

FIGURE 5.10   A three-machine, two-job flow shop.

M1 → M2 → M3 → M4

Job number	Processing time on machine			
	M1	M2	M3	M4
1	1	4	6	2
2	4	1	1	6

a. Processing times on machines M1, M2, M3, M4

Schedule number	Job sequence on machine				Makespan	Mean flow time
	M1	M2	M3	M4		
1	1 - 2	1 - 2	1 - 2	1 - 2	19	16
2	1 - 2	1 - 2	1 - 2	2 - 1	20	19
3	1 - 2	1 - 2	2 - 1	1 - 2	21	18
4	1 - 2	1 - 2	2 - 1	2 - 1	(15)	(14)
5	1 - 2	2 - 1	1 - 2	1 - 2	24	21
6	1 - 2	2 - 1	1 - 2	2 - 1	25	24
7	1 - 2	2 - 1	2 - 1	1 - 2	24	21
8	1 - 2	2 - 1	2 - 1	2 - 1	18	15,5
9	2 - 1	1 - 2	1 - 2	1 - 2	23	20
10	2 - 1	1 - 2	1 - 2	2 - 1	24	23
11	2 - 1	1 - 2	2 - 1	1 - 2	25	22
12	2 - 1	1 - 2	2 - 1	2 - 1	19	18
13	2 - 1	2 - 1	1 - 2	1 - 2	23	20
14	2 - 1	2 - 1	1 - 2	2 - 1	24	23
15	2 - 1	2 - 1	2 - 1	1 - 2	23	20
16	2 - 1	2 - 1	2 - 1	2 - 1	17	14,5

b. All possible nonpreemptive schedules

FIGURE 5.11   A four-machine, two-job flow shop.

In Johnson's problem, there are two machines and n jobs simultaneously available at time zero. A schedule is sought to complete all the jobs within a minimum makespan.

Let p_{ik} denote the time required to process job i on machine k, where $i = 1, 2, \ldots, n$, and $k = 1, 2$. By consequence 1 given above, makespan is minimized by a permutation schedule. Johnson's scheduling rule is:

In an optimal schedule job i precedes job j if:

$$\min(p_{i1}, p_{j2}) \leqslant \min(p_{j1}, p_{i2}).$$

The original paper also presents a working procedure for implementing the rule:

1. List the jobs in a table:

Job number	Processing time on machine	
	M1	M2
1	p_{11}	p_{12}
2	p_{21}	p_{22}
$\vdots$	$\vdots$	$\vdots$
n	p_{n1}	p_{n2}

2. Find the smallest processing time in the table.
3. If the smallest processing time is for the first machine, place the corresponding job in the first available position in sequence. If it is for the second machine, place the corresponding job in the last available position in sequence. Ties between jobs may be broken arbitrarily or, if a rule is required, order the job with the smallest job subscript first. In case of a tie between p_{i1} and p_{i2}, determine the position of job i according to p_{i1}.
4. Remove the assigned job from the table. If the table is empty, stop. Otherwise, go to step 2.

In Figure 5.12 an example is worked out to illustrate Johnson's procedure in a two-machine, six-job flow shop. It is apparent that the rule constructs the schedule from both ends toward the middle. The optimal permutation schedule 4-6-2-3-5-1 has a makespan of 36.

We should note that Johnson's procedure lends itself to an intuitive interpretation. Put the smallest p_{i1} first so the second machine can start processing as soon as possible. Put the smallest p_{i2} last so the total processing can be completed as early as possible after the last operation on machine 1 is finished. And, indeed, this is reasonable to do, as suggested by the two

Job number	Processing time on machine	
	M1	M2
1	5	4
2	6	6
3	11	7
4	1	3
5	7	5
6	2	8

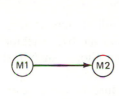

a. Processing times on machines M1, M2

Pass	Unscheduled jobs	Minimum processing time among unscheduled jobs	To which job does it belong?	On which machine?	Partial schedule
1	1, 2, 3, 4, 5, 6	1	4	M1	4 ☐ ☐ ☐ ☐ ☐
2	1, 2, 3, 5, 6	2	6	M1	4 6 ☐ ☐ ☐ ☐
3	1, 2, 3, 5	4	1	M2	4 6 ☐ ☐ ☐ 1
4	2, 3, 5	5	5	M2	4 6 ☐ ☐ 5 1
5	2, 3,	6	2	M1, M2	4 6 2 ☐ 5 1
6	3	Irrelevant	Irrelevant	Irrelevant	4 6 2 3 5 1

b. Applying Johnson's working rule

FIGURE 5.12   Scheduling to minimize makespan in a two-machine, six-job flow shop.

inequalities that bound the makespan from below:

$$M = F_{\max} \geq \sum_{i=1}^{n} p_{i1} + p_{[n]2},$$

$$M = F_{\max} \geq p_{[1]1} + \sum_{i=1}^{n} p_{i2},$$

where $p_{[1]1}$ is the time required to process on machine 1 the first job in sequence, and $p_{[n]2}$ the time on machine 2 of the last job in sequence. As $\sum p_{i1}$ and $\sum p_{i2}$ are sequence-independent, one would set $p_{[1]1} = \min p_{i1}$ or $p_{[n]2} = \min p_{i2}$ in order to reduce the two bounds. Then one would proceed the same way with the diminished list of jobs at every pass through the scheduling algorithm. Szwarc [1981] investigates the extreme solutions of the two-machine flow shop problem.

5.2.4.2 The three-machine flow shop problem (makespan criterion)

Although in this case permutation schedules are still dominant with respect to minimizing makespan, it is not possible to extend the two-machine algorithm presented above to the general three-machine shop. Analytical results exist, however, for particular situations.

Johnson [1954] provides an extension of his procedure to the case in which either $\min p_{i1} \geqslant \max p_{i2}$ or $\min p_{i3} \geqslant \max p_{i2}$ —that is, all of the second machine processing times are smaller than any of either the first or the third machine processing times. The implication is that the second machine could not possibly become a bottleneck.

Then the optimal scheduling rule for minimal makespan is:

In an optimal schedule job, i precedes job j if

$$\min(p_{i1} + p_{i2}, p_{j3} + p_{j2}) \leqslant \min(p_{j1} + p_{j2}, p_{i3} + p_{i2}).$$

The working rule is identical to the one for the two-machine shop, provided that in that rule we replace p_{i1} by $(p_{i1} + p_{i2})$, and p_{i2} by $(p_{i3} + p_{i2})$.

To put it otherwise, the three-machine $(M1) \rightarrow (M2) \rightarrow (M3)$ flow shop is reduced to an equivalent two-dummy machine $(M1 + M2) \rightarrow (M2 + M3)$ flow shop.

Burns and Rooker [1978] show that Johnson's algorithm also produces an optimal schedule in a three-machine flow shop when each job $i = 1, \ldots, n$ satisfies the condition $p_{i2} \leqslant \min(p_{i1}, p_{i3})$.

Another special case is presented by Jackson [1956a] who establishes optimality of Johnson's procedure for the three-machine flow shop in which all jobs use a common machine for their first operation and a common machine for their third operation; for the second operation the machine differs with each job.

For general flow shops in which condition $\min p_{i1} \geqslant \max p_{i2}$ or $\min p_{i3} \geqslant \max p_{i2}$ is not satisfied, Johnson's scheduling rule is not necessarily optimal. However, Giglio and Wagner [1964] show that it can still produce good schedules which would, at least, constitute initial solutions upon which further improvement may be carried on.

Other approaches to minimizing makespan in the general three-machine flow shop include integer programming formulations, combinatorial procedures (branch-and-bound), and heuristics. Story and Wagner [1963] and Giglio and Wagner [1964] formulate the scheduling problem as an integer program in which a binary variable Z_{ij} is defined to take on a value of 1 if job i is assigned position j in sequence and a value of 0 otherwise. The objective function is to minimize the total idle time on machine 3. Unfortunately, the computational experience is not very favorable, as even for moderate numbers of jobs and machines the number of constraints and integer variables becomes too large for the computational capability of existing integer programming codes.

The most successful approaches seem to be the branch-and-bound procedures. Application of branch-and-bound to scheduling is based on the fact that the building of a permutation schedule has the structure of a tree. The tree starts from an initial node at which no job has been scheduled yet. Then, at each node an additional job is appended to the sequence until all jobs are scheduled. The tree has a total of $1 + n + n(n-1) + \cdots + n!$ nodes. Each node represents a partial schedule (Figure 5.13).

Branch-and-bound for scheduling in flow shops was originally developed by Ignall and Schrage [1965] and Lomnicki [1965]; for a survey on the technique itself, see Elmaghraby and Elshafei [1976].

Two issues have to be addressed when searching through the tree:

- A branching rule for making a decision on which node to choose next to branch from.
- An elimination rule by which a certain node and all the nodes that emanate from it may be removed from further consideration. When elimination takes place, it reflects the fact that the partial sequence corresponding to the node being eliminated is dominated by some other partial sequence. Domination means that the dominated partial sequence, if completed to a full schedule, cannot possibly lead to a smaller makespan than the dominating sequence, and therefore it need not be considered. Without the elimination mechanism, one would have to enumerate the large number of nodes equal to the total of partial sequences.

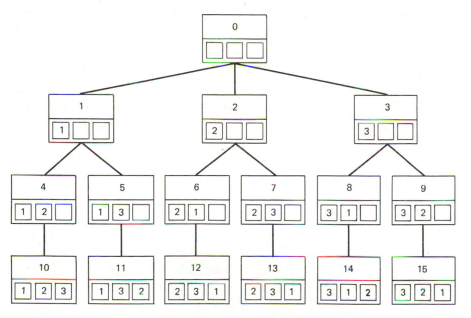

FIGURE 5.13   Enumeration tree for three-job, flow shop problem (permutation schedules).

The branch-and-bound technique starts from the initial node along the n branches corresponding to the n possible jobs that can occupy the first position in the sequence. Every time a new node is created, a lower bound on the makespan is computed. Further branching is usually performed from the node with the smallest lower bound.

Dominance checks are made to establish whether a node can be discarded. As an example, suppose two nodes represent partial sequence s_1 and s_2, respectively. The two sequences contain the same jobs in different order. Let $T2(s)$, and $T3(s)$ be the times at which machines 2 and 3, respectively, complete processing on the jobs in some partial sequence s. Then, if $T2(s_1) \leqslant T2(s_2)$ and $T3(s_1) \leqslant T3(s_2)$ the node associated with partial sequence s_2 may be discarded since s_2 is dominated by s_1.

Ashour [1970], Gupta [1970], Gupta and Reddi [1978], McMahon and Burton [1967], and Szwarc [1971, 1973, 1978], to mention a few, have worked on developing sharper bounds and more powerful dominance conditions, in order to reduce the search for optimality. Baker [1975] and Lageweg et al. [1977] have performed comparative computational studies of the relative efficiency of various bounding and elimination strategies. Lageweg et al. found that an algorithm with a lower bound based on Johnson's two-machine problem, combined with an elimination criterion of Szwarc [1971], was able to solve reasonably quickly problems with up to 50 jobs as long as the number of machines was small (three machines). As the number of machines increased, lower bounds became less reliable and solution times increased drastically.

Heuristics are discussed in the context of large flow shops, where they become an important schedule generation alternative, as optimal techniques get out of the realm of computational feasibility.

5.2.4.3 Large flow shop problems (m > 3 and large n)

As mentioned earlier, scheduling to minimize makespan in the flow shop is NP-complete. Over a quarter of a century after Johnson's results, analytical work has not overstepped the three-machine case.

Undoubtedly, Johnson's pioneering work has strongly influenced scheduling research on flow shops. His adoption of the makespan criterion has probably prompted most researchers to resort to the same criterion. Therefore, results for other measures of performance are comparatively scarce. For instance, Ignall and Schrage [1965] apply branch-and-bound to the problem of minimizing mean flow time and find out that the problem is very difficult even for the two-machine flow shop. The computational effort required increases with 2^n. Gupta [1972] tries heuristic procedures for minimizing the mean flow time. Integer programming formulation is still another approach, but it is computationally infeasible for any real-sized problem.

In what follows we are limiting our presentation to research work treating the makespan criterion.

A distinguishing trait of the research on large flow shops is the emphasis on permutation schedules. Although for $m \geqslant 4$ permutation schedules are not dominant, it is reasonable to believe that the best permutation schedule, even if not necessarily optimal, cannot be too far away from the true optimum. Indeed, consider the job which is first in sequence on machine k. If on machine $k-1$ this job is in the ith position, jobs in positions $1, 2, \ldots, i-1$, although completed by machine $k-1$, have to be delayed at machine k until this particular job completes processing on both machine $k-1$ and machine k. Intuition says that this change of ordering might increase the maximum flow time (makespan) and, therefore, constructing an order preserving schedule (permutation schedule) could be a good way to go. Moreover, permutation schedules constitute a substantially smaller set containing $n!$ sequences versus $(n!)^m$ nonpermutation schedules.

Evidently, complete enumeration of the $n!$ permutation schedules is out of the question. Implicit enumeration by branch-and-bound as described for the three-machine shop can be extended to large flow shops, but it may become computationally prohibitive. Therefore, paralleling the work on optimal procedures has been work on heuristics. Noteworthy heuristics for the makespan criterion are those of Campbell et al. [1970] and Dannenbring [1977].

Campbell et al. [1970] use Johnson's procedure to solve a series of two-machine approximations to the actual problem. The first two-machine problem considered contains only machines #1 and #m of the original problem. The intervening $m-2$ machines are ignored. Johnson's rule is applied to find the optimal permutation schedule. The second step of the heuristic pools together machines #1 and #2 to form a dummy machine on which job i requires a processing time $p_{i1'} = p_{i1} + p_{i2}$. Also, machines #$(m-1)$ and #m form a second dummy machine with processing time $p_{i2'} = p_{i,m-1} + p_{im}$. Johnson's rule is applied and the best permutation schedule for this two-dummy machine flow shop is produced. At step s the first dummy machine contains the original machines #1 through #s, while the second dummy machine includes machines #$(m-s+1)$ through #m. Johnson's rule again finds the optimal schedule. In total $m-1$ steps are required. Consequently, $m-1$ sequences are generated (some of them may be identical). With each sequence, the makespan for the original problem is computed, and the best sequence is chosen as the solution.

Dannenbring [1977] also uses Johnson's procedure to solve a two-machine approximation to the critical problem. The resulting schedule is then improved as much as possible by switching adjacent jobs in the sequence. In an extensive evaluation of a wide set of heuristics, Dannenbring [1977] finds that his heuristic is able to obtain the true optimum in more cases than the heuristic of Campbell et al. [1970], but the latter is considerably faster.

For other heuristics see Palmer [1965], Gupta [1972], and Smith and Dudek [1967], who modified an earlier algorithm by Dudek and Teuton [1964].

An important issue concerning approximation algorithms is the question about how far from optimality are their solutions. Traditionally, researchers have run heuristic procedures on selected test problems for which the optimal solution was known. Then inferences were drawn with respect to the performance of the algorithm. Clearly, the major difficulty lies in designing a representative set of test problems. A recent approach is to develop bounds on the worst case behavior of a particular heuristic. Gonzalez and Sahni [1978] present heuristics for the flow shop and show how to compute such bounds on their performance.

5.2.5   The General Job Shop

The general job shop consists of $m \geqslant 2$ machines. Unlike the flow shop, work flow is not unidirectional, that is, a job can enter the job shop at any machine and leave the shop from any machine (see example of Table 5.1 and Figure 5.1). Jobs are in general multistage and can have any number of operations. Most researchers, however, assume that each job has exactly m operations and uses each machine only once.

There are two dominant classes of job shop models that have been studied in the literature: the static deterministic and the dynamic probabilistic job shop, which are all extremely hard computationally.

The sole exception is the static deterministic problem with $m = 2$, and no job having more than two operations, in which case Jackson's [1956] optimal algorithm constructs the minimum makespan schedule. Otherwise, if $m > 2$ or if some job has more than two operations, scheduling in the static shop is NP-complete (Lenstra et al. [1977]) and, therefore, no polynomial-bounded optimizing algorithm is expected to be found.

The dynamic probabilistic job shop represents a network of queues, and in its turn defies attempts to attack the problem analytically, leaving heuristics and simulation as the only approaches.

5.2.5.1   The static deterministic job shop

Although real job shops in industrial settings are dynamic probabilistic, studying the static deterministic job shop model is expected to provide a first understanding of the nature of scheduling in job shops.

In the static deterministic job shop n jobs are available at time zero, and all processing times are known with certainty. The problem is to construct the schedule which minimizes a given measure of performance. The measures of performance almost exclusively resorted to are the makespan and the mean flow time, used with nonpreemptive schedules. A survey of the static general job shop problem, for the makespan criterion, is given by Bakshi and Arora [1969].

The Two-Machine Job Shop Problem (makespan criterion). The simplest job shop problem contains only two machines, with all jobs having at most two operations. An optimizing procedure exists, due to Jackson [1956a], with respect to the makespan criterion.

There are four kinds of jobs in Jackson's algorithm:

- Set {1} contains the jobs which consist of only one operation, to be performed on machine #1, M1.
- Set {2} contains the jobs which consist of only one operation, to be performed on machine #2, M2.
- Set {12} contains the jobs which consist of two operations, of which the first is to be processed on M1, and the second on M2.
- Set {21} contains the jobs which consist of two operations, of which the first is to be processed on M2, and the second on M1.

First, use Johnson's [1954] two-machine flow shop algorithm to sequence the jobs in {12} optimally, disregarding all other jobs. Then, with the same procedure, sequence the jobs in {21}. Jobs in {1} may be sequenced arbitrarily; similarly, jobs in {2}. To obtain the solution to the original problem, concentrate the four sets of jobs as follows, preserving the orderings achieved above within each set:

- on M1 schedule jobs in {12} first, then jobs in {1}, and at the end jobs in {21}
- on M2 schedule jobs in {21} first, followed by jobs in {2}, followed by jobs in {12}

The algorithm optimizes the makespan by minimizing the total idle time between operations. Intuitively, the algorithm works as follows (see Figure 5.14): schedule first compactly on M1 jobs in {12}. Meanwhile, process on M2 the first operation of all jobs in {21}. Now think of the time when jobs in {12} move to M2. By processing the jobs in {2} first, it is possible that when the jobs in {12} arrive at M2 for their second operations they will have already had all

FIGURE 5.14
Principle of Jackson's (1956a) algorithm.

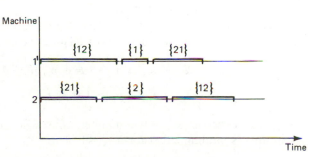

processing on M1 completed and, therefore, can be scheduled compactly on M2. Thus, deferring on M2 jobs in {12} until after jobs in {2} can only be beneficial in terms of reducing idle time. A similar reasoning applies for M1.

The n job, m machine job shop problem. As mentioned, the problem is NP-complete, and no exact specialized solution procedures are known. Optimization approaches include integer programming formulation and branch-and-bound algorithms. In general, however, they cannot be carried out to the final optimal solution because of the computational infeasibility associated even with small-sized problems. Indeed, an upper bound on the total number of schedules is $(n!)^m$ and, although some schedules are infeasible because of routing requirements, the total number of feasible schedules is still extremely large. Other approaches consist of heuristics.

A. *The integer programming formulation* of the job shop scheduling problem (Manne [1960]) offers the advantage of versatility in choosing the measure of performance.

Assume job i $(i = 1,...,n)$ requires processing by machine k $(k = 1,...,m)$ exactly once in its operation sequence (thus, each job has m operations). Let:

p_{ik} = processing time of job i on machine k

X_{ik} = starting time of job i on machine k

q_{ijk} = indicator which takes on a value of 1 if operation j of job i requires machine k, and zero otherwise

Y_{ihk} = variable which takes on a value of 1 if job i precedes job h (not necessarily directly) on machine k, and zero otherwise.

The formulation has routing constraints of the following form:

$$\sum_{k=1}^{m} q_{ijk}(X_{ik} + p_{ik}) \leqslant \sum_{k=1}^{m} q_{i,j+1,k} X_{ik}, (i = 1,...,n; j = 1,...,m-1),$$

which says that for a given job i, the $(j+1)^{st}$ operation may not start before the jth operation is completed.

Notice that the X_{ik}'s are decision variables whose values will fully determine an optimal Gantt chart.

To prevent scheduling two different jobs at the same time on the same machine, one has to formulate a set of disjunctive constraints:

$$X_{hk} - X_{ik} \geqslant p_{ik} - (H + p_{ik})(1 - Y_{ihk}),$$
$$X_{ik} - X_{hk} \geqslant p_{hk} - (H + p_{hk})Y_{ihk},$$

where H is a very large positive number, chosen so that only one of the above constraints is binding either for $Y_{ihk} = 1$ or for $Y_{ihk} = 0$.

To summarize the entire set of constraints:

$$\sum_{k=1}^{m} q_{ijk}(X_{ik} + p_{ik}) \leqslant \sum_{k=1}^{m} q_{i,j+1,k} X_{ik} \qquad (i = 1, \ldots, n; \ j = 1, \ldots, m-1)$$

$$X_{hk} - X_{ik} \geqslant p_{ik} - (H + p_{ik})(1 - Y_{ihk}),$$

$$X_{ik} - X_{hk} \geqslant p_{hk} - (H + p_{hk})Y_{ihk}, \qquad \begin{aligned} &(i = 1, \ldots, n \\ &h = 1, \ldots, n \\ &k = 1, \ldots, m.) \end{aligned}$$

$$X_{ik} \geqslant 0,$$

$$Y_{ihk} = 0 \text{ or } 1.$$

Notice that Y_{hik} need not be defined if Y_{ihk} is in the formulation.

The objective function for the minimization of the mean flow time can be written as:

Minimize
$$\sum_{i=1}^{n} \sum_{k=1}^{m} q_{imk} X_{ik},$$

that is, one minimizes the sum of the starting times of the last operation of each job.

If one minimizes the makespan M, the completion time of the last operation of each job should be constrainted as follows:

$$\sum_{k=1}^{m} q_{imk}(X_{ik} + p_{ik}) \leqslant M, \qquad (i = 1, \ldots, n),$$

and the objective function is: Minimize M.

Other measures of performance can also be modeled.

If a solution to the model may be found for a given problem, it will constitute a reference point in testing various approximation algorithms. However, there are computational difficulties, given that the number of $(mn^2 - n)$ constraints and $mn(n-1)/2$ integer variables grows rather fast with m and n, relative to the capability of existing integer programming codes. For instance, a five-job, five-machine problem involves 120 constraints and 50 integer variables, while a 10-job, 10-machine formulation has 990 constraints and 450 integer variables.

Greenberg [1968] gives a branch-and-bound technique for solving the above mixed integer programming problem. Fisher [1973a, 1973b] proposes a different integer programming formulation. Limited computational experience is presented with a branch-and-bound solution technique in which lower bounds are obtained by the use of Lagrange multipliers.

B.   *Schedule construction algorithms* generate schedules by performing a sequence of steps. Such an algorithm starts from an empty *partial* schedule. With each step the partial schedule is augmented by scheduling one more

Job	Operation 1		Operation 2		Operation 3	
number	Machine	Processing time	Machine	Processing time	Machine	Processing time
1	3	1	2	1	1	1
2	1	0.5	2	2	—	—

a. Operation processing times

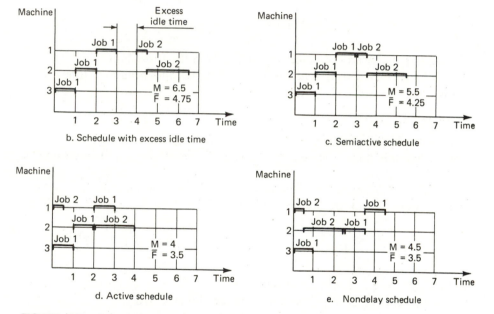

b. Schedule with excess idle time

c. Semiactive schedule

d. Active schedule

e. Nondelay schedule

FIGURE 5.15 Scheduling in two-job, three-machine job shop.

operation or job.* When all operations of all jobs have been scheduled, we have a *complete* schedule.

Available schedule generation algorithms span the full spectrum, ranging from the exhaustive enumeration of all possible schedules, out of which the best may be selected, to techniques by which a single feasible schedule, not necessarily the optimum, is obtained.

Ba. *Exhaustive enumeration algorithms* are important from a theoretical point of view rather than from a practical point of view. The important issue that has to be addressed regards the types of schedules that can be constructed. There are four classes: schedules with excess idle time, semiactive, active, and nondelay schedules. Schedules with idle time (Figure 5.15b) may be discarded

---

*In a partial schedule, only part of the entire set of operations of all jobs have been assigned starting and completion times.

right from the outset since surplus idle time cannot be beneficial under any measure of performance.

A semiactive schedule contains no excess idle time. It can be obtained by compacting a schedule with excess idle time. Intuitively, on a Gantt chart all operations are pushed to the left, without changing their sequence on any machine, until the surplus idle time is "squeezed" out (Figure 5.15c).

A given semiactive schedule can be improved if, on the Gantt chart, it is possible to shift to the left some operations without causing other operations to start later than scheduled initially. When a schedule allows no such shift to be made, it is an active schedule (Figure 5.15d). The active schedules constitute the smallest dominant set with respect to any regular measure of performance.

The nondelay schedules are a subset of active schedules. In a nondelay schedule, a machine is never kept idle if some operation is scheduleable, that is, ready for processing. We say that an operation is scheduleable if all operations which precede it on the job are completed. Thus, the starting time of an operation is the earliest time at which the operation is scheduleable *and* the corresponding machine is available (Figure 5.15e). Notice that the schedule in Figure 5.15d is not nondelay, since at time 0.5, machine 2 is kept idle although it could start processing operation 2 of job 2.

The tree of Figure 5.16 classifies the schedules that can be constructed for a static deterministic job shop problem.

As already mentioned, the smallest dominant set of schedules are the active schedules. Indeed, the best schedule is not necessarily nondelay, as is obvious from Figure 5.15. However, there is empirical evidence (Conway et al. [1967, chap. 6-8]) that the best nondelay schedule, even if not optimal, is likely to provide a very good solution (a situation similar to the case of permutation schedules in flow shops). Since nondelay schedules constitute a set smaller than all active schedules, and as they are not more difficult to generate, it is reasonable to limit one's search to the set of nondelay schedules whenever constructive algorithms for the optimal schedule do not exist.

Giffler and Thompson [1960] provide an algorithm for the generation of all active schedules for a job shop problem, and Baker [1974, chap. 7] presents a modification of this algorithm to generate all nondelay schedules.

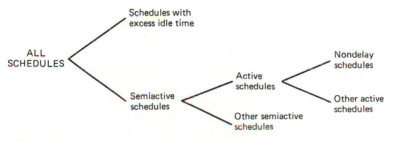

FIGURE 5.16 Classification of job shop schedules.

Constructing a schedule has a tree-like structure, in which each node represents a partial schedule. Branching from one node to the next means that one more scheduleable operation is appended to the last partial schedule. To perform a branching, two sequential decisions have to be made:

- Select the machine to which an operation is to be assigned next.
- Out of the scheduleable operations requiring that machine, select one to be scheduled next.

After selecting the operation, its assigned starting time is the earliest time at which it may be scheduled. Figure 5.17 shows the enumeration tree for the two active schedules of Figure 5.15d and 5.15e.

If, while constructing a schedule, the algorithm generates starting times in a nondecreasing sequence of numbers, it is a *dispatching* procedure. Giffler and Thompson's algorithm and its modification mentioned above are of the dispatching type. To illustrate, the sequence of start times that lead to the active schedule of node 7 in Figure 5.17 is: 0-0-1-2-2. The series of start times for the active (also nondelay) schedule of node 8 is: 0-0-0.5-2.5-3.5. This means that no operation is inserted in a time slot before an already scheduled operation on the same machine or, to put it differently, start time decisions are made in the same order that they would be implemented if the schedule were executed. The implication is that start times do not have to be specified all at the beginning; scheduling decisions can be made sequentially over time.

We should mention that the full significance of dispatching procedures is achieved only with dynamic probabilistic job shops where, because of the lack of precise information on job arrivals, a procedure which makes starting time decisions as they are needed (i.e., when a machine becomes idle) is the only viable option.

We do not insist on the algorithms themselves because exhaustive enumeration is obviously computationally prohibitive for large problems. To curtail the search through the enumeration tree, some researchers have employed branch-and-bound techniques. Others have renounced optimality and resorted to heuristics to cut down the search even more. We briefly review both approaches below.

Bb.   *Branch-and-bound procedures* have received substantial attention from numerous researchers, with emphasis on the makespan criterion. Early work was performed by Brooks and White [1965], followed by Balas [1969], Charlton and Death [1970], Florian et al. [1971], Ashour et al. [1974], and Lageweg et al. [1977], to name a few. The various procedures differ primarily with respect to the branching strategy and the generation of bounds. In spite of some progress, however, branch-and-bound remains ineffective in solving larger problems. Indeed, in a recent study Lageweg et al. [1977] report solving a six-job, six-machine problem within a few seconds on a Control Data Cyber 73-28, but they fail to produce an optimal schedule for a 10-job, 10-machine job shop within five minutes of CPU time.

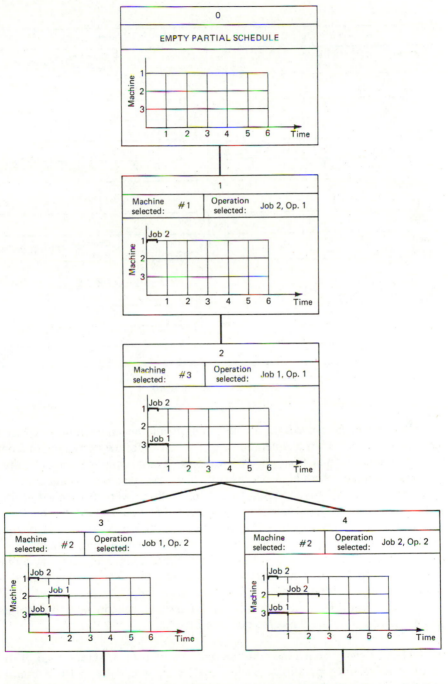

FIGURE 5.17   Enumeration tree by Giffler and Thompson (1960) algorithm for job shop problem of Figure 5.15.

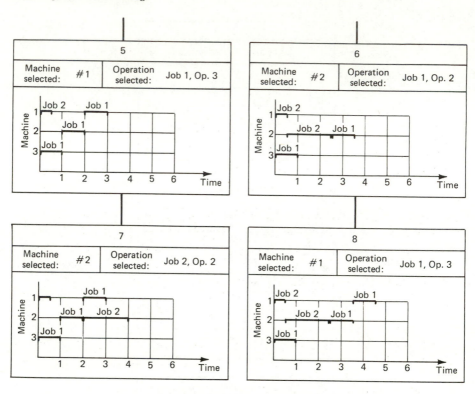

FIGURE 5.17 *(Continued)*

Bc. *Heuristic procedures* are different from the enumeration schemes seen earlier in that in an enumeration tree, heuristics follow a single path from the initial node to some final node corresponding to a complete schedule, thus building a unique schedule in one pass through the tree. For instance, in the enumeration tree of Figure 5.17, after node 2 there were two scheduleable operations—Job 1/Op. 2 and Job 2/Op. 2—that could enter the enlarged partial schedule to be constructed next. The exhaustive enumeration algorithm of Giffler and Thompson [1960] followed both branches and obtained two complete schedules. A branch-and-bound procedure might have to probe along each branch up to a certain depth before deciding that a particular branch is not promising and that it should be abandoned. Opposite these, a heuristic procedure would select one and only one of the two scheduleable operations and then proceed along the corresponding branch.

Thus, at every branching point an operation has to be selected out of the set of scheduleable operations. Such a procedure would be called *operation oriented*. The selection can be conducted in two distinct ways.

One way is to make the selection by the use of a *deterministic priority rule* that takes into account some attribute of the operations or of their associated

jobs. A study by Jeremiah et al. [1964] is the classical reference in this respect.*
Active and nondelay schedules were generated, and several priority rules were
tested.

For the mean flow time criterion, although no rule was consistently
superior, it was found that rules which select light unprocessed work loads
tended to produce better schedules such as:

- SPT (*S*hortest *P*rocessing *T*ime). At the branching point, select the operation
  with the shortest processing time.

- LWKR (*L*east *W*ork *R*emaining). Select the operation whose associated job
  has the least work remaining to be done.

When makespan was considered, better schedules were produced when
jobs with heavy unprocessed work loads were selected, such as using the rule:

- MWKR (*M*ost *W*ork *R*emaining). Select the operation whose associated job
  has the most work remaining to be done.

It is interesting to draw a parallel to results reviewed earlier. Indeed,
Jeremiah et al.'s findings remind us of the static single and parallel machine
shops where arranging jobs in nondecreasing order of their work load (SPT
ordering) minimized mean flow time, while minimization of makespan in the
parallel machine shop was approached with heuristics which scheduled jobs in
order of nonincreasing processing time (LPT ordering).

Another way of selecting an operation is by use of a *probabilistic priority
rule* or random sampling mechanism. Giffler et al. [1963] assign all scheduleable
operations at a given branching point equal probabilities of being selected.
Then they draw one operation at random out of this probability distribution.
By making one pass through the enumeration tree one schedule is generated.
Usually several passes are performed, with the possibility that the random
sampling mechanism will result every time in other operations being chosen at
the branching points. Thus, a sample of feasible schedules is constructed, from
which the best schedule is selected in terms of some given measure of
performance.

A somewhat more sophisticated random sampling mechanism can be
devised if the selection of the operation is biased by some attribute of the
operation or of the associated job. It is called probabilistic dispatching and
Conway et al. [1967, chap. 6-9] cover it in fair detail. Probabilistic dispatching
leads, in general, to better schedules than the corresponding deterministic
priority rule. However, from the available studies, it is not clear whether the
improvement warrants the substantially increased computational requirements.

Another category of heuristics completely treats one job at a time rather
than working with individual operations, that is, all the operations of a job are
scheduled in succession. Therefore, we call this class of procedures *job oriented*.

---

*The study is largely summarized by Conway et al. [1967, chap. 6-8].

The techniques for loading orders onto machines, used by most schedulers in actual industrial settings, are of this type. In general, they are applied in an adjusting manner, meaning that, in order to better accommodate new jobs, one might have to modify starting time assignments made for operations scheduled before.

A study by Crabill [1964]* experiments with such a procedure, which admits the alternative of inserting operations of the job being scheduled into an existing schedule, rather than only appending them at the end. If the insertion requires adjusting the starting times of previously scheduled operations, this is done so as to obtain an active schedule. After some limited experimental testing, the heuristic compared favorably with several dispatching procedures with respect to the minimization of makespan.

Magee and Boodman [1967, p. 255] present a job-at-a-time heuristic procedure for practitioners. The procedure tries to fit the operations of a given job in the time slots left available on each machine by the work load scheduled previously. The order in which jobs are considered is not specified but, from other sections of their book, it can be inferred that jobs are selected, for instance, according to the number of days they have been held on the scheduler's desk before being released periodically to the shop floor. The procedure is as follows:

1. For every operation j of the job under consideration determine:
   1.1. Time t_j as the sum of the processing time at operation j and the processing times thereafter to complete the job.
   1.2. The earliest time T_j at which processing of the operation can be started on the corresponding machine.
   1.3. The sum $T_j + t_j$, which represents the possible completion time as dictated by operation j.
2. Find the operation which determines the latest completion time, that is, $\max(T_j + t_j)$. This is the "bottleneck."
3. Schedule the bottleneck operation as early as possible, that is, at the time under 1.2.
4. Schedule subsequent operations as early as possible, and prior operations as late as possible, consistent with the routing of the job.

Although the algorithm has no stated measure of performance, it seems that, for the given job, it aims at reducing the holding cost of work-in-process inventory and completing the job as early as possible.

As an example, see Figure 5.18, where the shaded segments represent previously scheduled work load. The open segments represent the operations of the job being scheduled (the arrows are drawn to show the routing of the job more clearly). It is apparent that the operation on machine 3 is the bottleneck.

---

*The main results are also reported by Conway et al. [1967, pp. 130–131].

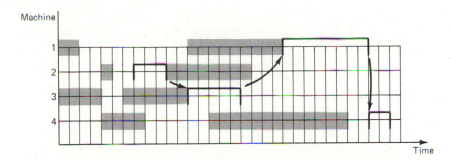

FIGURE 5.18   Job-at-a-time scheduling (Magee and Boodman (1967)).

5.2.5.2   The dynamic probabilistic job shop

In the dynamic probabilistic job shop, which consists of m functionally related machines, jobs arrive at random and continuously over time. In general, processing times are considered known at the time jobs arrive in the shop. There have been, however, studies which assumed nondeterministic operation times.*

In front of each machine there is a queue of jobs awaiting processing. After processing on the machine in whose queue it has been waiting, the job moves sequentially to other queues and, eventually, it is completed and discharged from the system. Such a system has been visualized as a *network of queues*. The vast majority of real industrial shops are dynamic probabilistic.

In this context, it is no longer possible to construct a schedule in the sense of assigning each operation a start time and a completion time on the corresponding machine.† Rather, the problem is partitioned into sequencing problems at each machine. Thus, when a machine becomes idle, one has to select out of its queue the next job for processing on this particular machine. This sort of decision making was earlier termed dispatching. By the use of a *dispatching rule*, also called *queue discipline*, *priority rule*, or *selection discipline*,

---

*These features are most often associated with open job shops. In the closed job shop the release of jobs to the shop floor is more predictable, due to the fact that the jobs are generated by a disaggregation mechanism, which is controllable. But, when processing times are nondeterministic (and this is the case with real industrial shops), this relative advantage is lost once the job progresses beyond the machine through which it entered the shop, so that arrivals at other machines become stochastic. Since jobs may exhibit a large variety of routings, and also because the shop under consideration itself might be just one of the stages in a more complex multistage system of job shops, virtually at all the machines jobs arrive randomly, even in the closed job shop case.

†A schedule may still be constructed if we limit ourselves to a finite number of jobs, such as the jobs existing in the shop at the time the schedule is drawn, and if processing times or their estimates are known. However, since this constitutes a static approach to a dynamic problem, the schedule will certainly suffer from swift obsolescence. The scheduling problem, then, becomes a rescheduling problem, in which frequent updating by computer is essential. Systems of this sort are reported by Reiter [1966], Moodie and Novotny [1968].

a priority index is assigned to each job in a queue and then processing takes place in increasing or decreasing order of the indices. These priorities move the jobs through the shop instead of a schedule. In a paper by Panwalkar and Iskander [1977], over 100 dispatching rules are inventories and presented within a classification framework.

In this light, the essence of studying the dynamic probabilistic job shop problem is to determine the effectiveness of various priority rules in terms of optimizing a predetermined measure of performance. Researchers have approached the problem analytically, using queueing network theory, and experimentally.

A.   *The analytical approach.* One of the main concerns of analytical studies is to derive the steady state joint probability distribution of the queue sizes at the various machines in the shop, and to determine the impact of different dispatching rules upon the behavior of the queueing network. This has proved to be extremely difficult and, therefore, only limited results exist.

With few exceptions, systems of queues have been analyzed under the assumptions that external sources of jobs are Poisson, and service times at all machines are generated from exponential distributions. The basic model was developed by Jackson [1957, 1963]. His result, which is the most powerful analytical result available, is known as Jackson's decomposition principle. It establishes sufficient conditions under which a network of m queues behaves probabilistically as m-independent individual machine queues. These conditions are:

- The arrival of jobs from outside the shop is Poisson.
- The routing of jobs depends only on a fixed probability transfer matrix (see Figure 5.3).
- Processing times at each machine are exponentially distributed.
- The priority rule at each machine depends neither on the routing of the jobs nor on the processing times (such as the FCFS queue discipline).

Under these assumptions the queue sizes at the various machines, expressed as numbers of jobs, are independent random variables at each point in time. Hence, the job shop may be broken down into m single-machine systems. Unfortunately, by virtue of the restrictive fourth assumption, Jackson's decomposition is inapplicable in the case of some important dispatching rules (to be presented later) because many of these rules either depend on the jobs' processing times or take into account look-ahead information about subsequent queues to which the jobs are moving.

Other studies following Jackson's early work aimed at expanding his basic model. The interested reader is referred to the paper by Lemoine [1977] for an overview of available results and a discussion of important and still unresolved issues in queueing network models.

B. *The experimental approach*. In the face of the difficulties associated with analytic techniques, there are several alternatives open for attack upon the problem. These are shown below.

Ba. *Experimentation with real shops* by implementing various queue disciplines and then evaluating their relative merits based on actual performance. Although this approach holds the advantage of realism, it is usually impractical and would entail a considerable loss of generality. However, short of conducting proper said experiments with alternative dispatching rules, there have been studies reporting on results obtained in real job shops operating on the basis of dispatching rules. For example, Elmaghraby and Cole [1963] describe a production control system developed and implemented in a small job shop at the Western Electric Company. As far as sequencing at the various work stations in the shop was concerned, it was done using a priority rule which depended on the job's due data and on the processing time in the remaining operations through which the job had to pass. The benefits claimed for the system after several months of operation are reduced manufacturing lead time, reduced work-in-process inventories, and better customer relations.

Bb. *Simulation conducted in real shops for operational purposes* is designed to project ahead the operation of the shop in order to provide foremen and department heads with estimates on work load expected for the next time interval, and to evaluate the probable effect of dispatching decisions. As an example, consider the computer-monitored job shop control system at the El Segundo Division of Hughes Aircraft Company, reported by Bulkin et al. [1966]. In this application, the simulation starts from a current status description of the queues in the shop. A dispatching rule based on the job's due date and on its remaining number of operations is utilized to assign priorities to jobs waiting at the various machine groups. Then, at each machine group processing of the jobs in order of their priorities is simulated, using estimated operation processing times. After completion of an operation, the job's priority index is updated and moved to the next queue (according to the routing). The simulation stops after enough work has been processed to cover one shift's operation. Several reports are generated, among which the "order schedule report" showing, by machine groups, the jobs already waiting at the beginning of the shift as well as the jobs expected to arrive during the shift. Benefits claimed for the system include reduced manufacturing intervals and better customer service. We should note that, although the papers presented above and several other similar papers* report on successful scheduling systems, not too much of a general conclusion may be drawn with respect to the efficacy of the particular scheduling techniques and queue disciplines employed. As is usually the case,

---

*Other reports on implemented job shop control systems are summarized by Buffa and Taubert [1972, chap. 12].

much of the claimed improvement is brought about by the availability of better and up-to-date information as well as by the systematic approach that comes along with formal systems. Therefore, applicative studies of this sort are dependent on more research oriented work for the development and testing of dispatching procedures.

Bc. *Simulation conducted for research purposes* tests a given set of priority rules in the context of various job shop processes under alternative measures of performance.

A general simulation study starts by generating a hypothetical job file, in which the job interarrival times are included, along with job routings, operation processing times, and due dates. Arrival times and processing times are sampled from stated probability distributions.* In most studies arrivals are Poisson and processing times are exponentially distributed.† For operational feasibility, the average arrival rate of jobs must be smaller than the average processing capability of the shop. Otherwise, queues would gradually grow over all bounds.

The routines of the jobs are defined in the context of a specified shop setting, stating the number and types of machines, and whether any of them are interchangeable. The shop setting may be either hypothetical or the representation of a real job shop. The size of the shop is highly variable in various studies, ranging from five machines up to a thousand. Nevertheless, it was found (Baker and Dzielinski [1960]) that the influence of the shop size is not significant. This is important because it permits experimentation with relatively small shop models and generalization of the results.

Other parameters can also be considered such as the values of the jobs, the cost of processing, setup times (if taken separately from processing times), lot sizes, and, of course, the queue disciplines to be tested.

Then the simulation starts—that is, once a job is recorded as having arrived in the shop it is moved from one queue to the next according to the routing, corresponding processing times, and priority rule.

After the simulation stops, the performance measures of interest are computed and statistical tests are done to compare the influence of the different priority rules on shop performance. The statistics of interest are usually collected under steady state conditions, that is, when the mean departure rate from the shop equals the mean arrival rate to the shop.

---

*There is a difference, though: in general, after sampling, processing times are transferred to the scheduling procedure (thus becoming known), while arrival times are not made available in advance (thus remaining nondeterministic).

† However, a study by Harris [1965] conducted in a large machine shop finds that the shop did not conform to an Erlang model. Thus, it appears that the Poisson-type distribution is not sufficient to describe job arrivals, service times are not exponentially distributed, and actual queue behavior differs from the predictions of Erlang models. Therefore, when simulating real shops, the types of distributions specific to the shop should be determined and used rather than the "standard" modeling assumptions.

The typical underlying assumptions of job shop simulation models parallel, in general, the assumptions mentioned earlier (section 5.2.1) for the basic job shop process:

1. The operations of a job are strictly ordered, alternate routings not being considered. Also, consecutive operations on the same machine are not permitted.
2. Jobs consist of operations in series.
3. Due dates and processing times are known at the time jobs arrive in the shop.
4. Setup times are sequence-independent and are included in the processing times.
5. Jobs move instantaneously between machines.
6. Each machine is continuously available for assignment. Labor, tools, materials, and other resources are always in ample supply, and machines never break down.
7. There is only one of each type of machine in the shop.
8. A machine can process only one operation at a time.
9. Machines are not interchangeable; that is, a given operation can be performed by only one machine in the shop.
10. Operation preemption is not allowed.
11. Operation overlapping is not permitted.
12. No provisions are made for scrap or rework.

A large diversity of conditions may be modeled by observing some of the above assumptions while relaxing others.

The majority of simulation studies focus on measures of performance related to:

- shop congestion, as reflected by the amount of work-in-process inventories, job flow time, waiting time in queues
- satisfaction of preassigned due dates, as shown by the number (or fraction) of tardy jobs, and by job lateness

However, other approaches to characterizing shop performance have also been advanced, although much fewer. For example, Jones [1973] evaluates two dispatching rules in terms of the cost of idle machines, cost of carrying work-in-process inventory, cost of long due dates, and cost of missing due dates. Steudel et al. [1977] use multivariate autoregressive time-series analysis to detect changes in the behavior of a queueing network as a result of operating it under priority rule.

In the balance of this section, we will examine a few dispatching rules and their effect on shop performance. A word of caution, though: Since the priority rules for general job shops have been developed and tested in the context of some well-defined (usually hypothetical) conditions, generalization of the results with respect to the relative efficacy of the rules in terms of a given criterion should be carefully made (where generalization is possible at all). For a more complete and detailed study, the survey papers by Day and Hottenstein [1970], Panwalkar and Iskander [1977], and Chapter 11 of the book by Conway et al. [1967] are recommended for consideration.

Priority rules for relieving shop congestion

A shop is congested when it has a high level of work-in-process inventory, which can be measured either by the number of jobs or by their work content (see section 5.2.1.4). Equivalently, due to the flow time–inventory relationship (equation 5.6), the average job flow time is widely used to reflect shop congestion.

Conway [1965a], in an extensive study comparing a large number of queue disciplines, concludes that the overall best performance is shown by the SPT rule. Therefore, he recommends that it "should be considered the standard in scheduling research, against which candidate procedures must demonstrate their virtue." A similar result is given by Baker and Dzielinski [1960], who find that SPT dispatching is best for the minimization of the mean flow time.

Under the SPT rule, when a machine becomes idle in the shop, the job with the shortest imminent operation is selected for processing out of the queue waiting at that particular machine. Thus, the priority index of a job is the impending operation processing time itself. It is apparent that, in order to apply this rule, it is sufficient to have information only about the jobs in the individual machine queue. Therefore, these sorts of selection disciplines are classified as *local*.

It is remarkable that the Shortest Processing Time concept which, in various versions, minimizes mean flow time in the single and parallel machine shops, also exhibits an excellent performance in queueing networks under the mean flow time criterion. The explanation is that, by favoring short jobs, SPT forces more jobs through the shop than other rules in a given time interval.

However, a shortcoming of SPT is that an individual job having a long operation might have to wait at the corresponding machine inordinately long until all short operation jobs are cleared out. In the extreme, when short operation jobs keep arriving to the queue, the long operation job will never be done. It is interesting to note, nevertheless, that this fact does not necessarily imply that SPT maximizes the variance of flow time. This follows from the comparison of SPT with other rules such as:

FCFS (*First Come, First Served*): job which arrives at the machine queue first is processed first on that machine.

FASFS (*First Arrived at the Shop, First Served*): of the jobs awaiting processing at a machine, highest priority is given to the job which arrived at the shop earliest.

RANDOM: at the time of arrival to a particular queue, the job is assigned a random number. The job associated with the smallest random number is given highest priority.

TABLE 5.6   Results of Experiments by Conway and Maxwell [1962]

RULE	MEAN FLOW TIME	VARIANCE OF FLOW TIME
SPT	283.1	388.672
RANDOM	344.4	93.074
FCFS	344.4	61.785

Tables 5.6 and 5.7 confirm that SPT achieves minimum flow time. But, while in Table 5.6 SPT has the highest flow time variance, in Table 5.7 only FASFS yields a lower variance than SPT.

To correct for the unacceptably long flow times that might be experienced by long operation jobs, various schemes have been advanced. Conway and Maxwell [1962], Conway [1964],* and Conway [1965a] investigate the following variants of the SPT rule:

- *Truncated SPT.* A limit is imposed on the waiting time for individual jobs in each queue. From jobs having to wait for more than the specified limit, select according to FCFS. If no job exceeds the limit, assign priorities by SPT.
- *Alternation of SPT with FCFS.* This procedure was implemented in two ways:

  - FCFS is used until the number of jobs in queue attains a certain limit. Then switch to SPT for that particular queue until the number of jobs is reduced below the specified limit. Repeat the procedure.
  - Switch from SPT and FCFS and vice-versa on a cyclical basis. Out of the total cycle duration, use SPT for a certain time, then uses FCFS for the rest of the cycle.

It is intuitively clear, and the studies confirmed it, that none of these schemes can be as effective as simple SPT at reducing the mean flow time or mean number of jobs in queue.† Lowering the flow time variance is achieved at the expense of increased work-in-process inventory. However, the efficacy of the above procedures is not uniform. Alternating SPT with FCFS turned out to be more successful in preserving much of the low mean flow time performance of simple SPT, while the truncated SPT lost much of the SPT advantage before an important reduction in flow time variance could be achieved.

Aside from the class of local rules mentioned earlier, there is the class of *global* priority rules. They are termed global because, in selecting the next job

---

*Largely summarized in Chapter 11 and Appendix C3 of Conway et al. [1967].
†Recall (section 5.2.1.4) that the mean number of jobs in the shop consists of the mean number of jobs in queue plus the mean number of jobs being processed on the machines.

TABLE 5.7   Results of Experiments by Conway [1965b]

RULE	MEAN FLOW TIME	VARIANCE OF FLOW TIME
SPT	(34.0)	2,318
FASFS	72.5	(1,565)
FCFS	74.4	5,739
RANDOM	74.7	10,822

for processing, they also use information from other machines in the shop besides that available at the machine under consideration. Global rules appear like a natural generalization when, instead of single-operation jobs, we deal with jobs that have to visit several machines before being completed.

For example, the following two rules (Conway [1964, 1965a]) look ahead to the work load of the queue to which the job will move next after leaving the machine at which it is currently waiting:

- WINQ (*W*in *N*ext *Q*ueue). Highest priority is given to the job that will join the queue with the smallest work load. The work load is computed as the sum of the imminent operation processing times of the jobs waiting in the queue.
- XWINQ (*E*xpected *W*ork *i*n *N*ext *Q*ueue). Similar to the above, except that the expected work load is relevant. This means that, besides the jobs already in the next queue, one has to consider all jobs which are expected to arrive there (from other machines) before the job under discussion.

Simulation results show (see Table 5.8) that neither of the two global rules performed better than simple SPT with respect to mean number of jobs in queue.

In quest for superior performance, combinations of simple rules were tried, thus obtaining composite queue disciplines. For instance, both WINQ and XWINQ were linearly combined with SPT in the idea that SPT's outstanding behavior could further benefit from the addition of some global information. The composite priority index was computed as the weighted sum of the priority indices given by the two simple rules. Results turned out to be disappointing because improvement over SPT accomplishment (Table 5.8) could be obtained only for certain weighting factors, and when it was obtained it was rather marginal. Moreover, one should not forget that global rules require an information retrieval and processing system whose cost should be weighted against the potential benefits.

TABLE 5.8   Results of Experiments with Local, Global, and Composite Results (Conway [1964])

RULE	MEAN NUMBER OF JOBS IN QUEUE
SPT	23.25
WINQ	40.43
XWINQ	34.03
0.5 (SPT) + 0.5 (WINQ)	30.14
0.9 (SPT) + 0.1 (WINQ)	23.76
0.95 (SPT) + 0.05 (WINQ)	23.00
0.97 (SPT) + 0.03 (WINQ)	22.83
0.94 (SPT) + 0.06 (XWINQ)	23.26
0.96 (SPT) + 0.04 (XWINQ)	22.67
0.98 (SPT) + 0.02 (XWINQ)	22.74

The conclusion is, in general, accepted that SPT is the best rule for reducing shop congestion, due both to its good and robust* performance and to its ease of implementation.

Priority rules for improving the satisfaction of preassigned due dates

The extent to which preassigned due dates are adhered to can be characterized by the distribution of job lateness. Queue disciplines differ in their effect on the mean and variance of lateness, and on other measures of performance, such as fraction of jobs tardy and mean tardiness.

The added complication in these simulations is that one has to study the selection rules in conjunction with the manner in which job due dates are assigned, because "scheduling procedures of sufficient power to enforce a completely arbitrary set of due dates do not yet exist" (Conway et al. [1967, p. 230]).

Conway [1965b] describes four methods of setting due dates. Thus, due dates can be obtained by adding to the job arrival time either a constant

---

*Here, robustness refers to the sensitivity to the quality of processing time information. Tests by Conway [1965a] show that, even when processing time estimates are affected by substantial errors, SPT still retains much of its advantage over RANDOM and FCFS dispatching.

manufacturing lead time (CON), such as is often quoted by salesmen, or a lead time determined at random (RDM), as if due dates were set by customers and accepted by shop management. Other methods determine the manufacturing lead time either proportional to the total work content of the job (TWK), or proportional to the job's number of operations (NOP), the way shop management itself would probably assign due dates. NOP looks reasonable for cases where actual processing represents only a minor portion of the total manufacturing lead time, with the balance being waiting time at the various machines on the job's routing.

Conway [1965b] identifies four priority rules that consider due date information and that are used in industry:

- DDATE (due date): highest priority is given to the job due earliest, that is, the job priority index is made equal to its due date.
- SLACK (slack time): slack time for a given job equals the difference between the time currently remaining until due date and the remaining processing time.* The job with minimum slack receives highest priority.
- OPNDD (operation due date): in a given queue, the highest priority is assigned to the job due earliest at that particular machine. To determine the due dates for the operations of a job, space them equally in the time interval between the job arrival and its due date.
- SLACK/OPN (slack per operation): the job with the smallest ratio between the slack time (as defined above) and the number of operations still remaining to be performed receives the highest priority.

Of all, SLACK/OPN is the most complex selection discipline.

Simulation results for a hypothetical shop with nine machines and 8,700 jobs are presented in Table 5.9. Besides due-date-oriented rules, the mean flow time "champion" SPT and the "neutral" FCFS are also included. Due dates were assigned by the TWK method, and machines were loaded at 88.4% of their capacities.

As reflected in the fraction of jobs tardy and, as expected, using due date information results in better observance of due dates than under FCFS. SLACK/OPN rule performed best, but we should also point to the excellent behavior of SPT, which came very close to SLACK/OPN, although it completely ignores due date considerations. The explanation can be found in the characteristics of the lateness distributions:

- Under SPT rule:

  - mean lateness is very much reduced as a consequence of the reduction in the mean flow time, see equation (5.7)
  - variance of lateness is sizeable since SPT does not make any effort to follow the due dates
  - lateness distribution is highly skewed (Figure 5.19a); its tail results from long operation jobs which tend to become tardy because of their long flow times

---

*SLACK is the dynamic sort of slack time. There is also the static slack, STSLACK, defined as due date minus time of job arrival at that machine.

TABLE 5.9   Results of Experiments with Due Date Criteria (Conway [1965b])

RULE	FRACTION OF JOBS TARDY	MEAN JOB LATENESS	VARIANCE OF JOB LATENESS	MEAN FLOW TIME
DDATE	15.75%	−15.5	432	63.7
SLACK	22.02%	−13.1	433	65.8
OPNDD	10.36%	−9.9	14,560	69.0
SLACK/OPN	3.71%	−12.8	266	66.1
SPT	5.02%	−44.9	2,878	34.0
FCFS	44.79%	−4.5	1,686	74.4

- the combination of the extremely small mean lateness with the skewness compensates for the large variance of the distribution, thus producing only a small fraction of jobs tardy
- SLACK/OPN cannot match SPT in reducing mean lateness. However, being due date oriented, it yields a much lower variance (Figure 5.19b). The reduced variance offsets the larger mean, leading to a small proportion of jobs missing their due dates.

It is interesting to mention that under heavier shop loads, SPT surpassed SLACK/OPN, yielding a substantially smaller proportion of jobs tardy. This happened because a heavier load tends to increase mean flow time, hence mean lateness too. But SPT is less sensitive because it only extends the tail of the lateness distribution into the tardiness region, while the more compact SLACK/OPN shifts a larger portion of its distribution into the positive quadrant.

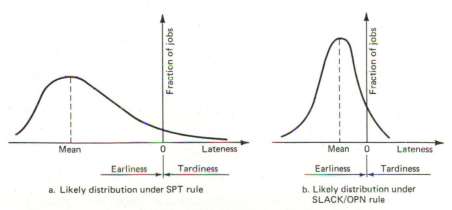

a. Likely distribution under SPT rule

b. Likely distribution under SLACK/OPN rule

FIGURE 5.19   Job lateness distributions in general job shop.

To further complicate things and to confirm that there is no universal due-date-oriented priority rule, results show that under CON and RDM ways of setting due dates SLACK/OPN's performance becomes inferior to DDATE's and FCFS's (results not available for OPNDD and SLACK). Obviously, SPT is least affected by the due-date-setting mechanism and remains very good.

In concluding this discussion, "one could offer SPT as an alternative to simple due-date rules with considerable confidence that it would reduce the fraction of jobs that were tardy, the mean lateness and even the mean tardiness. However, under very general conditions one could not deny the price that would be exacted in terms of lateness variance" (Conway et al. [1967, p. 237]).

Clearly, using processing time information is instrumental in lowering mean lateness, and due dates should be considered if a reduction in lateness variance is desired. Conway [1965b] tests a composite rule obtained by linearly combining SPT with SLACK/OPN. The composite queue discipline outperformed both component rules in terms of the proportion of tardy jobs, producing the best result when the two terms were equally weighted. Conway et al. [1966] develop a more complex composite rule which, besides considering processing times and job due dates, also includes global information about the status of the shop. While it did not surpass SPT for the percentage of jobs tardy, it did provide a smaller mean tardiness and a lower variance of lateness than the simple rules. Certainly, practical application of these composite rules requires the setting of weighting factors appropriate for the particular job shop situation, and if global information is also needed it will entail some costs.

A study by Carroll [1965] proposes a selection discipline by which the highest priority in a queue is given to the job with the highest value of the following ratio:

$$\frac{\text{Delay } cost \text{ for the job}}{\text{Processing } time \text{ for the imminent operation}}.$$

The rule is mnemonically termed C over T, or COVERT. It tries to retain the good features of SPT, by favoring jobs with short imminent operations, and at the same time to avoid the extreme lateness of long operation jobs, by imputing a cost to any anticipated tardiness in the completion of the job.

For a given job i, the dynamic slack time S_i is computed (as in SLACK above), the expected waiting time $E(W_i)$ is estimated, and the delay cost is defined as follows (values outside the $[0, 1]$ interval are not allowed):

$$\text{Delay cost} = \begin{cases} 1 & \text{if } S_i \leqslant 0 \\ 0 & \text{if } S_i > 0 \text{ and } S_i > E(W_i) \\ \dfrac{kE(W_i) - S_i}{kE(W_i)} & \text{otherwise,} \end{cases}$$

where k is a parameter. COVERT's performance was found to be sensitive to variations in the value of k.

TABLE 5.10   Results of Experiments for Mean Tardiness Criterion (Carroll [1965])

RULE	MEAN JOB TARDINESS
FCFS	36.6
FASFS	24.7
STSLACK/OPN	16.2
SPT	11.3
TRUNCATED SPT	4.6
COVERT (with $k=1$)	(2.5)

Table 5.10 shows comparative results under the mean tardiness criterion. STSLACK/OPN is similar to SLACK/OPN except that it uses the static slack, which was defined in the preceding footnote.

It is apparent that COVERT performed best, but it is more complicated and more difficult to implement than the other queue disciplines.

Other aspects

There are simulation studies in which some of the 12 assumptions stated earlier are relaxed, and additional issues of scheduling in job shops are investigated. Several of the problems which have been treated are noted here.

- *Alternate routing.* If shop conditions require it, one may perform some of the operations in a different order than specified on the job's routing (relaxation of assumption 1); Neimeier [1967] and Eilon [1969].
- *Job structures other than serial* (relaxation of assumption 2). Jobs containing assembly operations are considered by Trilling [1966] and Maxwell and Mehra [1968].
- *Double resource shops.* In which not only machine capacity but also available labor is limited (relaxation of assumption 6); Nelson [1967] and Allen [1963].
- *Interchangeable machines.* Some operations can be processed on several alternate machines (relaxation of assumption 9). This might enable the scheduler to avoid an already congested machine by selecting an alternate machine which has a smaller work load; Allen [1963], Russo [1965], and Wayson [1965].
- *Expediting.* It is the action by which rush or "hot" jobs are identified and given special priority in front of other jobs that compete for the same facilities. Jobs can be expedited for a number of reasons: they are overdue, the stock replenished by the job is depleted or running out, the customer has requested his job to be delivered earlier than initially scheduled and shop management has found it important to do so, and so on. Expediting can be carried out with or without preempting the lower priority job which is in process when the rush job arrives at the machine (relaxation of assumption 10); Hottenstein [1969, 1970].
- *Multiple criteria performance measure.* The effectiveness of various queue disciplines is evaluated with an aggregate measure of performance constituted by combining several simple performance criteria; LeGrande [1966].

5.2.6 Closing Notes

From the preceding review it is evident that, since the 1950s, a tremendous effort has been spent and significant progress has been made in scheduling research. Despite all these, we are witnessing a relative lack of application of theoretical developments to actual industrial settings.

In an attempt to search for the causes of this situation, Panwalkar et al. [1973] have conducted a survey designed to collect data on various aspects of scheduling. Their findings show that current operations research techniques may be inadequate for many production environments on several grounds.

- Existing optimal scheduling algorithms can handle problems of only limited size, while the survey indicated that 81% of the cases involved more than 10 jobs and 10 machines at a given time.
- There is a marked discrepancy between the "preferred" measures of performance used in research and the industrial scheduling objectives. Thus, the majority of responses to the survey pointed to the meeting of due dates as the most important criterion. When that was achieved, most companies also took into account secondary criteria such as minimizing total setups or minimizing total processing time.

Unfortunately, as our review revealed, scheduling research was not quite successful in finding optimization procedures to respond to the primary industrial scheduling concern, that is, satisfaction of due dates. At the same time setups, the secondary concern, are not even considered separately from processing times in the majority of studies. As for total processing time, although one would be tempted to identify it with makespan (the popular measure of performance in research), most likely it has a different meaning because real job shops are dynamic, in which case the makespan concept does not make sense. By minimization of total processing time, industry probably understood the minimization of flow time for each job, or the minimization of processing time alone. The latter is, however, an engineering problem rather than something to be achieved by better scheduling.

Finally, one of the main themes of scheduling research, reducing shop congestion and cutting down work-in-process inventory, appeared not to be a current objective for the industrial scheduler.

The above results suggest that, if scheduling theory is to improve scheduling practice, future research for the development of better algorithms and heurisitics should be paralleled by efforts directed toward closer links with the industries in order to better understand their problems.

As we have mentioned at the start of this chaper, operations scheduling decisions should be part of a larger hierarchical production planning system, We would like to emphasize that proper allocation, at the aggregate planning level, of the production capacity among product types, and proper balancing of the capacities among the stages of the production process are prerequisites

TABLE 5.11 Job Shop Scheduling Models

SHOP CONFIG-URATION	JOB ARRIVAL PROCESS	NATURE OF PROCESSING TIMES	SCHEDULING PROBLEM	RULE OR ALGORITHM	REMARKS
SINGLE MACHINE SHOP	Static	Deterministic	Minimize mean flow time	SPT	Optimal
			Minimize max. job tardiness and max. job lateness	EDD	Optimal
			Minimize number of tardy jobs	Moore's algorithm	Optimal
			Tardiness problem	Combinatorial techniques	NP-complete problem
			Sequence-dependent setups, minimum makespan	Algorithms for the traveling salesman problem	
	Dynamic deterministic	Deterministic	Minimize mean flow time	SPT, nonpreemptive	Optimal
				SRPT, preempt–resume	Optimal
			Minimize max. lateness	EDD, preempt–resume	Optimal
			Minimize number of tardy jobs	Optimal algorithms for special cases	General problem is NP-complete
	Dynamic probabilistic	Deterministic	Minimize mean flow time	SPT, nonpreemptive	Optimal
				SRPT, preempt–resume	Optimal
		Probabilistic	Minimize mean flow time	SEPT, nonpreemptive	Optimal

TABLE 5.11 *(Continued)*

SHOP CONFIG- URATION	JOB ARRIVAL PROCESS	NATURE OF PROCESSING TIMES	SCHEDULING PROBLEM	RULE OR ALGORITHM	REMARKS
PARALLEL MACHINE SHOP	Static	Deterministic	Minimize makespan	Heuristics (LPT, MULTIFIT)	NP-complete problem
			Minimize mean flow time	SPT-type sorting procedure	Optimal
			Tardiness problem	Optimal procedures for special cases	
FLOW SHOP Two machines	Static	Deterministic	Minimize makespan	Johnson's algorithm	Optimal
Three machines			Minimize makespan	Optimal procedures for special cases	
Large flow shops			Minimize makespan	Heuristics	NP-complete problem
GENERAL JOB SHOP Two machines	Static	Deterministic	Minimize makespan	Jackson's algorithm	Optimal
Large job shops	Static	Deterministic	Minimize makespan Minimize mean flow time	Integer programming, schedule construction algorithms	NP-complete problem
	Dynamic probabilistic	Deterministic	Reducing shop congestion Satisfaction of due dates	Dispatching by queue disciplines	Studies by computer simulation

for the successful implementation of any job shop scheduling system. At the same time, operations scheduling affects the parameter values assumed by the aggregate planning, such as lead times, production rates, service levels, machine and labor utilization, and so on. To date, there are few models which recognize this and other sorts of interactions. As illustrations, see Shwimer [1972b] and Gelders and Kleindorfer [1974, 1975] who present procedures for coupling capacity (i.e., manpower) planning decisions with detailed job scheduling decisions.

In conclusion, Table 5.11 summarizes the models which are presented in the job shop scheduling section.

5.3   Project Management

A particular instance of an intermittent system is the one-time project. Such a project can be directed toward the realization of various objectives, of which we mention a few:

- construction of a power plant, a highway, a spaceship, and so on
- repair and maintenance of a nuclear plant, an oil refinery, a ship, and so on
- design, development, and marketing of a new project
- research and development work

In general, this kind of project is complex and large scale, involves a large number of component activities that must be time-phased according to specified precedence requirements, and entails a considerable financial effort.

The main concern in managing such a project is how to schedule the component activities in order to achieve a certain goal: to complete the project by a specified deadline, or to minimize the cost of meeting the target date, or to minimize the total project completion time, and so on.

The class of techniques used for analyzing, planning, and scheduling large-scale projects have an important feature in common: all of them are based on the representation of the project as a network of activities. Therefore, they are often referred to as network analysis, network planning, and network planning and scheduling. The most widely used names, however, are the acronyms PERT and CPM, which stand for two techniques that evolved in the late 1950s.

PERT (*P*rogram *E*valuation and *R*eview *T*echnique)* was developed in 1957–1958 by a research team set up by the Navy Special Projects Office, the Booz, Allen, and Hamilton consulting firm, and the Missiles Systems Division of Lockheed Aircraft Company in order to efficiently plan and produce the Polaris missile system. The methodology was published in 1959 (Malcolm et al.

*Subsequently also known as Project Evaluation and Review Technique, or Performance Evaluation and Review Technique.

[1959]), and further discussed by Murray [1963], MacCrimmon and Ryavec [1964], Clark [1964], Grubbs [1962], and Hartley and Wortham [1966].

CPM (*C*ritical *P*ath *M*ethod) is a development independent of PERT. It was the result of a joint effort of the DuPont Company and Remington Rand Univac Division, originally aimed at better planning in controlling the overhaul and maintenance of chemical plants. The project was started in 1957 and the CPM method was released in 1959 (Kelley and Walker [1959]).

From the point of view of the network representation and activity scheduling, there are no essential differences between PERT and CPM. This is why today, more often than not, the two names are used interchangeably. However, as originally developed, they bore the mark of the environments from which they stemmed.

Thus, as the outgrowth of an R&D undertaking, PERT had to cope with the uncertainties that accompany R&D activities. Hence, PERT regards the total project duration as a random variable, and performs probabilistic calculations in order to characterize it.

CPM was developed in the context of a project which consisted, in general, of routine operations whose durations were more or less well established. Therefore, CPM is basically deterministic. But a major concern of the originators of CPM was to reduce the total time during which the facility had to be shut down for overhaul, because plant downtime meant lost production capacity. Starting from the idea that some activities may be shortened if additional resources were allocated to them, CPM was associated with a time–cost tradeoff feature by which an optimum balance was sought between the duration and the cost of the project.

We have mentioned that a project consists of a number of activities. An *activity* (also called by other authors *job* or *task*) is a portion of a project having the following properties:

- It has a beginning and an ending point, clearly identifiable, called *events*.
- It has a *duration*, which is the time interval elapsed between the moment the activity starts and the moment the activity is completed.
- It consumes resources.

The application of the network planning and scheduling methods typically goes through the following steps:

- *Project planning and construction of the network*. The activities involved in the project are identified, their precedence constraints are specified and the network is developed.
- *Scheduling*. This step needs estimates for the durations of the activities. Based on these estimates, activities are assigned start times. The scheduling process must observe all predecessor–successor relationships.
- *Resource analysis and allocation*. To perform resource analysis and allocation one has to know the resource requirements of every activity, on the one hand,

and the resource constraints, on the other. Then various problems may arise. For example, in view of the resources available to the project, the schedule obtained at the previous step may be infeasible, in which case a rescheduling is called for in order to align the project requirements to the resource restrictions. Or, if the total project duration obtained in the scheduling step is considered too long, one could try to reduce it by allocating sufficient additional resources to certain activities to speed them up and thus shorten the execution of the project.

- *Project control.* It is a function which is carried on after the project has started. Essentially, project control refers to checking actual performance against the plan. If important differences are found, a rescheduling becomes necessary by updating and revising the uncompleted portion of the project.

Issues such as project selection under limited resources and the organizational aspects of applying PERT/CPM, will not be treated here or will be touched upon only peripherally. The interested reader, however, can consult the following references to gain insight into these problems:

- *Process selection.* As the process by which one determines which of several alternative projects to initiate and pursue: the survey paper of Souder [1978];
- *Project planning and organizational issues.* Moder and Phillips [1970, chap. 3], Archibald and Villoria [1967], Martin [1976], and several papers focusing on organizational problems in the book edited by Davis [1976];
- *Project control.* NASA PERT/Cost System [1962], Paige [1963], Moder and Phillips [1970, chap. 10], and Wiest and Levy [1977, chap. 6].

5.3.1   Constructing the Network

We will consider this topic in the context of an example. Suppose we are setting up the project of building a new barn and a garage in place of the old wooden barn existing on a farm.

We start by identifying all activities that must be performed in order to complete the project successfully. Then, by taking into account the technological constraints, we specify the predecessor–successor relationships; see Table 5.12. We should stress that no scheduling considerations should influence the establishment of the precedence relations. For instance, we did not and should not condition the start of activity H by the completion of G only because we might reason that the same crew will have to pour all concrete structures. If this is the case, we will be faced at a later stage of the project with a resource (labor) allocation problem which is not to be thought over and resolved now.

Notice that the duration estimates and activity resource requirements have not been determined yet. It is advisable (Moder and Phillips [1970, chap. 4]) to first develop a draft version of the project network, which can help the project team focus on the logic of the activity interrelationships, and spot possible inconsistencies, false dependencies, and redundancies before addressing issues of scheduling and resource allocation.

We find it appropriate to mention at this point the PERT/CPM classical assumptions, some of which have already been considered in putting together our example above:

- The activities of a project are known before the project starts.
- Two activities may be interrelated by a finish-to-start predecessor–successor relationship which can be specified beforehand. For instance, activity *A* precedes *C* in a finish-to-start relationship, which means that *C* may not begin before *A* is completed. In this example, we say that *A* is a *predecessor* of *C*, while *C* is a *successor* of *A*. A job may have more than one predecessor or successor, or none.
- If two activities are not interrelated by a predecessor–successor relationship they are independent, that is, they may be started and stopped independently of each other.
- The duration of an activity has no bearing on the durations of any other project activities.

In some cases, it becomes necessary to relax some of these assumptions in order to build more realism into the model. Some brief references will be made later on this issue.

Before proceeding further, the following definition is adapted from Ford and Fulkerson [1974]:

A project network is a directed graph which consists of a finite collection *N* of *n* elements *i*, *j*,..., called nodes, together with a subset *A* of the ordered

TABLE 5.12   Activity Analysis for Reconstruction Project

ACTIVITY SYMBOL	ACTIVITY DESCRIPTION	PREDECESSORS
A	Demolish old barn	—
B	Procure materials for brickwork and reinforcements for concrete structures	—
C	Sort reuseable materials resulting from demolition	A
D	Excavate for foundations	A
E	Dig path of driveway	A
F	Make list of other necessary materials and procure them	C
G	Pour reinforced concrete foundations	B, D
H	Pour concrete driveway	E
I	Erect brick walls	B, G
J	Level floor with gravel and pour rough concrete floor	F, G
K	Install wiring for electrical system	F, I
L	Finish walls	K, M, N
M	Erect roof	F, I
N	Finish concrete floor	J
O	Mount gutters and downspouts	F, M
P	Clean up	H, L, O

pairs (i, j) of nodes called arcs. To draw the network, one selects a point corresponding to each node i of N and directs an arrow from i to j if the ordered pair (i, j) is in A.

Since in the project management literature the arcs of a network are called arrows, we will use the *arrow – node* terminology throughout this section.

Both the CPM and PERT developers chose the arrows of the network to represent the activities of the project. An arrow (i, j) extends between two nodes: the tail node i, representing the starting event of the associated activity, and the head node j, which stands for the ending event.

Under CPM, specifications are written on arrows, describing activities. PERT writes descriptions inside nodes to define events (see Figure 5.20). It is apparent that CPM focuses on controlling the activities of the project, while PERT monitors the achievement of events at planned points in time. In general, CPM types of networks are easier to read and seem to parallel better the manager's concern for activities rather than for events. This probably explains why they are more popular. For this reason we will use CPM networking in what follows. For simplicity, we shall write on arrows activity symbols rather than entire descriptions.

There are several rules that have to be observed while constructing a network, imposed either by logical considerations or by the requirements of existing computer software for network problems:

1. The length of an arrow has no significance.
2. The logical significance of a node is that the activities represented by the outgoing arrows may not start before all the activities represented by the incoming arrows have been completed.
3. A network may have only one *initial node* (the starting event of the project) and only one *terminal node* (the completion event of the project). The activities whose arrows leave the initial node are the *initial activities* (they have no predecessor), and those entering the terminal node are the *terminal activities* (they have no successor).
4. An activity must be uniquely identified by its starting and ending events, which implies that:

    - Node numbers may not be duplicated.
    - Two nodes may be directly connected by at most one arrow. This allows us to refer to activities either by their symbols or by the corresponding ordered pair of tail-head nodes; for example, in Figure 5.20a activity "Sort reusable materials" may be called either activity C or activity $(3,4)$.
5. Nodes should be numbered such that for every arrow (i, j), $i < j$.

Rule 5 has the virtue of helping identify the occurrence of cycles (closed loops) in a network. For example, in Figure 5.21 activities U, V, and Z form a cycle, which is an inconsistency of logic. Indeed, by the transitivity of the precedence relationships, it turns out that every activity in the cycle is a

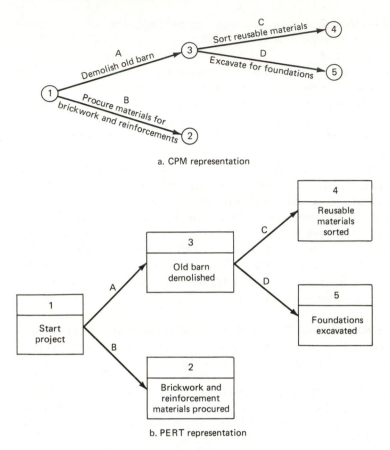

a. CPM representation

b. PERT representation

FIGURE 5.20 **Comparative network representations of activities *A*, *B*, *C*, and *D* of Table 5.12.**

predecessor of itself. This situation is signaled by the impossibility of numbering the three nodes associated with U, V, and Z so as to satisfy rule 5.

There are cases in which the observance of the above rules requires the use of *dummy* activities. A dummy activity has zero duration and consumes no resources (has zero cost). Its only purpose is to express logical interrelationships. For instance, activities K and M in Table 5.12 have I as a common predecessor. At the same time, they have activity L as a common successor. Figure 5.22a expresses these interconnections, but the diagramming violates the second part of rule 4. A correct solution is to use an extra node for the ending event of M, and to introduce a dummy activity to show that L may not start before both M and K are completed (Figure 5.22b). For graphical differentiation we shall depict dummy activities by dashed lines.

Figure 5.23 contains a first draft of our project network, in which the activities in Table 5.12 are represented according to the aforementioned rules.

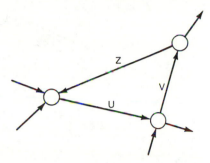

FIGURE 5.21   Cycle in network.

In order to conform to rule 5, the number of the nodes was done by a procedure given by Fulkerson [1962]:

1. Number the initial node with 1.

2. Delete all arrows leaving the nodes which have already been numbered.

3. Continue the numbering by identifying all nodes with no incoming arrows and by assigning them consecutive numbers in any order.

4. Repeat steps 2 and 3 until the terminal node is numbered.

Because of its important role in network scheduling, we will now define the notion of *path* (Ford and Fulkerson [1974]):

Let $N_1, N_2, \ldots, N_i, \ldots, N_n$ ($n \geqslant 2$) be a sequence of distinct nodes such that every pair (N_i, N_{i+1}), $i = 1, \ldots, n-1$, is an arrow of the network. Then the sequence of nodes and arrows $N_1 - (N_1, N_2) - N_2 - \cdots - (N_{n-1}, N_n) - N_n$ forms a path from node N_1 to node N_n. For instance, in Figure 5.23, 1-*A*-3-*D*-5 is a path between nodes 1 and 5, while 1-*B*-2-(2,5)-5 is another path between the same two nodes. Obviously, a path may be fully identified in a simpler way by specifying either only the sequence of nodes through which it passes or the sequence of activities which lie along it; for example, 1-3-5 or *A*-*D* instead of 1-*A*-3-*D*-5.

As the network contains no inconsistency of logic, we will inspect it now for possible redundancies. Thus, it is pretty easy to locate at least one redundant predecessor relationship: dummy activity (2,9) is not necessary in order to impose *B* as a predecessor of *I*, because activity *B* precedes *I* anyway along path 1-2-5-7-9. Hence, dummy (2,9) and the implied precedence are redundant.

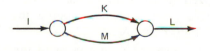

a. Representation in violation
   on rule 4

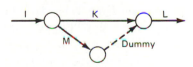

b. A correct representation

FIGURE 5.22   Use of dummy activity.

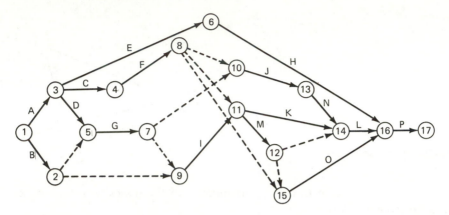

FIGURE 5.23   First draft of project network.

We should point to the fact that, although both *B* and *G* are predecessors of *I*, activity *G* is an *immediate predecessor* while *B* is a *distant predecessor*.

In general, redundancies lead to an unnecessarily increased number of dummy activities,* thus making the network less readable and adding to computer costs. Therefore, it is desirable to remove them from the network. By removing all redundancies, we keep on the predecessor list only the immediate predecessors. To do this we adopt a procedure by Wiest and Levy [1977, chap. 2]:

1.   Make a list of the project activities in topological order, that is, include an activity in the list only if all its predecessors have already been listed. One way to achieve this is to order the activities by nondecreasing *i* or *j* numbers. Ties may be broken arbitrarily. In general, there may be several topological orderings for a given set of activities. One is presented in Table 5.13. Notice that the original Table 5.12 was not topologically ordered, since *L* was out of topological sequence.

2.   Construct a matrix with as many rows as there are activities in the project. Open a column for each activity except the terminal ones. Fill in the row and column headings with the activities in topological order (see Figure 5.24).

3.   Every activity, starting with the first in the topological list, will be inspected for redundant precedence requirements. While it is under inspection, call it the "Analyzed activity." Then:

3a.   Extract from Table 5.13 the analyzed activity's predecessors shown in its row. Call them "original predecessors"; for example, suppose the analyzed activity is 0; its original predecessors are *F* and *M*.

3b.   In the analyzed activity's row of the matrix, place a cross in the columns corresponding to its original predecessors.

*Exceptions, however, exist and one will be illustrated later.

TABLE 5.13   Activities of Reconstruction Project in Topological Order

ACTIVITY	TAIL NODE	HEAD NODE	PREDECESSORS
A	1	3	—
B	1	2	—
C	3	4	A
D	3	5	A
E	3	6	A
F	4	8	C
G	5	7	B, D
H	6	16	E
I	9	11	B, G
J	10	13	F, G
K	11	14	F, I
M	11	12	F, I
N	13	14	J
L	14	16	K, M, N
O	15	16	F, M
P	16	17	H, L, O

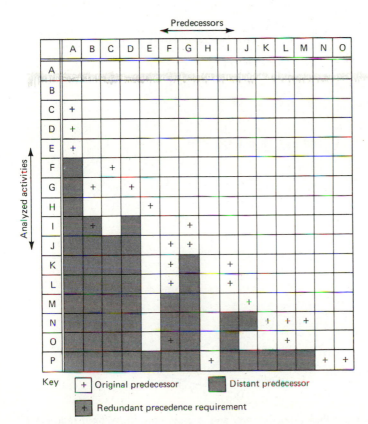

Key:
[+] Original predecessor   ▓ Distant predecessor

[▓+] Redundant precedence requirement

3c.   Inspect the row of each of the original predecessors to find its own predecessors. There are "distant predecessors" to the analyzed activity. Shade those cells in the analyzed activity's row which are in the distant predecessors' columns; for example, the predecessors of *F* (both original and distant) are *A* and *C*; similarly, the predecessors of *M* are *A*, *B*, *C*, *D*, *F*, *G*, and *I*. Hence, the distant predecessors of 0 are *A*, *B*, *C*, *D*, *F*, *G*, and *I*.

4.   After all activities have been inspected, any cross which is shaded indicates a redundant original predecessor to the activity heading that row. The redundant predecessors may be removed from that activity's predecessor list in Table 5.13. The network should also be modified accordingly.

After the redundancy check two original predecessors turn out to be, in fact, distant predecessors: activity *B* as a predecessor of *I*, and activity *F* as a predecessor of 0. Figure 5.25 shows the table with only the immediate predecessors retained, and the resulting network.

The network of Figure 5.25 may be simplified even further by merging nodes 6 and 8, thus suppressing dummy activity (6,8). The result is shown in

Activity	Immediate predecessors
A	—
B	—
C	A
D	A
E	A
F	C
G	B, D
H	E
I	G
J	F, G
K	F, I
M	F, I
N	J
L	K,M, N
O	M
P	H,L, O

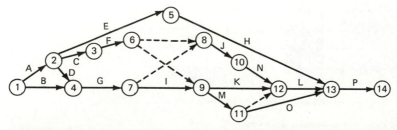

FIGURE 5.25   List of immediate predecessors, and project network without redundant precedence relationships.

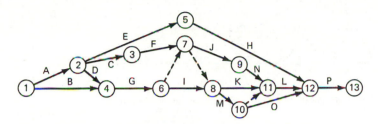

FIGURE 5.26 Simplified project network.

Figure 5.26. It should be noticed that, by simplifying the network, a redundant predecessor relationship has been introduced: dummy activities (6, 7) and (7, 8) require *G* to be completed before *K* starts. This is obviously not necessary since *G* precedes *K* anyway along path *G-I-K*. Nevertheless, we may not remove the two dummy activities because they are there to express other precedence requirements related to *J* and *K*.

5.3.2 Project Activity Scheduling

The objective of scheduling is to determine how long the project will take and to assign starting and finishing times to all activities involved. Clearly, in order to be able to do this, one needs estimates for the durations of the individual activities.* The resources involved in the performance of the activities are of no concern yet.

To get a better grasp of the basic scheduling concepts, let us consider first a simple network (Figure 5.27a). The number written at the right of the activity symbol represents its duration, say in days. For simplicity, we will work with whole days (no fractions).

There are three paths through the network between the initial and the terminal nodes: path *B-E-F* having a length of 7 days, path *A-C-F* of 9 days, and path *A-D-E-F* of 8 days. Path *A-C-F* is the longest and imposes, therefore, the shortest time within which the project could be completed, that is, 9 days. It is called the *critical path*, and *A*, *C*, and *F* are *critical activities*. They are drawn in heavier lines.

Figures 5.27b through 5.27i give time-scaled representations of all the schedules that can be constructed for the simple network we have taken as an example. Each arrow's projection on the horizontal axis spans a time interval equal to the corresponding activity's duration. By analyzing these figures, we will build up several important scheduling concepts.

In Figure 5.27b it is arbitrarily assumed that the project starts at time zero and that every activity is scheduled to begin as early as possible, at a

---

*While with CPM a unique duration estimate has to be produced for each activity, PERT, which regards activity durations as random variables, involves the use of three time estimates out of which the expected duration is computed (to be seen in section 5.3.3).

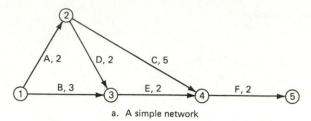

a. A simple network

Note: The numbers on the time axis mark the closing of the day.

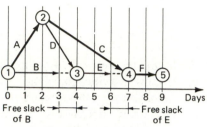

Free slack of B → ← → ← Free slack of E

b. All activities scheduled at earliest start times

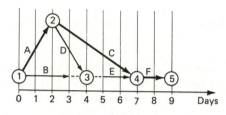

c. Activity E Scheduled at latest start time (total slack of E used up)

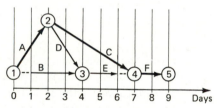

d. Free slack of B used up

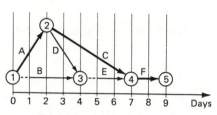

e. Total slack of E and free slack of B used up

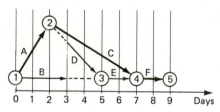

f. Total slack of E and total slack of D used up

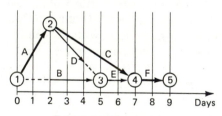

g. Total slack of E and total slack of B used up

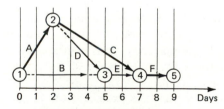

h. Total slack of E and total slack of D used up; B's start delayed by one day within its total slack

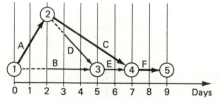

i. All activities scheduled at latest start times (all total slack times used up)

FIGURE 5.27 Time-scale representations for illustration of critical path and slack time concepts.

moment called the *earliest start time*. Denote the earliest start time for activity (i, j) by $ES_{i,j}$.

In general, it is reasonable to complete projects as early as possible. Hence, let us set our project's deadline for day 9. Then, it is obvious that no critical activity may be delayed* beyond its earliest start time if the project is to be completed on time.

Noncritical activities, however, allow some scheduling flexibility. For instance, from Figure 5.27b it is apparent that B and E may be delayed each by 1 day without causing the project to run late (see figures 5.27c, 5.27d, and 5.27e). We say that activities B and E have slack time.

As far as D is concerned, it does not necessarily have to start on day 3, as initially scheduled in Figure 5.27b. It may begin on day 4 (Figure 5.27f), with the effect that E has to be scheduled 1 day later than its earliest start time. Nevertheless, this will not delay the completion of the project beyond the preestablished deadline. Hence, activity D has slack time too.

Another situation which should be brought to the reader's attention is the possibility that activity B will be delayed by 2 days (Figure 5.27g), with the project still being completed on time. As opposed to the case mentioned earlier, when B was delayed by 1 day only, this time the delay affects activity E which may start no earlier than day 6.

Finally, in Figure 5.27i, every activity (i, j) is planned to start as late as the deadline for completing the project would allow. We say that it is scheduled at its *latest start time*, $LS_{i,j}$.

To summarize, we note that two instances of slack time have been identified:

- The case in which some activity (i, j) may be delayed without affecting the earliest start times of any of its successors (e.g., activities B and E in Figure 5.27e). The slack time associated with this case is called *free slack*, $FS_{i,j}$. Free slack may be visualized on the time-scaled representation of the network with all activities scheduled at their earliest start times; see the dotted lines in Figure 5.27b.
- The case in which, although the scheduled completion of the project is not affected by delaying activity (i, j) beyond its $ES_{i,j}$, some of the (i, j)'s successors are compelled to begin later than their earliest start times (e.g., activity D in Figure 5.27f and activity B in Figure 5.27g). Clearly, activity (i, j) has no free slack, yet it presents another kind of scheduling flexibility relative to the project deadline, called *total slack*, $TS_{i,j}$.

It follows immediately that an activity which has free slack also has at least as much total slack (see Table 5.14), that is,

$$0 \leqslant FS_{i,j} \leqslant TS_{i,j}.$$

Let us note that the critical activities have the least total slack.

---

*When we say that an activity is "delayed," we refer to the fact that it starts later than its earliest start time. In the context of this section, "delaying" does not include stretching out the activity by interrupting it or by slowing down its execution.

To help formalize our graphical developments, let us review the notations used so far and introduce some more:

$ES_{i,j}$ = earliest start time for activity (i, j)

$LS_{i,j}$ = latest start time for activity (i, j)

$EF_{i,j}$ = earliest finish time for activity (i, j)

$LF_{i,j}$ = latest finish time for activity (i, j)

$Y_{i,j}$ = duration of activity (i, j)

T_i = earliest occurrence time for the event represented by node i

$FS_{i,j}$ = free slack for activity (i, j)

$TS_{i,j}$ = total slack for activity (i, j)

n = generic index for the terminal node of the network.

From Figure 5.27b it is apparent that, in order to determine the earliest start times, one should begin by considering the start time of the project, and then schedule every activity to start as soon as all of its predecessors are completed. This is known as the *forward pass* because, in making the calculations, one traverses the network from node 1 to node n. The following procedure is carried out:

1. Set the earliest start time of all initial activities equal to the start time of the project (common practice is to set it equal to zero).

2. Consider the activities one by one in topological order. For each activity (i, j) compute:*

$$ES_{i,j} = \max\left[EF_{\text{all immediate predecessors of } (i,j)} \right] \qquad (5.8)$$

$$EF_{i,j} = ES_{i,j} + Y_{i,j}. \qquad (5.9)$$

3. The earliest finish time for the project, that is, the earliest occurrence time T_n for the completion event, is given by:

$$T_n = \max[EF_{\text{all terminal activities}}]. \qquad (5.10)$$

Figure 5.27i suggests that the latest finish times can be determined if one crosses the network from the terminal node to the initial node while scheduling each activity as late as possible. This is the *backward pass* and it consists of the following steps:

1. Set the latest finish time of all terminal activities equal to the scheduled completion time for the project.

---

*Obviously, (5.8) is not applicable to the initial activities whose earliest start times have already been established by step 1.

2. Consider the topologically ordered activities in reverse order, and calculate for each:

$$LF_{i,j} = \min\left[LS_{\text{all immediate successors of } (i,j)} \right] \qquad (5.11)$$

$$LS_{i,j} = LF_{i,j} - Y_{i,j}. \qquad (5.12)$$

It is now rather straightforward to determine the slack times. All we have to do is to formalize their definitions:

- The free slack represents the activity's scheduling flexibility with respect to its immediate successors (i.e., delaying the activity will not delay any successor):

$$FS_{i,j} = \min\left[ES_{\text{all immediate successors of } (i,j)} \right] - EF_{i,j}; \qquad (5.13)$$

- The total slack represents the activity's scheduling flexibility relative to the preestablished project completion time (i.e., the activity may be delayed without causing any delay in finishing the project on time):

$$TS_{i,j} = LS_{i,j} - ES_{i,j} = LF_{i,j} - EF_{i,j}. \qquad (5.14)$$

Table 5.14 shows activity scheduling results for the simple network of Figure 5.27a, under the assumptions that the project starts at time zero and must be completed by day 9.

We will apply scheduling calculations (5.8)–(5.14) to our reconstruction project, whose network was drawn in Figure 5.26. In the absence of a computer, the calculations may be made by hand, using numerical entries placed directly on the network to show activity times and slack (see Figure 5.28). We chose to place next to each activity a box containing scheduling results. To avoid confusion, the activity symbol is also included in the box. The free and total slacks are written above or under the box. The literature offers various other ways of representing the scheduling computations graphically; see for instance Levy et al. [1963], Moder and Phillips [1970, pp. 71–77], and Wiest and Levy [1977, p. 32].

Let us note the following points:

- For the purpose of performing scheduling calculations, the concept of immediate predecessor or successor was adapted accordingly. For example, although by network logic F is an immediate predecessor to M (see the table in Figure 5.25), the intervening dummy activity $(7,8)$ leads to regarding F as being rather an immediate predecessor to $(7,8)$, and $(7,8)$ being an immediate predecessor to K. Based on this sort of interpretation and by computing the earliest and latest times for the dummy activities one can apply relations (5.8)–(5.13) mechanically. Slack times, which give a measure of scheduling flexibility (essential to resource allocation), have not been determined for the dummy activities, because they are unnecessary.
- If the scheduled completion time for the project is later by Δt than T_n, all total activity slacks in the network and the free slack times of the terminal activities become larger by Δt.

The critical path may be determined either by using only the forward pass results or by considering total slack time information.

TABLE 5.14   Scheduling Results for Network in Figure 5.27a (1 time unit = 1 day)

ACTIVITY	DURATION	IMMEDIATE PREDECESSORS	IMMEDIATE SUCCESSORS	EARLIEST START TIME	EARLIEST FINISH TIME	LATEST START TIME	LATEST FINISH TIME	FREE SLACK	TOTAL SLACK
A	2	—	C, D	0	2	0	2	Critical activity $FS_{1,2} = TS_{1,2} = 0$	
B	3	—	E	0	3	2	5	1	2
C	5	A	F	2	7	2	7	Critical activity $FS_{2,4} = TS_{2,4} = 0$	
D	2	A	E	2	4	3	5	0	1
E	2	B, D	F	4	6	5	7	1	1
F	2	C, E	—	7	9	7	9	Critical activity $FS_{4,5} = TS_{4,5} = 0$	

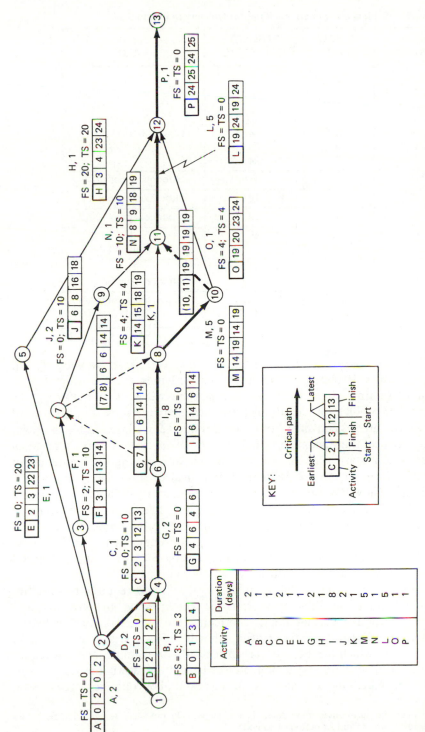

FIGURE 5.28 Reconstruction project network after scheduling computations (project start time = 0; scheduled project completion time = 25).

341

TABLE 5.15 Critical and Subcritical Paths for Network in Figure 5.27

ACTIVITY	TOTAL SLACK	EARLIEST START TIME	PATH
A	0	0	
D	0	2	
G	0	4	
I	0	6	Critical path
M	0	14	1-2-4-6-8-10-11-12-13
L	0	29	
P	0	24	
B	3	0	Subcritical path 1–4
K	4	14	Subcritical path 8–11
O	4	19	Subcritical path 10–12
C	10	2	
F	10	3	Subcritical path 2-3-7
J	10	6	
N	10	8	Subcritical path 7-9-11
E	20	2	Path of least criticality
H	20	3	2-5-12

Thus, suppose we have completed the forward pass, so we know T_n and all earliest times. If there are several terminal activities, the one which has its earliest finish time equal to T_n is critical. Then we work our way up the network. The problem of identifying the critical activity arises at nodes toward which several arrows converge (for example, node 12 in Figure 5.28). In such a case, it is critical that incoming activity which has its earliest finish time equal to the earliest start time of the critical activity leaving the node under consideration (in Figure 5.28, activity L is critical because $EF_{11,12} = ES_{12,13}$).

Suppose now that we have completed both the forward and the backward passes. Sort the activities into groups by total slack, then arrange the groups in nondecreasing order of total slack time. Within each group, order the activities by increasing earliest start times. The first group contains the critical path, while the next groups form subcritical paths* (Table 5.15). The larger the total slack, the lower the degree of criticality.

From our presentation above, it follows that if it is required to speed up project execution, one has to shorten the activities on the critical path. However, beyond a certain point, shortening the current critical activities becomes ineffective because the critical path will change course to another path in the network which has been so far subcritical. For example, one can reduce the duration of our reconstruction project by cutting down the duration of activity M. When the duration of M comes to be equal to 1 day path,

*A network may contain more than one critical path (Figure 5.29). A subcritical path does not necessarily have to run from node 1 to node n.

and the corresponding approximate normal density function is shown in the upper part of Figure 5.30c. This function enables us to make probabilistic statements about the chances of completing the project. For example, if the scheduled completion time is $S_5 = 10$ days, there is a probability of about 89% of meeting this deadline. Or, there is even a chance of 11% of completing the project within as few as 8 days.

It should be straightforward to perform similar probabilistic calculations for other paths in the network. In general, one could consider paths running from node 1 to various nodes representing milestones in the project. Obviously, if we refer to some node i, variance computations have to be made along that path connecting it to node 1, which has the largest expected length. Then, the resulting probability distribution vis-à-vis scheduled time S_i will allow us to assess the probabilities of interest.

Let us now look into the problem of completing the project of Figure 5.30b in time. If we chose to be more careful we should investigate, besides the critical path, also the next longest path A-D-E-F. The lower part of Figure 5.30c presents for comparison the approximate normal distribution of path A-D-E-F. It is immediately apparent that the 89% chance, estimated initially, of completing the project within 10 days is optimistically biased. The overstatement comes from neglecting subcritical path A-D-E-F which, although it has an expected length of only 8 days, shows quite a sizable variance mainly because of activities D and E. As a result, if we are to judge by path A-D-E-F the project would be completed by the end of day 10 with a probability of only 85%.

We realize now that the use by PERT of deterministic activity scheduling, including the assumption that the critical path is fixed and given once and for all, is wrong in principle because of the variability in activity durations. Indeed, it is quite possible that upon execution of the project represented in Figure 5.30b, activity C will take, say, 5 days and activities D and E 3 days each. In this case, the critical path would be A-D-E-F rather than A-C-F.*

Thus, in general, PERT tends to yield optimistic estimates for expected path lengths and for the probabilities of achieving events by their scheduled dates. An extensive investigation of this bias and of the assumptions underlying the PERT calculations has been made by MacCrimmon and Ryavec [1964]. Other authors like Clark [1961], Fulkerson [1962], Clingen [1964], Martin [1965], Elmaghraby [1967], and Robillard and Trahan [1977], to mention a few, have studied the problem in search for improved estimates of path length distribution functions. Based on Clark's [1961] work, Moder and Phillips [1970, pp. 304–305] give rules-of-thumb for bias correction.

---

*As already mentioned, the earliest occurrence time for node i is dictated by the longest of all paths connecting it to node 1. Since path lengths are random variables, the statistical problem is one of finding the expected maximum of a set of random variables which, in project networks, are generally not independent (Clark [1961]). In our example, if we refer to the terminal node 5 the set of dependent random variables consists of the lengths of paths A-C-F, A-D-E-F, and B-E-F.

However, the dependency among path lengths renders the analytical treatment of correcting for the PERT bias quite difficult. Therefore, as we have already seen it happening before when analytical tools failed or were inefficient, Monte Carlo simulation represents an alternative approach to this sort of problem. Van Slyke [1963] uses this simulation procedure to establish the unbiased distribution of the critical path length. In principle, each simulation run consists of drawing at random, for every project activity, a duration time from the associated distribution function and then establishing the critical path. After a suitable number of runs (Van Slyke performed 10,000 of them) one computes, besides estimates of the mean and variance of the project duration, an index of criticality for every activity. The criticality of an activity is defined as the ratio between the number of times the activity turns out to be critical and the total number of simulation runs. It estimates the probability that, upon execution of the project, the activity under consideration will end up on the critical path. The larger the index of criticality, the higher the degree of attention management should give to the activity in question.

To get a better feel for the problem, let us give an example: assume we have performed five Monte Carlo simulation runs for the network in Figure 5.30. Table 5.16 contains the sampled activity durations and the critical path determined with each run. Table 5.16b shows the resulting criticality indices on the basis of this limited sample.

5.3.4   Resource Analysis and Allocation

The only restrictions considered by us so far in scheduling project activities have been technological; resources have not been our concern. We are now considering the resource analysis and allocation issue under which we include several classes of problems. A feature common to these problems is the recognition that the resources involved in carrying out a project can influence scheduling either by their limited availability or by other kinds of restrictions.

Obviously, to perform resource analysis and allocation we assume as known the requirements of each activity for various types of productive resources, and the resource restrictions.

The execution of a project involves two categories of costs (Moder and Phillips [1970, p. 184]):

- activity direct costs: the costs of material, equipment, and direct labor for the performance of the activity (payroll, overtime, hiring and firing costs)
- project indirect costs: overhead costs, late completion penalties, early completion bonuses, and so on

It is clear that the indirect costs increase with the duration of the project. As for the direct costs it is true, in general, that it is more expensive to perform

TABLE 5.16 Monte Carlo Simulation for Network in Figure 5.30

a. Sampled activity durations and resulting critical paths

SIMULATION RUN	SAMPLED DURATION TIMES FOR ACTIVITY:						LENGTH OF PATH:			CRITICAL PATH
	A	B	C	D	E	F	A-C-F	A-D-E-F	B-E-F	
1	1.41	2.46	5.16	3.92	2.93	1.72	8.29	9.98	7.11	A-D-E-F
2	3.07	2.95	5.04	1.05	.56	2.14	10.25	6.82	5.65	A-C-F
3	2.47	3.20	4.90	.87	.73	2.29	9.66	6.36	6.22	A-C-F
4	1.18	3.58	5.52	2.10	3.75	2.24	8.94	9.27	9.57	B-E-F
5	2.02	3.54	4.64	.84	2.68	2.07	8.73	7.61	8.29	A-C-F

b. Criticality indices

Activity	A	B	C	D	E	F
Criticality index	4/5	1/5	3/5	1/5	2/5	5/5

an activity in a shorter time than to complete it in a longer period. Hence, if we want to finish a project quickly, we have to accept high direct costs while economizing on indirect costs. A project performed at a slower pace takes longer and entails smaller direct but higher indirect costs.

The literature contains a number of resource related problems, and an overall presentation is given in Table 5.17.

Resource loading produces, for a given project schedule, time charts regarding the usage of the various resources required by the project activities (for an example, see Figure 5.31). One way to utilize the charts is to check them against resource availabilities to establish whether the project is feasible. Or, an analysis of alternative loading profiles resulting from different project schedules may suggest ways to further improve resource utilization.

Resource leveling focuses on the time pattern of resource usage. In optimizing scheduling decisions, no explicit costs are considered. Rather, it is implicitly assumed that varying the usage of a specific resource from one period to the next entails significant costs and, therefore, it is reasonable to look for a schedule which prevents such important variations from happening. The typical example is that of labor: having period-by-period fluctuations in labor usage induces such charges as hiring, firing, overtime, and idle labor costs.

Hence the problem: given a prespecified project completion time and ample resources, determine the activity schedule which will meet the project due date with minimal period-by-period variations in resource utilization.

In Figure 5.31, the example network of Figure 5.27 is reconsidered. The numbers written between square brackets under arrows show manpower requirements, in mandays, of the corresponding activities. The early start

TABLE 5.17   A Bird's-Eye View of Resource Related Problems

CLASS OF PROBLEMS	PROBLEM SPECIFICS	OBJECTIVE
RESOURCE LOADING		For a given project schedule, resource loading determines the implied time profile of the requirements for various types of resources.
RESOURCE ALLOCATION — Resource leveling problems	Unlimited resources Fixed activity durations Preestablished project due date	Project due date must be met; schedule activities such that resource usage over time shows minimal period-by-period variations.
Resource constrained problems focusing on project duration	Fixed resource limits Fixed activity duration	Find the project schedule of minimum duration.
Resource constrained problems focusing on total costs	Multiple projects considered Fixed resource limits Variable activity durations Desired project completion times	Schedule all activities so as to minimize total costs.
Time–cost tradeoff problems	Unlimited resources Variable activity durations Preestablished project duration	Find the project schedule which minimizes the direct costs.

schedule (Figure 5.31a) exhibits considerable fluctuations in labor usage, with a peak on the third day. By making use of activity slack, a new schedule is drawn (Figure 5.31b), in which activities D and E begin at their latest start times. The result is a flatter manpower loading diagram.

For moderately sized project networks in which only one type of resource is involved, resource leveling may be performed manually by use of mechanical loading and scheduling devices. For more complex cases (large networks and several resource types), the aid of a computer is needed. In general, as the combinatorial nature of the problem precludes optimal solutions, leveling procedures are heuristically based (for further reference see Burgess and Killebrew [1962], Levy et al. [1962], De Witte [1964], Moder and Phillips [1970, pp. 163–170]).

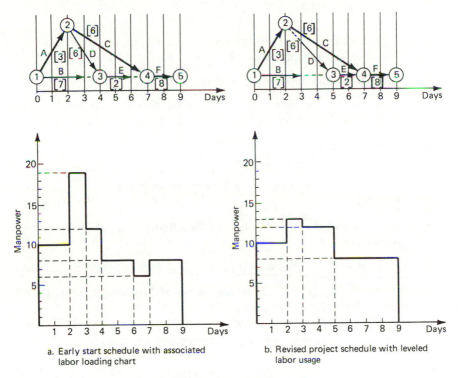

a. Early start schedule with associated labor loading chart

b. Revised project schedule with leveled labor usage

FIGURE 5.31 **Scheduling to level manpower requirements.**

Resource constrained problems address the issue of allocating limited resources to competing activities in order to achieve one of the following two objectives:

- Construct the schedule which results in the minimal project completion time among all possible completion times.
- Construct the schedule which has the minimal total cost.

We realize that, in general, fixed resource constraints and fixed project due dates are not compatible. Therefore, when resource restrictions are imposed, one can try either to minimize project duration or to minimize total costs. In the latter case, a desired project due date may still be established, with the provision that the total cost function should contain late completion penalties when it is impossible to observe the deadline.

We are now giving a conceptual mathematical programming formulation (Talbot and Patterson [1978]) to help us best understand the nature of the resource constrained scheduling problem. A few additional notations are required:

$F_{i,j}$ = scheduled finish time for activity (i, j); a project schedule is defined by a complete set of $F_{i,j}$

$P_{i,j}$ = set of immediate predecessors of activity (i, j)

t = time, assumed divides into integer periods (hours, days, weeks, etc.); $t = 1, \ldots, T$, where T is a known completion time for the project $\left(\text{e.g., } T = \sum_{(i,j) \,\in\, \text{network}} Y_{i,j} \right)$

A_t = set of activities in progress, call them active, in time period t

$r_{i,j}^k$ = usage rate of the kth resource type by activity (i, j) when it is active, $k = 1, \ldots, K$

R_t^k = amount of the kth resource type available in time period t.

Assume all $r_{i,j}^k$, R_t^k, and $Y_{i,j}$ fixed and measured in integer units. Recall that $Y_{i,j}$ denotes the activity duration.

Suppose we want to minimize total project duration. Then the optimal schedule is the solution to the following mathematical program:

Minimize $\quad\quad\quad\quad\quad \max_{(i,j)\,\in\,\text{network}} \left[F_{i,j} \right]$ $\quad\quad\quad\quad\quad\quad$ (5.18)

subject to:

$$\max_{(h,i)\,\in\,P_{i,j}} \left[F_{h,i} \right] + Y_{i,j} \leqslant F_{i,j} \quad\quad (i, j) \in \text{network} \quad\quad (5.19)$$

$$\sum_{(i,j)\,\in\,A_t} r_{i,j}^k \leqslant R_t^k, \quad\quad \begin{matrix} (k = 1, \ldots, K; \\ t = 1, \ldots, T). \end{matrix} \quad\quad (5.20)$$

The combinatorial nature of the problem is immediately apparent if we think of A_t. Indeed, in a given time period t, different project schedules may have different sets A_t. To identify the elements of A_t one can use 0–1 integer variables (see Pritsker et al. [1969], Wiest and Levy [1977, pp. 130–132]), yielding an integer programming model. Clearly, the problem is inherently difficult.

One conceivable approach is to enumerate all possible schedules, retain the feasible ones by checking (5.20), and select the best. However, this is computationally infeasible.

Another approach is based on the realization that constructing a project schedule has a tree-like structure (Johnson [1967] gives a good pictorial representation of it) originating in the sequential nature of the decisions, that is, scheduling decisions are made first for time period 1, then for time period 2, and so on. Hence, various implicit enumeration schedules have been devised to produce optimal schedules (Davis [1973]). Unfortunately, to date, these techniques remain ineffective for all but small problems, reasonable computational times being reported for networks with no more than 50 activities (Talbot and Patterson [1978]).

For these reasons we have to fall back on heuristic procedures which, although they cannot guarantee mathematical optimality and show variable performance depending on the type of problem, are able to handle very large networks and produce schedules that are, in general, good enough to serve the operational needs of the users. The surveys by Davis [1966, 1973] can give the interested reader a picture of the achievements in the field. The sample of commercially available computer programs in Davis [1978, p. 382] illustrates their capabilities of attacking resource constrained problems involving multiple projects with tens of thousands of activities and hundreds of resource types. Finally, a study by Davis and Patterson [1975] provides a comparison of the relative effectiveness of various solution techniques; see also Jenette [1976].

The speed of a heuristic method comes from the fact that in traversing the enumeration tree from the initial node to some final node, corresponding to a complete project schedule, it follows only one route, as opposed to an optimum seeking algorithm, which tries several routes in search for the best. Then the heart of the matter is the rule (or rules) by which one decides in every time period which activity (or activities) to schedule for execution. Making such a decision is equivalent to selecting at the branching point the branch along which one continues the development of the project schedule.

For the *resource constrained problem focusing on project duration*, Kelley [1963] is one of the first to have proposed such a method. His approach is to start with a topologically ordered list of activities within which a new ranking is obtained by some measure of the activity's urgency, such as the total slack resulting from the critical path scheduling. Activities are thus scheduled in order of nondecreasing total slack as soon as resources become available. He also suggests repeating the process with several different rankings and choosing the shortest project schedule.

Apparently, the "least slack first" (equivalent to the "minimum latest start time first") criterion has gained wide acceptance, as it is embedded in almost all solution methods for this problem. We find it, for instance, in a heuristic procedure by Wiest [1966] (presented in great detail by Wiest and Levy [1977, pp. 112–120]), and in the one illustrated by Moder and Phillips [1970, pp. 158–162]. The former allows for rescheduling active noncritical activities if the freed resources can help scheduling critical activities, while the latter uses within the "least slack first" a secondary ordering criterion of "shortest activity duration first" to reduce the average time activities have to wait for resources.

Weglarz [1981] deals with a project scheduling problem in which not only the resource usage rate at every moment but also the total resources available

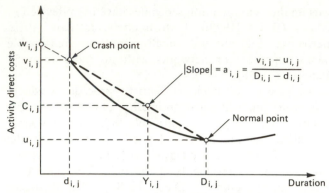

FIGURE 5.32 **Direct costs versus time curve for activity (i, j).**

for the whole project duration are constrained. These resources are said to be doubly constrained. A typical example of such doubly constrained resources is money, when the rate of expenditure as well as the total budget allocated must be observed.

The *resource constrained problem focusing on total costs* has an increased degree of complexity. It is also called "long range resource planning" by Moder and Phillips [1970], as it may encompass multiple projects that compete for some limited resources, and consists of allocating them to the activities involved with the objective of scheduling all activities such as to minimize the total of direct and indirect costs.

Activity durations are no longer regarded as fixed; rather, the execution may be speeded up by allocating more resources to the activity in question. To illustrate, we will mention two of the more widely referenced heuristics: SPAR-1 (*S*cheduling *P*rogram for *A*llocating *R*esources) developed by Wiest [1967], and RAMPS (*R*esource *A*llocation and *M*ulti-*P*roject *S*cheduling) by Moshman et al. [1963]. Both procedures consider that an activity may be performed either at a normal pace, may be crashed,* or stretched out by using a normal, maximum, or minimum amount of resources, respectively.

The *time – cost tradeoff problem*, as explained in the introduction to section 5.3, is centered on the idea that the durations of some activities can be cut down if additional resources are allocated to them. This can be visualized graphically as a cost versus time curve which is, at least on a limited portion, downsloping (Figure 5.32). The widely accepted convex shape shows that it is marginally costlier to induce the last percentages of reduction in activity duration than the first percentages.

For technical reasons, the duration may not be reduced indefinitely. We call the limit "crash point." There is also a most cost efficient duration called

---

*"Crashing" an activity means performing it in the shortest technically possible time by allocating to it all the necessary resources.

"normal point"; stretching the activity beyond it may lead to a rise in direct costs. It is clear that we shall be interested only in the central region of the curve contained between the two significant points.

In the first formulation of the time–cost tradeoff problem, Fulkerson [1961] and Kelley [1961] made the simplifying assumption of continuous linear direct cost functions. We shall adopt this approximation to the convex cost curve (see the dashed chord in Figure 5.32) throughout the balance of this section.

Suppose now that we have a project schedule with all activities at their normal durations. If it becomes necessary to speed up project execution then, as shown in section 5.3.2, we have to shorten the activities on the critical path. As we do so, the critical path might change. The important thing, however, is to stay cost-efficient, that is, always to expedite that activity on the current critical path which entails the smallest marginal increase in direct costs. It is only in this way that we can move, for the entire project, along the most efficient direct cost versus time curve.

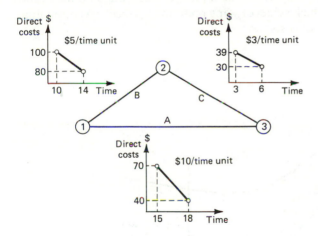

Step	Activity duration			Critical activities	Project duration	Project direct costs
	A	B	C			
1	18	14	6	B, C	20	150
2	18	14	4	A, B, C	18	156
3	17	14	3	A, B, C	17	169
4	16	13	3	A, B, C	16	184

FIGURE 5.33 Network with time-cost trade-off curves; incremental costs per time unit are shown for each curve.

To illustrate, consider the network in Figure 5.33. At normal activity durations the project lasts 20 time units and the critical path is *B-C*. Assume we want to cut down the project to 16 time units. Obviously, we should start by shortening *C*. When the duration of *C* is 4 units, activity *A* also becomes critical. We continue to reduce *C* up to 3 units, the crash point, and *A* to 17. To reach the desired project duration, we will have to shorten *B* down to 13 units and *A* to 16. These steps are summarized in the Table in Figure 5.33.

Figure 5.34 shows the cost curves associated with a project. The lack of smoothness of the direct cost curve reflects the fact that reducing the project length is achieved up to some point by shortening a certain critical activity and from that point on by shortening another critical activity.

The mathematical problem is, then, to find the project schedule which minimizes the total costs, that is, shorten project duration (if it is too long) up to the point where the increase induced in direct costs is just balanced by the reduction in indirect costs.

There are situations in which either the indirect cost curve may not be determined with sufficient accuracy, or the duration of the project is imposed contractually or by other means. Then one no longer seeks the minimum total cost, rather the schedule which achieves some prescribed project execution time $\mathcal{D}$ at minimum project direct costs.

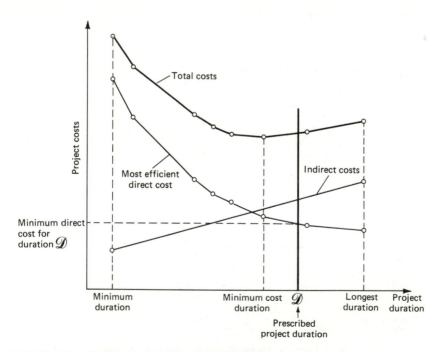

FIGURE 5.34 Project costs versus project duration.

Thus, the time–cost tradeoff is: given a prespecified project duration $\mathcal{D}$ and ample resources,* determine the set of activity durations and the schedule which minimizes the project direct costs.

By formulating the problem as a linear program we can provide a refined treatment to it. In Figure 5.32, the cost function is defined over the range bounded by $d_{i,j}$ and $D_{i,j}$. The linear approximation we are using exhibits a cost increase of $a_{i,j}$ per time unit reduction in the activity duration. The unknown activity duration is $Y_{i,j}$ associated with a cost $C_{i,j}$.

The total direct project cost is the sum of individual costs and can be written as:

$$\text{Total direct project cost} = \sum_{(i,\,j)\,\in\,\text{network}} C_{i,j} = \sum_{(i,\,j)\,\in\,\text{network}} \left(w_{i,j} - a_{i,j} Y_{i,j} \right).$$

As all $w_{i,j}$ are constant, costs are minimized if $\sum_{(i,\,j)\,\in\,\text{network}} a_{i,j} Y_{i,j}$ is maximized.

Then the formulation of the time–cost tradeoff problem becomes:

Maximize
$$Z = \sum_{(i,\,j)\,\in\,\text{network}} a_{i,j} Y_{i,j} \tag{5.21}$$

subject to:

$$T_i + Y_{i,j} - T_j \leqslant 0, \tag{5.22}$$
$$Y_{i,j} \leqslant D_{i,j} \qquad \text{all } (i,\,j) \in \text{network} \tag{5.23}$$
$$-Y_{i,j} \leqslant -d_{i,j}, \tag{5.24}$$
$$T_n - T_1 \leqslant \mathcal{D}. \tag{5.25}$$

Inequalities (5.22), in which T_i is the unknown earliest occurrence time for the event represented by node i, impose the predecessor–successor relationships. The difference $T_n - T_1$ represents the total project duration. If the project starts at time zero (5.25) becomes simply $T_n \leqslant \mathcal{D}$. If (i, j) is a dummy activity $Y_{i,j} = d_{i,j} = D_{i,j} = 0$. Notice that resources are not explicitly considered, rather the composite cost of using them enters the decision making.

By solving the model, one obtains the optimal activity durations and the earliest node occurrence times. These provide all the necessary information for constructing an optimal project schedule.

By inspecting the linear program (5.21)–(5.25) it becomes apparent that, for sizable networks, it cannot be solved by the simplex method because of the excessive number of constraints. Other solution techniques have been sought. Thus, we have the well-known procedure developed independently by Fulkerson [1961] and Kelley [1961] (also in Ford and Fulkerson [1974, pp. 151–162]) by

---

*If resources are limited, we are facing a resource constrained problem and will have to use one of the procedures referred to earlier.

which the dual problem to the above primal linear program is established, interpreted as a network flow problem, and then solved by a flow augmenting algorithm. The procedure can handle large networks with thousands of activities. An alternative solution technique by Phillips and Dessouky [1977] uses a minimal cut search algorithm in a flow network resulting from appropriately interpreting the original project network. This appears to have favorable computational times.

If the cost versus time curve has a more pronounced convexity and the linear approximation of Figure 5.32 proves to be too coarse, a finer piecewise linear representation can be provided (Bradley et al. [1977, chap. 9.2], Moder and Phillips [1970, pp. 213–214]), in which case Fulkerson's network flow algorithm is still applicable. General nonconvex continuous and more complicated discontinuous tradeoff cost functions can also be handled (Meyer and Shaffer [1963], Moder and Phillips [1970, pp. 215–218]), but the resulting models are integer programs which, unfortunately, are computationally infeasible even for small networks. One way to go would be to decompose the network into smaller portions, treating them separately and then putting together the partial results.

5.3.5   Closing Notes

Before concluding, we would like to point to some developments related to problems we have already presented. These developments will not be treated here but may be of interest to the reader. The relevant original references will be provided. Moder and Phillips [1970] and Wiest and Levy [1977] may also be consulted for textbook presentations of the topics.

- An alternative way of diagramming a project is to represent activities in the nodes of the network with the arrows expressing precedence relationships. Called "precedence diagram" by Fondahl [1962], its developer, it does not require the use of dummy activities; an example may be found in Levy et al. [1963], and in Figure 5.35.
- Classical CPM and PERT recognize only finish-to-start precedence requirements (mentioned in section 5.3.1). A later development by IBM, called precedence diagramming or precedence networking, permits other kinds of precedence relationships to be expressed: finish to finish, start to start, and start to finish. It also allows for lag intervals between start or finish points of interdependent activities.
- Decision CPM (DCPM) is a generalization of the usual CPM by Crowston and Thompson [1967], to consider the possibility of performing some of the activities by several alternative methods. Each method has a different cost, a different activity performance time, and possibly different predecessor–successor relationships. Rather than selecting one alternative in advance, DCPM includes them all in the project network and then chooses those which minimize the total cost of completing the project. The problem can be formulated as an integer programming model for whose solution branch-and-bound algorithms have been written (Crowston and Wagner [1970], Crowston [1970]).

Task T_j	Immediate predecessors	Duration t_j
T1	—	6
T2	—	9
T3	T1	4
T4	T1	5
T5	T2	4
T6	T3	2
T7	T3, T4	3
T8	T6	7
T9	T7	3
T10	T5, T9	1
T11	T8, T10	10
T12	T11	1
Total duration: 55		

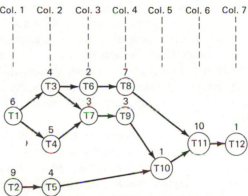

FIGURE 5.35 Precedence diagram for a production process.

- Probabilistic project networking represents another extension of classical PERT–CPM in order to incorporate cases in which the way a project continues from some point on may depend on the uncertain outcome of one or several activities. Such situations are typical with R&D projects. One of the best known systems is GERT (*G*raphical *E*valuation and *R*eview *T*echnique) originally developed by Pritsker and Happ [1966], Pritsker and Whitehouse [1966], and Whitehouse [1973]. It features probabilistic branching (nodes with multiple uncertain outcomes), feedback loops in the network, multiple node realizations, and probabilistic activity durations. Usually GERT network analysis is carried out by simulation during which statistics on project times and costs are collected. The interested reader can find a multiteam, multiproject R&D application in Moore and Taylor [1977].

- *V*enture *E*valuation and *R*eview *T*echnique (VERT), an extension of GERT, is a mathematically oriented network-based simulation technique which analyzes times, costs, and performances. Usually GERT can analyze times and costs only; hence, VERT is a more powerful technique than GERT. The interested readers should see Moeller [1972] and Moeller and Digman [1981].

5.4 Line Balancing

When a product or a family of technologically similar products exhibit high volume and stable demand* over lengthy periods of time, it becomes economical to design and lay out a special facility dedicated exclusively to the product or family of products under consideration. In order to cut down on work-in-process inventory and on such nonproductive times as loading, unloading, and transportation between successive operations, the work stations (consisting either of machines or of workers performing manual operations) are physically arranged in a contiguous sequence according to the technological ordering of the manufacturing stages. The resulting facility is called a *fabrication line* if the

---

*High volume and stable demand are required in order to ensure a minimal capacity load factor.

production process is fabrication, or *assembly line* if it is assembly. As will become clear soon, in the context of this section it makes conceptually no difference whether the process is fabrication or assembly. Therefore, we will be referring to either of the layouts as *production line* or simply *line*.*

A product line consists of a sequence of N *work stations*. The product proceeds serially from station 1 to station N. At each work station an *operation* takes place. N product units are simultaneously in process in different stages of completion.

In most cases the product is transferred between stations by means of specialized devices such as inclined planes, conveyors, belts, and transfer machines. However, the presence of transfer devices is not a prerequisite for a production line layout. Rather, the disposition of the workers and equipment in conformity with the ordering of the manufacturing process *and* the simultaneous processing of N units, each at a different station, constitutes the distinguishing traits.

To the scheduler a production line represents an important simplification: since its inner working is regulated by design, for scheduling purposes it may be treated as just a single integrated machine which automatically executes the entire sequence of operations required for turning some raw material into a part or a product, or for assembling some component parts and subassemblies into a finished product.

An operation is a grouping of tasks, a *task* being the smallest work element that can be separated and performed relatively independently of other activities in the same production process.

The *cycle time* of the line is the amount of time elapsed between two successive units entering or leaving the line.

In order to set up a production line, the total work required for the manufacturing of the product has to be divided first into tasks and then grouped into operations. The arrangement of the tasks into work stations is called a *balance*. The grouping of the tasks has to observe various restrictions. The most numerous class of constraints are the precedence relations which limit, on technological groups, the order in which the tasks are to be performed. Other restrictions such as station position relative to the front or back of the unit, tasks that must be performed on particular equipment whose location is fixed and given, tasks that must be kept at separate work stations, and so on, add further complexity to the problem (see, for example, Wester and Kilbridge [1962a, 1962b]). This section will treat only problems constrained by precedence relations.

---

*Production lines are in the category of product layout, typical of high-volume production. At the other end of the spectrum we find the process layout, in which the manufacturing facilities (equipment, machine tools, etc.) are grouped according to the general functions they perform, with no regard to any particular product. Thus, in a machine shop serving a made-to-order business one would find a lathe department, milling machine department, grinding machine department, etc.

Let c be the cycle time of the line and p_i, $i = 1, \ldots, N$, the duration of the ith operation. Duration p_i consists of the entire time interval required at station i to receive, position, actually work on, release, and transport the unit to the next station. If we succeed in grouping the tasks such that all operation durations are equal ($p_i = p$ for all i), the line is perfectly *balanced*; then $c = p$. A perfectly balanced line can also be obtained when some operation time p_i is such that $p_i = k_i c$, with k_i positive and integer. Obviously, in order to still be able to maintain a cycle time of c, k_i identical machines or workers have to perform simultaneously operation i upon k_i different and successive units. This is a line with *multiple work stations* (Buxey [1974]). We shall limit, however, our presentation to the cases where $c \geq \max p_i$.

As the product moves serially from one station to the next, it follows that the average cycle time must be the same at any one work station* and equal to c.

In the most general case one cannot obtain a perfectly balanced line, so station i is associated with an idle time $(c - p_i)$ in every cycle c. If we total these idle times for the entire line, a quantity d called *balance delay* results:

$$d = Nc - \sum_{i=1}^{N} p_i.$$

We can also express the balance delay in relative terms, percentagewise:

$$d_\% = \frac{Nc - \sum_{i=1}^{N} p_i}{Nc} \cdot 100. \tag{5.26}$$

Since idle time is expensive in terms of labor and equipment costs, it is regarded, in general, as reasonable to seek an arrangement of tasks into work stations with minimum balance delay. This objective is equivalent to minimizing product Nc.

5.4.1 Problem Definition

From the preceding discussion it is apparent that, in the context of high-volume production, scheduling is implicitly achieved once the production line is laid out. By grouping tasks into operations and then by physically setting them up as work stations, one decides upon the flow of the product, the sequence in

---

*The station average cycle time is the average time elapsed between two successive units starting or completing processing at the particular work station. With perfect balance, a unit remains at every station for exactly a time interval c. Consider now an unbalanced line having some operation i out of balance with $p_i < c$. We can run station i continuously, which means that as soon as a unit arrives, the station becomes busy for a duration p_i, after which it is idle for the interval $(c - p_i)$ until the following unit arrives. Notice that the product flows smoothly, with no stops, along the line. However, we might choose to consolidate several idle intervals $(c - p_i)$ into larger time slices by running operation i part time and by storing the product alternately before and after the station. The flow of the product becomes intermittent and work-in-process inventory accumulates. By taking into account the consolidated idle and running periods of the station, we shall find that the average time elapsed between two successive product units is still c.

which activities are performed, and the times at which they start and get completed. Operations scheduling turns into the problem of establishing the production line.

To illustrate, let us consider a production process consisting of J tasks. A task is denoted Tj and has a performance time of t_j. Our example in Figure 5.35 has $J = 12$ tasks with total task duration of 55. As stated, the objective is to group the tasks into N work stations to become a production line. Evidently $\sum_{i=1}^{N} p_i = \sum_{j=1}^{J} t_j = 55$.

The table in Figure 5.35 contains the basic data:* precedence relations and task performance times. The precedence diagram, whose nodes represent the tasks, summarizes by the use of arrows the technological sequencing restrictions.

In the construction of the precedence diagram we have followed a procedure given by Jackson [1956b]:

Step 1.   In column 1, on the left side of the page, represent all tasks which need not follow any tasks.

Step m (start with $m = 2$; repeat this step until all tasks have appeared on the diagram; with each repetition increase m by 1).

      (a) In column m, to the right of column $m - 1$, represent all tasks not already on the diagram which need not follow any task which is not already on the diagram.

      (b) Draw all arrows from tasks in column $m - 1$ to tasks in column m which must follow them. Repeat this procedure replacing column $m - 1$ by columns $m - 2, \ldots, 1$ successively. To avoid redundancy, no arrow is drawn from one task to another if it is possible to go from the first task to the second following arrows already drawn.

Constructing the precedence diagram of the production process brings several advantages: it is probably the most suggestive guide to the logical and systematic analysis of the precedence relationships of the tasks, might bring to light improvements in the manufacturing technology itself, is useful in training industrial engineering personnel (Prenting and Battaglin [1964]).

We shall assume in what follows that the performance durations of the tasks are always integer. This can be easily achieved by using a suitable time unit.

Figure 5.36 shows for our example the way in which the balance delay depends on the number of stations and the cycle time. The two graphs are based exclusively on relation (5.26) and do not account for the fact that some (N, c) combinations might be infeasible because of the impossibility of grouping the tasks accordingly.

---

*These data can be extracted from engineering documents such as the route sheet, the assembly chart, and the operation process chart (see Buffa [1972, pp. 80–89] for an example). In our discussion here, when defining the problem, we shall not be concerned with its industrial engineering aspects about how to divide the work into tasks and how to identify precedence relations and other constraints.

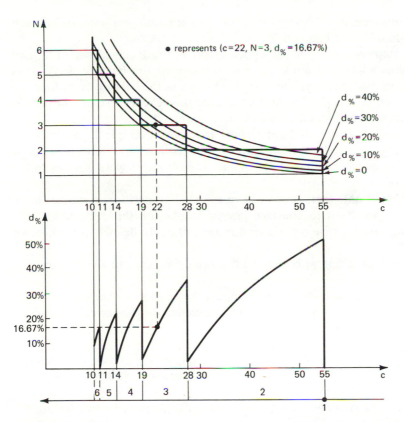

FIGURE 5.36 Balance delay, cycle time, and number of stations for example of Figure 5.35.

The upper graph contains a family of curves of the form $Nc = (\sum_{j=1}^{J} t_j)/(1 - d_\% /100)$ having $d_\%$ as parameter. Recall that we have already decided to limit ourselves to the case of $c \geqslant \max p_i$. Since by definition tasks may not be split, it follows that $\max p_i \geqslant \max t_j$. Hence, $c \geqslant \max t_j$. Therefore, we do not have to consider cycle times smaller than 10. It is also clear that when $N = 1$ all tasks are put in the same work station and $c = 55$; so, there is no need to consider a cycle time larger than $\sum_{j=1}^{J} t_j = 55$.

In view of the pursued balance delay minimization, we would like to pair N and c such as to stay all the time on the $d_\% = 0$ curve. This is obviously not possible because the number of stations must be integer. For a given c, in order to achieve the smallest value of the product Nc, the minimum required number of stations, $N_{\min}$, is given by:

$$N_{\min} = \min\left(N \geqslant \frac{\sum_{j=1}^{J} t_j}{c} \right) \text{ and } N \text{ integer.} \quad (5.27)$$

For instance, if we choose $c = 22$ we need at least three stations, in which case $d_{\%} = 16.67\%$ (see Figure 5.36).

The stepwise curve in the upper graph is the locus of such $(N_{\min}, c)$ combinations which guarantee the minimization of the balance delay. It is transposed in the lower graph into what is known as the balance delay function (Kilbridge and Wester [1961]). Again, these are theoretical curves. By neglecting all technological restrictions, they do not address the issue of whether the implied balances may be obtained. Indeed, take as an example the point $c = 11$, $N = 5$, having $d_{\%} = 0$. This would mean perfect balance but, unfortunately, it proves impossible to group the tasks of our example into 5 work stations with a cycle time of 11.

We should note that, once we have assumed all performance times to be integer, we only have to consider integer values for the cycle time. This explains why the stepwise curve does not touch the zero delay hyperbola at all values of N.

To establish a line with minimal balance delay one can go two ways:

(a) Either set the cycle time and minimize the number of work stations, or
(b) Set the number of work stations and then find the balance which minimizes the cycle time.

In general, in the context of a hierarchical planning process (see chapters 3 and 6), production rates constitute aggregate planning decisions, so the cycle time has to be set such as to ensure the achievement of the preestablished production rate. However, there is still some flexibility left in selecting the value of the cycle time. Thus, for instance, if a required production rate may be attained operating in one shift a line with cycle c, the same output can result from a slower line (i.e., with a larger c) working overtime or in two shifts, or by running two parallel identical lines. Or, if a faster line is in operation (i.e., having a smaller c) it will have to run only part time. Obviously, these alternatives affect the aggregate costs related to overtime, idle time, inventory, overhead coming with additional shifts, and so on.

In any case, we aim at selecting such a cycle time as to be as close as possible to one of the minima of the balance delay function. For our example Figure 5.36 shows that the best theoretical values for c are 11, 14, 19, and 28.

Sometimes approach (b) has to be followed, as might be the case when rebalancing an old fabrication line. Suppose the existing work stations contain such fixed location machines which make it uneconomical to start shuffling them. Then the number of stations is imposed by the old layout and optimizing means minimizing the cycle time.

A survey of the research work in the field (for an excellent review, see Ignall [1965]) would reveal that almost all available techniques take alternative (a) to the problem because minimizing cycle time directly, given the number of stations, is quite difficult. Therefore, our presentation will also focus on approach (a).

It is possible to find a minimum cycle time for N work stations indirectly, in an iterative fashion (Ignall [1965]):

1. Compute the theoretical minimum cycle time for the given N:

$$c = \left(\sum_{j=1}^{J} t_j \right) / N.$$

2. Use some method for approach (a) with cycle c and see if an N station balance can be constructed; if yes, the perfect balance, with zero delay, has been obtained.
3. If not, increase c in relatively large steps Δ until an N station balance is obtained.
4. Reduce c in smaller steps δ until the number of stations increases back to $N+1$.
5. Repeat steps 3 and 4 with different Δ and δ until c can no longer be reduced for the given N.

At this point, we are ready to give a formal definition of the *line balancing problem* (Gutjahr and Nemhauser [1964]):

Given a finite set $\mathfrak{T}$, a partial order on $\mathfrak{T}$, a positive real valued function f defined on $\mathfrak{T}$, and a number c, find a collection of subsets of $\mathfrak{T}$, $(S_1, S_2, \ldots, S_N)$ satisfying the following conditions:*

1. $\displaystyle\bigcup_{i=1}^{N} S_i = \mathfrak{T}$,   All tasks must be assigned to stations.

2. $\displaystyle S_i \cap_{i \neq j} S_j = \varnothing$,   Each task must be assigned only once.

3. $\displaystyle f(S_i) = \sum_{x \in S_i} f(x) \leqslant c, i = 1, \ldots, N$ The work content of any single station should not exceed the cycle time.

4. If x precedes y, $x \in S_i$, $y \in S_j$, then $i \leqslant j$,   A task x preceding task y may not be performed in a station subsequent to the station to which y is assigned.

5. $\displaystyle \left[Nc - \sum_{i=1}^{N} f(S_i) \right]$ be minimized.

Note that we are considering task performance times to be additive, which is the assumption customarily made.[†]

---

*$\mathfrak{T}$ is the set of tasks $(T1, T2, \ldots, Tj, \ldots, TJ)$, the partial order on $\mathfrak{T}$ are the precedence relations, function f yields the performance times [i.e., $t_j = f(Tj)$ and later, at condition 3, $p_i = f(S_i)$], and c is the cycle time.

†Ignall [1965] discusses briefly a situation of nonadditivity in which a task with a long performance time can be broken into several shorter tasks with a longer total performance time.

We should mention that a production line is, by configuration, a flow shop (see section 5.2.1.3). There are, however, differences stemming from the various degrees of equipment specialization: while the general flow shop processes many different products, a production line is devoted, in the extreme, to a unique product (the single product line) which is manufactured time and again. Also, on a line N product units are processed simultaneously, while in a flow shop the various products usually move in batches from operation to operation. From here follows the concern for equating the work content of the stations along the line balancing problem, which is absent in the case of the general flow shop where other optimization criteria, such as the makespan, are pursued (see section 5.2.4).

Scheduling the single-product line as a flow shop is complete once a solution to the line balancing problem is found, because the sequence and timing of the operations are controlled by design.

When a family of products shares the facility (the multiproduct line), as is the case in the automobile industry where a variety of models are assembled interspersed on the same line, scheduling is more involved:

- First, tasks have to be assigned to stations. As the products in the family, although technologically similar, are distinct, they will require different amounts of work at some of the stations. We are facing here what is known as the *mixed model line balancing problem*. In order to use labor and equipment efficiently we still want to minimize idle time. To do this Thomopoulos [1967, 1970] selects a time interval T—for instance, a shift—against which the balancing is done. Consider now all the product units, of all models in the family, which have to be manufactured during time T. Station i is a collection of tasks from all these units, assigned to the station in conformity with the precedence restrictions, and adding up to a total performance time P_i which must not exceed T. Grouping the tasks into stations should be done so as to minimize $\sum_{i=1}^{N}(T - P_i)$, the total idle time along the line.

- Second, a *model-mix sequencing problem* has to be solved. As mentioned above, the various products, or models, in the family load the individual stations differently. Therefore, a sequence of product models has to be found which will minimize station idle time and, at the same time, prevent congestion (Wester and Kilbridge [1964]). In this stage the problem may be viewed as a flow shop scheduling problem in which each unit to be produced counts as a "job," and each station is a "machine." Obviously, given the manner in which the line operates only permutation schedules make sense, and minimizing the makespan for, say, all the units to be produced in time T will also minimize idle time on all stations. Unfortunately, the large flow shop problem still requires progress to be made toward efficient solution techniques (see section 5.2.4.3). However, assuming that a solution is found, an immediate check has to be made whether the resulting makespan exceeds the value of T. If so, then back-and-forth iterations will be required between the mixed model line balancing and the model-mix sequencing problems.

A distinct instance of the multiproduct line assumes that the products in the family are manufactured intermittently in batches for stock rather than being intermixed on the line. The line is set up based on the group technology concept (Starr [1978, p. 187]), which means that the products are of similar design and technology, showing only differences in size or in other nonessential elements. Lines of this sort are met in the fabrication of families of such parts as pistons, cylinder heads, gears, cams, and so on. To shift the line from one family member to another, a changeover of nonnegligible cost is required, which makes it economical to resort to batch manufacturing. In spite of the batch processing, the facility continues to be a production line and not a general flow shop. This is true because the facility is fully dedicated to one product at a time. Under this light, the multiproduct line with batch processing appears in operation as a sequence of single-product lines. If the facility were to be run as a general flow shop, products would move in batches (rather than unit by unit) between operations (stations) and up to N different batches might be present in the shop at any given moment. Also, the conversion from one product to the next would be done by individual operations and not necessarily for the entire shop at a time.

If we are interested in determining the optimum lot sizes to be sequenced on the multiproduct line, we can think of the line as a single machine and apply one of the models for multiple items sharing the same equipment (see section 4.2.3.1). Meal [1978] presents a classification of assembly lines from the viewpoint of detailed planning, and develops rules for allocating assembly capacity among the items produced on the line. Young [1967] also discusses the lot sizing aspect and assumes that the cost of conversion from one product to the next is sequence-dependent.

We hope that by the preceding discussion we managed to make clear why production lines have gained separate status in the literature. In what follows we shall be preoccupied by the methods that were developed for solving the line balancing problem for single-product lines.

5.4.2   Solving the Line Balancing Problem

By far the largest body of research work has been produced for the deterministic line balancing, which makes the assumptions that all performance times are fixed and given, and that stations do not experience breakdowns.

From the definition it is evident that we are confronted by a combinatorial problem, for whose examination and solution various approaches have been investigated. We shall indicate some references without attempting to be exhaustive:

- Integer programming: Salveson [1955], Bowman [1960], White [1961], and Thangavelu and Shetty [1971];
- Dynamic programming: Held et al. [1963];
- Feasible sequences enumeration algorithms

- Optimal tree search procedures: Jackson [1956b], Mansoor [1964], Nevins [1972], and Dar-El [1973];*
- Shortest path algorithm: Gutjahr and Nemhauser [1964];
- Heuristic techniques: Kilbridge and Wester [1961a], Helgeson and Birnie [1961], Tonge [1961, 1965], Hoffmann [1963], Held et al. [1963], Mansoor [1964], Moodie and Young [1965], Arcus [1966], Nevins [1972], and Dar-El [1973].

An experimental study by Mastor [1970] compares Held et al.'s dynamic programming technique, four heuristics, and four bench mark rules for assigning tasks to stations on a sample of 20 task problems, 40 task problems, and some actual industrial problems. The results point to Arcus' COMSOAL and Held et al.'s algorithm as the most effective in finding minimum delay balances, although Held et al.'s technique required substantially longer computer time. A subsequent comparison by Dar-El [1973] shows that his MALB algorithm, applied to a set of problems with 50 to 140 tasks, reduces the average balance delay below Arcus' COMSOAL performance in less computation time. In the domain of exact methods, the integer programming approach of Thangavelu and Shetty appears to be about 50% faster than Held et al.'s dynamic programming with moderately sized problems (50 tasks or less).

It comes as no surprise to find that, in general, optimal algorithms become computationally infeasible way before reaching the domain of realistic problems with 100 tasks or more, and tens of work stations. This explains the predominance of heuristic procedures, and not even these can efficiently handle very complex balancing problems involving multiple work stations, fixed location equipment, workpiece reorientation, workers shared by several work stations, and so on.

A discussion on most of the aforementioned algorithms is provided by Ignall [1965]. He suggests that, rather than pursuing a time-consuming algorithm in search of the mathematical optimum, it is better to try to find a good approximate balance first for two reasons: first, because a range of cycle times might have to be investigated requiring several balances to be produced; second, because the balance generated by whatever formal technique we choose can be improved upon by experienced engineering personnel who would incorporate complexities which could not be handled by the model.

The reader can also find good textbook presentations of balancing techniques. Thus, Buffa and Taubert [1972] give extensive illustrations on numerical examples of two well-known heuristics: the Kilbridge and Wester [1961a] and Arcus [1966] techniques. Zimmermann and Sovereign [1974] actually solve a classical line balancing problem due to Jackson [1956b] by Bowman's [1960] integer programming, Gutjahr and Nemhauser's [1964] network model, Held et al.'s [1963] dynamic programming, and Kilbridge and Wester's [1961a] and Helgeson and Birnie's [1961] heuristics. Johnson and

---

*Held et al., Mansoor, Nevins, and Dar-El give procedures that may be applied in either an optimal or an approximate manner.

Montgomery [1974] describe in detail the Thangavelu and Shetty [1971] integer programming model. Plane and McMillan [1971] also give an integer programming formulation.

We choose not to present again the same techniques. Rather, we will illustrate how to produce a balance using heuristic rules for assigning tasks to stations. This, we believe, will give the reader a general understanding of heuristics in production line balancing. Then we shall present the more recent Nevin's [1972] best bud search procedure.

To generate a balance implies finding an executable ordering of tasks, called *feasible sequence* (Ignall [1965]), and then assigning the tasks in that order to work stations up to a total time per station not to exceed the cycle time. Constructing all feasible sequences would guarantee that all possible balances are enumerated and in the end the best, in terms of minimum idle time, can be selected. But, because of the extremely large number of sequences this approach is computationally impractical even if, by a result of Jackson [1956b], one were able to identify and eliminate early enough the dominated (i.e., nonpromising) sequences.

A heuristic procedure avoids the thorny dimensionality issue by constructing only one feasible sequence and, therefore, only one balance. This is achieved by selecting the next task to include in a station using some relatively simple rule,* or a combination of rules, which is applied repeatedly until all tasks have been assigned. Clearly, the approach has its own difficulties related to finding assignment procedures that would produce with a reasonable, if not an optimal, amount of computational effort at least a good balance. This is, in principle, the concern of the authors referenced earlier under heuristic techniques: they propose various algorithms and then seek to evaluate their effectiveness and computational efficiency by experimenting with them on selected test problems.

To illustrate the heuristic approach, suppose we are given a cycle time $c = 12$, for which we are asked to balance a line for the production process in Figure 5.35. By relation (5.27), the smallest number of work stations required is 5. Consider the following two simple rules for constructing a feasible sequence:

1. From among the scheduleable tasks[†] choose first the task with the largest total number of successors.
2. Break ties by ranking first the task with the longest performance time.

The essence of rule 1 is that in the long run it tends to make a larger number of tasks (i.e., successors) scheduleable, thus offering a wider choice for

---

*Selection rules have been suggested by several authors, for instance, Tonge]1965] and Arcus [1966].

[†]A task is scheduleable if it has not yet been assigned, and all of its immediate predecessors have already been assigned positions in the sequence or allocated to work stations.

grouping into stations. Rule 2 is intended to bring more flexibility by leaving shorter tasks toward the end when the remaining time in the station decreases.

Below we show the 12 tasks, their total number of successors, and the durations:

Tasks	T1	T2	T3	T4	T5	T6	T7	T8	T9	T10	T11	T12
Number of all successors	9	4	7	5	3	3	4	2	3	2	1	0
Duration	6	9	4	5	4	2	3	7	3	1	10	1

This is the way the two rules operate:

- At the beginning, tasks T1 and T2 are scheduleable; T1 is selected by rule 1.
- Update the scheduleable list; it will contain T2, T3, and T4; T3 is chosen because it has the most successors.
- Next, tasks T2, T4 and T6 are scheduleable; T4 comes first because it has the largest number of successors, and so on.

The resulting feasible sequence is shown here:

$$T1, T3, T4, T2, T7, T5, T9, T6, T8, T10, T11, T12$$

From this sequence, tasks are then loaded into work stations up to the cycle time limit:

T1, T3	T4	T2, T7	T5, T9, T6	T8, T10	T11, T12
Station 1	Station 2	Station 3	Station 4	Station 5	Station 6

The procedure produced a non-optimal line with a balance delay of 23.6%. However, an optimal five-station balance exists and one is shown in Figure 5.37.

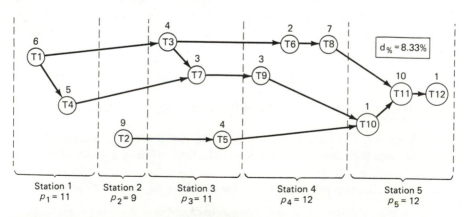

FIGURE 5.37 Optimal five-work station balance.

Of course, while the same rule applied to another problem might yield the optimum solution, it is also true that solving our problem by other rules might lead to another balance. Take, for instance, these two rules:

1. From the set of scheduleable tasks, select first the task with the most immediate successors.
2. Break ties at random.

Following are the tasks listed, along with their number of immediate successors:

Tasks	T1	T2	T3	T4	T5	T6	T7	T8	T9	T10	T11	T12
Number of immediate successors	2	1	2	1	1	1	1	1	1	1	1	0

A few steps of the procedure will make its modus operandi evident:

- The first scheduleable list consists of tasks T1 and T2; with rule 1, select T1.
- After this, the updated scheduleable set includes T2, T3, and T4, of which T3 has the largest number of immediate successors and, therefore, becomes the second in sequence.
- Now T2, T4, and T6 are scheduleable and by rule 1 they are at a tie; a random drawing picks T4, and so on.

The feasible sequence thus generated is:

$$T1, T3, T4, T6, T8, T2, T7, T9, T5, T10, T11, T12$$

Then tasks are assigned to work stations in this order. The result is represented in Figure 5.38. Notice that this heuristic technique was unable to find an optimal five-station balance for the given cycle time of 12.

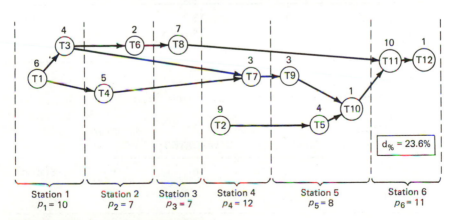

FIGURE 5.38 A six-work station line.

In the two examples given above, feasible sequences were constructed first, and only after that were tasks assigned to stations. There is another alternative by which the sequence of tasks is created as they are assigned, as in the heuristic method which follows (based on Arcus' [1966] COMSOAL):

1. Make the list of scheduleable tasks.
2. From the scheduleable list, pick those tasks which have individual durations not in excess of the time left available at the station currently being assigned work; call these tasks "candidates." If no candidate can be found, it means that the station is as full as it can be and a new one is started.
3. Select a candidate at random and assign it to the current station.
4. Repeat steps 1 through 3 until all tasks have been allocated.

Again, describing a few iterations performed for our problem should suffice:

- We start station 1, so the available time is 12.

SCHEDULEABLE LIST	DURATIONS	CANDIDATES	RANDOMLY SELECTED	
T1	6	T1	T1 →	Station 1
T2	9	T2		

- After T1 is assigned to station 1, the available time is reduced to 6.

UPDATED SCHEDULEABLE LIST	DURATIONS	CANDIDATES	RANDOMLY SELECTED	
T2	9	T3	T3 →	Station 1
T3	4	T4		
T4	5			

- With both T1 and T3 in station 1, the available time is 2.

UPDATED SCHEDULEABLE LIST	DURATIONS	CANDIDATES	RANDOMLY SELECTED	
T2	9	T6	T6 →	Station 1
T4	5			
T6	2			

Moder and Rodgers [1968] suggest that a more robust variance estimator may be obtained if, instead of the extreme time estimates o and p, one uses estimates of the 5 and 95 percentiles of the activity duration distribution.

Confidence intervals for path lengths in the network.   Having the expected activity durations calculated by (5.15), we can perform all scheduling computations as shown in section 5.3.2. At this point, we are mostly interested in the forward pass that yields at each node i the earliest occurrence time* T_i for the associated event:

$$T_i = \max\left[EF_{\text{all activities whose arrows converge to node } i}\right].\qquad (5.17)$$

In particular, the length of the critical path determines the earliest expected finish time for the project, T_n.

Events which are important for progress on the project (often called "milestones") may be assigned scheduled occurrence times. Let S_i be the scheduled time for event at node i.

Then, knowing T_i and S_i, the natural question is to what extent can we assert that the scheduled time will be met. This is simply the problem of determining a confidence interval around the estimated length of a particular path in the network.

A path, as defined earlier, is a concatenation of activities. Therefore, its length, as the sum of uncertain durations, is itself a random variable. Probability theory results for sums of random variables help us determine the probabilistic characteristics of the path length:

- The expected length of the path is the sum of the expected durations of the component activities (Feller, Vol. 1 [1968, p. 222]).
- The variance of the path length equals the sum of the individual variances, given that in section 5.3.1 activity durations were assumed mutually independent (Feller, Vol. 1 [1968, p. 230]).
- A central limit theorem due to Lindeberg (see Feller, Vol. 2 [1971, p. 262]) allows us to establish that the sum of a number of mutually independent activity durations, hence the path length, is asymptotically normally distributed if individual activity variances are small as compared to the variance of the path (i.e., no component activity should dominate the path).[†]

---

*If initial activities start at time zero, the earliest occurrence time T_i is given by the longest path from node 1 to node i.

[†]Finiteness of all expected activity durations and of all activity variances is also required. We made no mention of this because the nature of the problem guarantees it.

An implication of the theorem is that the larger the number of activities along the path, the better the normal approximation to the distribution of the path length. We realize that the examples we will be giving, having to be kept small in order to serve instructive purposes, will be wanting in this respect.

To illustrate, let us reconsider in Figure 5.30 the network of Figure 5.27a. Each activity is provided with the three duration estimates o, m, and p. Next to each arrow the corresponding $\hat{\mu}$ and $\hat{\sigma}^2$ are shown. Notice that values were chosen such as to yield average durations equal to the original duration estimates used in performing activity scheduling in Figure 5.27. Therefore, the critical path remains A-C-F and the earliest finish time for the project is $T_5 = 9$ days.

According to the probability results just mentioned, we compute:

$$\text{Expected length of critical path} = 2+5+2 = 9,$$

$$\text{Variance of critical path length} = .44+.11+.11 = .66,$$

Activity	o	m	p
A	1	1.5	5
B	2	3	4
C	4	5	6
D	.5	1	7.5
E	.5	.75	8.5
F	1	2	3

a. System of three time estimates for project activities

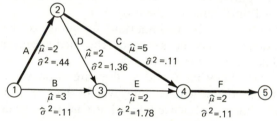

b. PERT estimates of expected activity durations and variances

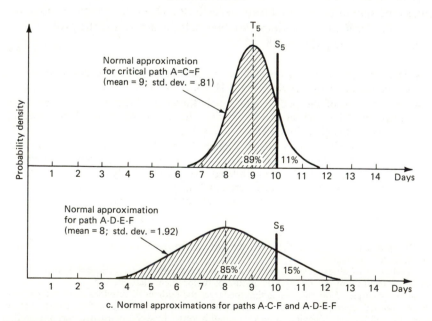

c. Normal approximations for paths A-C-F and A-D-E-F

FIGURE 5.30 PERT probabilistic calculations.

● Station 1 contains T1, T3, and T6 and is full; start station 2, so available time is again 12.

UPDATED SCHEDULEABLE LIST	DURATIONS	CANDIDATES	RANDOMLY SELECTED	
T2	9	T2	T8 →	Station 2
T4	5	T4		
T8	7	T8		

If the assignment process is repeated in the same fashion, the feasible sequence that follows is generated simultaneously with the six-station balance shown in Figure 5.39:

$$T1, T3, T6, T8, T4, T7, T9, T2, T5, T10, T11, T12$$

The selection rules, these and others, may be combined in various ways to yield more complex, and hopefully more effective, rules. For instance, Tonge [1965] combines them probabilistically in the sense that, every time an assignment decision is asked for, a random mechanism decides which selection rule, out of a given set, has to be used.

Let us present now an optimizing procedure* by Nevins [1972], called the best bud search, which we shall apply to our example problem. The imposed cycle time is the same, $c = 12$.

Let:

D' = sum of durations of all tasks

D = sum of durations of those tasks which so far have been assigned

N' = upper bound on the number of stations allowed in any balance

s = number of work stations already generated.

In our problem, $D' = 55$. Since an optimal five-station solution is known to exist, the best bud search should also be able to produce one, so we set $N' = 5$.

A bud is represented as a list $(s, T1, T2, ..., Tn)$ indicating that tasks $T1, T2, ..., Tn$ have already been assigned to the first s work stations of the production line. The problem associated with this bud is to assign the remaining J-n tasks to the remaining N'-s stations.

---

*For a given cycle time, an optimizing procedure will always find a balance with the minimum possible number of stations. This number, however, might differ (in the sense of being larger) from the theoretical N_{min} given by relation (5.27).

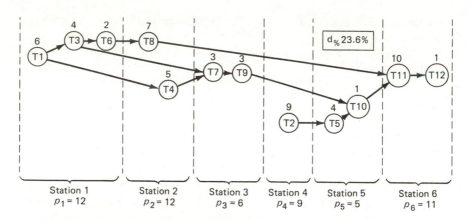

FIGURE 5.39   Alternative six-work station line.

A bud called "parent bud" may sprout "immediate descendant buds." In going from the parent to the immediate descendant bud a number, say m, of new tasks are added to the set of tasks corresponding to the parent bud. These m tasks constitute a new work station. For example, bud A sprouts bud B in Figure 5.40 by adding one new task, T2. Task T2 constitutes a station.

Figure 5.40 shows that the search starts with bud A represented by an empty list, as no assignments have been made yet. Construct a list of all scheduleable tasks arranged in order of nonincreasing duration. Move down the list looking for a task—call it A_1—whose duration will not exceed the time left available at the station currently being assigned work. Assign A_1 to the station. From here on, until all the immediate descendant buds are generated, keep both the assigned tasks and the scheduleable tasks in a small table simply called LIST. To know that some of the tasks have already been assigned we shall use a special notation. For example, the first task assigned to the station was denoted A_1, so the notation will be Task: A_1. Insert all of the tasks made scheduleable by the assignment of A_1 on the LIST after A_1 so that the portion of the LIST after A_1 will remain in order of nonincreasing duration.

Continue down the LIST to the end of it, adding new tasks $A_2, A_3, \ldots, A_m$ to the work station until it is as full as it can be. Tasks $A_1, A_2, \ldots, A_m$ will be combined with the tasks in the parent bud to form a descendant bud, provided that this work station is not a subset of some other work station constructed in this iteration.*

Then:

1. Remove from the station just generated the last task assigned A_m.
2. Delete from the LIST the immediate successors of A_m.

*An iteration refers to the sprouting of a bud.

3. Locate on the LIST task A_m and continue on that portion of the LIST after this task trying to generate a new work station.

If the LIST after task A_m is empty, repeat steps 1 through 3 with task A_{m-1} instead, and if the same happens again repeat with A_{m-2}, A_{m-3}, and so on. If we reach task A_1 and the LIST after it is still empty, no new stations may be found at this stage, that is, the parent bud will sprout no more immediate descendants.

Now another bud has to be selected for sprouting in the next iteration. To make the selection, every bud is assigned a score defined by the ratio $(D' - D)/(N' - s)$. The score is simply the average processing time left to be assigned to the remaining work stations. The unsprouted bud with the lowest score is chosen as the new parent bud and the procedure is repeated by starting again with a list of scheduleable tasks in order of nonincreasing performance time, and so on.

Two checks might prove useful during the execution of the search:

- If $D' - D \leqslant c$ and $s < N'$, an immediate solution is at hand: assign all the remaining tasks to one work station.
- If $(D' - D)/(N' - s) > c$, no solution can be obtained along that branch of the search tree.

We shall illustrate with a few iterations, after which Figure 5.40 should become self-explanatory. With every bud we have inscribed the following information: the symbol of the bud, its score, and the associated list representation.

The initial bud A has a score of $(55 - 0)/(5 - 0) = 11$. Finding its immediate descendants means enumerating all feasible #1 stations.

Step 1

ORDERED SCHEDULEABLE LIST	DURATIONS	
T2	9	→ Assign T2 to station 1.
T1	6	Insert task T5 on the LIST.

LIST	DURATIONS	↙
T2:A_1	9	
T1	6	→ No other assignment possible within cycle time.
T5	4	Bud *B* has been generated.

Step 2

Remove task T2:A_1 from station 1. Remove from the LIST task T2's successor, T5. Station 1 is empty.

LIST	DURATIONS
T2	
↓T1	6↓

→ Search portion* of the LIST after task T2.
Assign T1 to station 1.
Insert tasks T3 and T4 on the LIST.

LIST	DURATIONS
T2	
↓T1:A_1	6↓
T4	5
T3	4

→ Assign T4 to station 1.
No other task becomes scheduleable.

LIST	DURATIONS
T2	
T1:A_1	6↓
T4:A_2	5
T3	4

→ No other assignment possible within cycle time.
Bud *C* has been generated.

Step 3

Remove task T4:A_2 from station 1. Keep T1 in station 1 and try to assign to it other tasks.

LIST	DURATIONS
T2	
T1:A_1	6
T4	
↓T3	4↓

→ Search portion of the LIST after task T4.
Assign T3 to station 1.
Insert task T6 on the LIST.

LIST	DURATIONS
T2	
T1:A_1	6
T4	
T3:A_2	4↓
T6	2

→ Assign T6 to station 1.
Insert task T8 on the LIST.

LIST	DURATIONS
T2	
T1:A_1	6
T4	
↓T3:A_2	4↓
T6:A_3	2
T8	7

→ No other assignment possible within cycle time.
Bud *D* has been generated.

*By shading part of the LIST, we intend to show that the portion is excluded from being searched.

Step 4

Remove task T6:A$_3$ from station 1. Remove from the LIST task T6's successor, T8. Keep T1 and T3 in station 1 and try to assign to it other tasks.

LIST	DURATIONS		
T2			
T1:A$_1$	6	→	Search portion of the LIST after task T6.
T4			It is empty.
T3:A$_2$	4		
T6			
↓	↓		

Step 5

Remove task T3:A$_2$ from station 1. Remove from the LIST task T3's successor, T6. Keep T1 in station 1 and try to assign to it other tasks.

LIST	DURATIONS		
T2			
T1:A$_1$	6	→	Search portion of the LIST after task T3.
T4			It is empty.
T3			
↓	↓		

Step 6

Remove task T1:A$_1$ from station 1. Remove from the LIST task T1's successors, T4 and T3. Station 1 is empty.

LIST	DURATIONS		
T2		→	Search portion of the list after task T1.
T1			It is empty.
↓	↓		

No other #1 station can be generated, so bud *A* cannot sprout any more immediate descendant buds.

At this point bud *D* has the lowest score. Therefore, it becomes the parent bud to sprout next.

Step 7

ORDERED SCHEDULEABLE LIST	DURATIONS	
T2	9	
T8	7	Assign T2 to station 2.
T4	5	Insert task T5 on the LIST, and so on.

The search tree developed during the execution of the procedure is presented in Figure 5.40.

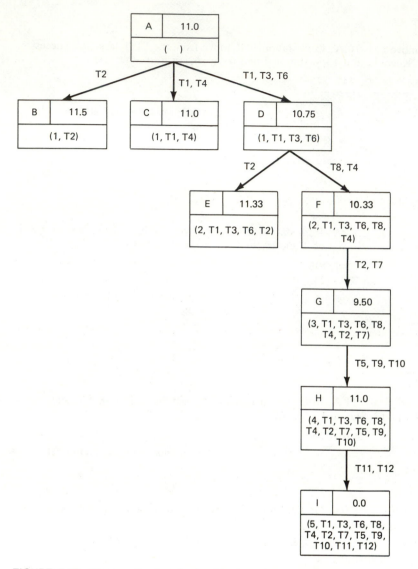

FIGURE 5.40   Enumeration tree for best bud search procedure.

Below we have the feasible sequence and the optimal five–work station balance that have been generated:

$$\underbrace{T1, T3, T6}_{\text{Station 1}} \mid \underbrace{T8, T4}_{\text{Station 2}} \mid \underbrace{T2, T7}_{\text{Station 3}} \mid \underbrace{T5, T9, T10}_{\text{Station 4}} \mid \underbrace{T11, T12}_{\text{Station 5}}$$

$p_1 = 12 \quad p_2 = 12 \quad p_3 = 12 \quad p_4 = 8 \quad p_5 = 11$

A comparison with the balance in Figure 5.37 shows that the optimal solution is not necessarily unique.

Nevins presents comparative computational results of his method and Tonge's [1965] from which the former appears superior. Unfortunately, no account is given of the computer time required by the application of the best bud search.

A heuristic version of the technique is also included in Nevins' paper.

5.4.3 Closing Notes

Our limited treatment of the production line balancing problem has skipped a number of issues, some of which will be briefly brought to the reader's attention.

- One aspect which has been only tangentially mentioned is the use of storage units or bunkers between work stations. Three basic uses of interstation storage have been identified in the literature. One is to limit the transfer of station downtime along the line, which occurs because of station breakdowns. A second is to absorb stochastic variations in operation performance times. It can be proven that the provision of bunkers increases the output of the production line. The problem has been studied under various modeling assumptions by different authors, addressing such issues as the number of storage units on the line, their location and size (Hunt [1956], Young [1967], Kraemer and Love [1970]; a survey is given by Koenigsberg [1959]). A third use is with unbalanced lines. Bunkers would store the product alternately before and after some operation which works faster than the cycle time, allowing that station to be run only for a few hours each shift. Thus, one worker would be able to service two or several such stations operating part time by turns.

- The probabilistic version of the line balancing problem has also other implications than just the aforementioned interstation storage issue. When operation times are stochastic, specific questions, in addition to the ones we have analyzed thus far, are asked: Should the line be mechanically paced or not and, if yes, what should be the speed of the belt or conveyor and how far apart should consecutive product units be spaced? A discussion of this aspect may be found in Buffa [1961]; also summarized in Buffa [1976].

  Brown [1971] suggests that some buffering should be provided in the form of time allowed between operations to compensate in case one station takes more than the standard time. Successive stations down the line require larger buffer times. This is to say that, in order to prevent the buildup of excess operation times, which can lead to saturation and shutting down the line, the average performance rate should increase with successive stations. Or, as Ignall [1965] puts it: "It may be desirable to assign work more loosely at the beginning of the line." Starr [1978] finds that, in order to cope with the variable operation time problem, managers frequently load production lines within 90% of their full capacity.

- The search for the best production line configuration tacitly implies the idea that the associated division of labor and the corresponding specialization automatically bring efficiency and high productivity. In reality, the social aspect of job specialization versus job enrichment might prove to match in importance the problem of finding a good line balancing technique.

- Finally, a word of caution and, at the same time, a direction for future efforts: the gap between research and industrial practice in the domain of balancing production lines. A survey, to which 95 companies responded (Chase and Aquilano [1973, p. 125]), showed that only five of those firms used any formalized techniques. Among the reasons invoked were the inflexibility of the techniques, especially in handling multiproduct lines, and the general complexity and unavailability of the programs themselves.

BIBLIOGRAPHY

ABDEL-WAHAB, H. M. and T. KAMEDA, "Scheduling to Minimize Maximum Cumulative Cost Subject to Series-Parallel Precedence Constraints," *Operations Research*, Vol. 26, No. 1, January–February 1978.

ALLEN, M., "The Efficient Utilization of Labor Under Conditions of Fluctuating Demand," in J. F. Muth and G. L. Thompson (editors), *Industrial Scheduling*, Prentice-Hall, Englewood Cliffs, N.J., 1963.

ARCHIBALD, R. D. and R. L. VILLORIA, *Network-Based Management Systems (PERT/CPM)*, Wiley, New York, 1967.

ARCUS, A. L., "COMSOAL: A Computer Method of Sequencing Operations for Assembly Lines," in E. S. Buffa (editor), *Readings in Production and Operations Management*, Wiley, New York, 1966.

ASHOUR, S., "A Branch-and-Bound Algorithm for Flow-Shop Scheduling Problems," *AIIE Transactions*, Vol. 2, No. 2, June 1970, pp. 172–176.

ASHOUR, S., T. E. MOORE, and K.-Y. CHIU, "An Implicit Enumeration Algorithm for the Nonpreemptive Shop Scheduling Problem," *AIIE Transactions*, Vol. 6, No. 1, March 1974, pp. 62–72.

BAKER, C. T. and B. P. DZIELINKSI, "Simulation of a Simplified Job Shop," *Management Science*, Vol. 6, No. 3, April 1960, pp. 311–323.

BAKER, K. R., *Introduction to Sequencing and Scheduling*, Wiley, New York, 1974.

BAKER, K. R., "A Comparative Study of Flow Shop Algorithms," *Operations Research*, Vol. 23, No. 1, January–February 1975, pp. 62–73.

BAKER, K. R. and A. C. MERTEN, "Scheduling with Parallel Processors and Linear Delay Costs," *Naval Research Logistics Quarterly*, Vol. 20, No. 4, December 1973, pp. 793–804.

BAKER K. R. and L. E. SCHRAGE, "Finding an Optimal Sequence by Dynamic Programming: An Extension to Precedence-Related Tasks," *Operations Research*, Vol. 26, No. 1, January–February 1978, pp. 111–120.

BAKSHI, M. S., and S. R. ARORA, "The Sequencing Problem," *Management Science*, Vol. 16, No. 4, December 1969, pp. B247–B263.

BALAS, E., "Machine Sequencing via Disjunctive Graphs: An Implicit Enumeration Algorithm," *Operations Research*, Vol. 17, No. 6, November–December 1969, pp. 941–957.

BARNES, J. W. and J. J. BRENNAN, "An Improved Algorithm for Scheduling Jobs on Identical Machines," *AIIE Transactions*, Vol. 9, No. 1, March 1977, pp. 25–31.

BELLMORE, M. and G. L. NEMHAUSER, "The Traveling Salesman Problem: A Survey," *Operations Research*, Vol. 16, No. 2, May–June 1968, pp. 538–558.

BOWMAN, E. H., "Assembly Line Balancing by Linear Programming," *Operations Research*, Vol. 8, No. 3, May–June 1960, pp. 385–389.

BRADLEY, S. P., A. C. HAX, and T. L. MAGNANTI, *Applied Mathematical Programming*, Addison-Wesley, Reading, Mass., 1977.

BROOKS, G. H. and C. R. WHITE, "An Algorithm for Finding Optimal or Near-Optimal Solutions to the Production Scheduling Problem," *Journal of Industrial Engineering*, Vol. 16, No. 1, January 1965, pp. 34–40.

BROWN, R. G., *Management Decisions for Production Operations*, Dryden Press, Hinsdale, Ill., 1971.

BRUCKER, P., J. K. LENSTRA, and A. H. G. RINNOOY KAN, "Complexity of Machine Scheduling Problems," Matematisch Centru, Amsterdam, Report BW43/75, April 1975.

BUFFA, E. S., "Pacing Effects in Production Lines," *Journal of Industrial Engineering*, Vol. 12, No. 6, November–December 1961, pp. 383–386.

BUFFA, E. S., *Operations Management*: *Problems and Models*, Wiley, New York, 1972.

BUFFA, E. S., *Operations Management*: *The Management of Productive Systems*, Wiley, New York, 1976.

BUFFA, E. S. and W. H. TAUBERT, *Production-Inventory Systems*: *Planning and Control*, Irwin, Homewood, Ill., 1972.

BULKIN, M. H., J. L. COLLEY, and H. W. STEINHOFF, JR., "Load Forecasting, Priority Sequencing, and Simulation in a Job-Shop Control System," in E. S. Buffa (editor), *Readings in Production and Operations Management*, Wiley, New York, 1966.

BURGESS, A. R. and J. B. KILLEBREW, "Variation in Activity Level on a Cyclical Arrow Diagram," *Journal of Industrial Engineering*, Vol. 13, No. 2, March–April 1962, pp. 76–83.

BURNS, F. and J. ROOKER, "Three-Stage Flow-Shops with Recessive Second Stage," *Operations Research*, Vol. 26, No. 1, January–February 1978, pp. 207–208.

BUXEY, G. M., "Assembly Line Balancing with Multiple Stations," *Management Science*, Vol. 20, No. 6, February 1974, pp. 1010–1021.

CAMPBELL, H. G., R. A. DUDEK, and M. L. SMITH, "A Heuristic Algorithm for the *n* Job *m* Machine Sequencing Problem," *Management Science*, Vol. 16, No. 10, June 1970, pp. 630–637.

CARROLL, D. C., "Heuristic Sequencing of Single and Multiple Component Jobs," unpublished Ph.D. thesis, M.I.T., Cambridge, Mass., 1965.

CHARLTON, J. M. and C. C. DEATH, "A Generalized Machine Scheduling Algorithm," *Operational Research Quarterly*, Vol. 21, No. 1, March 1970, pp. 127–134.

CHASE, R. B. and N. J. AQUILANO, *Production and Operations Management*, Irwin, Homewood, Ill., 1973.

CHO, Y. and S. SAHNI, "Preemptive Scheduling of Independent Jobs with Release and Due Times on Open, Flow and Job Shops," *Operations Research*, Vol. 29, No. 3, May–June 1981, pp. 511–522.

CLARK, C. E., "The Greatest of a Finite Set of Random Variables," *Operations Research*, Vol. 9, No. 2, March–April 1961, pp. 145–162.

CLARK, C. E., "The PERT Model for the Distribution of an Activity Time," *Operations Research*, Vol. 10, No. 3, May–June 1962, pp. 405–406.

CLINGEN, C. T., "A Modification of Fulkerson's PERT Algorithm," *Operations Research*, Vol. 12, No. 4, July–August 1964, pp. 629–632.

COFFMAN, E. G., JR. (editor), *Computer and Job-Shop Scheduling Theory*, Wiley, New York, 1976.

CONWAY, R. W., "An Experimental Investigation of Priority Assignment in a Job Shop," Memorandum RM-3789-PR, RAND Corporation, Santa Monica, Calif., February 1964.

CONWAY, R. W., "Priority Dispatching and Work-in-Process Inventory in a Job Shop," *Journal of Industrial Engineering*, Vol. 16, No. 2, March–April 1965a, pp. 123–130.

CONWAY, R. W., "Priority Dispatching and Job Lateness in a Job Shop," *Journal of Industrial Engineering*, Vol. 16, No. 4, July–August 1965b, pp. 228–237.

CONWAY, R. W., B. M. JOHNSON, and W. L. MAXWELL, "An Experimental

Investigation of Priority Dispatching," *Journal of Industrial Engineering*, Vol. 11, No. 3, May–June 1960, pp. 221–230.

CONWAY, R. W. and W. L. MAXWELL, "Network Dispatching by the Shortest Operation Discipline," *Operations Research*, Vol. 10, No. 1, January–February 1962, pp. 51–73.

CONWAY, R. W., W. L. MAXWELL and L. W. MILLER, *Theory of Scheduling*, Addison-Wesley, Reading, Mass., 1967.

CONWAY, R. W., W. L. MAXWELL, and J. W. OLDZIEY, "Sequencing Against Due Dates," Proceedings of the 4th IFORS Conference, Cambridge, Mass., September 1966.

CRABILL, T. B., "A Lower-Bound Approach to the Scheduling Problem," Research Report, Department of Industrial Engineering, Cornell University, Ithaca, N.Y., 1964.

CROWSTON, W. B., "Decision CPM: Network Reduction and Solution," *Operational Research Quarterly*, Vol. 21, No. 4, December 1970, pp. 435–452.

CROWSTON, W. B. and G. L. THOMPSON, "Decision CPM: A Method for Simultaneous Planning, Scheduling, and Control of Projects," *Operations Research*, Vol. 15, No. 3, May–June 1967, pp. 407–426.

CROWSTON, W. B. and M. H. WAGNER, "A Comparison of Tree Search Schemes for Decision Networks," Technical Report No. 380-69, Sloan School of Management, M.I.T., Cambridge, Mass., 1969 (revised September 1970).

DANNENBRING, D. G. "An Evaluation of Flow Shop Scheduling Heuristics," *Management Science*, Vol. 23, No. 11, July 1977, pp. 1174–1182.

DAR-EL, E. M. (MANSOOR), "MALB—A Heuristic Technique for Balancing Large-Scale Single-Model Assembly Lines," *AIIE Transactions*, Vol. 5, No. 4, December 1973, pp. 343–356.

DAVIS, E. W., "Resource Allocation in Project Network Models—A Survey," *Journal of Industrial Engineering*, Vol. 17, No. 4, April 1966, pp. 177–188.

DAVIS, E. W., "Project Scheduling Under Resource Constraints—Historical Review and Categorization of Procedures," *AIIE Transactions*, Vol. 5, No. 4, December 1973, pp. 297–313.

DAVIS, E. W. (editor), *Project Management: Techniques, Applications, and Managerial Issues*, Publication No. 3 in the Monograph Series, Production Planning and Control Division, American Institute of Industrial Engineers, Atlanta, Georgia, 1976.

DAVIS, E. W., "Project Management: Network-Based Scheduling Techniques," in A. C. Hax (editor), *Studies in Operations Management*, North Holland, Amsterdam, 1978.

DAVIS, E. W. and J. H. PATTERSON, "A Comparison of Heuristic and Optimum Solutions in Resource-Constrained Project Scheduling," *Management Science*, Vol. 21, No. 8, April 1975, pp. 944–955.

DAY, J. E. and M. P. HOTTENSTEIN, "Review of Sequencing Research," *Naval Research Logistics Quarterly*, Vol. 17, No. 1, March 1970, pp. 11–40.

DeWITTE, L., "Manpower Leveling of PERT Networks," *Data Processing for Science/Engineering*, Vol. 2, No. 2, March–April 1964, pp. 29–37.

DISNEY, R., "Random Flow in Queueing Networks: A Review and Critique," *AIIE Transactions*, Vol. 7, No. 3, September 1975, pp. 268–288.

DOGRAMACI, A. and J. SURKIS, "Evaluation of a Heuristic for Scheduling Independent Jobs on Parallel Identical Processors," *Management Science*, Vol. 25, No. 12, December 1979, pp. 1208–1216.

DUDEK, R. A. and O. F. TEUTON, JR., "Development of M-Stage Decision Rule for Scheduling m Jobs Through m Machines," *Operations Research*, Vol. 12, No. 3, May–June 1964, pp. 471–497.

EASTMAN, W. L., S. EVEN, and I. M. ISAACS,   "Bounds for the Optimal Scheduling of *n* Jobs on *m* Processors," *Management Science*, Vol. 11, No. 2, November 1964, pp. 268–279.

EILON, S.,   "Multi-Product Scheduling in a Chemical Plant," *Management Science*, Vol. 15, No. 6, February 1969, pp. B267–B279.

ELMAGHRABY, S. E.,   "On the Expected Duration of PERT Type Networks," *Management Science*, Vol. 13, No. 5, January 1967, pp. 299–306.

ELMAGHRABY, S. E.,   "The Machine Sequencing Problem—Review and Extensions," *Naval Research Logistics Quarterly*, Vol. 15, No. 2, June 1968, pp. 205–232.

ELMAGHRABY, S. E. and R. T. COLE,   "On the Control of Production in Small Job Shops," *Journal of Industrial Engineering*, Vol. 14, No. 4, July–August 1963, pp. 186–196.

ELMAGHRABY, S. E. and A. N. ELSHAFEI,   "Branch-and-Bound Revised: A Survey of Basic Concepts and Their Applications in Scheduling," in W. H. Marlow (editor), *Modern Trends in Logistics Research*, M.I.T. Press, Cambridge, Mass., 1976.

ELMAGHRABY, S. E. and S. PARK,   "On the Scheduling of Jobs on a Number of Identical Machines," *AIIE Transactions*, Vol. 6, No. 1, March 1974, pp. 1–13.

EMMONS, H.,   "One-Machine Sequencing to Minimize Certain Functions of Job Tardiness," *Operations Research*, Vol. 17, No. 4, July–August 1969, pp. 701–715.

FELLER, W.,   *An Introduction to Probability Theory and Its Applications*, Wiley, New York, Vol. 1, Third Edition, 1968, Vol. 2, Second Edition, 1971.

FISHER, M. L.,   "Optimal Solution of Scheduling Problems Using Lagrange Multipliers: Part I," *Operations Research*, Vol. 21, No. 5, September–October 1973a, pp. 1114–1127.

FISHER, M. L.,   "Optimal Solution of Scheduling Problems Using Lagrange Multipliers, Part II," in S. E. Elmaghraby (editor), *Symposium on the Theory of Scheduling and Its Applications*, Springer-Verlag, Berlin, 1973b.

FISHER, M. L.,   "A Dual Algorithm for the One-Machine Scheduling Problem," *Mathematical Programming*, Vol. 11, No. 3, December 1976, pp. 229–251.

FISHER, M. L. and R. JAIKUMAR,   "An Algorithm for the Space-Shuttle Scheduling Problem," *Operations Research*, Vol. 26, No. 1, January–February 1978, pp. 166–182.

FLORIAN, M., P. TRÉPANT, and G. McMAHON,   "An Implicit Enumeration Algorithm for the Machine Sequencing Problem," *Management Science*, Vol. 17, No. 12, August 1971, pp. B782–B792.

FONDAHL, J. W.,   "A Non-Computer Approach to the Critical Path Method for the Construction Industry," Technical Report No. 9, Construction Institute, Stanford University, 1961 (revised 1962).

FORD, L. R., JR. and D. R. FULKERSON,   *Flows in Networks*, Princeton University Press, Princeton, N.J., 1974.

FULKERSON, D. R.,   "A Network Flow Computation for Project Cost Curves," *Management Science*, Vol. 7, No. 2, January 1961, pp. 167–178.

FULKERSON, D. R.,   "Expected Critical Path Lengths in PERT Networks," *Operations Research*, Vol. 10, No. 6, November–December 1962, pp. 808–817.

GAREY, M. R., R. L. GRAHAM, and D. S. JOHNSON,   "Performance Guarantees for Scheduling Algorithms," *Operations Research*, Vol. 26, No. 1, January–February 1978, pp. 3–21.

GAREY, M. R., D. S. JOHNSON, and R. SETHI,   "Complexity of Flow Shop and Job Shop Scheduling," *Mathematics of Operations Research*, Vol. 1, No. 2, May 1976, pp. 117–129.

GELDERS, L. and P. R. KLEINDORFER,   "Coordinating Aggregate and Detailed

Scheduling Decisions in the One-Machine Job Shop: Part I. Theory," *Operations Research*, Vol. 22, No. 1, January–February 1974, pp. 46–60.

GELDERS, L. and P. R. KLEINDORFER, "Coordinating Aggregate and Detailed Scheduling Decisions in the One-Machine Job Shop: Part II. Computation and Structure," *Operations Research*, Vol. 23, No. 2, March–April 1975, pp. 312–324.

GERE, W. S., "Heuristics in Job Shop Scheduling," *Management Science*, Vol. 13, No. 3, November 1966, pp. 167–190.

GERTSBAKH, I. and H. I. STERN, "Minimal Resources for Fixed and Variable Job Schedules," *Operations Research*, Vol. 26, No. 1, January–February 1978, pp. 68–85.

GIFFLER, B. and G. L. THOMPSON, "Algorithms for Solving Production Scheduling Problems," *Operations Research*, Vol. 8, No. 4, July–August 1960, pp. 487–503.

GIFFLER, B., G. L. THOMPSON, and V. VAN NESS, "Numerical Experience with the Linear and Monte Carlo Algorithms for Solving Production Scheduling Problems," in J. F. Muth and G. L. Thompson (editors), *Industrial Scheduling*, Prentice-Hall, Englewood Cliffs, N.J., 1963.

GIGLIO, R. J. and H. M. WAGNER, "Approximate Solutions to the Three-Machine Scheduling Problem," *Operations Research*, Vol. 12, No. 2, March–April 1964, pp. 305–324.

GOLDBERG, H. M., "Analysis of the Earliest Due Date Scheduling Rule in Queueing Systems," *Mathematics of Operations Research*, Vol. 2, No. 2, May 1977, pp. 145–154.

GOLOVIN, J., "A Survey of the Inventory Control–Detailed Scheduling Problem," Technical Report No. 84, Operations Research Center, M.I.T., Cambridge, Mass., September 1973.

GONZALEZ, T. and S. SAHNI, "Flowshop and Jobshop Schedules: Complexity and Approximation," *Operations Research*, Vol. 26, No. 1, January–February 1978, pp. 36–52.

GRAVES, S. C., "A Review of Production Scheduling," *Operations Research*, Vol. 29, No. 4, July–August 1981, pp. 646–675.

GREENBERG, H., "A Branch and Bound Solution to the General Scheduling Problem," *Operations Research*, Vol. 16, No. 2, March–April 1968, pp. 353–361.

GRUBBS, F. F., "Attempts to Validate Certain PERT Statistics, or: Picking on PERT," *Operations Research*, Vol. 10, No. 6, November–December 1962, pp. 912–915.

GUPTA, J. N. D., "*M*-Stage Flow Shop Scheduling by Branch and Bound," *Operations Research*, Vol. 7, No. 1, January–February 1970, pp. 37–43.

GUPTA, J. N. D., "Heuristic Algorithms for Multistage Flow Shop Problem," *AIIE Transactions*, Vol. 4, No. 1, March 1972, pp. 11–18.

GUPTA, J. N. D. and R. A. DUDEK, "Optimality Criteria for Flow Shop Schedules," *AIIE Transactions*, Vol. 3, No. 3, September 1971, pp. 239–245.

GUPTA, J. N. D. and S. S. REDDI, "Improved Dominance Conditions for the Three-Machine Flowshop Scheduling Problem," *Operations Research*, Vol. 26, No. 1, January–February 1978, pp. 200–203.

GUTJAHR, A. L. and G. L. NEMHAUSER, "An Algorithm for the Line Balancing Problem," *Management Science*, Vol. 11, No. 2, November 1964, pp. 308–315.

HARRIS, R. D., "An Empirical Investigation and Model Proposal of a Job Shop-Like Queueing System," Western Management Science Institute, UCLA, Working Paper No. 84, Los Angeles, July 1965.

HARTLEY, H. D. and A. W. WORTHAM, "A Statistical Theory for PERT Critical Path Analysis," *Management Science*, Vol. 12, No. 10, June 1966, pp. 469–481.

HASTINGS, N. A. J. and J. B. PEACOCK, *Statistical Distributions*, London Butterworths, London, 1975.

HELD, M., R. M. KARP, and R. SHARESHIAN, "Assembly Line Balancing—Dynamic Programming with Precedence Constraints," *Operations Research*, Vol. 11, No. 3, May–June 1963, pp. 442–459.

HELGESON, W. P. and D. P. BIRNIE, "Assembly Line Balancing Using the Ranked Positional Weight Technique," *Journal of Industrial Engineering*, Vol. 12, No. 6, November–December 1961, pp. 394–398.

HOFFMANN, T. R., "Assembly Line Balancing with a Precedence Matrix," *Management Science*, Vol. 9, No. 4, July 1963, pp. 561–563.

HOLTZMAN, J. M., "Bounds for a Dynamic Priority Queue," *Operations Research*, Vol. 19, No. 2, March–April 1971, pp. 461–468.

HORN, W. A., "Minimizing Average Flow Time with Parallel Machines," *Operations Research*, Vol. 21, No. 3, May–June 1973, pp. 846–847.

HOTTENSTEIN, M. P., "A Simulation Study of Expediting in a Job Shop," *Production and Inventory Management*, Vol. 10, Second Quarter 1969, pp. 1–11.

HOTTENSTEIN, M. P., "Expediting in Job-Order-Control Systems: A Simulation Study," *AIIE Transactions*, Vol. 2, No. 1, March 1970, pp. 46–54.

HUNT, G. C., "Sequential Arrays of Waiting Lines," *Operations Research*, Vol. 4, No. 6, December 1956, pp. 674–683.

IGNALL, E. J., "A Review of Assembly Line Balancing," *Journal of Industrial Engineering*, Vol. 15, No. 4, July–August 1965, pp. 244–254.

IGNALL, E. J. and L. E. SCHRAGE, "Application of the Branch-and-Bound Technique to Some Flow-Shop Scheduling Problems," *Operations Research*, Vol. 13, No. 3, May–June 1965, pp. 400–412.

JACKSON, J. R., "An Extension of Johnson's Results on Job-Lot Scheduling," *Naval Research Logistics Quarterly*, Vol. 3, No. 3, September 1956a, pp. 201–224.

JACKSON, J. R., "A Computing Procedure for a Line Balancing Problem," *Management Science*, Vol. 2, No. 3, April 1956b, pp. 261–271.

JACKSON, J. R., "Networks of Waiting Lines," *Operations Research*, Vol. 5, No. 4, August 1957, pp. 518–521.

JACKSON, J. R., "Some Problems in Queueing with Dynamic Priorities," *Naval Research Logistics Quarterly*, Vol. 7, No. 3, September 1960, pp. 235–250.

JACKSON, J. R., "Queues with Dynamic Priority Disciplines," *Management Science*, Vol. 8, No. 1, October 1961, pp. 18–34.

JACKSON, J. R., "Waiting-Time Distribution for Queues with Dynamic Priorities," *Naval Research Logistics Quarterly*, Vol. 9, No. 1, March 1962, pp. 31–36.

JACKSON, J. R., "Job Shop-Like Queueing Systems," *Management Science*, Vol. 10, No. 1, October 1963, pp. 131–142.

JENETTE, E., "Experience with and Evaluation of Critical Path Methods," in E. W. Davis (editor), *Project Management: Techniques, Applications and Managerial Issues*, Publication No. 3 in Monograph Series, Production Planning and Control Division, American Institute of Industrial Engineers, Atlanta, Georgia, 1976.

JEREMIAH, B., A. LALCHANDANI, and L. SCHRAGE, "Heuristic Rules Toward Optimal Scheduling," Research Report, Department of Industrial Engineering, Cornell University, Ithaca, N.Y., 1964.

JOHNSON, L. A. and D. C. MONTGOMERY, *Operations Research in Production Planning, Scheduling, and Inventory Control*, Wiley, New York, 1974.

JOHNSON, S. M., "Optimal Two- and Three-Stage Production Schedules with Setup Times Included," *Naval Research Logistics Quarterly*, Vol. 1, No. 1, March 1954, pp. 61–68.

JOHNSON, T. J. R., "An Algorithm for the Resource Constrained Project Scheduling Problem," unpublished Ph.D. thesis, Sloan School of Management, M.I.T., Cambridge, Mass., August 1967.

JONES, C. H., "An Economic Evaluation of Job Shop Dispatching Rules," *Management Science*, Vol. 20, No. 3, November 1973, pp. 293–307.

KARP, R. M., "Reducibility Among Combinatorial Problems," in R. E. Miller and J. W. Thatcher (editors), *Complexity of Computer Computations*, Plenum Press, New York, 1972.

KARP, R. M., "On the Computational Complexity of Combinatorial Problems," *Networks*, Vol. 5, 1975, pp. 45–68.

KELLEY, J. E., JR., "Critical Path Planning and Scheduling: Mathematical Basis," *Operations Research*, Vol. 9, No. 3, May–June 1961, pp. 296–320.

KELLEY, J. E., JR., "Scheduling Activities to Satisfy Constraints on Resources," in J. F. Muth and G. L. Thompson (editors), *Industrial Scheduling*, Prentice-Hall, Englewood Cliffs, N.J., 1963.

KELLEY, J. E., JR. and M. R. WALKER, "Critical Path Planning and Scheduling," in *Proceedings of the Eastern Joint Computer Conference*, Boston, December 1959.

KILBRIDGE, M. D. and L. WESTER, "A Heuristic Method of Assembly Line Balancing," *Journal of Industrial Engineering*, Vol. 12, No. 4, July–August 1961a, pp. 292–298.

KILBRIDGE, M. D. and L. WESTER, "The Balance Delay Problem," *Management Science*, Vol. 8, No. 1, October 1961b, pp. 69–84.

KISE, H., T. IBARAKI, and H. MINE, "A Solvable Case of the One-Machine Scheduling Problem with Ready and Due Times," *Operations Research*, Vol. 26, No. 1, January–February 1978, pp. 121–126.

KOENIGSBERG, E., "Production Lines and Internal Storage—A Review," *Management Science*, Vol. 5, No. 4, July 1959, pp. 410–433.

KRAEMER, S. A. and R. F. LOVE, "A Model for Optimizing the Buffer Inventory Storage Size in a Sequential Production System," *AIIE Transactions*, Vol. 2, No. 1, March 1970, pp. 64–69.

LAGEWEG, B. J., J. K. LENSTRA, and A. H. G. RINNOOY KAN, "Job-Shop Scheduling by Implicit Enumeration," *Management Science*, Vol. 24, No. 4, December 1977, pp. 441–450.

LAWLER, E. L., "On Scheduling Problems with Deferral Costs," *Management Science*, Vol. 11, No. 2, November 1964, pp. 280–288.

LeGRANDE, E., "The Development of a Factory Simulation System Using Actual Operating Data," in E. S. Buffa (editor), *Readings in Production and Operations Management*, Wiley, New York, 1966.

LEMOINE, A. J., "Networks of Queues—A Survey of Equilibrium Analysis," *Management Science*, Vol. 24, No. 4, December 1977, pp. 464–481.

LENSTRA, J. K., A. H. G. RINNOOY KAN, and P. BRUCKER, "Complexity of Machine Scheduling Problems," *Annals of Discrete Mathematics*, Vol. 1, 1977, pp. 343–362.

LENSTRA, J. K. and A. H. G. RINNOOY KAN, "Complexity of Scheduling Under Precedence Constraints," *Operations Research*, Vol. 26, No. 1, January–February 1978, pp. 22–35.

LEVY, F. K., G. L. THOMPSON, and J. D. WIEST, "Multi-ship, Multi-shop, Workload Smoothing Program," *Naval Research Logistics Quarterly*, Vol. 9, No. 1, March 1962, pp. 37–44.

LEVY, F. K., G. L. THOMPSON, and J. D. WIEST, "The ABC's of the Critical Path Method," *Harvard Business Review*, Vol. 41, No. 5, September–October 1963, pp. 98–108.

LEWIN, D. E., "On Assembly Line Balancing and Related Topics," unpublished master's thesis, Alfred P. Sloan School of Management, M.I.T., Cambridge, Mass, 1967.

LOMNICKI, Z., "A Branch-and-Bound Algorithm for the Exact Solution of the Three-Machine Scheduling Problem," *Operational Research Quarterly*, Vol. 16, No. 1, March 1965, pp. 89–100.

MacCRIMMON, K. R. and C. A. RYAVEC, "An Analytical Study of the PERT Assumptions," *Operations Research*, Vol. 12, No. 1, January–February 1964, pp. 16–37.

MAGEE, J. F. and D. M. BOODMAN, *Production Planning and Inventory Control*, McGraw-Hill, New York, 1967.

MALCOLM, D. G., J. H. ROSEBOOM, C. E. CLARK, and W. FAZAR, "Applications of a Technique for Research and Development Program Evaluation," *Operations Research*, Vol. 7, No. 5, September–October 1959, pp. 646–669.

MANNE, A. S., "On the Job—Shop Scheduling Problem," *Operations Research*, Vol. 8, No. 2, March–April 1960, pp. 219–223.

MANSOOR, E. M., "Assembly Line Balancing—An Improvement on the Ranked Positional Weight Technique," *Journal of Industrial Engineering*, Vol. 15, No. 2, March–April 1964, pp. 73–77.

MARTIN, C. C., *Project Management — How to Make It Work*, AMACOM, New York, 1976.

MARTIN, J. J., "Distribution of the Time Through a Directed Acyclic Network," *Operations Research*, Vol. 13, No. 1, January–February 1965, pp. 46–66.

MASTOR, A. A., "An Experimental Investigation and Comparative Evaluation of Production Line Balancing Techniques," *Management Science*, Vol. 16, No. 11, July 1970, pp. 728–746.

MAXWELL, W. L., "On Sequencing *n* Jobs on One Machine to Minimize the Number of Late Jobs," *Management Science*, Vol. 16, No. 5, January 1970, pp. 295–297.

MAXWELL, W. L. and M. MEHRA, "Multiple-Factor Rules for Sequencing with Assembly Constraints," *Naval Research Logistics Quarterly*, Vol. 15, No. 2, June 1968, pp. 241–254.

McMAHON, G. B. and P. G. BURTON, "Flow Shop Scheduling with the Branch-and-Bound Method," *Operations Research*, Vol. 15, No. 3, May–June 1967, pp. 473–481.

McNAUGHTON, R., "Scheduling with Deadlines and Loss Functions," *Management Science*, Vol. 6, No. 1, October 1959, pp. 1–12.

MEAL, H. C., "A Study of Multi-Stage Production Planning," in A. C. Hax (editor), *Studies in Operations Management*, North Holland, Amsterdam, 1978.

MELLOR, P., "A Review of Job Shop Scheduling," in G. K. Groff and J. F. Muth (editors), *Operations Management — Selected Readings*, Irwin, Homewood, Ill., 1969.

MEYER, W. L. and L. R. SHAFFER, "Extensions of the Critical Path Method Through the Application of Integer Programming," Report issued by the Department of Civil Engineering, University of Illinois, Urbana, July 1963.

MODER, J. J. and C. R. PHILLIPS, *Project Management with CPM and PERT*, Van Nostrand Reinhold, New York, 1970.

MODER, J. J., and E. G. RODGERS, "Judgement Estimates of the Moments of PERT Type Distributions," *Management Science*, Vol. 15, No. 2, October 1968, pp. B76–B83.

MOELLER, G. L., "VERT," *Technical Papers: Twenty-Third Institute Conference and Convention*, American Institute of Industrial Engineers, Atlanta, Georgia, 1972.

MOELLER, G. L. and L. A. DIGMAN, "Operations Planning with VERT," *Operations Research*, Vol. 29, No. 4, July–August 1981, pp. 676–697.

MOODIE, C. L. and D. J. NOVOTNY, "Computer Scheduling and Control Systems for Discrete Part Production," *Journal of Industrial Engineering*, Vol. 19, No. 7, July 1968, pp. 336–341.

MOODIE, C. L. and H. H. YOUNG, "A Heuristic Method of Assembly Line

Balancing for Assumptions of Constant or Variable Work Element Times," *Journal of Industrial Engineering*, Vol. 16, No. 1, January–February 1965, pp. 23–29.

MOORE, J. M.,   "An *n*-Job, One-Machine Sequencing Algorithm for Minimizing the Number of Late Jobs," *Management Science*, Vol. 15, No. 1, September 1968, pp. 102–109.

MOORE, J. M. and R. C. WILSON,   "A Review of Simulation Research in Job Shop Scheduling," *Production and Inventory Management*, Vol. 8, No. 1, 1967, pp. 1–10.

MOORE, L. J. and B. W. RAYLOR, III,   "Multiteam, Multiproject Research and Development Planning with GERT," *Management Science*, Vol. 24, No. 4, December 1977, pp. 401–410.

MORTON, T. E. and B. G. DHARAN,   "Algoristics Single-Machine Sequencing with Precedence Constraints," *Management Science*, Vol. 24, No. 10, June 1978, pp. 1011–1020.

MOSHMAN, J., J. JOHNSON, and M. LARSEN,   sponsored by American Federation of Information Processing Societies "RAMPS—A Technique for Resource Allocation and Multi-Project Scheduling," in *Proceedings*: *Joint Computer Conference Proceedings*, Vol. 23, Baltimore: Spartan 1963.

MUNTZ, R. R. and E. G. COFFMAN,   "Optimal Preemptive Scheduling on Two-Processor Systems," *IEEE Transactions on Computers*, Vol. C-18, No. 1, November 1969, pp. 1014–1020.

MURRAY, J. E.,   "Considerations of PERT Assumptions," *IEEE Transactions*, EM-10, 1963, pp. 94–99.

NATIONAL AERONAUTICS AND SPACE ADMINISTRATION,   *PERT and Companion Cost System*, U.S. Government Printing Office, Washington, D.C., October 1962.

NEIMEIER, H. A.,   "An Investigation of Alternative Routing in a Job Shop," unpublished master's thesis, Cornell University, Ithaca, N.Y., June 1967.

NELSON, R. T.,   "Labor and Machine Limited Production Systems," *Management Science*, Vol. 13, No. 9, May 1967, pp. 648–671.

NEVINS, A. J.,   "Assembly Line Balancing Using Best Bud Search," *Management Science*, Vol. 18, No. 9, May 1972, pp. 529–539.

NUNNIKHOVEN, R. S. and H. EMMONS,   "Scheduling on Parallel Machines to Minimize Two Criteria Related to Job Tardiness," *AIIE Transactions*, Vol. 9, No. 3, September 1977, pp. 288–296.

PAIGE, H. W.,   "How PERT-Cost Helps the General Manager," *Harvard Business Review*, Vol. 41, No. 6, November–December 1963, pp. 87–95.

PALMER, D. S.,   "Sequencing Jobs Through a Multi-Stage Process in the Minimum Total Time—A Quick Method of Obtaining a Near Optimum," *Operational Research Quarterly*, Vol. 16, No. 1, March 1965, pp. 101–107.

PANWALKAR, S. S., R. A. DUDEK, and M. L. SMITH,   "Sequencing Research and the Industrial Scheduling Problem," in S. E. Elmaghraby (editor), *Symposium on the Theory of Scheduling and Its Applications*, Springer-Verlag, Berlin, 1973.

PANWALKAR, S. S. and W. ISKANDER,   "A Survey of Scheduling Rules," *Operations Research*, Vol. 25, No. 1, January–February 1977, pp. 45–61.

PAPADIMITRIOU, C. H. and K. STEIGLITZ,   "Some Examples of Difficult Traveling Salesman Problems," *Operations Research*, Vol. 26, No. 3, May–June 1978, pp. 434–443.

PARKER, R. G., R. H. DEANE, and R. A. HOLMES,   "On the Use of a Vehicle Routing Algorithm for the Parallel Processor Problem with Sequence Dependent Changeover Costs," *AIIE Transactions*, Vol. 9, No. 2, June 1977, pp. 155–160.

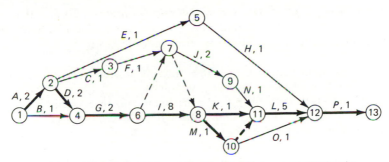

a. Activity *M* shortened to 1 day; project duration 21 days; two critical paths

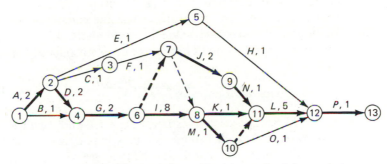

b. Activity *M* shortened to 1 day, activity *I* shortened to 2 days; project
duration 15 days; three critical paths

FIGURE 5.29   Shortening the reconstruction project by speeding up critical activities.

1-2-4-6-8-11-12-13 becomes critical and imposes a minimum length of 21 days
upon the project (Figure 5.29a). Notice that the subcritical path of 8–11 has
turned into critical. If a further reduction is sought, activity *I* may be
shortened to 2 days, at which point a new critical path 1-2-4-6-7-9-11-12-13 of
15 days emerges (Figure 5.29b). Subcritical path 7-9-11 has been "activated."
Obviously, any attempt to shorten the project by further reducing the duration
of *I* is bound to be fruitless. The topic will be taken up later in section 5.3.4.

5.3.3   The PERT Probabilistic Calculations

As mentioned earlier, in the case of projects in which activity durations are
uncertain, the activity scheduling calculations of section 5.3.2 are performed
using the expected values of the durations. One question to raise is how are the
expected durations estimated and, more generally, how can one describe
uncertain activity performance times. Then, after activity scheduling is
completed, one would like to know how much credibility can be attached to
results obtained by a deterministic technique applied to a probabilistic problem.
In this section, we show the answers the PERT probabilistic approach offers to
these and other related questions.

Probabilistic Characterization of Activity Durations. Rather than trying to estimate directly the expected performance time of an activity, PERT developers chose to estimate three duration times instead:

- The optimistic duration, o, is the shortest possible time to complete the activity, assuming most favorable conditions.
- The pessimistic duration, p, is the maximum time that would be necessary to perform the activity under most unfavorable conditions.*
- The most likely duration, m.

To use these values, one must specify the kind of probability distribution associated with the activity duration. Clark [1962] proposed to use the beta distribution[†] for this purpose. His proposal has become extensively accepted. Under this assumption, the expected value of the activity duration can be approximated by a linear combination of the three times introduced above:

$$\text{Estimated average activity duration} = \hat{\mu} = \frac{o + 4m + p}{6}. \qquad (5.15)$$

Notice that the PERT approach to estimate expected performance time is most useful in the case of skew distributions where it is easier to produce a judgment of what the most probable duration is, together with the optimistic and pessimistic values, rather than to think in terms of average duration times.

To determine the duration variance, PERT makes use of the unimodality property of the beta distribution. With unimodal probability distributions, one can always find an interval of variate values of six standard deviations to contain the great majority of the distribution. Hence, PERT approximates the standard deviation as one-sixth of the range assumed by the variate:

$$\text{Estimated standard deviation of activity duration} = \hat{\sigma} = \frac{p - o}{6}. \qquad (5.16)$$

---

*Unfavorable conditions do not include unusual acts of nature such as floods, earthquakes, etc.

[†]The beta probability density function for random variable Y contained in the interval $[o, p]$ is:

$$\frac{1}{(p - o)B(v, w)}\left[\frac{Y - o}{p - o}\right]^{v-1}\left[\frac{p - Y}{p - o}\right]^{w-1},$$

where $v > 0$, $w > 0$ are shape parameters and $B(v, w)$ is the complete beta function:

$$B(v, w) = \int_0^1 u^{v-1}(1 - u)^{w-1} \, du.$$

The beta distribution is particularly fit for the probabilistic description of activity durations as it is defined on a finite and nonnegative interval of variate values, is unimodal for $v > 1$ and $w > 1$, and can attain a wide variety of different shapes, both skewed and symmetrical, depending on v and w (see Hastings and Peacock [1975]).

PHILLIPS, S., JR. and M. I. DESSOUKY, "Solving the Project Time/Cost Tradeoff Problem Using the Minimal Cut Concept," *Management Science*, Vol. 24, No. 4, December 1977, pp. 393–400.

PICARD, J.-C. and M. QUEYRANNE, "The Time-Dependent Traveling Salesman Problem and Its Application to the Tardiness Problem in One-Machine Scheduling," *Operations Research*, Vol. 26, No. 1, January–February 1978, pp. 86–110.

PLANE, D. R. and C. McMILLAN, JR., *Discrete Optimization*, Prentice-Hall, Englewood Cliffs, N.J., 1971.

POGGIOLI, P., Pratique de la Méthode PERT, Les Editions d'Organisation, Paris, 1970.

POUNDS, W. F., "The Scheduling Environment," in J. F. Muth and G. L. Thompson (editors), *Industrial Scheduling*, Prentice-Hall, Englewood Cliffs, N.J., 1963.

PRENTING, T. D. and R. M. BATTAGLIN, "The Precedence Diagram: A Tool for Analysis in Assembly Line Balancing," *Journal of Industrial Engineering*, Vol. 15, No. 4, July–August 1964, pp. 208–213.

PRITSKER, A. A. B. and W. W. HAPP, "GERT: Graphical Evaluation and Review Technique, Part I: Fundamentals," *Journal of Industrial Engineering*, Vol. 17, No. 5, May 1966, pp. 267–274.

PRITSKER, A. A. B., L. S. WATTERS, and P. M. WOLFE, "Multi-Project Scheduling with Limited Resources: A Zero-One Programming Approach," *Management Science*, Vol. 16, No. 1, September 1969, pp. 93–108.

PRITSKER, A. A. B. and G. E. WHITEHOUSE, "GERT: Graphical Evaluation and Review Technique, Part II: Probabilistic and Industrial Engineering Applications," *Journal of Industrial Engineering*, Vol. 17, No. 6, June 1966, pp. 293–299.

REITER, S., "A System for Managing Job-Shop Production," *Journal of Business*, Vol. 39, No. 3, July 1966, pp. 371–393.

RINNOOY KAN, A. H. G., B. J. LAGEWEG, and J. K. LENSTRA, "Minimizing Total Costs in One-Machine Scheduling," *Operations Research*, Vol. 23, No. 5, September–October 1975, pp. 908–927.

ROBILLARD, P. and M. TRAHAN, "The Completion Time of PERT Networks," *Operations Research*, Vol. 25, No. 1, January–February 1977, pp. 15–29.

ROOT, J. G., "Scheduling with Deadlines and Loss Functions on k Parallel Machines," *Management Science*, Vol. 11, No. 3, January 1965, pp. 460–475.

ROTHKOPF, M., "Scheduling Independent Tasks on Parallel Processors," *Management Science*, Vol. 12, No. 5, January 1966, pp. 437–477.

RUSSO, F. J., "A Heuristic Approach to Alternate Routing in a Job Shop," master's thesis, M.I.T., Cambridge, Mass., June 1965.

SAHNI, S., "Preemptive Scheduling with Due Dates," *Operations Research*, Vol. 27, No. 5, September–October 1979, pp. 925–934.

SALVADOR, M. S., "Scheduling and Sequencing," in J. J. Moder and S. E. Elmaghraby (editors), *Handbook of Operations Research: Models and Applications*, Van Nostrand Reinhold, New York, 1978.

SALVESON, M. E., "The Assembly Line Balancing Problem," *Journal of Industrial Engineering*, Vol. 6, No. 3, May–June 1955, pp. 18–25.

SCHRAGE, L. E., "Some Queueing Models for a Time-Shared Facility," unpublished Ph.D. thesis, Cornell University, Ithaca, N.Y., February 1966.

SCHRAGE, L. E., "A Proof of the Optimality of the Shortest Remaining Service Time Discipline," *Operations Research*, Vol. 16, No. 3, May–June 1968, pp. 687–690.

SCHRAGE, L. E. and K. R. BAKER, "Dynamic Programming Solution of

Sequencing Problems with Precedence Constraints," *Operations Research*, Vol. 26, No. 3, May–June 1978, pp. 444–449.

SETHI, R.   "On the Complexity of Mean Flow Time Scheduling," *Mathematics of Operations Research*, Vol. 2, No. 4, November 1977, pp. 320–330.

SHWIMER, J.,   "On the *n*-Job, One-Machine Sequence-Independent Scheduling Problem with Tardiness Penalties: A Branch-and-Bound Approach," *Management Science*, Vol. 18, No. 6, February 1972a, pp. B301–313.

SHWIMER, J.,   "Interaction Between Aggregate and Detailed Scheduling in a Job Shop," unpublished Ph.D. thesis, M.I.T., Cambridge, Mass., June 1972b.

SMITH, D. R.,   "A New Proof of the Optimality of the Shortest Remaining Processing Time Discipline," *Operations Research*, Vol. 26, No. 1, January–February 1978, pp. 197–199.

SMITH, R. D. and R. A. DUDEK,   "A General Algorithm for the Solution of the *n*-Job, *m*-Machine Sequencing Problem of the Flow Shop," *Operations Research*, Vol. 15, No. 1, January–February 1967, pp. 71–81.

SMITH, W. E.,   "Various Optimizers for Single-State Production," *Naval Research Logistics Quarterly*, Vol. 3, No. 1, March 1956, pp. 59–66.

SOUDER, W. E.,   "Project Selection, Planning and Control," in J. J. Moder and S. E. Elmaghraby (editors), *Handbook of Operations Research*, Van Nostrand Reinhold, New York, 1978.

SRINIVASAN, V.,   "A Hybrid Algorithm for the One-Machine Sequencing Problem to Minimize Total Tardiness," *Naval Research Logistics Quarterly*, Vol. 18, No. 3, September 1971, pp. 317–327.

STARR, M. K.,   *Operations Management*, Prentice-Hall, Englewood Cliffs, N.J., 1978.

STEUDEL, N. J., S. M. PANDIT, and S. M. WU,   "A Multiple Time Series Approach to Modeling the Manufacturing Job-Shop as a Network of Queues," *Management Science*, Vol. 24, No. 4, December 1977, pp. 456–463.

STORY, A. E. and H. M. WAGNER,   "Computational Experience with Integer Programming for Job-Shop Scheduling," in J. F. Muth and G. L. Thompson (editors), *Industrial Scheduling*, Prentice-Hall, Englewood Cliffs, N.J., 1963, chap. 14.

SU, Z. S. and K. C. SEVCIK,   "A Combinatorial Approach to Dynamic Scheduling Problems," *Operations Research*, Vol. 26, No. 5, September–October 1978, pp. 836–844.

SZWARC, W.,   "Elimination Methods in the $m \times n$ Sequencing Problem," *Naval Research Logistics Quarterly*, Vol. 18, No. 3, September 1971, pp. 295–305.

SZWARC, W.,   "Optimal Elimination Methods in the $m \times n$ Flow Shop Scheduling Problem," *Operations Research*, Vol. 21, No. 6, November–December 1973, pp. 1250–1259.

SZWARC, W.,   "Special Cases of the Flow-Shop Problem," *Naval Research Logistics Quarterly*, Vol. 24, No. 3, September 1977, pp. 483–492.

SZWARC, W.,   "Dominance Conditions for the Three-Machine Flow-Shop Problem," *Operations Research*, Vol. 26, No. 1, January–February 1978, pp. 203–206.

SZWARC, W.,   "Extreme Solutions of the Two Machine Flow-Shop Problem," *Naval Research Logistics Quarterly*, Vol. 28, No. 1, March 1981, pp. 103–114.

TALBOT, F. B. and J. H. PATTERSON,   "An Efficient Integer Programming Algorithm with Network Cuts for Solving Resource-Constrained Scheduling Problems," *Management Science*, Vol. 24, No. 11, July 1978, pp. 1163–1174.

THANGAVELU, S. R. and C. M. SHETTY,   "Assembly Line Balancing by Zero-One Integer Programming," *AIIE Transactions*, Vol. 3, No. 1, March 1971, pp. 61–68.

THOMOPOULOS, N. T.,   "Line Balancing—Sequencing for Mixed Model Assembly," *Management Science*, Vol. 14, No. 2, October 1967, pp. B59–B75.

THOMOPOULOS, N. T.,   "Mixed Model Line Balancing with Smoothed Station Assignments," *Management Science*, Vol. 16, No. 9, May 1970, pp. 593–602.

TONGE, F. M., *A Heuristic Program for Assembly Line Balancing*, Ford Foundation Doctoral Dissertation Series 1960 Winner, Prentice-Hall, Englewood Cliffs, N.J., 1961.

TONGE, F. M., "Assembly Line Balancing Using Probabilistic Combinations of Heuristics," *Management Science*, Vol. 11, No. 7, May 1965, pp. 727–735.

TRILLING, D. R., "Job Shop Simulation of Orders That Are Networks," *Journal of Industrial Engineering*, Vol. 17, No. 2, February 1966, pp. 59–91.

VAN SLYKE, R. M., "Monte Carlo Methods and the PERT Problem," *Operations Research*, Vol. 11, No. 5, September–October 1963, pp. 839–860.

WAYSON, R. D., "The Effects of Alternate Machines on Two Priority Dispatching Disciplines in the General Job Shops," master's thesis, Cornell University, Ithaca, N.Y., February 1965.

WEGLARZ, J., "Project Scheduling with Continuously-Divisible, Doubly Constrained Resources," *Management Science*, Vol. 27, No. 9, September 1981, pp. 1040–1053.

WESTER, L. and M. D. KILBRIDGE, "Heuristic Line Balancing—A Case," *Journal of Industrial Engineering*, Vol. 13, No. 3, May–June 1962a, pp. 139–149.

WESTER, L. and M. D. KILBRIDGE, "A Review of Analytical Systems of Line Balancing," *Operations Research*, Vol. 10, No. 5, September–October 1962b, pp. 626–638.

WESTER, L. and M. D. KILBRIDGE, "The Assembly Line Model-Mix Sequencing Problem," in *Proceedings of the Third International Conference on Operational Research*, Oslo (Norway), Dunod, Paris, 1964.

WHITE, W. W., "Comments on a Paper by Bowman," *Operations Research*, Vol. 9, No. 2, March–April 1961, pp. 274–276.

WHITEHOUSE, G. E., *Systems Analysis and Design Using Network Techniques*, Prentice-Hall, Englewood Cliffs, N.J., 1973.

WIEST, J. D., "Heuristic Programs for Decision Making," *Harvard Business Review*, Vol. 44, No. 5, September–October 1966, pp. 129–143.

WIEST, J. D., "A Heuristic Model for Scheduling Large Projects with Limited Resources," *Management Science*, Vol. 13, No. 6, February 1967, pp. B359–B377.

WIEST, J. D. and F. K. LEVY, *A Management Guide to PERT/CPM: with GERT/PDM/DCPM and Other Networks*, Prentice-Hall, Englewood Cliffs, N.J., 1977.

WILKERSON, L. J. and J. D. IRWIN, "An Improved Algorithm for Scheduling Independent Tasks," *AIIE Transactions*, Vol. 3, No. 3, September 1971, pp. 239–245.

YOUNG, H. H., "Optimization Models for Production Lines," *Journal of Industrial Engineering*, Vol. 18, No. 1, January 1967, pp. 70–78.

ZIMMERMANN, H.-J. and M. G. SOVEREIGN, *Quantitative Models for Production Management*, Prentice-Hall, Englewood Cliffs, N.J., 1974.

6

Hierarchical Production Planning Systems

6.1 Introduction

Production can be defined as the process of converting raw materials into finished products. An effective management of the production process should provide the finished products in appropriate quantities, at the desired times, of the required quality, and at a reasonable cost.

As we indicated in Chapter 1, production management encompasses a large number of decisions that affect several organizational echelons. These decisions can be grouped into three broad categories:

1. strategic decisions, involving policy formulation, capital investment decisions, and design of physical facilities
2. tactical decisions, dealing primarily with aggregate production planning
3. operational decisions, concerning detailed production scheduling issues

These three categories of decisions differ markedly in terms of level of management responsibility and interaction, scope of the decision, level of detail of the required information, length of the planning horizon needed to assess the consequences of each decision, and degree of uncertainties and risks inherent in each decision. These considerations have led us to favor a hierarchical planning system to support production management decisions, which guarantees an appropriate coordination of the overall decision-making process, but, at the same time, recognizes the intrinsic characteristics of each decision level.

Early motivation for this approach can be found in the pioneering work of Holt, Modigliani, Muth, and Simon [1960], and in Winters [1962]. The work reported in this chapter is based on a long-term research effort undertaken at M.I.T. Hax and Meal [1975] were the first in formalizing a hierarchical production planning structure and proposed a set of coordinated heuristics for its implementation. Bitran and Hax [1977] interpreted these heuristics in terms of optimization subproblems, suggested iterative procedures to optimize the subproblems, and discussed the linking mechanisms that relate the subproblems to one another. Further refinements were developed by Bitran, Haas, and Hax [1981, 1982], who also extended the hierarchical planning methodology to a two-stage production process. Bradley, Hax, and Magnanti [1977] described an application of hierarchical production systems to a continuous manufacturing process (in Chapter 6), and to a job shop activity (in Chapter 10). Additional references to this methodology can be found in the works by Hax [1974, 1976], Hax and Golovin [1978], Golovin [1975], Gabbay [1975, 1979], Candea [1977], Shwimer [1972], and Newson [1971, 1975]. Related material developed outside M.I.T. has been published by Jaikumar [1973, 1974], Ritzman et al. [1979], Zoller [1971], and Dempster et al. [1981].

This chapter discusses the methodology associated with the design of hierarchical production planning (HPP) systems. Section 6.2 describes the development of such systems for single-stage production facilities in a batch-processing setting. Section 6.3 expands this methodology to cover two-stage production facilities. The *Material Requirements Planning* (MRP) approach to plan production for multistage processes is described in section 6.4. Finally, section 6.5 provides some preliminary computational results to compare the efficiency of MRP against that of HPP.

6.2   Hierarchical Production Planning: A Single-Stage System—The Regular Knapsack Method

Production decisions involve complex choices among a large number of alternatives. These choices have to be made by trading off conflicting objectives under the presence of financial, technological, and marketing constraints. Such decisions are not trivial and model-based systems have proven to be of great assistance in supporting managerial actions in this field. In fact, one could argue that, in this respect, production is the most mature field of management. A great many contributions have been made in this field by operations research, systems analysis, and computer sciences. But now we believe it is both significant and feasible to attempt a more comprehensive and integrative approach to production management.

The optimal planning and scheduling of multiple products has received much attention in the operations research literature. Several attempts (Manne [1958], Dzielinski, Baker, and Manne [1963], Dzielinski and Gomory [1965],

Lasdon and Terjung [1971]) have been made to formulate the overall problem as a single mixed-integer mathematical programming model to be solved on a rolling horizon basis. However, these approaches require data such as the forecast demand for every item over a complete seasonal cycle, usually a full year. When these systems involve the scheduling of several thousands of items, these data requirements become overwhelming and the resulting planning process becomes unrealistic due to the magnitude of the forecast errors inherent in such detailed long-term forecasts.

The obvious alternative to a detailed monolithic approach to production planning is a hierarchical approach, where decisions are made in sequence. Aggregate decisions are made first and impose constraints within which more detailed decisions are made. In turn, detailed decisions provide the feedback to evaluate the quality of aggregate decision making. Each hierarchical level has its own characteristics, including length of the planning horizon, level of detail of the required information and forecasts, scope of the planning activity, and type of manager in charge of executing the plan.

6.2.1 The Hierarchical Structure
of the Single-Stage Production System

The basic design of a hierarchical planning system includes the partitioning of the overall planning problem, and the linkage of the resulting subproblems. An important input is the number of levels recognized in the product structure. Hax and Meal [1975] identify three different levels:

1. *Items* are the final products to be delivered by the customers. They represent the highest degree of specificity regarding the manufactured products. A given product may generate a large number of items differing in characteristics such as color, packaging, labels, accessories, size, and so on.

2. *Families* are groups of items which share a common manufacturing setup cost. Economies of scale are accomplished by jointly replenishing items belonging to the same family.

3. *Types* are groups of families whose production quantities are to be determined by an aggregate production plan. Families belonging to a type normally have similar costs per unit of production time, and similar seasonal demand patterns.

These three levels are required to characterize the product structure in many batch-processing manufacturing environments. In some practical applications, more or fewer levels might be needed. In this chapter, we will propose hierarchical planning systems based on these three levels of item aggregation. The systems can be extended to different numbers of aggregation levels by defining adequate subproblems linking these levels.

The first step in our hierarchical planning approach is to allocate production capacity among product types by means of an aggregate planning model. The planning horizon of this model normally covers a full year in order to take into proper consideration the fluctuation demand requirements for the products. We advocate the use of a linear programming model at this level. The advantages of using such a model will be discussed in the next section. The major drawback is that a linear programming model does not take setup costs into consideration. The implications of this limitation will be examined in a later section.

The second step in the planning process is to allocate the production quantities for each product type among the families belonging to that type by disaggregating the results of the aggregate planning model only for the *first* period of the planning horizon. Thus, the required amount of data collection and data processing is reduced substantially. The disaggregation assures consistency and feasibility among the type and family production decisions and, at the same time, attempts to minimize the total setup costs incurred in the production of families. It is only at this stage that setup costs are explicitly considered.

Finally, the family production allocation is divided among the items belonging to each family. The objective of this decision is to maintain all items with inventory levels that maximize the time between family setups. Again, consistency and feasibility are the driving constraints of the disaggregation process.

An extensive justification of this approach is provided by Hax [1974, 1976] and by Hax and Meal [1975]. Figure 6.1 shows the overall conceptualization of the hierarchical planning effort. A computer-based system has been developed to facilitate its implementation. The details of such a system are reported elsewhere (Hax et al. [1976], Hax and Golovin [1978b]). In this section we will summarize the basic features of the single-stage hierarchical planning system developed by Bitran and Hax [1977], which will be referred to as the *Regular Knapsack Method* (RKM). The origin of this name is due to the fact that the family and item disaggregation subsystems are both represented by means of knapsack problems.

6.2.2 Aggregate Production Planning for Product Types

Aggregate production planning is the highest level of planning in the production system, addressed at the product-type level. Any aggregate production planning model discussed in Chapter 3 can be used as long as it adequately represents the practical problem under consideration. We consider the following simplified linear program at this level.

Problem P

Minimize $\sum_{i=1}^{I} \sum_{t=1}^{T} (c_{it}X_{it} + h_{i,t+L}I_{i,t+L}) + \sum_{t=1}^{T} (r_t R_t + o_t O_t)$

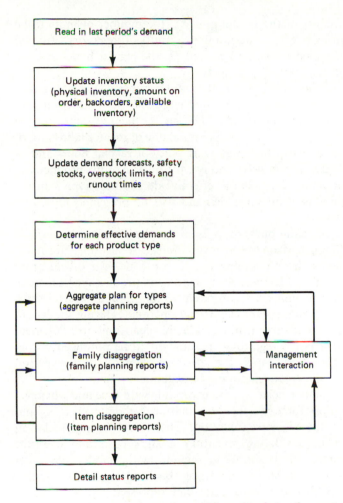

FIGURE 6.1   Conceptual overview of hierarchical planning system.

subject to:

$$X_{it} - I_{i,t+L} + I_{i,t+L-1} = d_{i,t+L}, \qquad i=1,\ldots,I; \; t=1,\ldots,T$$

$$\sum_{i=1}^{I} m_i X_{it} \leqslant O_t + R_t, \qquad t=1,\ldots,T$$

$$R_t \leqslant (rm)_t, \qquad t=1,\ldots,T$$

$$O_t \leqslant (om)_t, \qquad t=1,\ldots,T$$

$$X_{it}, I_{i,t+L} \geqslant 0, \qquad i=1,\ldots,I; \; t=1,\ldots,T$$

$$R_t, O_t \geqslant 0, \qquad t=1,\ldots,T.$$

The decision variables of the model are: X_{it}, the number of units to be produced of type i during t; $I_{i,t+L}$, the number of units of inventory of type i left over at the end of period $t + L$: and R_t and O_t, the regular hours and the overtime hours used during period t, respectively.

The parameters of the model are: I, the total number of product types; T, the length of the planning horizon; L, the length of the production lead time; c_{it}, the unit production cost (excluding labor); h_{it}, the inventory carrying cost per unit per period; r_t and o_t, the cost per manhour of regular labor and of overtime labor; $(r_m)_t$ and $(om)_t$, the total availability of regular hours and of overtime hours in period t, respectively; and m_i, the inverse of the productivity rate for type i in hours/unit. $d_{i,t+L}$ is the effective demand for type i during period $t + L$. (A definition of effective demand will be presented in a later section of this chapter.)

Whenever seasonal variations are present in the demand pattern of product types, the planning horizon has to cover a full seasonal cycle. Normally, aggregate planning models have planning horizons of one year divided into equally spaced time intervals. If there is a significant production lead time, there should be a frozen planning horizon equal to the production lead time. Changes in production schedules cannot normally be made during the length of the frozen horizon since it takes a full production lead time to implement the changes. Thus, the decision regarding the amount to be produced during period t, X_{it}, has as primary input the effective demand during period $t + L$, $d_{i,t+L}$. Figure 6.2 illustrates the timing implications.

Whenever the production costs, c_{it}, are invariable with time and whenever the payroll of regular work force is a fixed commitment, then terms $c_{it}X_{it}$ and $r_t R_t$ are deleted from the objective function. The model simply seeks an optimum aggregate plan considering inventory holding costs and overtime costs as the basic tradeoffs. It is simple to include in the model other cost factors and decisions, such as hiring and firing, backorders, subcontracting, lost sales, and so on. Also, the constraints can represent any number of technological, financial, marketing, and other considerations.

Linear programming is a convenient type of model to use at this aggregate level because of its computational efficiency and the wide availability of linear programming codes. Linear programming also permits sensitivity and

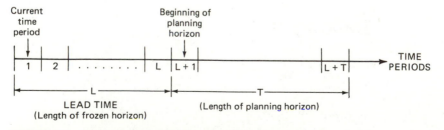

FIGURE 6.2 Timing implications in aggregate planning.

parametric analysis to be performed quite easily. The shadow price information that becomes available when solving linear programming models can help to identify opportunities for capacity expansions, market penetrations, introduction of new products, and so on.

Notice that manufacturing setup costs are purposely ignored in the aggregate model formulation. Normally, setup costs have a secondary impact on determining the total production cost. Moreover, the inclusion of setup costs would force the model to be defined at a family level and would imply a high level of detail which would invalidate all the advantages of aggregate planning to be discussed in the next section. Consequently, setup costs are considered only at the second level of the hierarchical planning process.

Because of the uncertainties present in the planning process, only the first time period results of the aggregate model are implemented. At the end of every time period, new information becomes available that is used to update the model with a rolling planning horizon of length T. Therefore, the data transmitted from the type level to the family level are the resulting production and inventory quantities for the first period of the aggregate model. These quantities will be disaggregated among the families belonging to each corresponding type.

6.2.3 The Advantages of Aggregate Planning

The advantages of the aggregate approach as compared to a detailed one may now be clearer. These advantages can be divided into three distinct categories.

The first category considers the costs of data collection to support the model as well as the computational cost of running the model. A major information system may be required to collect the demand, productivity, and cost data as well as to prepare forecasts for thousands of individual items, a more costly project than building the production planning system itself. This data must then be reviewed by management. As the number of items increases, this effort can become unwieldy, leading to deterioration of the data used in the planning process and therefore the output. In most cases, this cost of data collection and preparation will far outweigh the cost of computation. This is important to note as the cost of computation continues to decrease and it becomes feasible to solve enormous linear or nonlinear programming problems. Aggregation of items can significantly reduce the cost and effort in demand forecasting and data preparation in addition to decreasing the computational costs.

The second category considers the accuracy of the data. Unless all items are perfectly correlated, an aggregate forecast of demand will have reduced variance. In general, we are able to employ more sophisticated techniques such as econometric models or autoregressive moving average statistical models and spend more time in obtaining managerial judgment, given the smaller number of forecasts required. Since decisions on regular time, overtime, hiring and firing, and other production rate changes are based on the *total* production quantity demanded, increased forecast accuracy on total demand should improve the decision-making process.

Finally, and perhaps from an implementation standpoint, most importantly, aggregation leads to more effective managerial understanding of the model's result. When 10,000 items are being planned simultaneously, the sensitivity of the results to changes in individual item demands may be complex. There are too many combinations of changes to consider. The manager may never be able to see the overall picture but, instead, be lost in the details.

In addition, at this level of managerial planning, most marketing forecasts are made by product group and decisions made by product line or manpower class. These are the budgeting decisions, not lot sizing decisions for next week. It is crucial that the decision variables and sensitivity analysis that can be carried out correspond to those with which the manager deals.

6.2.4 The Family Disaggregation Model

The central condition to be satisfied at this level for a coherent disaggregation is the equality between the sum of the productions of the families in a product type and the amount dictated by the higher level for this type. This equality will assure consistency between the aggregate production plan and the family disaggregation process. This consistency is achieved by determining run quantities for each family that minimize the total setup cost among families.

The disaggregation methodology to be described was originally developed by Bitran and Hax [1977, 1981]. For alternative disaggregation approaches, see Hax and Golovin [1978a]. A comparison among various disaggregation procedures is offered in Bitran, Haas, and Hax [1981].

Bitran and Hax propose the following model for family disaggregation, which has to be solved for every product type i and gives rise to a continuous knapsack problem.

Problem P_i

Minimize
$$\sum_{j \in J^\circ} \frac{s_j d_j}{Y_j},$$

subject to:

$$\sum_{j \in J^\circ} Y_j = X_i^*$$
$$lb_j \leqslant Y_j \leqslant ub_j, \qquad\qquad j \in J^\circ, \qquad\qquad (6.1)$$

where Y_j is the number of units of family j to be produced; s_j is the setup cost for family j; d_j is the forecast demand (usually annual) for family j; lb_j and ub_j are lower and upper bounds for the quantity Y_j; and, X_i^* is the total amount to be allocated among all the families belonging to type i. X_i^* has been determined by the aggregate planning model and corresponds to the optimum value of the variable X_{i1} since only the first-period result of the aggregate model is to be implemented.

The lower bound lb_j, which defines the minimum production quantity for family j, is given by:

$$lb_j = \max\left[0, \left(d_{j,1} + d_{j,2} + \cdots + d_{j,L+1}\right) - AI_j + SS_j\right],$$

where $d_{j,1} + \cdots + d_{j,L+1}$ is the total forecast demand for family j during the production lead time plus the review period (assumed equal to one); AI_j is the current available inventory for family j (equal to the sum of the physical inventory and the amount on order minus the backorders); and SS_j is the required safety stock. The lower bound lb_j guarantees that any backorders will be caused by forecast errors beyond those absorbed by the safety stock SS_j.

The upper bound ub_j is given by:

$$ub_j = OS_j - AI_j,$$

where OS_j is the overstock limit of family j. When family j has a terminal demand at the end of its season, OS_j can be calculated by means of a newsboy model (see Chapter 4, section 4.2.2.3).

The objective function of problem P_i assumes that the family run quantities are proportional to the setup cost and the annual demand for a given family. This assumption (which is the basis of the economic order quantity formulation) tends to minimize the average annual setup cost. Notice that the total inventory carrying cost has already been established in the aggregate planning model; therefore, it does not enter into the current formulation.

The first constraint of problem P_i,

$$\sum_{j \in J^\circ} Y_j = X_i^*,$$

assures the equality between the aggregate model input X_i^* and the sum of the family run quantities. It can be shown (Bitran and Hax [1981]) that this condition can be substituted by

$$\sum_{j \in J^\circ} Y_j \leqslant X_i^* \tag{6.2}$$

without changing the optimum solution to problem P_i. In what follows the equality constraint will be relaxed into inequality.

Initially, J° contains only those families which trigger during the current planning period. A family is said to trigger whenever its current available inventory cannot absorb the expected demand for the family during the production lead time plus the review period, that is, those families whose current available inventory is such that

$$AI_j < \left(d_{j,1} + d_{j,2} + \cdots + d_{j,L+1}\right) + SS_j.$$

Equivalently, one can define $J°$ as containing all those families whose runout times are less than one time period, that is,

$$ROT_j = \frac{AI_j - SS_j}{\sum_{t=1}^{L+1}d_{j,t}} < 1.$$

It is necessary to start production for these families in order to avoid future backorders. All other families are put on a secondary list and will be scheduled only if extra capacity is available.

Bitran and Hax [1977] propose an efficient algorithm to solve problem P_i through a relaxation procedure. The algorithm consists of initially ignoring the bounding constraints (6.1) and of solving the objective function subject to the knapsack restriction (6.2). Then a check is made to verify that the optimum values Y_j^* satisfy the bounds (6.1). If they do satisfy the bounds, the Y_j^*'s constitute the optimal solution for problem P_i. If they do not satisfy the bounds, at least some of the Y_j^*'s are shown to be optimal and a new iteration takes place. Optimality and convergence proofs are presented in Bitran and Hax [1981] and will be omitted here.

The algorithm (for each product type)

Let $s_j d_j = a_j$; $\beta = 1, 2, \ldots$ be the counter of iterations; and J^β be the set of families whose run quantities have not been determined up to the beginning of iteration β.

In case $\sum_{j \in J°} ub_j \leqslant X_i^*$, the optimal solution is $Y_j^* = ub_j, j \in J°$. This case could happen only if (even by scheduling at their upper bounds all those families which trigger in the current planning period) one could not fill all the production amount assigned to the corresponding type by the aggregate planning model. In this case, the remaining capacity is filled by producing families in the secondary list (up to their upper bounds) ordered in increasing runout time.

When $\sum_{j \in J°} lb_j > X_i^*$, problem P_i is infeasible. This case can happen only when the aggregate production planning model is infeasible since there is not enough capacity to satisfy the minimum demand requirements of a given product type. In this case, one has backorders. To distribute the possible backorders among the families in product type i, the following disaggregation is adopted:

$$Y_j = lb_j + \frac{\left(X_i^* - \sum_{j \in J°} lb_j\right)lb_j}{\sum_{j \in J°} lb_j}, j \in J°.$$

This formulation allocates the backorders in proportion to the lower bound lb_j of each family.

The authors will describe the algorithm, assuming $\sum_{j \in J^0} lb_j \leqslant X_i^* \leqslant \sum_{j \in J^0} ub_j$.

Initialization

Let $\beta = 1$, $P^1 = X_i^*$, and $J^1 = J^0$.

Step 1. Compute for all $j \in J^\beta$:

$$Y_j^\beta = \frac{\sqrt{a_j}}{\sum_{j \in J^\beta} \sqrt{a_j}} P^\beta, \text{ and go to step 2.}$$

Step 2. Check, for all $j \in J^\beta$, if $lb_j \leqslant Y_j^\beta \leqslant ub_j$.
If yes, $Y_j^* = Y_j^\beta$, $j \in J^\beta$, is optimal; stop.
If no, go to step 3.

Step 3. Determine $J_+^\beta = \{ j \in J^\beta : Y_j^\beta \geqslant ub_j \} = \langle$set of families which have exceeded their upper bounds$\rangle$;
$J_-^\beta = \{ j \in J^\beta : Y_j^\beta \leqslant lb_j \} = \langle$set of families which have run quantities lower than their lower bounds$\rangle$.

Compute:

$$\Delta = \sum_{\substack{j \in J_+^\beta \\ \text{(total excess)}}} \left(Y_j^\beta - ub_j \right); \quad \nabla = \sum_{\substack{j \in J_-^\beta \\ \text{(total deficit)}}} \left(lb_j - Y_j^\beta \right).$$

Go to step 4.

Step 4. If $\Delta \geqslant \nabla$, define $Y_j^* = ub_j$, $j \in J_+^\beta$.
If $\Delta < \nabla$, define $Y_j^* = lb_j$, $j \in J_-^\beta$.
Let $J^{\beta+1} = J^\beta - \langle$indices of families defined at their upper or lower bound of iteration $\beta \rangle$.
$P^{\beta+1} = P^\beta - \langle$sum of run quantities of the families deleted from $J^\beta \rangle$.
If $J^{\beta+1} = \phi$, stop; Y_j^* is optimal. Otherwise, go to step 1.
The algorithm is finite because at each iteration the run quantity of at least one family is determined.

6.2.5 *The Item Disaggregation Model*

For the period under consideration, all the costs have already been determined in the former two levels, and any feasible disaggregation of a family run quantity has the same total cost. However, the feasible solution chosen will establish initial conditions for the next period and will affect future costs. In order to save setups in future periods, one could distribute the family run quantity among its items in such a way that the runout times of the items coincide with the runout time of the family. A direct consequence is that all items of a family will trigger simultaneously. To attain this objective, the authors propose the following strictly convex knapsack problem for each family j.

Problem P_j

Minimize $\quad \dfrac{1}{2} \displaystyle\sum_{k \in K^\circ} \left[\dfrac{Y_j^* + \sum_{k \in K^\circ}(AI_k - SS_k)}{\sum_{k \in K^\circ}\sum_{t=1}^{L+1} d_{k,t}} - \dfrac{Z_k + AI_k - SS_k}{\sum_{t=1}^{L+1} d_{k,t}} \right]^2$

subject to:

$$\sum_{k \in K^\circ} Z_k = Y_j^*$$

$$Z_k \leqslant OS_k - AI_k$$

$$Z_k \geqslant \max\left[0, \sum_{t=1}^{L+1} d_{k,t} - AI_k + SS_k\right]$$

where Z_k is the number of units to be produced of item k; AI_k, SS_k, and OS_k are, respectively, the available inventory, the safety stock, and the overstock limit of item k; $d_{k,t}$ is the forecast demand for item k in period t; $K^\circ = \{1,2,\dots\}$ is the set of indices of all the items belonging to family j; and, Y_j^* is the total amount to be allocated for all items belonging to family j. Y^* was determined by the family disaggregation model.

The first constraint of problem P_j requires consistency in the disaggregation from family to items. The last two constraints are the upper and lower bounds for the item run quantities. These bounds are similar to those defined for the family disaggregation model in the previous section.

The two terms inside the square bracket of the objective function represent, respectively, the runout time for family j and the runout time for an item k belonging to family j (assuming perfect forecast). The minimization of the square of the differences of the runout times will make those quantities as close as possible. (The term $1/2$ in front of the objective function is just a computational convenience.)

The following transformation will help in simplifying the problem formulation:

$$h_k = Z_k + AI_k - SS_k;$$

$$D_k = \sum_{t=1}^{L+1} d_{k,t};$$

$$D = \sum_{k \in K^\circ} D_k;$$

$$h = Y_j^* + \sum_{k \in K^\circ} (AI_k - SS_k);$$

$$ub_k = OS_k - SS_k; \text{ and,}$$

$$lb_k = \max\left[0, \sum_{t=1}^{L+1} d_{k,t} - AI_k + SS_k\right] + AI_k - SS_k.$$

The problem P_j is equivalent to the following problem.

Problem P_j

Minimize
$$\frac{1}{2} \sum_{k \in K^\circ} \left(\frac{h}{D} - \frac{h_k}{D_k} \right)^2$$

subject to:

$$\sum_{k \in K^\circ} h_k = h$$

$$lb_k \leqslant h_k \leqslant ub_k, k \in K^\circ.$$

The following algorithm can be proved to be optimal to solve problem P_j (see Bitran and Hax [1981]).

Initialization
Let:

$$h_k^\circ = \frac{D_k h}{D}, k \in K^\circ;$$

$$K_+^\circ = \{k \in K^\circ : h_k^\circ \geqslant ub_k\}; \ K_-^\circ = \{k \in K^\circ : h_k^\circ \leqslant lb_k\};$$

$$\Delta^\circ = \sum_{k \in K_+^\circ} (h_k^\circ - ub_k); \text{ and, } \nabla^\circ = \sum_{k \in K_-^\circ} (lb_k - h_k^\circ).$$

Case 1. $\Delta^\circ \geqslant \nabla^\circ$.

It can be shown that $h_k^* = ub_k, k \in K_+^\circ$, together with the solution to (P1) below, will solve problem P_j:

Minimize
$$\frac{1}{2} \sum_{k \in K^1} \left(\frac{h}{D} - \frac{h_k}{D_k} \right)^2, \tag{P1}$$

subject to:

$$\sum_{k \in K^1} h_k = h^1$$

$$lb_k' \leqslant h_k \leqslant ub_k, k \in K^1$$

where:

$$K^1 = K^\circ - K_+^\circ; \ lb_k' = lb_k, k \in K_-^\circ$$

$$lb_k' = \frac{D_k h}{D}, k \in (K^\circ - K_+^\circ - K_-^\circ)$$

$$h^1 = h - \sum_{k \in K_+^\circ} ub_k.$$

An algorithm to solve (P1)
Let $lb_k' = lb_k, k \in K_-^\circ$; $lb_k' = D_k h/D, k \in (K^1 - K_-^\circ)$; and $h_k^*, k \in K^1$ be the optimal solution to (P1).

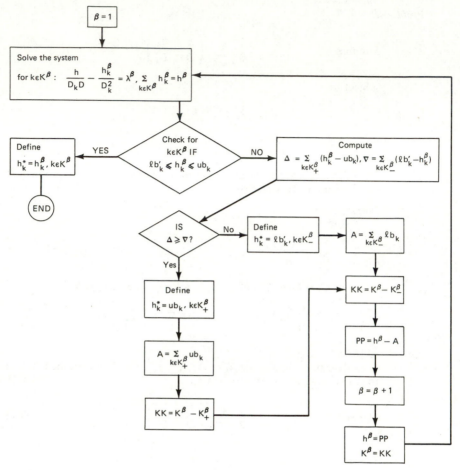

Case 2. $\nabla° > \Delta°$.

It can be shown that $h_k^* = lb_k, k \in K^o_-$ together with the solution of (P2) below will solve problem P_j.

Minimize
$$\frac{1}{2} \sum_{k \in K^1} \left(\frac{h}{D} - \frac{h_k}{D_k} \right)^2 \qquad (P2)$$

subject to:

$$\sum_{k \in K^1} h_k = h^1$$

$$lb_k \leqslant h_k \leqslant ub'_k, k \in K^1$$

where:

$$K^1 = K^o - K^o_-; ub'_k = ub_k, k \in K^o_+$$

$$ub'_k = \frac{D_k h}{S}, k \in (K^1 - K^o_+)$$

$$h^1 = h - \sum_{k \in K^o} lb_k.$$

An algorithm to solve (P2)
    Solve in the same way as the flow chart (P1), but use ub'_k instead of ub_k and use lb_k instead of lb'_k.

6.2.6 Issues of Infeasibility and Demand Forecasts

The rolling horizon aggregate planning procedure combined with disaggregation may lead to infeasibility. This section will illustrate how the infeasibilities can occur and will suggest a way to eliminate them. To simplify the explanation, one may assume that a perfect forecast exists and that every family is composed of a unique item, that is, the disaggregation consists of passing directly from the aggregate solution to detail schedules.

A simple problem consisting of 1 product type ($i = 1$), 2 items ($k = 1, 2$), a planning horizon of 3 time periods ($t = 1, 2, 3$), and zero production lead time, will be considered.

The aggregate constraints are:

$$I_0 + X_1 - I_1 \qquad\qquad\qquad = d_1$$
$$I_1 + X_2 - I_2 \qquad\qquad = d_2$$
$$I_2 + X_3 - I_3 = d_3.$$

(Nonnegativity constraints)

The detailed constraints are:

$$I_{k,0} + Z_{k,1} - I_{k,1} \qquad\qquad\qquad = d_{k,1} \qquad k = 1, 2$$
$$I_{k,1} + Z_{k,2} - I_{k,2} \qquad\qquad = d_{k,2} \qquad k = 1, 2$$
$$I_{k,2} + Z_{k,3} - I_{k,3} = d_{k,3} \qquad k = 1, 2.$$

(Nonnegativity constraints)

Feasibility conditions require that these two constraint sets are satisfied and that:

$$\sum_{k=1}^{2} Z_{k,t} = X_t \quad t = 1, 2, 3.$$

Assume the following demand and inventory conditions.

ITEM	DEMAND			INITIAL INVENTORY
	PERIOD $t = 1$	PERIOD $t = 2$	PERIOD $t = 3$	
$k = 1$	$d_{11} = 5$	$d_{12} = 17$	$d_{13} = 30$	$I_{10} = 9$
$k = 2$	$d_{21} = 3$	$d_{22} = 12$	$d_{23} = 30$	$I_{20} = 20$
Total	$d_1 = 8$	$d_2 = 29$	$d_3 = 60$	$I_0 = 29$

The reader can verify that, although

$$X_1 = 8, X_2 = 0, X_3 = 60, I_1 = 29, I_2 = 0, I_3 = 0$$

is a feasible solution to the aggregate problem, it does not have a corresponding feasible disaggregation. The reason for this infeasibility is that the aggregate model ignores the fact that inventory for item 2 cannot be used to satisfy demand for item 1.

This type of infeasibility can be avoided by working with *effective demands*. If the initial inventory of an item is not zero, subtract it from the demand requirements in the first period to obtain the effective demand for that period. If the initial inventory exceeds the first-period demand, continue with this adjustment process until all the inventory is used up. The following are the effective demands of the example:

ITEM	EFFECTIVE DEMAND			INITIAL INVENTORY
	PERIOD $t=1$	PERIOD $t=2$	PERIOD $t=3$	
$k=1$	$d_{11} = 0$	$d_{12} = 13$	$d_{13} = 30$	0
$k=2$	$d_{21} = 0$	$d_{22} = 0$	$d_{23} = 25$	0
Total	$d_1 = 0$	$d_2 = 13$	$d_3 = 55$	0

It can be shown (Gabbay [1979]) that if one works with effective demands, any feasible solution to the aggregate model generates a feasible solution to the disaggregate model.

In general, if $\bar{d}_{k,t}$ is the forecast demand for item k in period t, AI_k is its corresponding available inventory and SS_k is its safety stock, the effective demand $d_{k,t}$ of item i for period t is given by

$$d_{k,t} = \begin{cases} \max\left[0, \sum_{l=1}^{t} \bar{d}_{k,l} - AI_k + SS_k\right], & t = 1,\ldots,T \text{ if } \bar{d}_{k,t-1} = 0 \\ \bar{d}_{kt} \text{ otherwise.} \end{cases} \quad (6.3)$$

The effective demand for a type i is given by the sum of the effective demands of all items belonging to a given type, that is,

$$d_{i,t} = \sum_{k \in K} d_{k,t}. \quad (6.4)$$

The hierarchical planning system operates as follows:

1. An aggregate forecast is generated for each product type for each time period in the planning horizon. Since the number of types normally is reasonably small, these forecasts can be produced by using fairly sophisticated forecasting models (such as regression analysis) which would be prohibitively expensive to employ at the item level due to the extensive number of items present in most manufacturing environments. In addition, these forecasts can

be reviewed by experienced managers in order to introduce judgmental inputs which the models cannot capture.

2.   The type forecasts are disaggregated into item forecasts by forecasting the proportion of the total type demand corresponding to each item. These proportions can be updated by using exponential smoothing techniques which are appropriate to apply at a detailed level. Item and family forecasts only are required for a single time period in the models presented.

3.   After updating the available inventory for each item, the effective item demand is obtained by applying expression (6.3) above. Whenever the initial inventory exceeds the first-period demand, expression (6.3) requires item forecasts for successive periods in the planning horizon. Using exponential smoothing techniques, one can obtain these by making trend and/or seasonality adjustments to the initial period forecast.

4.   The effective demand for types is obtained from expression (6.4). Computer programs that carry out the necessary calculations are discussed in Hax et al. [1976].

6.2.7   Measuring Performance of the Single-Stage Hierarchical Planning System

Bitran and Hax [1977] conducted a series of experiments to examine the performance of the single-stage hierarchical system just described to determine the size of forecast errors, capacity availability, magnitude of setup costs, and nature of the planning horizon.

The data used for these tests were taken from a manufacturer of rubber tires. The product structure characteristics and other information are given in Figure 6.3. Table 6.1 exhibits the demand pattern for both product types. Product type 1 has a terminal demand season (corresponding to the requirements of snow tires) and consists of two families and five items. Demand for product type 2 is highly fluctuating throughout the year. Product type 2 has three families and six items. Families are groups of items sharing the same molds in the curing presses and, therefore, sharing a common setup cost. The items are, for instance, white wall and regular wall tires of a given class. Families and items have the same cost characteristics and the same productivity rates as their corresponding types.

The experiments consisted of applying the single-stage hierarchical planning system to a full year of simulated plant operations. Production decisions were made every four weeks, at which time a report was generated identifying aggregate as well as detailed decisions. The model was then updated, normally using a one-year rolling planning horizon. The process was repeated 13 times. At the end of the simulation, total setup costs, inventory holding costs, overtime costs, and backorders were accounted for. A summary

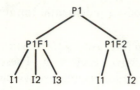

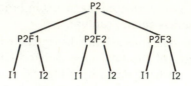

Family setup cost = $90
Holding cost = $.31/unit a month
Overtime cost = $9.5/hr.
Productivity factor = .1 hr./unit
Production lead time = 1 month

Family setup cost = $120
Holding cost = $.40/unit a month
Overtime cost = $9.5/hr.
Productivity factor = .2 hr./unit
Production lead time = 1 month

Regular work force costs and unit production costs are considered fixed costs

Total regular work force = 2,000 hrs./month
Total overtime work force = 1,200 hrs./month

FIGURE 6.3   Product structure and other relevant information.

of 11 different simulation runs is provided in Table 6.2. The simulations were implemented in the *C*omputer Based *O*perations *M*anagement *S*ystem (COMS) developed at M.I.T. (Hax et al. [1976]).

Run 1 can be regarded as the *base case*. It has no forecast errors, a planning horizon of one year divided into 13 periods of four-week durations each, a normal capacity (defined as 2,000 hours of regular time and 1,200 hours of overtime per period), on a normal setup cost ($90 per family belonging to product type 1 and $120 per family belonging to product type 2). All other runs include some variation of the characteristics of run 1.

TABLE 6.1   Demand Patterns of Product Types

TIME PERIOD t	PRODUCT TYPE 1 P1	PRODUCT TYPE 2 P2
1	12,736	6,174
2	7,813	2,855
3	0	4,023
4	0	4,860
5	0	7,131
6	0	9,665
7	1,545	17,603
8	7,895	14,276
9	10,982	11,706
10	15,782	15,056
11	16,870	8,232
12	15,870	7,880
13	9,878	10,762
Total	99,371	120,223

TABLE 6.2 Summary of Computational Results with Proposed Hierarchical Planning System

RUN COST COMPONENTS	1 BASE CASE NO FORECAST ERRORS	2 10% FORECAST ERRORS	3 30% FORECAST ERRORS	4 HIGH SETUP COST CASE I P1: 5,000, 50 P2: 400, 400, 1,000 NO FORECAST ERROR	5 HIGH SETUP COST CASE II P1: 6,000, 4,500 P2: 400, 5,000, 3,000 NO FORECAST ERROR	6 TIGHT CAPACITY 1,600 REG. HRS. NO FORECAST ERROR
SETUP HOLDING OVERTIME	5,360 72,510 81,111	5,360 73,611 81,425	5,250 76,577 82,365	67,050 72,374 81,111	104,800 72,597 81,102	4,480 115,072 117,439
TOTAL COST BACKORDERS	158,981 2	160,396 1,513	164,192 6,243	220,535 10	258,499 4	236,991 144

TABLE 6.2 Summary of Computational Results with Proposed Hierarchical Planning System (continued)

RUN COST COMPONENTS	7 LOOSE CAPACITY 2,500 REG. HRS. NO FORECAST ERROR	8 6-MONTH PLANNING HORIZON NORMAL CAPACITY NO FORECAST ERROR	9 6-MONTH PLANNING HORIZON TIGHT CAPACITY NO FORECAST ERROR	10 6-MONTH PLANNING HORIZON NORMAL CAPACITY 10% FORECAST ERROR	11 1-1-1-3-6 PLANNING HORIZON NORMAL CAPACITY NO FORECAST ERROR
SETUP HOLDING OVERTIME	5,910 56,002 48,507	5,690 67,212 88,597	5,030 83,983 103,332	5,690 64,971 90,773	5,250 78,052 75,440
TOTAL COST BACKORDERS	110,419 0	161,499 0	192,345 16,658	161,434 2,951	158,742 73

6.2.7.1   Sensitivity to forecast errors

Runs 1, 2, and 3 show the impact of forecast errors in production planning decisions. Forecast errors are uniformly distributed in intervals of the type $[-a, +a]$ and are introduced in all three levels. Moreover, the demands of families in a same product type and the demands of items in a family add to the demand of the product type, and the demands of items in a family add to the demand of the product type and of the family, respectively. Increasing forecast errors causes the quality of the decisions to deteriorate. Both cost and size of backorders increase when forecast errors begin to escalate. However, the system performs reasonably well even under forecast errors of up to 30%. (The 6,243 units backordered in run 3 represent a 97% service level.) These results show that aggregate forecasts can be more accurate than detailed forecasts, and thus provide an important justification for the hierarchical approach.

6.2.7.2   Sensitivity to changes in setup costs

The values imputed to the setup costs in the base case (run 1) were realistic measures of actual setup costs incurred in normal manufacturing operations. They included direct setup costs (manpower and materials) as well as opportunity costs for having the machines idle while performing the changeover. It was intended to test the system's performance under extreme setup cost conditions. Thus, runs 4 and 5 were made with the following setup cost characteristics.

	TYPE 1		TYPE 2		
	FAMILY 1	FAMILY 2	FAMILY 1	FAMILY 2	FAMILY 3
Run 4	5,000	50	400	400	1,000
Run 5	6,000	4,500	400	5,000	3,000
Base case—run 1	90	90	120	120	120

Naturally, the total cost associated with runs 4 and 5 increases significantly. It can be observed that runs 1, 4, and 5 are almost identical in terms of inventory holding costs and overtime costs, which indicates that the overall production strategies for these runs do not change much. This suggests a limitation of this particular hierarchical approach when applied to situations with extremely high setup costs since, under these conditions, one could have expected higher inventory accumulation to obtain a better balance between inventory and setup costs. Section 6.2.9.3 describes a modification introduced in the hierarchical planning system to deal with high setup costs.

6.2.7.3 Sensitivity to capacity availability

Runs 6 and 7 evaluate the performance of the system under different capacity conditions. Run 6 uses only 1,600 hours of regular capacity per period; run 7 expands the regular capacity to 2,500 hours. As indicated in the results in Table 6.2, the system's performance is quite sensitive to capacity changes. Under tight capacity there is a significant increase in both costs and backorders; the opposite is true under loose capacity. Clearly, the system can be useful in evaluating proposals for capacity expansion.

6.2.7.4 Sensitivity to changes in planning horizon characteristics

Runs 8, 9, 10, and 11 experiment with various lengths of the planning horizon under different conditions. Shortening the planning horizon from 13 periods to 6 periods does not affect the system's performance under normal capacity conditions. (Compare runs 1 and 8 and runs 2 and 10.) However, the size of backorders begins to increase significantly when the planning horizon is shorter and under tight capacity conditions (run 9).

Run 11 deals with an aggregation of time periods in the planning horizon. The length of the planning horizon is a full year divided into six time periods of uneven lengths. Each of the first four periods has a four-week duration; the fifth period covers 12 weeks (an aggregation of three four-week periods); and the sixth period covers 24 weeks (an aggregation of six four-week periods). Run 11 shows a performance similar to that of the base case. This result indicates that this type of aggregation of the planning horizon could be useful in many situations since it improves the forecasting accuracy in more distant time periods and reduces the computational effort of processing the system without experiencing a decline in performance.

6.2.7.5 Degree of suboptimization

Although the proposed hierarchical planning system provides optimum solutions to the subproblems that deal with individual decisions at each level, it is not an overall optimum procedure. Setup costs are ignored at the aggregate planning level and, thus, suboptimization possibilities are introduced. To determine how serious this suboptimization problem can be, a detailed mixed integer programming (MIP) model was developed at a detailed item level to identify the true optimal solution to the test problem. The MIP model was implemented by means of IBM's MPSX/MIP code, which is a general purpose branch-and-bound algorithm.

Due to the expensive computational cost of solving MIP models, the comparisons between the hierarchical planning system and the MIP model were limited to situations which contained no forecast errors and for which the optimum yearly cost could be obtained by solving the MIP model only once.

(If forecast errors had been introduced, each run would have required solving the MIP model 13 times.)

MIP solutions were computed for three of the previous runs: the base case (run 1'), the first high setup cost run (run 4'), and the tight capacity run (run 6'). The MIP results are given in Table 6.3. The existing limits on the node tables of the branch-and-bound code used did not allow one to determine the true optimum in the MIP runs. Therefore, the solutions reported in Table 6.3 might be improved. Table 6.3 also provides the continuous lower bounds obtained when the computations were interrupted. For all practical purposes, one could consider the solutions corresponding to runs 1' and 6' to be optimal. Run 4' could possibly be improved.

By comparing the total costs of the three runs, one can see that the hierarchical planning system is extremely efficient. Only under abnormally high setup costs might the system's performance begin to depart significantly from the overall optimal solution.

	HIERARCHICAL SYSTEM	BEST KNOWN MIP SOLUTION
Base case	158,981	158,339
High setup cost	220,535	203,360
Tight capacity	236,733	237,232

In summary, the proposed hierarchical system seems to perform quite near the optimum when moderate setup costs are present. The base case cost, which reflected the operating data of the tire industry, is only 0.4 percent higher than the best known optimum solution obtained by the MIP formulation. However, each run of the hierarchical system costs about $5, while the corresponding MIP run costs about $50. The MIP approach would be computationally impossible to carry out for large problems. Moreover, the

TABLE 6.3   Summary of Computational Results with Mixed Integer Programming Models

	1'	4'	6'
RUN COST COMPONENTS	BASE CASE NO FORECAST ERROR	HIGH SETUP COST CASE I P1: 5,000, 50 P2: 400, 400, 1,000	TIGHT CAPACITY 1,600 REG. HR.
Setup Holding Overtime	4,590 75,953 77,796	48,050 79,880 75,430	3,930 115,872 117,430
Total Cost (best known solution)	158,339	203,360	237,232
Lower Bound	153,926	162,783	233,665

hierarchical system appears to offer coherent solutions for reasonable changes in forecast errors, for capacity availabilities, and for planning horizon lengths.

Extremely high setup costs could affect the performance of the system. In practice, families with very high setups are candidates for continuous production (as opposed to batch production) if they have a high level of demand. In such cases, families can be handled independently of the prescribed system. In situations in which there are few high-setup families with low demand, special constraints can be imposed on the family disaggregation model to produce those families in large enough quantities by setting the lower bound of the family to its unconstrained economic order quantity. When all of the families in the product structure have high setup costs and low demand levels, it may not be desirable to eliminate setup costs at the aggregate level. In such a situation, one could eliminate the aggregate planning model for product types, allocate production quantities at the family level by using an approach similar to that proposed by Lasdon and Terjung [1971], and apply the item disaggregation model to allocate the family production quantities among items.

Some additional refinements to the methodology proposed in these sections, together with further computational results, have been treated by Bitran, Haas, and Hax [1981]. Their findings are reported in section 6.2.9.

6.2.8   Comparing Disaggregation Procedures

An important determinant for the performance of hierarchical production planning systems is the procedure used to disaggregate earlier decisions at each hierarchical level. The Regular Knapsack Method just presented identifies one possible alternative for hierarchical designs. The knapsack nature of the subproblems is very appealing because of its great computational advantage. However, it is imperative that we gain some theoretical understanding of the impact of different disaggregation schemes on the production planning costs. Such an understanding will help us in evaluating and comparing alternative disaggregation mechanisms, and in judging the improvements to be obtained by introducing modifications to the RKM.

This section will describe two fundamental theorems which provide important insights into the strengths of various disaggregation methodologies. Let the superscript u denote a generic disaggregation procedure applied to problem P of section 6.2.2. (To simplify the notation, we will be assuming that the lead time, L, is equal to 0 in problem P.) The effective demands can be expressed as a function of the real demands (or forecasted demands) and the disaggregation procedure used as follows:

$$d_{it} = \bar{d}_{it} - g_{it}^u \qquad \text{for } i = 1, 2, \dots, I; \ t = 1, 2, \dots, T.$$

The quantity g_{it}^u represents the total contribution of all items belonging to product type i to determine the effective demand of that product type in period t, using the disaggregation procedure u. The g_{it}^u's can also be interpreted as that part of the initial inventory carried forward to meet future demands. Different disaggregation procedures will affect the initial inventory, I_{k0}, of each item and, thus, the effective demand of the product types. Therefore, $\sum_{t=1}^{\tau} g_{it}^u$, $\tau = 1, \ldots, T$ indicate the sum of the real or forecasted demands of the items in product type i that can be satisfied directly by the initial inventory up to period τ.

Problem P can be rewritten as a function of disaggregation u as follows:

Problem P^u

$$z^u = \min \sum_{i=1}^{I} \sum_{t=1}^{T} \left(c_{it} X_{it}^u + h_{it} I_{it}^u \right) + \sum_{t=1}^{T} \left(r_t R_t^u + o_t O_t^u \right)$$

$$+ \sum_{i=1}^{I} \sum_{t=1}^{T-1} h_{it} \sum_{k=t+1}^{T} g_{ik}^u$$

subject to:

$$I_{it-1}^u + X_{it}^u - I_{it}^u = \bar{d}_{it} - g_{it}^u \qquad i = 1, 2, \ldots, I;\; t = 1, 2, \ldots, T$$

$$\sum_{i=1}^{I} m_i X_{it}^u \leqslant R_t^u + O_t^u \qquad t = 1, 2, \ldots, T$$

$$R_t^u \leqslant (rm)_t \qquad t = 1, 2, \ldots, T$$

$$O_t^u \leqslant (om)_t \qquad t = 1, 2, \ldots, T$$

$$X_{it}^u, I_{it}^u, R_t^u, O_t^u \geqslant 0 \qquad i = 1, 2, \ldots, I;\; t = 1, 2, \ldots, T.$$

where the last term in the objective function represents the holding cost of the initial inventory of all product types, which is a function of the disaggregation procedure used. This term has been omitted in problem P since, given a disaggregation procedure, the initial inventory cost is constant. However, it is important to include it in problem P^u because our purpose is to compare the performance of various disaggregation procedures.

The quantities g_{it}^u satisfy the following condition:

$$\sum_{t=1}^{T} g_{it}^u = I_{io} \qquad i = 1, 2, \ldots, I,$$

where I_{io} is the initial inventory of product type i.

A disaggregation procedure u is said to be feasible if problem P^u is feasible.

Theorem 6.1.   Let u_1 and u_2 be two generic feasible disaggregation procedures such that:

$$\sum_{k=1}^{t} g_{ik}^{u_1} \geqslant \sum_{k=1}^{t} g_{ik}^{u_2} \qquad i = 1, 2, \ldots, I;\; t = 1, 2, \ldots, T. \tag{6.5}$$

Then $z^{u_1} \leqslant z^{u_2}$.

The proof of this theorem is provided in Appendix 6.1, and its implications are discussed below.

Define $u = 0$ to be the case where $g_{i1}^o = I_{io}$ and $g_{it}^o = 0$, $i = 1, 2, \ldots, I$; $t = 2, \ldots, T$. This implies the allocation of all initial inventory to the first period of the planning horizon, even if the demands during that period become negative. Moreover, since $g_{i1}^o = I_{io} = \sum_{k=1}^T g_{ik}^{u_j}$ for $i = 1, 2, \ldots, I$ and for every feasible disaggregation u_j, it follows that:

$$\sum_{k=1}^t g_{ik}^o \geqslant \sum_{k=1}^t g_{ik}^{u_j}$$

for every $t = 1, 2, \ldots, t$; $i = 1, 2, \ldots, I$ and every u_j. Hence, if we let z^o be the optimal value of problem P^o corresponding to $u = 0$ the corollary below is directly implied by theorem 6.1.

Corollary 6.1. Assume problem P^o is feasible. Then, $z^o \leqslant z^{u_j}$ for every feasible disaggregation u_j.

Theorem 6.1 provides a mechanism for comparing two disaggregation procedures u_1 and u_2. If conditions (6.5) are met, u_1 is preferred to u_2. In this sense, conditions (6.5) can be viewed as establishing a partial order structure in the space of feasible disaggregations.

The key question to ask at this point is whether a feasible disaggregation procedure exists which is optimal, that is, which attains the lower bound z^o. The answer to the question is provided by theorem 6.2 below, which establishes the conditions under which the disaggregation procedure known as "*E*qualization of *R*unout *T*imes" (EROT) becomes optimal.

EROT allocates the production amount determined at the aggregate planning level for a given product type, X_{i1}, in such a way as to equalize the runout times of all the items belonging to that type. The runout time for a product type is defined as the number of periods (possibly a fractional number) that will elapse until the inventory of that item reaches the safety stock level.

Theorem 6.2. Let u_E denote the EROT disaggregation procedure. Then, if all disaggregations are made with the EROT disaggregation method, if $I_{io} \geqslant 0$ for all product types, and if the aggregate product-type problem P^o is feasible, it follows that:

$$z^o = z^{u_F}.$$

The proof of this theorem is provided in Appendix 6.2.

Recognizing that the aggregate plan ignores setup costs, there are two important conclusions that are derived from theorems 6.1 and 6.2.

First, a qualitative interpretation of theorem 6.1 is that the larger the g_{it}'s are for small values of t, the better it is in terms of total primary costs. That is, the longer the initial inventories are carried into the future, the higher will be the total cost. Consequently, the best disaggregation scheme must allocate the initial inventory of each product type uniformly, in terms of runout time, among all its items. This interpretation makes clear that the EROT disaggregation is optimal, as proved in theorem 6.2. However, when setup costs grow in importance, it is desirable to allocate larger inventories to the items that have the highest setup costs. The motivation for a nonuniform allocation of inventories among items in a product type is the desire to minimize total setup costs. Therefore, we face a tradeoff between using the EROT disaggregation procedure and consequently minimizing total primary costs while incurring high setup costs, and choosing a disaggregation that allocates the inventories in a manner that considers setup cost levels, reducing these costs while incurring higher primary costs. Our computational experience, to be discussed in section 6.2.10, has shown that when the total setup costs are 5% or less of the total production costs, EROT performs quite efficiently. The RKM, enhanced by modifications to be introduced in the next section, is one of those methodologies that are more effective than EROT when setup costs are significant.

Second, EROT is a "myopic" disaggregation rule. The aggregate planning model covers a long planning horizon, usually a full year, to allow for an efficient allocation of facilities, manpower, and inventory under fluctuating demand conditions. However, once the aggregate plan has been established, we need just to look for a few periods ahead (the length of which is represented by the runout time) to determine an appropriate disaggregation. Although EROT is an optimal disaggregation procedure only under the absence of setup costs, the qualitative implications of this approach support the essence of hierarchical planning, which advocates the use of long planning horizons at the highest planning level while drastically decreasing the planning horizons at the lower planning levels.

6.2.9 Modifications Introduced in Regular Knapsack Method

Concerns about the performance of disaggregation procedures under high setup costs, and the myopic nature of disaggregation rules, led Bitran, Haas, and Hax [1981] to incorporate some modifications in the single-stage hierarchical planning system referred to as the Regular Knapsack Method. Computational results evaluating the performance of EROT, RKM, and the modified knapsack will be discussed in section 6.2.10. This section will cover three important changes made to RKM.

6.2.9.1 A myopic objective formulation for the family subproblem

The objective function proposed originally in the RKM (see section 6.2.4) was:

$$\text{Minimize} \sum_{j \in J^\circ} \frac{s_j d_j}{Y_j}$$

The definition of d_j, covering demand over the entire planning horizon, contradicts the myopic nature of the disaggregation process referred to in the previous section. As a consequence, the resulting solution Y_j of problem Pi will not be sensitive to the difference among the demand patterns of the families belonging to a given product type in the immediate future. Inspired by the results of theorems 6.1 and 6.2, d_j was redefined as a demand for family j over the runout time of its corresponding product type; that is to say, over the time interval that would exhaust the production quantity X_{i1} of the product type i containing family j when that quantity is disaggregated according to the EROT scheme.

6.2.9.2   *The look-ahead feasibility rule*

Another important problem that led us into modifying the RKM was the generation of infeasibilities that could be introduced in the aggregate problem by the disaggregation procedure used. Golovin [1975] detected this problem and illustrated its occurrence by means of a numerical example. Gabbay [1975] suggested a set of constraints to be introduced in the family subproblem that would provide necessary and sufficient conditions for the existence of feasible disaggregations over the entire planning horizons. However, his results were restricted to the static case; that is, when problem P is solved only at the beginning of the first period and no rolling horizon is used. Moreover, Gabbay's constraints destroy the special knapsack structure of the family subproblems, thus eliminating the computational advantages of such a structure.

To overcome the potential presence of infeasibilities, we developed a simple rule that looks ahead just one period, attempting to prevent the next period's disaggregation from becoming infeasible. We designated this as the "Look-Ahead Feasibility Rule." The essence of the computations needed to carry out this rule is presented in Figure 6.4.

A numerical example might facilitate an understanding of the applications of this rule.

Assume that the aggregate schedule for product type P1, composed of families F1 and F2, is:

PRODUCT TYPE P1	INITIAL INVENTORY	PRODUCTION	DEMAND	ENDING INVENTORY
Period 1	10 units	25 units	20 units	15 units
Period 2	15 units	5 units	20 units	0 units

Demand and inventory data for families F1 and F2 are as follows:

	F1	F2
INITIAL INVENTORY IN PERIOD 1	0 UNITS	10 UNITS
DEMAND IN PERIOD 1	10 UNITS	10 UNITS
DEMAND IN PERIOD 2	10 UNITS	10 UNITS

The inventory figures do not include safety stocks.

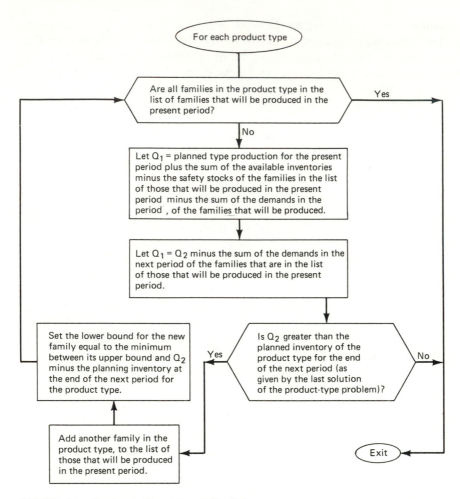

FIGURE 6.4   The Look-Ahead Feasibility Rule.

According to this data, only F1 will trigger in the first period. Therefore, under RKM, only F1 will be produced and its production quantity will be 25 units (for simplicity, we are assuming no upper bounds for both families). In the second period, only F2 will trigger, since its initial inventory will be zero units and its demand will be 10 units. However, since the production scheduled for P1 is 5 units, a shortage of 5 units for family 2 will result. If the Look Ahead routine in Figure 6.4 is applied, the value of Q_1 will be $Q_1 = 25 - 0 - 10 = 15$ and $Q_2 = 15 - 10 = 5$. The planned inventory for the product type P1 at the end of period 2 will be zero units. Hence, $Q_2 = 5 > 0$. Therefore, the "Look-Ahead Feasibility Rule" adds to the list of families to be produced in the present period (period 1), composed just of F1, the family F2 with a lower bound of 5 units for its production quantity. This modification will eliminate the infeasibility created by RKM. It is important to note that this adjustment routine does not preclude the use of the efficient knapsack algorithm to solve the family subproblem *Pi*.

6.2.9.3   Modifications of regular knapsack method for case of high setup costs

We have already addressed the role of setup costs in hierarchical production planning systems. The initial approaches introduced by Hax and Meal [1975] and Bitran and Hax [1977] ignore the setup costs at the product-type level, and include them in the decision rules at the family level. The resulting algorithms proved to be effective when setup costs did not exceed 10% of the total production costs, as reported in section 6.2.7.

The cases that still deserve consideration are those in which setup costs represented a percentage higher than 15 of the total production cost. Figure 6.5 describes a subroutine that we introduced to the RKM for those situations with fairly high setup costs. This routine can be easily modified to allow for managerial inputs which reflect their judgment regarding changes to be incorporated in the aggregate schedule in order to save setup costs. These changes will invariably represent tradeoffs between the linear costs identified in the aggregate production level and the setup costs incurred at the family level.

The routine briefly described in Figure 6.5 works as follows. Initially, the family subproblems *Pi* are solved and the production quantities Y_j for each family are obtained. The integer number of periods of demand, for each family *j*, that can be satisfied by Y_j, is computed and denoted by $N(j)$. Next, Silver–Meal's lot sizing method [1973] is applied, for each family *j*, considering the stream of demands starting with the present period. The output of the method is denoted by $L(j)$ and we refer to it as the ideal quantity to be produced for family *j* in the present period. We have chosen Silver–Meal's procedure instead of the Wagner–Whitin [1958] algorithm because the first is much more efficient computationally and gives satisfactory results (see Peterson and Silver [1979] for a comparison of the two methods). The next step is to compute the integer number $M(j)$ of periods of demand that can be totally satisfied by $L(j)$. It is important to note that $N(j)$, $L(j)$, and $M(j)$ are computed considering effective family demands. For each family, the difference between the capacity allocated by the family subproblems and the capacity needed to cover the demand for more than minimum $[M(j), N(j)]$ periods is considered freed. The sum of the freed capacities of each family, independently of the product type to which it belongs, is denoted by Z. After removing the free capacity from each family, we denote the remaining production quantity by $Q(j)$. All families are ordered according to "increasing marginal costs," $MC(J) = -1/Q(j)[s_j d_j/Q(j) - h_i Q(j)/2]$, where s_j is the setup cost for

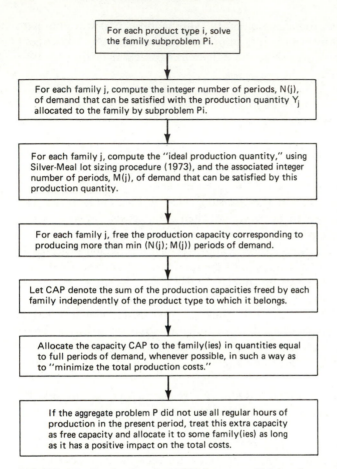

For each product type i, solve the family subproblem Pi.

For each family j, compute the integer number of periods, N(j), of demand that can be satisfied with the production quantity Y_j allocated to the family by subproblem Pi.

For each family j, compute the "ideal production quantity," using Silver-Meal lot sizing procedure (1973), and the associated integer number of periods, M(j), of demand that can be satisfied by this production quantity.

For each family j, free the production capacity corresponding to producing more than min (N(j); M(j)) periods of demand.

Let CAP denote the sum of the production capacities freed by each family independently of the product type to which it belongs.

Allocate the capacity CAP to the family(ies) in quantities equal to full periods of demand, whenever possible, in such a way as to "minimize the total production costs."

If the aggregate problem P did not use all regular hours of production in the present period, treat this extra capacity as free capacity and allocate it to some family(ies) as long as it has a positive impact on the total costs.

FIGURE 6.5   Routine to adapt RKM for case of high setup costs.

family j, d_j is the demand of family j over the myopic planning horizon (as defined in section 6.2.9.1), and h_i is the cost of holding one unit in stock for one period. The capacity Z is then allocated to the families in quantities equal to full periods of demand [whenever possible, starting with the one with minimum $MC(j)$]. After allocating one period of demand to a family j, its marginal cost is recomputed with $Q(j)$ increased by the corresponding amount. If after allocating the capacity Z there exists at least one family with negative marginal cost, and there are regular hours of production available that the aggregate problem P did not use for the present period, the routine allocates the time available to those families. We would like to point out that variants of the marginal criterion, $MC(j)$, have been tested and none performed better than the one reported here. This approach effectively alters the aggregate schedule as long as the expected savings in setup costs more than compensate for changes in the costs considered by the aggregate schedule.

6.2.10 *Computational Results*

A series of experiments were conducted by Bitran, Haas, and Hax [1981] to examine the performance of the modifications introduced in the hierarchical knapsack method and to compare this method with others. The data used for these tests was taken from the manufacturer of rubber tires reported in section 6.2.7. The product structure characteristics, together with relevant information, were given in Figure 6.3.

The experiments were divided into two sets. In the first set, the production planning methods were applied to a full year of simulated plant operations. Production decisions were made every four weeks. The model was then updated, using a one-year planning horizon. The process was repeated 13 times. At the end of the simulation, total setup costs, inventory holding costs, overtime costs, and backorders were calculated. Direct manufacturing costs and regular work force costs were omitted because they were considered fixed costs for this application.

The methods compared are:

1. The RKM modified by considering the myopic horizon for the demand at the family level (subsection 6.2.9.1) and the "Look-Ahead Feasibility Rule" (subsection 6.2.9.2). In Table 6.4 this method corresponds to the column "K12."

2. The RKM with the three modifications, that is, the modifications considered in point 1 above, plus the adjustment routine for high setup costs (subsection 6.2.9.3). In Table 6.4 this method corresponds to the column "K123."

3. EROT, which consists in disaggregating the product-type production quantities directly into item quantities, using as a criterion the equalization of runout times—that is, the production quantity of each product type—is allocated among the items in such a way that they last for an equal number of periods (assuming a perfect forecast). In Table 6.4, this method corresponds to the column "EROT."

Seventy-two experiments were performed. The base case corresponds to the data taken from the manufacturer of rubber tires. The data for the other 71 experiments were constructed by perturbing the data of the base case in order to explore the effects of the production capacity, magnitude, and relative values of the setup costs and forecast errors. Global statistics will be provided for the 72 experiments. Due to space limitations, we report in Table 6.4 the results of 17 problems solved. This subset is representative of the results obtained throughout the 72 experiments performed insofar as identifying meaningful combinations of available capacities, forecast errors, and setup costs. For the purpose of comparison, we have also solved the 17 problems by the RKM. The corresponding results are shown in column "RKM" in Table

TABLE 6.4   A Comparison of the Costs Resulting When the Various Approaches Were Tested on Sample Points

CASE	COST TYPE*	RKM	K12	K123	EROT	BEST MIP SOLUTION FOUND
Base case C1F1S1	Holding	29,920	30,651	45,476	29,923	
	Setup	5,580	5,360	5,030	5,910	
	Overtime	81,684	81,113	72,319	81,681	
	Total	117,184	117,120	122,825	117,514	115,616
	Setup/total	4.8%	4.6%	4.1%	5.0%	
	% difference in cost from MIP	1.4	1.3	6.2	1.6	
	Backorders	—	—	—	—	
C1F1S8	Holding	31,221	33,195	30,739	29,923	
	Setup	11,910	12,610	12,210	13,910	
	Overtime	82,382	79,302	81,682	81,682	
	Total	125,513	125,107	124,631	125,515	122,790
	Setup/total	9.5%	10.1%	9.8%	11.1%	
	% difference in cost from MIP	2.2	1.9	1.5	2.2	
	Backorders	71 units	—	—	—	
C1F1S5	Holding	31,922	32,028	35,921	29,923	
	Setup	67,050	67,050	54,650	68,850	
	Overtime	81,682	80,926	79,714	81,681	
	Total	180,654	180,004	170,285	180,454	165,550
	Setup/total	37.1%	37.2%	32.1%	38.2%	
	%difference in cost from MIP	9.1	8.7	2.9	9.0	
	Backorders	4 units	—	—	—	
C2F1S5	Holding	13,583	14,042	47,784	13,584	
	Setup	67,850	67,050	53,850	68,850	
	Overtime	48,577	48,878	24,681	47,578	
	Total	130,010	129,970	126,315	130,012	124,236
	Setup/total	52.2%	51.6%	42.6%	53.0%	
	% difference in cost from MIP	4.9	4.6	1.7	4.6	
	Backorders	—	—	—	—	
C1F2S1	Holding	64,380	65,473	65,386	63,806	
	Setup	4,740	5,070	5,030	5,730	
	Overtime	80,957	78,907	78,657	79,709	
	Total	150,077	149,450	152,073	149,245	
	Setup/total	3.2%	3.4%	3.3%	3.8%	
	Backorders	5 units	—	—	—	
C1F3S1	Holding	83,034	86,315	94,553	78,197	
	Setup	4,300	5,180	5,070	5,910	
	Overtime	88,396	83,491	80,303	90,412	
	Total	175,730	174,986	179,926	174,519	
	Setup/total	2.5	3.0	2.8	3.4	
	Backorders	—	—	—	—	

TABLE 6.4   A Comparison of the Costs Resulting When the Various Approaches Were Tested on Sample Points (continued)

CASE	COST TYPE*	RKM	K12	K123	EROT	BEST MIP SOLUTION FOUND
C1F3S7	Holding	85,343	90,295	89,088	78,197	
	Setup	194,000	171,300	152,200	203,700	
	Overtime	88,753	77,729	85,709	90,412	
	Total	368,096	339,324	326,997	372,309	
	Setup/total	52.7	50.5	46.5	54.7	
	Backorders	6 units	—	—	—	
C2F1S1	Holding	13,584	13,584	21,849	13,584	
	Setup	5,910	5,910	5,310	5,910	
	Overtime	48,878	47,578	42,237	47,578	
	Total	68,371	67,072	68,396	67,072	
	Setup/total	8.6	8.8	7.8	8.8	
	Backorders	—	—	—	—	
C2F1S7	Holding	13,583	14,066	59,739	13,584	
	Setup	200,500	195,300	134,100	203,700	
	Overtime	48,878	48,878	28,047	47,578	
	Total	262,961	258,244	221,881	264,862	
	Setup/total	76.2	75.6	60.4	76.9	
	Backorders	—	—	—	—	
C2F2S1	Holding	49,856	49,856	53,721	49,856	
	Setup	5,730	5,730	5,400	5,910	
	Overtime	50,269	48,523	47,503	48,523	
	Total	105,855	104,109	106,624	104,289	
	Setup/total	5.4	5.5	5.1	5.7	
	Backorders	—	—	—	—	
C3F1S1	Holding	73,016	76,157	82,455	77,584	
	Setup	3,930	4,480	4,480	5,910	
	Overtime	118,560	117,326	111,320	112,560	
	Total	195,506	197,963	198,255	196,054	
	Setup/total	2.0	2.3	2.3	3.0	
	Backorders	5,522 units	—	—	—	
C3F1S7	Holding	71,584	92,752	92,678	77,584	
	Setup	198,500	192,700	172,100	203,700	
	Overtime	118,560	98,960	99,830	112,560	
	Total	388,645	384,412	364,608	393,844	
	Setup/total	51.1	50.1	47.2	51.7	
	Backorders	6,942 units	—	—	—	
C3F2S1	Holding	84,620	100,304	106,213	80,986	
	Setup	4,300	4,920	4,810	5,910	
	Overtime	118,560	92,930	88,600	108,243	
	Total	207,480	198,154	199,623	195,139	
	Setup/total	2.1	2.5	2.4	3.0	
	Backorders	8,159 units	301 units	301 units	1,412 units	

TABLE 6.4   A Comparison of the Costs Resulting When the Various Approaches Were Tested on Sample Points (continued)

CASE	COST TYPE*	RKM	K12	K123	EROT	BEST MIP SOLUTION FOUND
C3F2S7	Holding	84,842	97,526	108,409	82,986	
	Setup	202,900	195,300	178,700	203,700	
	Overtime	118,560	91,634	91,450	108,243	
	Total	406,302	384,460	378,559	392,929	
	Setup/total	49.9	50.8	47.2	51.8	
	Backorders	6,178 units	—	—	—	
C3F3S1	Holding	87,030	120,364	117,426	86,926	
	Setup	4,300	4,920	4,920	5,910	
	Overtime	118,560	87,192	90,257	118,531	
	Total	209,900	212,476	212,603	211,367	
	Setup/total	2.1	2.3	2.3	2.8	
	Backorders	10,302 units	—	—	—	
C3F3S7	Holding	86,570	120,349	145,205	86,926	
	Setup	190,600	188,800	174,700	203,700	
	Overtime	118,559	92,219	74,385	118,531	
	Total	395,729	400,368	394,290	409,157	
	Setup/total	48.2	47.2	44.3	49.8	
	Backorders	10,158 units	—	—	—	
C3F1S5	Holding	71,584	90,084	90,826	77,584	
	Setup	60,050	50,450	54,650	68,850	
	Overtime	118,559	104,864	100,560	112,560	
	Total	250,193	255,398	246,038	258,994	
	Setup/total	24.0	19.8	22.2	26.6	
	Backorders	6,942 units	—	—	—	

*CODE   Holding cost—dollars
Setup cost—dollars
Overtime cost—dollars
Total cost—dollars
Setup/total—percentage
Backorders—units

6.4. The data structure used in the computational experiments is given below:

Capacity (3 cases)

- C1: 2,000 hrs./month   regular time
- C2: 2,500 hrs./month   regular time
- C3: 1,600 hrs./month   regular time

Overtime is 60% of the regular hours in all three cases.

Forecast errors (3 cases)

- F1: zero forecast error
- F2: $.02 + .01t^{1.3}$ with no bias
- F3: $.02 + .01t^{1.3}$ all positive forecast errors

where t denotes the period in the planning horizon of the aggregate problem. F2 and F3 assume that the forecast error increases in absolute value as t increases. That is, the further away a period is, the higher the average absolute value of the forecast error is. For F2, the probabilities of positive and negative forecast errors were assumed to be equal to .5.

Setup Costs (8 cases)

		Product type 1	Product type 2
S1	Family 1	90	110
	Family 2	90	110
	Family 3	—	110
S2	Family 1	900	1,100
	Family 2	900	1,100
	Family 3	—	1,100
S3	Family 1	900	110
	Family 2	1,800	110
	Family 3	—	110
S4	Family 1	500	1,000
	Family 2	2,000	100
	Family 3	—	50
S5	Family 1	5,000	400
	Family 2	50	400
	Family 3	—	1,000
S6	Family 1	3,000	110
	Family 2	4,000	110
	Family 3	—	110
S7	Family 1	6,000	400
	Family 2	4,500	5,000
	Family 3	—	3,000
S8	Family 1	300	300
	Family 2	90	100
	Family 3	—	400

The notation used in Table 6.4 is as follows: $CiFjSk$ indicates that the capacity data used in Ci, the forecast error structure is Fj, and the setup cost structure is Sk. C1F1S1 corresponds to the base case.

Some conclusions that can be drawn from the computational experiments are:

1. Independent of capacity limitations and forecast errors, under low setup costs, K123 does not perform as effectively as K12. However, as expected, under high setup costs the routine is effective and should be used.
2. Although the backorders observed are not significant in the experiments performed, they are always lower in K12 and K123 than in the EROT method. In all cases with tight capacity and forecast error (either biased or unbiased), the EROT procedure carried backorders.
3. All three methods react as expected to high forecast errors and capacity constraints.

4. The cases in which the EROT procedure performed better than the other two methods were characterized by extremely low setup costs. However, the improvement over K12 is not significant even in those few cases.

5. In 13 out of the 17 cases, K12 outperformed RKM in terms of total cost. In the four cases where the reverse occurs, the regular knapsack method presents a significant number of backorders.

6. It is interesting to observe that, except in one case with significant forecast error (C3F2S7), the sum of holding and overtime costs are smaller for the EROT than for other methods. This fact is a direct consequence of theorem 6.2.

To test if the observed differences in the total costs obtained with the four methods are statistically significant, the Wilcoxon signed rank test was performed. The test was used to compare the methods, pairwise. The null hypothesis is that the total costs of the first approach are less than or equal to those of the second. Table 6.5 shows the results obtained for the Wilcoxon test. *WI* is the Wilcoxon statistics and σ is its standard deviation.

The Wilcoxon statistics indicate that, overall, the adjusted knapsack with feedback is superior to all other approaches. However, our detailed analysis suggests that if the setup costs are very small—that is, less than 10% of the total cost—the feedback algorithm should not be used.

The second set of experiments consisted in solving a selected sample of the 72 problems as mixed integer programming problems (MIP). The formulation of the production planning problems as MIPs can be seen as an optimal representation. The four problems shown in Table 6.6 were solved using the Land and Powell package on the computer Prime 400 at M.I.T. Unfortunately, although each problem contains only 65 zero-one variables, no "true optimal" solution was found within 40 hours of connect time for each of the four problems. In Table 6.6, we indicate the best solution available at time of interruption of the computer programs. Due to the poor performance of the mixed integer package, we limited the experiments to only four problems which were solved just once (rather than on a rolling horizon basis). This last fact favors the MIP formulations. To facilitate the comparison between the methods, the results corresponding to the four problems obtained in Table 6.4 for the RKM, K12, K123, and EROT algorithms are repeated in Table 6.6.

TABLE 6.5   Results Obtained for Wilcoxon Test

METHODS COMPARED	WILCOXON STATISTICS	SAMPLE SIZE	CONFIDENCE WITH WHICH NULL HYPO-THESIS CAN BE REJECTED (%)
RKM vs. K12	$WI = 1.81\sigma$	17	96
RKM vs. K123	$WI = 1.90\sigma$	17	97
K12 vs. K123	$WI = 5.36\sigma$	72	> 99
EROT vs. K123	$WI = 5.53\sigma$	72	> 99

The results in Table 6.6 indicate that when the setup costs are less than 5% of total costs and K12 is used, or when the setup costs are greater than 5% and K123 is used, the total annual costs were never more than 3% greater than the best MIP solution found after 40 hours of connect time. Finally, we point out that none of the 72 problems solved by the RKM, K12, K123, and EROT algorithms on a rolling horizon basis—that is, solved 13 times over the horizon of one year—exceeded 10 minutes of connect time on the M.I.T. computer Prime 400.

The experimentation reported herein tends to confirm our belief that hierarchical planning systems provide a very effective alternative for supporting production planning decisions at a tactical and operational level. When contrasted with a mixed integer programming formulation, hierarchical planning methods produce near-optimal solutions with significantly smaller computational efforts and data collection requirements. The hierarchical planning approach represents a feasible alternative for the solution of large-scale real life problems which will be unthinkable to tackle with an MIP–based model. Moreover, and most important from a pragmatic point of view, the hierarchical approach parallels the hierarchy of production planning decisions within the firm.

From a methodological point of view, our experiments seem to indicate that the modifications introduced to the Regular Knapsack Method clearly improve the performance of previous algorithms. The K123 method, under the wide variety of situations tested, outperforms statistically all other methodological alternatives considered. However, a closer examination of those cases where setup costs account for less than 10% of the total production cost indicates that K12 or EROT might br preferred over K123. EROT and K12 tend to perform quite closely under low-setup cost conditions.

6.3 Hierarchical Production Planning: A Two-Stage System

In the previous sections, we have addressed the issue of designing hierarchical production planning (HPP) systems for batch processing in a single-stage manufacturing environment. We will now turn our attention to discuss extensions of this approach to support two-stage production processes. This is

TABLE 6.6 Total Costs

	C1F1S1	C1F1S5	C1F1S8	C2F1S5
RKM	117,184	180,654	125,513	130,010
K12	117,120	180,004	125,107	129,970
K123	122,825	170,285	124,631	126,315
EROT	117,514	180,454	125,515	130,012
Best MIP solution	115,616	165,550	122,790	124,236

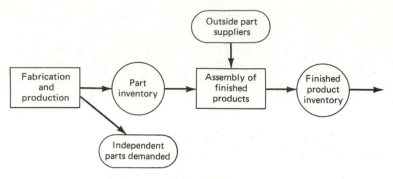

FIGURE 6.6   The two-stage production setting.

an important area of concern since many manufacturing environments can be described in these terms. The most relevant of such environments involve fabrication and assembly operations, where activities have to be planned in a coordinated way. Figure 6.6 illustrates a simplified representation of a two-stage setting. A conceptual overview of a two-stage HPP system is given in Figure 6.7. The essence of the approach can be summarized as follows:

- First, individual parts and finished products are grouped into aggregate parts and aggregate finished products.
- Second, an aggregate model is used to schedule the corresponding production quantities for those aggregate parts and finished products. The model addresses this decision jointly, thus guaranteeing the appropriate coordination of the two-stage process.
- Third, the aggregate part production and finished product production plans are disaggregated to determine the detailed schedules for individual parts and finished products.
- Fourth, a reconciliation of possible differences at the detail level is performed via part inventories.

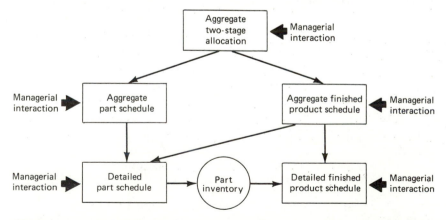

FIGURE 6.7   Conceptual overview of hierarchical production planning system for fabrication and assembly process.

We will now proceed to describe the methodology proposed by Bitran, Haas, and Hax [1982] for the development of two-stage hierarchical production planning systems.

6.3.1   Hierarchical Structure
for the Two-Stage Production System

The highest level of planning in the hierarchical approach determines production schedules for aggregate parts and aggregate finished products (see Figure 6.7). Thus, the first design decision to be made concerns the way in which individual parts and finished products are to be aggregated.

The criterion for the aggregation of finished products follows quite closely the one adopted for the single-stage hierarchical planning system. The aggregation used for finished products in the two-stage setting is as follows:

- *Product items*: are end finished products delivered to customers.
- *Product types*: are groups of finished product items having similar direct production costs (excluding labor), holding cost per unit per period, productivities (number of units that can be produced per unit of time), and seasonalities.
- *Product families*: are groups of finished product items sharing a major setup cost and requiring an identical number of the same parts.

The aggregation criterion for parts recognizes only one level of aggregation:

- *Part items*: are individual parts either required as a component to a product item or having an independent demand as a service or spare part.
- *Part types*: are groups of part items having similar direct production costs, holding costs per part per period, and productivities. Part items also share common fabrication facilities. For parts, two levels of aggregation were sufficient as no two items shared a setup cost.

This aggregation of finished products and parts is applicable to many industrial settings encountered in practice. This framework can be adjusted to fit several variants of the proposed aggregation structure and should not be seen as a limitation of the hierarchical methodology to be presented.

6.3.2   Aggregate Production Planning
for Product Types and Part Types

The aggregate two-stage allocation model introduced here is formulated as a linear program. This representation is chosen because in the vast majority of practical instances, production allocation decisions lend themselves quite naturally to be treated by linear programming. However, any of the aggregate production models suggested in Chapter 3 could have been used as long as they provide an acceptable formulation of the process being considered.

The Aggregate Two-Stage Linear Programming Model

Problem P'

Minimize
$$\sum_{t=1}^{T} \sum_{i=1}^{I} \left(h_{it} I_{it} + r_t R_{it} + o_t O_{it} \right)$$

$$+ \sum_{t=1}^{T-L} \sum_{k=1}^{K} \left(\hat{h}_{kt} \hat{I}_{kt} + \hat{r}_{kt} \hat{R}_{kt} + \hat{o}_{kt} \hat{O}_{kt} \right)$$

subject to:

$$I_{it-1} + m_i(R_{it} + O_{it}) + I_{it} = d_{it} \qquad i = 1,2,\ldots,I; t = 1,2,\ldots,T \qquad (6.6)$$

$$\sum_{i=1}^{I} R_{it} \leqslant (rm)_t \qquad t = 1,2,\ldots,T$$

$$\sum_{i=1}^{I} O_{it} \leqslant (om)_t \qquad t = 1,2,\ldots,T$$

$$ss_{it} \leqslant I_{it} \leqslant os_{it} \qquad i = 1,2,\ldots,I; t = 1,2,\ldots,T$$

$$\sum_{k=1}^{K} \hat{R}_{kt} \leqslant (\widehat{rm})_t \qquad t = 1,2,\ldots,T - L$$

$$\sum_{k=1}^{K} \hat{O}_{kt} \leqslant (\hat{o}_m)_t \qquad t = 1,2,\ldots,T - L$$

$$\widehat{ss}_{kt} \leqslant \hat{I}_{kt} \leqslant \widehat{os}_{kt} \qquad k = 1,2,\ldots,K; t = 1,2,\ldots,T - L$$

$$\hat{I}_{kt-1} + \hat{m}_k(\hat{R}_{kt} + \hat{O}_{kt}) - \hat{I}_{kt} = \sum_{i=1}^{I} f_{ik} m_k(R_{it+L} + O_{it+L}) \qquad (6.7)$$

$$k = 1,2,\ldots,K; t = 1,2,\ldots,T - L$$

$$R_{it}, O_{it}, I_{it}, \hat{R}_{kt}, \hat{O}_{kt}, \text{ and } \hat{I}_{kt} \geqslant 0 \qquad i = 1,\ldots,I; k = 1,2,\ldots,K;$$

$$t = 1,2,\ldots,T.$$

The indices i, k, and t represent, respectively, product types, part types, and time periods. The parameters h_{it}, r_t, o_t, m_i, d_{it}, $(rm)_t$, $(om)_t$, ss_{it}, and os_{it} denote, respectively, the cost of holding one unit of inventory of product type i from period t to period $t + 1$, the cost of one hour of regular labor in period t, the cost of one hour of overtime in period t, the productivity of product type i, the effective demand of units of product type i in period t, the number of regular labor hours in period t, the number of overtime hours in period t, the safety stock of product type i in period t, and the overstock limit of product type i in period t. The parameters with a "`^`" have the same meaning for part types.

The number of units of part type k required per unit of product type i is represented by f_{ik}. This parameter is discussed later in this section. The variables R_{it}, O_{it}, and I_{it} denote the number of hours of regular labor time, the number of hours of overtime, and the number of units in inventory for product type i in period t. The variables with a "`^`" have the same meaning for part type k in period t. The fabrication lead time of parts is denoted by L. The labor unit cost for part types has been assumed to be a function of each part type, while the labor unit cost for assembly, r_t and o_t, are taken equal for all product types. These assumptions do not cause a loss of generality in the results discussed in the paper.

Effective demands for product types are computed by netting out the available inventory of each item belonging to the product type. Therefore, in our model formulation, $I_{io} = 0$ for $i = 1, 2, \ldots, I$. For the computation of the effective demand see section 6.2.6.

Problem P′ is solved with a rolling horizon of length T. At the end of each time period, new information becomes available and is used to update the model. Only the results pertaining to the first $L + 1$ periods for product types, and to the first period for part types, are implemented. Constraints (6.7) couple part-type requirements and product-type production. The other set of constraints involves either part types or product types, but not both. The first L constraints in (6.6) are included in order to take into consideration the revised forecasts made at the beginning of each period. Although the corresponding parts are already being manufactured, or have already been ordered, minor variations can be absorbed either by expediting the part production or having a supplier make a special delivery.

To simplify the formulation of problem P′, we have intentionally omitted planned backorders, hiring and firing, lost sales, and subcontracting. If needed, these can easily be incorporated.

A critical point in the two-stage model is the definition of the parameters f_{ik}. Theorem 6.3 below shows how those parameters are computed. It also demonstrates that, under certain hypotheses, the definition adopted implies the existence of a feasible disaggregation scheme.

Let j denote a generic product family of product type i, let n be a generic part in part type k, and define f_{ik} as a weighted average of the f_{ijkn} as:

$$f_{ik} = \frac{\sum_{j \in J(i)} \sum_{n \in N(k)} \bar{d}_j f_{ijkn}}{\sum_{j \in J(i)} \bar{d}_j} \qquad i = 1, 2, \ldots, I; k = 1, 2, \ldots, K \qquad (6.8)$$

where $J(i)$ is the set of indices of the product families in product type i, $N(k)$ is the set of indices of parts in part type k, $\bar{d}_j$ is the annual demand of family j, and f_{ijkn} is the number of units of part n required by each unit of product family j. Note that f_{ijkn} is well defined since, by definition, the families in a product type require the same number of units of the same parts. Although problem P′ is solved on a rolling horizon basis, the f_{ik}'s need not be recomputed at every period unless the forecasts of the annual demand vary significantly.

It is important to realize that the parameter f_{ik} represents a weighted average of the parts required by individual items. Thus, the solution of the aggregate problem P′ does not assure the existence of feasible disaggregation even with perfect forecasts. Fortunately, under mild conditions feasibility can be achieved, as is shown in the following theorem. The main thrust of the theorem is to provide a qualitative insight into this difficult problem.

Theorem 6.3.   Assume that a perfect forecast is available, that the initial inventory of every product family is equal to zero, and that problem P is solved just once (i.e., it is not solved on a rolling horizon basis). The first L constraints in (6.6) are deleted. Then the initial inventory of part type k plus the production scheduled by problem P′ for this part type up to period τ is sufficient to satisfy the sum of the demands, corresponding to the interval $[1, \tau]$, of all parts in part type k for every τ, such that, $1 \leqslant \tau \leqslant T - L$.

Proof.   Denote $m_i(R_{it+L} + O_{it+L})$ by X_{it+L}. The production of part type k from periods 1 to τ plus its initial inventory, for a generic τ in the interval $[1, T - L]$, is:

$$\hat{I}_{ko} + \sum_{t=1}^{\tau} \hat{m}_k(\hat{R}_{kt} + \hat{O}_{kt}) = \hat{I}_{k\tau} + \sum_{t=1}^{\tau} \sum_{i=1}^{I} f_{ik} X_{it+L} = \hat{I}_{k\tau} + E_k, \quad (6.9)$$

where $E_k = \sum_{t=1}^{\tau} \sum_{i=1}^{I} f_{ik} X_{it+L}$, and the first equality follows from (6.7). The sum of the demands of all parts, corresponding to the interval $[1, \tau]$, in part type k is:

$$\sum_{i=1}^{I} \sum_{t=1}^{\tau} \sum_{j \in J(i)} \sum_{n \in N(k)} f_{ijkn} \bar{d}_{jt+L} = B_k, \quad (6.10)$$

where $\bar{d}_{jt+L}$ denotes the demand of product family j in period $t + L$. Recall that, by assumption, the initial inventories of each finished product family are zero.

We first show that $E_k \geqslant B_k$. Since all items in a given product type i have the same seasonality, it follows that the ratio of cumulative family demands within a product type remains constant:

$$\frac{\sum_{t=1}^{} \bar{d}_{jt+L}}{\sum_{j \in J(i)} \sum_{t=1}^{\tau} \bar{d}_{jt+L}} = \frac{\bar{d}_j}{\sum_{j \in J(i)} \bar{d}_j} . \quad (6.11)$$

Hence, from (6.8) and (6.11),

$$f_{ik} = \frac{\sum_{j \in J(i)} \sum_{n \in N(k)} \sum_{t=1}^{\tau} f_{ijkn} \bar{d}_{jt+L}}{\sum_{j \in J(i)} \sum_{t=1}^{\tau} \bar{d}_{jt+L}},$$

and:

$$\sum_{j \in J(i)} \sum_{t=1}^{\tau} f_{ik} \bar{d}_{jt+L} = \sum_{j \in J(i)} \sum_{n \in N(k)} \sum_{t=1}^{\tau} f_{ijkn} \bar{d}_{jt+L},$$

or, equivalently, since $\bar{d}_{it+L} = \sum_{j \in J(i)} \bar{d}_{jt+L}$, we have:

$$\sum_{i=1}^{I} \sum_{t=1}^{\tau} f_{ik} \bar{d}_{it+L} = \sum_{i=1}^{I} \sum_{j \in J(i)} \sum_{n \in N(k)} \sum_{t=1}^{\tau} f_{ijkn} \bar{d}_{jt+L}. \qquad (6.12)$$

The aggregate problem P′ implies that:

$$\sum_{t=1}^{\tau} X_{it+L} \geqslant \sum_{t=1}^{\tau} \bar{d}_{it+L}. \qquad (6.13)$$

Therefore, by substituting (6.13) in (6.12) we obtain:

$$E_k \geqslant B_k. \qquad (6.14)$$

Since $\hat{I}_{k\tau} \geqslant 0$, it follows by (6.9), (6.10), and (6.14) that:

$$\hat{I}_{ko} + \sum_{t=1}^{\tau} \hat{m}_k (\hat{R}_{kt} + \hat{O}_{kt}) \geqslant \sum_{i=1}^{I} \sum_{j \in J(i)} \sum_{n \in N(k)} \sum_{t=1}^{\tau} f_{ijkn} \bar{d}_{jt+L}.$$

Since theorem 6.3 assumes perfect forecasts, it might seem that a feasible disaggregation is a trivial matter. However, this is not the case because of the complexity of the bill of materials which contains families within product types with different parts.

Moreover, although theorem 6.3 establishes feasibility conditions for the case of no forecast error and a stationary horizon, our computational experience indicates that good results are obtained even in the absence of these conditions. There are two reasons to support this fact. First, in our computational work, we have observed that the rolling production schedules obtained are quite stable. Second, it can be shown that if the initial inventories are nonzero, but the product families' initial inventories are well balanced, that is, if:

$$\frac{I_{jo}}{\sum_{j \in J(i)} I_{jo}} = \frac{\bar{d}_j}{\sum_{j \in J(i)} \bar{d}_j}, \qquad \text{for } i = 1, 2, \ldots, I \text{ and } jJ(i), \qquad (6.15)$$

then theorem 6.3 holds.

It is important to realize that, although the aggregate linear programming problem treats the demand of products and parts as being deterministic, uncertainties and forecast errors are reorganized and captured by safety stock constraints. The magnitude of the safety stock lower bounds depends on the characteristics of each application. Managers can use shadow prices provided by linear programming and sensitivity analyses, in addition to their experience and knowledge of the operation, to establish convenient values for safety stocks. These quantities can also be used to provide a protection against inaccuracies that might be present in the bill of materials.

We conclude this section by pointing out that the setup costs have been intentionally ignored in problem P'. They are considered during the disaggregation process. This procedure is acceptable whenever setup costs are not a significant portion of total costs. When this is not the case, a procedure similar to the one described in subsection 6.2.9.3 for adjusting the hierarchical method for high setup costs can be developed.

6.3.3 Two-Stage Hierarchical Production Planning System—The Disaggregation Procedure

The disaggregation of the solution of the aggregate problem P' is performed in two steps. Initially, product family requirements over the first $L+1$ periods and part requirements for period 1 are determined. In the second step, the production quantities for product items in period 1 are obtained by disaggregating the corresponding production quantities of the product families to which they belong. Let X_{it} and $\hat{X}_{kt}$ denote, respectively, $m_i(R_{it} + O_{it})$ and $\hat{m}_k(\hat{R}_{kt} + \hat{O}_{kt})$.

Step 1: Product Families and Part Requirements. To determine the production quantities for product families and parts, the following problem needs to be solved:

Problem PD

Minimize
$$\sum_{t=1}^{L+1} \sum_{i=1}^{I} \sum_{j \in J(i,t)} (s_j D_{jt}/Q_{jt}) + \sum_{k=1}^{K} \sum_{n \in N(k,1)} (\hat{s}_k \hat{D}_{k1}/\hat{Q}_{n1}) \quad (6.16)$$

subject to:

$$\sum_{i=1}^{I} \sum_{j \in J(i,t)} f_{ijkn} Q_{jt} \leq \widehat{ai}_{nt} - \widehat{ss}_{nt}$$
$$k = 1,\ldots,K; n \in N(k); t = 1,\ldots,L \quad (6.17)$$

$$\sum_{i=1}^{I} \sum_{j \in J(i,L+1)} f_{ijkn} Q_{jL+1} \leq \widehat{ai}_{nL+1} - \widehat{ss}_{nL+1} + \hat{Q}_{n1}$$
$$k = 1,\ldots,K; n \in N(k) \quad (6.18)$$

$$\sum_{j \in J(i,t)} Q_{jt} = X_{it} \qquad i = 1,\ldots,I; t = 1,\ldots,L+1 \quad (6.19)$$

$$\sum_{n \in N(k,1)} \hat{Q}_{n1} = \hat{X}_{k1} \qquad k = 1,\ldots,K \quad (6.20)$$

$$lb_{jt} \leq Q_{jt} \leq ub_{jt} \qquad i = 1,\ldots,I; j \in J(i,t); t = 1,\ldots,L+1 \quad (6.21)$$

$$\hat{lb}_{n1} \leq \hat{Q}_{n1} \leq \hat{ub}_{n1} \qquad k = 1,\ldots,K; n \in N(k,1). \quad (6.22)$$

The setup cost of product family j is denoted by s_j. The demand of family j over the runout time of the product type to which it belongs is represented by D_{jt}. The runout time is the number of time periods in which the available inventory plus the production quantity X_{it} minus the safety stock of the product type is expected to last. The lower and upper bounds lb_{jt} and ub_{jt} are defined as follows:

$$lb_{jt} = \max\left(0, \bar{d}_{jt} - ai_{jt} + ss_{jt}\right) \qquad (6.23)$$

$$ub_{jt} = \max\left(0, os_{jt} - ai_{jt}\right) \qquad (6.24)$$

where $\bar{d}_{jt}$, ai_{jt}, and ss_{jt} are, respectively, the demand, the available inventory, and the safety stock in period t. The variable Q_{jt} denotes the production quantity of family j in period t. The parameters and variables with a "~" have the same meaning for parts instead of product families. $\widehat{ai}_{nt}$ includes the numbers of units of part n on order or being fabricated that will become available in period t. $J(i, t)$ and $N(k, t)$ are, respectively, the set of indices of families in product type i and the set of indices of parts in part type k that have a strictly positive lower bound in period t. These are the families and parts that are triggered in period t.

The objective function (6.16) assumes that the family-run quantities are proportional to the setup costs and to the annual demand for a given family. This assumption, which is the basis of the economic order quantity formulation, tends to minimize the average annual setup cost. Notice that the demand terms in the objective function, D_{jt} and $\hat{D}_{k1}$, cover a planning horizon equal to the runout time. This is consistent with the myopic rules developed in subsection 6.2.9.2. Constraint (6.17) could have been omitted and the productions corresponding to the lead time "frozen." However, we have chosen not to freeze the production over the horizon L since some corrections can be accommodated in practice either by expediting production or by having special deliveries made by suppliers. Problem PD has a convex objective function with linear constraints. It has been solved by the Frank and Wolfe [1956] algorithm. This method solves the problem through a sequence of linear programs and can be applied to the large-scale problems encountered in practice.

Theorem 6.4 below shows that under certain conditions a disaggregation problem, intimately related to problem PD, can be decomposed into continuous convex knapsack subproblems of the same type as those that arise in the single-stage hierarchical model. The advantage is that the knapsack problems can be solved by the efficient algorithm reported in subsection 6.2.4.

The lower and upper bounds (6.23) and (6.24) for $t = 2, \ldots, L+1$ are a function of the disaggregation procedures used in periods 1 to L, since the available inventories are affected by those disaggregations. However, because the rolling horizon production schedules tend to be quite stable, it is possible to estimate the lower and upper bounds using the results obtained from the disaggregation of the last aggregate schedule available. We denote these estimates by lbe_{jt} and ube_{jt} and rewrite (6.21) as:

$$\begin{cases} lb_{j1} \leqslant Q_{j1} \leqslant ub_{j1} & i = 1, \ldots, I; \ j \in J(i,1) \\ lbe_{jt} \leqslant Q_{jt} \leqslant ube_{jt} & i = 1, \ldots, I; \ j \in J(i,t); \ t = 2, \ldots, L+1. \end{cases}$$

$$(6.21')$$

Problem PD with (6.21') instead of (6.21) is denoted by problem PDe.

Theorem 6.4. Assume that a perfect forecast is available for the first $L+1$ periods, and that the product families in each product type require the same number of units of each part, that is, $f_{ijkn} = q_{ikn}$ for $i = 1, 2, \ldots, I; \ j \in J(i)$, $k = 1, \ldots, K$, and $n \in N(k)$. The Problem PDe can be decomposed in $[I(L+1) + k]T$ continuous convex knapsack problems.

Proof. Due to the assumption of perfect forecasts, safety stocks can be deleted and constraints (6.17) and (6.19) become:

$$\sum_{i=1}^{I} \sum_{j \in J(i,t)} f_{ijkn} Q_{jt} = \sum_{i=1}^{I} q_{ikn} X_{it} \leqslant \widehat{ai}_{nt}$$

$$k = 1, \ldots, K; \ n \in N(k); \ t = 1, \ldots, L \qquad (6.25)$$

and:

$$\sum_{i=1}^{K} \sum_{j \in J(i,L+1)} f_{ijkn} Q_{jL+1} = \sum_{i=1}^{I} q_{ikn} X_{iL+1} \leqslant \widehat{ai}_{nL+1} + \hat{Q}_{n1}$$

$$k = 1, \ldots, K; \ n \in N(k), \qquad (6.26)$$

where the first equalities in (6.25) and (6.26) follow from (6.19). The terms in the left-hand sides of the inequalities in (6.25) and (6.26) are known from the aggregate schedule obtained from problem P'. Moreover,

$$\widehat{ai}_{nt+1} = \widehat{ai}_{nt} - \sum_{i=1}^{I} q_{ikn} X_{it} \quad t = 1, \ldots, L.$$

Hence, all terms on the right-hand side of (6.25) and $\widehat{ai}_{nL+1}$ are not dependent on the method of disaggregation. Consequently, constraints (6.25) can be deleted. Therefore, problem PDe can be rewritten as:

Problem PDe

Minimize $\displaystyle \sum_{t=1}^{L+1} \sum_{i=1}^{I} \sum_{j \in J(i,t)} \left(s_j D_{jt} / Q_{jt} \right) + \sum_{k=1}^{K} \sum_{n \in N(k,1)} \left(\hat{s}_k \hat{D}_{k1} / \hat{Q}_{n,1} \right)$

subject to

$$\sum_{i=1}^{I} q_{ikn} X_{iL+1} \leq \widehat{ai}_{nL+1} + \hat{Q}_{nl} \quad k=1,\ldots,K; n \in N(k)$$

$$\sum_{j \in J(i,t)} Q_{jt} = X_{it} \qquad i=1,\ldots,I; t=1,\ldots,L+1$$

$$\sum_{n \in N(k,1)} \hat{Q}_{nl} = \hat{X}_{k1} \qquad k=1,\ldots,K$$

$$lb_{j1} \leq Q_{j1} \leq ub_{j1} \qquad i=1,\ldots,I; j \in J(i,1)$$

$$lbe_{jt} \leq Q_{jt} \leq ube_{jt} \qquad i=1,\ldots,I; j \in J(i,t); \qquad t=2,\ldots,L+1$$

$$\widehat{lb}_{nl} \leq \hat{Q}_{nl} \leq \widehat{ub}_{nl} \qquad k=1,\ldots,K; n \in N(k,1).$$

Problem PDe can be decomposed in the following $[I(L+1)+K]$ continuous convex knapsack problems:

Problem PK(i, 1)

For $i=1,2,\ldots,I$

Minimize
$$\sum_{j \in J(i,1)} s_j D_{j1}/Q_{j1}$$

subject to:

$$\sum_{j \in J(i,1)} Q_{j1} = X_{i1}$$

$$lb_{j1} \leq Q_{j1} \leq ub_{j1} \qquad j \in J(i,1).$$

Problem PK(i, t)

For $i=1,2,\ldots,I$ and $t=2,\ldots,L+1$

Minimize
$$\sum_{j \in J(i,t)} s_j D_{jt}/Q_{jt}$$

subject to:

$$\sum_{j \in J(i,t)} Q_{jt} = X_{it}$$

$$lbe_{jt} \leq Q_{jt} \leq ube_{jt} \qquad j \in J(i,t).$$

Problem PD(k)

For $k=1,2,\ldots,K$

Minimize
$$\sum_{n \in N(k,1)} \hat{s}_k \hat{D}_{k1}/\hat{Q}_{nl}$$

subject to:

$$\sum_{n \in N(k,1)} \hat{Q}_{n1} = \hat{X}_{k1}$$

$$\text{Maximum} \left(\widehat{lb}_{n1} ; \sum_{i=1}^{I} q_{ikn} X_{iL+1} - \widehat{ai}_{nL+1} \right) \leqslant \hat{Q}_{n1} \leqslant \widehat{ub}_{n1} \qquad n \in N(k,1).$$

The assumption of perfect forecast during the first $L+1$ periods allows us to decompose the problem into a set of knapsack problems that can be solved quite easily. Even if this assumption does not strictly hold, we can expect that moderate forecast errors can be absorbed by appropriate levels of safety stocks and the problem can still be decomposed without severe departures from optimality.

Step 2: Product Item Requirements. The last production quantities to be determined are the number of units of each product item to be assembled in the present period. That is, we need to disaggregate the quantities Q_{j1} obtained from either problem PD or problem PK($i, 1$). The disaggregation is performed through the following knapsack problem for each family j in $J(i, 1)$, $i = 1, 2, \ldots, I$.

Problem F(j, 1)

$$\text{Minimize} \sum_{v \in V(j)} \left[\frac{Q_{j1} + \sum_{v \in V(j)} (ai_{v1} - ss_{v1})}{\sum_{v \in V(j)} \bar{d}_{v1}} - \frac{z_{v1} + ai_{v1} - ss_{v1}}{\bar{d}_{v1}} \right]^2$$

subject to:

$$\sum_{v \in V(j)} z_{v1} = Q_{j1}$$

$$lb_{v1} \leqslant z_{v1} \leqslant ub_{v1} \qquad v \in V(j).$$

The parameters $\bar{d}_{v1}$, ai_{v1}, ss_{v1}, lb_{v1}, and ub_{v1} denote, respectively, the demand, available inventory, safety stock, lower bound, and upper bound of product item v in time period 1. $V(j)$ is set of indices of the product items in product family j. The lower and upper bounds lb_{v1} and ub_{v1} are computed in the same way as in (6.23) and (6.24). The objective function in problem $F(j, 1)$ attempts to equalize the runout time of each item in family j and the runout time of family j. Problem $F(j, 1)$ is a continuous convex knapsack problem with bounded variables. An effective algorithm to solve it has been provided in subsection 6.2.5.

6.4   Material Requirements Planning

Material Requirements Planning is the most widely used design philosophy to deal with multistage production planning (see Orlicky [1975]). MRP is essentially an information system and a simulation tool that generates proposals for production schedules which managers can evaluate in terms of their feasibility and cost effectiveness. MRP, in its present structure, does not deal directly with optimization criteria associated with multilevel production issues. Moreover, there is no single MRP design. In practice, one can observe a wide spectrum of MRP systems with which managers interact in different ways.

An MRP system is a collection of logical procedures for managing, at the most detailed level, inventories of component assemblies, subassemblies, parts, and raw materials in a manufacturing environment. It is a modern and, by necessity, improved version of an older technique utilized for quite a while in scheduling multistage production operations, called "parts explosion," used in determining the amounts of components required in the manufacturing of some *end item*.

A key element to the determination of component requirements is the *bill of material*, which is an engineering document and can be represented as a symbolic exploded view of the end item structure. Figure 6.8 shows a bill of material with six levels. An item on level *l* is a *parent item* to every item on level *l* + 1 to which it is connected by a line. These are called *component items*. Thus, subassembly S2 is a parent to subassembly S3, which is its component. In turn, subassembly S3 is a parent to components P6, P7, P8, and so on. The item on the highest level in such a tree-like structure, usually denoted "level zero," is the end item. Each level involves some action that requires a lead time to accomplish: purchasing of materials, fabrication, assembly, and so on.

A parts explosion implies computing the necessary amounts of every component material, part, subassembly, and so on required for the manufacturing of a given number of end item units. For this we have to know the "quantity per" factors, that is, the amounts required of each component item in order to obtain one parent item. Then, conceptually, it is quite simple: multiply the desired quantity of a parent item by the "quantity per" factor to obtain the needed number of component item units, called *gross requirements*. Repeat while going from level zero to the bottom of the bill of material.

With complex products, where large amounts of data have to be handled and processed, the older procedures performed manually were hardly able to do more than just the simple calculations mentioned above. The advent of large-storage, high-speed data processing equipment made it possible for the old technique to be reconsidered, made operational, and enhanced by the addition of a number of new and useful features, and so MRP evolved. It gained rapidly in popularity, especially after the APICS (*A*merican *P*roduction and *I*nventory *C*ontrol *S*ociety) MRP "crusade," conducted by its fervent proponents (e.g., Orlicky [1973, 1975], Orlicky, Plossl, and Wight [1972], Plossl [1980], Plossl and Wight [1971], Wight [1974], Berry, Vollman, and Whybark [1979]).

Our section here is intended to describe the basic logic of MRP. It is suggested that those interested further in the topic consult the following additional references: Smith [1978], Meal [1975], Chase and Aquilano [1981],

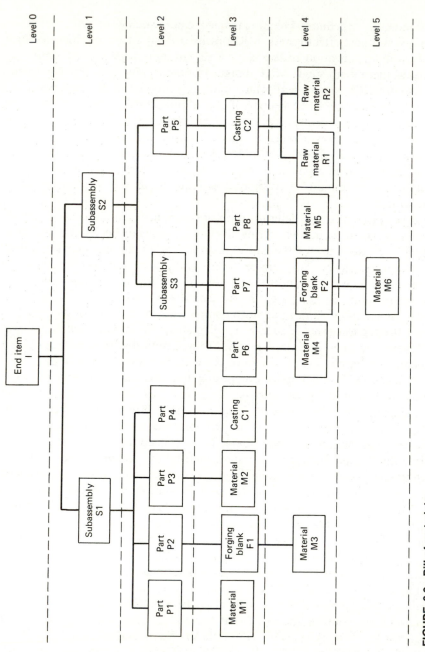

FIGURE 6.8   Bill of material

and McClain and Thomas [1980]. For an in-depth coverage of technical details, the book by Orlicky [1975] is probably the best source. On the application side, the COPICS manual outlines a computer based integrated manufacturing control system, including MRP, implemented by IBM.

In the context of multistage production, we distinguish between independent demand and dependent demand. The *independent demand* originates in market demand for an item. The demand by a parent item for its components is *dependent demand*. If an item is needed both as a component and as a spare part, we say that it experiences both dependent and independent demand.

An MRP system is designed to deal with dependent demand items. In the case of component items also having independent demand, the forecast quantity is added to the gross requirements in the same time period.

As far as the end-items are concerned, they are forecast and their production is planned outside MRP. This action results in what is called a *master production schedule*. MRP accepts the master schedule as an input, assumes that it is feasible from the viewpoint of the resource requirements, and plans orders of component items accordingly. If planned work load exceeds available capacity in some work centers, the problem is referred for solution to someone else. The system signals it but cannot deal with this problem (to be seen later).

The processing logic of MRP, involves the following sequence of calculations:

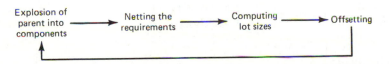

The *explosion* has already been mentioned as the mechanism by which gross requirements for component items are computed. First, one explodes period by period the quantities of level zero items (end items) planned for production by the master schedule. Figure 6.9 shows this process for our example of Figure 6.8. Then, after netting, lot sizing, and offsetting at level 1, the planned orders (to be seen) for level 1 items are exploded into gross requirements for level 2 components, and so on.

Net requirements are determined by netting the gross requirements against any amount on hand or already on order. Table 6.7 applies the netting computations to item S1. Suppose that now it is right at the beginning of time period 1, and we have an initial inventory of 20 units of subassembly S1; 80 units will be arriving in period 2 from an order released in the period just ending* (the arrow in the table is meant to suggest this).

*For greater clarity, let us agree on the following: quantities shown as inventory on hand or projected are considered to exist in stock at the end of the period; the scheduled receipts are always due at the beginning of the period; planned orders are released at the beginning of the period.

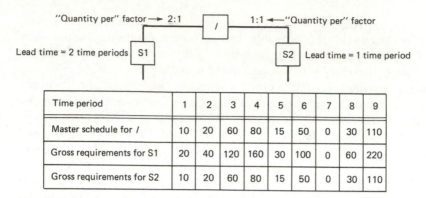

FIGURE 6.9 Explosion of planned production of *I* into gross requirements for S1 and S2.

Let index t denote the period ($t = 1, 2, 3, \ldots$). We calculate:

$$\begin{pmatrix} \text{Projected} \\ \text{inventory} \end{pmatrix}_1 = \begin{pmatrix} \text{Initial} \\ \text{inventory on hand} \end{pmatrix} + \begin{pmatrix} \text{Scheduled} \\ \text{receipts} \end{pmatrix}_1 - \begin{pmatrix} \text{Gross} \\ \text{requirements} \end{pmatrix}_1$$

$$\begin{pmatrix} \text{Projected} \\ \text{inventory} \end{pmatrix}_{\substack{t \\ t \geq 2}} = \begin{pmatrix} \text{Projected} \\ \text{inventory} \end{pmatrix}_{t-1} + \begin{pmatrix} \text{Scheduled} \\ \text{receipts} \end{pmatrix}_t - \begin{pmatrix} \text{Gross} \\ \text{requirements} \end{pmatrix}_t$$

$$\begin{pmatrix} \text{Net} \\ \text{requirements} \end{pmatrix}_1 = \max\left\{ 0, \left[-\begin{pmatrix} \text{Projected} \\ \text{inventory} \end{pmatrix}_1 \right] \right\}$$

$$\begin{pmatrix} \text{Net} \\ \text{requirements} \end{pmatrix}_{\substack{t \\ t \geq 2}}$$
$$= \max\left\{ 0, \left[\begin{pmatrix} \text{Gross} \\ \text{requirements} \end{pmatrix}_t - \begin{pmatrix} \text{Scheduled} \\ \text{receipts} \end{pmatrix}_t - \max\left(0, \begin{array}{c} \text{Projected} \\ \text{inventory}_{t-1} \end{array} \right) \right] \right\}.$$

TABLE 6.7 Computing Net Requirements for Subassembly S1

	CURRENT TIME ↓									
TIME PERIOD	JUST ENDING	1	2	3	4	5	6	7	8	9
Gross requirements		20	40	120	160	30	100	0	60	220
Initial inventory on hand	20									
Scheduled receipts		0	80							
Projected inventory (if no orders are released)		0	40	−80	−240	−270	−370	−370	−430	−650
Net requirements		0	0	80	160	30	100	0	60	220

Lot sizing in the MRP context requires the construction of a dynamic multistage inventory model as each stage experiences a deterministic time-varying demand. Unfortunately, lot sizing in multistage systems is a difficult and as yet unsatisfactorily unsolved problem. For a comprehensive discussion of lot sizing, see Berry [1972].

The approach taken by the MRP developers is to neglect the multistage nature of the production process and to determine lot sizes for each stage sequentially starting with level 1, then level 2, and so on. Of the 10 techniques listed below, only the Wagner–Whitin algorithm is optimal (it was presented in section 3.4.1), all others being heuristics:

1. Wagner–Whitin algorithm
2. fixed order quantity
3. economic order quantity
4. lot-for-lot ordering
5. fixed period requirements
6. period order quantity
7. least unit cost
8. least total cost
9. part-period balancing
10. Silver–Meal heuristic procedure

Rules 2 and 3, by neglecting the specific discrete pattern of requirements, are not a recommended choice.

Probably the simplest of all is the lot-for-lot approach by which each production order (i.e., a batch) is limited to one period's net requirements. The method is fit for expensive items, given that it minimizes inventory holding costs, for items that are ordered seldom, and for high-volume components that are manufactured with specialized equipment which requires inexpensive setup operations or no setups at all.

But, when the setup cost cannot be neglected, the lot-for-lot may become expensive because it orders too often. If a simple lot sizing rule is still desired, one can resort to number 5 above. This method intends to economize on setups by combining into one production order the net requirements of a preestablished number of periods, thus reducing the number of setups. A similar approach is the period order quantity rule, except that it computes the ordering interval, while the fixed period requirements approach sets arbitrarily the number of periods to be covered by a lot.

The least unit cost, least total cost, part-period balancing, and Silver–Meal algorithm present a higher degree of complexity because they involve the minimization of the total of setup and inventory carrying costs in the context of the discrete time-varying demand pattern experienced by the item under consideration.

TABLE 6.8 Lot Sizing and Planning Orders for Subassembly S1

TIME PERIOD	PAST JUST ENDING	CURRENT TIME 1	2	3	4	FUTURE 5	6	7	8	9
Gross requirements		20	40	120	160	30	100	0	60	220
Initial inventory on hand	20									
Scheduled receipts (from orders released in the past)		0	80							
Net requirements		0	0	80	160	30	100	0	60	220
Lot quantities*				240		130			280	
Planned orders		240		130			280			
Planned receipts (from future orders)		0	0	240	0	130	0	0	280	220
Projected inventory		0	40	160	0	100	0	0	220	0

*Shown in period when required.

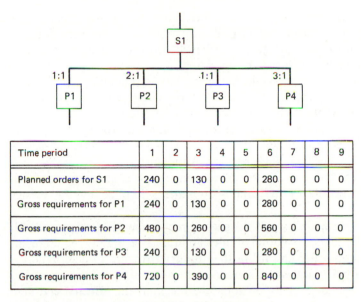

FIGURE 6.10   Explosion of level 1 planned orders.

Technical details on procedures 2 through 9 can be found in the book by Orlicky [1975, chap. 6]; the Silver–Meal heuristic technique is extensively presented by Peterson and Silver [1979, chap. 8.6].

Offsetting implies subtracting the lead time from the date at which the order is supposed to be delivered. By the offsetting mechanism, one determines the times at which orders should be released to the shop floor or placed with the vendors. Lead time values may depend on order quantity. The MRP system must be given the necessary formulas or tables for determining the appropriate lead times.

In Table 6.8, the net requirements for subassembly S1 have been grouped into production batches using the fixed period requirements rule. Each lot quantity sums the net requirements of two consecutive time periods.* Then, given the 2-period lead time, orders have been planned for release in periods 1, 3, and 6.

After completing the calculations for level 1, we resume the cycle for level 2 starting from the planned orders for level 1 items. We shall illustrate only the explosion process (Figure 6.10).

From our discussion thus far, it appears that MRP was conceived as an inventory control alternative better fitted to multistage production than statistical inventory control. The reason for this is that, given a master

---

*The first period included in the batch should have nonzero net requirements. This is why period 7 is skipped.

schedule, the uncertainties associated with predicting future requirements for components are very much reduced. The period-to-period variations in requirements are no longer a sign of stochastic demand behavior, rather, a predictable effect of the batch type of operation.

It should be clear that, while being an aid to planning, MRP itself (despite the "planning" connotation) is not a planning technique because it cannot generate, evaluate, and select scheduling alternatives in the face of limited productive resources. In fact, the total of planned orders generated by MRP might result in unacceptable or even infeasible work loads* in various work centers and in different time periods. Although unable to resolve such situations itself, the system can be of assistance by calculating for each resource the time profile of the total requirements implied by the master production schedule.

Also, a special capability called "pegged requirements" (Orlicky [1975]) is a means to facilitate the resolution of infeasibilities. Pegging the requirements means tracing a shop order upward in the product structure to determine the end item and the time period which generated the order. Thus, if one or several planned orders cause an overload in some work center, the affected end-item quantity is readily identified and tentative changes to the master schedule can be suggested by managers. Then these are tested by generating new load profiles and, if the situation continues to be unsatisfactory, the trial-and-error procedure can be reiterated. Obviously, modifications are not limited to changing the master schedule. There can also be experimentation with trial fitting of orders of component items with the purpose of redistributing work loads. In this function, MRP appears as a simulation tool which allows managers to examine the consequences of their production planning decisions.

Several requirements have to be met (Orlicky [1975], Plossl and Wight [1971]) in order to given an MRP implementation project a chance of success:

- Availability of a computer is a must. Although it is possible to obtain a material requirements plan manually, it would be impossible to keep it up to date because of the highly dynamic nature of manufacturing environments. And because we brought up the issue of updating the requirements plan, let us mention the two approaches available as options: the *regenerative* method by which, when the master schedule changes, the old plan is discarded and the material requirements are exploded all over again, and the *net change* system, which reworks the old plan by exploding only the items affected by changes.

- A feasible master production schedule must be drawn up, or else the accumulated planned orders of components might "bump" into the resource restrictions and become infeasible. Smith [1978] points out that the lack of appropriate support for managers to produce good master schedules is a major weakness of MRP, and probably the biggest source of disappointment in the performance of such systems. As shown earlier, the MRP response to this is resorting to trial-and-error and using the system in its simulation capacity.

---

*The cause is an infeasible master schedule with which the explosion started.

- The bills of material should be accurate. It is essential to update them promptly to reflect any engineering changes brought to the product. It is clear that if a component part is omitted from the bill of material it will never be ordered by the system.
- Inventory records should be a precise representation of reality, or else the netting process and the generation of planned orders become meaningless.
- Lead times for all inventory items should be known and given to the MRP system.
- Shop floor discipline is necessary to ensure that orders are processed in conformity with the established priorities. Otherwise, the lead times passed to MRP will not materialize (Smith [1978]).

On the benefit side of using an MRP system, one can count the following:

- Reduced inventories resulting from a better match between order quantities and requirements, and from better timing of inventory replenishments.
- Improved customer service (fewer stockouts and less late orders) by early warning of possible trouble spots such as insufficient capacity, late deliveries of components, and so on.
- Lower manufacturing costs coming from the previous two benefits as well as from reductions in such personnel as clerks, expediters, and storekeepers.

Before closing this section, we would like to mention briefly the controversial issue of safety stocks in MRP systems. The opinions expressed by various authors span a wide spectrum: one extreme is that "safety stock is properly applied only to inventory items subject to independent demand" (Orlicky [1975, p. 79]); others consider that safety stocks should also be maintained at component item levels since they are affected by uncertainties too (Meal [1975], New [1975], and Whybark and Williams [1976]). A very good discussion of pros and cons is given by Smith [1978], who recommends carrying safety stocks of components, a point of view we share.

In a more recent paper, Meal [1979] utilizes a classification given by Whybark and Williams [1976] for the uncertainties affecting the component item levels. They show that there are supply and demand, and quantity and timing uncertainties. By simulation, they establish that safety stocks are most effective in protecting against quantity uncertainties while safety time is most effective in dealing with timing uncertainties. Starting from here, Meal [1979] estimates a variance associated with the quantity uncertainty, resulting from both the supply and demand process and a variance characterizing the combined effect of lead time variability and requirement timing uncertainty. He then computes a safety stock intended for quantity protection and a safety time for timing protection, both determined as multiples of the respective standard deviations. Notice that the approach is similar to the establishment of safety stocks for fast-moving items by the use of safety factors (section 4.4.2).

6.5 Comparing Hierarchical Production Planning with Material Requirements Planning

In this section we report the results of extensive computational experiments conducted by Bitran, Haas, and Hax [1982] to assess the performance of the proposed two-stage hierarchical planning system. Since MPR is so widely used to deal with production planning and inventory control in multistage settings, we have contrasted the two approaches.

As we pointed out in the previous section, there is no single MRP design. Therefore, it is hard to make any comparison between "MRP" and any alternative support system. In spite of this, we would like to present some computational results contrasting the performance of HPP and an MRP system we have identified for these purposes. The reader should be warned not to make definite conclusions on the relative merits of these two approaches. Our objective is simply to establish a reference against which we can evaluate the HPP methodology. In fact, HPP should not be viewed as an alternative to MRP. We believe that some elements of the hierarchical framework can be constructively used to enhance the MPR system.

6.5.1 The MRP Model Tested

The essential features of MRP are illustrated in Figure 6.11. Although we have already reviewed the basic MRP concepts in section 6.4, it is important to emphasize the framework of MRP so as to facilitate a proper comparison between that methodology and the HPP system.

First, MRP defines the production quantities for individual product items through a planning horizon at least equal to the maximum lead time of the parts needed for the assembly of finished products. This production plane becomes the master schedule.

The master schedule of production item quantities is then exploded to compute requirements for all the part items. When all the requirements for a given part item have been consolidated, an individual production schedule is developed for each item.

At this step, no effort has been made to take into account the economics of joint part production; in fact, total aggregate parts scheduled for production might result in unacceptable or infeasible work load fluctuations. To correct for these possibilities, MRP calculates the work load profiles by major fabrication centers. These profiles are examined by operating managers and, if undesirable patterns are detected, changes are introduced either at the master schedule level, or at the part item scheduling level.

When MRP is conceived within the framework just described, it is, in essence, a simulation tool which allows managers to test some suggested production programs and identify their consequences.

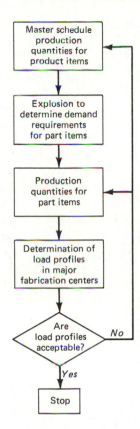

FIGURE 6.11
The essence of MRP computations.

If we contrast MRP with the proposed HPP system, we can identify several areas of fundamental differences. HPP determines a joint product type–part type aggregate schedule. That schedule is both feasible and attempts to optimize primary costs. Moreover, the fact that it is an aggregate schedule clearly facilitates genuine understanding of its implications. The HPP disaggregation process that leads to part item and finished product item scheduling is focused only on the immediate relevant time period. This avoids an excessive amount of data and computational work, because long-term consequences have already been accounted for at the aggregate planning level.

Figure 6.12 depicts the way in which we modeled the MRP system for the purpose of experimental comparison. Our primary concern was to implement computational rules for MRP that could provide unbiased groups for evaluation. The master schedule was determined by disaggregating the solution of an aggregate linear programming model for product types for the full planning horizon. The disaggregation procedure used was Equalization of Runout Time. As discussed in subsection 6.2.8, this disaggregation rule allows for an effective and consistent detailed schedule when the full planning horizon is involved.

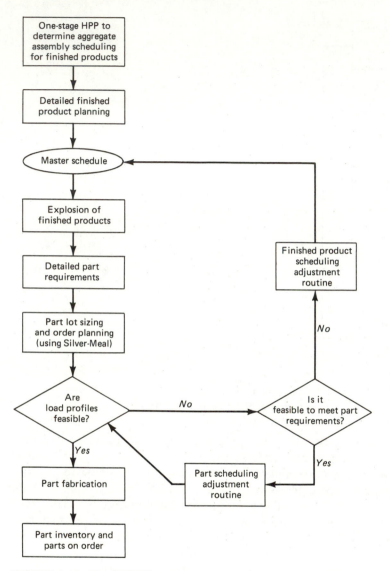

FIGURE 6.12   The "MRP'" method used for comparative purposes.

After the individual product item quantities were exploded to determine part item requirements, the Silver–Meal algorithm was used to determine part item production schedules. As reported in Peterson and Silver [1979], that method performs quite effectively when compared with alternative lot sizing methodologies.

The last element that we introduced in modeling MRP was the ability to correct for unattractive or infeasible production schedules. The consolidated production schedule for part items was examined and adjusted.

For the sake of brevity, we are referring to that system as "the MRP system." The reader should recognize that it is not in the spirit of our work to make definite comments on another methodology. This would have been an impossible task since MPR can be viewed as a broad approach to production planning rather than a specific, well-defined methodology.

In the remaining part of this section we will present the product structure used in the comparison, and the computational results comparing HPP with the MRP system outlined above.

6.5.2 Product and Part Structure

The data used in the experiments were scaled down from a pencil manufacturing company. This firm assembles a variety of pencils requiring a number of distinct components which are shown in Table 6.9. Individual pencils are the product items. Identical-sized pencils were grouped into a single product type, requiring similar assembly times. Within a product type, items sharing common

TABLE 6.9 The Finished Product/Part Structure

The Product—Pencils	
Variations —Sizes–Product Types	
Insignias on the Side–Product Families	
Colors–Items	
The Parts —Wood	
Lead	
Erasers (not all pencils require this)	

THE NUMBER OF PARTS REQUIRED PER UNITS OF FINISHED PRODUCT

		PART TYPE 1	PART TYPE 2	PART TYPE 3	
FINISHED PRODUCT/PART		WOOD	ERASER	LEAD 1	LEAD 2
PENCIL					
Size 1 (Product Type 1)					
Insignia 1 (Family 1)	Color 1	1	1	1	0
	Color 2	1	1	1	0
Insignia 2 (Family 2)	Color 1	1	1	0	1
	Color 2	1	1	0	1
Size 2 (Product Type 2)					
Insignia 1 (Family 1)	Color 1	1	1	1	0
	Color 2	1	1	1	1
Insignia 2 (Family 2)	Color 1	1	1	1	0
	Color 2	1	1	1	0
Insignia 3 (Family 3)	Color 1	1	0	0	1
	Color 2	1	0	0	1

setup costs and having the same inscriptions were grouped into product families. Parts sharing common production facilities were classified into part types. This resulted in three part types: wood, erasers, and lead (this last part type was composed of two part items, lead 1 and lead 2).

In order to test the robustness of the HPP and MRP methodologies, a number of critical parameters were selected to be varied within appropriate ranges. The parameters selected were: finished product capacity, part capacity, forecast errors, seasonality of demands, finished product setup costs, part setup costs, part holding costs, seasonality of finished product demand, and overtime costs. Appendix 6.3 describes the details of the values tested for each parameter and their corresponding measurements. The total combination of the values of the parameters tested results in 100 different runs.

6.5.3 Computational Results

We compared the performance of MRP and HPP, in terms of costs and backorders. When total annual costs were used as a measure of performance, 93% of the tests favored hierarchical production planning. The maximum cost advantage in these cases was 144%. In those tests favoring MRP, the maximum cost advantage was 3%.

When total backorders as a percent of annual demand were used as the measure of performance, 22% of the tests favored hierarchical production planning, 5% of the tests favored MRP, and the remaining 73% resulted in no backorders under either methodology. In the 5% of the tests favoring MRP, the maximum difference in backorders was 2% of annual demand. In the 22% of the tests favoring hierarchical production planning, the maximum difference was 8%. A summary of the differences in methods for all 100 tests simulated is illustrated in Figure 6.13.

For the purpose of a more complete comparison, we attempted to identify distinguishing features of the tests which favored MRP and those which most strongly favored the hierarchical approach.

Of the seven tests which favored MRP in terms of costs, none favored MRP in terms of backorders. In two tests, the MRP approach had higher backorders than the hierarchical approach. Of the remaining five tests, two had exceedingly high part capacity and zero forecast error, and very high part–setup costs. The remaining three tests which favored MRP did so by small amounts and all had medium forecast errors with a positive bias, very high part–setup costs, and high part capacity. This indicates that the MRP approach outperforms HPP in terms of cost only if (1) part capacity is unlimited and forecast error is low, or (2) part capacity is loose, and finished product forecasts are always high and part setup costs are steep.

The five tests that favored MRP in terms of backorders strongly favored hierarchical production planning in terms of cost. The average difference in total annual cost was 68%. Simultaneously, they all had high seasonality, low

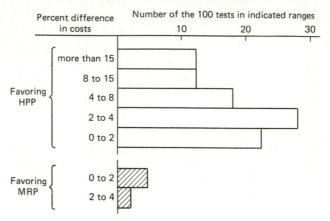

PERCENTAGE DIFFERENCE IN TOTAL
COSTS OF TWO METHODOLOGIES

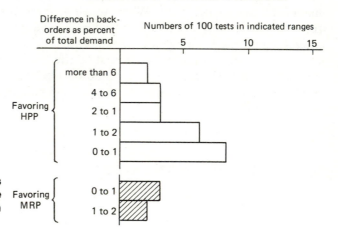

DIFFERENCE IN TOTAL BACKORDERS
AS PERCENTAGE OF TOTAL ANNUAL DEMAND

FIGURE 6.13
A summary of the results
comparing the two-stage
hierarchical model with
MRP.

finished product capacity, very high part setup costs, and medium or high part capacity. This indicates that if seasonality is high, capacity relatively tight, part setup costs very high, and backorders very costly, the MRP approach is preferable to HPP.

In examining the 11 tests in which the total costs associated with the HPP method were at least 15% smaller than those associated with MRP, no overall conclusions regarding point characteristics can be drawn. It is worth noting that none of the 11 tests had either very high part capacity or very strong positive biases in the forecasts.

In the two cases in which the backorders associated with MRP were greater than the backorders associated with HPP by more than 6% of annual demand, part capacity was low, forecast errors were unbiased, and seasonality was high.

In general, when parts are fabricated internally, the HPP approach appears superior to the MRP method of planning in all but the very unusual cases. This finding is further supported by comparing these two approaches with the Wilcoxon Statistic (Mosteller and Rourke [1973]). This test indicates that the probability that the difference in total cost of the HPP and the MRP approaches comes from a distribution centered at zero is less than .0001 (the normalized Wilcoxon statistic is greater than 7 1/2 standard deviations). The statistic supports our conclusion that the HPP methodology is superior to MRP for the cases tested.

6.5.4 Conclusions

The HPP system proposed in this text represents a novel and systematic way to deal with complex production planning decisions faced in a two-stage manufacturing environment. When tested in a relatively simple setting, it provided encouraging results which lead us to believe that the methodology has interesting potentials that could be exploited.

Given the importance of coordinating effectively fabrication and assembly operations, we feel that serious attention should be focused on hierarchical production planning systems per se or in combination with MRP as a topic for future research.

Appendix 6.1   Proof of Theorem 6.1

Theorem 6.1. Let u_1 and u_2 be two generic feasible disaggregation procedures such that:

$$\sum_{k=1}^{t} g_{ik}^{u_1} \geqslant \sum_{k=1}^{t} g_{ik}^{u_2} \qquad i = 1, 2, \ldots, I; \, t = 1, 2, \ldots, T. \tag{6.8}$$

Then $z^{u_1} \leqslant z^{u_2}$.

Proof. Let $(X^{u_2}, I^{u_2}, R^{u_2}, O^{u_2})$ be a feasible solution of problem P^{u_2}. Hence,

$$X_{it}^{u_1} = X_{it}^{u_2}, \, R_t^{u_1} = R_t^{u_2}, \, O_t^{u_1} = O_t^{u_2} \quad \text{and} \quad I_{it}^{u_1} = I_{it}^{u_2} + \sum_{k=1}^{t} g_{ik}^{u_1} - \sum_{k=1}^{t} g_{ik}^{u_2}$$

$i = 1, 2, \ldots, I; \, t = 1, 2, \ldots, T$ is feasible in problem P^{u_1}. Moreover, the objective

function value of problem P^{u_1} for this feasible solution is:

$$
z^{u_1} \leqslant \sum_{i=1}^{I} \sum_{t=1}^{T} \left(c_{it} X_{it}^{u_1} + h_{it} I_{it}^{u_1} \right) + \sum_{t=1}^{T} \left(r_t R_t^{u_1} + o_t O_t^{u_1} \right) + \sum_{i=1}^{I} \sum_{t=1}^{T-1} h_{it} \sum_{k=t+1}^{T} g_{ik}^{u_1}
$$

$$
= \sum_{i=1}^{I} \sum_{t=1}^{T} \left(c_{it} X_{it}^{u_2} + h_{it} I_{it}^{u_2} \right) + \sum_{t=1}^{T} \left(r_t R_t^{u_2} + o_t O_t^{u_2} \right)
$$

$$
+ \sum_{i=1}^{I} \sum_{t=1}^{T} h_{it} \left(\sum_{k=1}^{t} g_{ik}^{u_1} - \sum_{k=1}^{t} g_{ik}^{u_2} \right) + \sum_{i=1}^{I} \sum_{t=1}^{T-1} h_{it} \sum_{k=t+1}^{T} g_{ik}^{u_1}
$$

$$
= \sum_{i=1}^{I} \sum_{t=1}^{T} \left(c_{it} X_{it}^{u_2} + h_{it} I_{it}^{u_2} \right) + \sum_{t=1}^{T} \left(r_t R_t^{u_2} + o_t O_t^{u_2} \right) + \sum_{i=1}^{I} \sum_{t=1}^{T-1} h_{it} \sum_{k=t+1}^{T} g_{ik}^{u_2}
$$

$$
- \sum_{i=1}^{I} \sum_{t=1}^{T-1} h_{it} \sum_{k=t+1}^{T} g_{ik}^{u_2} - \sum_{i=1}^{I} \sum_{t=1}^{T} h_{it} \sum_{k=1}^{t} g_{ik}^{u_2} + \sum_{i=1}^{I} \sum_{t=1}^{T} h_{it} \sum_{k=1}^{t} g_{ik}^{u_1}
$$

$$
+ \sum_{i=1}^{I} \sum_{t=1}^{T-1} h_{it} \sum_{k=t+1}^{T} g_{ik}^{u_1}
$$

$$
= \sum_{i=1}^{I} \sum_{t=1}^{T} \left(c_{it} X_{it}^{u_2} + h_{it} I_{it}^{u_2} \right) + \sum_{t=1}^{T} \left(r_t R_t^{u_2} + o_t O_t^{u_2} \right) + \sum_{i=1}^{I} \sum_{t=1}^{T-1} h_{it} \sum_{k=t+1}^{T} g_{ik}^{u_2}.
$$

$$(6.9)$$

The last inequality in (6.9) follows from the fact that $\sum_{k=1}^{T} g_{ik}^{u_1} = \sum_{k=1}^{T} g_{ik}^{u_2} = I_{io}$ $i = 1, 2, \ldots, I$. The conclusion that can be drawn from (6.9) is that the optimal value of problem P^{u_1} is not higher than the value of the objective function of problem P^{u_2} for any feasible solution in problem P^{u_2}, that is, $z^{u_1} \leqslant z^{u_2}$.

Theorem 6.1 indicates that any two feasible disaggregation procedures are not necessarily comparable in terms of total aggregate production costs. It is important to note, however, that the optimal value z^u of problem P^u used to compare disaggregation schemes is a proxy for the total production cost of the hierarchical method.

Appendix 6.2   Proof of Theorem 6.2

Theorem 6.2.   Let u_E denote the EROT disaggregation procedure. Then, if all disaggregations are made with the EROT disaggregation method, if $I_o \geqslant 0$ for all product types, and if the aggregate product-type problem P^o is feasible, it follows that:

$$
z^o = z^{u_E}.
$$

Proof.   Every summation $\sum_{t=a}^{b}$ with $b < a$ is defined as being zero. Let u_E denote the EROT disaggregation procedure and assume that all disaggregations are made using this method. Let $I_{io} \geqslant 0$, $i = 1, 2, \ldots, I$, be the initial inventory of product type i before the computations of the effective demands. Recall that safety stocks are not included in the I_{io} for $i = 1, 2, \ldots, I$. Denote by $\bar{d}_{it}$ that real demand of product type i in time period t for $i = 1, 2, \ldots, I$ and $t = 1, 2, \ldots, T$. Since the EROT disaggregation procedure is being used, each inventory I_{io} will last for $R(i)$ periods where:

$$R(i) = r(i) + \frac{I_{io} - \sum_{t=1}^{r(i)} \bar{d}_{it}}{\bar{d}_{ir(i)+1}} \qquad i = 1, 2, \ldots, i, \tag{6.10}$$

$r(i)$ is the smallest nonnegative integer satisfying

$$I_{io} - \sum_{t=1}^{r(i)+1} \bar{d}_{it} < 0.$$

Moreover, the product-type problem P^{u_E} that we need to solve at the beginning of period 1 is such that $g_{it}^{u_E}$ are nonnegative and satisfy for each $i = 1, 2, \ldots, T$ the condition $I_{io} = \sum_{i=1}^{T} g_{it}^{u_E}$. The first term in (6.10) is the smallest integer less than or equal to $R(i)$.

The EROT disaggregation method implies that for each product type $i = 1, 2, \ldots, I$ one of the two following cases occur:

(a) If $r(i) \geqslant 1$, then $g_{it}^{u_E} = \bar{d}_{it}$, $t = 1, 2, \ldots, r(i)$, and $\qquad$ (6.11)

$$0 \leqslant I_{io} - \sum_{k=1}^{r(i)} \bar{d}_{ik} = g_{ir(i)+1}^{u_E} \leqslant \bar{d}_{ir(i)+1} \tag{6.12}$$

(b) If $r(i) < 1$ then $I_{io} = g_{i1}^{u_E} < \bar{d}_{i1}$. $\qquad$ (6.13)

Assume that problem P^o is feasible and that (X^o, I^o, R^o, O^o) is one of its optimal solutions. Define:

$$X^{u_E} = X^o, R^{u_E} = R^o, O^{u_E} = O^o, \quad \text{and} \quad I_{it}^{u_E} = \sum_{k=1}^{t} X_{ik}^o - \sum_{k=1}^{t} d_{ik} + \sum_{k=1}^{t} g_{ik}^{u_E}$$

$$t = 1, 2, \ldots, T; i = 1, 2, \ldots, I. \tag{6.14}$$

To show that $(X^{u_E}, I^{u_E}, R^{u_E}, O^{u_E})$ is feasible in problem P^{u_E} we still need to prove that it satisfies the mass balance constraints and that $I^{u_E} \geqslant 0$. First, we prove that the mass balance constraints hold at $(X^{u_E}, I^{u_E}, R^{u_E}, O^{u_E})$.

$$I_{it-1}^{u_E} + X_{it}^{u_E} - I_{it}^{u_E} = \sum_{k=1}^{t-1} X_{ik}^o - \sum_{k=1}^{t-1} \bar{d}_{ik} + \sum_{k=1}^{t-1} g_{ik}^{u_E} + X_{it}^o - \sum_{k=1}^{t} X_{ik}^o$$

$$+ \sum_{k=1}^{t} \bar{d}_{ik} - \sum_{k=1}^{t} g_{ik}^{u_E} = \bar{d}_{it} - g_{it}^2 \quad i = 1, 2, \ldots, I; t = 1, 2, \ldots, T. \tag{6.15}$$

The first equality in (6.15) follows from (6.14). Next, we prove that $I^{u_E} \geqslant 0$.

Note that:

1. for $1 \leqslant t \leqslant r(i)$, $I_{it}^{u_E} = \sum_{k=1}^{T} X_{ik}^o \geqslant 0$, $i = 1, 2, \ldots, I$ by (6.11)
2. for $t = r(i) + 1$

$$I_{ir(i)+1}^{u_E} = \sum_{k=1}^{r(i)+1} X_{ik}^o - \sum_{k=1}^{r(i)+1} \bar{d}_{ik} + \sum_{k=1}^{r(i)+1} g_{ik}^{u_E}$$

$$= \sum_{k=1}^{r(i)+1} X_{ik}^o - \sum_{k=1}^{r(i)+1} \bar{d}_{ik} + I_{io} = I_{ir(i)+1}^o \geqslant 0 \qquad i = 1, 2, \ldots, I;$$

the second equality follows from (6.11), (6.12), and (6.13) since they imply that $I_{io} = \sum_{k=1}^{r(i)+1} g_{ik}^{u_E}$;

3. for $t > r(i) + 1$,

$$I_{it}^{u_E} = \sum_{k=1}^{t} X_{ik}^o - \sum_{k=1}^{t} \bar{d}_{ik} + \sum_{k=1}^{t} g_{ik}^{u_E} = \sum_{k=1}^{t} X_{ik}^o - \sum_{k=1}^{t} \bar{d}_{ik} + I_{io}$$

$$= I_{it}^o \geqslant 0. \quad i = 1, 2, \ldots, I;$$

the second equality follows from (6.11), (6.12), and (6.13) since they imply that $I_{io} = \sum_{k=1}^{r(i)+1} g_{ik}^{u_E}$ and hence $g_{ik}^{u_E} = 0$, $k = r(i) + 2, \ldots, T$. From items 1, 2, and 3 we have it that $(X^{u_E}, I^{u_E}, R^{u_E}, O^{u_E})$ is feasible in problem P^{u_E}. Therefore,

$$z^{u_E} \leqslant \sum_{i=1}^{I} \sum_{t=1}^{T} (c_{it} X_{it}^{u_E} + h_{it} I_{it}^{u_E}) + \sum_{t=1}^{T} (r_t R_t^{u_E} + o_t O_t^{u_E}) + \sum_{i=1}^{I} \sum_{t=1}^{T-1} h_{it} \sum_{k=t+1}^{T} g_{ik}^{u_E}$$

$$= \sum_{i=1}^{I} \sum_{t=1}^{T} \left[c_{it} X_{it}^o + h_{it} \left(\sum_{k=1}^{t} X_{ik}^o - \sum_{k=1}^{t} \bar{d}_{ik} + \sum_{k=1}^{t} g_{ik}^{u_E} \right) \right]$$

$$+ \sum_{t=1}^{T} (r_t R_t^{u_E} + o_t O_t^{u_E}) + \sum_{i=1}^{I} \sum_{t=1}^{T-1} h_{it} \sum_{k=t+1}^{T} g_{ik}^{u_E}$$

$$= \sum_{i=1}^{I} \sum_{t=1}^{T} \left[c_{it} X_{it}^o + h_{it} \left(\sum_{k=1}^{t} X_{ik}^o - \sum_{k=1}^{t} \bar{d}_{ik} + I_{io} \right) \right] + \sum_{t=1}^{T} (r_t R_t^o + o_t O_t^o)$$

$$+ \sum_{i=1}^{I} \sum_{t=1}^{T-1} h_{it} \sum_{k=t+1}^{T} g_{ik}^{u_E} - \sum_{i=1}^{I} \sum_{t=1}^{T} h_{it} \left(I_{io} - \sum_{k=1}^{t} g_{ik}^{u_E} \right)$$

$$= \sum_{i=1}^{I} \sum_{t=1}^{T} (c_{it} X_{it}^o + h_{it} I_{it}^o) + \sum_{t=1}^{T} (r_t R_t^o + o_t O_t^o) = z^o,$$

hence, $z^{u_E} \leqslant z^o$. However, from corollary 6.1, $z^o \leqslant z^{u_E}$. Consequently, $z^o = z^{u_E}$.

Appendix 6.3   The Data Base for Comparing HPP and MRP Methodologies

Given the large number of possible input parameters, we varied those we felt were most important to test and held constant the finished product holding cost, annual demand, the product structure, and productivity. All variables held constant were set to values representative of the actual pencil manufacturer used as a base for our study.

We did not consider it necessary to vary both the finished product and part holding costs, since it is their relative magnitudes that are of primary importance for the purpose of our simulation.

The product/part structure we chose to use throughout the simulation was discussed in subsection 6.5.2 and illustrated in Table 6.9.

Productivity was not varied in the tests simulated. The effects generated by altering productivity are equivalent to those observed when changing capacity. They influence the number of finished products and parts that the system can produce at any moment in time. We felt it unnecessary to vary both parameters.

The measure used for capacity was the minimum fraction of demand that can be satisfied with regular time. The capacity was varied between 20% and 100% for finished products and 20% and 250% for parts and was measured in the following manner.

(a) Determine the period where the highest average demand per period occurs (based on cumulative demand–see Figure 6.14). Let us call this period N.

(b) At period N, compute the average demand per period, or:

$$\text{Average demand}_N = (\text{Cumulative demand up to period } N)/N.$$

(c) If capacity with no overtime is equal to Average demand$_N$, then capacity is set to 100%. If capacity with the maximum allowable overtime is equal to Average demand, then capacity is set at 0%. At all points between these two extremes, capacity is scaled appropriately.

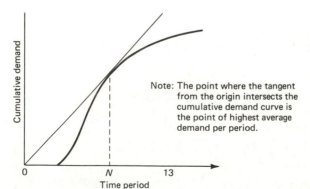

FIGURE 6.14
Determination of the highest average demand per period.

Note: The point where the tangent from the origin intersects the cumulative demand curve is the point of highest average demand per period.

To define high setup costs, we relied upon the impact of those costs on the length of the economic order quantities runs. We defined a high (very high) setup cost to be one associated with a run length greater than two (three) periods. Within the production environment in which we conducted these tests, a three-period setup cost was high.

Despite the assumption in the HPP approach that setup costs are secondary, we tested points with high part and finished product setup costs in an attempt to identify situations in which the MRP approach outperformed our hierarchical model.

The forecast error, which was expressed as a percentage of demand, was an increasing function of time. The following three scales for forecast error magnitude were used:

$$0,$$
$$0.01 + 0.02t^{1.3},$$
$$\text{and } 0.05 + 0.02t^{1.1},$$

where t represents time. Given the magnitude of the forecast error, the probability of an error being positive was defined as the positive bias of the forecast and ranged from zero to one in the tests. Exponentially increasing forecast errors correspond to what we have observed in practice.

Each demand pattern was treated as two connected opposite direction sine waves (as represented in Figure 6.15). Changes in seasonal patterns were controlled by modifying the coefficient of variation of the seasonal factors ranging from 1.3 to 5.2.

Part holding costs were measured as a percentage of finished product holding costs and varied between 30% and 80%.

Overall, finished product and part capacity and setup costs, part holding costs, forecast errors, and seasonalities assumed a variety of realistic possible values in the tests simulated.

FIGURE 6.15
Representation of demand patterns.

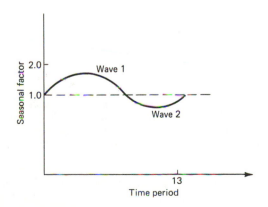

BIBLIOGRAPHY

BERRY, W. L., "Lot Sizing Procedures for Requirements Planning Systems: A Framework for Analysis," *Production and Inventory Management*, Second Quarter 1972, pp. 19–34.

BERRY, W., T. VOLLMAN, and C. WHYBARK, *Master Production Scheduling: Principles and Practice*, American Production and Inventory Control Society, Washington, D.C., 1979.

BITRAN, G. R., E. A. HAAS, and A. C. HAX, "Hierarchical Production Planning: A Single Stage System," *Operations Research*, Vol. 29, No. 4, July–August 1981, pp. 717–743.

BITRAN, G. R., E. A. HAAS, and A. C. HAX, "Hierarchical Production Planning: A Two Stage System," *Operations Research*, Vol. 30, No. 2, March–April 1982.

BITRAN, G. R. and A. C. HAX, "On the Design of Hierarchical Production Planning Systems," *Decision Sciences*, Vol. 8, No. 1, January 1977, pp. 28–54.

BITRAN, G. R. and A. C. HAX, "Disaggregation and Resource Allocation Using Convex Knapsack Problems with Bounded Variables," *Management Science*, Vol. 27, No. 4, April 1981, pp. 431–441.

BRADLEY, S. P., A. C. HAX, and T. L. MAGNANTI, *Applied Mathematical Programming*, Addison-Wesley, Reading, Mass., 1977. Chapter 6 based on the technical paper by A. C. Hax, "Integration of Strategic and Tactical Planning in the Aluminum Industry," Working Paper No. 026-73, Operations Research Center, M.I.T., Cambridge, Mass., September 1973; Chapter 10 based on the paper by R. J. Armstrong and A. C. Hax, "A Hierarchical Approach for a Naval Tender Job-Shop Design," Technical Report No. 101, Operations Research Center, M.I.T., Cambridge, Mass., August 1974.

CANDEA, D., "Issues of Hierarchical Planning in Multi-Stage Production Systems," Technical Report No. 134, Operations Research Center, M.I.T., Cambridge, Mass., July 1977.

CHASE, R. B. and N. J. AQUILANO, *Production and Operations Management*, Irwin, Homewood, Ill., 1981, chap. 16, pp. 513–548.

COPICS (*Communications Oriented Production Information and Control System*), IBM, Form No. GBOF-4115, White Plains, New York, 1972.

DEMPSTER, M. A. H., M. L. FISHER, L. JANSEN, B. J. LAGEWEG, J. K. LENSTRA, and A. H. G. RINNOOY KAN, "Analytical Evaluation of Hierarchical Planning Systems," *Operations Research*, Vol. 29, No. 4, July–August 1981, pp. 707–716.

DZIELINSKI, B. P., C. T. BAKER, and A. S. MANNE, "Simulation Tests of Lot Size Programming," *Management Science*, Vol. 9, No. 2, January 1963, pp. 229–258.

DZIELINSKI, B. P., and R. E. GOMORY, "Optimal Programming of Lot Sizes, Inventory and Labor Allocations," *Management Science*, Vol. 11, No. 9, July 1965, pp. 874–890.

FRANK, M. and P. WOLFE, "An Algorithm for Quadratic Programming," *Naval Research Logistics Quarterly*, Vol. 3, Nos. 1 and 2, March–June 1956, pp. 95–110.

GABBAY, H., "A Hierarchical Approach to Production Planning," Technical Report No. 120, Operations Research Center, M.I.T.,Cambridge, Mass., 1975.

GABBAY, H., "Optimal Aggregation and Disaggregation in Hierarchical Planning," in P. Ritzman et al. (editors), *Disaggregation: Problems in Manufacturing and Service Organizations*, Martinus Nijhoff, Boston, 1979.

GOLOVIN, J. J., "Hierarchical Integration of Planning and Control," Technical Report No. 116, Operations Research Center, Cambridge, Mass., M.I.T., 1975.

HAX, A. C., "A Comment on the Distribution System Simulator," *Management Science*, Vol. 21, No. 2, October 1974, pp. 233–236.

HAX, A. C., "The Design of Large Scale Logistics Systems: A Survey and an Approach," W. H. Marlow (editor), in *Modern Trends in Logistics Research*, M.I.T. Press, Cambridge, Mass., 1976.

HAX, A. C. and J. J. GOLOVIN, "Hierarchical Production Planning Systems," A. C. Hax (editor), in *Studies in Operations Management*, North Holland, Amsterdam, 1978a.

HAX, A. C. and J. J. GOLOVIN, "Computer Based Operations Management System (COMS)," A. C. Hax (editor), in *Studies in Operations Management*, North Holland, Amsterdam, 1978b.

HAX, A. C., J. J. GOLOVIN, M. BOSYJ, and T. VICTOR, "COMS: A Computer-Based Operations Management System," Technical Report No. 121, Operations Research Center, M.I.T., Cambridge, Mass., January 1976.

HAX, A. C. and H. C. MEAL, "Hierarchical Integration of Production Planning and Scheduling," in M. Geisler (editor), *TIMS Studies in Management Science, Vol. 1, Logistics*, North Holland/American Elsevier, New York, 1975.

HOLT, C. C., F. MODIGLIANI, J. F. MUTH, and H. A. SIMON, *Planning Production Inventories and Work Force*, Prentice-Hall, Englewood Cliffs, N.J., 1960.

JAIKUMAR, R., "An Imputed Cost Approach to Resource Constrained Scheduling Problems," in *Algorithms for Production Control and Production Scheduling Proceedings*, Karlovy Vary, Czechoslavakian Academy of Sciences, Karlovgvary, Czechoslavakia, 1973, pp. 169–178.

JAIKUMAR, R., "An Operational Optimization Procedure for Production Scheduling," *Journal of Computational Operations Research*, Vol. 1, No. 2, August 1974, pp. 191–200.

KANODIA, A. S., "Material Requirements Planning: A Study," Technical Report No. 128, Operations Research Center, M.I.T., Cambridge, Mass., November 1976.

LASDON, L. S. and R. C. TERJUNG, "An Efficient Algorithm for Multi-Item Scheduling," *Operations Research*, Vol. 19, No. 4, July–August 1971, pp. 946–969.

MANNE, A. S., "Programming of Economic Lot Sizes," *Management Science*, Vol. 4, No. 2, January 1958, pp. 115–135.

McCLAIN, J. O. and L. J. THOMAS, *Operations Management — Production of Goods and Services*, Prentice-Hall, Englewood Cliffs, N.J., 1980, pp. 301–332.

MEAL, H. C., "Manufacturing Control and Material Requirements Planning," presented at the *Seventh Annual Meeting of the American Institute for Decision Sciences*, Cincinnati, November 5, 1975.

MEAL, H. C., "Safety Stocks in MRP Systems," Technical Report No. 166, Operations Research Center, M.I.T., Cambridge, Mass., July 1979.

MEHTA, N., "How to Handle Safety Stock in an MRP System," *Production and Inventory Management*, Vol. 21, No. 3, Third Quarter 1980, pp. 16–22.

MOSTELLER, F. and R. E. K. ROURKE, *Sturdy Statistics*, Addison-Wesley, Reading, Mass., 1973.

NEW, C., "Safety Stocks for Requirements Planning," *Production and Inventory Management*, Vol. 16, No. 2, Second Quarter 1975, pp. 1–18.

NEWSON, E. P., "Multi-Item Lot Size Scheduling by Heuristic, Part I: With Fixed Resources, Part II: With Variable Resources," *Management Science*, Vol. 21, No. 10, June 1975, pp. 1186–1203.

ORLICKY, J. A., "Net Change Material Requirements Planning," *IBM Systems Journal*, Vol. 12, No. 1, 1973, pp. 2–29.

ORLICKY, J. A., *Material Requirements Planning: The New Way of Life in Production and Inventory Management*, McGraw-Hill, New York, 1975.

ORLICKY, J. A., G. PLOSSL, and O. W. WIGHT, "Structuring the Bill of Material for MRP," *Production and Inventory Management*, Vol. 13, No. 4, 1972, pp. 19–42.

PETERSON, R. and E. A. SILVER, *Decision Systems for Inventory Management and Production Planning* Wiley, New York, 1979.

PLOSSL, G. W., "MRP Yesterday, Today, and Tomorrow," *Production and Inventory Management*, Vol. 21, No. 3, Third Quarter 1980, pp. 1–10.

PLOSSL, G. W. and O. W. WIGHT, *Material Requirements Planning by Computer*, Special Report of the American Production and Inventory Control Society, Washington, D.C., 1971.

RITZMAN, L. P., L. J. KRAJEWSKI, W. L. BERRY, S. H. GOODMAN, S. T. HARDY, and L. D. VITT (editors), *Disaggregation Problems in Manufacturing and Service Organizations*, Martinus Nijhoff, Boston, 1979.

SHWIMER, J., "Interactions Between Aggregate and Detailed Scheduling in a Job Shop," unpublished Ph.D. thesis, Sloan School of Management, M.I.T., June 1972.

SILVER, E. A. and H. C. MEAL, "A Heuristic for Selecting Lot Size Quantities for the Case of a Deterministic Time Varying Demand Rate and Discrete Opportunities for Replenishment," *Production and Inventory Management*, Vol. 14, No. 2, Second Quarter 1973, pp. 64–74.

SMITH, D. J., "Material Requirements Planning," in A. C. Hax (editor), *Studies in Operations Management*, North Holland, Amsterdam, 1978.

WAGNER, H. M. and T. M. WHITIN, "A Dynamic Version of the Economic Lot Size Model," *Management Science*, Vol. 5, 1958, pp. 89–96.

WHYBARK, D. C. and J. G. WILLIAMS, "Material Requirements Planning Under Uncertainty," *Decision Sciences*, Vol. 7, No. 4, October 1976, pp. 595–606.

WIGHT, O. W., *Production and Inventory Management in the Computer Age*, Cahners, Boston, 1974.

WINTERS, P. R., "Constrained Inventory Rules for Production Smoothing," *Management Science*, Vol. 8, No. 4, July 1962, pp. 470–481.

ZOLLER, K., "Optimal Disaggregation of Aggregate Production Plans," *Management Science*, Vol. 17, No. 8, April 1971, pp. B533–B547.

$$7$$

Diagnostic Analysis of A Production and Distribution System

7.1 Introduction

So far in our book, we have covered a wide variety of methodologies whose purpose is to assist managers in *solving problems* encountered in the fields of production and inventory. We believe the book would be incomplete if we were not to dedicate some attention to the perhaps harder question of problem *identification*. We can argue that prior to embarking into expensive data collection, model development, and implementation efforts which characterize most system design activities in industrial logistics, it is mandatory to undertake a careful diagnosis of the existing operations. Such diagnosis will allow one to detect areas which are worthy of detailed analysis, representing the largest available opportunities measured in terms of costs and benefits.

A review of the literature in operations management and operations research reveals a significant gap in the development of methodology appropriate to assess the performance of logistics systems. Most of the work reported concentrates on models for optimal configuration or control of such systems, including simulation models to test inventory allocation policies (Bowersox et al. [1972], Connors et al. [1972], and Porter [1972]), and mathematical programming optimization models for physical configuration design (most notably the Benders decomposition approach of Geoffrion et al. [1974, 1978]).

Unfortunately, these very large models are not appropriate for diagnostic study, where the analyst needs to rely on simpler descriptive statements of the logistic system, more in line with the reduced time and budget allocations usually enforced. In a diagnostic study, the set of models used must be varied in nature, smaller, more aggregate in detail, and less data-hungry than the design and control support tools. The main purposes of an exploratory study are to uncover potential areas for improvement and to determine if the application of more formal large-scale optimization and simulation models is a worthwhile undertaking.

It is hard for us to understand the reasons for the continuous neglect of diagnostic studies in the literature. Are they so trivial that their reporting seems unnecessary, or so complex that they have escaped genuine efforts for structuralization? Certainly we do not think that diagnostic studies are simple, but we think that they have not been given the attention they ought to receive.

The tendency to overstudy techniques for solving problems, while the process of defining those problems is given little attention, is a bias that seems to pervade most of the research work in operations management and operations research. Long ago, Pounds [1969] conducted a study on "The Process of Problem Finding," and he suggested that we should concentrate our effort in the construction of models to define the relevant problems. This message seems to have gone unnoticed, but it is the essence of a diagnostic study. There are many areas of attention, and we should define models to establish sound benchmarks against which actual performance can be measured. A problem is considered to exist whenever a change in actual practices can lead to a substantially improved state of affairs. Most of the time, this improvement can be measured in total dollars saved or earned, and the firm should be able to define, for each situation, a threshold over which a potential improvement will be considered attractive.

The diagnostic study reported in this chapter adheres to that line of thinking. A first step in this process is the selection of broad areas of attention, and a second step is the construction of models to judge actual performance. Issues of interest for managers emerge in a very natural way from this analysis.

Since we are not in a position to propose a general methodology for diagnosing logistics systems, we will limit ourselves to describe an actual diagnostic study undertaken for a large firm in the consumer goods sector. The study was originally conducted by Hax, Majluf, and Pendrock [1981]. It focuses on the methodologies that were developed to fit the particular situation under consideration. However, we believe that the approaches presented in this chapter have some potential to be generalized to other situations. For additional work in this direction, see Bitran, Hax, and Valor [1981, 1982].

7.2　The Scope of the Study

At the time of the study, the firm was manufacturing and distributing more than £1 billion per year. According to its managerial team, their logistic system was performing satisfactorily, except for minor problems that had started to emerge. In general, they considered the development of all production and distribution activities to be very much under control. This was viewed as a substantial achievement, considering the size of the operation.

The main reason for starting this study on logistics was a "feeling of discomfort" expressed by the managerial team. They explained to us that the firm has been using the same system for so many years that they were unable to see the problems or inefficiencies of the system. Thus, the managers of the firm decided to have an external look at their operation.

From the outset, four major areas were identified as the scope of the diagnostic analysis. These areas were chosen in conjunction with the firm's managers as being critical to the overall performance of the distribution operations, and also as being areas which could be adequately investigated by an outside team. These areas are the following:

1. *Production and distribution planning and scheduling system.* The firm had developed and implemented a fairly sophisticated system to support production and distribution planning decisions. The first task that was required of us was to provide a critique of the existing system leading to a proposed framework for improvements. The work performed in this area is described in section 7.4.

2. *Quality of forecasting.* Another concern expressed by the managers was related to the overall quality of the demand forecasts. Most of the products sold by the firm were subject to heavy seasonalities and promotional activities, which created fairly erratic demand patterns. Therefore, a relevant question to be asked was whether or not the unavoidable resulting forecast errors were within reasonable limits. In section 7.5 an analysis of variance is performed which identifies the sources of bias in the sales branch forecasting, as well as the overall quality of the forecasting data. The forecasts analyzed are for each sales branch, for each product, and for each four-week period.

3. *Inventory management.* The third major area of concern was centered on the overall inventory levels. We were asked to attempt to assess whether the inventories accumulated were too high, and what potential benefits could be derived by enforcing better control mechanisms for these inventories. The managers were using aggregate indicators such as turnover ratios, which had presented a historical erosion pattern. They realized that these measurements were too simplistic to provide an effective diagnostic tool, and they wanted us to examine this matter more carefully. Section 7.6 examines the aggregate inventory situation for the firm, and analyzes the specific components of the inventory carried in the sales branches. A model is developed to understand the magnitude of the sales branches' inventory, and this model is used to estimate potential changes in inventory with improvements in forecasting, lead times, and inventory service levels.

4. *Consolidation of sales branches.* The last area of interest concentrated on exploring cost reductions opportunities by consolidating some of the existing sales branches used to distribute goods throughout the United States. In section 7.7, a model is developed to understand the nature of the costs incurred in the operation of the sales branches. The model is used to estimate

the magnitude of cost savings from consolidation of sales branches. The analysis considers several scenarios of sales growth and change in the product line which has different weight and volume characteristics.

Prior to discussing the diagnostic work in the four areas, we will proceed to describe, in the next section, the basic characteristics of the logistics system in the firm.

7.3   Physical Characterization of the Existing Logistics System

An essential part of this descriptive effort is to identify a minimum data base which allows us to identify in quantitative terms the major parameters of the logistics system. This is important for two reasons. First, qualitative opinions collected from the managers of the firm are very often confusing and contradictory in nature, based on subjective, biased inputs. Second, the data base will provide the essential inputs for the development of the aggregate models to be used in the diagnostic phase.

In brief, the firm is a consumer goods manufacturer operating in a highly competitive market where sales promotions are prominent. Yearly sales are in the high nine-digit range. Facilities are located throughout the United States. The firm owns plants, distribution centers, sales branches, and the truck fleet used for delivery to retail stores; common carriers are used for transportation between distribution centers and sales branches. There are relays between the distribution centers, but no transshipment activity between sales branches.

One important aggregation in a logistics system is the ABC analysis, which presents the level of contribution to sales. This was determined for both products and for sales branches (see figures 7.1 and 7.2). There are 200

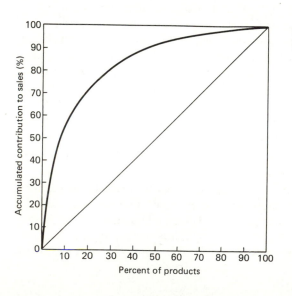

FIGURE 7.1
Distribution of sales by products.

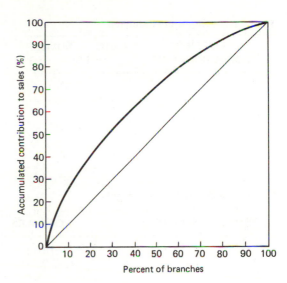

FIGURE 7.2
Distribution of sales by branches.

distinguishable products and 200 sales branches. Not surprisingly, the ABC analysis for products shows a high contribution by a minority of the products, while the sales branches are fairly homogeneous, with little variation in size except for a few large and a few small branches. In the forecasting analysis, we will emphasize the need to provide a different treatment to A and non-A products. Class A items are those that account for the top 50 to 60% of sales.

The firm has 10 plants, each having its own distribution center. Not all of the 200 products are manufactured in all the plants. This is because their production requires some special equipment which is expensive to duplicate everywhere. Table 7.1 describes the distribution of sources of production per product. It is important to realize that 76% of the products are manufactured in only 1 plant, and 87% have either one or two production sources. This is an important fact since it greatly simplifies the decision pertaining to the assignments of plants to serve a particular sales branch for a given product. Given the information in Table 7.1, this decision is trivial for about 87% of the products because even when two sources of production exist, they tend to be geographically separated so as to cover distinct natural territories.

The intensity of promotional activity can also be described in quantitative terms. End-of-year promotions are the major complicating factor for inventory management in this firm. Table 7.2 shows the severity of the situation. Roughly 50% of the products are promoted, with some products as often as six four-week periods per year. It should be added that not only A-level, but also B- and C-level items are being promoted, creating severe demand peaks during the year for low-volume items, which should normally receive less managerial attention than the higher volume items.

One final quantitative characterization which will be of interest is the loading profile for plants. This measures the fluctuation in capacity utilization

TABLE 7.1   Origins of Production

NUMBER OF PRODUCTION POINTS	TOTAL NUMBER OF PRODUCTS	%	CUMULATIVE %
1	152	76.0	76.0
2	22	11.0	87.0
3	11	5.5	92.5
4	9	4.5	97.0
5	3	1.5	98.5
6	2	1.0	99.5
7	1	0.5	100.0
Total	200	100.0	

Dollar contribution of each category:

NUMBER OF PRODUCTION POINTS	% OF SALES	CUMULATIVE %
1	37.0	37.0
2	23.3	60.3
3	1.1	61.4
4	16.0	77.4
5	12.2	89.6
6	5.3	94.9
7	5.1	100.0
	100.0	

at plants in the most aggregate terms, in this case the number of production shifts per working day per month. There are multiple production lines in each plant, and three shifts per day per line are possible. In total, there can be 240 production line shifts per day for the company. Table 7.3 shows the production loading, normalized to a base of percent of yearly average; for example, in January there were 3% more production shifts per day than the yearly average. (Note that loadings reflected the end-of-year and January promotions.) While the promotional sales peaks were quite high, the production loadings were not

TABLE 7.2   Summary of Promotional Activities

Number of products promoted: 83 out of 200
Average number of periods promoted: 2.8

NUMBER OF PERIODS PROMOTED	NUMBER OF PRODUCTS	%
1	27	32.5
2	18	21.7
3	11	13.3
4	8	9.6
5	13	15.7
6	6	7.2
	83	100.0

TABLE 7.3   Production Loading (index: % of yearly average)

MONTH	SYSTEM TOTAL
January	103
February	95
March	94
April	97
May	98
June	94
July	95
August	102
September	108
October	111
November	103
December	101
Average	100

overly dramatic, ranging from 94% to 111 percent of average. This indicates that the firm relies more heavily on early production than on overtime or seasonal workers. Early production places a strong emphasis on forecasting for detailed item demands.

It should be emphasized, though, that the fluctuation of production levels for individual plants is higher than the overall average. Also, there are four plants whose production levels exceeded or fell short of the yearly plant average by more than 20 percent. Therefore, the conclusions derived for the overall set of plants have to be analyzed carefully when studying the performance of individual plants.

7.4   Production and Distribution Planning and Scheduling System

7.4.1   Basic Characteristics of the Existing System

The company has developed over about ten years a vast computer based system intended to support planning and scheduling decisions in the areas of production and distribution. This system is a centrally controlled function, consisting of a set of computer tools, the heart of which is a large-scale mathematical programming model. A schematic overview of the system is presented in Figure 7.3, and a brief description follows.

Production and distribution decisions are reviewed weekly on the basis of sales branch forecasts covering four four-week periods (16 weeks is the total horizon). Planning is begun for the week after the next; that is to say, week 1 is frozen.

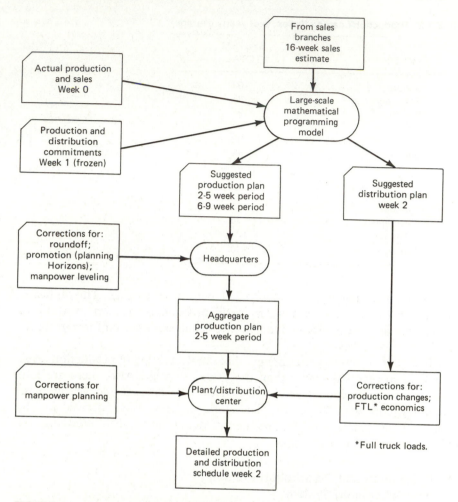

FIGURE 7.3 **Current planning and scheduling production and distribution system.**

The 16-week sales estimates generated by sales branches, the actual production and distribution levels for week 0, and the corresponding commitments for week 1, are input to the large-scale mathematical programming system. The outputs of this system are a suggested distribution plan for week 2, and a suggested production for two four-week periods (weeks 2 through 5, and 6 through 9), which are supposed to minimize the total production and distribution costs. The large-scale model consists of a linear program of about 84,000 constraints and 1 million variables.

The production plan suggests the total production, for each individual item in each plant, aggregated in two four-week periods. A managerial group at headquarters has assumed the responsibility for adapting the plan in two major ways: the time frame is halved and is decomposed into four individual weeks, and the individual items are aggregated into families of similar items which can be processed in the same work station at a given plant.

The group at headquarters makes three additional modifications to the suggested plan. First, they round off the fractional allocation of shifts proposed by the mathematical programming model for every working station. Second, corrections are introduced in order to smooth the total manpower requirements through time. And, third, the production quantities are occasionally modified to take into account significant increases in sales requirements resulting from promotions and seasonalities occurring beyond the 16-week planning horizon considered by the model.

The corrected production plan for week 2 (which has been aggregated for products in the same family), and the suggested distribution plan for the same week, are finally received by plant and distribution center managers. They disaggregate the production plan into individual items and introduce additional corrections due to manpower leveling, full truck load economies, and a host of factors affecting daily operations. Finally, a detailed production and distribution schedule for week 2 emerges from this process.

7.4.2 Critique of the Existing System: Myopic Planning Horizon and External Corrections to the Model

The first observation that one could make regarding the operation of the existing system is the inadequacy of its planning horizon. Due to the fluctuating nature of the demand pattern for most products, which results from both intense promotional activities and strong seasonalities, a 16-week planning horizon is not sufficient to decide effectively on the allocation of production and manpower sources. This is confirmed by frequent corrections that are made to the production plans suggested by the model, both by managers at headquarters as well as by plant and distribution center managers. These corrections are designed to obtain smoother levels of manpower and to take into account the effect of promotions and other peaks in demand not covered in the 16-week forecasts. Note that the short planning horizon was dictated in part by the combinatorial nature of the problem, which could be alleviated by removing the origin of production decisions from the weekly model run.

Moreover, it is important to notice that the corrections are introduced *after* the model is processed, thus disrupting the optimality criterion that the model uses to allocate production capacity. The major reason why the existing model cannot work with a longer planning horizon is the enormous dimensionality of the large-scale model that seeks to optimize the production allocation process at a great level of detail. This optimization effort, however, is destroyed by the mandatory external corrections that have to be introduced into the model's suggested plans due to the myopic planning horizon.

Another important correction that has to be input externally by headquarters managers is the roundoff of the fractional solution yielded by the system. After all these corrections are introduced, the original solution sought be the model has been substantially modified, and its "optimal" character has been largely lost.

7.4.3 Critique of the Existing System: Excessive Level of Detail for Planning Decisions and Inadequate Support for Scheduling Decisions

The existing system attempts to provide support for decisions that involve the appropriate planning of production and distribution resources, as well as the detailed utilization of these resources. Although these two types of decisions—planning and scheduling—have very different characteristics, they are handled in a single monolithic model. It is our opinion that this is an inappropriate design concept, which will produce unsatisfactory support for both types of decisions.

Let us be more specific. There are planning decisions that pertain to the overall corporation, which need a corporate scope to be resolved properly, as well as planning decisions that can be addressed at each plant independently. Among the most important corporate decisions we can cite are the allocation of products to plants and branches; that is to say, what products will be produced in which plants to serve which specific sales branches. These decisions have important consequences for the deployment of physical facilities and manpower resources, and frequently involve tradeoffs in labor costs, transportation costs, in-transit inventories, and capital investments. Such decisions neither need to be revised every week nor should they be based on very detailed information (as currently performed), but they need to be examined with long planning horizons from a corporate perspective.

After products have been assigned to plants and sales territories, an additional set of planning decisions has to be resolved within each plant. These decisions pertain to the levels of production, work force, and inventories to satisfy the fluctuating requirements for each product group in an effective manner. Again a long planning horizon, covering at least a full seasonal cycle, is required to determine the values of those quantities. Also, in this case, too much detail becomes counterproductive to understand the implications of one's actions.

Once appropriate plans have been generated, we are left with the operational decisions that require the detailed scheduling of production at each plant and the detailed shipment of trucks from distribution centers to sales branches. The production scheduling decisions need to take into account setup costs for each batch, interactions among successive batches, and costs related to changes in production levels (such as overtime, idle time, and changes in number of shifts). The shipment decisions should consider full truck load economies and balanced allocation of inventories among the sales branches. These decisions are not properly handled by the existing system, which again forces external corrections to the model to be made without adequate support.

After these comments, it should be clear that the major paradox of the actual system is that it contains far too much detail for planning purposes, and not enough for scheduling reasons. Planning should be based on fairly aggregate information covering long-time horizons. This will decrease the large amount of data manipulation currently needed, increase the accuracy of the forecasting inputs (since it is easier to forecast aggregate rather than detailed quantities), and improve the quality of planning decisions. On the other hand, scheduling should be based on short-term detailed information which is not currently available in the computerized data bank.

7.4.4 An Alternative Production and Distribution Planning and Scheduling System

The problems described so far tend to be generated by the monolithic character of the current computer support system, which attempts to describe, by means of a single model, a process which is intrinsically hierarchical in nature. Clearly, there is not a single set of production and distribution decisions. Rather, there is a hierarchy of decisions, involving different echelons of the organizational structure. This hierarchy of decisions involves a wide range of managers, from top executives at the corporate level to plant, distribution center, and sales branch managers; and it covers a range of issues that go from the corporate allocation of resources to the detailed scheduling of trucks. One of the major fallacies of the current system is that it tries to capture all of these issues with a single mathematical model. We have already analyzed the problems that this approach creates due to the different planning horizons, and the distinct levels of aggregation of the information required to support the various types of decisions involved. But there is an additional problem which is even more critical.

A model is just a simplified representation of a problem that generates suggestions for managerial actions. These suggestions should be assessed and evaluated by the managers that the model is intended to support. Making these interactions viable is a major element in every model design. As we have already indicated, the production and distribution decisions of the firm involve several managerial levels; therefore, a system that deals with these decisions should recognize all of these hierarchical levels and provide the means to allow for effective managerial interactions from one decision level to the next. It is interesting to note that the actual implementation of the large-scale approach has been modified over the years until it conforms more closely with the standards of the hierarchical approach.

These considerations have led us to propose an alternative production and distribution planning and scheduling system. The essence of the proposed system, described in Figure 7.4, consists of a hierarchy of small models, each one intending to capture one critical aspect of the planning and scheduling process. The outputs of these models would be subject to the review of the managers in charge of the corresponding decisions, prior to transferring that decision to the lower hierarchical level.

As can be seen from Figure 7.4, there are four different models that have different scopes, planning horizons, degrees of detail, and frequency of updating. The first model deals with the plant–product–branch assignment issue. It represents, from a corporate perspective, all plants, sales branches, and products in an aggregate model covering a planning horizon of a full year. The result of the model should be updated semiannually. The second model, also spanning a full-year planning horizon, deals with aggregate production and distribution decisions at each plant, and is updated once every four-week period. The third approach assures consistency in the hierarchical set of decisions throughout the organizational structure.

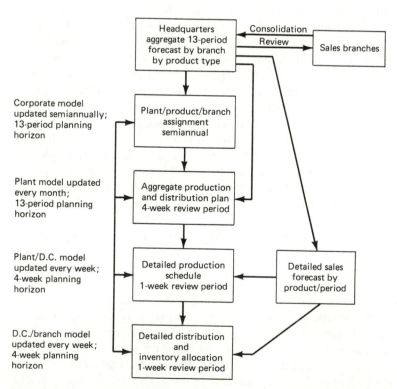

FIGURE 7.4 Proposed production and distribution planning and scheduling system.

The methodological details pertaining to the development of hierarchical planning systems have already been covered in Chapter 6. This study allows us to illustrate a setting where hierarchical planning systems present a natural approach to support logistics systems.

7.5 Forecasting

Forecasts are undated weekly by the 200 sales branch managers for each product for the next 16 weeks. The discussion in previous sections highlights the importance of this data; it is the only forecasting input and drives the planning process.

The initial review of the forecasting data is aimed at analyzing aggregate performance. The total forecast in dollars for all products for all branches for each period is compared to the actual sales recorded for the period. In each of the 13 periods for the base year of analysis, the forecast exceeds actual sales. Table 7.4 shows the bias for each period. The bias is easily explained by the responsibility assigned to the sales branch manager who makes the forecast. The sales manager is responsible only for sales and revenue performance and is not accountable for inventory costs; hence, the tendency to overforecast and accumulate surplus inventory.

The upward bias alone is not a severe problem since its cause is explainable and its magnitude can probably be estimated. However, the bias complicates the evaluation of the forecast errors, which is essential for inventory management. An *Analysis of Variance* (ANOVA) model was used to separate the bias from the forecast errors.

TABLE 7.4 Aggregate Forecasting Performance

PERIOD	FORECAST BIAS
1	28.8%
2	10.8
3	8.2
4	12.4
5	21.5
6	18.4
7	14.6
8	15.3
9	18.1
10	14.4
11	21.6
12	26.3
13	18.2
Average	17.5%

$$\text{Forecast bias} = \left(\frac{\text{Forecast}}{\text{Actual sales}} - 1 \right) \times 100$$

The hypothesis of the model is that distinguishable biases can be attributed to an overall factor for all forecasts and individual factors for each product, for each sales branch, and for each time period. Further, the size of the forecast errors should be proportional to the size of the forecast. The following multiplicative model was tested:

$$D_{pbt} = F_{pbt} \times M \times P_p \times B_b \times T_t \times e_{pbt} \tag{7.1}$$

subject to:

$$\prod_p P_p = 1 \tag{7.2}$$

$$\prod_b B_b = 1 \tag{7.3}$$

$$\prod_t T_t = 1 \tag{7.4}$$

where:

D_{pbt} = actual sales demand for product p, in sales branch b, in time period t

F_{pbt} = the associated forecast

M = the overall bias factor

P_p, B_b, T_t = the bias terms for each product, branch, time period

e_{pbt} = error term for the model; the error for the unbiased forecast $F_{pbt} \times M \times P_p \times B_b \times T_t$.

The model was calibrated with 234,000 data points representing 200 sales branches, each carrying about 90 products, for 13 time periods. The calibration was performed by a least squares linear regression on the log term of equations (7.1) to (7.4).

After the first calibration 200 P_p terms, 200 B_b terms, and 13 T_t terms were found. The outliers in the P_p data set were identified through exploratory data analysis techniques (Steam-and-Leaf and Schematic Plots; see Tukey [1977]). These all corresponded to low-volume products, new products, or perfect substitutes for other products. These products were believed to be sufficiently removed from the general problem to be eliminated from the ANOVA. The model was recalibrated with about 220,000 data points.

The results of the ANOVA are represented in the distribution of the bias terms, and in the quality of the forecasts. The overall bias term, M, is 0.17 or 17% of actual, confirming the data in Table 7.4. The product and branch bias terms are represented in figures 7.5–7.7. The product biases exhibit a much larger spread than the branch biases, indicating that variations in forecasting accuracy are due more to differentiation between products than to differentiation in the skills or circumstances of the sales branch managers.

1.4*	0 1
1.3*	0 6
1.2*	0 1 2 2 3 4 4 5 5 6 6 7 7 8
1.19	9
1.18	
1.17	0
1.16	
1.15	1 1 8
1.14	1 2
1.13	6 7 8 9
1.12	5
1.11	0 2 4 9
1.10	
1.09	0 0 5
1.08	0 1 4 5 5 9 9 9
1.07	1 3 9
1.06	3 4 5 6 6 7
1.05	2 8 8 9
1.04	1 6 6
1.03	2 3 4 6 7
1.02	0 3 5 8 9 9
1.01	0 3 6 7 7 8 9
1.00	1 3 6 6
0.99	2 2 3 4 6 7 8 8
0.98	4 7 8
0.97	2 2 2 5 6 8
0.96	1 1 6 6 7 8 9
0.95	1 1 3 4
0.94	1 2 2 3 4
0.93	1 3 9
0.92	0 1 2 4 5 5 5 5 6 6 7 7 8 8 9 9 9
0.91	1 1 4 8
0.90	1 1 1 1 2 7 8
0.89	
0.88	4 4 6 6 7 8
0.87	1 6 7
0.86	3 8
0.85	3 3 6 8
0.84	0 2 2 2 4 7
0.83	4 5
0.82	5 6
0.81	7
0.80	1 2
0.79	0
0.75	8
0.73	8

FIGURE 7.5

Stem-and-Leaf for product bias (P_p term in ANOVA).

1.23	1
1.16	1 3
1.15	
1.14	2
1.13	3 3
1.12	1 3 6 1
1.11	5 7
1.10	7
1.09	0 2
1.08	2 3 7
1.07	1 2 2 3 5 5 8 9
1.06	2 2 2 2 4 4 5 7
1.05	0 1 2 2 6 6
1.04	2 4 5 6 7 8 9
1.03	2 3 3 6 8 8
1.02	0 0 3 3 7 8
1.01	0 1 1 1 1 2 2 2 3 4 5 6 6 6 7 7 8 8 9
1.00	1 3 4 6 8 8 9
0.99	0 0 3 4 5 5 5 5 6 6 9
0.98	0 1 1 4 4 6 6 6 7 7 7 8 8 8 9
0.97	0 1 1 2 2 3 3 5 6 7 7
0.96	0 0 1 1 2 2 3 6 6 8 8 9
0.95	1 2 3 4 4 5 7 7 7 8 9 9
0.94	0 1 7 7 7 7 9 9 9
0.93	0 1 2 4 6 9
0.92	1 3 3 8 8
0.91	6 7
0.90	4 4 4 5 6 6
0.89	3
0.88	1 3 4 7 7
0.87	
0.86	
0.85	0

FIGURE 7.6

Stem-and-Leaf for branch bias (B_b term in ANOVA).

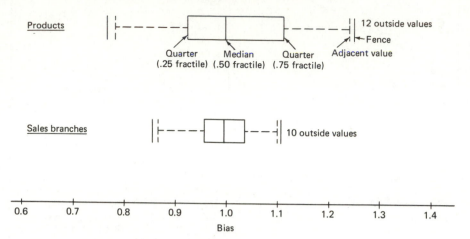

FIGURE 7.7 Schematic plot of product and sales branch biases.

These observations from the Exploratory Data Analysis are crucial to a forecasting diagnosis. First, the outliers could be found easily. Time-series forecasting models are generally hindered by the fact that not all items follow the same behavioral patterns. Finding the outliers, and confirming that they are indeed special case products with low sales, leads to more confident estimates of the variance in demand. Second, Exploratory Data Analysis achieved a confirmation of the fact that forecasting problems are created by heterogeneity in the products rather than among branches. Improvements to forecasting should be achieved by developing product-oriented techniques for nationwide application, rather than by focusing on individual branch sales forecasts.

The essential parameter used to measure the quality of the forecasts is the standard deviation of the forecast errors. This is equal to 0.5, representing an error equivalent to 1/2 of actual sales.

Assuming that the forecast errors follow a log-normal distribution, it may be concluded that it is not uncommon to find actual demand exceeding an unbiased forecast by 100%, or being only 50% or less of this forecast. (The chance of either of these two events happening is approximately 10%.)

This conclusion is extremely important, because this range corresponds to the best approximation that may be achieved with this forecasting procedure after removing all identifiable biases. The high forecasting error increases the safety stock required to maintain a given service level. The actual impact of this volatility over inventories is discussed later in greater detail. What is important to consider now is that there seems to be ample opportunity for modeling support of the eyeballing forecasting procedures used by sales branch managers.

7.6   Inventory Management

7.6.1   Basic Characteristics

The majority of the finished goods inventory is stored in the sales branches, with additional supplies in the distribution centers and in transit between the distribution centers and sales branches. Accordingly, the analysis in this section is focused on the sales branch inventory.

The inventory in sales branches was examined initially in an aggregate manner. Table 7.5 shows the inventory in sales branches, and in transit to sales branches as a percentage of the four-week sales forecasts. Over the year, the sales branch inventory averages 76.2% of the four-week forecast (15.2 days) and in transit averages 15.2% (3.0 days).

Since there is a bias in the forecasts when the inventory is measured against the actual sales, the average inventory is 89% of actual sales (17.9 days of demand). The highest inventory occurs in periods 1, 12, and 13, which are also the periods of the heaviest promotional activity. This pattern is expected because of the higher priority given to inventory for products which are being promoted.

We will now examine the potential savings resulting from a reduction of inventory levels, by making a very aggregate representation of the inventory problem. This is to be accomplished by building a single model that can be validated against the existing situation, and then determining the inventory improvements resulting from changes in the current operational policies.

TABLE 7.5   Sales Branch Inventory and Forecast Demand

PERIOD	% OF 4-WEEK FORECAST		DAYS OF FORECAST DEMAND	
	INVENTORY	IN-TRANSIT	INVENTORY	IN-TRANSIT
1 1976	85.49	12.80	17.1	2.6
2	69.22	16.56	13.8	3.3
3	75.61	13.82	15.1	2.8
4	72.70	13.84	14.5	2.8
5	70.38	13.10	14.1	2.6
6	74.40	14.62	14.9	2.9
7	77.74	14.09	15.6	2.8
8	70.31	14.93	14.1	3.0
9	71.60	13.93	14.3	2.8
10	71.60	14.25	14.3	2.9
11	76.75	18.01	15.4	3.6
12	85.58	18.89	17.1	3.8
13	86.19	17.89	17.2	3.6
Total	76.20	15.20	15.2	3.0

Probabilistic models in the literature usually relate inventory levels with stockout of backorder policies (see section 4.4). This same approach is used here with one basic difference; while most models treat products individually, we examine aggregate levels of inventories. The firm under study did not have sufficient data (in machine readable form) to facilitate the development of probabilistic models at the disaggregate level, and resources were not available for a data collection effort.

7.6.2 Components of Inventory at Sales Branches

There are several reasons why a company needs to carry inventory. It is important to identify each of these reasons for the firm and try to estimate the magnitude of the inventory which is required. The components of inventory which are pertinent in this case are summarized in Table 7.6. There are three major components of inventory at the sales branches: cycle stock, promotional stock, and safety stock.

Cycle stock. These stocks arise when shipments occur in lots rather than in a continuous supply. On average, cycle stock should be equal to one-half of the replenishment quantity. Sales branches are generally served weekly from each supply distribution center. This would lead to a cycle stock of 2.5 days of demand. Since a few branches receive some products less frequently than weekly, the overall average cycle stock is estimated at 3.0 days.

TABLE 7.6   Components of Inventory at Sales Branches

SALES BRANCH INVENTORY COMPONENTS	AVERAGE NO. OF DAYS	OF INVENTORY	COMMENTS
Cycle		3	1-week replenishment time
Promotion		1	Average for year
Safety stock			
Variability in production lead time	2.5		Production available at end of week
Variability in distribution lead time	3.0		Distribution available in sales branch at beginning of week
Cushion stock	4.0		Given by firm
Forecast bias	2.7		Difference between using forecast as base and sales as base
Other	1.7		
Total safety stock		13.9	
Total		17.9	

Promotional stock. These stocks arise as a method of smoothing production levels in the face of variations in demand due to promotional activities. The average contribution to inventory was estimated at no more than 1 day of sales, by considering the increases in inventory in periods 12, 13, and 1, and in-transit inventories in months 11, 12, and 13, which are clearly linked to promotional activities. By doing this calculation with the numbers presented in Table 7.5 (corrected for the forecast error), we obtain an average per period of something less than 1 day, but this number was rounded up to 1 because there is some extra stock explained by promotional activities in other periods of the year.

Safety stock. This stock protects against uncertainty in demand over the lead time. There are several facets to this uncertainty which include variations in demand during that lead time (resulting in cushion stock and forecast bias). Table 7.6 shows the components of the safety stock that the company was actually having at the time of the study, and it also shows in the column labeled "Comments" the reasons for this inventory buildup. For example, variability in production lead time is taken as 2.5, because although items are produced continuously over a five-day week, the system counts on the items being available only at the end of the week. A similar reasoning justifies the 3.0 assigned to variability in distribution lead time. A cushion stock of 4 days is an inventory the firm was trying to maintain as an extra protection for demand variability. Finally, the forecast bias of 2.7 days corresponds to the inventory increase resulting from a permanent upward bias in sales forecast. The total safety stock adds up to 13.9 days of demand.

This number, which is an empirical measure justified by common administrative routines, has been checked with an analytical model for demand over the lead time. It has been assumed, based on the analysis of forecast errors in the ANOVA study, that this demand follows a log-normal distribution, whose density function is:

$$f(\tilde{d}; \mu, \sigma) = \left(1/\sqrt{2\pi}\,\sigma_d\right) e^{-(1/2)[(\ln \tilde{d} - \mu)/\sigma]^2}$$

where:

$\tilde{d} =$ Demand over lead time (random variable)

$\mu =$ Expected value of $\ln \tilde{d}$

$\sigma =$ Standard deviation of $\ln \tilde{d}$.

The parameters μ and σ may be determined from the expected value and standard deviation of the demand over the lead time, which are designated by $\bar{d}$ and σ_d, respectively. The relations that link these four parameters are:

$$\mu = \ln\left[\bar{d}/\sqrt{1 + (\sigma_d/\bar{d})^2}\,\right]$$

$$\sigma^2 = \ln\left[1 + (\sigma_d/\bar{d})^2\right].$$

To compute the inventory required to guarantee a service level, a standard table of the normal distribution is necessary. Suppose that the service level (defined as one minus the probability of stockout) is designated by p, and that the corresponding normal deviate obtained from the table is k_p. In this case, the resulting inventory (S) may be computed from:

$$Pr(\tilde{d} \leqslant S) = p$$

or:

$$\frac{\ln S - \mu}{\sigma} = k_p$$

or:

$$S = \left[\bar{d} / \sqrt{1 + \left(\sigma_d / \bar{d} \right)^2} \right] e^{k_p \sqrt{\ln[1 + (\sigma_d/\bar{d})^2]}}.$$

This expression allows us to represent inventory levels as a function of service level (p), expected demand over lead time $(\bar{d})$, and the coefficient of variation $(\sigma_d/\bar{d})$. To validate this model, we gave to these parameters the values that characterize the existing situation and observed the resulting inventory. Current service levels were set at 90%, implying a value of $k_p = 1.282$. The coefficient of variation, which is a measure of the forecasting quality, was obtained from the ANOVA model to be 0.5. With these substitutions, the above expression reduces to:

$$S = 1.64 \times \bar{d}.$$

To obtain a measure of the safety stock, one should subtract from the inventory level S the average demand over the lead time. Therefore,

$$SS = 0.64 \times \bar{d}.$$

Here $\bar{d}$ is expressed in terms of *days* of demand, currently equal to 22, the average lead time in days. Consequently, the model would predict for the existing conditions the presence of a safety stock of 14 days (0.64×22). This is perfectly consistent with the actual safety stock of 13.9 days presented in Table 7.6.

7.6.3 Potential Improvements in Sales Branch Inventory

The largest component of inventory is the safety stock. This component can be reduced through improvements in the accuracy of the forecasting data or in reduction of the lead time for meeting sales branch orders. Improvements in forecasting are represented by reductions in the standard deviation of forecast errors over the lead time. These reductions will tend to decrease that portion of the safety stock linked to the cushion stock and the forecast bias. An improvement representing a 40% reduction in the standard deviation was taken as a scenario, because the managers of the firm suggested this was a goal that could be achieved over a reasonable period of time without incurring any sizable expense. All that was required was to provide appropriate training in forecasting to the sales branch managers as well as giving them some central support. The total replenishment lead time to the sales branch was 22 days. This included production and distribution lead times as well as order processing lead times. To examine the impact of lead time reduction on inventory savings, we assumed that the 22-day lead time would realistically be reduced to 15.

The two effects, reduction in forecast errors and reduction in lead times, are not additive because with shorter lead times the impact of improved forecasting is diminished. The model was then used to calculate safety stock levels for improved forecasting accuracy and reduced lead times. The results are shown in Table 7.7.

To appreciate fully the extent of the potential improvements in inventory, the numbers in Table 7.7 should be compared with the actual level of 18 days of inventory. Each day of inventory corresponds approximately to a cash retention of $5 million and an extra cost $1 million per year (at a 20% cost of capital). Under any standard of comparison, the potential reductions are very attractive. What is interesting in this result is that the two variables controlling this conclusion are forecasting accuracy and lead time, and that both of them seem to exhibit a wide latitude for managerial intervention.

7.7 Consolidation of Sales Branches

There are several optimization models for strategic planning of warehouse and sales branch configuration. Notably, the recent work by Geoffrion and Graves [1974] offers an attractive large-scale mathematical programming approach to this problem. However, given that the existing system has 200 sales branches and 10 plants, any macromodel would involve prohibitive data collection and computing costs for a diagnostic study. At this stage, managers are merely attempting to assess the magnitude of the potential cost savings to determine whether a further study is worthwhile. An alternative approach would be the

TABLE 7.7 Potential Improvements in Sales Branch Inventory (days inventory)

PROBABILITY OF STOCKOUT	LEAD TIME	FORECASTING ACCURACY	
		EXISTING	40% IMPROVEMENT
10%	4.4 weeks	0*	−5.4 days
10%	3.0 weeks	−4.1 days	−7.8 days
5%	4.4 weeks	+6.2 days	−2.1 days
5%	3.0 weeks	+0.3 days	−5.6 days

*The actual level of inventory is 18 days of demand.

TABLE 7.8   Consolidation of Sales Branches: Components of Operating Costs and Causal Factors

1.	Labor costs
	Office labor
	Warehouse labor
	Truck labor
	Selling salaries
	Managerial salaries
	Employee benefits
2.	Expenses
	Miscellaneous controllable expenses
	Truck expenses
	Selling expenses
3.	Rent, depreciation, and taxes
4.	Other expenses
	Advertising costs
	General administrative costs
	Cash and trade discounts
5.	Total cost = Sum of items 1 through 4

NOTE: Changes in inventory costs are excluded from this analysis, but their inclusion would tend to favor consolidation.

development of a simple, aggregate model for a broad understanding of the potential cost savings resulting from consolidation of sales branches. Geoffrion [1976] has also advocated the use of minimodels as a way to gain insight into facilities location problems.

Several components of sales branch costs which would vary with the number of branches, and hence with the volume of activity at each branch, were identified, as well as the basic causal cost factors. Table 7.8 lists these components and factors. For each component, we fitted a model using data from a representative sample of five of the sales branches. The total cost was the sum of these cost factors over all sales branches.

The functional forms of the relations used are summarized in Table 7.9. To maintain the confidentiality of the study, we are not providing the resulting values of the coefficients. These relations should be considered only tentative representations of cost items, because they have been built on a thin data base. Nonetheless, they represent a good summary of the qualitative and quantitative information we obtained, and we believe they serve the purpose of assessing the order of magnitude of savings that may be expected by pursuing a consolidation strategy.

7.7.1   Total Cost in Terms of Number of Sales Branches Only

The specific question asked with regard to sales branches is if there is some room for consolidation. This issue must be pursued under different scenarios for business growth and product mix, which were signaled by managers of the firm as sensitive parameters in this problem.

TABLE 7.9 Functional Forms of Cost Components at Sales Branches

1. *Labor Costs*
   Office labor: $L_0 = a_0 + a_1 N_b + a_2 N_b^2 + a_3 U_b$
   Warehouse labor: $L_W = b_0 + b_1 A_b + b_2 A_b^2 + b_3 U_b$
   Truck labor: $L_T = c_0 + c_1 T_b$
   Selling salaries: $L_S = d_0 + d_1 S_b$
   Management salaries and employment benefits: $L_{MB} = e_0(L_0 + L_W + L_T + L_S)$

2. *Expenses*
   Miscellaneous controllable expenses: $E_M = f_0 + f_1 A_b + f_2 A_b^2$
   Truck expenses (poor relation): $E_T = (\$/\text{stop})N_b$;
   $$(\$/\text{stop}) = g_0 + g_1/d_b + g_2 d_b$$
   Selling expenses: $E_S = h_0 + h_1 D_b$

3. *Rent, Depreciation, and Taxes*: Typical values are $1/sq. ft. for old
   branches and $2/sq. ft. for new branches, the average
   being $1.72/sq. ft. Therefore, the estimation of this
   item is made as: $R = 1.72 \times A$

4. *Other Expenses*: Total advertising costs, general administrative costs,
   and cash and trade discount costs for one year
   were taken at fixed costs, determined by the actual
   expenditures in those items for all sales branches.
   Therefore:
   Advertising costs: $O_A = i_0$ (total for all sales branches)
   General administration cost: $O_C = j_0$ (total for all sales branches)
   Cash and trade discounts: $O_D = k_0 S_0$

5. *Total Cost*: Adding labor costs, all expenses, and rent, depreciation,
   and taxes, the following relation is obtained for total cost:

$$TC = I_0 + I_1 B + I_2 \sum_b A_b + I_3 \sum_b A_b + I_4 \sum_b D_b$$
$$+ I_5 \sum_b N_b + I_6 \sum_b N_b^2 + I_7 \sum_b S_b + I_8 \sum_b T_b$$
$$+ I_9 \sum_b U_b + I_{10} \sum_b \frac{1{,}000 U_b}{N_b} + I_{11} \sum_b \frac{N_b^2}{D_b}$$

Nomenclature:

L_0	= Office labor cost (000 $/year)	O_D	= Cash and trade discounts (000 $/year)
L_W	= Warehouse labor cost (000 $/year)	b	= Index to identify a sales branch
L_T	= Truck labor cost (000 $/year)	B	= Number of sales branches
L_S	= Selling salaries (000 $/year)	A_b	= Area of sales branch b (000 sq. ft.)
L_{MB}	= Management salaries and employee benefits (000 $/year)	D_b	= Distance covered by sales branch b in delivery trips (000 miles/year)
E_M	= Miscellaneous controllable expenses	N_b	= Number of stops made by sales branch b in delivery trips (000/year)
E_T	= Truck expenses	S_b	= Sales in branch b (000 $/year)
E_S	= Selling expenses	T_b	= Number of trucks in branch b
R	= Rent, depreciation, and taxes	U_b	= Units delivered in branch b (000,000/year)
O_A	= Advertising costs (000 $/year) for all sales branches)		
O_C	= General administrative cost (000 $/year for all sales branches)	d_b	$= D_b N_b$ = miles per stop in branch b
		u_b	$= 1{,}000 U_b/N_b$ = units delivered per stop in branch b

A truly detailed analysis of branch consolidation is outside the scope of this study. The approach used, instead, is to isolate in the total cost the impact that may be traced back exclusively to the number of sales branches. In this way, the cost function is expressed only in terms of one decision variable (number of sales branches) and two scenario variables (business growth and product mix).

The specific variables chosen in the formulation of the total cost are the following:

Decision variable:

$$B = \text{Number of sales branches}$$

Scenario variables:

$$g = \text{Business growth favor (the base value is 1.0)}$$

$$\delta = \text{Product mix factor (the base value is 1.0).}$$

The average volume per pound goes up with the value of δ.

For the cost function to be derived, it is necessary to introduce certain simplifying assumptions, the most important ones being:

- Sales branches are assumed to be homogenous.
- Total distance traveled and total number of trucks required in retail distribution go down when number of sales branches is increased.
- Total warehouse space goes up proportionally with g and δ.
- Total distance traveled goes up proportionally with g and δ.
- Total number of stops does not change. (Number of clients and frequency of service remains approximately the same.)
- Dollar sales go proportionally to the growth factor (in constant dollars).
- Total number of trucks goes up proportionally to g and δ.
- Total number of units delivered goes up proportionally to g. (Pounds per unit remain the same.)
- Number of units delivered per stop goes up proportionally to g.
- Service constraints are not considered.

The resulting functional form for the total cost expression in terms of B, g, and δ is as follows:

$$TC = \alpha_0 + \alpha_1 g + \alpha_2 \delta g + \alpha_3 B + \alpha_4 gB + \alpha_5 B^{-1} + \alpha_6 \frac{B^{\frac{1}{2}}}{\delta g} + \alpha_7 \delta^2 g^2 B + \alpha_8 \frac{\delta^2 g^2}{B}$$

$$+ \alpha_9 \frac{\delta g}{B^{\frac{1}{2}}} + \alpha_{10} B^{\frac{5}{2}}$$

By computing the total cost for different values of the number of sales branches, and under different combinations of growth and product mix, it may be concluded that the optimum number of sales branches is somewhere between 150 and 175 but that the savings generated by this transformation are not very impressive (see Table 7.10).

TABLE 7.10 Annual Cost of Operation of Sales Branch Network
(100 represents actual cost for base case with existing number of sales branches)

NUMBER OF SALES BRANCHES	TOTAL COST (000 $)			
	BASE CASE ($g=1.0, \delta=1.0$)	MOST LIKELY PRODUCTION FOR 1986 ($g=1.2, \delta=1.05$)	1986 WITHOUT INCREASE IN LOW-DENSITY LINE ($g=1.2, \delta=1.0$)	EXTREME CASE FOR A 1986 SITUATION ($g=1.3, \delta=1.1$)
135	98.8	121.1	118.9	134.1
140	98.7	120.9	118.7	133.8
145	98.7	120.7	118.6	133.5
150	98.6*	120.6	118.5	133.3
155	98.7	120.5	118.4	133.1
160	98.7	120.4	118.3*	133.0
165	98.8	120.3*	118.4	132.9
170	98.9	120.4	118.5	132.8
175	99.0	120.5	118.6	132.7*
180	99.2	120.6	118.7	132.8
185	99.4	120.7	118.3	132.9
190	99.6	120.8	119.0	133.0
195	99.8	120.9	119.1	133.1
200	100.0	121.1	119.2	133.2

*Minimum total cost.

TABLE 7.11 The Case of Three Small Branches Consolidated in a Large One

ANNUAL COST ESTIMATES (000 $)	FOR THREE SMALL BRANCHES	FOR CONSOLIDATED BRANCH	SAVINGS FROM CONSOLIDATION
Labor costs	1,103	927	176
Expenses	312	316	−4
Rent, depreciation, & taxes	30	60	−30
Total	1,445	1,303	142
Cost per dollar of sales	16.0¢	14.4¢	1.6¢

DATA	SMALL BRANCHES	CONSOLIDATED BRANCH
Area (000 sq. ft.)	10	30
Number of stops (000)	15	45
No. of units delivered (000,000)	.5	1.5
Total distance traveled (000 miles)	100	300 + 25% penalty = 375
Sales (000 $)	3,000	9,000
Number of trucks	5	15
Rent cost ($/sq. ft.)	1	2

NOTE: Advertising, general expenses, and cash and trade discounts are assumed the same for both situations. They are not included in the cost estimates. Rental costs are assumed to double for a new facility.

490

TABLE 7.12 The Case of Two Average Branches Consolidated in a Large One

ANNUAL COST ESTIMATES (000 $)	FOR 2 AVERAGE BRANCHES	FOR CONSOLIDATED BRANCH	SAVINGS FROM CONSOLIDATION
Labor costs	1,219	1,116	103
Expenses	308	364	−56
Rent, depreciation, & taxes	40	80	−40
Total	1,567	1,560	+ 7
Cost per dollar of sales	15.7¢	15.6¢	+ 0.1¢

DATA	AVERAGE BRANCHES	CONSOLIDATED BRANCH
Area	20	40
Number of stops (000)	18	36
No. of units delivered (000,000)	1	2
Total distance traveled (000 miles)	150	300 + 25% penalty = 375
Sales (000 $)	5,000	10,000
Number of trucks	10	20
Rent cost ($/sq. ft.)	1	2

NOTE: Advertising, general expenses, and cash and trade discounts are assumed the same for both situations. They are not included in the cost estimates. Rental costs are assumed to double for a new facility.

7.7.2   Consolidation of Subset of Sales Branches

The results in the previous subsection indicate that, in general, branch and consolidation has some attraction, and that the firm should try to go toward a smaller number of sales branches. We will now explore the benefits to be derived from some specific consolidations, in order to suggest the patterns that may be more profitable. It should be emphasized that each particular case must be analyzed independently because the patterns to be presented are derived from relations which are valid as an average, but which may not be good approximations in particular cases.

Table 7.11 presents the consolidation of three small branches of 10,000 square feet each into one of 30,000 square feet. The result obtained is that this particular case generates $142,000 savings per year, which represents 1.6 cents per dollar of sales. (The actual savings are dependent on the area for sales branches, as well as the values given to the other parameters such as number of stops, number of units delivered, total distance traveled, sales, number of trucks, and rent cost.)

Table 7.12 presents the consolidation of two 20,000 square feet branches into one 40,000 square feet branch. In this case, the savings in labor costs are almost totally wiped out by the increased expenses and rent.

The conclusion that this exercise seems to suggest is that in the consolidation of small branches there is room for savings generated in the large reduction in labor costs; but when branches become too large, the increase in other costs dominates this reduction, making the consolidation unattractive.

7.8   Conclusions of the Study

In this chapter, we intended to present puzzling questions we faced when developing a diagnostic study of a logistics system. Our initial search in the literature did not produce a wealth of publications on which we could confidently base our study, so we had to explore some new avenues in the attack on the problem. In this section, we want to summarize the main conclusions we derived from this professional experience in the general approach to a diagnostic problem, and the managerial recommendations stemming from this particular study.

7.8.1   Diagnostic Study of Ongoing Logistics System

To draw general conclusions from a unique experience may be somewhat risky. Nevertheless, we feel that there are two important suggestions that seem to have a more permanent value, though we cannot offer sufficient empirical evidence to sustain this claim at this point.

In the first place, a diagnostic study is more properly completed by developing many small models rather than a big one. Our observation in this particular case is that managers of the firm were fully aware of the problems that the small models conceptualized, so there was no instance in which an aversion to the idea of modeling was expressed. On the contrary, these models, in many cases, were valuable in supporting some intuitive notions that managers had on specific problems.

The second fundamental recommendation is the use of the hierarchical approach to decision making as a framework for the study. This case happens to provide a very interesting validation of the basic ideas in that framework, because the planning and control system, as operated in practice at the time of the study, exhibited a substantial deviation from its formal centralized and monolithic design. Some necessary interventions to the large-scale approach were required to make it more responsive to the immediate needs of managers at different levels in the hierarchical chain. It is interesting to realize that many of the problems that we uncovered in this particular application were born in the tension between the need for managers to conduct their tasks in the terms which are more natural and familiar to them, and the constraints that a large-scale centralized system necessarily imposes upon them.

7.8.2   Managerial Recommendations

A great deal of attention was given to the formulation of suggestions for managerial action, including the definition of priorities and timetables. Due to space constraints, we will limit ourselves to listing the most important of these suggestions for each of the issues presented in earlier sections.

Production and Distribution Planning and Scheduling

1. Recognize the implications of the hierarchical nature of the managerial process.
2. Consider the establishment of profit centers at the sales branch level.

Forecasting

1. Assign responsibilities for aggregate forecasting to a headquarters group.
2. Improve procedures for sales branch forecasting.

Inventory Management

1. Attempt to reduce lead time and improve forecasting accuracy.
2. Make sales branch managers accountable for inventory performance.

Consolidation of Sales Branches

1. Continue the reduction in the number of sales branches.
2. Concentrate attention where the consolidated sales branch would be large enough to overcome the increased rental cost of a new facility.

BIBLIOGRAPHY

BITRAN, G. R., A. C. HAX, and J. VALOR-SABATIER, "Diagnostic Analysis of Inventory Systems: A Statistical Approach," Working Paper No. 1272-81, Sloan School of Management, M.I.T., Cambridge, Mass., October 1981.

BITRAN, G. R., A. C. HAX, and J. VALOR-SABATIER, "Diagnostic Analysis of Inventory Systems: An Optimization Approach," *Naval Research Logistics Quarterly*, Vol. 29, No. 1, March 1982.

BOWERSOX, D. J. et al., *Dynamic Simulation of Physical Distribution Systems*, Michigan State University Press, East Lansing, 1972.

CONNERS, M. M. et al., "The Distribution System Simulator," *Management Science*, Vol. 18, No. 8, April 1972, pp. B425–B453.

GEOFFRION, A. M., "The Purpose of Mathematical Programming Is Insights Not Numbers," *Interfaces*, Vol. 7, No. 1, Part 1, November 1976, pp. 81–92.

GEOFFRION, A. M. and G. W. GRAVES, "Multi-Commodity Distribution System Design by Benders Decomposition," *Management Science*, Vol. 20, No. 5, January 1974, pp. 822–844.

GEOFFRION, A. M., G. W. GRAVES, and S. LEE, "Strategic Distribution System Planning: A Status Report," in A. C. Hax (editor) *Studies in Operations Management*, North Holland, Amsterdam, 1978.

HAX, A. C., N. S. MAJLUF, and M. PENDROCK, "Diagnostic Analysis of a Production and Distribution System," *Management Science*, Vol. 26, No. 9, September 1980, pp. 871–889.

PORTER, T. W., "Management of Multiple Warehouse Systems," *Automation*, Vol. 19, No. 1, January 1972, pp. 52–56.

POUNDS, W. F., "The Process of Problem Finding," *Industrial Management Review*, Vol. 11, No. 1, Fall 1969, pp. 1–19.

TUKEY, J. W., *Exploratory Data Analysis*, Addison-Wesley, Reading, Mass., 1977.

Author Index

Subject Index